DATE DUE FOR RETURN

The Constitution
OF THE
Federal Republic of Germany

THE
Constitution
OF THE
Federal Republic
OF
Germany

David P. Currie

THE UNIVERSITY OF CHICAGO PRESS

Chicago and London

DAVID P. CURRIE is Edward H. Levi Distinguished Service Professor and Arnold and Frieda Shure Scholar in the Law School at the University of Chicago.

The University of Chicago Press, Chicago 60637
The University of Chicago Press, Ltd., London
© 1994 by The University of Chicago
All rights reserved. Published 1994
Printed in the United States of America
03 02 01 00 99 98 97 96 95 94   1 2 3 4 5
ISBN: 0-226-13113-0 (cloth)

Library of Congress Cataloging-in-Publication Data

Currie, David P.
    The Constitution of the Federal Republic of Germany / David P.
Currie.
        p.   cm.
    Includes bibliographical references and index.
    1. Germany--Constitutional law.   I. Title.
KK4450.C87   1994
342.43--dc20
[344.302]   94-12206

The paper used in this publication meets the minimum requirements of the American National Standard for Information Sciences – Permanence of Paper for Printed Library Materials, ANSI Z39.48-1984.

"Denn nur durch Vergleichung un-
terscheidet man sich und erfährt,
was man ist, um ganz zu werden,
was man sein soll."

THOMAS MANN[*]

---

[*] "For only by making comparisons can we distinguish ourselves from others and discover who we are, in order to become all that we are meant to be." The quotation is taken from Joseph in Ägypten (1933), the second volume of Mann's epic novel Joseph und seine Brüder.

Contents

Preface

The rapid reunification of Germany in the wake of the East German revolution of 1989 has awakened new interest in that country, coupled with no little anxiety in some quarters. What can we expect from this powerful nation of nearly eighty million people? How is it governed? Can it be trusted? Is it firmly committed to the values of democracy and freedom? Will it be a threat to its own citizens, or to its neighbors?

There is no crystal ball in which to find answers to such questions. So long as nations are composed of fallible mortals, there can be no guarantee of a rosy future. Absent some cataclysmic event, however, the past may have value in predicting what is to come; and the recent constitutional history of Germany is reassuring.

Germany was divided for forty-five years. The East – the German Democratic Republic – was a typical Communist state modeled after the Soviet Union until the people put an end to it in 1989. The West – the Federal Republic of Germany – adopted a Basic Law (Grundgesetz) based upon democracy, freedom, and the rule of law, which for more than forty years it has respected and enforced. This Basic Law is now the constitution of all Germany. The experience under its provisions deserves to be better understood for its own sake, for the comparative insights it affords into our own Constitution, and not least for its significance in assessing the consequences of reunification.

Germany is a particularly fertile field for the student of comparative constitutional law. Not only does Germany have a written constitution that embodies many of the basic principles – including federalism – that also underlie our own. It also has a Constitutional Court (Bundesverfassungsgericht) with broad powers of judicial review. Since its establishment in 1951 this tribunal has produced nearly ninety volumes of reported decisions. Those decisions, together with the text of the Basic Law itself (which is reprinted in English, as amended, in the Appendix), provide the raw material on which the present study is based.[1]

---

[1] The official reports, entitled Entscheidungen des Bundesverfassungsgerichts, are cited throughout this book under the abbreviation BVerfGE by volume, page number, and date. Unfortunately for ready identification, cases are given no

Secondary sources on German constitutional law are inexhaustible, and they have played an important role in shaping the meaning of the Basic Law. In the interest of finishing this book within the present century, I have relied largely on three comprehensive multivolume treatises selected in order to afford a variety of views: the mainstream and influential commentary on the Basic Law [Grundgesetz Kommentar] first published by Theodor Maunz and Günter Dürig in 1958 [cited throughout this book as Maunz/Dürig]; the less conventional and avowedly less conservative volumes edited by Erhard Denninger and others and published in 1984 as part of a series of "alternative" commentaries [Kommentar zum Grundgesetz für die Bundesrepublik Deutschland (Reihe Alternativkommentare), hereafter cited as AK-GG]; and the thorough and scholarly new Handbuch des Staatsrechts der Bundesrepublik Deutschland, edited by Josef Isensee and Paul Kirchhof [hereafter cited as Handbuch des Staatsrechts]. The standard brief introduction to the subject is Konrad Hesse, Grundzüge des Verfassungsrechts der Bundesrepublik Deutschland, a popular textbook that was uncommonly influential even before its author became a highly respected (and since retired) Justice of the Constitutional Court.[2]

Both primary and secondary sources on the Basic Law are increasingly available in English as well. Donald Kommers has made a major contribution by publishing edited versions of many of the leading decisions, with enlightening commentary, in his excellent casebook, The Constitutional Jurisprudence of the Federal Republic of Germany (1989), and the Constitutional Court has published the first of a series of volumes of translations of major opinions on its own.[3] Ulrich Karpen has edited a collection of introductory essays by German experts in English entitled The Constitution of the Federal

---

official name in the reports; where popular designations have attained currency, they are given in parentheses or in the text (e.g., *Gruppenuniversität, Elfes, Lüth*). Decisions not yet officially published (together with some that never appear in the official compilation) often are reported in various legal periodicals, notably the Neue Juristische Wochenschrift [hereafter cited as NJW]; others that have not been picked up there are cited to slip opinions printed by the Constitutional Court itself.

Unfortunately for the academic voyeur, opinions of the Court are unsigned. Cases are commonly assigned to individual Justices on the basis of subject matter, and no secret is made of each Justice's fields of interest. See Donald P. Kommers, Judicial Politics in West Germany 182-83 (1976). Nevertheless it is relatively difficult for an outsider to form a picture of the jurisprudence or style of individual members of the Court. Signed concurring and dissenting opinions, first authorized in 1970, remain far less prevalent than those of Justices of the U.S. Supreme Court. See § 30(2) BVerfGG; Theodor Maunz, Bruno Schmidt-Bleibtreu, Franz Klein, & Gerhard Ulsamer, Bundesverfassungsgerichtsgesetz, § 30, Rdnr. 4-6 (2d ed. 1985).

[2] These and other shorthand citations are explained in a separate table of Abbreviations and Shortened Titles that immediately follows this Preface.

[3] Decisions of the Bundesverfassungsgericht – Federal Constitutional Court – Federal Republic of Germany (vol. 1, pts. I-II, 1992).

Republic of Germany (1988). Professor Christan Starck has edited two collections of essays: Main Principles of the German Basic Law (1983) and New Challenges to the German Basic Law (1991). Professor Kommers, in conjunction with Justice Paul Kirchhof of the Constitutional Court, has recently published a series of papers by both German and American observers entitled Germany and Its Basic Law (1993). Professor Blair has published a book on German federalism,[4] Professor Kommers one on the Constitutional Court,[5] Professor Koch one on German constitutional history.[6] Scholarly articles in English on particular aspects of German constitutional law now appear regularly in American journals; a number of them are cited where pertinent throughout this book.

A word about form: There are footnotes. Some of them are long and textual. They reflect the conviction that some material is too tangential to be permitted to interrupt the text but too important to be left out entirely.

Two chapters of this book have been previously published in article form.[7] Permission to reprint this material is gratefully acknowledged. Thanks are also due to Viola Manderfeld, George Metcalf, Max Putzel, and their colleagues at the University of Chicago, who introduced me to Germany and its language many years ago; to Gerhard Casper, who fostered my interest in comparative law and was my indispensable adviser on this project; to the Law Faculties of the Universities of Frankfurt, Hannover, and Heidelberg, where the research leading to this study was begun; to the Fritz Thyssen Stiftung, which underwrote some of the associated travel costs; to the Raymond and Nancy Goodman Feldman Fund, the Kirkland and Ellis Faculty Research Fund, the Mayer, Brown and Platt Faculty Research Fund, the Morton C. Seeley Fund, the Sonnenschein Faculty Research Fund, the Frieda and Arnold Shure Research Fund, and the Russell Baker Scholars Fund, which helped support the continuance of the project; to Maurits Beerepoot, Jay Feist, Tanja Hens, Clemens Ladenburger, and David Lyle, who checked the citations; to Michael Bothe, Anne-Marie Slaughter Burley, Barbara Flynn Currie, Erhard Denninger, Abner Greene, Dieter Grimm, Lawrence Lessig, Knut Wolfgang Nörr, Thomas Oppermann, Jost Pietzcker, Ingo Richter, Eberhard Schmidt-Aßmann, Hans-Peter Schneider, Helmut Steinberger, Geoffrey Stone, Cass Sunstein, and Reinhard Zimmermann, who furnished invaluable advice and encourage-

---

[4] Philip M. Blair, Federalism and Judicial Review in West Germany (1981).

[5] See note 1 supra.

[6] H. W. Koch, A Constitutional History of Germany in the Nineteenth and Twentieth Centuries (1984).

[7] See David Currie, Lochner Abroad: Substantive Due Process and Equal Protection in the Federal Republic of Germany, 1989 Sup. Ct. Rev. 333, copyright © 1990 by The University of Chicago; David Currie, Separation of Powers in the Federal Republic of Germany, 41 Am. J. Comp.L. 201 (1993), copyright © 1993 by the American Society of Comparative Law, Inc.

ment; to President Roman Herzog of the Constitutional Court, who kindly provided copies of opinions not yet published; to Donald Kommers, who graciously permitted use of translations from his casebook;[8] and to John Ultmann, without whom there would have been no book at all.

The aim of this book is to explain the essential features of the Basic Law as illuminated by the decisions of the Federal Constitutional Court and compared with the Constitution of the United States.[9]

---

[8] The English version of the Basic Law itself, which appears in the Appendix, is adapted from an official publication of the Press and Information Office of the German Federal Government; most other translations in this book are my own.

[9] Decisions of the U.S. Supreme Court noted in this volume are discussed in David P. Currie, The Constitution in the Supreme Court: The First Hundred Years (1985) [hereafter cited as The First Hundred Years] and David P. Currie, The Constitution in the Supreme Court: The Second Century (1990) [hereafter cited as The Second Century].

Abbreviations and Shortened Titles

a.F.

alte Fassung (old version)

AK-GG

Kommentar zum Grundgesetz für die Bundesrepublik Deutschland (Reihe Alternativkommentare 1984) ("Alternative" Commentary on the Basic Law)

Akten und Protokolle

Der Parlamentarische Rat, 1948-1949: Akten und Protokolle (Kurt G. Wernicke & Hans Booms, eds.) (Collected records of the constitutional convention (Parliamentary Council))

AöR

Archiv des öffentlichen Rechts (Archive of Public Law) (periodical)

BArbGE

Entscheidungen des Bundesarbeitsgerichts (Decisions of the Federal Labor Court)

BayRS

Bereinigte Sammlung des bayrischen Landesrechts (Official report of Bavarian decisions and laws)

Bericht der VerfKomm

Bericht der Gemeinsamen Verfassungskommission (Report of the Joint Commission on the Constitution), BT/Drucksache 12/6000 (1993).

BGB

Bürgerliches Gesetzbuch (Civil Code)

BGBl

Bundesgesetzblatt (Official publication of federal session laws)

BGH

Bundesgerichtshof (Federal Court of Justice)

BVerfG

Bundesverfassungsgericht (Federal Constitutional Court)

BVerfGE	Entscheidungen des Bundesverfassungs-gerichts (Decisions of the Federal Constitutional Court)
BVerfGG	Bundesverfassungsgerichtsgesetz (Statute respecting the Federal Constitutional Court)
BVerwGE	Entscheidungen des Bundesverwaltungs-gerichts (Decisions of the Federal Administrative Court)
BWG	Bundeswahlgesetz (Federal Election Law)
DöV	Die öffentliche Verwaltung (Public Administration) (periodical)
DRiG	Deutsches Richtergesetz (Statute defining the status of German judges)
EAEC	European Atomic Energy Community
ECSC	European Coal and Steel Community
EEC	European Economic Community
EGBGB	Einführungsgesetz zum Bürgerlichen Gesetzbuch (Introductory law to the Civil Code)
Einigungsvertrag	Vertrag zwischen der Bundesrepublik Deutschland und der Deutschen Demokratischen Republik über die Herstellung der Einheit Deutschlands (Unification Treaty between West and East Germany)
The First Hundred Years	David P. Currie, The Constitution in the Supreme Court: The First Hundred Years (1985)
GG	Grundgesetz (Basic Law)
GVBl	Gesetz- und Verordnungsblatt (Register of Laws and Regulations)
Handbuch des Staatsrechts	Josef Isensee and Paul Kirchhof (eds.), Handbuch des Staatsrechts der Bundesrepublik Deutschland (Multivolume treatise on constitutional law)

Herrenchiemsee Bericht	Bericht über den Verfassungskonvent auf Herrenchiemsee vom 10. bis 23. August 1948 (Report of the conference of experts who prepared a first draft of the Basic Law)
JöR (n.F.)	Jahrbuch des öffentlichen Rechts (neue Folge) (Yearbook of Public Law (New Series))
JuS	Juristische Schulung (Legal Education) (periodical)
JZ	Juristenzeitung (Lawyers' News)
Maunz/Dürig	Theodor Maunz and Günter Dürig, Grundgesetz Kommentar (Commentary on the Basic Law)
Maunz/Schmidt-Bleibtreu	Theodor Maunz, Bruno Schmidt-Bleibtreu, Franz Klein, and Gerhard Ulsamer, Bundesverfassungsgerichtsgesetz Kommentar (Commentary on the statute respecting the Constitutional Court)
NJW	Neue Juristische Wochenschrift (New Law Journal)
OLG	Oberlandesgericht (High Court of a Land (state))
PrOVG	Entscheidungen des Preußischen Oberverwaltungsgerichts (Decisions of the Prussian Administrative High Court)
Quellen zum Staatsrecht	Ernst Rudolf Huber (ed.), Quellen zum Staatsrecht der Neuzeit (1951) (Collection of source materials on the constitutional law of postwar Germany)
RGBl	Reichsgesetzblatt (Official publication of session laws before adoption of the Basic Law)
RGZ	Entscheidungen des Reichsgerichts in Zivilsachen (Decisions of the Reich Supreme Court in Civil Matters)
Rdnr.	Randnummer (marginal number)

RV   Reichsverfassung (Constitution of the Reich)

S.   Seite (page)

The Second Century   David P. Currie, The Constitution in the Supreme Court: The Second Century (1990)

Sten. Ber.   Stenographischer Bericht des Parlamentarischen Rates (transcript of debates in the Parliamentary Council)

StGB   Strafgesetzbuch (Criminal Code)

StPO   Strafprozeßordnung (Code of Criminal Procedure)

VBl   Verordnungsblatt (Register of Regulations)

von Mangoldt/Klein/Starck   Hermann von Mangoldt, Friedrich Klein, and Christian Starck, Das Bonner Grundgesetz (3d ed. 1985) (Commentary on the Basic Law)

WRV   Weimarer Reichsverfassung (Weimar Constitution)

ZPO   Zivilprozeßordnung (Code of Civil Procedure)

1

Introduction

I. A LITTLE HISTORY

In the legal sense, Germany did not become a nation until 1871. For centuries it was a profusion of generally autocratic states, large and small, loosely associated within the framework of the so-called Holy Roman Empire of the German Nation (Heiliges Römisches Reich Deutscher Nation). The Emperors traced their rights back to Charlemagne and beyond, and many of them were actually crowned in Rome. The title, however, was largely a conceit of the Hapsburg rulers, whose seat of power lay in Austria; and centrifugal forces assured a substantial decentralization of authority, especially after the Peace of Westphalia in 1648. The Empire was thus by no means a nation in the modern sense, and it had nothing remotely resembling a modern constitution.[1]

In the first decade of the nineteenth century Napoleon overran Germany, annexing the Rheinland and dominating much of the south and west through a league of puppet states known as the Rheinbund (Confederation of the Rhine). Napoleon's victories finally put an end to the increasingly nominal Empire; the last Emperor formally abdicated in 1806.[2]

But Napoleon had bitten off more than he could swallow, and once he was driven out the old order was to a considerable extent restored. The Empire was replaced in 1815 by the Deutscher Bund (German Confederation), which despite the existence of a permanent deliberative body composed of representatives of the member states

---

[1] See, e.g., Otto Kimminich, Der Bundesstaat, 1 Handbuch des Staatsrechts 1113, Rdnr. 28; Fritz Hartung, Deutsche Verfassungsgeschichte vom 15. Jahrhundert bis zur Gegenwart 148-51 (8th ed. 1964); Dieter Grimm, Deutsche Verfassungsgeschichte 1776-1866, pp. 43-46 (1988); Gerhard Anschütz in 1 Gerhard Anschütz & Richard Thoma (eds.), Handbuch des Deutschen Staatsrechts 17, 18-21 (1930).

[2] See id. at 21-23; Golo Mann, Deutsche Geschichte des 19. und 20. Jahrhunderts 62-64 (1958) (14. Auflage der Sonderausgabe, printed 1979). German constitutional history from the time of the French Revolution is comprehensively recounted in Ernst Rudolf Huber's monumental multi-volume Deutsche Verfassungsgeschichte seit 1789, vol. 1 of which appeared in 1957. For a more manageable but still thorough account beginning with Charlemagne see Otto Kimminich, Deutsche Verfassungsgeschichte (2d ed. 1987).

(the Bundesversammlung or Bundestag) was largely a defensive alliance among autonomous autocrats – antiliberal, antinational, and
dominated once again by Austria.[3]

This alliance proved insufficient to contain the energies un-
leashed by an expanding economy and by the French Revolution.
Prussia responded by drawing most of the German-speaking world
except Austria into a new customs union ("Zollverein") that moved in
the direction of economic unity.[4] A number of individual princes responded by granting their subjects "oktroyierte" constitutions – charters imposed from above, not adopted by the people. Typically these
charters gave ordinary subjects some say in the governmental process (through representation in one house of a legislature), and some
contained elements of a Bill of Rights. Their principal purpose may
well have been to forestall more radical change and thus to
strengthen the position of the monarch; but as a practical matter they
established the principle that autocratic power was not unlimited.[5]

The Revolution of 1848, spilling over from France, intimidated the
German princes into agreeing to the election of a national assembly
("Nationalversammlung") to promulgate a constitution for the entire
nation. The resulting Paulskirchenverfassung of 1849[6] (so called after the church in Frankfurt where the Assembly met) was the
blueprint for radical change in three fundamental respects. It provided for the first time for the creation of a real German state, a federation whose central government was to have power over not only
such obvious subjects as foreign, military, and monetary affairs,
transportation, and communication, but also the law of associations
and of business generally ("das Gewerbewesen"), as well as authority
to adopt uniform laws for such arguably local matters as contracts,
torts, judicial procedure, and crime.[7] In addition, the 1849 constitution institutionalized democracy by vesting lawmaking power in a bi-
cameral legislature, one branch of which (the Reichstag) was to be
popularly elected, the other to represent the legislatures and executives of the individual states ("Länder").[8] Finally, the new constitu-

---

[3] See Mann, supra note 2, at 95-96, 118-19, 123-24; Grimm, supra note 1, at 65-68;
Kimminich, supra note 2, at 316-26; Ernst Rudolf Huber, Das Kaiserreich als
Epoche verfassungsrechtlicher Entwicklung, 1 Handbuch des Staatsrechts 35,
Rdnr. 8; Godehard Josef Ebers in 1 Anschütz & Thoma, supra note 1, at 26-31.

[4] See Kimminich. supra note 2, at 402-06; Mann, supra note 2, at 139-41.

[5] See Rainer Wahl, Die Entwicklung des deutschen Verfassungsstaates bis
1866, 1 Handbuch des Staatsrechts 3, Rdnr. 12-16; Grimm, supra note 1, at 71-75, 110-
13.

[6] Verfassung des Deutschen Reichs vom 28. März 1849, RGBl. S. 101 [hereafter
cited as RV 1849], reprinted in Rudolf Schuster (ed.), Deutsche Verfassungen (17th
ed. 1985) at 29-56.

[7] RV 1849, §§ 6-47, 59, 64. § 62 also contained a necessary and proper clause that
read, not coincidentally, very much like that found in U.S. Const., Art. I, § 8.

[8] RV 1849, §§ 85-94, 100, 102. Section 101 gave the Cabinet ("Reichsregierung") a
suspensive veto that could be overridden only by enacting the same measure in

tion took a giant step in the direction of establishing what the Germans call the Rechtsstaat (a state characterized by the rule of law) by including a Bill of Rights binding on all branches of state authority[9] and enforceable by independent judges[10] – and in so doing the National Assembly repeatedly invoked the American model.[11]

Notwithstanding its liberal pedigree, the Paulskirchenverfassung vested executive authority in a hereditary emperor ("Kaiser")[12] – not simply out of tradition or political necessity but – with a look over the shoulder at recent French misfortunes – as a check on the excesses of popular government.[13] Thus the first significant step toward German democracy was also a decisive step toward separation of powers – in contrast to nineteenth-century England, where the realities of Cabinet government had long since democratized the executive and reduced to a legal fiction the separation that Montesquieu had so admired.

The 1849 constitution was never put into force; as revolutionary fervor waned, the old order reasserted itself, and unity was postponed.[14] Prussia, the dominant power in what is now Germany, imposed a new constitution of its own from above to solidify the monarchy.[15] Even this document made significant concessions to modern liberal ideas. Legislation (including the budget) required the consent not only of King and nobles but also of a chamber elected by the people.[16] Although this popular chamber was skewed according to wealth[17] and could not legislate on its own, it could effectively prevent legislation; and that was an important step toward democ-

---

three consecutive sessions. Within the Länder the executive was also to be "responsible" to the popularly elected Parliament ("Landtag"). Id., §§ 186-87.

[9] Id., §§ 130-73.

[10] Id., §§ 125-28, 177, 181-82.

[11] See Helmut Steinberger, Bemerkungen zu einer Synthese des Einflusses ausländischer Verfassungsideen auf die Entstehung des Grundgesetzes mit deutscher verfassungsrechtlichen Traditionen, in Klaus Stern (ed.), 40 Jahre Grundgesetz: Entstehung, Bewährung und internationale Ausstrahlung 41, 66-67 (1990); Peter Schulz, Ursprünge unserer Freiheit 115-30 (1989).

[12] RV 1849, §§ 68-70. Under § 73 the Kaiser exercised his powers through ministers of his own choosing but who were described as "responsible," suggesting some degree of parliamentary and thus popular control. Under § 74 all governmental acts of the Kaiser required the countersignature of a responsible minister.

[13] See Wahl, supra note 5, Rdnr. 6, 18.

[14] The story is concisely and effectively told in Mann, supra note 2, ch. 4. See also Grimm, supra note 1, at 175-207; Günter Mick, Die Paulskirche (1988), passim.

[15] Verfassungsurkunde für den Preußischen Staat vom 31. Januar 1850, Preuß. Ges. Sammlung S. 17 [hereafter cited as Prussian Constitution of 1850], reprinted in part in Schuster, supra note 6, at 57-70. See Wahl, supra note 5, Rdnr. 21.

[16] Prussian Constitution of 1850, Art. 62, 65, 69-72.

[17] Id., Art. 71.

racy.[18] In addition, the Prussian constitution contained an extensive
Bill of Rights.[19] Most of the rights it afforded could be limited by
legislation, but that required approval by the popularly elected
Reichstag, and thus the people's rights could be restricted only with
their consent. Thus "on paper," it has been said, the Prussian
constitution "did not look so bad." In practice, however, the
"plutocratic" voting system, coupled with the general political
discouragement of the people, produced a "reactionary and
submissive" Parliament, and the proudest achievements of the
revolution – from fundamental rights to the ministerial
responsibility suggested elsewhere in the constitution[20] – "were
watered down or abolished."[21]

   As Bismarck's Prussian forces won a series of military victories
over Denmark, Austria, and France, the pressure for unification increased. The first fruit of this development was the Norddeutscher
Bund (1867),[22] which in 1871 gave way to a new Deutsches Reich that
brought together all German states except Austria. The constitution
of this new Germany ("Bismarcksche Reichsverfassung"),[23] like that
of Prussia, was reactionary in comparison to the visionary
constitution of 1849. It contained no Bill of Rights and no provision for
judicial review of legislation,[24] and the popularly elected Parliament[25] could not exercise its broad legislative powers[26] without the
approval of the largely nondemocratic states represented in the
Bundesrat (Federal Council).[27] As in Prussia, however, no legislation could be passed without parliamentary (and thus popular) consent.[28] Thus the essential principle of the 1871 constitution, it has

---

[18] During the budget crisis of the 1860s Chancellor Bismarck raised money
without legislative authorization on the theory that the Constitution did not say what
happened if Parliament rejected a proposed budget, but he afterwards sought (and
obtained) immunity for his actions. See Wahl, supra note 5, Rdnr. 23-26; Kimminich, supra note 2, at 371-76.

[19] Prussian Constitution of 1850, Art. 3-42.

[20] See id., Art. 44 (once again requiring the countersignature of a "responsible"
Minister for acts of the King).

[21] Mann, supra note 2, at 259-61.

[22] See Verfassung des Norddeutschen Bundes vom 16. April 1867, BGBl. S. 2),
reprinted in part in Schuster, supra note 6, at 95-98.

[23] Verfassung des Deutschen Reichs vom 16. April 1871, RGBl. S. 63 [hereafter
cited as RV 1871], reprinted in Schuster, supra note 6, at 71-93.

[24] See also 9 RGZ 232, 235-36 (1883) (rejecting the argument that judicial review
was implicit); Steinberger, supra note 11, at 67.

[25] RV 1871, Art. 20.

[26] The list of imperial legislative powers resembled that of the 1849 constitution.
See RV 1871, Art. 4; text at notes 6-7 supra. It was under the 1871 constitution (as
amended in 1873) that the famous Bürgerliches Gesetzbuch (BGB) was adopted – a
codification of the civil law that (with amendments) is still in force today.

[27] RV 1871, Art. 5, 6. The Kaiser, on the other hand, had no veto power.

[28] See id., Art. 5.

been said, was the division of authority among three distinct organs representing the monarchical, parliamentary, and federative principles respectively, in order to prevent the concentration of power in any single body.[29]

Bismarck's 1871 constitution survived until the country collapsed in revolution at the end of World War I. From the ashes arose the Weimar Republic, a democratic federal state with a liberal constitution promulgated by a popularly elected assembly.[30] Central legislative powers were even further extended,[31] but administrative authority remained decentralized; even federal laws were generally enforced by the Länder, subject to federal supervision.[32] As under the 1871 constitution, a general federal court ("Reichsgericht") was established to assure uniformity of interpretation;[33] for the first time in recent history a special tribunal ("Staatsgerichtshof") was set up to resolve intergovernmental disputes.[34] Nothing was said about judicial review of legislation, but in an opinion reminiscent of *Marbury v. Madison* the Reichsgericht found it implicit in the nature of a written constitution.[35] Tucked away at the end was an extensive Bill of Rights[36] – subject in many cases to limitation by simple legislation[37]

---

[29] See Huber, supra note 3, Rdnr. 33-36, 55, 63. In theory the requirement of countersignature by a "responsible" prime minister (RV 1871, Art. 17), also borrowed from the Paulskirche and Prussian constitutions (see notes 12, 20 supra), appeared to afford a measure of popular control of executive acts as well, and Professor Huber (supra, Rdnr. 45) concluded that the Parliament actually exercised considerable influence on the composition of the Cabinet. But as Golo Mann has noted, the constitution failed to specify to whom the Chancellor was responsible; and "in fact until 1918 German Chancellors were responsible to no one but the King and Emperor who appointed and discharged them." Mann, supra note 2, at 368-69.

[30] Verfassung des Deutschen Reiches vom 11. August 1919, RGBl. S. 1383 [hereafter cited as WRV], reprinted in Schuster, supra note 6, at 99-131.

[31] See Art. 6-11 WRV. For comparison of these provisions with those of the 1871 constitution see Gerhard Anschütz, Die Verfassung des Deutschen Reichs 79-80 (4th ed. 1933). The Länder, as represented in the Reichsrat, were given a veto that could be overridden by referendum or by a two-thirds vote of the Reichstag, as the President might choose. See Art. 74 WRV.

[32] Id., Art. 14-15. Exceptions were listed in Art. 78-101.

[33] Id., Art. 103.

[34] Id., Art. 108. See generally Ernst Friesenhahn, Die Staatsgerichtsbarkeit, 2 Anschütz & Thoma, supra note 1, 523-45. This authority had previously been exercised by the Bundesrat. See id. at 528-29; RV 1871, Art. 76. Cf. Articles of Confederation (U.S.), Art. IX; U.S. Const., Art. III, § 2.

[35] 111 RGZ 320 (1925). See also Ernst von Hippel in, 2 Anschütz & Thoma, supra note 1, at 556: "Only the power of judicial review can assure the supremacy of the constitution." Cf. Marbury v. Madison, 5 U.S. 137 (1803). For criticism of the Reichsgericht's decision see Anschütz, supra note 31, at 370-75.

[36] Art. 109-65 WRV.

[37] See, e.g., id., Art. 118 (guaranteeing freedom of expression "within the limits of the general laws"); Art. 152 (freedom of contract in accordance with law ("nach Maßgabe der Gesetze")); Art. 153 (requiring just compensation for takings

– including a number of specific provisions imposing affirmative
duties on the state (such as the right to education, social insurance,
and the like)[38] influenced no doubt by similar provisions in the
French constitution of 1791.[39]

Crippled by economic woes exacerbated by burdensome reparations provisions in the hated Treaty of Versailles, the Weimar Republic lasted only fourteen years. Hindsight has identified several critical weaknesses in its otherwise exemplary constitution. Unalloyed
proportional representation[40] led to the splintering of Parliament,
and efforts to require a certain threshold of popular support for representation were struck down as contrary to the requirement of equal
elections.[41] Unable to muster a stable majority, the Reichstag delegated broad powers to the executive to issue regulations having the
force of law, while others were issued without statutory authority on
the basis of the broad emergency powers granted the Reichspräsident
by the constitution itself.[42] The President could dissolve the Reichstag
virtually at will[43] and often did; seven parliaments sat in twelve
years, and for significant periods the Republic had no parliament at
all.[44] Conversely, it was generally understood that the Reichstag
could vote the Cabinet out of office without agreeing on its successor,
and this led to a power vacuum in the executive.[45] This gap too
tended to be filled by an increasingly autocratic President, who
derived additional legitimacy by virtue of his direct election by the
people.[46]

"insofar as no imperial statute otherwise provides"). For a classification of the various basic rights provisions of the Weimar Constitution on the scale of their relative
insulation from restriction by various organs of government see Anschütz, supra
note 31, at 517-19.

[38] See, e.g., WRV, Art. 119 (state support of maternity and of families with
multiple children), 143-146 (public education), 161 (social insurance), 163
(employment and unemployment insurance). See also Anschütz, supra note 31, at
514-16, 740-41, and Carl Schmitt in 2 Anschütz & Thoma, supra note 1, at 595 (both
dismissing these provisions as mere programmatic guidelines that created no individual rights). Both the Paulskirchenverfassung of 1849 (§ 155) and the Prussian
constitution of the following year (Art. 21) had required the state affirmatively to
provide for public education, as do the constitutions of many of our states. E.g., Ill.
Const., Art. X, § 1 (1970).

[39] See text at notes 109-10 infra.

[40] Art. 22 WRV.

[41] See Hans Schneider, Die Reichsverfassung vom 11. August 1919, 1 Handbuch
des Staatsrechts 85, Rdnr. 47-49.

[42] Art. 48 WRV. See Schneider, supra note 41, Rdnr. 53-56.

[43] Art. 25 WRV. The only limitation was that he not do so more than once for the
same reason.

[44] See Schneider, supra note 41, Rdnr. 51.

[45] Art. 54 WRV. See Kimminich, supra note 2, at 495-96 (noting that the Weimar
Republic had twenty governments in fourteen years).

[46] Art. 41 WRV. See also Schneider, supra note 41, Rdnr. 64.

Constitutional amendments required an extraordinary majority,[47] and most of the explicit amendments that were adopted were trivial.[48] An ominous precedent was set, however, when the constitution was amended to extend President Ebert's term for fear that the reactionary Hindenburg would succeed him[49] (as he ultimately did) – a questionable tampering with the basic rules of the game for naked partisan purposes. More troublesome still was the practice that came to be known as breaking through the constitution (Verfassungsdurchbrechung). Simply by passing an unconstitutional law by the requisite two-thirds vote, the legislature could depart from the Constitution – and often did – without explicitly amending it. The result was, among other things, that the Constitution could be altered entirely by accident and that no one could determine what the Constitution provided by reading it – a state of affairs scarcely compatible with the rule of law.[50]

The basic difficulty, however, was not so much with the constitution as with the people; as was commonly said, the Weimar Republic was a democracy without democrats. The voters never managed to agree on a stable parliamentary majority, and when things got really tough they ended up by handing the state over to its enemies.[51] The latter responded naturally enough by abrogating the major features of the constitution itself.[52] A variety of strong-arm tactics helped to produce the overwhelming majorities by which some of these measures were approved;[53] but it became a cause for regret that

---

[47] Art. 76 WRV.

[48] See Schneider, supra note 41, Rdnr. 78.

[49] See id., Rdnr. 79.

[50] See id., Rdnr. 81-82; Anschütz, supra note 31, at 401-02; Richard Thoma in 2 Anschütz & Thoma, supra note 1, at 155-57; Walter Jellinek in id. at 187-88.

[51] A majority of the members elected to the Reichstag in 1932 were either Nazis or Communists, and neither party had made a secret of its opposition to parliamentary democracy. See Schneider, supra note 41, Rdnr. 86-89.

[52] See, e.g., the so-called Reichstagsbrandverordnung (Verordnung des Reichspräsidenten zum Schutz von Volk und Staat vom 28. Februar 1933), RGBl. I S. 83, which set aside a number of Bill of Rights provisions "until further notice"; the infamous Ermächtigungsgesetz of March 24, 1933, RGBl. I S. 141, which authorized legislation by decree and without regard to most constitutional limitations; Gesetz über den Neuaufbau des Reichs vom 30. Januar 1934, RGBl. I S. 75, which subordinated the Länder governments to federal control; Deutsche Gemeindeordnung vom 30. Januar 1935, RGBl. I S. 49, which did the same for local governments. See generally Rolf Grawert, Die nationalsozialistische Herrschaft, 1 Handbuch des Staatsrechts 143; Kimminich, supra note 2, at 567-72; Mann, supra note 2, at 814-37.

[53] The vote on the Ermächtigungsgesetz, for example, was highly suspect, as Communist deputies had been excluded from the Reichstag and Länder representatives on the Reichsrat replaced by agents of the central government. The later vote on neutralization of state governments was unanimous. See Grawert, supra note 52, Rdnr. 5, 13.

there were no explicit substantive limits to the extent to which the
constitution could be amended.[54]

II. THE BASIC LAW

From the beginning the Allied Powers were determined not to repeat the mistakes of the Versailles Treaty. In the Atlantic Charter of
1941 Roosevelt and Churchill agreed to seek "a peace which will afford to all nations the means of dwelling in safety within their own
boundaries, and which will afford assurance that all the men in all
lands may live out their lives in freedom from fear and want."[55] At
the Potsdam Conference in 1945 this approach was made concrete
with regard to Germany. It was no part of Allied policy "to destroy or
to enslave the German people, but rather to give them the opportunity
to rebuild their country and their lives on a democratic and peaceful
basis."[56]

To this end the American authorities, under the leadership of
General Lucius Clay, began almost at once to reestablish the democratic process. Indigenous prime ministers were appointed for the
states of Hesse, Bavaria, und Württemberg-Baden in 1945, and municipal elections were held the following year. Democratic constitutions for the Länder were drafted by popularly elected assemblies and
ratified by the people, and elections were held at the state level. Thus
by 1947 Germans in the American occupation zone had already re-
gained a significant measure of democratic self-government.[57]

There was as yet no Federation. The French, fearful of a strong
Germany, preferred to decentralize authority as much as possible.
The Americans, well aware of the virtues of federalism, were
nonetheless convinced that a dismembered Germany would be a
recipe for trouble. "A self-supporting and self-responsible Germany,"
General Clay later wrote, "is essential to the restoration of stability,
and without a stable Europe lasting peace is impossible."[58]

In January 1948, following a six-power conference in London, the
Western Allies presented to the prime ministers of the eleven Ger-

---

[54] For conflicting views as to whether there were implicit limits on amendment
see Schneider, supra note 41, Rdnr. 83; Anschütz, supra note 31, at 402-06; Carl
Schmitt, Verfassungslehre 25-26, 102-06 (1928) (denying, i.a., that Germany could
be turned into an absolute monarchy or a soviet republic by a two-thirds vote of the
Reichstag).

[55] See Lucius Clay, Decision in Germany 11 (1950).

[56] See id. at 40.

[57] See Michael Stolleis, Besatzungsherrschaft und Wiederaufbau deutscher
Staatlichkeit 1945-1949, 1 Handbuch des Staatsrechts 173, Rdnr. 54-67; Wolfgang
Benz, Von der Besatzungsherrschaft zur Bundesrepublik 41-42 (1984). Develop-
ments in the British and French zones were less rapid. See id.; Stolleis, supra,
Rdnr. 44, 68-94.

[58] See Clay, supra note 55, at ix.

man states within their spheres of influence three documents (the so-called Frankfurt Documents) setting forth a framework for the establishment of a German federal state. The first and most important of these documents authorized the prime ministers to call a constitutional convention and laid down the conditions for eventual Allied approval:

> The constituent assembly will draft a democratic constitution which will establish for the participating states a governmental structure of federal type which is best adapted to the eventual re-establishment of German unity . . . , and which will protect the rights of the participating states, provide adequate central authority, and contain guarantees of individual rights and freedoms.[59]

Thus the Allied conditions were very general: democracy, federalism, and fundamental rights. If the new constitution was to succeed, it had to be the work of the Germans. As General Clay wrote in a related context, "reform obtained by order of the occupation authorities is not likely to be lasting, and our hope is that it can be brought about by the German people."[60] In fact the minimum requirements laid down by the Allies coincided fully with the ideas of the Germans themselves.[61]

Working from a draft produced by a conference of experts at the palace of Herrenchiemsee, a Parliamentary Council ("Parlamentarischer Rat") elected by the newly reestablished state parliaments set to work to develop a new Basic Law. The aim of the delegates was to reconstitute the free democratic system envisioned by the Weimar Constitution while correcting the weaknesses thought to have contributed to its demise.[62]

The Allies followed the proceedings of the Parliamentary Council closely, and they were not entirely satisfied with what they saw. As early as November 1948 an Allied "aide-mémoire" had attempted to narrow the delegates' discretion by spelling out the general requirements of the Frankfurt Documents in greater detail,[63] and in an

---

[59] See Ernst Rudolf Huber (ed.), 2 Quellen zum Staatsrecht der Neuzeit [hereafter cited as Quellen zum Staatsrecht] 197-200 (1951). The English text can be found in 1 Jahrbuch des öffentlichen Rechts (n.F.) [hereafter cited as 1 JöR (n.F.)] 1, 2 (1951).

[60] See Clay, supra note 55, at 302.

[61] See Parlamentarischer Rat, Stenographischer Bericht [hereafter cited as Sten. Ber.] 18 (1948) (Delegate Süsterhenn); Helmut Steinberger, 200 Jahre amerikanische Bundesverfassung 33 (1987); Schulz, supra note 11, at 217-18; Stolleis, supra note 57, Rdnr. 116; Reinhard Mußgnug, Zustandekommen des Grundgesetzes und Entstehen der Bundesrepublik Deutschland, 1 Handbuch des Staatsrechts 219, Rdnr. 71.

[62] See id., Rdnr. 42; Steinberger, supra note 11, at 53: "Weimar and the terrifying example of National Socialism stood clearly in the foreground."

[63] See 2 Quellen zum Staatsrecht at 208-09.

April 1949 memorandum the military governors objected that the
Council's developing draft departed from the prescribed criteria in
several significant respects.[64] The heart of the Allied complaint went
to the question of federalism. As General Clay put it, from the Allied
standpoint the draft provided for "too much centralization of
authority," especially with respect to legislative and financial powers.[65]

Eventually a compromise was reached that was acceptable to both
parties. As a former Justice of the Constitutional Court has written,
"Allied intervention did not succeed in branding the Basic Law with
the stain of an instrument imposed by the occupying powers."[66] At
the same time, in approving the final draft the Allies were able to say
that in their opinion it "happily combine[d] the German democratic
tradition with the concepts of republican government and of a legal
order such as the world now considers essential to the life of a free
people."[67]

Within a few days the Basic Law was ratified by the Parliaments
of more than two-thirds of the Länder, and it took effect on May 23,
1949.[68]

A. Fundamental Rights

The Basic Law begins with a Bill of Rights (Grundrechtskatalog)
in order to emphasize that human rights are not a mere appendage

---

[64] See id. at 210. These later interventions provoked no little annoyance in the
Parliamentary Council. See Sten. Ber. at 173 (Delegate Schmid), 206 (Delegate
Menzel).

[65] See Clay, supra note 55, at 421-22.

[66] See Steinberger, supra note 61, at 33.

[67] See 2 Quellen zum Staatsrecht at 217-18. The day on which the Parliamentary
Council approved the Basic Law, said Konrad Adenauer in closing the convention
over which he had presided, was "the first happy day for Germany since 1933." Sten.
Ber. at 242.

[68] Ratification by the people themselves was proposed in the Parliamentary
Council on grounds of democratic legitimacy but rejected for the same reason the
document was not entitled a "constitution": that it would give too much symbolic
significance to an act meant to be only provisory. See Sten. Ber. at 230 (Delegates
von Brentano and Schmid). Bavaria rejected the Basic Law because, as one of its
delegates had explained at the convention, it gave the Federation too much authority. Like the delegate himself, however, Bavaria at the same time pledged adherence to the new union. See Sten. Ber. at 237 (Delegate Schwalber), 272. For further
details respecting the genesis of the Basic Law see Mußgnug, supra note 61; Peter
Merkl, The Origin of the West German Republic (1963); John Ford Golay, The
Founding of the Federal Republic of Germany (1958). The proceedings of the Herrenchiemsee conference and of the convention itself are reprinted in a multi-volume collection entitled Der Parlamentarische Rat, 1948-1949: Akten und Protokolle (Kurt G. Wernicke & Hans Booms, eds.) [hereafter cited as Akten und
Protokolle]; the entire proceedings are summarized in 1 JöR (n.F.), passim.

to the Constitution[69] but (as Article 1(2) expressly provides) the very "basis of every community, of peace, and of justice throughout the world." At the head of the list, in Article 1(1), stands human dignity, the most fundamental of all rights, which as the framers were well aware had been utterly trampled by the Nazis, which the state is directed both to respect ("achten") and affirmatively to protect ("schützen"), and which Article 79(3) protects even against constitutional amendment.[70]

There follows a detailed catalog of specific rights expressly binding all legislative, executive, and judicial organs of government (Art. 1(3)), state and local as well as federal.[71] Included are life, bodily in-

---

[69] See the remarks of Delegate Carlo Schmid in the Parliamentary Council, reported in 1 JöR (n.F.) at 42.

[70] See id. at 48 (Dr. Bergsträßer), 52 (Dr. von Mangoldt). For a general introduction to the fundamental rights provisions of the Basic Law see Klaus Stern, Idee und Elemente eines Systems der Grundrechte, 5 Handbuch des Staatsrechts 45.

[71] Plainly only *German* governmental organs are bound. See, e.g., 27 BVerfGE 253, 272 (1969) (excluding damage caused by the Allies during postwar occupation); 84 BVerfGE 90, 122-23 (1991) (excluding confiscations by Soviet authorities in East Germany). See also 58 BVerfGE 1, 27-28 (1981) (no right of action under Art. 19(4) against act of international organization); 66 BVerfGE 39, 56-57 (1983) (no constitutional complaint under Art. 93(1) cl. 4a against decisions of non-German authorities respecting stationing of missiles in Germany).

Interpretive difficulties arise when German courts are asked to enforce foreign law or to extradite a criminal suspect to another country for a trial that will not meet German constitutional standards. The Constitutional Court began by declining to impose German standards on other nations in the latter case, finding the prohibition of capital punishment in Art. 102 no obstacle to extradition to a country in which the death penalty might be imposed. 18 BVerfGE 112, 116-21 (1964). Later opinions have taken a less dogmatic position, declaring extradition impermissible when it would expose the accused to inhumane punishment or to action inconsistent with some other central principle of the Basic Law. See 75 BVerfGE 1, 16-17 (1987); 60 BVerfGE 348, 354 (1982) (leaving open the question whether the death-penalty decision would still be followed); Isensee, Grundrechtsvoraussetzungen und Verfassungserwartungen an die Grundrechtsausübung, 5 Handbuch des Staatsrechts 353, Rdnr. 95-101 (questioning the more recent decisions). Moreover, the Court has made clear that a German tribunal cannot escape the limitations of the basic rights simply by applying foreign law. Everything a German court does is an exercise of German authority; whether a particular basic right is offended must be determined by interpretation of its geographical scope, regardless of which law is applied. Otherwise, said the Court, the legislature could limit the reach of the Constitution by enacting choice of law rules. 31 BVerfGE 58, 70-77 (1971). Cf. Shelley v. Kraemer, 334 U.S. 1 (1948) (holding the state responsible for discrimination when it enforced a private racial covenant). See also the provision in Art. 6 of the Introductory Law to the Civil Code [hereafter cited as EGBGB], which forbids any application of foreign law incompatible with basic rights; Wolfgang Rüfner, Grundrechtsadressaten, 5 Handbuch des Staatsrechts 525, Rdnr. 38.

Art. 1(3) says nothing about the geographical reach of the basic rights, and the issue is both controversial and unsettled. See Isensee, supra, Rdnr. 77-94 (concluding in essence that the Basic Law protects Germans everywhere but foreigners only

tegrity, and freedom from bodily restraint (Art. 2(2)); freedom of religion (Art. 4), expression (Art. 5), assembly (Art. 8), association (Art. 9), and petition (Art. 17);[72] marriage, the family, and the right to private schooling (Art. 6–7); privacy of the home (Art. 13) and of the mails (Art. 10); the right to travel (Art. 11), occupational freedom (Art. 12), and the right to property (Art. 14). Beyond these specific provisions are Article 3, which contains both general and particular guarantees of equality, and Article 2(1), which protects the right to free development of personality ("die freie Entfaltung der Persönlichkeit"), and which has been interpreted as a general guarantee of freedom of action ("allgemeine Handlungsfreiheit").[73]

---

when they are subject to German authority, which basically means within Germany). Cf. the Supreme Court's disappointing conclusion that the fourth amendment's ban on unreasonable searches and seizures – which one might have thought a basic rule of decent behavior for the United States in all its actions – was inapplicable to acts directed toward noncitizens abroad. United States v. Verdugo-Urquidez, 494 U.S. 259 (1990).

The surprisingly complicated question of the impact of basic rights on the relations between private parties ("Drittwirkung") is discussed in chapter 4 infra.

[72] See also Art. 21(1), not technically a part of the Bill of Rights, which (with an interesting exception discussed in chapter 4) guarantees the right to form political parties.

[73] Many of the fundamental rights are guaranteed to everyone ("Jeder" or "Jedermann") (e.g., Art. 2(1), (2), 5(1), 17), or without restriction as to those protected (e.g., Art. 1(1), 4(1), (2), 5(3), 6, 10, 14). See also Art. 3(1) ("alle Menschen"), 3(3) ("Niemand"). Others – primarily of a political or economic nature – are expressly limited to Germans ("alle Deutschen") (Art. 8(1), 9(1), 11(1), 12(1)). See also Art. 33(2) (eligibility for public office). The legislature remains free to extend economic rights to non-Germans, as it has generally done – and as the European Communities treaties require with respect to citizens of other member states. See generally Rüfner, Grundrechtsträger, 5 Handbuch des Staatsrechts 485, Rdnr. 3-16. There is no explicit limitation to German citizens in Art. 38(1)'s guarantee of "general, direct, free, equal, and secret elections," but in 1990 the Court went so far as to strike down an attempt to extend the right to vote to noncitizens in reliance on the general declaration of Art. 20(2) that all state authority is derived from the people ("geht vom Volke aus") – which the Court interpreted in light of the principle of self-government to mean citizens of the state to be governed. 83 BVerfGE 37 (1990). This decision was modified by constitutional amendment in 1992. Political rights need not be extended to foreigners in the United States either (see Foley v. Connelie, 435 U.S. 291, 297 (1978)), but they have been in the past, and except for explicit limitations respecting eligibility for elective federal office nothing in our Constitution seems to stand in the way.

Under Art. 19(3) the basic rights apply to domestic corporations or associations ("inländische juristische Personen") to the extent consistent with the nature of the right ("soweit sie ihrem Wesen nach auf diese anwendbar sind"). In practice this means that most rights can be exercised by associations; life, marriage, and freedom from imprisonment are among the obvious exceptions. See Rüfner, supra, Rdnr. 30-53. Though the language of Art. 19(3) is compendious enough to embrace bodies organized under public law, it is read sensibly enough not to protect one gov-

None of the enumerated freedoms is absolute. Several of them (e.g., life and bodily integrity, freedom from bodily restraint, expression, outdoor assembly, occupational freedom) are expressly made subject to restriction by or on the basis of statute, as in Weimar. The right to free development of personality is explicitly limited by the rights of others, the constitutional order, and the moral code ("die Rechte anderer, . . . die verfassungsmäßige Ordnung, [und] das Sittengesetz"). Even those liberties not expressly subject to restriction (e.g., religious, artistic, and academic freedoms) are understood to be implicitly limited by other constitutional provisions, most conspicuously by the guarantee of human dignity in Article 1(1).[74]

On the other hand, the legislature's power to limit basic rights is never unrestricted either. Under Article 19(1) and (2) a statute limiting basic rights must be a general one, must identify the rights affected, and may not impinge upon the essence ("Wesensgehalt") of the right. As we shall see, the Constitutional Court has found other important restrictions on legislative power to limit basic rights implicit in the rule of law ("Rechtsstaat") or in the basic rights themselves.

As in the United States, the fundamental rights provisions of the Basic Law perform the traditional defensive or negative function of protecting the individual against interference by the state. Thus, for example, the guarantee of occupational freedom in Article 12(1) has been held to forbid limitation of the number of drugstores[75] and the personal liberty provision of Article 2(2) to preclude commitment to a mental institution for purposes of mere "improvement."[76] The German provisions, however, have sometimes been held to have a positive dimension as well: They impose a variety of affirmative duties on the state to protect one citizen against another and even on occasion to overcome organizational, technical, or financial obstacles to the exercise of a fundamental right. In the most famous and most controversial of these decisions – recently revised without disturbing the basic conclusion that the state had an affirmative duty to protect unborn life – the Constitutional Court held that constitutional provisions protecting human dignity and the right to life *required* the leg-

---

ernmental body from another. When a public-law organization serves as a medium for the exercise of individual rights, on the other hand, it may enjoy comparable rights of its own. See id., Rdnr. 63-84 (citing churches, broadcasting companies, and institutions of higher learning); see also chapters 4, 6 infra.

[74] See, e.g., 30 BVerfGE 173, 193-96 (1971) (*Mephisto*), discussed in chapter 4 infra.

[75] 7 BVerfGE 377 (1958). See chapter 6 infra.

[76] 22 BVerfGE 180 (1967). See chapter 6 infra. See Sten. Ber. at 44 (Delegate Heuss) (noting the argument that the individual needed protection against the state because "power itself is evil").

islature in most instances to make abortion a crime.[77] Similarly, the guarantee of broadcasting freedom in Article 5(1) has been held to require the state to establish a legal framework in which all significant interests can make themselves heard,[78] and the provision of Article 7(4) protecting the right to establish private schools has been found to require in some cases that they be subsidized by the state.[79]

Affirmative constitutional rights and duties are not entirely unknown in the United States. The New Hampshire Constitution of 1784 went so far as to constitutionalize Locke's understanding of the social compact by conferring on every citizen "the right to be protected . . . in the enjoyment of his life, liberty and property;"[80] the Supreme Court once held that a state had deprived an employer of property without due process of law by denying him an injunction against picketing by striking workers.[81] Nevertheless our Constitution has been held to be basically, as Judge Posner wrote not long ago, "a charter of negative rather than positive liberties."[82] The Supreme Court reaffirmed this understanding in *DeShaney v. Winnebago County Dept. of Social*

---

[77] 39 BVerfGE 1 (1975). This decision graphically illustrates the fact that the state can commonly fulfill its affirmative duty to protect one person only by restricting the rights of another. See Dieter Grimm, Die Zukunft der Verfassung 222 (1991); Rainer Wahl & Johannes Masing, Schutz durch Eingriff, 45 Juristenzeitung [JZ] 553, 556 (1990). See also 88 BVerfGE 203 (1993). Both abortion decisions are discussed in chapter 6 infra.

[78] 12 BVerfGE 205 (1961). See chapter 4 infra.

[79] 75 BVerfGE 40 (1987). See chapter 6 infra. The affirmative right to protection against third parties and to the establishment of institutions essential to the exercise of a fundamental right is widely accepted by German commentators; the affirmative right to social services is much more controversial, not least because of the deliberate decision of the framers of the Basic Law to omit most of the affirmative social rights explicitly guaranteed by the Weimar Constitution. See Josef Isensee, Das Grundrecht als Abwehrrecht und als staatliche Schutzpflicht, 5 Handbuch des Staatsrechts 143, Rdnr. 19, 23; Erhard Denninger, Staatliche Hilfe zur Grundrechtsausübung durch Verfahren, Organisation und Finanzierung, id. at 291, Rdnr. 7, 28, 35-36; Dietrich Murswiek, Grundrechte als Teilhaberechte, soziale Grundrechte, id. at 243, Rdnr. 90-96.

[80] N.H. Const., Pt. I, Art. 12 (1784). Similar provisions appeared in contemporaneous constitutions of Massachusetts, Vermont, and Virginia. See Isensee, supra note 79, Rdnr. 25. Indeed the original purpose of the equal protection clause, confirmed by its language, was to impose on the states the conditional affirmative duty to afford blacks the same protection against acts of third parties as they afforded whites. See David Currie, Positive and Negative Constitutional Rights, 53 U. Chi. L. Rev. 864, 880-81 (1986).

[81] Truax v. Corrigan, 257 U.S. 312 (1921) (alternative holding). For other actual or arguable instances see Currie, supra note 80, passim.

[82] Jackson v. City of Joliet, 715 F.2d 1200, 1203 (7th Cir. 1983). For an impressive effort to demonstrate that history supports the opposite view see Steven J. Heyman, The First Duty of Government: Protection, Liberty and the Fourteenth Amendment, 41 Duke L.J. 507 (1991).

Services[83] in 1989, concluding flatly that the state had no constitutional duty to protect a child against violence by its own parent:

> [N]othing in the language [or history] of the Due Process Clause . . . requires the State to protect the life, liberty, and property of its citizens against invasion by private actors. . . . Its purpose was to protect the people from the State, not to ensure that the State protected them from each other. The Framers were content to leave the extent of governmental obligation in the latter area to the democratic political processes.[84]

Differences in phrasing arguably make positive constitutional rights and duties somewhat easier to justify under the German constitution than under our own. Freedom of broadcasting, for example, is simply "guaranteed [wird gewährleistet]," not merely protected against official abridgement; Article 1(1), as noted above, expressly requires the state to "protect" human dignity.[85] Such textual handholds, however, have played relatively little visible part in the decisions.[86] The Constitutional Court is as likely to employ the teleological argument that the rights guaranteed cannot be effectively exer-

---

[83] 489 U.S. 189 (1989).

[84] Id. at 195-96. See also Harris v. McRae, 448 U.S. 297, 316 (1980) (concluding that "although government may not place obstacles in the path of a woman's exercise of her freedom" to have an abortion in many cases, "it need not remove those not of its own creation" by providing a subsidy for the poor). See W. Cole Durham, General Assessment of the Basic Law – An American View, in Paul Kirchhof & Donald P. Kommers (eds.), Germany and its Basic Law 37, 45 (1993): "The German approach is fundamentally more sympathetic to a conception in which the state plays a role in facilitating the actualization of freedom. Rather than being the key power that needs to be constrained if liberty is to be preserved, the state is seen as the vehicle for achieving freedom."

[85] Contrast U.S. Const., Amdt. 14: "No state shall . . . deprive any person of life, liberty, or property without due process of law."

[86] See Isensee, supra note 79, Rdnr. 80. Examples include the two *Abortion* cases, supra note 77, and the famous *Mephisto* decision, 30 BVerfGE 173, 194 (1971), where in upholding an injunction against defamation of a deceased actor the Constitutional Court paraphrased Art. 1(1)'s requirement that the state affirmatively "protect" human dignity. In its first decision on the subject the Constitutional Court had interpreted Art. 1(1) to impose a duty on the state to protect human dignity only from third parties, not from objective want. 1 BVerfGE 97, 104 (1951). Later decisions, as noted, have occasionally enunciated affirmative duties of "social" protection as well, but without invoking the explicit terms of Art. 1(1). See also Peter Häberle, Die Menschenwürde als Grundlage der staatlichen Gemeinschaft, 1 Handbuch des Staatsrechts 815, Rdnr. 77 (stating the common contemporary understanding that Art. 1(1) requires the state to guarantee everyone the minimum conditions necessary for survival ("Existenzminimum")).

cised without affirmative state assistance[87] or the general principle
(developed in an early opinion respecting freedom of expression)[88]
that the Bill of Rights embodies an objective order of values ("eine objektive Wertordnung") that pervades all areas of the law[89] – reinforced on occasion, in cases involving social benefits, by the social
state principle discussed in the next section.[90] Finally, the difference
in interpretation may be explained in part by the different social and
political climates in which the German and American constitutions
were adopted: Notwithstanding their many virtues, James Madison
and his friends could hardly be described as modern social
democrats.[91]

The practical difference between the two countries in regard to
positive rights and duties should not be exaggerated. On the one
hand, the unlikelihood that such affirmative services as welfare
payments and criminal laws will be abandoned may make our traditional equal protection principle the practical equivalent in many
cases of an absolute duty to provide them.[92] On the other hand, the
German court has exercised a considerable degree of restraint in determining the scope of such affirmative duties as it has discovered in
the Basic Law. Only in rare cases has that court so far found the government's affirmative action wanting. In other instances, while
enunciating a general governmental duty, it has emphasized the
broad discretion of the political branches in determining, for example, how much money to invest in educational facilities, or how best
to protect against terrorism, or how to resolve competing interests in
environmental disputes.[93] The extent of the state's affirmative obli-

---

[87] See, e.g., the groundbreaking First Television Case, 12 BVerfGE 205, 261
(1961), discussed in chapter 4 infra. For a concise and powerful statement of this
argument see Grimm, supra note 77, at 227-34.

[88] See 7 BVerfGE 198, 203-07 (1958) (*Lüth*), discussed in chapter 4 infra.

[89] See 35 BVerfGE 79, 112-14 (1973) (*Gruppenuniversität*), discussed in chapter 4
infra. For a general defense of the connection between the "objective order of values" and the duty to protect against third parties see Erhard Denninger in 1 AK-GG,
vor Art. 1, Rdnr. 33.

[90] See also Isensee, supra note 79, Rdnr. 32-36, 83-85 (justifying the duty to protect
one citizen against another on the basis of the implicit social compact). Accord
Eckart Klein, Grundrechtliche Schutzpflicht des Staates, 1989 NJW 1633, 1635-36.

[91] See also Grimm, supra note 77, at 224-27 (arguing that in Europe the *original*
conception of fundamental rights – though often lost sight of in the intervening
years – was an objective one that imposed affirmative obligations on the state).

[92] See Currie, supra note 80, 53 U. Chi. L. Rev. at 880-82.

[93] See chapter 6 infra. See also Isensee, supra note 79, Rdnr. 160-67 (adding that
the rule of law ordinarily requires that decisions as to how to protect one citizen
against another be made by the legislature); Konrad Hesse, Grundzüge des Verfassungsrechts der Bundesrepublik Deutschland (18th ed. 1991), Rdnr. 289 (denying,
even under the decisions just noted, that the Basic Law recognizes *any* fundamental rights that can properly be characterized as participatory rights
("Teilhaberechte") in the sense of individual rights to government benefits independent of those provided by existing law).

gations in practice seems to depend less upon the reigning theory than upon the aggressiveness or deference with which it is applied.

Indeed there are observers who suggest that, practically speaking, affirmative constitutional rights are inherently unlikely ever to be much more than pious exhortations to the political branches of government. In contrast to traditional defensive rights, it is argued, rights to participate in the provision of government services have such imprecise boundaries that their implementation is not to be expected without legislative and executive definition: "For this reason social rights such as the right to protection of the family, motherhood, and youth cannot be captured by an enforceable, abstract norm."[94] This conclusion was backed up by the observation that (as of 1954), despite the worldwide proliferation of constitutional provisions explicitly imposing affirmative social duties, "[n]o constitution recognizing the rule of law has yet actually succeeded in practice" in transcending the classical negative understanding of fundamental rights.[95]

---

[94] Ernst Forsthoff, Begriff und Wesen des sozialen Rechtsstaates, 12 Veröffentlichungen der Vereinigung der Deutschen Staatsrechtslehrer 8, 11-12, 20 (1954). See also Murswiek, supra note 79, Rdnr. 44, 49-56, 61-65 (adding that explicit rights to social services in the Weimar Constitution had proved largely ineffective). But see Grimm, supra note 77, at 238-40 (arguing that the courts should determine and enforce the minimum level of government support necessary to make each basic right a reality).

[95] Forsthoff, supra note 94, at 12, 33. See also Ill. Const., Art. XI, § 2 (1970), which bravely assures every person a "right to a healthful environment" enforceable against "any party, governmental or private," but which has had no perceptible impact on official decisions. Similar provisions have begun to appear in the constitutions of individual German Länder. See, e.g., Landesverfassung der Freien Hansestadt Bremen vom 21. Oktober 1947, SaBremR 100-a-1, geändert durch Gesetz vom 8.9.1987, GBl. S. 233, Art. 11a; Verfassung des Saarlandes vom 15. Dezember 1947, BS Saar 100-1, in der Fassung des Gesetzes Nr. 1183 vom 25.1.1985 (ABl. S. 106), Art. 59a. The Italian Corte Costituzionale, in contrast, has taken some modest steps toward judicial enforcement of affirmative social rights. See Luis María Díez-Picazo & Marie-Claire Ponthoreau, The Constitutional Protection of Social Rights: Some Comparative Remarks, European University Institute Working Paper Law No. 91/20, pp. 10-13.

In contrast to the Weimar Constitution, the Basic Law – like the U.S. Constitution – imposes few affirmative obligations on individuals. Examples include the duty of parents to care for and bring up their children (Art. 6(2)), compulsory military or alternative service for men (Art. 12a)), the social obligations of property (Art. 14(2)), discussed in chapter 6 infra), and the civil servant's obligation of fidelity (Art. 33(4), (5)). See generally Hasso Hoffmann, Grundpflichten und Grundrechte, 5 Handbuch des Staatsrechts 321, passim (noting (Rdnr. 42) that most constitutional duties of the individual, like those of the state, can be effectuated only through legislation). Contrast Mass. Const. of 1780, pt. I, Art. 10: "Each individual . . . . is obliged . . . to contribute his share to the expence of this protection; to give his personal service, or an equivalent, when necessary."

B. Basic Structural Principles

Article 20 of the Basic Law enumerates a series of fundamental principles that identify the essential features of the German state and that, like the human dignity provision of Article 1, are protected even against constitutional amendment by Article 79(3). "The Federal Republic of Germany," Article 20(1) declares, "is a democratic and social federal state [ein demokratischer und sozialer Bundesstaat]." The paragraphs that follow specify that all public authority is derived from the people; that it shall be exercised by elections and voting and through the agency of particular ("besondere") legislative, executive, and judicial organs; that the legislature is bound by the constitutional order and the other branches by "Gesetz und Recht" – an ambiguous formulation that can be interpreted to mean either "statute and law" or "law and justice," which is by no means the same thing.

Article 28(1) expressly applies the essence of these principles to the constituent states (Länder), and in two respects it is more explicit: "The constitutional order in the Länder must conform to the principles of a republican, democratic, and social state characterized by the rule of law [des republikanischen, demokratischen und sozialen Rechtsstaates]." The republican principle is suggested by the nation's very name, which is repeated in Article 20(1), and implied by the provision for elected legislative bodies. Some aspects of the rule of law are explicitly mentioned in later paragraphs of the same Article, and the general principle – which Article 28(1) seems to presuppose – is often said to be implicit in Article 20 as a whole.[96]

Federalism, separation of powers, and republican democracy will be discussed in detail in later chapters, but they are familiar concepts that require no initial explanation to the Anglo-American reader. Two of the basic principles found in Articles 20 and 28, however, deserve a brief explication at this point: the rule of law ("Rechtsstaat") and the social state ("Sozialstaat").

1. The Rechtsstaat. In the Anglo-American sense the rule of law is likely to be understood to mean that public officials are bound by law. Article 20(3) expressly embodies this principle. But the German concept of the Rechtsstaat – a state in which the rule of law prevails

---

[96] See, e.g., Roman Herzog in 2 Maunz/Dürig, Art. 20, pt. VII, Rdnr. 30-42. The significance of finding the general Rechtsstaat principle implicit in Art. 20 is that Art. 79(3) protects "the principles laid down in Article . . . 20" even against constitutional amendment. The Constitutional Court once denied in an important opinion that Art. 20 was the locus of the general Rechtsstaat principle (30 BVerfGE 1, 24-25 (1970)), but the idea survives. See Herzog, supra, Rdnr. 35; Eberhard Schmidt-Aßmann, Der Rechtsstaat, 1 Handbuch des Staatsrechts 987, Rdnr. 90. For detailed criticism of the traditional learning on this subject see Philip Kunig, Das Rechtsstaatsprinzip 49-110 (1986).

– has come to embrace a great deal more.[97] Even in the absence of express provisions such as those applicable to bodily restraint, condemnation of property, and occupational freedom, the Rechtsstaat principle generally permits liberty to be restricted only in accordance with statute, and it imposes limits on delegation of policymaking authority going far beyond those made explicit elsewhere in the Basic Law.[98] It requires fair warning[99] and fair procedure[100] and imposes meaningful limitations on retroactivity.[101] It has been said to embody the essence of judicial review of administrative action guaranteed by Article 19(4) and even (by emphasizing the alternative meaning of "Recht" as justice rather than law) substantive provisions of the Bill of Rights.[102] Finally, it has been held to embrace a pervasive

---

[97] The origins, development, and contours of the Rechtsstaat principle are traced by Herzog in 2 Maunz/Dürig, Art. 20, pt. VII. See also Schmidt-Aßmann, supra note 96, passim; Leonard Krieger, The German Idea of Freedom 252-61 (1957); Kunig, supra note 96, passim.

[98] See chapter 3 infra.

[99] See 5 BVerfGE 25, 31-34 (1956). Cf. United States v. Cohen Grocery Co., 255 U.S. 81 (1921). See Herzog in 2 Maunz/Dürig, Art. 20, pt. VII, Rdnr. 63 (observing that the need for general clauses limits application of this principle to exceptional cases).

[100] E.g., 26 BVerfGE 66, 71-72 (1969) (permitting the victim to intervene in a criminal proceeding); 38 BVerfGE 105, 111-18 (1974) (affirming a witness's right to counsel under certain circumstances); 57 BVerfGE 117, 120-21 (1981) (relying on the rule of law in conjunction with the explicit guarantee of a judicial hearing in Art. 103(1) to hold that a filing deadline was satisfied when the document arrived at court); 64 BVerfGE 135, 145-57 (1983) (discussing to what extent proceedings must be translated for a defendant who cannot communicate in German); 65 BVerfGE 171, 174-78 (1983) (forbidding appellate argument in the absence of defense counsel).

[101] See, e.g., 13 BVerfGE 206, 212-14 (1961) (invalidating a law increasing the tax on land sales previously made); 21 BVerfGE 173, 182-84 (1967) (holding that a prohibition on combining tax counseling with certain other activities could not be applied immediately to persons who had been engaged in both before the statute was passed). Retroactivity in the first of these cases was in the Court's terms genuine ("echt"), since the law attached consequences to past acts themselves. In the second it was spurious ("unecht"), since the law merely disappointed expectations by diminishing the value produced by past actions. Not surprisingly, the Court has been considerably more lenient in passing upon spurious than upon genuine retroactivity. See, e.g., 19 BVerfGE 119, 127-28 (1965) (permitting taxation of securities that had been tax-exempt when purchased). Also not surprisingly, there have been difficulties in distinguishing genuine from spurious retroactivity. E.g., 72 BVerfGE 175, 196-200 (1986) (upholding an increase in interest payable in the future on preexisting loans). For criticism of the distinction as engendering more confusion than clarity see 48 BVerfGE 1, 23 (1978) (Steinberger, J., dissenting); Herzog in 2 Maunz/Dürig, Art. 20, pt. VII, Rdnr. 65-70; for the perception of increased clarity in more recent decisions see Schmidt-Aßmann, supra note 96, Rdnr. 86. Retroactive *criminal* punishment is expressly prohibited by Art. 103(2).

[102] See Herzog in 2 Maunz/Dürig, Art. 20, pt. VII, Rdnr. 23, 27, 40; Hesse, supra note 93, Rdnr. 202-05; Wahl, supra note 5, Rdnr. 19. For the concept of justice

principle of proportionality ("Verhältnismäßigkeit"), which had its origins in a provision of the general statutes commissioned by Frederick the Great that limited the discretion of the administration in executing its police powers[103] and which has come to represent a major restriction on legislative as well as executive authority to limit fundamental rights.

The basic idea behind the proportionality principle is that, even when the legislature is specifically authorized to restrict basic rights, the restriction must be reasonable.[104] The decisions have broken down this general principle into three elements reminiscent of the American tests both for substantive due process and for the necessity and propriety of federal legislation: The limitation must be adapted ("geeignet") to the attainment of a legitimate purpose; it must be necessary ("erforderlich") to that end; and the burden it imposes must not be excessive ("unzumutbar").[105] Necessity for this purpose is narrowly defined: As in certain instances of strict scrutiny in the United States, the legislature must select the least burdensome means of achieving its goal.[106] The upshot is intensive scrutiny of the reasonableness of measures impinging upon the interests protected by the Bill of Rights, even when the legislature is expressly authorized to enact them.

We shall have more than one occasion to return to the Rechtsstaat principle in the chapters that follow.

2. *The Sozialstaat.* Though no single principle of the U.S. Constitution embraces all aspects of the Rechtsstaat, many of its compo-

---

("Gerechtigkeit") as an element of the rule of law see 28 BVerfGE 264, 277-79 (1970) (discussing double jeopardy).

[103] Allgemeines Landrecht für die Preußischen Staaten, pt. II, tit. 17, § 10 (making it the duty of the administration (Polizei) to take *necessary* measures ("[d]ie nöthigen Anstalten") to preserve the public peace, order, and security). The process by which this principle found its way into decisions interpreting the Basic Law is adumbrated in chapter 6 infra.

[104] See 30 BVerfGE 1, 20 (1970); Denninger in 1 AK-GG, vor Art. (1), Rdnr. 12.

[105] See 78 BVerfGE 232, 245-47 (1988); Herzog in 2 Maunz/Dürig, Art. 20, pt. VII, Rdnr. 71-76. The third element is sometimes called proportionality in the narrow sense ("Verhältnismäßigkeit im engeren Sinne"); the entire principle is often referred to as the "Übermaßverbot," or prohibition of excessively intrusive means. Cf. McCulloch v. Maryland, 17 U.S. 316, 421 (1819) (necessary and proper clause); Mugler v. Kansas, 123 U.S. 623, 661-62 (1887) (due process) (both stressing the legitimacy of the end and the appropriateness of the means).

[106] E.g., 78 BVerfGE 232, 245 (1988); see Herzog in 2 Maunz/Dürig, Art. 20, pt. VII, Rdnr. 75 ("Prinzip der Wahl des mildesten Mittels"). Cf. Shelton v. Tucker, 364 U.S. 479, 488 (1960) (freedom of association); Dean Milk Co. v. Madison, 340 U.S. 349, 354 (1951) (discrimination against interstate commerce). This general formulation does not exclude varying levels of scrutiny according to the seriousness and intimacy of the intrusion. See Denninger in 1 AK-GG, vor Art. 1, Rdnr. 12, and chapter 6 infra, discussing the *Pharmacy* case.

nents have counterparts of one sort or another in American constitutional law. The same can hardly be said of the Sozialstaat principle, also anchored in Articles 20 and 28 of the Basic Law, which essentially commits the Federal Republic to the social welfare state.

The Sozialstaat provisions, which had no precise antecedents in earlier German constitutions, reflect the growing conviction – expressed by Montesquieu as early as 1748 – that it was not enough for the state to protect citizens from one another and to protect the individual from the state; the state should also be required affirmatively to promote the public weal.[107] The preamble to our Constitution recognizes this goal,[108] but the text leaves its implementation to legislative discretion: Congress is authorized but not required to tax and accordingly to spend in order "to provide for . . . the general welfare."[109] The French Constitution of 1791 went further, imposing a duty on the state to establish not only a system of free public education (as do many of our state constitutions) but also a system of public assistance "to bring up abandoned children, relieve poor invalids, and furnish work to the able-bodied poor who cannot obtain it for themselves."[110] The Weimar Constitution, as already noted, contained a number of similar provisions, as do the postwar constitutions of a number of individual Länder.[111]

---

107 2 Baron de Montesquieu, Spirit of the Laws, bk. XXIII, ch. XXVI, at 514 (Thomas Nugent ed. 1900) (first published in 1748) (arguing that the state "owes to every citizen a certain subsistence, a proper nourishment, convenient clothing, and a kind of life not incompatible with health"). See generally Hans F. Zacher, Das soziale Staatsziel, 1 Handbuch des Staatsrechts 1045.

108 See U.S. Const., Preamble: "In order . . . to promote the general welfare . . . ."

109 U.S. Const., Art. I, § 8.

110 Constitution tit. Ier. (France 1791). "Social rights," however, "are not conceived as genuine subjective rights in France" today; "[t]hey are programmatic principles whose implementation and concrete scope depends on the legislature." Díez-Picazo & Ponthoreau, supra note 95, at 16.

111 See text at notes 37-38 supra. See also, i.a., Landesverfassung der Freien Hansestadt Bremen vom 21. Oktober 1947, SaBremR 100-a-1, Art. 8 (right to work), 14 (housing), 49 (unemployment assistance), 57 (social insurance), 58 (assistance for those unable to work); Verfassung des Landes Brandenburg vom 20. August 1992, GV. BB. I, S. 122, 298, Art. 29 (education), 45 (social insurance and public assistance), 47 (housing), 48 (employment). Cf. Costituzione della Repubblica Italiana (1948), Art. 3, 32, 34, 38. The Spanish Constitution of 1978 (Art. 39-52) follows the Italian model. Art. 53(3) adds, however, that while the social and economic principles laid down in these provisions shall be taken into account by all three branches of government, "they can be claimed before the courts only in accordance with legislation passed for their implementation." See Díez-Picazo & Ponthoreau, supra note 95, at 21-22. Cf. Verfassung des Landes Sachsen-Anhalt vom 16. Juli 1992, GVBl S 600, Art. 34-40, containing a list of official goals ("Staatsziele") ranging from de facto gender equality to housing and full employment, which the state must strive within its ability to attain ("nach Kraften anzustreben") and toward

The Parliamentary Council made the deliberate decision not to follow this route.[112] The Basic Law contains only one clear example of a specific right to government social services: Article 6(4)'s provision that "every mother has a claim to the protection and support of the community."[113] But the underlying principle of social welfare was by no means abandoned; it was generalized by the new formulation declaring Germany and its Länder bound to the principles of the social state.

Unlike the Rechtsstaat principle, the Sozialstaat provisions have never yet been held, standing alone, to invalidate governmental action or inaction.[114] But this does not mean they have been a dead letter. In the first place, they are understood to impose a duty on legislators and administrators affirmatively to promote the public welfare.[115] Although it is generally agreed that considerations of democracy and separation of powers preclude judicial efforts to define and enforce this duty in ordinary cases,[116] public servants may nevertheless take it seriously. For as Madison emphasized in presenting the Bill of Rights to Congress in 1789, written constitutional provisions appeal both to their consciences and to their con-

---

which its actions are to be directed ("sein Handeln danach auszurichten"). Id., Art. 3.

[112] See Sten. Ber. at 44 (Delegate Heuss), 172 (Delegate Schmid), 215 (Delegate Wessel) (regretting the decision); 1 JöR (n.F.) at 43-44; Murswiek, supra note 79, Rdnr. 46-47. See also id., Rdnr. 90-96 (taking this history as a convincing argument against interpreting basic rights provisions purely defensive on their face to confer the right to affirmative social services). Accord Wolfgang Martens, Grundrechte im Leistungsstaat, in 30 Veröffentlichungen der Vereinigung der Deutschen Staatsrechtslehrer 7, 29-32 (1972).

[113] Cf. Art. 119 WRV. See also Art. 6(5) of the Basic Law [hereafter often cited as GG], which affirmatively requires the enactment of legislation to assure practical equality of opportunity for illegitimate children. These provisions are discussed in chapter 6 infra.

[114] See, e.g., 1 BVerfGE 91, 105 (1951): "Only the legislature can do what is essential to the realization of the social welfare state." Only if the lawmakers "arbitrarily neglected" to perform their obligation, the Court added, might the individual arguably be heard to complain. Id.

[115] See id.; 22 BVerfGE 180, 204 (1967); 27 BVerfGE 253, 283 (1969) (duty to spread losses inflicted by Allied forces during occupation after World War II); 40 BVerfGE 121, 133 (1975) (duty to assure adequate care of the handicapped who cannot provide for themselves and to seek to integrate them into society). See also Hesse, supra note 93, Rdnr. 213; Zacher, supra note 107, Rdnr. 1, 106; Roman Herzog in 2 Maunz/Dürig, Art. 20, pt. VIII, Rdnr. 6; Michael Kittner in 1 AK-GG, Art. 20, Abs. 1-3, pt. IV, Rdnr. 1, 47; Denninger in 1 AK-GG, vor Art. 1, Rdnr. 23, and authorities cited.

[116] See, e.g., 22 BVerfGE at 204; 27 BVerfGE at 283; Hesse, supra note 93, Rdnr. 289; Herzog in 2 Maunz/Dürig, Art. 20, pt. VIII, Rdnr. 28, 49-51; Denninger, supra note 79, Rdnr. 43.

stituents.[117] While history and human nature make it plain that not every public official invariably obeys the law, they also caution us against the equally implausible conclusion that persons in public positions do nothing but violate their trust. Even independent judges have been known on occasion to subordinate their personal preferences to what they perceived to be the law,[118] and as Madison suggested the ballot box provides an additional check against abuses of legislative or executive authority.

Moreover, from the very beginning, the Sozialstaat principle has exerted a powerful influence on the interpretation and application of the laws.[119] Within a month after denying that an individual could sue to enforce rights created by the social state clause itself, the Court invoked the same provision in drawing upon the Code of Civil Procedure to fill a gap in the statutes by providing for court-appointed counsel in controversies before the Constitutional Court: To permit poverty to hinder a party in asserting his rights would contradict the principle of a democratic and social state characterized by the rule of law.[120] Six years later the Court relied upon the Sozialstaat principle to help sustain a price control statute against the argument that it infringed the freedom of contract guaranteed by Article 2(1): Contractual freedom itself, said the Court, was defined and limited by the social state principle.[121] Later decisions have relied upon the Sozialstaat provisions to heighten the level of scrutiny with respect to inequalities in eligibility for aid to the blind,[122] to reinforce the conclusion that human dignity required restrictive interpretation of a law providing for life imprisonment,[123] and to strengthen the argument that positive or participatory rights ("Teilhaberechte") may be

---

[117] 1 Annals of Congress 455. See also Letter of James Madison to Thomas Jefferson, Oct. 17, 1788, in J. Boyd., ed., 14 Papers of Thomas Jefferson 16, 20 (1958).

[118] See, e.g., West Virginia Board of Education v. Barnette, 319 U.S. 624, 646-47 (1943) (Frankfurter, J., dissenting); Ogden v. Saunders, 25 U.S. 213, 264 (1827) (opinion of Washington, J.) (as explained in The First Hundred Years at 151).

[119] See Zacher, supra note 107, Rdnr. 107; Grimm, supra note 77, at 323; Herzog in 2 Maunz/Dürig, Art. 20, pt. VIII, Rdnr. 27. Cf. the functions of social rights explicitly delineated in the Spanish Constitution, supra note 111.

[120] 1 BVerfGE 109, 111 (1952).

[121] 8 BVerfGE 274, 329 (1958). Similar cases are legion. See, e.g., 21 BVerfGE 245, 251 (1967) (state monopoly of employment agency business); 44 BVerfGE 70, 89 (1977) (compulsory health insurance for farmers). See generally Kittner in 1 AK-GG, Art. 20, Abs. 1-3, pt. IV, Rdnr. 56. The idea behind these decisions is codified in part by the provisions in Art. 14(2) that "property imposes duties" and that its use "shall also serve the public weal." See chapter 6 infra. This is not to say that the social state principle automatically trumps any defensive right with which it comes into conflict; there must be a balancing of competing constitutional values. See Herzog in 2 Maunz/Dürig, Art. 20, pt. VIII, Rdnr. 41-45.

[122] See 37 BVerfGE 154, 164-65 (1974).

[123] 45 BVerfGE 187, 228-29 (1977).

found in constitutional provisions phrased simply as defenses against the state.[124]

Commentators have suggested additional ways in which the Sozialstaat principle might possibly affect judicial decisions: as a prohibition of affirmatively "unsocial" state actions[125] and as a barrier to the dismantling of social programs already in force:[126] Even if as an original matter a court cannot legitimately determine the appropriate level of expenditure for old-age insurance, it might conceivably be able to say that once such a program is enacted it may not be significantly reduced or repealed.[127]

---

[124] See 33 BVerfGE 303, 331-32 (1972) (*Numerus Clausus*); 75 BVerfGE 40, 65 (1987) (private schools), both discussed in chapter 6 infra. See also Denninger in 1 AK-GG, vor Art. 1, Rdnr. 23-25; Hans-Peter Schneider, Eigenart und Funktionen der Grundrechte im demokratischen Verfassungsstaat, in Joachim Perels, Grundrechte als Fundament der Demokratie 11, 33 (1979).

[125] See Herzog in 2 Maunz/Dürig, Art. 20, pt. VIII, Rdnr. 26, and authorities cited; Peter Badura, Arten der Verfassungsrechtssätze, 7 Handbuch des Staatsrechts 33, Rdnr. 15-16 (arguing that any legal norm inconsistent with a declaration of state goals ("Staatszielbestimmung") such as the Sozialstaat clauses is unconstitutional).

[126] See Kittner in 1 AK-GG, Art. 20, Abs. 1-3, pt. IV, Rdnr. 29, 79 (noting that to some extent this result has already been achieved by finding vested property rights in existing benefit programs; see chapter 6 infra). Cf. the similar argument made with respect to the repeal of laws fulfilling the state's duty to protect one citizen against another in Isensee, supra note 79, Rdnr. 160. For the suggestion that social rights may already perform such a ratchet function in both France and Spain see Díez-Picazo & Ponthoreau, supra note 95, at 17, 22 (citing the Secretary-General of the Conseil Constitutionnel for the view that "the most positive aspect of the constitutional case-law in this field" is that "it prevents any attempt to go back as far as social conquests are concerned").

[127] Obviously not every reduction of an existing benefit program offends the social state principle. See, e.g., 36 BVerfGE 73, 84 (1973) (making this point explicitly); 24 BVerfGE 220, 235 (1968) (upholding a cutback of social insurance against a Sozialstaat objection with the observation that the persons excluded from coverage were generally able to take care of themselves); 82 BVerfGE 60, 80 (1990) (upholding a reduction of payments to relatively well-to-do families with children because the recipients were not left without "the minimal requirements for an existence consistent with human dignity"); 14 BVerfGE 288, 304-05 (noting the legislature's latitude for judgment even with respect to those in need of protection). For a more sweeping rejection of the ratchet theory see Christian Starck, Die Verfassungsauslegung, 7 Handbuch des Staatsrechts 189, Rdnr. 55: "A general prohibition of retrogression [Rückschrittsverbot] cannot be derived from the Sozialstaat principle."

The entire subject of programmatic constitutional provisions was thoroughly canvassed not so long ago by a blue-ribbon panel of academic experts of various political persuasions appointed by the federal Ministers of Interior and Justice. The upshot was a unanimous recommendation for the adoption of objective provisions analogous to the Sozialstaat clauses making it the duty of the state to promote employment and culture and to protect the environment, in the hope of stimulating additional action to those ends. Subjective rights to employment, culture, or a clean environment, in contrast, were unanimously rejected as either illusory or unduly

C. The Allocation of Powers

Two fundamental principles of German federalism should have a familiar ring to anyone from the United States: All powers not granted to the central government (Bund) by the Basic Law are reserved to the states (Länder), and in case of conflict federal law prevails.[128] In other respects, however, the federal structures of the two countries differ greatly.

Most lawmaking authority in Germany is federal, as has been true since 1871.[129] Most federal laws, however, are still carried out by the Länder,[130] which also retain a significant voice in the determination of federal legislative as well as executive policy.[131] Separate financial provisions sharply restrict state taxing authority, assure the Länder a substantial share of federal revenues, and require the wealthier states to help support the poorer.[132] These provisions for financial equalization ("Finanzausgleich") promise to provide a major avenue for renewal of the states that once were East Germany.

Judicial authority too is distributed differently than in the United States. Instead of separate federal and state systems crowned by a single Supreme Court with jurisdiction essentially limited to federal matters, the Basic Law provides principally for state trial courts whose decisions are subject to review by federal courts at the highest level – in rare cases on questions of state as well as federal law.[133]

Both state and federal courts are organized on subject-matter lines; there are specialized courts for taxation, social security, and labor, as well as more general tribunals for administrative and civil or criminal law.[134] Judicial review of administrative invasion of alleged rights is constitutionally guaranteed,[135] as are the existence, independence, and jurisdiction of a Federal Constitutional Court (Bundesverfassungsgericht) with broad authority to resolve

---

restrictive of the democratic process, or both. See Staatszielbestimmungen/Gesetzgebungsaufträge (Bericht der Sachverständigenkommission) 13-15, 48-49, 67, 82, 84, 90-92, 100-07, 130-32 (1983).

[128] Art. 30, 31 GG. Cf. U.S. Const., Art. VI & amend. X.

[129] See Art. 70-75 GG. Cf. notes 26, 31 supra and accompanying text.

[130] Art. 83-90 GG. Cf. text at notes 31-32 supra.

[131] See, e.g., Art. 77, 80(2), 84(1), (2). Cf. notes 27, 31 supra, and accompanying text.

[132] Art. 104a-15 GG. These provisions were substantially revised in 1969. See Act of May 12, 1969, 1 BGBl 359.

[133] Art. 92, 95-96 GG. See the discussion of this latter point in chapter 3 infra.

[134] Art. 95 GG.

[135] Art. 19(4) GG.

constitutional questions without regard to many of the "case or controversy" limitations of our Article III.[136]

Federal legislative power is entrusted to the popularly elected Bundestag,[137] whose enactments are subject to suspensive veto by the Bundesrat, a separate body composed of members of the executive branch of the Länder governments,[138] and in many cases conditioned upon its assent.[139] Constitutional amendments, which must be explicit, require a two-thirds vote of each body; in several critical respects, as we have seen, the Constitution may not be amended at all.[140]

Germany has a President ("Bundespräsident"), but his functions are largely ceremonial.[141] Real executive discretion at the federal level is lodged in the Bundesregierung (Cabinet or "Government" in the British sense), headed by a Chancellor ("Bundeskanzler") whom the Bundestag as a practical matter elects but can remove only if it simultaneously names his successor. Other members of the Cabinet, whom the Chancellor appoints, have considerable autonomy to run their own ministries within general principles ("Richtlinien") laid down by the Chancellor.[142] The Basic Law establishes independent agencies to supervise the currency and to audit public accounts;[143] otherwise the general understanding is that significant political authority must be subject to ministerial and thus to democratic parliamentary control.[144] On the other hand, as already noted, most actual enforcement of federal law is done by state rather than federal officials; federalism makes up to a significant extent for the incomplete separation of legislative and executive powers inherent in a parliamentary system.

---

[136] Art. 93-94, 97, 100 GG. See also text at notes 145-63 infra.

[137] Art. 38(1), 77(1) GG.

[138] Art. 51, 77 GG.

[139] E.g., Art. 84(1) GG.

[140] Art. 79 (1) - (3) GG. Though Art. 79(3) does not expressly say so, it has been argued that it cannot itself be amended; for otherwise it could not effectively serve its purpose. See Hesse, supra note 93, Rdnr. 707; Peter Badura, Verfassungsänderung, Verfassungswandel, Verfassungsgewohnheitsrecht, 7 Handbuch des Staatsrechts 57, Rdnr. 28. For the argument that for this reason the substantive and procedural limitations of Art. 79 (1)-(3) also apply to the adoption of a new constitution by the people under Art. 146 as revised upon reunification, see Josef Isensee, Schlußbestimmung des Grundgesetzes: Artikel 146, 7 Handbuch des Staatsrechts 271, Rdnr. 61.

[141] Art. 54, 58-60 GG.

[142] See Art. 62-67 GG.

[143] Art. 88, 114 GG.

[144] See chapter 3 infra.

D. The Constitutional Court

Since this book is largely focused upon decisions of the Constitutional Court, it seems appropriate to spell out the nature and functions of that body in somewhat greater detail.[145]

As noted above, the Constitutional Court is a tribunal, entirely separate from the ordinary courts, whose virtually sole function is to interpret and apply the constitution. Other courts may and must construe and obey the Basic Law in cases that come before them, but only the Constitutional Court has authority to reject a statute passed since 1949 on the ground that it offends the Basic Law.

In recognition of the political significance of the Court's task, its Justices are not appointed but elected – half by the Bundestag (indirectly) and half by the Bundesrat – for an unrenewable term of twelve years.[146] Once elected, they are "independent" and "subject only to the law"; like most other judges, they can be removed only by judicial decision and only on grounds specified by statute.[147]

The jurisdiction of the Constitutional Court is largely specified by the Basic Law itself.[148] Most cases reach the Court by way of constitutional complaint ("Verfassungsbeschwerde"), a challenge to executive, judicial, or (less commonly) legislative action by a person claiming infringement of his constitutional rights. This procedure is entirely familiar to those who know something of United States courts; it is closely analogous to an action attacking the constitutionality of state action under 42 U.S.C. § 1983.[149]

Equally familiar in principle, and also frequently (though not *so* frequently) invoked, is the incidental power of the Court to pass upon the constitutionality of statutes that other tribunals are asked to apply. This is the type of judicial review recognized by *Marbury v. Madison*,[150] with one interesting difference. As indicated above, only the Constitutional Court has this power; Article 100(1) requires other courts, if they believe a statute determinative of the case unconstitutional, to certify the question to the Constitutional Court. The reasons for this monopoly include uniformity of decision as well as respect for legislative dignity and judgment; the procedure is known

---

[145] Additional specificity and documentation are provided in chapter 3 infra.

[146] See Art. 94 GG; §§ 4(1)-(2), 6 BVerfGG (the statute establishing the Constitutional Court). A two-thirds vote is required for election. Id., §§ 6(5), 7. § 4(3) of the statute sets an outside retirement date of 68 years.

[147] Art. 97(1)-(2) GG.

[148] Art. 93(1), 100(1) GG. The legislature may add to the Court's jurisdiction but may not reduce it below the constitutional minimum. See Art. 93(2).

[149] Because of the volume of constitutional complaints, Parliament has authorized the Court to set up panels of three Justices to screen out those which are frivolous or undeserving, but the Court still does not have the broad discretion enjoyed by our Supreme Court over petitions for certiorari. See chapter 3 infra.

[150] 5 U.S. 137 (1803).

as judicial reference ("Richtervorlage") or concrete norm control ("konkrete Normenkontrolle").

But the Constitutional Court has additional powers of a more abstract nature, with longstanding historical roots, that place that tribunal much closer to the center of political action than our Supreme Court. To begin with, the Court is empowered to determine controversies between various organs of government with respect to their relative rights and powers. Thus the Court can determine the boundaries between executive and legislative authority ("Organstreite"), between federal and state competence ("Bund-Länder Streitigkeiten"), and between the spheres of the several states ("föderalistische Streitigkeiten"). In Germany, in contrast to the United States, a governmental body is viewed as the most appropriate defender of its own prerogatives.[151]

Finally, and in most vivid contrast to the Supreme Court, the Constitutional Court is authorized to pass upon "differences of opinion or doubts on the procedural and substantive compatibility of federal or state law with this Basic Law . . . at the request of the Federal Government, of a state government, or of one third of the members of the Bundestag." In other words, the Court has the power to pass on the validity of state or federal laws in the abstract; the procedure is known as abstract norm control ("abstrakte Normenkontrolle"). The Basic Law thus pushes the principle of judicial review pretty close to its logical conclusion: The Court is given all powers necessary to ensure that it can function, in accord with the framers' intentions, as guardian of the Constitution ("Hüter der Verfassung"); and every one of the procedures noted in this section is guaranteed by the Basic Law itself.[152]

Decisions of the Constitutional Court, which are mostly declaratory in form, are binding on all organs of government, and many of them are given the force of law.[153] But the Court has developed a panoply of pragmatic tools to reduce the friction inherent in the exercise of judicial review. First, like our Supreme Court, the German court often goes out of its way to construe a questionable statute so as to assure its conformity with the constitution ("verfassungskonforme Auslegung").[154] The result is often the same as if the statute had been struck down, but legislative feelings are spared by indulging the

---

[151] Contrast Massachusetts v. Mellon, 262 U.S. 447 (1923).

[152] Unlike the French Conseil constitutionnel, however, the Constitutional Court is not authorized to render opinions as to the constitutionality of a proposed law *before* its promulgation. Cf. Constitution de la France du 3 juin 1958, Art. 61.

[153] See §§ 31, 67, 72, 78, 81, 95 BVerfGG; Donald P. Kommers, The Constitutional Jurisprudence of the Federal Republic of Germany 57 (1989). The Court does have authority, however, to issue preliminary injunctions ("einstweilige Anordnungen") pending its final decision, under § 32 BVerfGG.

[154] See, e.g., 8 BVerfGE 274, 324 (1958) (*Price Control*); 36 BVerfGE 1, 20 (1973) (*East German Treaty*); Hesse, supra note 93, Rdnr. 79-81. Cf. Mossman v. Higginson, 4 U.S. 12, 14 (1800).

presumption that the lawmakers are sensitive to their constitutional obligations. Even when a statute is found unconstitutional, it is not always immediately declared void; as on occasion in this country, the Court sometimes gives the legislature a grace period in which to revise the law in order to avoid even greater harm.[155] In other cases the Court has gone so far as to uphold a statute while warning that it may soon become unconstitutional; the effect is once more to leave time for orderly reconsideration and to avoid a troublesome gap in the law.[156] Finally, in the famous *Saarland* case the Court expressly upheld an agreement providing for government of that region in a manner concededly incompatible with various provisions of the Basic Law on the ground that the only available alternative was even worse; the Court's obligation was to reach a result as nearly in accord with the constitution as possible.[157]

At the same time, however, the Constitutional Court commonly embellishes its decisions with specific instructions to the legislature as to how to assure future compliance with the Basic Law.[158] This practice too will strike a familiar chord for readers conversant with such Supreme Court decisions as *Miranda v. Arizona*[159] and *Roe v. Wade*.[160]

Pursuant to statute, the Constitutional Court is divided into two separate panels ("Senate") of eight Justices each. Under current law the allocation of cases between the two panels is determined partly by the procedural posture of the case, partly by the substantive issues presented, and partly by alphabetical order. Thus the Second Senate is responsible, among other things, for intergovernmental disputes and most abstract norm-control proceedings, for matters of criminal procedure, and for complaints filed by parties whose names begin with the letters L-Z in which questions of civil procedure predomi-

---

[155] This approach is often taken when the omission of some group from a provision for government benefits is held to violate the equality guarantee of Art. 3(1) GG, for in such a case the legislature has a choice whether to extend the benefit to the disfavored class or to abolish it entirely. See 22 BVerfGE 349, 360-63 (1967) (detailing the procedure to be followed in these cases). See generally Wiltraut Rupp-von Brünneck, Admonitory Functions of Constitutional Courts (Germany), 20 Am. J. Comp. L. 387, 393-95 (1972). Cf. Northern Pipeline Construction Co. v. Marathon Pipe Line Co., 458 U.S. 50 (1982).

[156] See, e.g., 39 BVerfGE 169, 185-95 (1975) (sex discrimination in law respecting private pensions); Rupp-von Brünneck, supra note 155, at 396-99. For a defense of this practice (attacked by some observers as an exercise in obiter dictum) as "an act of judicial self-restraint" in comparison with immediate invalidation, see id. at 399-403.

[157] 4 BVerfGE 157, 168-78 (1955). See chapter 2 infra.

[158] E.g., 24 BVerfGE 299, 351 (1968) (*Party Finance*); 39 BVerfGE 1, 49-50 (1975) (*Abortion*). See Kommers, supra note 153, at 61-62; Mathias Kleuker, Gesetzgebungsaufträge des Bundesverfassungsgerichts (1993).

[159] 384 U.S. 436 (1966).

[160] 410 U.S. 113 (1973).

nate.[161] The built-in potential for deadlock within each panel is countered by requiring a majority vote of participating Justices for a finding of unconstitutionality,[162] the risk of conflicting decisions between panels by requiring each Senate to call a session of the Court en banc ("Plenum") if it wishes to depart from a position taken by the other.[163]

Thus in an organizational sense the Constitutional Court is essentially two courts rather than one; we shall treat it as one for purposes of the present study.

E. Unification and Beyond

In the first forty years of its existence the Basic Law was amended no fewer than thirty-five times – more frequently than the U.S. Constitution during its first 200 years.[164] Many of the amendments have been relatively minor; a number have added to the list of federal legislative powers. Major amendment packages in 1956 and 1968, providing for national defense and internal security respectively, were necessitated by earlier limitations on sovereignty imposed by the Allies after World War II; the most significant actual reform yet undertaken by constitutional amendment was an extensive revision of the financial powers of the Bund and the Länder in 1969.[165]

Far more significant for German constitutional law than any of these formal amendments was the sudden and unexpected reunification of East and West Germany in October 1990.[166] No constitutional amendment was necessary to effect this epochal metamorphosis; the Federal Republic was conceived from the first as only one part of a larger Germany still intact in principle though divided in fact.[167] The Basic Law envisioned alternative means of achieving reunification:

---

[161] See § 14 BVerfGG; Beschluß des Plenums gemäß § 14 Abs. 4 vom 6. Oktober 1982 (BGBl. I S. 1735); Theodor Maunz, Bruno Schmidt-Bleibtreu, Franz Klein, & Gerhard Ulsamer, Bundesverfassungsgerichtsgesetz [hereafter cited as Maunz/Schmidt-Bleibtreu], § 14 (2d ed. 1985).

[162] § 15(3) BVerfGG.

[163] Id., § 16. The latter provision has proved essentially a dead letter. See Maunz/Schmidt-Bleibtreu, supra note 161, § 16 (reporting that it had been invoked only once as of 1985 (citing 4 BVerfGE 27 (1954)) and listing several instances in which it should have been invoked but was not). Fortunately, outright conflicts between the two panels are comparatively rare. On institutional aspects of the Court generally see Donald P. Kommers, Judicial Politics in West Germany: A Study of the Federal Constitutional Court (1976).

[164] For the argument that too frequent resort to the amending process may endanger the symbolic force of the Basic Law see Schulz, supra note 11, at 230-31.

[165] See Grimm, supra note 77, at 376; Badura, supra note 140, Rdnr. 30-36.

[166] See chapter 2 infra.

[167] See the original versions of the Preamble and of Art. 23, 146 GG.

adoption of a new all-German constitution[168] or extension of the Basic Law itself to East Germany.[169] With the blessing of the West, the East chose the latter course: Five states newly reconstituted behind what had once been the Iron Curtain became constituent states of the Federal Republic.

Several constitutional amendments accompanied legislative approval of the reunification treaty, but they were essentially housekeeping provisions designed to conform the Basic Law to the realization of a united Germany. Subsequent political events have led to more significant amendments.

Ever since the beginning, the Basic Law had authorized the transfer of significant governmental powers to international organizations, and it was on the basis of this provision that the Federal Republic had become a member of the European Communities.[170] The additional transfers of power contemplated by the Maastricht Treaty prompted amendment of the Basic Law in 1992 to firm up the constitutional basis of further German participation,[171] and the Constitutional Court upheld the constitutionality of this amendment in October, 1993.[172] Significant restrictions on the generous right of political asylum afforded by Article 16 were adopted in June of the same year.[173]

Probably of greater significance in the long run was the establishment, upon reunification, of a Constitutional Commission ("Verfassungskommission"), composed of members of the Bundestag and Bundesrat, whose task it was to reexamine the entire Basic Law with a view toward additional amendments.[174] The work of this Commission fostered the most fundamental constitutional debate since the Basic Law itself was adopted in 1949. Its final report, filed in November 1993, recommended a number of alterations ranging from programmatic clauses committing the state to environmental protection and the promotion of sexual equality to a series of provisions designed to strengthen the authority of the Länder.[175] Because

---

[168] Art. 146 GG (a.F.).

[169] Art. 23 GG (a.F.)

[170] See chapter 2 infra; Art. 24 GG.

[171] Gesetz zur Änderung des Grundgesetzes vom 21. Dezember 1992, BGBl. I S 2086.

[172] See New York Times, Oct. 10, 1993, p. A6.

[173] Gesetz zur Änderung des Grundgesetzes vom 28. Juni 1993, BGBl. I S 1002; see chapter 6 infra. See also Gesetz zur Änderung des Grundgesetzes vom 14. Juli 1992, BGBl. I S. 1254 (amending Art. 87a to permit privatization of air traffic control); see chapter 3 infra.

[174] See Vertrag zwischen der Bundesrepublik Deutschland und der Deutschen Demokratischen Republik über die Herstellung der Einheit Deutschlands [hereafter cited as Einigungsvertrag], approved Sept. 23, 1990, BGBl. II S. 885, Art. 5.

[175] See Bericht der Gemeinsamen Verfassungskommission, BT/Drucksache 12/6000 [hereafter cited as Bericht der VerfKomm] 15-18 (1993). The amendments

the Commission's rules required a two-thirds vote (and thus the agreement of both major parties) for any recommendation, these proposals may soon become law.

More important than the modest amendments the Commission proposed was its emphatic rejection of a long list of more fundamental changes. Like our First Congress, the Commission was willing to endorse a number of improvements to the constitution, but not to tamper with its central principles.[176] Thus as Germany began to confront the challenges of unification and the new European Union, it gave a resounding vote of confidence to the Basic Law.

---

that accompanied approval of the Maastricht Treaty were also fruits of the work of the Constitutional Commission. See id. at 19-30.

[176] Cf. Kenneth R. Bowling, "A Tub to the Whale": The Founding Fathers and Adoption of the Federal Bill of Rights, 8 Journal of the Early Republic 223 (1988).

2

The Federal System

Federalism in the broad sense has a long history in Germany. The Empire that Napoleon destroyed was in its later stages essentially a loose confederation, and it was replaced by two others: the short-lived, French-dominated Rheinbund of 1806 and the indigenous Deutscher Bund of 1815. The abortive Frankfurt Constitution of 1849 ("Paulskirchenverfassung"), Bismarck's 1871 imperial constitution, and the Weimar Constitution of 1919 all provided for true central governments; but each of them reserved important powers to the constituent states.[1]

As the name of the present Republic suggests, the Basic Law builds upon this tradition. The Preamble confirms that the nation is divided into states (Länder), of which there are now sixteen. Article 20(1) expressly proclaims Germany a federal state ("Bundesstaat"); Article 79(3) goes so far as to place the basic principle of federalism and two of its specific attributes beyond the reach of constitutional amendment.[2] As we have seen, decentralization of governmental authority was one of the principal conditions for Allied approval of the Basic Law, but German and American commentators agree that federalism was not forced upon the Germans; they had seen more than enough of the dangers of a unitary state.[3]

---

[1] See generally Otto Kimminich, Der Bundesstaat, 1 Handbuch des Staatsrechts 1113, Rdnr. 25-35; Helmut Steinberger, Bemerkungen zu einer Synthese des Einflusses ausländischer Verfassungsideen auf die Entstehung des Grundgesetzes mit deutscher verfassungsrechtlichen Traditionen, in Klaus Stern (ed.), 40 Jahre Grundgesetz: Entstehung, Bewährung und internationale Ausstrahlung 41, 63 (1990): "Throughout its more than 1,000-year history, except for the years from 1933 to 1945, the political landscape of Germany always had a federal structure."

[2] The two entrenched attributes are "the division of the Federation into Länder" and their "participation . . . in [federal] legislation." As its legislative history confirms, Art. 79(3) does not freeze the details of the original distribution of federal and state authority, and in fact they have been amended a number of times. See 1 JöR (n.F.) at 579-84 (1951); Kimminich, supra note 1, Rdnr. 39. Contrast U.S. Const., Art. V, which for many years has permitted amendment of any provision, except that no state shall be deprived of "its equal suffrage in the Senate" without its consent.

[3] See Sten. Ber. at 203 (1949) (Delegate Menzel); Reinhard Mußgnug, Zustandekommen des Grundgesetzes und Entstehen der Bundesrepublik Deutschland, 1

As in the United States, in theory state authority is the rule and federal the exception: Under Article 30 all governmental power belongs to the constituent states except as the Basic Law otherwise provides.[4] The grants of authority to the central government ("Bund"), however, differ significantly from those in the United States. In accordance with longstanding tradition, the list of express federal legislative powers includes not only those subjects which have always been federal under our Constitution and most of the economic and social matters that we federalized during the New Deal, but also fields like contract, tort, and criminal law that in this country are still largely left to the states. Although the Constitutional Court has tended to construe these generous grants of federal power somewhat strictly, they have been extensively exercised; and as a result there is much less room for state legislation in Germany than in the United States.[5]

On the other hand, also in accord with longstanding tradition, federal executive and judicial powers are significantly narrower in Germany than they are in this country. Most federal legislation is carried out by the Länder, and federal courts are almost exclusively courts of last resort. Moreover, through the instrumentality of the Bundesrat (Council of State Governments), the Länder play an important role in the enactment of federal legislation. Comparison is difficult, but it may be that on balance the German Länder have no less power than their American counterparts – especially since, as a perceptive American observer pointed out over thirty years ago, the political check of state veto power is likely to be more effective than judicial enforcement of constitutional limitations on federal authority.[6]

Handbuch des Staatsrechts 219, Rdnr. 52-53, 71 ("The notion that federalism was forced on the Federal Republic by the Allies is a myth."). See also Michael Stolleis, Besatzungsherrschaft und Wiederaufbau deutscher Staatlichkeit 1945-1949, in id. 173, Rdnr. 116; John F. Golay, The Founding of the Federal Republic of Germany 41-44 (1958). One of the Nazis' first measures after taking power in 1933 was to abolish the Länder parliaments and subject Länder executives to control by the central government. Gesetz über den Neuaufbau des Reichs vom 30. Januar 1934, RGBl. I S. 75.

[4] "The exercise of governmental powers and the discharge of governmental functions shall be incumbent on the Länder in so far as this Basic Law does not otherwise prescribe or permit." Cf. U.S. Const., Amend. X.

[5] See Beratungen und Empfehlungen zur Verfassungsreform (Schlußbericht der Enquête-Kommission Verfassungsreform des Deutschen Bundestages) [hereafter cited as Schlußbericht der Enquête-Kommission], Zur Sache 2/77, Teil 2, S. 54 (1977): "Legislation has become a predominantly federal matter."

[6] See Golay, supra note 3, at 108-12. See also Sten. Ber. at 29 (Delegate Menzel); Konrad Hesse, Grundzüge des Verfassungsrechts der Bundesrepublik Deutschland (18th ed. 1991), Rdnr. 221: "What the Länder have lost in terms of autonomous power to formulate their own policy they have made up for in terms of influence on the central state."

In the United States the division of power between federal and state authorities exhausts the subject of federalism. In Germany, if one is not too strict about the definition, there are additional layers. Article 28(2) guarantees a certain degree of autonomy to local governments, which in this country (so far as the Constitution is concerned) are mere instrumentalities of the states. Moreover, even before reunification, various provisions of the Basic Law defined the relation of the Federal Republic to a larger Germany that was held to have survived the cataclysm of war, occupation, and partition. Finally, pursuant to the provisions of Article 24 and a new Article 23 the Federal Republic has transferred substantial sovereign powers to such supranational organizations as NATO and most significantly the European Communities, now known as the European Union. Thus the Federation is at the same time the central authority with respect to the Länder and a constituent part of what increasingly bears earmarks of a larger federal system.

I. LEGISLATIVE POWERS

Article 70 of the Basic Law applies the general principle of residual state competence to the legislative field: "The Länder shall have the right to legislate in so far as this Basic Law does not confer legislative power on the Federation." Other provisions, however, grant the Federation extensive legislative authority. In some instances that authority is exclusive; in others it is concurrent; in others it is only the power to enact framework legislation ("Rahmenvorschriften"), whose details are to be filled in by the states.

A. Exclusive Federal Authority

The basic list of exclusive federal legislative powers in Article 73 reads very much like the list of congressional powers in the U.S. Constitution: foreign affairs, defense, national citizenship, currency, weights and measures, free movement of goods and persons, postal and telecommunication services, patents and copyrights. Taxes are elsewhere provided for, and there is no necessary and proper clause.[7]

---

[7] Implicit and inherent powers have been only sparingly acknowledged. See, e.g., 3 BVerfGE 407, 421-22 (1954), explaining that implicit authority ("Gesetzgebungskompetenz kraft Sachzusammenhangs") would be found "only if a subject expressly entrusted to the Federation cannot sensibly be regulated without also regulating another subject that is not expressly so entrusted," inherent authority (Kompetenz "aus der Natur der Sache") at most for "those matters which arise directly from the existence and constitutional organization of the Federation," such as the location of the federal capital. Cf. Gerhard Anschütz, Die Verfassung des Deutschen Reichs 73-75, 95-96 (4th ed. 1933) (enunciating similar but subtly less hostile criteria for inherent and implied powers under the Weimar Constitution).

Federal civil service and "statistics for federal purposes," both of which we would find implicit, are expressly included; so are immigration, which our Supreme Court said was inherently federal,[8] and "federal railroads and air transport," which fall under our commerce clause.

Federal authority in many of these fields goes back to the 1871 constitution, exclusive authority to that of 1919; both were foreshadowed by the stillborn constitution of 1849.[9] The subjects included are those in which there is a strong argument for uniformity.[10] Several of them (e.g., foreign relations, most military affairs, and currency) are exclusively federal in the United States as well. The meaning of exclusivity is defined by Article 71: "In matters within the exclusive legislative power of the Federation the Länder shall have power to legislate only if, and to the extent that, a federal law explicitly so authorizes them." Thus the closest American analogies are not coinage or treatymaking, which are absolutely forbidden to the states, but interstate compacts, tariffs, and interstate commerce, over which state power is precluded or restricted in the absence of congressional consent.[11]

Most decisions of the Constitutional Court interpreting these provisions are straightforward and unsurprising.[12] A few are of sig-

---

A building code, the Court concluded, met neither of these tests: Land use and housing could both be regulated without prescribing such a code, and it was entirely imaginable to leave the matter to state law. See also id. at 428-29 (affirming the incidental power to determine the value of land when necessary to the accomplishment of tasks committed to the Federation); 84 BVerfGE 133, 148 (1991) (finding inherent federal authority to adopt regulations respecting employment relations in the public service of the East German states on their accession under Art. 23(2)); Maunz in 3 Maunz/Dürig, Art. 70, Rdnr. 45-49 (drawing a slippery distinction between the "breadth" and the "depth" of federal authority in concluding that incidental power ("Annexkompetenz") extends solely to "preparatory or executory measures," not to regulation of "independent subjects"). For a broader view see Hans-Werner Rengeling, Gesetzgebungszuständigkeit, 4 Handbuch des Staatsrechts 723, Rdnr. 56-58.

[8] See Chinese Exclusion Case, 130 U.S. 581 (1889).

[9] See RV 1849, §§ 6-47; RV 1871, Art. 4; Art. 6 WRV.

[10] See Sten. Ber. at 173 (Delegate Schmid).

[11] See U.S. Const., Art. I, § 10; Prudential Ins. Co. v. Benjamin, 328 U.S. 408 (1946). Federal permission for state regulation of exclusively federal matters is extremely rare in Germany. See Maunz in 3 Maunz/Dürig, Art. 71, Rdnr. 28 (listing two minor provisions respecting the island of Helgoland and one regarding initial arrangements in the newly admitted Saarland). For the suggestion that there may be implicit limits to the delegation of exclusive federal power to the Länder under this provision see Michael Bothe in 2 AK-GG, Art. 71, Rdnr. 6.

[12] See, e.g., 4 BVerfGE 60, 72-74 (1954) (revaluation of obligations in the wake of currency reform falls within exclusive federal authority over the currency); 26 BVerfGE 338, 367-79 (1969) (federal authority respecting the national railroad (Bundesbahn) supports federal statute concerning grade crossings along its

nificant interest, not least because they reflect a sensitivity toward reserved state authority that has been conspicuously missing from decisions of our Supreme Court for the past fifty-five years.

The first was one of the most celebrated decisions in the history of
the Constitutional Court, the great *Television* case of 1961.[13] For obvious reasons of efficiency, postal and telegraph service had been a
federal subject in Germany since the beginning and an exclusively
federal one since 1919. As technology advanced, the Weimar Constitution added telephone service to the list, and during the time these
provisions were in force the emerging radio medium was controlled
by a permit system set up and administered by the central government. Against this background it seemed logical enough that the Basic Law of 1949 extended exclusive federal legislative authority to telecommunications ("Fernmeldewesen") generally. Nevertheless, in the
first years after World War II both radio and television were controlled by a consortium of regional networks (the ARD) organized
under state rather than federal authority. The attempt of the Federation to break this monopoly by establishing a competing network of its
own precipitated a major confrontation over the boundary between
federal and state powers.[14]

The Land (state) of Hamburg had given the Norddeutscher Rundfunk a monopoly of radio and television broadcasting within its borders. Challenged by its new federal competitor, Hamburg sued to establish, among other things, the constitutionality of its monopoly.
Notwithstanding the flat grant of exclusive federal authority over
telecommunications, Hamburg won a substantial though incomplete
victory.

As a textual matter, said the Constitutional Court, the term
"telecommunications" embraced only "the technical processes of
transmitting . . . signals," not the field of broadcasting as a whole.
This conclusion was confirmed, the Court added, by the use of the
broader term broadcasting ("Rundfunk") in connection with freedom
of expression in Article 5(1).[15] Moreover, radio and television programming was a cultural matter, and the "fundamental decision" of

---

tracks); 62 BVerfGE 354, 366-67 (1982) (health insurance for military personnel
falls within authority to provide for national defense).

[13] 12 BVerfGE 205 (1961). For discussion of those portions of the opinion dealing
with freedom of broadcasting under Art. 5(1) see chapter 4 infra. This and many
other decisions noted in this chapter are also discussed, from a somewhat different
perspective, in Philip M. Blair, Federalism and Judicial Review in West
Germany (1981).

[14] The history of German broadcasting is recounted in 12 BVerfGE at 208-16.

[15] Broadcasting itself, the Court added, was "not an aspect but rather a 'user' of
telecommunication facilities." Id. at 226. This conclusion gains strength from the
Basic Law's parallel treatment of postal, telegraph, and telephone services, with respect to which the government's interest is clearly in the transmission rather than
the content of messages.

the Basic Law to leave cultural matters to the Länder (by omitting
them from the list of federal powers) made it impossible to uphold
federal authority over anything cultural in the absence of clear language. In addition, the reason for the grant of federal authority was
to prevent the "chaos" that might result from disuniform regulation
of such matters as the location and strength of transmitters and the
allocation of frequencies; there was no comparable need for uniformity with respect to the content of broadcasts. Tradition was not to
the contrary, since the Länder had disputed the exercise of federal
authority over programming throughout the Weimar period; and the
record of the constitutional convention ("Parlamentarischer Rat")
confirmed that the cultural side of broadcasting was not within the
new grant of federal power. Accordingly, the monopoly granted by
Hamburg was invalid as to the technical aspects of transmitting
radio and television signals but valid as to everything else; and for
similar reasons the competing federal network could be authorized
only to transmit signals, not to determine what was to be
transmitted.[16]

Thus in the opinion of the Court text, context, structure, purpose,
and history combined to give the provision for exclusive federal power
over telecommunications a narrower scope than an untutored observer might have expected. If the result suggests a rather rigorous
approach to the interpretation of federal authority, this is no accident. The fundamental premise of the Basic Law, the Court emphasized, was one of state authority. The reservation to the Länder of all
powers not granted to the Federation precluded any presumption of
federal authority in cases of doubt; "the structure of the Basic Law
demands instead a strict interpretation" (eine strikte Interpretation)
of federal powers.[17]

Similar statements are found in numerous decisions of the Constitutional Court. This is not to say that in the *Television* case or
anywhere else the Court strained to give federal authority an unnaturally narrow reading; a strict construction is not necessarily a hostile one.[18] But the German approach contrasts strikingly with Justice
Stone's familiar insistence that the tenth amendment's reservation
to the states of all powers not granted to the federal government was a
mere "truism."[19] Of course neither that amendment nor its German
counterpart takes away from the central authorities any powers
granted them by other provisions, but the German court seems on
solid ground in taking the reservation clause as evidence that federal

---

[16] Id. at 225-40, 248. Accord Hermann von Mangoldt, Das Bonner Grundgesetz
394-95 (1953). The deliberations of the constitutional convention, which do support
the Court's conclusion, are collected in 1 JöR (n.F.) at 476-78. Federal administrative authority in this field (Art. 87(1) GG), the Court added, was no broader than the
legislative authority conferred by Art. 73(7). 12 BVerfGE at 229-30, 248.

[17] Id. at 228-29.

[18] See Rengeling, supra note 7, Rdnr. 29-30.

[19] United States v. Darby, 312 U.S. 100, 123-24 (1941).

powers must not be construed so broadly that there is nothing left to reserve.[20]

A similar restraint in the interpretation of exclusive federal authority informed the Constitutional Court's 1969 decision striking down federal statutes immunizing the national railroad (Bundesbahn) and the post office (Deutsche Post) from fees assessed by state and local governments.[21] Article 73 gives the Federation exclusive legislative power over both federal railroads and the postal service. But grants of federal authority, the Court said once again, were to be interpreted strictly. Fees for processing an application for permission to clear timber or revise a bus schedule were a matter of state administrative procedure, not of railroad or postal regulation; and with exceptions not here applicable the procedure of state agencies was a matter reserved to the states.[22]

This decision illustrates another pervasive principle of German constitutional interpretation: Governmental powers tend to be construed as mutually exclusive.[23] Immunity of a railroad from administrative fees is either railroad law or administrative law; it cannot be both. Reminiscent of the short-lived American doctrine of dual federalism,[24] this approach can serve to limit the risk that state authority will be swallowed up by federal. At the same time, however, the theory of mutually exclusive powers poses a countervailing danger: If the reasoning of the fee decision were applied to hold the Federation without power to protect its instrumentalities from oppressive taxation or regulation, federal powers might be too narrow to achieve their goals.[25] Moreover, the exclusivity theory presents formidable

---

[20] See also Maunz in 3 Maunz/Dürig Art. 74, Rdnr. 15-16; Hesse, supra note 6, Rdnr. 236 (noting the Constitutional Court's tendency to interpret the division of authority between the Federation and its constituent states "with a decided emphasis on the autonomy of the Länder").

[21] 26 BVerfGE 281 (1969).

[22] Id. at 297-301.

[23] See 36 BVerfGE 193, 202-03 (1973): "[A] 'double competence,' on the basis of which the Federation and the Länder could regulate the same matter in different ways, is foreign to the constitutional system of allocation of powers and incompatible with its function of division of authority." See also Maunz in 3 Maunz/Dürig, Art. 73, Rdnr. 18; id., Art. 74, Rdnr. 9.

[24] This doctrine appeared to suggest that what lay within state authority was for that reason alone beyond federal reach. See, e.g., Hammer v. Dagenhart, 247 U.S. 251, 276 (1918).

[25] Cf. Bank v. Supervisors, 74 U.S. 26, 30-31 (1869) (upholding the power of Congress to immunize federal activities from state taxes). The German decision does not preclude this result. Nondiscriminatory fees for state administrative services present a weak case for intergovernmental immunity, and the applicability of the underlying permit requirements to federal instrumentalities was not questioned. Cf. Massachusetts v. United States, 435 U.S. 444, 453-63 (1978) (holding a state liable for federal aircraft registration charges on the ground that they were fees for administrative services despite the assumption that states retained a measure of immunity from federal taxation). Other decisions suggest that the Constitu-

classification problems.[26] It also contrasts sharply with the approach enunciated by Justice Johnson in *Gibbons v. Ogden* and widely accepted in the United States: Because transportation of contaminated goods affects both trade and health, it may generally be regulated under either commerce or police powers, and in case of conflict federal law prevails.[27]

A third case of interest with respect to exclusive federal powers was the Constitutional Court's 1972 decision upholding a federal law forbidding importation of subversive films.[28] The exclusive grant of federal authority over foreign affairs ("auswärtige Angelegenheiten"), the Court concluded, could not sustain the law; that power applied only to relations with other countries, not to regulations addressed to private parties.[29] Nevertheless the ban fell within the exclusive federal authority respecting "the free movement of goods" and "the exchange of goods . . . with foreign countries" granted by the fifth clause of Article 73: The history of comparable provisions in the Weimar Constitution showed that (as in modern American decisions) the power to regulate commerce could be exercised for police-

---

tional Court might well find a way to prevent one level of government from unduly interfering with the operations of another. See note 37 infra (discussing federal regulation of state salaries); note 112 infra (discussing taxation of state television fees); text at notes 225-44 infra (discussing the implicit principle of federal-state comity); 1 BVerfGE 14, 34-35 (1951) (holding that a federal law extending the term of two state legislatures offended, among other things, the federal principle). See also Paul Kirchhof, Staatliche Einnahmen, 4 Handbuch des Staatsrechts 87, Rdnr. 142 (suggesting that governments should generally be taxable only when they act in what we would call a proprietary capacity ("gewerbliche Betätigung")).

[26] Compare 7 BVerfGE 29, 38-41 (1957) (holding that a statute of limitations governing prosecution for illegal publications was a matter of "the general legal status of the press" (Art. 75 cl. 2) rather than of criminal law or judicial procedure (Art. 74 cl. 1) and thus not a proper subject of concurrent federal authority), with 36 BVerfGE 193, 202-09 (1973) (holding that testimonial privileges for journalists were a matter not of press law but of judicial procedure). Both opinions relied on tradition to support these classifications. The first, however, strengthened its conclusion by arguing that the short time allowed for prosecution of press offenses reflected considerations peculiar to the press (7 BVerfGE at 39). The second, conceding that the purpose of the privilege was to secure the free flow of information, stressed that the means of accomplishing this goal was "essentially of a procedural nature" (36 BVerfGE at 204-05). For discussion of the various factors considered in resolving such questions see Bothe in 2 AK-GG, Art. 70, Rdnr. 7-24 (criticizing the privilege decision in particular and the classification approach in general: "It is artificial and indeed impossible to interpret the legislative powers of the Federation and of the Länder . . . in such a way as to establish mutually exclusive preserves . . . . The limitation period for prosecution of press offenses is a matter of both criminal law and press law . . .").

[27] 22 U.S. 1, 234 (1824) (Johnson, J., concurring). See also id. at 209-210 (Marshall, C.J., for the Court).

[28] 33 BVerfGE 52 (1972).

[29] Id. at 60.

power reasons.[30] The latter holding demonstrates that the Constitutional Court is not always grudging in its interpretation of federal authority; the former gains support from the Court's interpretive principle that a specific provision should be construed as an exception to a more general one.[31]

The final decision of interest respecting exclusive federal powers was the Constitutional Court's 1981 conclusion that a state law entitling the state library to a free copy of works published within the state did not encroach upon the exclusive federal province of copyright law.[32] State law, the Court noted, allowed the library to obtain copies only of works that had already appeared; "the right of the author to determine whether and how his work is published is not affected."[33] Since another central function of copyright law is to define the author's right to compensation for the use of his intellectual product, an outsider may find this explanation incomplete.[34] This case thus seems to reaffirm the contrast between the German court's restrained approach to the interpretation of federal authority and the more expansive attitude of the U.S. Supreme Court during the same period.[35]

---

[30] Id. at 60-64. Cf. United States v. Darby, 312 U.S. 100, 112-17 (1941). The Constitutional Court went on to give the importation ban a narrow construction in conformity with the guarantee of informational freedom in Article 5(1) of the Basic Law. See 33 BVerfGE at 65-71; chapter 4 infra.

[31] See Bothe in 2 AK-GG, Art. 73, Rdnr. 1 (adding that a broad interpretation of the power over foreign affairs could render more specific grants such as that concerning foreign commerce superfluous). The decision that health insurance for military personnel fell within the power to provide for national defense rather than the power to determine the legal relations of persons in the public service (62 BVerfGE 354, 366-67 (1982), cited in note 12 supra) illustrates the difficulty as well as the application of the lex specialis doctrine; for although, as the Court said, the defense power was more specific as to the persons within its scope, it was more general as to the possible subjects of regulation. See Maunz in 3 Maunz/Dürig, Art. 74, Rdnr. 14.

[32] 58 BVerfGE 137, 145-46 (1981).

[33] Id. at 146. Cf. the Trade-Mark Cases, 100 U.S. 82, 93-94 (1879) (holding that the grant of congressional authority respecting copyrights did not support a federal trademark law because trademarks depended on prior appropriation rather than invention). The German Court went on to suggest, however, that the requirement of a free library copy would infringe the publisher's property rights as applied to a book published in small numbers at high cost. 58 BVerfGE at 147-52; chapter 6 infra.

[34] See 31 BVerfGE 229 (1971) (also noted in chapter 6 infra) (striking down as an infringement of property rights a provision authorizing free use of copyrighted works by schools).

[35] The Enquête-Kommission, a body of legislators, Länder officials, and scholars appointed to assess the desirability of amending the Basic Law during the 1970s, found no reason for dissatisfaction with the basic scheme of exclusive federal powers. See Schlußbericht der Enquête-Kommission, Teil 2, S. 62-63.

B. Concurrent Authority

The list of concurrent federal legislative powers in Article 74 is extensive. It embraces most of the authority over economic and social matters that our Supreme Court found implicit in the U.S. Constitution after President Roosevelt threatened to pack it in 1937:[36] welfare, social insurance, and labor law; economic regulation, including mining, manufacturing, energy, crafts and trades, banking, insurance, and exchanges; agriculture, fisheries, forests, and transportation; communicable diseases, medical licensing, the protection of plants and animals. Later amendments added air pollution, solid waste disposal, and noise and even (in Art. 74a) the power to regulate salaries of state and local officials.[37] Whatever the ostensibly narrower provisions of the U.S. Constitution may originally have meant, the United States Congress exercises most of these powers today.[38]

What Congress has not done, however, even though the Supreme Court might conceivably permit it to do so, is to promulgate a general civil or criminal code – much less a code of procedure for state courts, which even now should be beyond congressional power. The federal legislature did all three long ago in Germany, for civil, criminal, and procedural law were made federal subjects before 1900 and have remained so ever since.[39] Thus there are precious few matters that cannot be made the subject of federal legislation in the Federal Republic; most of them concern education and other cultural mat-

---

[36] See generally The Second Century, ch. 7.

[37] See 34 BVerfGE 9, 19-21 (1972), construing this amendment narrowly to conform with Art. 79(3), which forbids any amendment "affecting the division of the Federation into states":

> The Länder in a federation are "states" only if they retain an irreducible core of autonomous responsibility. Whatever the specific elements of this responsibility may be, at a minimum the Land must remain free to determine its own organization . . . and must be assured by the constitution of an appropriate share of overall tax revenues within the Federation.

Id. at 20. Cf. National League of Cities v. Usery, 426 U.S. 833 (1976).

[38] On regulation in general see Wickard v. Filburn, 317 U.S. 111 (1942); on social insurance see Steward Machine Co. v. Davis, 301 U.S. 548 (1937); on regulation of state and local employment see Garcia v. San Antonio Metropolitan Transit Authority, 469 U.S. 528 (1985).

[39] See RV 1871, Art. 4, Nr. 13, as amended by the statute of Dec. 20, 1873, RGBl. S. 379 (giving the Reich "die gemeinsame Gesetzgebung über das gesamte bürgerliche Recht, das Strafrecht und das gerichtliche Verfahren"). On the basis of this provision the famous Bürgerliches Gesetzbuch (BGB) or Civil Code was promulgated in 1896 (RGBl. S. 195).

ters, public health and safety ("Polizeirecht"), and the organization of state and local government.[40]

The breadth of concurrent federal legislative power was a source of grave Allied concern when the Basic Law was being considered. One of the three basic conditions for Allied approval laid down when the Länder governments were authorized to call a constitutional convention was that the new system be a federal one "that protects the rights of the participating states."[41] The military governors objected that the document drafted by the convention gave the Federation too much authority,[42] and at their insistence Article 72 was redrafted to ensure that concurrent federal powers could be exercised only upon a showing of special need:

> (2) The Federation shall have the right to legislate in these matters to the extent that a need for regulation by federal legislation exists because:
> 1. a matter cannot be effectively regulated by the legislation of individual Länder, or
> 2. the regulation of a matter by a Land law might prejudice the interests of other Länder or of the people as a whole, or
> 3. the maintenance of legal or economic unity, especially by the maintenance of uniformity of living conditions beyond the territory of any one Land, necessitates such regulation.[43]

If this provision had been taken seriously, it might significantly have limited federal authority. But it was not taken seriously; one of the first things the Constitutional Court did was essentially to read it out of the Basic Law.

There was no sign of trouble when, in its very first substantive decision, the Court enforced Article 72(2) by invalidating a federal law extending the terms of the legislatures of two states pending a referendum on reorganization of their territory: Even assuming that the subject fell within Article 118's authorization of federal laws respecting reorganization of the southwestern Länder, there was no

---

[40] See Hesse, supra note 6, Rdnr. 244; Sten. Ber. at 32-33 (Delegate Menzel), 37 (Delegate Schwalber). Menzel was a Social Democrat, Schwalber a Christian Socialist from Bavaria; both emphasized that there was no substantial disagreement over the proper scope of federal legislative powers.

[41] Frankfurter Dokument Nr. I, in 2 Quellen zum Staatsrecht 197, 198.

[42] See the Allied memoranda reprinted in id. at 208-14.

[43] The initial draft presented by the experts at Herrenchiemsee had provided more simply (in Art. 34) that in the realm of concurrent authority the Bund should regulate only that which required uniform regulation ("nur das . . . , was einheitlich geregelt werden muß"). See Bericht über den Verfassungskonvent auf Herrenchiemsee vom 10. bis 23. August 1948 [hereafter cited as Herrenchiemsee Bericht], 2 Akten und Protokolle 504, 584. That the final version was adopted in response to the Allied demand is documented in the convention debates, summarized in 1 JöR (n.F.) at 465-66.

need for federal legislation since the states could take care of the
problem for themselves.[44] In upholding a federal statute respecting
the retirement of chimney sweeps in 1952, however, the Court found
a need for uniformity under the third clause of Article 72(2) on the
less than satisfying ground that the Länder themselves had asked
the Federation to act.[45] More important, the opinion had begun by
doubting whether the question of need ("Bedürfnisfrage") was justiciable at all, or whether it was not – as had "generally been assumed"
with respect to a similar provision of the Weimar Constitution –
committed to the discretion of the legislature.[46] The next year, in
upholding a federal amnesty law on the basis of federal authority
over criminal procedure and the execution of sentences, the Court
answered its own question by withdrawing from the arena: "The
question whether there is a need for federal regulation is a question
for the faithful exercise of legislative discretion that is by its nature
nonjusticiable and therefore basically not subject to review by the
Constitutional Court."[47]

No reasons were given for this conclusion beyond another un-
elaborated reference to the Weimar Constitution.[48] There was indeed
precedent in the writings of Weimar scholars;[49] yet the Allies had
demanded, and the text seemed to give them, a meaningful limitation on legislative power.[50] One is reminded of our Supreme
Court's decision that whether a state's government was "republican"
was committed to the decision of Congress,[51] and of Chief Justice
Marshall's refusal to determine "the degree of necessity" for federal
legislation under the necessary and proper clause.[52] German
scholars tend to deny the existence of any political-question doctrine
in the Federal Republic; but the bulk of political-question decisions in

----

[44] 1 BVerfGE 14, 35-36 (1951) (alternative holding).

[45] 1 BVerfGE 264, 273 (1952). Contrast 1 BVerfGE 14, 35 (1951): "The Federation
cannot acquire legislative powers not granted it by the Basic Law through the consent of the states."

[46] 1 BVerfGE at 272-73.

[47] 2 BVerfGE 213, 224 (1953). Accord von Mangoldt, supra note 16, at 387.

[48] 2 BVerfGE at 224-25. A later opinion added that the need requirement was
"indefinite," 13 BVerfGE 230, 233-34 (1961); but that should only have meant, as one
influential commentator observed, that there was a need for judicial interpretation. See Maunz in 3 Maunz/Dürig, Art. 72, Rdnr. 19.

[49] See Anschütz, supra note 7, at 85 (arguing that whether there was a need for
uniform imperial laws respecting public safety, order, or welfare under Art. 9
WRV was a matter of legislative discretion).

[50] See Maunz in 3 Maunz/Dürig, Art. 72, Rdnr. 18 (arguing that to hold that the
legislature had discretion to determine the limit of its own power was to say that its
power was not limited at all); Bothe in 2 AK-GG, Art. 72, Rdnr. 12 (contrasting the
Court's willingness to determine the necessity for governmental action in deciding whether legislative limitations on constitutionally guaranteed rights satisfy
the requirement of proportionality).

[51] Pacific Tel. & Tel. Co. v. Oregon, 223 U.S. 118 (1912).

[52] McCulloch v. Maryland, 17 U.S. 316, 423 (1819).

this country can equally be explained on the ground that the matter was committed to the discretion or decision of another branch of government.[53]

To say that Article 72(2) placed the matter within legislative discretion, indeed, seemed to undermine the need requirement even more than a simple holding of nonjusticiability would have done; for the latter would have left the need provision binding though unenforceable, while the Court's theory seemed to be that the legislators had a right to do as they pleased. Later opinions have retreated somewhat from this position, first picking up on the suggestion that there might be review for abuse of discretion[54] and later declaring that the Constitutional Court was entitled to inquire "whether the legislature in principle correctly interpreted the terms employed in Art. 72(2) . . . and stayed within the framework that those terms describe."[55] Nevertheless, in the forty years since its withdrawal from the field the Court has reviewed a profusion of federal laws enacted on the basis of concurrent powers without once finding another violation of Article 72(2), and its investigation of the need for federal action even under the less deferential current standard can best be described as perfunctory.[56] Thus the need requirement has proved as ineffective in limiting federal authority in Germany as the enumeration of congressional powers has been in the United States.[57] One of the central recommendations of the Constitutional Commis-

---

[53] See Louis Henkin, Is There a "Political Question" Doctrine?, 85 Yale L.J. 597 (1976).

[54] E.g., 4 BVerfGE 115, 127-28 (1954) ("at most the Constitutional Court can determine whether the legislature has abused its discretion"). The initial decision had left the question of review for abuse of discretion open, 2 BVerfGE at 225.

[55] 13 BVerfGE 230, 234 (1961). The same formulation was repeated in 26 BVerfGE 338, 382-83 (1969), and more recently in 78 BVerfGE 249, 270 (1988).

[56] See also Blair, supra note 13, at 78-85. In general the Court tends to be content with finding that federal regulation was invited by the Länder or will promote uniformity. See, e.g., 13 BVerfGE 230, 234 (1961); 26 BVerfGE 338, 382-83 (1969); 78 BVerfGE 249, 270-71 (1988). Neither of these considerations seems to establish that uniformity was *required*; if the mere fact that federal law would promote uniformity were enough, Art. 72(2) would impose no limit at all. Cf. Art. 9 WRV (authorizing the enactment of federal legislation concerning welfare and the protection of public order and safety to the extent that there was a *need* for uniform laws ("ein Bedürfnis für den Erlaß einheitlicher Vorschriften"). For an effort to explicate what Art. 72(2) really requires see Maunz in 3 Maunz/Dürig, Art. 72, Rdnr. 21-23 (concluding that most federal legislation can be justified under the uniformity provision of Art. 72(2) cl. 3).

[57] One of the principal recommendations of the Enquête-Kommission in an effort to strengthen Länder authority was an attempt to put teeth in the need provision. See Schlußbericht der Enquête-Kommission, part 2, pp. 63-64. For doubts as to the effectiveness of such an attempt see Maunz in 3 Maunz/Dürig, Art. 72, Rdnr. 25.

sion in 1993 was an amendment to Article 93 making clear that the determination of need was subject to judicial review.[58]

On the other hand, the subject-matter limitations on federal legislation resulting from the reservation of unenumerated powers to the Länder have been as scrupulously observed in interpreting concurrent as in interpreting exclusive federal authority. The power to enact land law ("Bodenrecht") does not include authority to regulate building construction.[59] The authority over waterways ("Wasserstraßen") does not support a law against water pollution.[60] Regulation of admission ("Zulassung") to medical callings does not embrace regulation of the conduct of those who have already been admitted.[61] Civil law ("bürgerliches Recht") does not include rules respecting government liability, the rights of owners of condemned property, or damages for harm to publicly owned streets.[62]

In each of these cases the result was supported by impressive arguments from text, context, or tradition. The narrow language of the provision respecting medical licensing contrasted with a more commodious grant of authority over "the legal profession."[63] The waterways provision appeared in conjunction with other grants of power respecting transportation;[64] to give it a broad reading would have undermined the grant of authority to enact only framework leg-

---

[58] See Bericht der VerfKomm at 31, 33, 36. The Commission also proposed amending Art. 72(2) itself so as to make clear that uniformity of the law was not sufficient per se to justify federal legislation, but only when the national interest so required. See id. at 31, 33-34.

[59] 3 BVerfGE 407, 413-16 (1954) (invoking, inter alia, the legislative history of a similar provision in the Weimar Constitution).

[60] 15 BVerfGE 1, 7-24 (1962).

[61] See 17 BVerfGE 287, 292-94 (1964) (income support program for midwives); 33 BVerfGE 125, 152-55 (1972) (exclusion of specialists from general medical practice); 71 BVerfGE 162, 171-72 (1985) (prohibition of medical advertising). See also 4 BVerfGE 74, 82-85 (1954) (holding that regulation of disciplinary tribunals within the medical profession fell within neither the provision respecting admission to practice nor the federal power over judicial procedure).

[62] 61 BVerfGE 149, 174-202 (1982); 8 BVerfGE 229, 235-38 (1958); 42 BVerfGE 20, 28-32 (1976). The Constitutional Commission, perceiving a need for uniformity with respect to government liability, proposed an amendment to add this subject to the list of concurrent powers (subject to Bundesrat consent) in 1993. See Bericht der VerfKomm at 31, 34, 116.

[63] See Art. 74 cl. 1 GG ("die Rechtsanwaltschaft"); 17 BVerfGE at 292. Legislative history also supported this conclusion, for the conference of experts who drafted the provision had emphasized that health matters in general were largely reserved to the Länder, and the influential delegate Carlo Schmid assured the convention without contradiction that the proposed federal authority over medical licensing did not include the regulation of medical practice. See 1 JöR (n.F.) at 539, 542. Contrast Art. 7 cl. 8 WRV, which placed the entire subject of health ("das Gesundheitswesen") within concurrent federal power.

[64] Art. 74 cl. 21-23 (shipping, navigational aids, inland navigation, road traffic, highways, and railroads). See 15 BVerfGE at 12-14.

islation respecting water resource management ("Wasserhaushalt"), which clearly included pollution.[65] Civil law had traditionally been understood to deal with "the legal relationships between individuals," not between citizens and the state.[66] But the fact that these decisions may well have been correct does not detract from the striking contrast between the German court's approach to federalism and that of our own: The Supreme Court has made no serious effort to protect the reserved rights of the states for the past fifty-five years.[67]

One of the most challenging problems confronting the Constitutional Court has been to define the boundary between federal authority over "criminal law" and the traditional police powers of the Länder. If the Federation could regulate anything it liked by simply prescribing criminal sanctions, there would be nothing reserved to the states, contrary to the basic principle of state authority. Anticipating this danger, the experts who drafted the Basic Law had explained that criminal law embraced only matters that we would be inclined to call malum in se.[68] Invoking practice under similar provisions of earlier constitutions, however, the Constitutional Court held that federal authority extended to regulatory offenses as well.[69] Early decisions upholding federal power to punish the distribution of publications harmful to children,[70] the failure to keep records respecting the use of explosives,[71] and the construction of buildings without a permit[72] added that the activity made punishable need not be independently subject to federal regulation,[73] and in two of these cases the existence of federal regulatory authority was flatly denied.[74]

---

[65] Art. 75 cl. 4 GG; see 15 BVerfGE at 14-16.

[66] See 42 BVerfGE at 31.

[67] See, e.g., the decisions cited in note 38 supra. Rare exceptions include Oregon v. Mitchell, 400 U.S. 112 (1970), which by a 5-4 vote held that Congress could not alter the minimum age for voting in state elections; National League of Cities v. Usery, 426 U.S. 833 (1976) (overruled, Garcia v. San Antonio Metropolitan Transit Auth., 469 U.S. 528 (1985)), which dealt with the special question of federal power to regulate state government itself; and New York v. United States, 112 S. Ct. 2408 (1992), where the Court concluded that Congress could not require the states to regulate nuclear waste.

[68] "Criminal law is only the criminal law in the strict sense, with specific ethical content. It would be impermissible to undermine the authority of state legislatures indirectly by means of the power over criminal law." Herrenchiemsee Bericht, 2 Akten und Protokolle at 504, 531 .

[69] 27 BVerfGE 18, 32-33 (1969). See Anschütz, supra note 7, at 80-83 (arguing largely on the basis of history that the authority to enact criminal laws under Art. 7 cl. 2 WRV was not, as some commentators had recently argued, limited to matters otherwise subject to federal regulation).

[70] 11 BVerfGE 234, 237 (1960).

[71] 13 BVerfGE 367, 371-73 (1962).

[72] 23 BVerfGE 113, 122-26 (1968).

[73] See 11 BVerfGE at 237 (finding it unnecessary to decide whether the law protecting children from harmful publications fell within federal authority over "trade and commerce" (Art. 74 cl. 11) or "public welfare" (cl. 7)); 23 BVerfGE at

Each of these decisions, however, contained limiting language. The suppression of indecent publications, the Court said in the first case, was a traditional subject of criminal law.[75] In the other two instances federal law had prescribed punishment for the violation of regulations promulgated by the states themselves and thus could hardly be said to have undermined state authority.[76] The limit was confirmed in 1969, when the Court held unconstitutional a federal statute imposing criminal penalties for unauthorized use of the title "Engineer."[77] In this case, the Court emphasized, it was not state law but other provisions of the same federal statute that specified who was permitted to employ that title. The Federation had no authority to

---

124: "In defining criminal offenses . . . the federal legislature is not confined by the limits of authority otherwise conferred." Accord von Mangoldt, supra note 16, at 407. Cf. United States v. Butler, 202 U.S. 1 (1936) (reaching a similar conclusion that was destined to turn the power to tax in order to promote the general welfare into an instrument for regulating matters otherwise reserved to the states).

[74] See 13 BVerfGE at 371-72 (holding that the statute respecting explosives could not be sustained as an "economic law" within Art. 74 cl. 11 because its purpose was not to stimulate the economy but to protect public safety); 23 BVerfGE at 125 (citing the decision striking down the federal building code, note 59 supra, as authority that the subject of construction permits "belongs, with the general police power, within the competence of the Länder").

The narrow view of the permissible reasons for regulating the economy suggested by the first of these opinions is somewhat misleading. Although the Court initially suggested that a regulation of the economy could not be based *solely* on public safety, from the first it relied on pre-1949 tradition to hold that a concern for safety did not condemn a law serving economic ends as well; and later decisions have upheld "economic" regulations without saying that they served any purpose other than public safety. See, e.g., 8 BVerfGE 143, 148-54 (1958) (holding that a gun inspection requirement fell within the realm of economic regulation because it served to promote the weapons industry as well as to protect the public); 11 BVerfGE 6, 14 (1964) (concluding that a boiler permit requirement fell within federal authority over the economy *because* it promoted public safety); 41 BVerfGE 344, 355 (1976) (upholding federal safety requirements for elevators although their principal purpose was safety: "The law of occupations has always been in large part a specialized body of police regulations"). Cf. the similar decision respecting federal authority over foreign trade, text at notes 28-31 supra. A more convincing argument for holding the explosives provision not a legitimate regulation of the economy might have been that it was not limited to economic activities but was addressed to the public generally. See Maunz in 3 Maunz/Dürig, Art. 74, Rdnr. 151. Both weapons and explosives were later made federal subjects by constitutional amendment, Art. 74 cl. 4a GG.

[75] 11 BVerfGE at 237.

[76] See 13 BVerfGE at 373; 23 BVerfGE at 125. Cf. Clark Distilling Co. v. Western Md. Ry., 242 U.S. 311 (1917) (upholding a statute making it a federal crime to transport liquor in violation of state law at a time when Hammer v. Dagenhart, 247 U.S. 251 (1918), suggested doubts as to federal power to regulate the liquor trade directly).

[77] 26 BVerfGE 246, 257-58 (1969).

regulate the use of the engineer's title itself;[78] and "the federal legislature cannot regulate matters that lie within state authority through the back door of the criminal law."[79]

When federal legislative power is concurrent, the Länder are free to act to the extent the Federation does not.[80] This means that a federal statute preempts not only contrary state law (which would have been clear under the general supremacy principle of Article 31)[81] but also parallel state provisions – a result our Supreme Court has sometimes reached by statutory construction.[82] As in this country, there has been much litigation over whether particular state laws are preempted. The American observer would feel right at home reading most of these opinions.[83] Of greater analytical interest is the Constitutional Court's conclusion that the Federation could not preempt state regulation without regulating the matter itself.[84] It may be that this limitation is essentially formal; in keeping with the obvious fact that freedom from regulation may itself reflect a significant policy decision, the Court added that it would treat a declaration that certain activities should not be regulated as a substantive federal rule.[85]

---

[78] The authority over "economic law" granted by Art. 74 cl. 11, the Court said, would have permitted the Federation to regulate the practice of the engineering profession, but the mere specification of persons entitled to call themselves "engineers" bore "no relation to economic law." 26 BVerfGE at 254-56. See also 10 BVerfGE 141, 162-63 (1959) (holding that the specific reference to "private insurance" in Art. 74 cl. 11 showed that public insurance companies were not subject to federal regulation); 33 BVerfGE 206, 217 (1972) (concluding that a 1938 law punishing the unlicensed possession of firearms had become state rather than federal law under Art. 125 because it served not to regulate trade under Art. 74 cl. 11 but to protect public safety).

[79] 26 BVerfGE at 258. See generally Maunz in 3 Maunz/Dürig, Art. 74, Rdnr. 63-66.

[80] See Art. 72(1) GG. Thus, whether federal authority is exclusive or concurrent, the existence of state power lies in the hands of the federal legislature; inertia works against the Länder in one case and for them in the other. But see Bothe in 2 AK-GG, Art. 70, Rdnr. 5 (arguing that the distinction is of little practical significance because of the exhaustive degree to which the Bund has exercised its concurrent powers).

[81] See Art. 31 GG: "Federal law shall override Land law."

[82] See., e.g., Pennsylvania v. Nelson, 350 U.S. 497 (1956); Garner v. Teamsters Union, 346 U.S. 485 (1953).

[83] Early examples include 1 BVerfGE 283, 296-98 (1952) (federal law requiring stores to close at 7 p.m. precludes the Länder from setting an earlier as well as a later time); 2 BVerfGE 232, 235-36 (1953) (federal law requiring that employees be paid if they do not work on holidays does not preempt a state law requiring double wages if they do). See generally Jost Pietzcker, Zuständigkeit und Kollisionsrecht im Bundesstaat, 4 Handbuch des Staatsrechts 693.

[84] 34 BVerfGE 9, 27-28 (1972).

[85] Id. at 28; see also Maunz in 3 Maunz/Dürig Art. 74, Rdnr. 33-35. Cf. Teamsters Union v. Oliver, 358 U.S. 283 (1959) (concluding that federal labor law forbade

C. Framework Legislation

Framework laws ("Rahmenvorschriften") are supposed to lay down basic principles and leave their elaboration to the states. Federal laws passed pursuant to more plenary grants of power often do just that both in Germany and in the United States.[86] What is unusual about Article 75 of the Basic Law from an American point of view is that it empowers the Federation to enact *only* framework legislation in the fields to which it applies. Article 75 is thus an interesting compromise that requires significant decentralization of policymaking authority without sacrificing uniformity where uniformity is needed.[87] It has longstanding roots in German constitutional history.[88]

The list of possible subjects of framework legislation is relatively brief, but it includes much of what other provisions leave to the Länder: higher education, the press, and the film industry; hunting, conservation, and scenic preservation; land reform, regional planning, and water resource management; registration of residents and identity cards; and the legal status of state and local public servants in matters not within the concurrent authority granted by Article 74a. In contrast to exclusive and concurrent powers, this authority has been used somewhat sparingly, and the inclusion of several top-

---

application of state antitrust law to a collective-bargaining agreement on this ground).

[86] For the German situation see Maunz in 3 Maunz/Dürig, Art. 75, Rdnr. 10. American examples include the central provision of the Clean Air Act, 42 U.S.C. § 7410, which invites the states to determine in the first instance what control measures should be adopted in order to achieve compliance with federal standards for ambient air quality.

[87] Appropriately, framework laws may be enacted only where the need for federal legislation is established as provided in Art. 72(2); but the need requirement has played as insignificant a role in limiting framework legislation as it has in limiting the exercise of concurrent federal powers. See text at notes 40-57 supra; Maunz in 3 Maunz/Dürig, Art. 75, Rdnr. 35.

[88] See id., Rdnr. 20, citing Art. 4(4) of the 1871 constitution (authorizing enactment of general provisions ("allgemeine Bestimmungen") respecting banking) and Art. 10-11 of the Weimar Constitution (providing for the promulgation of principles ("Grundsätze") in various fields). As Maunz reveals, it was doubtful whether legislation under these earlier provisions could bind individual citizens (see also Anschütz, supra note 7, at 94-95, arguing that they could). There is no doubt that framework laws under the present Art. 75 may do so, but the Constitutional Commission has recommended that this power be limited to exceptional cases. See Maunz, supra, Rdnr. 21; 4 BVerfGE 115, 128-30 (1954); Bericht der VerfKomm at 31, 36. A handful of references to Grundsatz legislation are found in the Basic Law as well (see Art. 91a, 109(3), and 140 GG); they are understood to allow less intensive regulation than ordinary Rahmengesetze. See Rengeling, supra note 7, Rdnr. 283.

ics has been criticized as unnecessary.[89] Nevertheless framework legislation has been of considerable significance in the Federal Republic, and it has raised interesting analytical questions.

The fundamental requisite of framework legislation, the Constitutional Court has said, is that it leave significant leeway to the states in implementing its provisions.[90] It was the application of this principle in 1954 to strike down a statute forbidding the Länder to pay civil servants more than their federal counterparts that prompted the addition of concurrent authority over state salaries in Article 74a.[91] Like the converse question whether legislation leaves too much discretion to the executive,[92] the determination whether a framework law gives the Länder enough elbow room is highly subjective. Greater leeway is said to be required with respect to press and film, as to which Article 75 provides that framework legislation may concern only "general legal relations"; to higher education, for which it may establish only "general principles"; and to the public service, in which the Länder have a particular interest protected even against constitutional amendment by Article 79(3).[93]

Whether a particular statute leaves enough room for state policymaking can only be determined from case to case; in contrast to the question whether there is a need for federal regulation, this issue is subject to full judicial review.[94] On the one hand, after holding that the Federation could not tie state pay scales to federal, the Constitutional Court suggested that it could not require the participation of employees' representatives in decisions to discharge a particular class of civil servants.[95] On the other hand, the Court has permitted

---

[89] See Maunz in 3 Maunz/Dürig, Art. 75, Rdnr. 1, 42-43 (questioning the inclusion of hunting, press and film, and redistribution of land). The Constitutional Commission in 1993 proposed to eliminate university structure and films from the list of possible subjects of federal framework laws. See Bericht derVerfKomm at 31, 35-36.

[90] See 4 BVerfGE 115, 128-30 (1954). Cf. Anschütz, supra note 7, at 88-89 (giving a similar explanation of "Grundsätze" under Art. 10-11 WRV). For differing views as to whether the Länder are *required* to implement federal framework legislation see Maunz in 3 Maunz/Dürig, Art. 75, Rdnr. 14 (arguing that such an obligation would be inconsistent with state autonomy); Bothe in 2 AK-GG, Art. 75, Rdnr. 5 (arguing that otherwise the Länder would be able to frustrate the exercise of federal power). The Constitutional Commission has proposed to make state implementation mandatory. See Bericht der VerfKomm at 21,36.

[91] 4 BVerfGE 115, 135-38 (1954). See Maunz in 3 Maunz/Dürig, Art. 74a, Rdnr. 1.

[92] See Art. 80(1) GG (requiring the legislature to specify the content, purpose, and scope ("Inhalt, Zweck und Ausmaß") of delegated power); Schechter Poultry Corp. v. United States, 295 U.S. 595 (1935). For discussion of delegation issues in Germany see chapter 3 infra.

[93] See 4 BVerfGE 115, 136 (1954); Maunz in 3 Maunz/Dürig, Art. 75, Rdnr. 33.

[94] See 4 BVerfGE 115, 127-28 (1954). But see Anschütz, supra note 7, at 89 (arguing that this question too was committed to the legislature under Art. 10-11 WRV).

[95] 51 BVerfGE 43, 53-55 (1979) (finding that the framework law actually enacted left the states ample discretion in this regard).

framework legislation to limit the removal of such representatives from advisory committees,[96] to make proportional representation the general rule in the election of university governing bodies,[97] and even to prescribe the titles of state judges – because the statute left other aspects of their legal status to state law.[98] One may quibble about the results of particular cases, and there seems to have been a tendency toward more expansive interpretation of federal authority.[99] What is of interest here is that in this field as elsewhere – with the important exception of the need requirement of Article 72(2) – the Constitutional Court has not let the difficulty of drawing objectively defensible lines prevent it from making a sincere effort to preserve such state legislative authority as remains under the Basic Law.[100]

D. Financial Provisions

Conspicuously absent from the basic enumerations of federal power in Articles 73-75 are provisions respecting taxing and spending, which are collected in a separate part of the Basic Law devoted to financial matters (Art. 104a-115). In contrast to the corresponding

---

[96] 51 BVerfGE 77, 95 (1979).

[97] 66 BVerfGE 291, 306-07 (1984).

[98] 38 BVerfGE 1, 10-11 (1974). See also 43 BVerfGE 291, 343-44 (1977) (emphasizing – as the Constitutional Commission later urged be made explicit (see Bericht der VerfKomm at 31, 36) – that such definitive regulation of details is permissible only in cases of exceptional need). The authority to enact framework legislation respecting the legal status of state judges is given by Art. 98(3), not by the more general provision respecting civil servants in Art. 75, but the governing principles are the same.

[99] Most recently, however, without questioning its earlier decisions respecting the scope of federal power, the Court has emphasized that by its very nature framework legislation is presumed to invite state implementation and to confine the discretion of the Länder "no further than the language of the framework provision unavoidably requires." 80 BVerfGE 137, 158 (1989).

[100] Contrast the refusal of the U.S. Supreme Court since 1937 to police either the delegation of legislative power or the exercise of authority under the commerce clause, which present similar line-drawing problems. See, e.g., FEA v. Algonquin SNG, 426 U.S. 548 (1976) (upholding a grant of authority to take unspecified measures to prevent reliance on imports from jeopardizing national security); Wickard v. Filburn, supra note 38. The Enquête-Kommission (Schlußbericht, Teil 2, at 63-69) proposed to abolish the distinction between concurrent and framework legislative powers and to limit the Federation in all cases of nonexclusive authority to the enactment of guidelines ("Richtlinien") like the directives of the European Communities – which under Article 189 of the Common Market treaty bind the member states "as to the results to be achieved" while leaving them "the choice of form and methods" for so doing – in the absence of a showing that the legislative goal could not be attained without more intensive federal regulation. In light of the ineffectiveness of the analogous requirement of Art. 72(2) as a limit on federal power, it does not seem surprising that nothing has come of this proposal.

clauses of the U.S. Constitution, these provisions are notably detailed. They were comprehensively rewritten in 1969, and their interpretation has produced an extensive and complicated body of decisions.

Article 105(1) gives the Federation exclusive authority over export and import duties ("Zölle")[101] and fiscal monopolies ("Finanzmonopole") – traditional income-producing government enterprises involving matches and brandy.[102] In its original form, Article 105(2) proceeded to list particular categories of taxes that the Federation had concurrent authority to impose.[103] Since 1969, with the exception of certain local excise taxes (Art. 105(2a)), the Federation has had concurrent power over *all* taxes not within its exclusive authority, provided either that the Federation is entitled to at least part of the revenue under Article 106 or there is a need for federal legislation as defined by Article 72(2). Because the question of need is essentially unreviewable,[104] the upshot is that the Federation – like the United States Congress – may impose taxes on essentially whatever it likes.[105]

What differentiates the two systems sharply is that in Germany, as a general rule, anything taxed by the Federation is exempt from further taxation by the states. Because there is a federal sales tax, for example, the Länder may not tax the sale of wine.[106] The basis for this conclusion is the stringent preemption principle of Article 72(1), which permits the Länder to exercise concurrent powers only to the

---

[101] See 8 BVerfGE 260 (1958) (striking down a state law imposing charges for transporting goods across the international border). Cf. U.S. Const., Art. I, § 10, which similarly forbids state import or export taxes in the absence of congressional consent. Art. 73 cl. 5 envisions the Federal Republic as a unitary customs area; neither the Federation nor the Länder, it is said, can tax the movement of goods from one Land to another. See Maunz in 4 Maunz/Dürig Art. 105, Rdnr. 32. Since 1975, external tariffs have benefited the Common Market, not the Federal Republic. See id., Art. 106, Rdnr. 23.

[102] See id., Art. 105, Rdnr. 35-38 (arguing that the creation of additional state monopolies would offend the guarantee of occupational freedom in Art. 12(1) (see chapter 6 infra) and that the existing monopolies ought to be abolished because a modern state with adequate taxing authority has no need to engage in such unfair competition); Dieter Birk in 2 AK-GG, Art. 105, Rdnr. 8-9 (reporting the abolition of the match monopoly in 1983 and arguing that new monopolies in "isolated fields of little economic importance" would be permissible since otherwise the express provision of Art. 105(1) would be hollow). In light of all this and the tension between monopolies and the competitive principles of the Common Market, the provision respecting fiscal monopolies is essentially a dead letter.

[103] Included were taxes on income, property, inheritance, and gifts, along with most excises on consumption or sales – but only if the proceeds were applied at least in part to cover federal expenditures or the need requirement of Art. 72(2) was met. See 2 Quellen zum Staatsrecht at 247, 268.

[104] See text at notes 40-57 supra.

[105] See Maunz in 4 Maunz/Dürig Art. 105, Rdnr 39-40; Rudolf Wendt, Finanzhoheit und Finanzausgleich, 4 Handbuch des Staatsrechts 1021, Rdnr. 28-32.

[106] 7 BVerfGE 244, 258-65 (1958).

extent that the Federation does not.[107] To compensate for this severe limitation on their taxing authority, Article 106 guarantees the Länder a substantial share of the revenues from federal taxes,[108] and Article 105(3) gives them a say in determining the extent of federal taxation: No legislation relating to taxes whose revenues accrue even in part to state or local government may be enacted without Bundesrat consent.[109]

This last provision enables the Länder to block federal legislation that endangers their financial security, but it leaves them without authority to levy adequate taxes of their own. Concerned that financial independence was essential to the functioning of a federal system, the Allied authorities had insisted upon restricting federal authority in this field.[110] The 1969 reforms, however, reflect the original German concern that divergent tax schemes in different Länder might disrupt the operation of the national market;[111] the upshot is

---

[107] See id. at 258-59; Maunz in 4 Maunz/Dürig Art. 105, Rdnr 42a-44; Wendt, supra note 105, Rdnr. 33-37. The explicit authorization of "local excise taxes . . . not identical with those imposed by federal legislation" (Art. 105(2a) GG) permits the Länder to tax certain transactions also subject to federal taxation, provided that the state tax has only local effect and is similar to those traditionally imposed at the time the provision was adopted. See 40 BVerfGE 56, 60-64 (1975). This provision has given rise to considerable litigation. See, e.g., 69 BVerfGE 174, 183-84 (1985) (upholding a local tax on the sale of beer for on-premises consumption); 16 BVerfGE 306, 316-29 (1963) (striking down a local tax on the sale of ice cream because it was not so limited); Maunz in 4 Maunz/Dürig Art. 105, Rdnr. 55-60 (arguing that what made traditional local taxes not "identical" to the federal was that they applied only to a small subset of the transactions taxed under federal law).

[108] Revenues from income and corporation taxes are divided equally between the Bund and the Länder, except that local governments are entitled to a share of the former to be determined by law. Sales tax receipts are allocated by federal law requiring Bundesrat consent, with due regard to relative federal and state needs. Inheritance and real estate taxes, among others, are reserved to state and local governments respectively. See Birk in 2 AK-GG, Art. 106, Rdnr. 28, 30 (reporting that in recent years the Bund has been allotted roughly two-thirds of sales tax revenues and local governments 15 percent of payroll taxes).

[109] See Wendt, supra note 105, Rdnr. 21-22.

[110] See the memoranda of Nov. 22, 1948 and of March 2, 1949 from the military governors to the Parliamentary Council, in 2 Quellen zum Staatsrecht at 208-13. For recognition of this need in the Parliamentary Council see Sten. Ber. at 38-39 (Delegate Schwalber). See also id. at 33 (Delegate Menzel): "The money bag is the most important part of the body." Our experience under the Articles of Confederation, which left the central government dependent upon contributions from the states, lent force to the Allied objection, as did German experience under the 1871 and 1919 constitutions. See Wendt, supra note 105, Rdnr. 7-15.

[111] See 16 BVerfGE 306, 322-23 (1963); Sten. Ber. at 99 (Delegate Höpker-Aschoff); 1 JöR (n.F.) at 750-62. Cf. the intricate efforts of our Supreme Court under the commerce clause ever since the Case of the State Freight Tax, 82 U.S. 232 (1873), to protect interstate trade from undue interference by state taxes.

that both Bund and Länder are largely dependent upon uniform taxes whose enactment requires both federal and state consent.[112]

As in this country, taxes may serve social and economic purposes other than the production of revenue, and they often do.[113] This means, among other things, that through differential taxation the Federation may influence behavior it cannot regulate directly. The limiting principle, however, is that the exaction must in fact produce revenue; like our Supreme Court in former times,[114] the Constitutional Court does what it can to prevent the usurpation of other authority under the pretense of taxation.[115] On this basis the Court as recently as 1984 went so far as to strike down an exaction designed to provide funds for housing construction on the ground that all the money collected was ultimately to be refunded: A forced loan was not a tax because it resulted in no net revenue to the government.[116]

---

[112] See Schlußbericht der Enquête-Kommission, Teil 2, at 172 (praising the current financial provisions as a "happy medium" between extremes of state and federal power); Wendt, supra note 105, Rdnr. 43,103 (arguing for greater state authority); Maunz in 4 Maunz/Dürig Art. 105, Rdnr. 61 (finding the equal voice of the Bundesrat in tax matters under the circumstances an "indispensable condition" for the operation of the federal system). See also id., Rdnr. 25 (arguing that the independence of the Länder requires that state receipts from the registration of radio and television sets remain immune from federal taxes although the original ground for this conclusion – that the earlier grant of federal authority over sales taxes applied only to the provision of goods or services in the private market (31 BVerfGE 314, 323-33 (1971)) – was eliminated by the 1969 amendments).

[113] See, e.g., 16 BVerfGE 147, 160-62 (1963) (upholding a tax principally designed to discourage firms from transporting their own goods): "Taxes that encourage the taxpayer to take a specific economic course without legally requiring him to have always existed." See also 36 BVerfGE 66, 70-71 (1973) (upholding a tax whose principal purpose was to dampen inflation by reducing purchasing power); 38 BVerfGE 61, 79-81 (1974) (upholding a tax imposed on the transportation of goods by truck in order to reduce traffic and to improve the competitive position of the railroad).

[114] See, e.g., Child Labor Tax Case, 259 U.S. 20 (1922).

[115] See, e.g., 16 BVerfGE 147, 161 (1963): "One could speak of such an abuse [of authority] if the tax law contradicted its inherent revenue-raising purpose by plainly attempting to eliminate the occurrence of the taxable event, that is to say to suppress the activity entirely." See also 14 BVerfGE 76, 99 (1962) (stating a similar but somewhat more stringent test for determining when a state tax was forbidden because of its effect on an activity subject to federal regulation); Maunz in 4 Maunz/Dürig Art. 105, Rdnr. 9, 24; Klaus Vogel, Grundzüge des Finanzrechts des Grundgesetzes, 4 Handbuch des Staatsrechts 3, Rdnr. 51. For the argument that regulatory taxes should require regulatory competence see Kirchhof, supra note 25, Rdnr. 53-62.

[116] 67 BVerfGE 256, 281-90 (1984). The fact that the money was to be repaid without interest, the Court held, was immaterial; the money saved was not revenue obtained but expense avoided. Id. at 283. Nonrefundability was a traditional element in the German definition of taxes (see Wendt, supra note 105, Rdnr. 18), but the decision was rendered the more striking by the fact that the exaction raised money for spending in areas independently within federal competence – housing

The converse challenge has been to prevent either the Federation or the Länder from evading the carefully crafted financial provisions of the constitution by imposing what are in effect taxes under the guise of some other authority. Long before adoption of the Basic Law it was understood that not every duty to pay money to the state was a tax, and consequently the Constitutional Court has upheld a bewildering variety of exactions ("Gebühren," "Beiträge," "Sonderabgaben," etc.) without regard to the allocation of taxing power in Article 105. Thus charges assessed for investment in the depressed iron, steel, and coal industries[117] and to finance training positions for persons entering the work force[118] were sustained as exercises of federal authority over "economic law" (Art. 74 cl. 11), those in support of the domestic wine industry[119] under the power to promote agriculture (Art. 74 cl. 17). In contrast to ordinary taxes, these exactions fall upon a relatively narrow group rather than on the public at large;[120] like special assessments in this country, they therefore raise questions not only of federalism[121] but also of equality in the distribution of financial burdens.[122]

In accordance with tradition, the fundamental principle of decision has been that an exaction can be sustained apart from the tax provisions only if those on whom it is imposed can be said to bear some special responsibility for it, and that generally requires that the assessment be more or less balanced by some benefit conferred by the state.[123] Not only does the correspondence between benefit and

---

and the economy. For the fate of the argument that the exaction could be defended on the ground of the grants of authority over those subjects in Art. 74 see note 120 infra.

[117] 4 BVerfGE 7, 13-15 (1954).

[118] 55 BVerfGE 274, 309-18 (1980).

[119] 37 BVerfGE 1, 16-17 (1974).

[120] It was in part because the refundable surcharge to finance housing construction was imposed on the general public that it was held not to be sustainable as an economic or housing measure, although its refundability (see text at note 116 supra) kept it from being sustainable as a tax. See 67 BVerfGE 256, 274-80 (1984).

[121] See 55 BVerfGE 274, 300-02 (1980). The particular concern in that case was that taxes whose revenues benefited the Länder required Bundesrat consent, while economic measures under Art. 74 cl. 11 did not. See id. at 288-89, 297. Cf. the Head Money Cases, 112 U.S. 580 (1884), in which the Supreme Court sidestepped the question whether an exaction on the transportation of passengers met the uniformity requirement of Art. I, § 8 by holding that it was not a tax but a regulation of commerce.

[122] See, e.g., 55 BVerfGE 274, 302-04 (1980). Cf. Norwood v. Baker, 172 U.S. 269 (1898) (holding a special assessment disproportionate to the benefits accruing to the taxpayer a taking without compensation). To the extent that these exactions (as is typical of the so-called Sonderabgaben) flow into funds separate from the general treasury, they also endanger the integrity of the federal budget. See Art. 110 GG (providing for enactment of a balanced budget in statutory form); Kirchhof, supra note 25, Rdnr. 223-30.

[123] See, e.g., 55 BVerfGE at 308-18; Maunz in 4 Maunz/Dürig Art. 105, Rdnr. 12-20; Kirchhof, supra note 25, Rdnr. 231-38. Increasingly, however, special as-

burden go a long way toward eliminating any problem of inequality; it also suggests that the exaction is a price rather than a tax.[124] Thus wine producers bore the cost of promotional activities that enhanced their own profits, employers the cost of training workers they might later employ; businesses required to contribute to the recovery of the iron and coal industries were entitled to interest on their investment or to shares of stock in the benefited companies. Drawing lines in this area is a significant challenge,[125] but here as elsewhere the German Court has been far more willing to enforce limitations on federal authority than has its counterpart in the United States.

An even more pronounced solicitude for the interests of the Länder characterizes the Constitutional Court's jurisprudence with respect to federal spending. Article 104a(1), added by the 1969 amendments, provides that as a general rule both the Bund and the Länder must bear the costs of their own activities.[126] Paragraph (4) of the same Article nevertheless authorizes the Federation to "grant the Länder financial assistance for particularly important investments" under certain narrowly defined circumstances. The language of this provision is restrictive, and the Constitutional Court has interpreted it narrowly.

---

sessments have been levied on the basis of harm caused rather than benefits received, especially as a means of reducing pollution. They have not yet been tested before the Constitutional Court. See id., Rdnr. 251-55.

[124] This relationship is most evident in the case of the so-called Gebühren, which are usually fees for some governmental service rendered to the individual, such as the provision of electricity or education or the execution of a judgment. Even in this category, however, there are examples of assessments on those who have merely caused the state to incur costs, such as the fees charged persons convicted of crimes. See id., Rdnr. 185-97.

[125] See, e.g., Maunz in 4 Maunz/Dürig Art. 105, Rdnr. 21-23 (arguing that the exaction to pay for training positions was a tax and criticizing the decision (11 BVerfGE 105, 110-14 (1960)) upholding a requirement that employers pay for subsidies of employees with children, on the ground that in neither case did the exaction benefit the burdened class). See also 81 BVerfGE 156, 185-88 (1990) (relying on the fact that assessments on former employers were balanced by unemployment benefits paid to their former employees [!] to conclude that the stringent criteria governing special exactions did not have to be applied at all). In distinguishing the decision respecting vocational training on the ground that no corresponding state benefit had there been involved, the Court in the unemployment case appeared both to contradict the reasoning of the earlier opinion ("Taken in its entirety, therefore, the revenue produced by the exaction for vocational training is primarily employed in the interest of the employers" (55 BVerfGE at 316)) and to call into question the established criteria limiting the use of special exactions.

[126] Art. 104a(2) provides that the Federation bears the costs when the Länder enforce federal law as agents of the Federation ("im Auftrag des Bundes"), because in that situation the states are subject to federal direction (see text at notes 188-91 infra). The implication is that the Länder bear these costs when they administer federal law on their own responsibility. See Hans Herbert von Arnim, Finanzzuständigkeit, 4 Handbuch des Staatsrechts 987, Rdnr. 29-30.

"Federal financial assistance," said the Court in passing on federal grants for urban renewal in 1975, "creates the risk that the Länder may become dependent upon the Federation and thus endangers their constitutionally guaranteed autonomy."[127] Federal grants must therefore "remain the exception, and they must be so structured as not to become the means of influencing decisions of the constituent states in fulfilling their own responsibilities."[128] The constitutional criteria governing the existence of federal authority to make grants for this purpose, the Court concluded, were sufficiently vague that the legislature's decision to do so was subject only to limited judicial review, and there was no doubt that they had been met: Urban renewal was a particularly important investment that would significantly promote economic growth.[129]

However, in order to preserve state autonomy, the Court continued, implementation of the grant program must be left essentially to the states. The Federation might spend money to rebuild cities, but the Länder must be free to determine where and how to do it.[130] Since the urban renewal law could be construed to leave the choice of individual projects principally to the states, it was upheld;[131] a second program that did not meet this requirement was struck down the next year.[132]   Thus, unlike the modern Supreme Court, the German court polices federal spending to prevent usurpation of state or local authority by the attachment of conditions to the enjoyment of largesse.[133]

---

[127] 39 BVerfGE 96, 108 (1975). See also von Arnim, supra note 126, Rdnr. 14, 46.

[128] 39 BVerfGE at 107.

[129] Id. at 114-15. Art. 104a(4) authorizes federal grants only for investments of particular importance and only if "necessary to avert a disturbance of the overall economic equilibrium or to equalize differences of economic capacities within the Federal Republic or to promote economic growth." The standard of review here enunciated was identical to that employed in more recent decisions respecting the question of need for the exercise of concurrent federal authority under Art. 72(2). See text at notes 40-57 supra. For an explication of the constitutional standards see Maunz in 4 Maunz/Dürig, Art. 104a, Rdnr. 43-52.

[130] 39 BVerfGE at 115-21. Even general criteria for the selection of individual projects, the Court added, could be laid down only with state consent, either by administrative agreement or by legislation requiring Bundesrat consent under Art. 104a(4). Id. at 116-17, 121.

[131] Id. at 122-27.

[132] 41 BVerfGE 291, 310-13 (1976) (invalidating a program of financial aid for such infrastructure improvements as the preparation of industrial sites and the construction of waste disposal facilities). The Court added that state rights had also been infringed by establishing the program without either Bundesrat approval or formal agreement with the Länder (id. at 304-310) and by providing funds directly to local governments rather than to the states (id. at 313-14).

[133] Cf. United States v. Butler, 297 U.S. 1 (1936), where the Supreme Court made an unpersuasive effort to limit the regulatory effect of federal grants; Steward Machine Co. v. Davis, 301 U.S. 548 (1937), and South Dakota v. Dole, 483 U.S. 203 (1987), where the Court threw in the towel.

One important financial provision remains to be discussed: Article 107(2) provides for payments from one Land to another, and from the Federation to the Länder, in order to reduce inequalities of economic power among the states. There is no comparable provision in the U.S. Constitution, although various federal spending programs in this country may have the effect of redistributing wealth to less affluent states. As the Constitutional Court noted in upholding a law providing for equalization payments under a predecessor provision in 1952, the duty of one Land to subsidize another entails "a certain limitation of the financial autonomy of the Länder."[134] Thus the basic principle of federalism expressed in Articles 20(1) and 79(3) led the Court to conclude that no equalization statute would be permitted to "weaken critically the financial capacity [Leistungsfähigkeit] of the donor states or lead to a leveling [Nivellierung] of state finances."[135] But federalism, the Court continued, implied burdens as well as benefits; and one of them was the obligation of the stronger states to help the weaker ones.[136] Only if each state was financially able to fulfill its responsibilities, the Court later added, could the Länder be truly autonomous.[137]

In response to Allied concerns for the independence of the Länder,[138] the original authorization for equalization payments was narrowly drafted.[139] Yet the Constitutional Court declined to construe it narrowly, explaining that the sponsor of the provision had espoused a restrictive equalization system not because he liked it but only to satisfy Allied objections.[140] "The question of how far financial equalization among the Länder may be extended within the boundaries already drawn," the Court added, "is a question of finan-

---

[134] 1 BVerfGE 117, 131 (1952).

[135] Id. See also Josef Isensee, Idee und Gestalt des Föderalismus, 4 Handbuch des Staatsrechts 517, Rdnr. 149: "The constitutional maxim can only be that each Land must bear the consequences of its own financial decisions."

[136] 1 BVerfGE at 131.

[137] 72 BVerfGE 330, 383 (1986). See also Maunz in 4 Maunz/Dürig, Art. 107, Rdnr. 7.

[138] See 1 BVerfGE at 128-30 (noting among other things the initial Allied insistence that financial equalization be limited to modifying the dominant principle that allocated tax revenues to the state in which they were collected). Provisions to accomplish the limited equalization envisioned by the Allies are now found in the second and third sentences of Art. 107(1). For explanation of these provisions see Wendt, supra note 105, Rdnr. 67-70.

[139] The provision was found in Art. 106(4) of the original Basic Law, reprinted in 2 Quellen zum Staatsrecht at 268.

[140] 1 BVerfGE at 134-35. One is reminded once again of the old saw about leading horses to water. Cf. text at notes 40-57 supra (discussing the requirement that concurrent powers be exercised only when there is a need for federal legislation).

cial policy and not of constitutional law; it is not reviewable by the Constitutional Court."[141]

The 1969 amendments broadened the equalization provisions even further. The original authorization to provide assistance out of tax revenues accruing to the more affluent Länder became a duty, and the Federation was for the first time empowered to make additional payments out of its own funds.[142] Careful and detailed 1986 and 1992 opinions interpreting the revised provisions reveal both the extraordinary complexity of determining which Länder are entitled to what payments and – because these determinations are made by federal statute with the consent of the Bundesrat – the corresponding influence that Article 107 gives the Federation over the financial health of the Länder.[143]

---

[141] 1 BVerfGE at 134. John Marshall said much the same thing about the necessary and proper clause: "[W]here the law is not prohibited, and is really calculated to effect any of the objects intrusted to the government, to undertake here to inquire into the degree of its necessity, would be to pass the line which circumscribes the judicial department, and to tread on legislative ground." McCulloch v. Maryland, 17 U.S. 316, 423 (1819).

[142] See Maunz in 4 Maunz/Dürig, Art. 107, Rdnr. 45 (arguing that the latter provision poses a particular danger of unwanted federal influence on state policy).

[143] 72 BVerfGE 330, 383-423 (1986) (striking down various provisions of the implementing statute principally on the ground that they resulted in a miscalculation of the relative financial strength of the Länder and construing other provisions narrowly to avoid excessive leveling); 86 BVerfGE 148 (1992). See generally Wendt, supra note 105, Rdnr. 73-90. The equalization provisions promise to be a major vehicle for bringing the newly admitted East German Länder more nearly to the developmental level of the original states, but for practical reasons the unification treaty postponed their applicability until 1995. Einigungsvertrag, Art. 7(3).

Often mentioned as an alternative means to the goal of the equalization provisions in Art. 107(2) (see Maunz in 4 Maunz/Dürig, Art. 107, Rdnr. 10) is Art. 29, which as presently formulated empowers the Federation on the basis of referendum to reorganize state boundaries "to ensure that the Länder by their size and capacity are able effectively to fulfill the functions incumbent upon them." See Sten. Ber. at 16 (1948) (Delegate Schmid) (arguing that a "healthy federal system" was possible only if the Länder were reasonably comparable in size and wealth "and not purely accidental constructions that for the most part are no more than three years old and owe their existence to the happenstance of the line of demarcation between two infantry divisions." Originally obligatory, the authority conferred by Art. 29 has never been exercised, although the present Land of Baden-Württemberg was formed from three artificial entities created by the division of Germany into occupation zones after World War II on the basis of a special reorganization provision in Art. 118. Efforts at further reorganization were blocked first by Allied conditions attached to approval of the Basic Law (see 2 Quellen zum Staatsrecht at 217), then by rigorous standing limitations on proceedings before the Constitutional Court (13 BVerfGE 54 (1961)), and finally by increasing adaptation to originally arbitrary boundaries (see Maunz in 2 Maunz/Dürig, Art. 29, Rdnr. 19), as suggested by the refusal of voters to approve a proposed division of Baden-Württemberg into its traditional parts (see 37 BVerfGE 84 (1974)). The extraordinary power that Art. 29 and 118 gave the Federation over the very existence of its constituent states

E. The Role of the Bundesrat

Thus the list of federal lawmaking powers is impressively long; despite faithful judicial enforcement of many of the limits on federal authority, most significant legislation in Germany is federal. Yet it would be wrong to conclude that the Länder play a minor role in this field. Even though the Länder enact few important statutes of their own, they take a substantial part in the enactment of federal legislation. For while the members of the federal Parliament ("Bundestag") are directly elected by the people,[144] no federal law can be enacted without being submitted to a separate body called the Bundesrat (Council of State Governments), which represents the states themselves. It is not merely that, as was originally the case of the U.S. Senate, members are chosen by some branch of state government.[145] The members of the Bundesrat are *members* of state governments, appointed and subject to recall by the states;[146] they are there as representatives of the Länder.[147]

---

can be explained only by the arbitrariness of the initial division into Länder (see Maunz in 2 Maunz/Dürig, Art. 29, Rdnr. 5); their application to Baden-Württemberg in the very first case the Constitutional Court decided on the merits gave rise to the interesting notion that a provision of the Constitution itself might be unconstitutional. See 1 BVerfGE 14, 32-33 (1951); chapter 4 infra.

[144] See Art. 38(1) GG.

[145] See U.S. Const., Art. I, § 3 (providing that Senators be chosen by the state legislatures). Popular election of Senators dates from adoption of the seventeenth amendment in 1913.

[146] See Art. 51(1) GG. In fact the Prime Ministers of the Länder, along with their fellow Ministers, serve also as members of the Bundesrat; they and their alternates are said to be bound by instructions from the governments they represent. See Roman Herzog, Zusammensetzung und Verfahren des Bundesrates, 2 Handbuch des Staatsrechts 505, Rdnr. 2-9; for the Weimar understanding see Anschütz, supra note 7, at 346-47. For the vigorous debate in the Parliamentary Council on the question whether some or all members of the Bundesrat should be elected by the state legislatures (the so-called Senate alternative) see Sten. Ber. at 85-97.

[147] See Art. 50 GG: "The Länder shall participate through the Bundesrat in the legislation and administration of the Federation." The apportionment of seats in the Bundesrat deviates somewhat from the equality principle that applies to our Senate: The smallest Länder have three seats, those with two to six million inhabitants four, those with six to seven million five, and those with more than seven million six (Art. 51(2)). By rejecting a strict allocation according to population, the framers intended to prevent any single state from achieving a dominant position such as Prussia had enjoyed in the past. See Isensee, supra note 135, Rdnr. 140. Cf. Art. 61 WRV, which provided that no Land could have more than 40 percent of the seats in the Reichsrat, although on a strict population basis Prussia would have been entitled to more than half; Anschütz, supra note 7, at 339-40.

The details have varied over time, but every German constitution since 1849 has provided for a similar body through which the states play a role within the central government.[148] Under the Basic Law a variety of federal executive actions affecting the Länder require Bundesrat approval,[149] and the Bundesrat selects half the members of the Federal Constitutional Court.[150] The most important powers of the Bundesrat, however, are those respecting federal legislation.

The basic provision is Article 77, which gives the Bundesrat a suspensive veto over federal legislation generally. Normally the Bundestag may override this veto by a majority vote; but if the veto is passed by a two-thirds majority, a two-thirds vote is required.[151] In a number of instances, however, the Bundesrat has an absolute veto; no federal statute may become law without Bundesrat approval. Provisions to this effect are inconveniently scattered throughout the Basic Law. Predictably, they tend to involve matters of particular concern to the Länder: state finances,[152] state administrative agencies,[153] state boundaries,[154] amendment of the constitution itself.[155]

Originally it was expected that the requirement of Bundesrat consent would be the exception, not the rule. According to recent estimates, however, somewhere between fifty-five and sixty percent of all federal statutes now require such consent.[156] In part this high percentage is attributable to the fact that constitutional amendments giving the Federation additional powers commonly mitigate the in-

---

[148] See RV 1849, §§ 86, 88, 100, 102; RV 1871, Art. 5, 6; Art. 60, 63, 74 WRV. For antecedents dating back to the Holy Roman Empire see Jürgen Jekewitz in 2 AK-GG, vor Art. 50, Rdnr. 1-4.

[149] See, e.g., Art. 37(1), 84(3)-(5) (various measures to ensure faithful state enforcement of federal law), 80(2), 84(2) (federal regulations implementing federal statutes in certain cases).

[150] See Art. 94(1) GG. See also text at notes 208-09 infra (discussing new provisions giving the Bundesrat a significant role in affairs of the European Communities).

[151] See Art. 77(3), (4) GG.

[152] See, e.g., Art. 104a(4) (federal grants in aid), 105(3) (taxes from which Länder derive revenue), 106(3) (division of sales tax revenues between the Federation and the Länder), 107(2) (equalization payments to less affluent states). Cf. Art. 74a (compensation of state and local officers).

[153] See, e.g., Art. 84(1), 85(1), 108(2), (5) (regulation of state agency organization and procedure), 87(3) (establishment of additional federal agencies).

[154] See Art. 29(7) GG. Since 1976 more significant boundary changes have required approval by referendum instead, see Art. 29(2).

[155] Art. 79(2) GG (requiring a two-thirds vote in both Bundestag and Bundesrat). See generally Herzog, Aufgaben des Bundesrates, 2 Handbuch des Staatsrechts 489, Rdnr. 10-14. This allocation of responsibility represented a compromise. The Christian Democrats and their allies had wanted to require consent of the Bundesrat for all legislation; the Social Democrats had argued that the Bundestag should be permitted to override its veto in every case. See Sten. Ber. at 85-86 (Delegate Lehr), 89-90 (Delegate Dehler), 91 (Delegate Katz).

[156] See Herzog, supra note 155, Rdnr. 8.

cursion on state authority by giving the Bundesrat an absolute veto.[157] The most fertile source of laws requiring Bundesrat approval, however, is Article 84(1), whose interesting development merits closer examination.

As will be explained in the following section of this chapter, most federal laws in Germany are carried out by the Länder.[158] Because the Federation has an obvious interest in the execution of its laws, Article 84(1) permits it to regulate the organization and procedure of state agencies administering federal law. Because such regulations plainly impinge on the interests of the Länder, they may be enacted only with Bundesrat consent.

Many federal statutes contain provisions regulating state administrative organization and procedure. Moreover, the Constitutional Court very early concluded that a statute was to be treated as a unit for this purpose: If any provision of the statute regulated state administration, the entire statute required Bundesrat approval.[159] Thus the Bundesrat may base its rejection of a law regulating state procedure on objections to substantive provisions of the same statute; and thus the Bundesrat has veto power over many substantive provisions not independently requiring its approval.[160]

The reasoning in support of this conclusion was essentially formal: Article 84(1) provided that state agencies might be regulated in certain cases by "federal statute" with Bundesrat consent, and for purposes of determining whether a law had been enacted Article 78 seemed to treat each "statute" as a whole.[161] Nothing in the text of the latter provision, however, suggests it was meant to resolve the question of the extent of Bundesrat power. At first glance, moreover, the Court's interpretation appears to make little sense in terms of the division between federal and state authority, for the implication seems to be that the Bundestag can insulate its substantive provisions from Bundesrat rejection simply by placing them in one bill and the procedural provisions in another.[162] Indeed the same formalistic

---

[157] See id., Rdnr. 12.

[158] See Art. 83 GG.

[159] 8 BVerfGE 274, 294-95 (1958) (holding Bundesrat approval also required when the operation of a law requiring Bundesrat consent was extended: "Extension of the effective life of the price control statute was in effect the enactment of a new law with the same content").

[160] The law in question provided for price control and was enacted under Art. 74 cl. 11 (economic law), which does not require Bundesrat consent.

[161] 8 BVerfGE at 295. See Art. 78 GG: "A bill adopted by the Bundestag shall become a law if the Bundesrat consents to it . . . ." The Court added that its conclusion to treat the entire statute as a unit reflected the "consistent practice" of the affected institutions and that any other rule would produce "insuperable difficulties" (which were not defined) in the legislative process. Id.

[162] See 37 BVerfGE 363, 382 (1974) (dictum) (calling this a common practice); Herzog, supra note 155, at Rdnr. 15 (saying it has never happened). If Herzog is right, a possible explanation might be the fear that the Bundesrat might refuse to ap-

approach led the Court several years later to hold that a law *amending* a statute that regulated state procedure did not require Bundesrat approval unless it contained procedural provisions of its own; the amending law was itself a "statute," not a part of the statute it amended.[163]

In reaching this result, the Court developed an additional and more powerful argument based on the purpose of the consent requirement. Article 84(1) required Bundesrat approval because federal regulation of state administrative agencies was a major intrusion on the interests of the Länder; if the amending law contained no such regulation, there was no such intrusion and no reason to require Bundesrat consent.[164] The difficulty with this reasoning was that it seemed to cast doubt on the earlier decision to treat the initial statute as a unit: If only procedural provisions significantly impinge upon state interests, the consent requirement should not extend to substantive provisions just because they happen to be in the same statute.

A powerful dissenting opinion argued that this inconsistency cut the other way: To permit the Bundestag alone to amend substantive provisions that had initially required Bundesrat approval would undermine the requirement of initial Bundesrat consent. All the Bundestag would have to do to get its way would be to agree to the Bundesrat's original conditions and then, once the procedural provisions were safely enacted, alter the substantive part of the package by ordinary legislation.[165] The description in this passage of the original legislation as a "compromise" suggests a more convincing reason for the basically noncontroversial decision to treat the entire original statute as a unit: To allow substantive provisions to stand despite a Bundesrat veto of accompanying procedural ones might seriously distort the product of the legislative process, since the Bundestag

---

prove the procedural provisions until they were combined with the substantive ones in order to ensure its power to veto the latter.

[163] 37 BVerfGE 363, 379-83 (1974).

[164] Id. at 379-80. See also id. at 380-81 (adding that a contrary result would turn the requirement of Bundesrat consent from the exception into the rule).

[165] Id. at 408-09 (von Schlabrendorff, Geiger, and Rinck, JJ., dissenting). See also id. at 401-08 (neatly refuting other arguments of the majority). As the dissenters noted (id. at 409-10), the contrast was heightened by an intervening decision holding that the provision of Art. 80(2) for Bundesrat approval of federal regulations promulgated on the basis of laws requiring Bundesrat consent applied to *all* such regulations, whether or not the provisions they implemented would independently have required such approval. 24 BVerfGE 184, 194-201 (1968). See also the 5-to-3 decision (28 BVerfGE 66, 76-79 (1970)) concluding that a statute dispensing with the requirement of Bundesrat consent for the adoption of federal regulations (as Art. 80(2) permits) could itself be enacted only with Bundesrat approval, on the ground that it would be inconsistent to allow the Länder to be deprived of their veto power without their consent.

might not have adopted the substantive provisions without the contested procedure.[166] Thus the interpretation of the various provisions respecting Bundesrat approval of federal legislation has presented a continuing challenge, and the requirement of state participation in the enactment of federal laws remains an important safeguard for the interests of the Länder.[167] Because it is the *executive* branch of state government that is represented in the Bundesrat, moreover, this requirement also assures that practical questions of administration re-

---

[166] For exposition and criticism of this argument see Ossenbühl, Die Zustimmung des Bundesrates beim Erlaß von Bundesrecht, 99 Archiv des Öffentlichen Rechts [AöR] 369, 395-403 (1974) (terming it unlikely that the content of substantive provisions would be dependent upon the accompanying procedure).

It is not always easy to determine whether a federal statute regulates agency organization or procedure within the meaning of Art. 84(1). The American lawyer will be reminded at once of the difficulties that have arisen in distinguishing "substance" from "procedure" in various contexts in this country. See, e.g., Sibbach v. Wilson, 312 U.S. 1 (1941) (Rules Enabling Act); Guaranty Trust Co. v. York, 326 U.S. 99 (1945) (applying the rule of Erie R.R. v. Tompkins, 304 U.S. 64 (1938)); Levy v. Steiger, 233 Mass. 600, 124 N.E. 477 (1919) (interstate choice of law). For an example of difficulties of this nature in Germany see 37 BVerfGE 363, 383-95 (1974) (dividing 4-4 on the question whether a requirement that certain benefits be granted only upon application was procedural or substantive).

For the Constitutional Court the more difficult problem has been to determine whether a particular statute "otherwise provides" with respect to agency organization or procedure. That a statute might satisfy this criterion without expressly regulating those matters was recognized in 1974. It would be enough to require Bundesrat consent, the Court declared, if a proposed statute amended existing law in such a way as to "give an essentially different significance and scope" to procedural provisions that were not explicitly amended. 37 BVerfGE 363, 383 (1974). What this might mean was suggested by a decision four years later under the separate provision of Art. 87b(2), which requires Bundesrat consent to laws providing for federal administration of certain matters pertaining to national defense. The Bundesrat had already approved an earlier statute providing for federal administration of alternative service for conscientious objectors. Nevertheless, said the Court, consent was also required for a law dispensing with preexisting procedures for determining the good faith of persons claiming conscientious objector status, because the new provisions would so drastically increase the number of conscientious objectors as to amount to a new grant of federal authority. 48 BVerfGE 127, 177-84 (1978) (over two dissents). A 1987 decision, however, took a diffrerent tack with respect to Art. 84(1), without even citing the 1978 case. The extension of existing social insurance programs to include self-employed artists, the Court concluded, did not require Bundesrat approval; a mere quantitative increase in the caseload of state agencies was not enough, because the new statute did not *regulate* agency organization or procedure. 75 BVerfGE 108, 149-53 (1987).

[167] See also 1 BVerfGE 299, 310-11 (1952) (upholding a statute making the allocation of federal funds for public housing construction dependent upon unanimous agreement of the Länder themselves: the provision of Art. 50 regarding the role of the Bundesrat did not exhaust the possibilities for state participation in federal functions).

ceive adequate consideration in the legislative process.[168] Finally, because Bundestag and Bundesrat have often been controlled by different parties, the participation of the latter has sometimes provided a political check as well.[169] Like other guarantees of state interests in the Basic Law, the role of the Länder in federal legislation has been broadly construed by the Court; and Article 79(3) protects it in principle against constitutional amendment.[170]

II. OTHER POWERS

A. Executive Power

To an observer from the United States, one of the most startling aspects of the German Basic Law is that most federal laws are carried out by the states. Article 83 declares the basic principle: "The Länder shall execute federal laws as matters of their own concern insofar as this Basic Law does not otherwise provide or permit."[171] Article 83 is the administrative analog of the Article 70 provision respecting legislative power, which is riddled with exceptions; but the

---

[168] This knowledge was one of the advantages emphasized by advocates of the Bundesrat solution in the Parliamentary Council. See Sten. Ber. at 23-24 (Delegate Süsterhenn). See also Herzog, Stellung des Bundesrats im demokratischen Bundesstaat, 2 Handbuch des Staatsrechts 467, Rdnr. 21, 44 (concluding that the Bundesrat thus injects a modicum of reality into the legislative process). At the same time, however, the fact that it is the executive branch of state government that speaks through the Bundesrat means that any grant of legislative authority to the Bundestag subject to Bundesrat consent strengthens state executives at the expense of the state legislatures and thus diminishes direct popular control.

[169] See id. at Rdnr. 16, 19 (arguing that local interests (wine producers, less affluent states, etc.) tend to outweigh partisan considerations in most cases). See also id., Rdnr. 7 (noting that because the larger states are not fully represented in proportion to their population a coalition of the financially weaker Länder has controlled a majority of votes). Conversely, when the various organs are controlled by the same political party or coalition, the party system tends to undermine the division of authority, as it does in the United States.

[170] The Enquête-Kommission (Schlußbericht, pt. 1, at 203-04) expressed satisfaction with the basic provisions respecting the role and composition of the Bundesrat.

[171] See, e.g., 11 BVerfGE 6, 14-22 (1960) (holding that the central government could not constitutionally grant licenses under federal laws respecting boilers). The Court conceded that in exceptional cases the Federation might have unwritten authority to enforce federal laws that could not effectively be enforced by the Länder, but added that the mere fact that federal enforcement might be more expedient ("zweckmäßiger") did not justify a finding of implicit federal authority. Id. at 17-18; see also Peter Lerche in 3 Maunz/Dürig, Art. 83, Rdnr. 39-50.

exceptions to Article 83 are much less sweeping. Most legislative power in Germany is federal; most executive power is not.[172]

It is hard to imagine that Congress would ever trust the states to enforce federal law to the same extent in the United States. The usual reason federal laws are enacted is that the states have proved unwilling to tackle the problem; the same political pressures that produced legislative reluctance seem likely to produce executive footdragging as well.[173] In order to reduce federal bureaucracy and permit diversity, some federal statutes in this country do provide for state participation in their enforcement; but they generally provide for federal intervention in case the states do not do the job.[174]

The Federation is not without means of influencing the Länder in their execution of federal law.[175] As already noted, with Bundesrat consent the Bundestag may regulate the organization and procedure of state agencies administering federal law.[176] With Bundesrat consent the federal government may also confine state administrative discretion by issuing administrative regulations ("Verwaltungsvorschriften"),[177] and it may be authorized by statute to issue regulations binding third parties ("Rechtsverordnungen") as well.[178] Article 84(3) provides for federal supervision ("Bundesaufsicht") to ensure that the Länder faithfully carry out federal law and authorizes the dispatch of federal observers ("Beauftragte") to state agencies for this purpose.[179] If the state does not conform voluntarily, the

---

[172] See id. at Rdnr. 4, 53; Kimminich, supra note 1, at Rdnr. 50. Execution of state laws, as in this country, is reserved exclusively to the Länder. See Sten. Ber. at 173 (Delegate Schmid); 21 BVerfGE 312, 325 (1967) (holding the central government without power to grant permits for piers and other facilities in and about rivers under state law): "The execution of state laws by federal agencies is flatly precluded by the Basic Law."

[173] See Osborn v. Bank of the United States, 22 U.S. 738, 818-19 (1824): "All governments which are not extremely defective in their organization, must possess, within themselves, the means of . . . enforcing their own laws."

[174] E.g., Clean Air Act, § 110(a)(1)-(2), (c)(1), 42 U.S.C. § 7410(a)(1)-(2), (c)(1) (inviting the states to submit plans for implementing federal standards of ambient air quality but providing for federal action if state plans are inadequate).

[175] See Lerche in 3 Maunz/Dürig, Art. 83, Rdnr. 4.

[176] Art. 84(1) GG. See text at notes 158-66 supra.

[177] Art. 84(2) GG. The Bundesrat was recently said to have approved 699 of the 704 administrative regulations the Government had proposed. See Willi Blümel, Verwaltungszuständigkeit, 4 Handbuch des Staatsrechts 857, Rdnr. 39.

[178] Art. 80(1) GG. The Länder too may be authorized to adopt regulations with legislative force under this provision, and state agencies may adopt internally binding regulations in the absence of contrary federal law. See 76 BVerfGE 1, 76 (1987).

[179] If the agency is a subordinate one, consent of the agency or of the Bundesrat is required. The powers of federal observers are not further specified, but it is generally understood that they do not have authority to give orders to state officials or to take over the enforcement function. See, e.g., Lerche in 3 Maunz/Dürig, Art. 84, Rdnr. 165; Hans Peter Bull in 2 AK-GG, Art. 84, Rdnr. 60.

federal government may petition the Bundesrat for a determination that the state has failed in its duty, and the Bundesrat's decision is subject to review by the Constitutional Court (Art. 84(4)). With Bundesrat consent, the federal government may also be authorized to issue instructions ("Einzelweisungen") to state officials in particular cases (Art. 84(5)), and if all else fails it may take other "necessary measures" (the so-called "Bundeszwang") – also on condition of Bundesrat consent – in order to enforce state compliance (Art. 37).[180] Bundesrat consent means Länder consent, though not necessarily that of the offending Land; the Bundesrat has never been asked to find a state in violation of its duty or to approve coercive measures under Article 37.[181]

State administration of federal law in Germany is motivated in part by the same considerations that underlie our separation of legislative and executive powers. The dangers of an all-powerful federal executive were all too vividly illustrated during the Nazi period; the risk of inadequate enforcement is the price of protection against prosecutorial abuse. The Basic Law goes beyond our Constitution by taking enforcement not only out of legislative hands but largely out of federal hands as well; in a parliamentary system this may be necessary to assure effective freedom from legislative control.[182]

State enforcement of federal law had been the norm under earlier constitutions; the willingness of the framers of the Basic Law to reinstitute and even to strengthen it suggests that it had worked reasonably well.[183] Apparently it has also worked well enough since; al-

---

[180] Apart from instructions to the Länder and their officials, Art. 37 does not specify what measures may be taken; they are thought to include direct federal enforcement and the use of force. See Maunz in 2 Maunz/Dürig, Art. 37, Rdnr. 47-56; Michael Bothe in 2 AK-GG, Art. 37, Rdnr. 22-25. On the question of the degree to which less intrusive supervisory options under Art. 84 must be exhausted before Bundeszwang measures become "necessary" see Maunz, supra, Rdnr. 29; Lerche in 3 Maunz/Dürig, Art. 84, Rdnr. 135, 170.

[181] See Bothe in 2 AK-GG, Art. 37, Rdnr. 10. See also Bull in 2 id., Art. 84, Rdnr. 44 (adding that only sparing use has been made of the power to authorize federal instructions in particular cases). In approving adoption of the Basic Law, the Allied Military Governors had expressed misgivings lest this latter provision lead to an undue concentration of power. See 2 Quellen zum Staatsrecht at 217; Lerche in 3 Maunz/Dürig, Art. 84, Rdnr. 89 (concluding that so far these fears had not been realized).

[182] See 55 BVerfGE 274, 318 (1980); Kimminich, supra note 1, Rdnr. 45; Lerche in 3 Maunz/Dürig, Art. 83, Rdnr. 9, 10 (adding that decentralized enforcement also promotes understanding of particular cases and accommodation of varying local needs).

[183] See RV 1871, Art. 4 (giving the central authorities supervisory and legislative but not administrative powers over a long list of subjects); Art. 14 WRV (providing for state administration of federal law but permitting exceptions to be made by ordinary statute); Anschütz, supra note 7, at 109; Sten. Ber. at 38 (Delegate Schwalber) (declaring the general principle of Länder enforcement "practically uncontested"); 1 JöR (n.F.) at 624 (summarizing the discussions in the Parliamen-

though one hears periodic complaints about an enforcement deficit ("Vollzugsdefizit"), virtually no one seems to attribute it to the allocation of enforcement authority to the Länder.[184] The fact that so many federal laws can be enacted only with the consent of the Länder (though not necessarily of all of them) may help to reduce the danger of inadequate enforcement, as may the possibilities of federal intervention already described.[185] Another possible inference is that most Länder officials (presumably like most state officials in this country) take their constitutional obligations seriously.

Direct federal administration is provided for in areas in which unified administration is thought essential: foreign affairs, national defense, and currency; postal and telecommunications services, some federal taxes, some aspects of transportation.[186] Social insurance programs covering more than one Land are also federally administered,[187] as are the museums, archives, and libraries that once belonged to the former Prussian state.[188] Article 85 provides for an intermediate form of administration in which the Länder enforce federal law as agents of the Federation ("im Auftrag des Bundes") and subject to binding federal instructions.[189] Income and sales

---

tary Council); Lerche in 3 Maunz/Dürig, Art. 83, Rdnr. 7. Those who argued in the constitutional convention for federal collection of federal taxes emphasized the risks both of reluctant enforcement and of disuniform application, but they did not prevail. See Sten. Ber. at 33-34 (Delegate Menzel), 99-101 (Delegate Höpker-Aschoff) (adverting to unfortunate experiences under a 1913 statute).

[184] See Lerche in 3 Maunz/Dürig, Art. 83, Rdnr. 11 (reporting that "initially critical voices have rather receded" but attributing the general satisfaction in part to "bold interpretations" of federal administrative authority and to an increase in cooperative methods of state-federal enforcement); Isensee, supra note 135, Rdnr. 200. The Enquête-Kommission (Schlußbericht, pt. 2, pp. 86-87) expressed general satisfaction with the existing division of administrative authority between the Federation and the Länder.

[185] On the latter point see Lerche in 3 Maunz/Dürig, Art. 84, Rdnr. 130. See also Blümel, supra note 177, Rdnr. 41 (suggesting that judicial review had largely supplanted federal instructions as a means of controlling state administration of federal law).

[186] See Art. 32, 87(1), 87b, 87d, 88, 108(1) GG.

[187] See Art. 87(2) GG; 11 BVerfGE 105, 123 (1960) (upholding the establishment of a federal corporation to administer a fund for children's benefits under this provision).

[188] See 10 BVerfGE 20, 35-48 (1959) (upholding the establishment of a federal foundation for this purpose pursuant to Art. 135 GG, which provides in general that assets of states no longer existing belong to the Länder but permits the federal parliament to provide otherwise in case of "an overriding interest of the Federation").

[189] Federal supervision in such cases extends to the appropriateness ("Zweckmäßigkeit") as well as the legality of state administration. See Art. 85(4) GG; Bull in 2 AK-GG, Art. 85, Rdnr. 14-18. Although the affected Land must as a general rule be given an opportunity to comment before the Bund issues instructions, the decision to issue them lies within the discretion of federal officials, and

taxes and federal highways are to be administered in this way unless some other provision is made;[190] nuclear energy, aviation, and waterways may be.[191] Articles 91a and 91b, added in 1969 and amended the following year, designate such matters as the improvement of agricultural and economic structures and the construction of institutions of higher learning as joint tasks ("Gemeinschaftsaufgaben") of the Federation and the Länder.[192] Other forms of cooperative federal-state administration, not always explicitly provided for, have been of growing significance in recent years; at least one commentator finds in them a significant safety valve against the ordinary limitations of federal enforcement.[193]

Article 87(3) authorizes the creation of additional autonomous higher federal authorities ("selbständige Bundesoberbehörden") "for matters in which the Federation has the power to legislate." In light of the Basic Law's principle of the primacy of state administration, the further provision that federal agencies "at the intermediate and lower levels" may be set up only with Bundesrat consent and "in case of urgent need"[194] might be thought to suggest that "higher authorities" were supervisory bodies that did not administer the law di-

---

no substantive justification is required. 81 BVerfGE 310, 331-38 (1990) (upholding an instruction not to take the nuclear incident at Chernobyl as an occasion for applying new standards in passing on additional permits for a breeder reactor). This form of administration was first developed under the Weimar Constitution, which (as indicated in note 183 supra) permitted deviations from the general principle of autonomous state enforcement. See Bull, supra, Rdnr. 1. Although federal instructions to state agencies under these provisions have not been uncommon, the tendency is said to be toward a model of joint state-federal administration. See Lerche in 3 Maunz/Dürig, Art. 85, Rdnr. 17, 57, 89.

[190] See Art. 108(2)-(4), 90(2) GG.

[191] See Art. 87c, 87d, 89(2) GG. The first two provisions require a statute with Bundesrat consent, the third an application from the affected Land. For a complete list of possible areas of state administration "im Auftrag des Bundes" see Bull in 2 AK-GG, Art. 85, Rdnr. 5-8.

[192] For detailed discussion of these provisions see Maunz in 4 Maunz/Dürig, Art. 91a, 91b; Heiko Faber & Ingo Richter in 2 AK-GG, Art. 91a/91b; Blümel, supra note 177, Rdnr. 124-66.

[193] See, e.g., Art. 108(4) GG (authorizing the enactment of statutes providing for state-federal collaboration in tax administration); 32 BVerfGE 145, 152-56 (1971) (upholding Länder participation in the collection of taxes that the Federation was directed to administer, even before the above provision was in effect); 63 BVerfGE 1, 30-44 (1983) (upholding a federal statute entrusting management of a federal social security institution for chimney sweeps to a Bavarian state agency while stressing (id. at 41) that normally each level of government was expected to carry out its own functions); Lerche in 3 Maunz/Dürig, Art. 83, Rdnr. 84-123.

[194] Art. 87(3) GG. For explanation of the limitations on creation of inferior agencies under this provision and for a list of the few instances in which this authority had actually been exercised as of 1979 see Maunz in 3 Maunz/Dürig, Art. 87, Rdnr. 98-101.

rectly.[195] The Constitutional Court, however, has taken essentially the opposite position: Autonomous higher authorities are those which can administer the law without the aid of inferior agencies.[196] Thus under this provision the Court has upheld the establishment of federal agencies that supervise banks and determine which publications are harmful to minors – not despite but because of the fact that there was no state agency below them.[197] That Bundesrat consent is necessary before the Federation can set up a hierarchy of additional agencies should be a significant safeguard against wholesale displacement of state administration;[198] although an impressive variety of federal agencies have been set up under Article 87(3),[199] state execution of federal law remains the norm in fact as well as in theory.

Indeed, despite the general provision in Article 32(1) that "relations with foreign states shall be conducted by the Federation," the German Länder seem to have a more significant say in foreign affairs than their counterparts in the United States. That federal authority over "relations with foreign states" includes treaties is confirmed by Article 32(2), which requires consultation with any Land before conclusion of a treaty affecting its "special circumstances."[200]

---

[195] Earlier drafts would have required Bundesrat consent for the creation of higher authorities and corporations too, but this requirement was dropped without explanation during the constitutional convention. See 1 JöR (n.F.) at 646-52.

[196] See 14 BVerfGE 197, 211 (1962). Some support for this conclusion may be gleaned from the alternative provision in the same paragraph for federal corporations and institutions ("bundesunmittelbare Körperschaften und Anstalten des öffentlichen Rechtes") to carry out the same functions, since nothing in the text suggests that these organizations may act only in a supervisory capacity. See 37 BVerfGE 1, 24-25 (1974) (upholding the establishment of a federally administered fund to promote the wine industry under this provision).

[197] 14 BVerfGE 197, 210-15 (1962) (bank supervision); 31 BVerfGE 113, 117 (1971) (publications harmful to children). Cf. Morrison v. Olson, 487 U.S. 654 (1988) (holding that a special prosecutor was an "inferior officer" who need not be appointed by the President with Senate consent, although no superior officer had authority to control her actions). See also 14 BVerfGE at 213-14 (concluding that no showing of need in accordance with Art. 72(2) was required to justify establishment of a higher federal agency under Art. 87(3), despite the facts that such agencies were permitted only "for matters in which the Federation has the power to legislate" and that federal legislative authority over banks depended upon need).

[198] See Bull in 2 AK-GG, Art. 87, Rdnr. 23.

[199] See Maunz in 3 Maunz/Dürig, Art. 87, Rdnr. 89. In approving the Basic Law, the Allied Military Governors called particular attention to the breadth of authority conferred by Art. 87(3) and stated their intention to watch closely lest this provision or that of Art. 84(5) respecting federal instructions to state administrators "lead to an exaggerated concentration of power." See 2 Quellen zum Staatsrecht at 217. For German criticism along the same lines see Jakob Kratzer, Die Bundesoberbehörde, 3 DöV 529 (1950); Isensee, supra note 135, Rdnr. 203.

[200] Art. 78 of the Weimar Constitution, which contained a somewhat analogous provision, had gone further by expressly requiring the consent of a state before its

Article 32(3), however, expressly authorizes the Länder, with the consent of the Federal Government, to make treaties of their own with foreign states with respect to matters over which they have legislative authority.

Unlike the corresponding provision of our Constitution, this authority is not expressly restricted to nonpolitical "compacts" such as those determining boundaries or apportioning interstate streams; in this country states cannot make "treaties" even with congressional consent.[201] This difference may be more semantic than substantial, for the Basic Law limits the Länder to treaties respecting matters within their legislative authority, which is commonly said not to include political relations with foreign countries.[202] More significantly, the limitations on Länder authority in Article 32 apply only to relations with "foreign states"; unlike American states, German Länder may make agreements among themselves without federal permission.[203]

Most important in this connection is the widely though not universally accepted view that *only* the Länder may make treaties concerning matters within their exclusive domestic authority. Nothing in the text compels this conclusion. Article 32(1) on its face gives the Federation authority over everything affecting relations with foreign states, and Article 32(3) can be read to say that in certain matters within that category the Länder have concurrent power.[204] Similar language in the Weimar Constitution, however, had been commonly

---

boundaries could be altered by treaty. See Maunz in 2 Maunz/Dürig Art. 32, Rdnr. 23 (arguing that the same result should obtain under the Basic Law because it was implicit in "the nature of a state"). Cf. Geofroy v. Riggs, 133 U.S. 258, 267 (1890) (dictum) (making a similar argument for limiting the treaty power of the United States). Art. 59(2) requires legislative approval of treaties that "regulate the political relations of the Federation or relate to matters of federal legislation," but this is a separation of powers measure not directly relevant to the scope of federal treaty authority. See chapter 3 infra; Maunz, supra, Rdnr. 10.

[201] See U.S. Const., Art. I, § 10, as explained in Virginia v. Tennessee, 148 U.S. 503, 519 (1893). Indeed not every agreement between a German Land and a foreign governmental body even requires federal consent. See 2 BVerfGE 347, 371-75 (1953) (concluding that an agreement respecting administration of the harbor at Kehl was unaffected by Art. 32 because the other contracting party was a public corporation rather than a foreign state). Cf. Virginia v. Tennessee, 148 U.S. at 519 (narrowly defining "compacts" requiring congressional consent to include only those "tending to the increase of political power in the States").

[202] See Maunz in 2 Maunz/Dürig, Art. 32, Rdnr. 24-26.

[203] See id. at Rdnr. 64-65. See also id. at Rdnr. 12-14 (adding that for the same reason the Länder are free to deal with the Holy See on matters otherwise within their competence).

[204] In other respects the declaration in Art. 32(1) that foreign relations is "a federal matter" is understood to make federal authority exclusive, as it expressly was under Art. 78 of the Weimar Constitution. See id., Rdnr. 13, citing the convention records.

understood to give the Länder exclusive authority,[205] and commentators have drawn conflicting inferences from the records of the constitutional convention.[206] Somewhat suggestive in this regard, although not directly in point, is the famous 1957 *Concordat* decision, in which the Constitutional Court concluded that state law could constitutionally depart from a 1933 agreement between the former Reich and the Holy See guaranteeing Catholic education in public schools because the agreement dealt with a subject reserved to the Länder under the Basic Law.[207] Indeed, even those who argue that the Federation may make treaties on all matters affecting foreign relations tend to shy away from our Supreme Court's conclusion of implicit federal competence to implement treaties by statute, for fear that the central government might use its foreign affairs power as a means of determining matters reserved to the states.[208]

Finally, when the Maastricht Treaty looking toward a closer European Union was ratified in the closing days of 1992, the Basic Law was amended to give the Bundesrat – and therefore the Länder – an unprecedentedly influential part in European affairs. Whenever a

---

[205] See Art. 78 WRV; Wilhelm Grewe, Auswärtige Gewalt, 3 Handbuch des Staatsrechts 921, Rdnr. 84 ; Maunz in 2 Maunz/Dürig, Art. 32, Rdnr. 39.

[206] An earlier draft of the Basic Law that would have expressly tied the treaty powers of Bund and Länder to their respective spheres of legislative competence was altered in order to permit federal treaties on such matters as collective security and international arbitration, neither of which is within legislative authority at all. See 1 JöR (n.F.) at 301, 305 (1951). See also Maunz in 2 Maunz/Dürig, Art. 32, Rdnr. 29-41 (arguing that state authority is exclusive); Manfred Zuleeg in 1 AK-GG, Art. 32, Rdnr. 31-32 (arguing that it is not).

The practical difficulties of conducting foreign relations in this uncertain situation were alleviated by the so-called Lindauer Agreement of 1957, whereby the Federation agreed that it would conclude cultural treaties only with the consent of the Länder. See Grewe, supra note 205, Rdnr. 86; Maunz in 2 Maunz/Dürig, Art. 32, Rdnr.42-45; Zuleeg, supra, at Rdnr. 31 (noting the argument that this agreement was unconstitutional unless Art. 32 itself gave the Bund authority to make cultural treaties, since "the Länder may not give away their exclusive authority"). Art. 24(1a) GG, added in 1992, constitutionalizes the principle of joint Bund-Länder responsibility spelled out in the Lindauer Agreement.

[207] 6 BVerfGE 309, 340-67 (1957). The question presented was not federal power to make a new agreement on the subject but whether the agreement survived as federal or state law, and Art. 124 and 125 make that issue dependent upon the scope of federal legislative power. See id. at 343. Moreover, the Holy See is not considered a "foreign state" for purposes of Art. 32. See id. at 362; note 203 supra. But see the broader statement, id. at 365: "The Basic Law . . . denies the Federation lawmaking and administrative powers in the area of education and entrusts this subject to the exclusive responsibility of the Länder. . . . It also refrains from granting the Federation the constitutional authority to interfere in the exercise of this responsibility by the Länder."

[208] See, e.g., Zuleeg in 1 AK-GG, Art. 32, Rdnr. 33. Contrast Missouri v. Holland, 252 U.S. 416, 432 (1920): "If the treaty is valid there can be no dispute about the validity of the statute . . . as a necessary and proper means to execute the powers of the Government."

subject considered by the Union would be within Länder competence or subject to Bundesrat participation as an internal matter, a new Article 23 provides for Bundesrat participation in the formation of Germany's position. Insofar as Länder interests are affected, the Bundesrat's views must be considered ("berücksichtigt") even if the matter would normally fall within exclusive federal authority. If the principal focus ("Schwerpunkt") is on a matter subject to state legislative power, or on the composition or procedure of state agencies, the Bundesrat's position is to be given *controlling* weight ("maßgeblich zu berücksichtigen"), although without prejudice to the reponsibility of the Federation for the nation as a whole. Finally, when the measure under consideration principally affects a matter within the exclusive legislative power of the Länder, Germany is to be represented not by the Federal Government but by an appointee of the Bundesrat – who to be sure must exercise his authority in consultation and agreement with the Government ("unter Beteiligung und Abstimmung mit der Bundesregierung"), and once again with respect for the Federation's responsibility for the nation as a whole.[209]

Just how these apparently contradictory directions are to be reconciled remains to be seen. In any event the 1992 amendments give the constituent Länder a strikingly central share in the Federal Republic's participation in the future European Union.

B. Judicial Power

In the interest of uniformity and protection of federal rights, the Basic Law provides not only for a Federal Constitutional Court (Art. 92-94) but also for five federal supreme courts ("oberste Gerichtshöfe") whose jurisdiction is divided on subject-matter lines: the Federal Administrative Court, the Federal Fiscal Court, the Federal Labor Court, the Federal Social Court, and (for "ordinary" civil and criminal cases) the Federal Court of Justice ("Bundesgerichtshof") (Art. 95(1)). Even these courts are subject to state influence, for the Bundesrat elects half the members of the Constitutional Court (Art. 94(1)), while the Länder and the Bundestag are equally represented on a committee that selects judges of the other supreme courts in conjunction with the appropriate federal minister (Art. 95(2)).[210]

---

[209] The new provisions (Gesetz zur Änderung des Grundgesetzes vom 21. Dezember 1992, BGBl. I, S. 2086) can be found in 44 Sammelblatt für Rechtsvorschriften des Bundes und der Länder 309 (1993). They are explained in Rupert Scholz, Grundgesetz und Europäische Einigung, 1992 NJW 2593. For other provisions of the new Art. 23 respecting the transfer of powers to the European Union see text at notes 342-48 infra.

[210] The committee and the federal minister must agree before the appointment can be made. See Maunz in 4 Maunz/Dürig, Art. 95, Rdnr. 63. In a purely formal sense the appointment is made by the President of the Federal Republic (Art. 60(1)

In one significant respect the potential authority of federal courts is broader in Germany than in the United States. Nothing in the language of Article 95 suggests that they are limited to deciding matters of federal law, and Article 99 expressly permits the Länder to give them ultimate appellate jurisdiction over controversies arising under state law. The Land of Schleswig-Holstein, acting under this provision, has authorized the Bundesverfassungsgericht to act as final arbiter of controversies concerning its state constitution; it has established no constitutional court of its own.[211] The Constitutional Court has gone further, upholding a *federal* statute authorizing the Federal Administrative Court to review certain state court decisions turning entirely on state law, despite the argument that the Länder's reserved power to enact laws implied final authority to interpret them.[212] Thus, to the extent that federal or state law so provides, federal appellate review in Germany can promote uniformity even in areas outside the legislative authority of the Federation.[213]

Lower courts, on the other hand, are predominantly courts of the Länder. Apart from the Constitutional Court[214] and the "supreme" courts specified by Article 95(1), the Basic Law expressly contemplates federal courts only for military and civil-service controversies and for those concerning intellectual property.[215] All judicial power

---

GG), but as a largely ceremonial officer he is "normally bound" by their selection. See id., Rdnr. 62, 69-71.

[211] See Willi Blümel, Rechtsprechungszuständigkeit, 4 Handbuch des Staatsrechts 965, Rdnr. 7.

[212] 10 BVerfGE 285, 292-302 (1960) (persuasively marshaling the practice under similar provisions of earlier constitutions and finding the record of the constitutional convention inconclusive). A provision of the original draft expressly limiting federal courts to deciding federal questions had been dropped without explanation; individual delegates had expressed conflicting views as to the power of federal courts over state law. See also 1 JöR (n.F.) at 707-14 (showing that the central subject of debate had been whether federal jurisdiction should extend to cases involving state enforcement of *federal* law). Contrast Murdock v. Memphis, 87 U.S. 590 (1875). As a statutory matter, however, the authority of federal courts to determine state law in Germany remains the rare exception rather than the rule.

[213] On the other hand, although after extensive debate (see 1 JöR (n.F.) at 707-14) the Parliamentary Council decided not to leave the establishment of federal supreme courts to legislative discretion, it has been said that Art. 95(1) does not require that every state court decision be subject to federal appellate review even on matters of federal law. See, e.g., Maunz in 4 Maunz/Dürig, Art. 95, Rdnr. 28.

[214] The Constitutional Court is not strictly speaking an appellate court, but it often entertains constitutional challenges to the decisions of other courts, and private litigants challenging executive or legislative action must ordinarily exhaust other judicial remedies before filing a constitutional complaint. See Art. 94(2) GG; § 90(2) BVerfGG.

[215] Art. 96(1), (2), (4) GG. Federal patent and civil-service courts of first instance, whose judgments are reviewed by the Federal Court of Justice and the Federal Administrative Court respectively, have been established under these provi-

not given to federal courts, as Article 92 confirms,[216] is reserved to
the Länder by the general enumeration principle of Article 30. This
means that, in contrast to the situation in the United States, most
matters involving federal law are litigated initially in state court,
subject only to ultimate (and limited) federal appellate review.[217]

German observers do not appear to view the absence of lower federal courts as a threat to the supremacy of federal law.[218] Notwithstanding the force of John Marshall's argument that appeal was an
"insecure remedy" for possible state hostility to federal rights,[219] it
should be borne in mind that we got along under a somewhat similar
system until 1875.

Somewhat surprising to an outsider in light of the provisions just
described was the 1958 decision of the Constitutional Court upholding
a statute that gave the Federal Administrative Court original jurisdiction to review certain federal executive actions.[220] Normal jurisdictional practice in Germany tends to confirm the textual inference that "supreme courts" are to review lower courts, not to supplant them – as do explicit statements of supporters of the relevant
provisions in the constitutional convention, which the Court did not
cite.[221] Conceding that "higher" courts (for which the Basic Law
initially provided) basically ("grundsätzlich") meant appellate courts,

---

sions. See Maunz in 4 Maunz/Dürig, Art. 95, Rdnr. 7-10; Blümel, supra note 211,
Rdnr. 26-30.

[216] "Judicial power . . . shall be exercised by the Federal Constitutional Court, by
the federal courts provided for in this Basic Law, and by the courts of the Länder."

[217] See Blümel, supra note 211, Rdnr. 35. In contrast to the United States, federal
law regulates the jurisdiction and procedure of state courts and the compensation of
their judges, see id., Rdnr. 36-38; but state judges are appointed by state authorities.
See also Maunz in 4 Maunz/Dürig, Art. 95, Rdnr. 46, 49 (confirming that in
Germany too the courts of last resort are generally bound by findings of fact made
below).

[218] See, e.g., Isensee, supra note 135, Rdnr. 204 (arguing that the judicial powers
of the Länder are of "little significance" in the overall balance of federal and state
authority).

[219] Osborn v. United States, 22 U.S. 738, 822-23 (1824). See also England v.
Louisiana State Board of Medical Examiners, 375 U.S. 411, 416-17 (1964); 28 U.S.C.
§§ 1331, 1441(a).

[220] 8 BVerfGE 174, 176-81 (1958).

[221] See, e.g., Sten. Ber. at 173 (Delegate Schmid): "Adjudication is basically the
business of the Länder. Superior federal courts are established only at the highest
level in the interest of preserving uniformity of decision." See also 1 JöR (n.F.) at
713-14 (1951) (remarks of Delegate Zinn) (noting that the responsible committee had
"deliberately refrained from providing for federal administrative courts at the
middle and lower levels" because "the courts at the lower and middle levels should
be state courts"). See also the similar observations of Delegate Greve, id. at 710. One
must not push the textual argument too far; Art. III, § 2 expressly gives the
"Supreme" Court of the United States a limited original jurisdiction, and the
Supreme Court of New York is largely a trial court.

the Court found it sufficient that *most* of their jurisdiction was appellate, as it was under the challenged provisions.[222] The Justices buttressed this conclusion with extensive citations to the literature, adding that no one had objected on constitutional grounds when original jurisdiction was given to other "higher" federal courts or to the Reichsgericht established under Article 103 of the Weimar Constitution – which had lacked the crucial words "higher" or "highest."[223] The reader may recall the analogous decision permitting establishment of "higher" federal administrative agencies with nobody beneath them.[224] In both cases, however, the Court made clear that federal authority in the first instance must be the exception, not the rule.[225]

Thus although the great preponderance of legislative authority in Germany is federal, the executive and judicial powers of the Federation are significantly narrower. Unlike the United States, the Federation in the first instance may neither enforce nor expound every law it may constitutionally enact.

III. THE BUNDESTREUE PRINCIPLE

Independent of the detailed provisions dividing governmental authority between the Federation and the Länder, the Constitutional Court has held that the very existence of a federal system implies a duty of fidelity to the principle of federalism ("Bundestreue") – or, as it is sometimes stated, a duty to act in a way consistent with that principle ("Pflicht des bundesfreundlichen Verhaltens"). What this means is that in exercising their authority the Länder are bound to respect one another's interests and those of the Federation, and the Bund is required to respect the interests of the Länder.

The Bundestreue principle is a constitutional analog of the general civil-law duty of an obligor to act in good faith ("Treu und Glauben").[226] It had been discussed in the literature at least as early as 1916, and the Constitutional Court embraced it in one of its earliest opinions.[227] Though it is often described as an unwritten principle of constitutional law,[228] the Court's initial statement of the idea

---

[222] See 8 BVerfGE at 177-79.

[223] Id. at 179-81. See Anschütz, supra note 7, at 481-82 (concluding, as the Constitutional Court did with respect to Art. 92, 95 GG, that Art. 103 WRV required only that trial court jurisdiction lie *mostly* with the Länder).

[224] See text at notes 193-99 supra.

[225] See Maunz in 4 Maunz/Dürig, Art. 95, Rdnr. 43-48 (approving the Constitutional Court's decision in both its permissive and its restrictive aspects).

[226] See § 242 BGB.

[227] See 1 BVerfGE 299, 315 (1952) (citing Rudolf Smend, Ungeschriebenes Verfassungsrecht im monarchischen Bundesstaat, in Festgabe für Otto Mayer 247, 261 (1916)).

[228] See, e.g., 12 BVerfGE 205, 254 (1961).

understandably seems to trace it to the explicit declaration in Article
20(1) that the Federal Republic is a federal state ("Bundesstaat").[229]
The Bundestreue principle requires not only that one government
refrain from infringing the interest of another but also that it render
affirmative assistance when the occasion demands.[230] Whether the
duty has been violated is subject to judicial determination in an
appropriate case.[231]

Our Supreme Court has found no comparable general principle
in the Constitution of the United States. Article IV contains a variety
of provisions imposing particular duties on state and federal governments in the interest of the federal system: privileges and immunities for citizens of other states, respect for one another's judgments
and laws, extradition of fugitives, federal protection against despotism and violence.[232] Various intergovernmental immunities have
from time to time been found implicit in our federal system,[233] and
one of them is codified in the eleventh amendment. But the very existence of Article IV's explicit provisions has been taken as evidence
against the existence of any overall implicit requirement of federal
comity such as that recognized by the German court.[234]

The possible applications of the Bundestreue principle are both
interesting and varied. The case in which the doctrine was announced involved a request by Bavaria for an injunction against the
distribution of federal funds for public housing without unanimous
consent of the Länder, which the governing statute required. Upholding the power of the federal legislature to require such consent, the
Court went on to say that the Länder could not withhold their approval arbitrarily; the duty to respect the interests of other states re-

---

[229] "The constitutional principle of federalism that governs in a federal state
thus embraces the legal duty of the Federation and all its members to act in a manner consistent with the federal principle." 1 BVerfGE at 315. See also Roman Herzog in 2 Maunz/Dürig, Art. 20, Teil IV, Rdnr. 63. The conference of experts that
drafted the proposed Basic Law had described the Bundestreue principle as an essential element of federalism. Herrenchiemsee Bericht, 2 Akten und Protokolle at
504, 533.

[230] See Bothe in 1 AK-GG, Art. 20 Abs. 1-3, Rdnr. 39; text at notes 238-40, 242-44
infra.

[231] See 1 BVerfGE at 316; Herzog in 2 Maunz/Dürig, Art. 20, Teil IV, Rdnr. 62.

[232] Like the guarantee clause of our Art. IV, § 4, Art. 28(1) GG provides that "[t]he
constitutional order in the Länder must conform to the principles of republican,
democratic, and social government based on the rule of law." Unlike our Supreme
Court, the Constitutional Court regularly tests state laws against this provision.
See, e.g., 9 BVerfGE 268, 279 (1959) (finding the powers of an independent state
agency incompatible with the guarantee of a democratic state under the rule of
law); Bothe in 2 AK-GG, Art. 28 Abs. 1, Rdnr. 15-16.

[233] See, e.g., McCulloch v. Maryland, 17 U.S. 316 (1819); Collector v. Day, 78
U.S. 113 (1870); Hans v. Louisiana, 134 U.S. 1 (1890); National League of Cities v.
Usery, 426 U.S. 833 (1976); New York v. United States, 112 S. Ct. 2408 (1992).

[234] See Nevada v. Hall, 440 U.S. 410, 425 (1979).

quired the objecting Land to have some objective justification for its action.[235]

In the housing case the Bundestreue principle was invoked against the Länder; in the first *Television* case it was applied against the Federation. Before setting up a second network in 1960, the federal government had consulted the prime minister of a single state and had then promulgated the plan without responding to a counterproposal from the Länder. The Court held the Federation had violated its constitutional duty by dealing with only one Land on a matter concerning them all and by confronting the Länder with a fait accompli.[236]

Perhaps the most fascinating application of the Bundestreue principle came in connection with the controversy during the late 1950s over the stationing of nuclear weapons in Germany. Having failed to persuade the Bundestag to oppose atomic weapons, the Social Democratic Party (SPD) and its allies arranged for advisory referenda on the subject in various states and cities in which they enjoyed a majority. Striking enough was the Constitutional Court's decision that the Länder had encroached on federal authority by providing for referenda on this subject: National defense was an exclusively federal matter.[237] In this country the states commonly pass resolutions concerning military or foreign affairs, and nobody suggests that their doing so is unconstitutional; the resolutions are viewed as so much hot air. But the German court's argument gives food for thought: The whole purpose of the referenda was to bring pressure to bear on the central government to alter its policy respecting nuclear weapons and thus to interfere with the free exercise of exclusively federal authority.[238]

The conclusion that the Länder lacked power to conduct referenda on atomic weapons was based on the various provisions allocating defense authority to the Federation, not on the Bundestreue principle. In an even more interesting companion case, however, the Court held that fidelity to the federal system required the Länder not merely to refrain from infringing federal interests themselves but actively to prevent local governments from doing so; the state of Hesse was ordered to keep cities within its borders from holding referenda on the subject.[239] Like the Land itself, a city invaded federal authority by conducting such a vote; and since the Federation had no direct

---

[235] See 1 BVerfGE at 315-16. On the facts the Court found Bavaria's refusal justified and granted the injunction: Neither the unilateral decision of another Land to build housing beyond its means nor the allotment of other funds to Bavaria for a different purpose was a sufficient basis for the unfavorable allocation to which Bavaria objected. Id. at 316-22.

[236] 12 BVerfGE 205, 254-59 (1961).

[237] 8 BVerfGE 104, 116 (1958).

[238] Id. at 116-18.

[239] 8 BVerfGE 122 (1958).

means of preventing this infringement, it was the obligation of the Länder to do so.[240]

As these examples suggest, the Bundestreue principle leaves the Court a good deal of leeway in determining whether one government has failed to pay sufficient respect to the interest of another. Partly for this reason, care has been urged in applying it lest the Court encroach upon the discretion conferred upon various governmental bodies by the Basic Law.[241] Perhaps in response to such criticism, instances in which the Bundestreue principle has been invoked to support a finding of unconstitutionality have been relatively rare in recent years.[242]

However, the Bundestreue doctrine made a dramatic reappearance in the Spring of 1992. Since the Länder of Bremen and the Saarland were in serious financial difficulties, the Constitutional Court ruled, the Bund and the other Länder had a duty to help them that went beyond the normal limits of the equalization envisioned by Article 107.[243] There was no occasion to say anything about the eastern states that had joined the Federation after the disintegration of the German Democratic Republic. It cannot have escaped the Justices' attention, however, that the financial condition of those Länder was far worse than that of Bremen or of the Saarland. Thus the Bundestreue doctrine promises to reinforce the moral obligation of the more comfortable western Länder to share their resources with their compatriots in the east; and thus the doctrine provides yet another thriving example both of the creativity of the Constitutional Court and of its determination to enforce the fundamental constitutional decision in favor of a federal state.[244]

---

[240] See id. at 135-41. The third clause of Art. 93(1) gives the Constitutional Court jurisdiction of controversies over the respective rights of the Federation and the Länder, but not over those of the Federation and local governments. The coercive measures of the Bundeszwang under Art. 37 (see text at note 180 supra) are likewise available only against the states. See Maunz in 2 Maunz/Dürig, Art. 37, Rdnr. 12.

[241] See Hesse, supra note 6, Rdnr. 269-70 (also questioning whether an originally nonjusticiable principle of comity developed under a different regime should have been transformed into an enforceable limitation on authority under a constitution containing detailed provisions allocating power between the Federation and the states).

[242] See Donald P. Kommers, The Constitutional Jurisprudence of the Federal Republic of Germany 84-85 (1989).

[243] 86 BVerfGE 148, 258-70 (1992). See also id. at 271-76 (holding that by favoring the Saarland over Bremen in providing emergency assistance the Bund had offended the Bundestreue principle).

[244] See also 63 BVerfGE 1, 43-44 (1983) (dictum) (noting that it would offend the federal principle of Art. 20(1) for the Bund to conscript state agencies for federal purposes without their consent); 55 BVerfGE 274, 346 (1980) (dissenting opinion) (arguing that the Federation was obliged to consider the interests of the Länder before resorting to revenue measures in whose proceeds they would have no share); 81 BVerfGE 310, 337-38 (1990) (declaring that as a general rule the Bund was required to afford Länder administering federal law as agents of the Federation (im Auf-

IV. OTHER DIMENSIONS OF FEDERALISM

A. Local Government

The tradition of local autonomy in Germany goes back to the Middle Ages.[245] Revived by the reforms of Freiherr vom Stein in 1808,[246] it was written into the constitutions of 1849 and 1919[247] and is guaranteed by Article 28(2) of the Basic Law: "Local governments must be afforded the right to regulate all local affairs on their own responsibility, within the limits set by law." This guarantee serves both to enhance the right of self-determination and as an additional safeguard against the concentration of governmental power.[248] Apart from a few limited home rule provisions in state constitutions and a sometime implicit immunity from *federal* regulation, there is nothing even remotely like it in the United States.[249]

Local autonomy in Germany is far from absolute. Under Article 28(2) local governments are to exercise their powers "within the limits set by law." As the Constitutional Court made clear in its first opinion on the subject, this proviso permits the Länder (and in some cases also the Federation) to limit local self-determination to a considerable extent.[250] Yet the power of Bund and Länder to set limits to local government is not unbounded either. Building on the inter-

---

trag des Bundes) an opportunity for comment before exercising its authority to give them binding instructions).

[245] See Heiko Faber in 2 AK-GG, Art. 28 Abs. 2, Rdnr. 1-2. German scholars like to point out that local self-government is not strictly speaking an aspect of federalism, since local governments are not "states" but rather elements of the Länder. See, e.g., Günter Püttner, Kommunale Selbstverwaltung, 4 Handbuch des Staatsrechts 1171, Rdnr. 2.

[246] See id., Rdnr. 1.

[247] See RV 1849, § 184; Art. 127 WRV.

[248] See Maunz in 2 Maunz/Dürig, Art. 28, Rdnr. 48; Faber in 2 AK-GG, Art. 28 Abs. 2, Rdnr. 25. The 1935 decree subjecting local governments to central control described itself as one of the fundamental laws of the Nazi state. See Deutsche Gemeindeordnung vom 30. Januar 1935, RGBl. I S. 49; Rolf Grawert, Die nationalsozialistische Herrschaft, 1 Handbuch des Staatsrechts 143, Rdnr. 19.

[249] See, e.g., Ill. Const., Art. VII, § 6 (1970); National League of Cities v. Usery, 426 U.S. 833 (1976), overruled, Garcia v. San Antonio Mass Transit Auth., 469 U.S. 528 (1975). The U.S. Constitution says nothing about the relation between state and local governments.

[250] See 1 BVerfGE 167, 174-78 (1952). Although Art. 28(1) guarantees the existence of elected local councils ("Volksvertretungen") in the absence of an assembly of the citizens themselves ("Volksversammlung"), their functions are largely administrative rather than legislative. Most substantive matters, as well as many of the details of local government organization, are prescribed by state law. See Püttner, supra note 245, Rdnr. 7, 33, 41-42.

pretation of a similar provision in the Weimar Constitution, the Court in the same opinion declared that no law was valid if it invaded the core ("Kern") of local governmental authority.[251]

The notion of an inviolable core of local autonomy is obviously indeterminate, and it has given rise to a substantial body of decisions. Here as in so many other areas the Court (like our Supreme Court) has applied a balancing test, inquiring into the degree of intrusion into local self-determination as well as its justification.[252] On its face the test is reminiscent of the Supreme Court's formula for determining the immunity of state and local governments from federal regulation under the one-time doctrine of *National League of Cities v. Usery*;[253] but in practice the protection afforded by Article 28(2) has been relatively modest.

The tale begins with a 1952 decision upholding a federal statute that required local governments to employ former civil servants who had been displaced in the course or aftermath of World War II.[254] Article 131 gave the Federation explicit authority to make provision for such persons, the problem was extremely serious, and the burden imposed on local governments was temporary; the core of self-government, the Court concluded, was unaffected.[255] Later decisions have permitted the Länder to combine local governmental units,[256] to

---

[251] 1 BVerfGE at 174-76, 178. The opinion spoke also of the essence ("Wesensgehalt") of self-government, a synonymous concept that conjures up the requirement of Art. 19(2) that no law restricting fundamental rights ("Grundrechte") affect the essence of the right. See also Art. 93(1) cl. 4b GG, which authorizes local governments to file constitutional complaints to remedy infringements of their right to self-government. Strictly speaking, however, the right of self-determination is not one of the fundamental rights within the meaning of Art. 19(2); the analogous limitation respecting "core" functions of local government is derived from Art. 28(2) itself in light of its history. See Maunz in 2 Maunz/Dürig, Art. 28, Rdnr. 52, 56; Faber in 2 AK-GG, Art. 28 Abs. 2, Rdnr. 8. See also Püttner, supra note 245, Rdnr. 20 (arguing that if the legislature could enact any limitation it pleased on local self-government, the constitutional guarantee would be a hollow shell).

[252] See, e.g., 56 BVerfGE 298, 313-14 (1980); Maunz in 2 Maunz/Dürig, Art. 28, Rdnr. 51.

[253] See 426 U.S. at 851: "Our examination of the effect of the 1974 amendments . . . satisfies us that both the minimum wage and the maximum hour provisions [of the Fair Labor Standards Act] will impermissibly interfere with the integral governmental functions [of state and local governments]." See also id. at 856 (Blackmun, J., concurring) (interpreting the Court's opinion as employing "a balancing approach," as suggested by its treatment of the precedents, id. at 852-56).

[254] 1 BVerfGE 167 (1952).

[255] Id. at 174-80. Cf. Fry v. United States, 421 U.S. 542 (1975) (upholding an emergency freeze on state and local wages imposed by federal law).

[256] 26 BVerfGE 228, 237-41 (1969).

alter their boundaries,[257] to change their names,[258] to zone substantial portions of their territory for heavy industry.[259] In dicta the Court has gone so far as to affirm that individual governmental units may be abolished entirely;[260] Article 28(2) is generally said to guarantee the existence of local self-government as an institution, not the powers of individual governments.[261]

Yet there are limits to the authority of the Länder to invade the prerogatives even of individual localities. Procedurally, Article 28(2) has been held to require that a local government be afforded a hearing before action is taken that may be detrimental to its interests.[262] Substantively, Article 28(2) has been held to permit only such intrusions as promote some public interest; a Land cannot even change the name of one of its communities without giving some plausible reason.[263] Finally, the usual proportionality requirement has sometimes been applied;[264] one reason for setting aside a federal order severely limiting construction in the vicinity of an airport was the failure of federal authorities to determine whether their goals could be achieved by means less restrictive of local autonomy.[265]

Thus in the light of history the Constitutional Court has construed Article 28(2) to permit significant limitations of local self-gov-

---

[257] 50 BVerfGE 50, 52-56 (1978) (stressing that there were plausible reasons for the reorganization and that the complaining city was not left without effective ability to carry out its governmental tasks).

[258] 50 BVerfGE 195, 200-02 (1979).

[259] 76 BVerfGE 107, 117-24 (1987).

[260] See 50 BVerfGE 50, 50 (1978).

[261] See 76 BVerfGE 107, 119 (1987); Maunz in 2 Maunz/Dürig Art. 28, Rdnr. 45 (calling it the essence of Art. 28(2) that "autonomous local governments must always exist"). Accord Anschütz, supra note 7, at 583-84 (construing the comparable Weimar provision).

[262] The hearing requirement was announced in connection with a challenge to the renaming of a municipality, 50 BVerfGE 195, 202-03 (1979), where an adequate hearing was found to have been afforded. It was later applied as one ground for invalidating a federal order severely limiting construction in the vicinity of an airport, 56 BVerfGE 298, 320-23 (1980).

[263] 59 BVerfGE 216, 228-31 (1982).

[264] See 76 BVerfGE 107, 119-20 (1987). For an explanation of this concept see chapter 1 supra.

[265] See 56 BVerfGE 298, 323 (1980). In upholding a transfer of authority over solid-waste disposal from cities to counties in 1988, however, the Court was conspicuously silent about proportionality, leading some commentators to conclude that the Second Senate had decided to relegate that concept to the basic-rights context in which it originated. See 79 BVerfGE 127 (1988); Fritz Ossenbühl, Maßhalten mit dem Übermaßverbot, in Peter Badura & Rupert Scholz (eds.), Wege und Verfahren des Verfassungslebens: Festschrift für Peter Lerche 151, 160-61 (1993); Eberhard Schmidt-Aßmann, Kommunale Selbstverwaltung "nach Rastede," in Everhardt Franßen et al. (eds.), Bürger – Richter – Staat: Festschrift für Horst Sendler 121, 135-36 (1991) (noting also (at 123) the Court's new emphasis (79 BVerfGE at 149) on the democratic aspect of local government).

ernment that can be justified by some countervailing public interest. Nevertheless, unlike the United States Constitution, the Basic Law protects local governments against unreasonable limitation of their authority even on the part of the states; and as a practical matter local governments remain the basic enforcers of federal and state laws as well as of their own.[266]

B. The Federal Republic and Germany

The traditional subject of federalism in Germany is the division of authority between the Federal Republic and its constituent parts. But no modern study of German federalism can be complete without mention of the other side of the equation. Throughout most of its history the Federal Republic itself has been a part of not one but two larger entities: Germany and the European Communities.

The Basic Law was drafted on the fundamental premise that the postwar division of Germany was temporary. The Federal Republic was conceived from the start as only part of a larger entity called Germany that was unable to function as a state for the time being but that had survived unconditional surrender, occupation, and partition.

The continued existence of a larger Germany found expression in numerous provisions of the Basic Law. This term itself was chosen in preference to "Constitution" to avoid any implication that the West Germans meant to establish a separate nation.[267] The Preamble declared the intention "to give a new order to political life for a transitional period," recited that in so doing the German people in the Western zones "have also acted on behalf of those Germans to whom participation was denied," and called upon "the entire German people . . . to achieve in free self-determination the unity and freedom of Germany." Article 23, listing the western Länder in which the Basic Law was to be immediately applicable, provided that it should be put into force "in other parts of Germany . . . upon their accession [Beitritt]." Article 146 drove the point home by providing that the Basic Law itself should "cease to be in force on the day on which a constitution adopted by a free decision of the German people takes effect." On the basis of these provisions the Constitutional Court from the first recognized the continued existence of a larger Germany of which the Federal Republic was only a part.[268]

---

[266] See Faber in 2 AK-GG, Art. 28 Abs. 2, Rdnr. 16. In enforcing federal or state law, local governments are generally subject to supervision only as to the legality, not as to the desirability of their actions. See Püttner, supra note 245, Rdnr. 47.

[267] See, e.g., Sten. Ber. at 8-11 (1948) (remarks of Delegate Schmid); Mußgnug, supra note 3, Rdnr. 27-32.

[268] See, e.g., 5 BVerfGE 85, 126-28 (1956); 36 BVerfGE 1, 15-17 (1973). For criticism of the Court's position and for the alternative thesis that the Basic Law envisioned reunification of two separate states see Rudolf Bernhardt, Die deutsche

Though this larger entity was a "state without organization,"[269] its acknowledgement had significant practical consequences. Most fundamentally, the references to reunification in the Preamble and in Article 146 were held to make it the constitutional obligation of all governmental authorities both actively to promote that goal and to refrain from any action that would tend to interfere with its attainment.[270] The most severe test of this principle came in 1973, when in pursuit of its new policy of détente Willy Brandt's coalition government concluded a treaty with what had been commonly referred to as the "so-called" German Democratic Republic – in other words, with Communist East Germany.

Opponents of the treaty found it impossible to reconcile its acknowledgement of the existence of two German states with the Basic Law's premise that there was only one. A treaty recognizing the authority of a separate East Germany, they argued, was an obstacle to reunification and thus unconstitutional.[271] Invoking the American doctrine of judicial self-restraint without even translating it,[272] the Constitutional Court took a more pragmatic view. It was basically up to the political branches of government to determine how to achieve the constitutional goal of German unity. The Court could interfere only if those branches clearly abused their discretion, and they had not done so; for the treaty was susceptible of a construction that would preserve its constitutionality.[273]

To be sure, the Court reasoned, the treaty acknowledged that East Germany was a state in the sense of international law; but that was not to say that by concluding the treaty the Federal Republic had recognized the government of East Germany. Much less had the treaty in any way abandoned the constitutional goal of reunification, for it expressly declared that nothing in its provisions should be taken to affect obligations under preexisting international agreements, which flatly committed the Federal Republic to reunification.[274] In light of the Basic Law's theory of a single Germany, the treaty's acceptance of the existing border between East and West Germany was to be understood as essentially equating it for legal purposes with those separating the West German Länder.[275] Nothing in the treaty, the Court added, could be interpreted to permit any limitation of the right of East Germans to be treated as citizens in the Federal Republic or to

---

Teilung und der Status Gesamtdeutschlands, 1 Handbuch des Staatsrechts 321, Rdnr. 27-36.

[269] 36 BVerfGE 1, 16 (1973).

[270] See, e.g., 5 BVerfGE 85, 126-28 (1956); 36 BVerfGE 1, 17-19 (1973).

[271] See id. at 8-9.

[272] Id. at 14.

[273] Id. at 17-20.

[274] Id. at 21-24.

[275] Id. at 26-27.

deny them any of the fundamental rights guaranteed to "all Germans" by the Basic Law.[276]

Several of the fundamental rights are phrased in this way: freedom of assembly, freedom of association, freedom of movement, freedom to choose an occupation, freedom from extradition to a foreign country.[277] Article 116(1) defines Germans for purposes of the Basic Law to include "any person who possesses German citizenship,"[278] and the Constitutional Court made clear from the outset that this embraced those living in East Germany. In 1953, for example, the Court held that Article 11(1) gave East Germans the right to enter the Federal Republic, to establish their residence there, and to travel about freely like any West German citizen – subject only to possible statutory restrictions to protect against contagion, crime, or the inability to absorb additional arrivals.[279] This provision helps to explain why hundreds of thousands of migrants were accepted in the West once it became possible for them to leave East Germany in 1989.

Other decisions of the Constitutional Court drew additional practical consequences from the thesis of a single Germany. Article 16(2) forbade extradition of any German to a "foreign country" but not to East Germany, for even in its Communist days East Germany was not "foreign."[280] For the same reason commerce between East and West Germany was not foreign commerce,[281] and East German criminal convictions were enforceable in the Federal Republic – provided they did not infringe rights guaranteed by the Basic Law.[282] "The Soviet Zone," the Court reaffirmed in announcing this last con-

---

[276] Id. at 29-35. Thus in upholding the agreement the Court enunciated significant constitutional limitations on the treaty power; while formally losing their lawsuit, the complainants got a substantial part of what they had sued for.

[277] See Art. 8(1), 9(1), 11(1), 12(1), 16(2) GG.

[278] It also includes any person "who has been admitted to the territory of the German Reich within the frontiers of 31 December 1937 as a refugee or expellee of German stock or as the spouse or descendant of such person." Art. 116(2) makes separate provision for restoring German citizenship to persons who were deprived of it during the Nazi period "on political, racial, or religious grounds," and to their descendants.

[279] 2 BVerfGE 266, 272-84 (1953) (adding that in light of the deliberate decision of the constitutional convention to extend Art. 11 to East Germans a justification for limiting these freedoms would have to be demonstrated individually in every case). During the radical scare of the late 1960s Art. 11(2) was amended to add further grounds for limiting freedom of movement, most notably to protect against subversive activities.

[280] 37 BVerfGE 57, 64 (1974). See also 4 BVerfGE 299, 304-09 (1955) (permitting extradition to the Saarland before its accession to the Federal Republic in 1956 on the same ground after extensive discussion of the Parliamentary Council debates).

[281] 18 BVerfGE 353, 354 (1965).

[282] See, e.g., 1 BVerfGE 332, 341-43 (1952); 11 BVerfGE 150, 158-65 (1960) (finding East German convictions for economic crimes inconsistent with the right of free development of personality guaranteed by Art. 2(1) GG).

clusion, "belongs to Germany and cannot be considered a foreign country in relation to the Federal Republic."[283]

In conformity with the constitutional goal of reunification, Article 23 expressly provided for extending the Basic Law to "other parts of Germany . . . on their accession" to the Federal Republic. The Saarland, which had been under French domination since the end of the war, joined the Federation by this route in 1957.[284] The accession of the Saarland deserves brief comment both for the interesting constitutional issues it produced and for the example it set for the more significant accession of East Germany some thirty years later.

In 1955, following a period in which over vehement German objection the Saarland was being progressively digested by France, the two countries entered into an agreement looking toward "Europeanization" of the region until a peace treaty was concluded. Attacked as unconstitutional, this agreement was upheld on the pragmatic ground that the situation it contemplated was closer to what the constitution required than that which had previously existed.[285] To strike down the agreement because it did not conform to the Basic Law in all respects, the Court argued, would be to say that "the bad may not give way to the better because the best is unattainable," and the Basic Law could not be construed to require such an absurd result.[286]

Effectuation of the agreement, however, was conditioned upon approval by referendum. When the referendum was held, the Saarlanders rejected Europeanization and voted to join the Federal Republic. Instead of extending the entire Basic Law to the region immediately, federal authorities concluded a new treaty that reserved to France certain sovereign prerogatives for a three-year transition period and enacted a statute providing for election of interim federal legislators by the Saarland parliament. Neither of these provisions seemed to be in accord with the Basic Law, but the Court's pragmatic principle would appear to embrace them: Both the treaty and the statute did what was practicable to move in the direction of the constitution.[287]

Some observers contended that with the accession of the Saarland Article 23 had exhausted its function. The sole avenue for reunifying East and West Germany, in this view, was the adoption of a new constitution for all Germany under Article 146. In upholding the 1973 East German treaty, however, the Constitutional Court went out of its way to reject this interpretation. Nothing had happened to render Ar-

---

[283] Id. at 158. For the argument that the DDR should nevertheless be considered foreign for purposes of authority to prevent the export of cultural treasures (Art. 74 cl. 5) see Rengeling, supra note 7, Rdnr. 151.

[284] See Manfred Zuleeg in 1 AK-GG, Art. 23 et al., Rdnr. 27, 34.

[285] 4 BVerfGE 157, 168-78 (1955).

[286] Id. at 170.

[287] See Robert Leicht, Königsweg zur Einheit, Die Zeit, March 9, 1990, p. 5. (All citations to Die Zeit are to the overseas edition).

ticle 23 obsolete; the treaty must be construed not to interfere in any
way with the possible accession of East Germany under its provisions.[288] As a leading commentator pointed out, nothing in the
language of either Article 23 or Article 146 limited the applicability of
the former to the Saarland; the text spoke generally of accession by
"other parts of Germany."[289]

When reunification of East and West Germany became a realistic
possibility in 1989, the Germans thus faced the question whether to
pursue it by accession under Article 23 or by adoption of an all-German constitution under Article 146. The latter route would have had
the advantage of direct democratic legitimacy, for such a constitution
would have been adopted by "a free decision of the German people" –
presumably by referendum or by popularly elected convention, or
both.[290] The prospect of a new constitutional convention, however,
was as unsettling in Germany as it would be in the United States, for
in such a convention the entire Basic Law would have been subject to
reexamination. At best, tinkering with the terms of a document that
had served as the basis of an exemplary form of government for forty
years would have created uncertainty and delay; at worst it might
have weakened some of its desirable features.[291]

To avoid these risks both Germanys opted for accession under Article 23.[292] With a few special provisions to ease the transition,[293] the

---

[288] See 36 BVerfGE at 28-29.

[289] See Maunz in 2 Maunz/Dürig, Art. 23, Rdnr. 37. See also Sten. Ber. at 172
(Delegate Schmid) (explaining that Art. 23 provided for accession by "[a]ny part of
Germany"). Indeed, in contrast to the provision of U.S. Const., Art. IV, § 3 authoriz-
ing Congress to "admit" new states to the American Union, the term accession
("Beitritt") in Art. 23 suggested that other parts of Germany might join the Federal
Republic without even asking the consent of the Federation or the existing Länder.
See Maunz, supra, Rdnr. 40: "Whether another part of Germany becomes a part of
the Federal Republic depends upon its decision alone." The Basic Law's theory of a
single Germany supported this interpretation: It would hardly have been consistent
with the constitutional commitment to reunification to exclude any part of Germany that wished to accede.

[290] See Maunz in 4 Maunz/Dürig, Art. 146, Rdnr. 20. For a passionate argument
in favor of the Art. 146 approach see Jürgen Habermas, Der DM-Nationalismus,
Die Zeit, April 6, 1990, pp. 4-5.

[291] See Robert Leicht, Einheit durch Beitritt, Die Zeit, March 2, 1990, p. 3
(doubting for example that a new constitution would recognize a right of asylum for
political refugees as broad as that then afforded by Art. 16(2)).

[292] Alternatively, the Basic Law itself might perhaps have been submitted to a
national referendum under Art. 146 without the necessity for either accession or a
constitutional convention. Nevertheless the East German government formed after the March 1990 elections decided to achieve unification "promptly and responsi-
bly on the basis of Article 23." See Die Zeit, April 27, 1990, p. 1, col. 1; Unification
Treaty ("Einigungsvertrag"), Art. 1(1).

[293] Id., Art. 3-7. Art. 23 GG prescribed no specific timetable for putting the Basic
Law into force in areas that acceded to the Federal Republic, and the pragmatic
approach taken by the Court in the Saarland controversy suggested that the incorpo-

Basic Law became the constitution of all Germany; and the retention of a revised Article 146 arguably permits subsequent ratification by the people if additional legitimacy is desired.[294]

It remains to say a few words about the peculiar history of Berlin, which lay inside the Soviet occupation zone (later the German Democratic Republic) and was itself divided into eastern and western zones, not least by the notorious Berlin Wall. Article 23 listed "Greater Berlin" as one of the states in which the Basic Law was immediately applicable. Among the express conditions of Allied approval of the Basic Law, however, were that Berlin have no voting rights in either the Bundestag or the Bundesrat and that it not be "governed" by the Federation.[295] Article 144(2) reflected the first of these conditions by providing for (nonvoting) "representatives" from areas in which application of the Basic Law was "restricted." Application of the second condition raised a number of interesting questions.

On the one hand, it seemed obvious that the Federation would be "govern[ing]" Berlin if statutes enacted by the federal parliament were directly applicable there. Consequently, in approving a new constitution for Berlin in 1950, the Allies made clear that federal statutes could take effect within its borders only upon adoption by the local legislature.[296] Similarly, the Constitutional Court held it could not entertain constitutional challenges to legislative,[297] executive,[298]

---

ration of East Germany might be a gradual process. See Maunz in 2 Maunz/Dürig, Art. 23, Rdnr. 45; text at notes 283-87 supra .

[294] For the contention that it does not despite the plain intentions of its supporters see Josef Isensee, Schlußbestimmung des Grundgesetzes: Artikel 146, 7 Handbuch des Staatsrechts 271, Rdnr. 62-63 (arguing that Art. 79(3) protects the essential features of the Basic Law against alteration even under the revised Art. 146). The entire story of reunification is effectively related and analyzed, in English, in Peter Quint, The Constitutional Law of German Unification, 50 Md. L. Rev. 475 (1991). See also Rudolf Dolzer, The Path to German Unity: The Constitutional, Legal and International Framework, in Paul Kirchhof & Donald P. Kommers (eds.), Germany and Its Basic Law 365 (1993).

[295] See the approval letter of the Allied military governors (Genehmigungsschreiben) of May 12, 1949, in 2 Quellen zum Staatsrecht at 217; 1 BVerfGE 70, 72 (1951) (quoting Chancellor Adenauer's explanation that "continuing international tension" was the reason for the Allies' action). These conditions were unaffected by the treaty by which the Allies relinquished most of their occupation rights in 1954 and were reaffirmed by the Four Power Agreement of 1971. See 7 BVerfGE 1, 8 (1957) (citing BGBl. 1955 II S. 301, 306, 495, 498, 500); Scholz, Der Status Berlins, 1 Handbuch des Staatsrechts 351, Rdnr. 33. The Western Allies also reserved the right to govern Berlin themselves, but after 1955 they restricted their activity largely to matters affecting security. See id., Rdnr. 40.

[296] See 2 Quellen zum Staatsrecht at 551; 7 BVerfGE 1, 13 (1957).

[297] Id. at 13-17 (noting that the Allies had vetoed a Berlin law that would have given the Constitutional Court jurisdiction over Berlin).

[298] 7 BVerfGE 190, 192 (1957).

or judicial[299] acts of Berlin authorities; for to do so would subject Berlin to judicial governance by a constitutional organ of the Federation.[300]

On the other hand, the Court insisted, Berlin remained a Land of the Federal Republic despite the Allied reservations.[301] The fundamental rights recognized by the Basic Law itself, the Justices ruled, applied directly to Berlin; the limitations they imposed on Berlin authorities did not subject the city to governance by the Federation.[302] Furthermore, since the Allies had not objected when Berlin adopted the federal statute providing for federal review of state court decisions, judgments of Berlin courts could be appealed to federal tribunals other than the Constitutional Court.[303] Federal appellate judgments in such cases, the Court boldly added in 1966, could in turn be challenged before the Constitutional Court itself to the extent that they rested upon federal laws adopted by the Berlin legislature; for in such a case the Court was passing upon a federal court's application of federal law, not governing Berlin.[304] Indeed as early as 1952 a federal statute made it the duty of Berlin's parliament to adopt all federal laws, and the Allies did not complain – because, according to one commentator, the bare formality of local reenactment satisfied the purpose of ensuring an Allied opportunity to veto the application of any law that might embarrass their precarious relations with the Soviet Union.[305]

These hairline distinctions suggested an understandable determination on the part of West German authorities to do as much as they could get away with to give effect to the declaration of Article 23 that Berlin was one of the states of the Federal Republic.[306] As one

---

[299] 7 BVerfGE 192, 193 (1957).

[300] See 7 BVerfGE at 14-15.

[301] See id. at 7-13.

[302] 1 BVerfGE 70, 72 (1951).

[303] See 7 BVerfGE 1, 14, 16 (1957). However, the Court initially held that federal appellate judgments in Berlin cases could not be challenged on constitutional grounds in the Constitutional Court, because the Allies had not consented to that Court's jurisdiction. As the Court put it, intervention by the Constitutional Court would amount to a "politically significant intrusion upon Berlin authority." 10 BVerfGE 229, 232 (1959).

[304] 19 BVerfGE 377, 382-93 (1966). See also 20 BVerfGE 257, 266-68 (1966) (upholding jurisdiction over a constitutional challenge to the decision of a Berlin state court reviewing an action of the federal antitrust agency (Bundeskartellamt)); 37 BVerfGE 57, 60-64 (1974) (reaffirming jurisdiction to determine the validity of a federal law adopted in Berlin but not of the actions of Berlin officials or judges in applying it). For discussion of the delicate distinctions drawn in this area see Scholz, supra note 295, Rdnr. 65-67.

[305] See 19 BVerfGE 377, 385, 388-89 (1966); Scholz, supra note 295, Rdnr. 59-61.

[306] See id., Rdnr. 56 (invoking the Bundestreue principle and the doctrine of the Saarland case, text at notes 283-87 supra).

commentator aptly observed, the situation was untidy, but it worked.[307]

All of this became moot on October 3, 1990, when along with the newly reconstituted East German states of Brandenburg, Mecklenburg-Western Pomerania, Saxony, Saxony-Anhalt, and Thuringia a reunited Berlin became a full-fledged Land of the Federal Republic – as Article 23 from the outset had expressly if optimistically provided.[308]

C. The European Union

Finally, German federalism is complicated by yet another dimension of great and increasing significance, for almost since its inception the Federal Republic has been a member of three international organizations exercising substantial governmental powers: the European Coal and Steel Community, the European Atomic Energy Community, and the European Economic Community, which since approval of the Maastricht Treaty have been known collectively as the European Union.[309]

The three Communities were established by three separate treaties among their six original member states during the 1950s.[310] If German approval of these treaties had rested upon the ordinary treaty power, there might have been a serious question of their validity; for each entails the transfer of sovereign powers to a supranational organization.[311] In anticipation of just such an arrangement, however, Article 24 expressly authorized the Federation to "transfer sovereign powers to intergovernmental institutions"[312] –

---

[307] See id., Rdnr. 73.

[308] See Einigungsvertrag, Art. 1(1), 4 cl. 1 (revising the Preamble to the Basic Law accordingly). Art. 23 itself, having served its purpose, was repealed. Id., Art. 4 cl. 2.

[309] See generally Hans Peter Ipsen, Die Bundesrepublik Deutschland in den Europäischen Gemeinschaften, 7 Handbuch des Staatsrechts 767. The Maastricht Treaty, ratified in 1992, renamed the European Economic Community the European Community, in light of its increased responsibilities. See Treaty of Feb. 7, 1992 Respecting the European Union [hereafter cited as Maastricht Treaty], approved by Gesetz vom 28. Dezember 1992, BGBl. II S. 1251, Art. G.

[310] See Treaty of Rome of March 25, 1957, as amended [hereafter cited as EEC Treaty]; Treaty of Paris of April 18, 1951, as amended [ECSC]; Treaty of Rome of March 25, 1957, as amended [EAEC]. The three Communities have set up common institutions, and their membership has grown to twelve states. See Manfred Zuleeg in 1 AK-GG, Art. 24 Abs. 1, Rdnr. 6.

[311] See Grewe, supra note 205, Rdnr. 70-71.

[312] Art. 24(1) GG. Expressly mentioned during the constitutional debates as possible applications of this provision were international agencies to govern coal mining, electric power, and air transport. See 1 JöR (n.F.) at 224. The constitutional convention deliberately chose to require neither an extraordinary majority nor Bundesrat consent for the transfer of powers, "in order to declare unequivo-

as well as to agree to restrictions of German sovereignty incident to a system of collective security[313] and to abide by the decisions of an international tribunal respecting international disputes.[314]

The transfer of sovereign powers to the European Communities under this provision has been extensive. The treaty establishing the Economic Community, for example, not only curbs the authority of member states to discriminate against citizens of other member states and to interfere with the free flow of goods, services, and capi-

---

cally our readiness to play our part in the European order and in the peaceable world order." See id. at 226, 228 (remarks of Delegate Eberhard). In 1992, however, in connection with ratification of the Maastricht Treaty, a new Art. 23(1) was added to the Basic Law to require Bundesrat consent for further transfers of authority to the emerging European Union. See text at notes 342-48 infra.

[313] Art. 24(2) GG. See Grewe, supra n. 205, Rdnr. 77-78 (arguing that this provision required Germany to join the United Nations and permitted it to join NATO); 1 JöR (n.F.) at 222-28 (recounting debates in the constitutional convention suggesting that the reference to peace "in Europe and among the nations of the world" was designed to embrace both worldwide and regional security arrangements); 68 BVerfGE 1, 89-98 (1984) (upholding German consent to the stationing of NATO missiles in the Federal Republic under Art. 24(1) while leaving open the question whether it was also covered (as the government had contended) by Art. 24(2)); Rüdiger Wolfrum, Die Bundesrepublik Deutschland im Verteidigungsbündnis, 7 Handbuch des Staatsrechts 647, Rdnr. 17 (arguing that a system of collective defense (such as NATO) is not one of collective security). To an outsider these provisions would appear to lay to rest the burning controversy whether the employment of German troops outside the NATO area offends the provision of Art. 87a(2) that, "[a]part from defense, the Armed Forces may be used only to the extent expressly permitted by this Basic Law." Accord Karl Doehring, Systeme kollektiver Sicherheit, 7 Handbuch des Staatsrechts 669, Rdnr. 19-27. For additional arguments on this question see Hans-Georg Franzke, Art. 24 II GG als Rechtsgrundlage für den Außeneinsatz der Bundeswehr?, 1992 NJW 3075; Thomas Giegerich, The German Contribution to the Protection of Shipping in the Persian Gulf, 49 Zeitschrift für ausländisches öffentliches Recht und Völkerrecht 1 (1989). See also Art. 26(1) GG, which forbids among other things preparation for any "war of aggression."

In June 1993 the Constitutional Court held that the balance of hardship required a preliminary injunction against German participation in the humanitarian action in Somalia without parliamentary approval, in order to prevent irreparable harm to possible interests of the Bundestag; it left open for the time being the question whether Germany could participate at all. See BVerfG, Judgment of June 23, 1993, Case No. 2 BvQ 17/93, 1993 NJW 2038.

[314] Art. 24(3) GG. Germany has adhered to the statute establishing the International Court of Justice, but that tribunal does not meet the conditions of Art. 24(3) because its jurisdiction is neither "general, comprehensive, [nor] obligatory." See Zuleeg in 1 AK-GG, Art. 24 Abs. 3/ Art. 25, Rdnr. 83-84. Under the European Convention for the Protection of Human Rights and Fundamental Freedoms (213 U.N.T.S. 221), Germany is bound to respect decisions of the European Court of Human Rights respecting violations of that treaty; but such cases are not "disputes between states" within the meaning of Art. 24(3).

tal across their borders;[315] it also outlaws public and private restraints of interstate trade[316] and sets up a variety of supranational
institutions: a Council with broad legislative power to implement the
goal of a common market, a Commission with significant
enforcement authority, and a Court of Justice with jurisdiction to interpret the treaty as well as acts of Community institutions.[317] Acts of
the Council and the Commission, as well as decisions of the Court,
are declared to be binding and enforceable.[318] The net result has been
pungently described by a leading German observer:

---

[315] See EEC Treaty, Art. 7 (discrimination on grounds of nationality), 12-17
(import and export duties), 30-37 (quantitative restrictions on imports and exports),
48-51 (free movement of workers), 52-58 (freedom of establishment for firms and
self-employed persons), 59-66 (freedom to provide services), 67-73 (free movement
of capital), 92-94 (subsidies and other "state aids"), 95-99 (discriminatory and pro-
tectionist taxes). Cf. U.S. Const., Art. I, § 8 (commerce clause); Art. IV, § 2
(interstate privileges and immunities).

[316] EEC Treaty, Art. 85-94.

[317] See id., Art. 145-54 and Art. 2-8 of the Treaty establishing a Single Council
and a Single Commission of the European Communities, O.J. L152, July 13, 1967
(Merger Treaty) (setting up a Council composed of "representatives of the Member
States," i.e., of their executive governments); Art. 155-63 and Art. 9-19 of the
Merger Treaty (establishing a seventeen-member Commission "appointed by
common accord of the Governments of the Member States" and directing it to ensure application of the treaty and of measures taken under it); Art. 164-88 (creating
the European Court of Justice and defining its powers). Provisions authorizing legislation by the Council are scattered throughout the treaty. Of particular interest are
Art. 99 and 100, which empower the Council to promulgate measures promoting
harmonization of indirect taxes and of other laws or actions "directly affect[ing]
the establishment or functioning of the common market," and Art. 235, a sweeping
authorization to adopt upon request of the Commission measures "necessary to attain . . . one of the objectives of the Community." There is also a Parliament (now
popularly elected), whose powers are still largely but not entirely advisory. See,
e.g., Art. 137-44 and the Act concerning the election of the representatives of the Assembly by direct universal suffrage annexed to the Council Decision of Sept. 20,
1976 (O.J. L278, Oct. 8, 1976) (prescribing the Parliament's composition and procedure); Art. 149 (spelling out the details of a suspensive veto given the Parliament in
various matters by the Single European Act of 1986); Art. 237-38 (requiring Parliament assent to the addition of new member states and to association with non-
members). The same institutions have similar powers under the treaties establishing the other two Communities.

[318] See EEC Treaty, Art. 171 ("If the Court of Justice finds that a Member State
has failed to fulfill an obligation under this Treaty, the State shall be required to
take the necessary measures to comply with the judgment of the Court of Justice"),
187 ("The judgments of the Court of Justice shall be enforceable under the conditions laid down in Article 192"), 189 ("A regulation . . . shall be binding in its entirety and directly applicable in all Member States. A directive shall be binding, as
to the result to be achieved, upon each Member State to which it is addressed, but
shall leave to the national authorities the choice of form and methods. A decision
shall be binding in its entirety upon those to whom it is addressed"), 192 ("Decisions
of the Council or of the Commission which impose a pecuniary obligation on persons other than States, shall be enforceable").

The Communities possess a unitary, original sovereign authority of their own that permits them to take legislative, executive, and judicial actions that have immediate effects within the affected states and that may determine the legal relations of natural and artificial persons in the member states. The member states, for their part, have opened themselves to these incursions "to such an extent that the Federal Republic's claim to exclusive sovereignty within its own territory is withdrawn, and room is made for the immediate effectiveness and application of law from another source."[319]

The treaties contain no express supremacy clause, but the European Court of Justice has found the supremacy of Community over national law implicit in "the terms and the spirit of the Treaty."[320] That Community law is supreme as a matter of treaty interpretation is not enough to make it so; if the treaty rested on ordinary foreign-relations powers it too might well be subject to modification by subsequent legislation, as treaties are in the United States.[321] France has handled this problem in part by a constitutional provision giving treaties precedence over subsequent laws; Great Britain did so initially by a strong presumption that Parliament did not mean to infringe the treaty.[322] In Germany the Constitutional Court discovered a solution in Article 24(1): The Basic Law authorized the Federal Republic to relinquish its right to modify the treaty by later legislation, and it did so by approving a treaty implicitly making Community law supreme.[323]

Supremacy is strong medicine, especially when coupled, as it has been, with the obligation to accept decisions of the European Court of

---

[319] See Grewe, supra note 205, Rdnr. 70 (quoting 37 BVerfGE 271, 280 (1974)).

[320] Costa v. ENEL, [1964] ECR 585, 593. See also id. at 594: "The executive force of Community law cannot vary from one State to another in deference to subsequent domestic laws, without jeopardizing the attainment of the objectives of the Treaty set out in Article 5(2) and giving rise to the discrimination prohibited by Article 7." The Court added, id., that Community regulations would not be "binding," as Art. 189 says they are, if they could be nullified by national legislation.

[321] See 6 BVerfGE 309, 363 (1957) (allowing a Land to enact legislation conflicting with an agreement with the Holy See): Art. 25 GG subordinates statutes to "the general rules of public international law," but not to treaties. Cf. The Head Money Cases, 112 U.S. 580, 599 (1884).

[322] See T. C. Hartley, The Foundations of European Community Law 219-45 (2d ed. 1988). Despite the strong language of Art. 55 of the French constitution, however, the Conseil d'État is said to have been half-hearted in its acceptance of the supremacy of Community law. Id. at 234-36. One member of the House of Lords, in contrast, has recently stated without contradiction that in a case of direct conflict between an Act of Parliament and Community law the latter would prevail. Regina v. Secretary of State for Transport ex parte Factortame Ltd., [1991] 1 All ER 70, [1990] 3 CMLR 375 (1990) (opinion of Lord Bridge of Harwich).

[323] See 31 BVerfGE 145, 173-74 (1971); 73 BVerfGE 339, 374-75 (1986).

Justice as to the meaning of Community law.[324] Consequently the
Constitutional Court initially balked when asked to carry the
supremacy principle to its logical extreme in 1974.[325] It was true,
said the Court, that the Federal Republic had given the Communities
authority to adopt regulations having the force of law.[326] But there
were limits to the sovereign powers that could be transferred under
Article 24(1):

> Article 24 of the Basic Law provides for a transfer of sovereign pow-
> ers to intergovernmental organizations. This must not be taken lit-
> erally. Like any constitutional provision of similarly fundamental
> nature, Article 24 must be understood and interpreted in the context
> of the entire constitution. That is to say, the provision does not open
> the door to a change in the basic structure of the constitution, which
> constitutes its very identity, without constitutional amendment,
> through the mere promulgation of legislative acts by an intergov-
> ernmental institution.[327]

Among the "essential and inalienable" components of the German constitution, the Court continued, was its catalog of basic
rights. Article 24(1) was not a carte blanche empowering the Communities to override these rights; and the EEC treaty did not contain
a Bill of Rights of its own. Thus in any conflict between Community
law and the fundamental rights guaranteed by the Basic Law the latter must prevail; and so long as the Community did not provide corresponding safeguards the Constitutional Court would continue to
forbid German authorities to apply community law that conflicted
with the German provisions.[328]

Twelve years later, in light of significant changes in Community
law, the Constitutional Court receded from this conclusion.[329] Since
the 1974 decision, on the basis of the treaty's requirement that it
"ensure that in the interpretation and application of this Treaty the
law is observed,"[330] the European Court of Justice had asserted the
power to set aside Community law that infringed fundamental individual rights.[331] These rights, the European Court had declared,
were derived from "the common constitutional traditions of the

---

[324] See 31 BVerfGE 145, 173-74 (1971).

[325] 37 BVerfGE 271 (1974).

[326] Id. at 277-78.

[327] Id. at 279.

[328] Id. at 280-81, 285. The Italian Corte Costituzionale took a similar position.
See Antonio La Pergola & Patrick Del Duca, Community Law, International Law,
and the Italian Constitution, 79 Am. J. Int'l Law 598, 609 ff. (1985), cited in 73
BVerfGE 339, 376 (1986).

[329] 73 BVerfGE 339, 378-87 (1986).

[330] EEC Treaty, Art. 164.

[331] 73 BVerfGE at 379 (citing, inter alia, Stauder v. City of Ulm, [1969] ECR 419,
425, and J. Nold K.G. v. E.C. Commission, [1974] ECR 491, 507).

member states" and the European Convention on Human Rights.[332]
They included not only economic liberties but also freedom of
association and religion, protection of the family, equal treatment,
and a prohibition against arbitrary acts; they embraced the familiar
German principles of proportionality, nonretroactivity, and the right
to hearing.[333] Thus the current case law of the European Court
"guarantee[d] a minimum standard of substantive protection of
fundamental rights which in principle satisfie[d] the constitutional
requirements of the Basic Law";[334] and the willingness of that Court
to measure Community acts against these standards satisfied the
equally essential requirement of judicial review.[335] Accordingly the
German court reversed its position:

> So long as the European Communities, and in particular the case law
> of the European Court, generally ensure an effective protection of
> fundamental rights against the sovereign powers of the Communities
> that is to be regarded as substantially similar to the protection of
> fundamental rights that the Basic Law requires, . . . the Federal
> Constitutional Court . . . will no longer measure [Community] law
> against the standard of the fundamental rights contained in the Basic
> Law . . . .[336]

Notwithstanding this provisional withdrawal from the field, the
Constitutional Court adhered to the view that Article 24(1) did not authorize wholesale transfer of the power to act in contravention of fundamental rights.[337] Just what other limitations inhered in the
Court's insistence that no transfer of powers might alter the "basic
structure" or "essential" and "inalienable" features of the Basic Law
remained unsettled.[338] One common assumption was that at a
minimum the legislature could not accomplish by transfer under Ar-

---

[332] 73 BVerfGE at 379, 381. Art. F of the Maastricht Treaty now expressly binds
Community organs to respect both these common constitutional traditions and the
Convention. See Thomas Oppermann & Claus Dieter Classen, Europäische Union:
Erfüllung des Grundgesetzes, in Aus Politik und Zeitgeschichte, 9. Juli 1993, S. 11,
15.

[333] Id. at 380-81.

[334] Id. at 385-86.

[335] Id. at 384. See generally Hans-Werner Rengeling, Grundrechtsschutz in
der Europäischen Gemeinschaft (1993).

[336] 73 BVerfGE at 387. Because of their contrasting provisional "so long as"
formulations, the 1974 and 1986 decisions are familiarly known as "Solange Eins"
and "Solange Zwei."

[337] See id. at 375-76.

[338] See also 75 BVerfGE 223, 240-44 (1987) (holding German tribunals bound by a
decision of the European Court to the effect that Community directives directly
precluded the application of contrary national law, even though the treaty seemed to
say they were toothless until implemented by national legislation: The European
Court's interpretation remained within the limits of legitimate judicial creativity).

ticle 24(1) what it could not achieve by the more exacting process of constitutional amendment under Article 79.[339] That would mean that no transfer could empower an international organization to violate the dignity of the individual, destroy the essence of federalism, or depart materially from the guarantees of democracy, social responsibility, and the rule of law.[340] In its 1974 decision, for example, the Court expressed concern not only about the absence of an enforceable Community Bill of Rights but also about the democratic legitimacy of Community institutions, since lawmaking authority was basically vested in an unelected Council representing the governments of the member states.[341] A further unresolved question, given currency by proposals for Community action with respect to broadcasting, was whether Article 24(1) authorized the Federation to transfer powers that were reserved to the Länder.[342]

The Maastricht Treaty, finally ratified in 1993 after initial rejection in Denmark, envisions the transformation of the European Communities into a new European Union with a central bank, a common currency, and a common policy with respect to defense and foreign affairs. When this agreement came up for ratification in 1992, doubts were expressed whether Article 24(1) provided the necessary authority. The new Union, it was argued, was no longer an international organization within the meaning of that provision but a new federal state.[343]

To meet this objection, approval of the Maastricht Treaty was coupled with adoption of a new Article 23(1), which expressly authorizes the transfer of additional powers to the new European Union.[344]

---

[339] See, e.g., Zuleeg in 1 AK-GG, Art. 24 Abs. 1, Rdnr. 63; Maunz in 2 Maunz/Dürig, Art. 24, Rdnr. 16.

[340] See Art. 79(3) GG (protecting these essential features against constitutional amendment).

[341] See 37 BVerfGE at 280.

[342] See Maunz in 2 Maunz/Dürig, Art. 24, Rdnr. 18 (arguing that the Federation could transfer only its own powers); Grewe, supra n. 205, Rdnr. 72-74 (noting increasing support for the contrary position). Compare the equally unresolved question whether the general federal treaty authority embraces subjects on which only the Länder can legislate, text at notes 199-208 supra. See also Grewe, supra, Rdnr. 75 (arguing that only *individual* powers might be transferred, and that therefore Germany could not become part of "a unitary European state"). Similar arguments were made in an effort to limit the authority of our Constitutional Convention to propose "amendments" to the Articles of Confederation, but without success. See, e.g., 1 Max Farrand, Records of the Federal Convention of 1787, p. 262 (rev. ed. 1937). For the further argument that the essentially unamendable declaration in Art. 20(2) that "[a]ll state authority emanates from the people" guarantees not only democracy but the continued existence of a sovereign German nation see Hans Stöcker, Deutschland demnächst – eine europäische Unionsprovinz?, 1 Kritische Vierteljahresschrift für Gesetzgebung und Rechtswissenschaft 87, 98-100 (1991).

[343] See Scholz, supra note 209, 1992 NJW at 2594.

[344] Gesetz zur Änderung des Grundgesetzes vom 21. Dezember 1992, BGBl. I S. 2086, 44 Sammelblatt für Rechtsvorschriften des Bundes und der Länder 309 (1993).

In addition to removing the most obvious constitutional objections
to endorsement of the Maastricht Treaty, the new Article 23(1) codifies the essence of the Constitutional Court's decisions by pledging
German participation only in – and thus by authorizing the transfer
of powers only to – a Union that not only "provides protection for fundamental rights essentially comparable to that provided for by this
Basic Law" but is also "committed to the principles of democracy, federalism, social responsibility, and the rule of law" and to a new principle of "subsidiarity" understood (like the more detailed provision respecting concurrent powers of the Federation in Article 72(2), which
the Court has refused to enforce) to permit the Union to act only when
its member states cannot do so effectively on their own.[345]

The following sentence of Article 23(1) neatly answers two important questions by providing that both approval of the treaty itself and
any further transfers of authority that have the effect of altering or
authorizing alteration of the Basic Law may be accomplished only in
accordance with the procedural and substantive requirements for
constitutional amendments prescribed by Article 79(2) and (3). In
other words, any such transfer requires a two-thirds vote of both the
Bundestag and the Bundesrat, and it may not impair the essence of
human dignity, federalism, or the other values enshrined in Articles
1 and 20.[346] Precisely which transfers of authority would have the
effect of amending the Basic Law is not clear, and Article 23(1) does
not explicitly resolve the controversy over transfer of powers reserved
to the Länder. By requiring Bundesrat consent for *any* further transfer, however, the new provision undermines the strongest argument
against the transfer of state authority; for no longer can it be said that
the Bundestag would be unilaterally giving away powers it did not
possess.[347]

Defended by its supporters as another significant step toward the
goal of German participation in a united Europe as stated in the original Preamble to the Basic Law,[348] the Maastricht Treaty was attacked by others on the ground that the changes it wrought were so
massive that under Article 79(3) they could not be authorized even by
constitutional amendment, but only by recourse to the people.[349] The

---

[345] See Scholz, supra note 209, 1992 NJW at 2598-99 (arguing that the inclusion of
democracy in the list requires that the European Parliament finally be given
meaningful legislative authority).

[346] See id. at 2599.

[347] The additional provision of Art. 23(6) respecting representation of the
Federal Republic by a representative of the Länder when the European Union deals
with matters principally within their exclusive legislative authority seems to presuppose such a transfer and thus lends additional strength to this conclusion. See
text at notes 208-09 supra.

[348] See, e.g., Oppermann & Classen, supra note 332.

[349] See Hans Heinrich Rupp, Muß das Volk über den Vertrag von Maastricht
entscheiden?, 1993 NJW 38, 40.

inevitable constitutional challenge was filed; the Constitutional Court rejected it in a major 1993 decision.[350] The decision was narrow. The only argument considered was that the treaty infringed the rights of voters under Article 38 to participate in elections for the Bundestag. For it was implicit in that Article that by voting in those elections the people would exercise their democratic right of self-government. Thus Article 38 forbade any transfer of Bundestag powers that would leave German voters without the constitutional minimum of influence on those who exercised governmental authority over them; for even a constitutional amendment could not impair the essence of democracy.[351]

In light of the original constitutional commitment to European integration, said the Court, the transfer of governmental authority to a supranational institution could not per se be held inconsistent with democracy; the transfer found democratic legitimation in legislation passed by an elected assembly.[352] But an indispensable condition of German membership in such a community was that the influence of the sovereign people upon the acts of the community itself be assured.[353] In the long run it was not enough that basic Community decisions were made by executive officials of the member states who in turn were chosen by democratically elected parliaments. The democratic basis of the Union must be strengthened as its powers were extended, and those powers must be limited; for too great a preponderance of Community authority might weaken democracy in the constituent states.[354]

The Maastricht Treaty, the Court concluded, was consistent with these principles. It provided only for an association of sovereign states ("Staatenverbund"), not for a single European state.[355] It gave the Communities only limited enumerated powers, restricting them further by a subsidiarity requirement that (in glaring but unmentioned contrast to the comparable provision of Article 72(2) as interpreted by the Constitutional Court) the European Court of Justice

---

[350] BVerfG, Decision of Oct. 12, 1993, Case No. 2 BvR 2134/92 (not yet reported).

[351] Id., slip op. at 24-26, 40. In refusing to consider the additional claim that the treaty infringed various provisions of the Bill of Rights, the Court emphasized once again that the European Court of Justice would afford adequate protection against any such invasion (id. at 34), adding that if it did not the Constitutional Court itself would – surprisingly, even against organs of the Communities themselves (id. at 29-30).

[352] Id. at 42-43.

[353] Id. at 43.

[354] Id. at 45-46. See also id. at 44 (stressing the need to expand the role of the European Parliament). The specific provision for a European Central Bank independent of the normal political process (as envisioned by a simultaneous amendment to Art. 88 GG) was justified (like the Bundesbank itself) on the ground that experience had shown politicians incapable of ensuring a stable money supply. Id. at 77-79.

[355] See id. at 50-51.

was bound to enforce.[356] Democratic legitimation of any further extension of Community powers was assured by the provisions respecting amendment of the treaty; the Communities were given no authority to extend their own powers, and the Constitutional Court would – in yet another modification of its position – treat as invalid any Community action in excess of its authority.[357] Finally, the Court added without explanation in accents that would have warmed the heart of John C. Calhoun, Germany could unilaterally withdraw from the Union at any time.[358]

With friends like that, it might be argued, the European Union is hardly in need of adversaries. Like the earlier treaty between West and East Germany, the Maastricht Treaty is all right because it does very little, and the Court has promised to see to it that it does no more. Thus although the exact limits of the powers that may be given to the European Union under Article 23(1) remain uncertain, the bottom line is clear: Integration cannot proceed much further until the European Parliament is given a meaningful legislative role.

Nevertheless it is equally plain that very considerable authority has already been transferred to the European Union and that more may well be transferred in the near future. Where all this will ultimately lead is anybody's guess, but some years ago a knowledgeable observer was already able to draw interesting parallels between the increasing integration of Western Europe and the early development of federalism in the United States.[359] As the Constitutional Court emphasized in the Maastricht decision,[360] the European Union is not yet the United States of Europe; but the Federal Republic is already not only a central government with respect to the Länder but also a constituent part of a larger entity with significant governmental powers.

V. CONCLUSION

"Ground-level apartments," wrote the Israeli humorist Ephraim Kishon, "have one advantage and one disadvantage. The advantage is that there are no steps to climb. The disadvantage is that the ants have no steps to climb either." Federalism is like a flight of stairs: It

---

[356] Id. at 51, 79-83. See also id. at 66-74 (construing the powers granted by the treaty with respect to a currency union narrowly and insisting that it could not be put fully into effect without further action by the member states).

[357] Id. at 49, 53, 58-65. Any contrary interpretation by the European Court of Justice, the Court insisted, would not be binding. Id. at 81.

[358] Id. at 52.

[359] See Gerhard Casper, The Emerging European Constitution, in Proceedings of the 72d Annual Meeting of the American Society of International Law 166, 169-75 (1978).

[360] BVerfG, Decision of Oct. 12, 1993, Case No. 2 BvR 2134/92 (not yet reported), slip op. at 51.

makes it harder to accomplish legitimate governmental tasks, but it also makes it harder to infringe our freedom. Thus federalism fosters liberty – and democracy, diversity, and experimentation as well.[361] As one German scholar has remarked, federalism is difficult but rewarding ("nicht leicht, aber lohnend").[362]

Federalism is a central principle of the German Basic Law. Its contours differ in interesting ways from those of federalism in the United States. Legislation is more centralized in Germany; but execution and adjudication are less so, and the constituent states play a significant role in determining the policy of the Federation.

Although there seems to have been a general tendency toward increasing central authority in Germany,[363] constitutional limits on federal power remain a reality. Unlike our Supreme Court, the Constitutional Court – with the important exception of the Article 72(2) provision requiring a showing of need for the enactment of legislation within the concurrent authority of the Bund – has faithfully defended the prerogatives of the states.[364] Moreover, the increasing integration of Germany into the European Union – while widely viewed as posing a significant threat to federalism within Germany itself – affords significant additional protection against arbitrary or oppressive action by any level of German government.

As Learned Hand reminded us, no words on a piece of paper can preserve liberty unless it lives in the hearts of the people.[365] But the continuing importance attached to the decentralization of governmental authority in the Federal Republic over the past forty years is one of the many aspects of recent experience that give reason for optimism as to the future of liberty, democracy, and the rule of law in a no longer divided Germany.

---

[361] See Kimminich, supra note 1, at Rdnr. 22-24, 45-48. Cf. New State Ice Co. v. Liebmann, 285 U.S. 262, 311 (1932) (Brandeis, J., dissenting).

[362] See Kimminich, supra note 1, Rdnr. 22.

[363] See id., Rdnr. 56; Konrad Hesse, Der Unitarische Bundesstaat 14, 27 (1962) (adding that the principal function of the Länder is to check the actions of the central authorities through the Bundesrat). The last constitutional amendment significantly increasing Bund authority, however, dates from 1972.

[364] See Kimminich, supra note 1, Rdnr. 52; Blair, supra note 13, at 250. In adddition, the Constitutional Commission established pursuant to the Unification Treaty has proposed several amendments to strengthen the position of the Länder.

[365] Learned Hand, The Spirit of Liberty 190 (2d ed. 1954).

3

Separation of Powers

Like the Constitution of the United States, the German Basic Law is built upon the premise of popular sovereignty. "All governmental authority," says the second paragraph of Article 20, "emanates from the people." But the Federal Republic is after all a republic, not a direct democracy; the same paragraph goes on to say that the people shall exercise their power "by means of elections and voting" and through the organs of government.[1] Most important for present purposes, Article 20(2) also requires a separation of governmental powers; for it specifies that the people shall act through the agency of special, or particular, or separate ("besondere") legislative, executive, and judicial bodies.[2]

---

[1] In contrast to Art. 73-76 of the Weimar Constitution, the Basic Law provides for such devices as initiative or referendum only in connection with the rearrangement of state boundaries (Art. 29, 118 GG). The departure was deliberate: History had convinced the majority of delegates in the Parliamentary Council that direct democracy served principally as a tool of demagogues. For one of the many unsuccessful efforts of the Center Party to persuade the Parliamentary Council to include a general provision for direct democracy in the Basic Law see Sten. Ber. at 228-29 (Delegate Brockmann). See also Peter Krause, Verfassungsrechtliche Möglichkeiten unmittelbarer Demokratie, 2 Handbuch des Staatsrechts 313, and Roman Herzog in 2 Maunz/Dürig, Art. 20, Abschnitt II, Rdnr. 38-45 (both taking the conventional view that additional plebiscites at the federal level are impermissible); Ekkehart Stein in 1 AK-GG, Art. 20, Abs. 1-3, Abschnitt II, Rdnr. 39-40 (taking the contrary position); Bericht der VerfKomm at 83-86 (declining to propose amendments of the Basic Law to permit more direct democracy). Additional plebiscites at the state level are not forbidden by the Basic Law. See 60 BVerfGE 175, 207-08 (1982).

In reaching their conclusion neither Krause nor Herzog places any reliance on the term "Republik" in Art. 20(1). See Herzog in 2 Maunz/Dürig, Art. 20, Abs. III, Rdnr. 5-8 (arguing that (as in Art. 1 WRV, see Gerhard Anschütz, Die Verfassung des Deutschen Reichs 37 (4th ed. 1933)) the term is employed in opposition to monarchy, not to direct democracy). For a broader definition of "Republik" that still falls short of condemning direct democracy see Wilhelm Henke, Die Republik, 1 Handbuch des Staatsrechts 863, Rdnr. 7-8.

[2] See Art. 20(2) GG: "Alle Staatsgewalt geht vom Volke aus. Sie wird vom Volke in Wahlen und Abstimmungen und durch besondere Organe der Gesetzgebung, der vollziehenden Gewalt und der Rechtsprechung ausgeübt." See also Herzog in 2 Maunz/Dürig, Art. 20, Abschnitt V, Rdnr. 37-43.

Separation of powers can serve to promote rational government by optimizing the conditions for making various decisions:[3] Basic policy may be set by a deliberative assembly, administration may be entrusted to a unified executive, individual disputes may be resolved by independent judges.[4] No less significant, however, is Montesquieu's famous argument for separation of powers as a fundamental safeguard of liberty.[5] For when legislative, executive, and judicial powers are divided, three distinct bodies must abuse their authority before the citizen's rights can be infringed.[6]

The allocation of governmental powers in Germany differs from that in the United States in a number of interesting ways. The most striking difference is that the Federal Republic has a parliamentary rather than a presidential system; federal ministers serve at the pleasure of the legislature.[7] Thus at the outset there is less structural separation between legislative and executive organs in Germany than in the United States. The judges, on the other hand, are quite independent. Indeed in some respects they are better protected from executive or legislative influence than their counterparts in the United States.

Moreover, the lack of separation between the federal parliament and federal ministers is counterbalanced by a second interesting departure from the American model: a significant reduction in the powers of the ministers themselves. Most federal laws are carried out not by federal officials but by the constituent states ("Länder"), and even the federal administration is given a degree of independence from political pressure. Thus principles both of federalism and of civil service compensate to a significant extent for the structural symbiosis of the parliamentary model; even at the structural level there is more separation of powers in Germany than a first look at the parliamentary system might suggest.

Furthermore, the undeniable American advantage with respect to structural separation is matched by a marked German advantage

---

[3] See 68 BVerfGE 1, 86 (1984); Konrad Hesse, Grundzüge des Verfas-sungsrechts der Bundesrepublik Deutschland, Rdnr. 482 (18th ed. 1991) ("eine Frage sachgemäßer Bestimmung und Zuordnung der staatlichen Funktionen"); Eberhard Schmidt-Aßmann, Der Rechtsstaat, 1 Handbuch des Staatsrechts 987, Rdnr. 50.

[4] See Hesse, supra note 3, Rdnr. 488; cf. David Currie, The Distribution of Powers after Bowsher, 1986 Sup. Ct. Rev. 19.

[5] L'Esprit des Lois, bk. 11, ch. 6 (1748).

[6] For a German version of this theme see Herzog in 2 Maunz/Dürig, Art. 20, Abschnitt V, Rdnr. 2-12. For the analogous argument in support of federalism see chapter 2 supra. As we shall see, in Germany federalism significantly complements the horizontal separation of powers.

[7] The Länder constitutions likewise follow the parliamentary model, though the Basic Law does not require them to. See Matthias Herdegen, Strukturen und Institute des Verfassungsrechts der Länder, 4 Handbuch des Staatsrechts 479, Rdnr. 16-37.

Simler

in separation of functions. Only the legislature may make laws; only
the executive may enforce them; only judges may adjudicate. Not
only is the executive bound by the laws and in many respects permitted to act only on the basis of statutory authority; in Germany there
are meaningful and judicially enforced limits to the delegation of legislative power. With rare exceptions there are no independent agencies with executive powers; most enforcement authority is ultimately
subject to ministerial control. Finally, there are essentially no quasi-
judicial agencies in the American sense of the term; if administrators decide concrete individual disputes, their decisions must be subject to de novo judicial review on questions of fact as well as law.

difference

In sum, despite the parliamentary system there are significant
structural as well as functional limits to the concentration of authority in Germany. These limits provide significant additional safeguards against arbitrary governmental action, and Article 79(3) protects their essential features from constitutional amendment.[8]

I. LEGISLATIVE POWER

Federal statutes, Article 77(1) provides, are adopted by the Bundestag – the federal Parliament. Article 28(1) requires similar legislative bodies in the Länder.[9] Through the Bundesrat, the constituent states exercise a significant check on federal legislation – a
veto power that in a number of important instances cannot be overridden by the Bundestag itself.[10]

A. Elections and Equal Rights

In conformity with the democratic principle of Article 20(2), Article 38(1) prescribes that members of the Bundestag be chosen in

---

[8] See Art. 79(3) GG: "Amendments to this Basic Law affecting . . . the basic
principles laid down in Article . . . 20 shall be inadmissible."

[9] This requirement also applies to county and municipal governments ("Kreise
und Gemeinden"), except that in the latter the citizens themselves may act as a legislative assembly.

[10] See chapter 2 supra. Unlike the President of the United States (U.S. Const.,
Art. I, § 7), the executive in Germany has no general veto power. Laws increasing
expenditures or reducing revenues, however, can be adopted only with Cabinet approval. See Art. 113 GG. The theory is that neither the legislature nor the executive
can be trusted where the public's money is concerned; each branch therefore acts as
a check on the other. See Maunz in 4 Maunz/Dürig, Art. 113, Rdnr. 1; Gunter
Kisker, Staatshaushalt, 4 Handbuch des Staatsrechts, Rdnr. 35, 48-51. In addition,
legislative appropriations are interpreted only to authorize expenditures, not to require them. Id., Rdnr. 28, 52. Contrast Train v. City of New York, 420 U.S. 35
(1975). For an acerbic statement of the view that Art. 113 was doomed by political realities to be the dead letter it has apparently become see Heiko Faber in 2 AK-GG,
Art. 113, Rdnr. 1-4.

"general, direct, free, equal, and secret elections," and Article 28(1) applies the same requirements to the Länder.[11] The requirement that elections be "general" serves to prevent unjustifiable denial of the right to vote;[12] the requirements of freedom and secrecy are largely self-explanatory.[13] The requirements of directness and equality have proved more interesting and difficult to administer.

The Parliamentary Council made the deliberate decision neither to prescribe nor to preclude proportional representation but rather to leave the question to the ordinary political process.[14] But the Parliamentary Council was also called upon to adopt a statute specifying the system under which the first elections would take place. After debating the well-known merits and demerits of proportional representation, the Council settled upon a mixed system. Each voter would cast two ballots, one for an individual candidate, the other for a political party. Candidates receiving the highest number of votes in their districts would be elected, and the remaining seats would then be allotted in such a way that each party's total representation was essentially proportional to its total vote.[15]

---

[11] See also 1 BVerfGE 14, 33 (1951) (holding that the Bund had offended the democratic principle, among other things, by extending the terms of the legislatures of two Länder pending a referendum on their consolidation into a single southwestern state).

[12] See Art. 38(2) GG (prescribing a voting age of 18 years); 36 BVerfGE 139, 141-44 (1973) (noting the statutory exclusion of the mentally infirm and upholding a provision generally limiting voting rights to residents of the Federal Republic); 58 BVerfGE 202, 205-08 (1981) (warning that equality might soon require that a statutory exception for public servants employed abroad be extended to those working for the European Communities; Hans Meyer, Wahlgrundsätze und Wahlverfahren, 2 Handbuch des Staatsrechts 269, Rdnr.1-9 (questioning (at Rdnr. 3) the continuing denial of voting rights to persons convicted of certain crimes against the state); Maunz in 3 Maunz/Dürig, Art. 38, Rdnr. 39-40. In 1990 the Constitutional Court, relying on Art. 20(2) ("All state authority shall emanate from the people"), held that the right to vote could not constitutionally be extended to aliens. 83 BVerfGE 37, 50-59 (1990). Art. 28(1) was subsequently amended to permit citizens of other states within the European Communities to vote in local elections in accordance with Community law.

[13] See 59 BVerfGE 119 (1981) (rejecting the argument that absentee voting – which plainly promotes the generality of elections – created an unacceptable risk to either freedom or secrecy of the ballot); 66 BVerfGE 369, 380-84 (1984) (noting that Art. 38(1) forbade private as well as public interference with voting freedom but finding no violation in various warnings by employers that they would reduce hiring and investment in the event of a Social Democratic victory).

[14] See Sten. Ber. at 109 (Delegate Diederichs); 1 BVerfGE 208, 246 (1952). Contrast Art. 22 WRV, which prescribed proportional representation for elections to the Reichstag. For the argument that the decision not to write proportional representation into the Basic Law was not the equivalent of leaving the matter to legislative choice see Hans Meyer, Demokratische Wahl und Wahlsystem, 2 Handbuch des Staatsrechts 249, Rdnr. 31.

[15] See Sten. Ber. at 109-67; Wahlgesetz zum ersten Bundestag vom 15. Juni 1949, BGBl. S. 21, §§ 9-10, also printed in 2 Quellen zum Staatsrecht 277, 279 (1951).

Though intended as temporary, this dual system has persisted to the present day.[16] It was designed to ensure both that the Bundestag faithfully reflect the political makeup of the country and that the voters have an opportunity to select individual legislators of their choice.[17] It has provoked a number of important decisions of the Constitutional Court.

The first question was whether elections on the basis of the party ballot were "direct" within the meaning of Article 38(1). Originally, said the Court, the requirement of direct elections had been designed to prevent the interposition of electors ("Wahlmänner")[18] like those who were initially meant to choose the President of the United States; the Parliamentary Council was told that its purpose was to ensure that representatives were not elected by state legislatures,[19] as our Senators originally were. The principle was of course broader than these examples: Representatives should be elected by the people themselves.[20]

Thus it would offend the requirement of direct elections if representatives were effectively chosen by political parties,[21] and the election law gave them a considerable say in determining who would be elected. It was the parties, not the people, who determined which candidates were listed on their ballots, and in what order; the voter could not select a single candidate without voting for the whole list;[22] and each party's seats were filled in the order in which the names appeared.[23]

So long as the lists were fixed in advance, the Court said, there was no problem; the people made the actual decision who would become a member.[24] When a successful candidate withdrew or resigned after election, however, it was not permissible for a party either to name a substitute[25] or to change the order in which candi-

---

[16] The relevant provisions are now found in §§ 4-6 of the Bundeswahlgesetz [BWG], in der Fassung vom 1. September 1975, BGBl. I S. 2325, as subsequently amended.

[17] See Sten. Ber. at 110-11 (Delegate Diederichs).

[18] See 7 BVerfGE 63, 68 (1957); Meyer, supra note 12, Rdnr. 11 (tracing the requirement to the elections for the Frankfurt convention in 1848).

[19] See Sten. Ber. at 28 (Delegate Menzel).

[20] See 7 BVerfGE at 68; Meyer, supra note 12, Rdnr. 12.

[21] See 3 BVerfGE 45, 50 (1953).

[22] See 7 BVerfGE at 69-70 (concluding that this all-or-nothing feature did not offend the requirement that elections be "free").

[23] See id. at 70-71 (holding that this preference for candidates listed first did not violate the provision for "equal" elections).

[24] See id. at 68-69; 47 BVerfGE 253, 280-81 (1978) (adding that it was not even necessary that the names of the candidates appear on the ballot itself). Contrast Hermann von Mangoldt, Das Bonner Grundgesetz 231 (1953) (arguing that election by party list would offend the directness requirement).

[25] 3 BVerfGE at 49-52; 47 BVerfGE at 280.

dates appeared on the list;[26] for in either case it was the party, not the people, who made the final decision.

The requirement that elections be "equal" has proved even more productive of litigation. When the issue is government support of political parties, the guarantee of freedom to establish parties in Article 21(1), in conjunction with the general equality principle of Article 3(1), provides the principal standard; the relevant decisions, which apply a principle of equal opportunity ("Chancengleichheit"), are considered in the following chapter.[27] Article 38(1) has commonly been applied to require equality in the conduct of elections themselves.[28]

Because representation is basically proportional to overall party strength,[29] equality in the population of individual districts is of less concern in Germany than in the United States. Whenever a party wins more seats in individual districts than it would be entitled to on a strict proportional basis, however, it is permitted to keep them.[30] In this situation the existence of districts with smaller than average population will result in overrepresentation of that party.[31] Thus, not surprisingly, the Constitutional Court has held that Article 38(1) requires that districts be of approximately equal population.[32]

More interesting and more difficult are a group of decisions respecting the constitutionality of measures designed to counter the principal disadvantage of proportional representation: the risk of ungovernability resulting from the dispersal of votes among a multitude

---

[26] 7 BVerfGE 77, 84-86 (1957).

[27] See, e.g., 6 BVerfGE 273, 279-82 (1957) (nondeductibility of contributions to unrepresented parties); 7 BVerfGE 99, 107-08 (1957) (denial of public television time to unrepresented party); 44 BVerfGE 125, 144-66 (1977) (also invoking Art. 38(1)) (government propaganda for parties in ruling coalition). When the victim of discrimination in the distribution of largesse is not a political party, Art. 38(1) provides the governing standard. See 41 BVerfGE 399, 412-23 (1976) (exclusion of independent candidate from reimbursement of election expenses). See also chapter 4 infra.

[28] As noted above, limitations of the right to cast votes are usually tested against the requirement that elections be "general." See text at note 12 supra. The equality provision assures that each person has the same number of votes and that they are given equal effect. See Maunz in 3 Maunz/Dürig, Art. 38, Rdnr. 48.

[29] Double counting is avoided in most cases by subtracting the number of seats each party won in individual districts from the number to which it would be entitled under a strict proportional system. See § 10(2) of the 1949 statute (§ 6(4) of the current version).

[30] See § 10(3) of the 1949 statute (§ 6(5) of the current version).

[31] In Schleswig-Holstein, for example, where most districts were significantly smaller than the national average, the Christian Democrats won thirteen of the fourteen districts in the 1961 Bundestag election, although a proportional allocation would have given them only nine seats. See 16 BVerfGE 130, 137-38 (1963).

[32] Id. at 138-41 (approving the rather lenient statutory standard of thirty-three and one-third percent maximum deviation from the norm). Cf. Reynolds v. Sims, 377 U.S. 533 (1964).

of splinter parties – a risk that had materialized during the Weimar period, with most unfortunate results.[33]

One method employed to inhibit splintering was to require a specified number of petition signatures as a condition of ballot access, a second to exclude fringe parties from public support. The Constitutional Court has taken a very dim view of these devices. In 1953 it struck down a requirement that the candidate of a party not already significantly represented in the Bundestag or in the state legislature collect a mere 500 signatures in a district averaging 140,000 voters;[34] in 1968 it announced that any party that had amassed a piddling 0.5 percent of the vote in the preceding election was entitled to its share of government largesse.[35] By U.S. standards the requirements that were invalidated were quite modest.[36] In a system based substantially on proportional representation, however, a party can win seats without commanding anything like a plurality anywhere; thus it is more difficult to dismiss any party as insignificant, and virtually all are entitled to a chance to compete.

More successful was the attempt to regulate the results of the election directly by excluding parties that attracted less than a designated percentage of the vote from the allotment of seats on the party ballot. A 7.5 percent threshold, the Court held, was too high; it was out of line with tradition, and it excluded parties whose support could not be described as trivial.[37] But a five percent requirement was generally all right: It significantly reduced the danger of governmental paralysis without excessively disturbing the principle that the legislature should be a microcosm of society as a whole.[38]

---

[33] See chapter 1 supra.

[34] 3 BVerfGE 19, 23-29 (1953). See id. at 28 (noting the reluctance of German voters since the war to reveal publicly their support for any political party). The argument that the petition requirement impaired the secrecy of the election, however, was rejected (id. at 31-32), and a separate provision estimated to require a total of some 18,000 signatures to field entire slates of candidates throughout the country was upheld (id. at 29-31).

[35] 24 BVerfGE300, 340-43 (1968) (striking down a threshold of 2.5 percent). The only legitimate reason for any such limitation, the Court said, was to inhibit the formation of "parties" for the sole purpose of collecting government funds. Id. at 342.

[36] Contrast Jenness v. Fortson, 403 U.S. 431, 432 (1971) (upholding a requirement that independent candidates present petitions signed by five percent of eligible voters); Buckley v. Valeo, 424 U.S. 1, 96 (1976) (upholding a limitation of subsidies to parties that had obtained five percent or more of the present or previous vote). See Gerhard Casper, Williams v. Rhodes and Public Financing of Political Parties under the American and German Constitutions, 1969 Sup. Ct. Rev. 271.

[37] 1 BVerfGE 208, 241-60 (1952).

[38] See id. (dictum); 4 BVerfGE 31, 40 (1954); 6 BVerfGE 84 (1957). In holding that the legislature was not required to make an exception to the five percent rule for the Danish minority party in Schleswig-Holstein, the Court pointedly left open the question whether such an exception was permissible, and it was promptly enacted. See 4 BVerfGE at 42; Donald P. Kommers, The Constitutional Jurisprudence of the

This conclusion has been much criticized, not only because even before reunification the five percent threshold effectively disenfranchised as many as 1.8 million voters (enough to elect twenty-five members of the Bundestag), but also because a committee of the Parliamentary Council had dropped a provision that would expressly have authorized adoption of a five percent rule, on the ground that it was inconsistent with the principle of equal elections.[39] The interest in ensuring a Parliament capable of performing its functions, however, seems a strong one. Moreover, it is not altogether plain why the principle of equal elections is more seriously impaired by excluding parties with less than five percent (or 7.5 percent) of the vote than by adopting the winner-take-all system that prevails in Britain and the United States, which would effectively disenfranchise the voters of each losing party in every district – and which the Court conceded would be perfectly constitutional.[40]

It is implicit in Article 38(1) that each member of the Bundestag has an equal right to participate in its deliberations. Article 76(1) makes clear that members may introduce bills;[41] this right may be subjected to reasonable procedural regulations but not substantively limited, even by the Bundestag itself.[42] Full and equal membership

---

Federal Republic of Germany 186 (1989). Furthermore, before the first election following reunification the Court held it unreasonable to apply the usual five percent clause on a nationwide basis to parties that had grown up in East Germany and had had no opportunity to campaign for support elsewhere; it was enough that they commanded five percent of the vote in the new East German Länder. 82 BVerfGE 322, 339-42, 348-51 (1990). The inequality in this case was de facto rather than de jure; the Court required formally preferential treatment of East German parties in order to ensure them practical equality of opportunity. See chapter 6 infra.

[39] See Meyer, supra note 12, Rdnr. 26-29 (arguing that the Court displayed "an astonishing disrespect for the legislative history"); 1 JöR (n.F.) at 352.

[40] See note 14 supra and accompanying text. In rejecting this argument the Court said only that once the legislature opted for proportional representation it had to apply the principle consistently and equally. 1 BVerfGE at 246-47. Accord Maunz in 3 Maunz/Dürig, Art. 38, Rdnr. 50. Of course there are many instances in which the greater power does not include the lesser. See the general discussion of unconstitutional conditions in chapter 4 infra. In this case, however, the alternative less detrimental to equality seems not to impinge on any extraneous constitutional right, as the selective denial of a privilege would. Perhaps the best answer is that there is a stronger justification for the greater departure from equality inherent in abandoning proportional representation altogether: the greater ability of voters to select a representative of their own choosing.

[41] See Art. 76(1) GG: "Bills shall be introduced in the Bundestag by the Federal Government [Bundesregierung] or by members of the Bundestag [aus der Mitte des Bundestages] or by the Bundesrat."

[42] See 1 BVerfGE 144, 152-55, 158-61 (1952) (upholding a requirement that bills with significant impact on the federal budget be referred to committee before being considered on the floor but striking down a requirement that bills of this sort introduced by members of the Bundestag be accompanied by a proposal as to how to cover their costs). See also § 76 of the Bundestag's own Rules (Geschäftsordnung des

also entitles each member both to speak on the floor (subject once
again to reasonable time limitations in the interest of avoiding paralysis)[43] and in principle to serve on committees, where much of the
real work is done. Thus, for example, a representative may not be excluded from all committees simply because he is not a member of any
political party,[44] and in general it is said that parties must be represented on committees in proportion to their strength.[45] In one
significant recent decision, however, the Court held over two dissents
that the overriding need for confidentiality justified creation of a five-
member commission to consider the budget of secret service agencies
even though none of its members represented the unorthodox Green
Party.[46] This understandable limitation must be narrowly confined if
it is not to impair the principle of representative government.[47]

Article 44(1) further protects the interests of the minority by providing that the Bundestag's investigative machinery can be set in motion by as few as one fourth of its members. The Constitutional Court
has confirmed that this provision implicitly gives the same minority
the right to control the agenda of the investigating committee.[48]
These rights, as we shall see, provide an important means of control
of the executive in a parliamentary system.

Deutschen Bundestages, in der Fassung vom 25. Juni 1980, BGBl. I S. 1237, as
amended to 1990), reprinted in 3 Maunz/Dürig, Art. 38 (requiring in the interest of
efficiency that a bill be sponsored by at least five percent of the members); Schneider
in 2 AK-GG, Art. 38, Rdnr. 23.

[43] 10 BVerfGE 4, 12-20 (1959).

[44] 80 BVerfGE 188, 221-24 (1989) (over one dissent, id. at 241-44). See id. at 219:
"The principle of participation by every member must remain the standard" for
determining questions of legislative organization and proceedure. But see id. at
224-26 (holding over a different dissent (id. at 235-40) that the independent legislator need not be permitted to vote in committee, since that would give him more than
his share of power).

[45] 84 BVerfGE 304, 323-24 (1991). Art. 54(1) of the draft constitution proposed by
the experts at Herrenchiemsee had expressly so provided. See 2 Akten und Protokolle at 504, 590, 617 . See also 80 BVerfGE at 222 (arguing that in principle "each
committee must be a miniature copy of the whole body"). Contrast the first Congress
of the United States, in which committees were seen as the equivalent of a modern
party caucus from which opponents of the dominant faction were excluded. See
David Currie, The Constitution in Congress: The First Congress, 1789-91
(forthcoming).

[46] 70 BVerfGE 324, 362-66 (1986). See also id. at 372 (Mahrenholz, J., dissenting)
(complaining, inter alia, that the Greens had been excluded from the commission
on political grounds).

[47] Cf. Powell v. McCormack, 395 U.S. 486 (1969); Bond v. Floyd, 385 U.S. 116
(1966).

[48] 49 BVerfGE 70, 79-88 (1978) (construing a comparable state constitutional
provision).

B. Autonomy and Stability

Various provisions of the Basic Law protect the Bundestag from interference by other organs of government.[49] Members are elected for four-year terms[50] and entitled to "remuneration adequate to assure their independence."[51] In proper Burkean fashion, they are bound "only by their conscience."[52] For votes or debates in the Bundestag they may not be questioned elsewhere;[53] they may be prosecuted or arrested only with the consent of the Bundestag;[54] they may not be required to divulge information received in the course of their duties.[55] To avoid undue bureaucratic influence, civil servants and salaried public employees may be required to resign their offices before assuming a seat in Parliament.[56] The Bundestag decides for

---

[49] See generally Maunz in 2 Maunz/Dürig, Art. 40, Rdnr. 1-2; Schneider in 2 AK-GG, Art. 40, Rdnr. 2.

[50] Art. 39(1) GG.

[51] Art. 48(3) GG. The adequacy of their compensation is subject to review by the Constitutional Court. See 40 BVerfGE 296 (1975); 4 BVerfGE 144 (1955) (holding that individuals who are members of both federal and state legislatures need not be paid twice); 32 BVerfGE 157 (1971) (finding the retirement pension prescribed by law sufficient to satisfy Art. 48(3)); Maunz in 3 Maunz/Dürig, Art. 48, Rdnr. 14-16. For criticism of the decisions see Schneider in 2 AK-GG, Art. 38, Rdnr. 28 and Art. 48, Rdnr. 11-12 (arguing that the transformation of legislators into salaried officials, while freeing them from reliance on external sources of income, has made them dependent upon the political parties that determine their chances for reelection). Cf. U.S. Const., Art. I, § 6 ("a Compensation . . . to be ascertained by Law").

[52] Art. 38(1) GG. See generally Maunz in 3 Maunz/Dürig, Art. 38, Rdnr. 9-16. For glimpses into the ticklish relationship between this provision and Art. 21(1), which guarantees political parties a significant role in the political process, see Dieter Grimm, Die politischen Parteien, in Ernst Benda, Werner Maihofer, & Hans-Jochen Vogel (eds.), Handbuch des Verfassungsrechts 317, 352-56 (1983); Hesse, supra note 3, Rdnr. 598-603. As in the United States, the party system significantly limits the practical significance of the separation of powers in Germany. See Grimm, supra, at 360-65.

[53] Art. 46(1) GG; see Maunz in 3 Maunz/Dürig, Art. 46, Rdnr. 6. There is an exception for defamation. See also 60 BVerfGE 374 (1982) (holding that a representative might be subjected to censure ("Rüge") outside the Bundestag because the sanction had no legal effect). Cf. U.S. Const., Art. I, § 6: "[F]or any Speech or Debate in either House, they shall not be questioned in any other Place."

[54] Art. 46(2)-(4) GG; see Maunz in 3 Maunz/Dürig, Art. 46, Rdnr. 26. Prior consent is not required if the representative is apprehended "in the commission of the offense or in the course of the following day," but even then the proceeding must be suspended at Bundestag request. Cf. the narrower protection afforded to members of the U.S. Congress from arrest "in all Cases, except Treason, Felony and Breach of the Peace," U.S. Const., Art. I, § 6.

[55] Art. 47 GG; see Maunz in 3 Maunz/Dürig, Art. 47, Rdnr. 2.

[56] Art. 137(1) GG. The implementing statute effectively so provides. See Herzog in 2 Maunz/Dürig, Art. 20, Abschnitt V, Rdnr. 45 (arguing that repeal of this provision would be inconsistent with the general separation of powers requirement of Art. 20(2)). Although the text of the Basic Law speaks broadly of restrictions on

itself when to adjourn and reconvene,[57] chooses its own officers,[58] makes its own rules,[59] keeps its own order,[60] and resolves disputes respecting the election of its own members – subject in the last instance to review by the Constitutional Court.[61] In order to reduce its dependence on the executive for information necessary to the performance of its functions, the Bundestag has broad investigative powers.[62] Finally, in contrast to some other parliamentary systems,

---

"[t]he right to stand for election" (see Maunz in 4 Maunz/-Dürig, Art. 137, Rdnr. 15), the Constitutional Court has held that Art. 137 authorizes only incompatibility and not ineligibility provisions; since legislative autonomy is endangered only when an individual holds executive and legislative offices at the same time, the civil servant is permitted to serve once he has resigned his administrative position. 57 BVerfGE 43, 62, 66-69 (1981). See also 58 BVerfGE 177 (1981) (finding no incompatibility in simultaneous service in county and city government). Moreover, the German system being a parliamentary one, there is no comparable limitation with regard to cabinet ministers. See Art. 63, 64 GG; Herzog, supra, Rdnr. 46. The analogous U.S. provision is broader and leaves nothing to legislative discretion: "[N]o person holding any office under the United States shall be a member of either House during his continuance in office." U.S. Const., Art. I, § 6. The Basic Law contains no equivalent of the further provision of this section that serves the distinct purpose of preventing legislators from lining their own pockets by appointment to offices created or made more lucrative during their tenure.

[57] Art. 39(3) GG. The preceding paragraph requires the Bundestag to meet initially within 30 days after its election. Cf. U.S. Const., amend. XX, § 2 (requiring Congress to meet at least once a year and prescribing a presumptive date); Art. I, § 6 (limiting the power of one House to adjourn without consent of the other); Art. 2, § 3 (empowering the President to convene Congress "on extraordinary occasions" and to determine the date of adjournment if the two Houses cannot agree).

[58] Art. 40(1) GG. Cf. U.S. Const., Art. I, §§ 2, 3.

[59] Art. 40(1) GG. See 44 BVerfGE 308 (1977) (upholding a rule permitting action without the normal quorum in the absence of objection). Cf. U.S. Const., Art. I, § 5. The current Bundestag rules ("Geschäftsordnung") can be found in 3 Maunz/Dürig, Art. 38, p. 5.

[60] See Art. 40(2) GG, which vests "proprietary and police powers" in the presiding officer of the Bundestag and forbids searches and seizures on its premises without her consent.

[61] Art. 41(1)-(2) GG. This authority extends also to the question whether a member has lost his seat. See 5 BVerfGE 2 (1956) (upholding the Bundestag's decision to exclude a representative who had moved to East Berlin before it was a part of the Federal Republic). There is an obvious tension here between the principles of legislative independence and of democratic legitimacy. Contrast U.S. Const., Art. I, § 5 ("Each House shall be the judge of the elections, returns and qualifications of its own members"); Roudebush v. Hartke, 405 U.S. 15 (1972) (Senate decision respecting election not subject to judicial review); Powell v. McCormack, 395 U.S. 486 (1969) (qualifications subject to House determination limited to those listed in the Constitution).

[62] Art. 44(1) GG. See 67 BVerfGE 100 (1967); 76 BVerfGE 363 (1987); 77 BVerfGE 1 (1987); Schneider in 2 AK-GG, Art. 44, Rdnr. 2-3. Cf. Kilbourn v. Thompson, 103 U.S. 168 (1881); McGrain v. Daugherty, 273 U.S. 135 (1927). The investigative

the Basic Law sharply limits the power of the executive to dissolve the assembly.

Under the Weimar Constitution the Reichspräsident could dissolve the assembly at will, so long as he did not do so more than once for the same cause.[63] The results were instability, external control of Parliament, and impairment of representative democracy.[64] In reaction to this unsatisfactory state of affairs, Article 68(1) permits the Chancellor to bring about dissolution only if the Bundestag refuses his request for a vote of confidence, and then only if the President of the Federation ("Bundespräsident") agrees.[65]

The spirit of this provision was severely tested in 1982, when the Free Democratic Party (FDP), which held the balance of power in the Bundestag, decided to change horses in midstream – as in light of the express constitutional independence of the members it had a perfect right to do.[66] Abandoning the coalition with the Social Democrats (SPD) that both parties had promised the voters during the 1980 campaign, the FDP joined the so-called Union parties (CDU and CSU) in voting to replace Chancellor Helmut Schmidt with the Christian Democrat Helmut Kohl. All of this was in complete accord with the plain terms of Article 67(1).[67] The trouble began when the new coalition decided that it was desirable to hold new elections in order to obtain popular confirmation of the change.[68]

---

power serves also as an important check on executive abuse, see note 199 infra and accompanying text. In light of the experience in this country (cf. Watkins v. United States, 354 U.S. 178 (1957)) there might be cause to fear that in prescribing that "the decisions of investigative committees are not subject to judicial scrutiny" Art. 44(4) excessively subordinated individual rights to parliamentary autonomy; but fortunately the Constitutional Court has not taken this language at face value. See cases cited supra; Maunz in 3 Maunz/Dürig, Art. 44, Rdnr. 63-65 (explaining that this provision insulates only investigative findings, not sanctions against witnesses, from judicial review).

[63] Art. 25 WRV.

[64] See 62 BVerfGE 1, 41 (1983) (noting that not one Reichstag during the entire Weimar period had been permitted to serve out its full constitutional term).

[65] The Chancellor is the head of the Cabinet ("Bundesregierung"); the President's duties, except in this instance, are largely ceremonial. See text at notes 171-92 infra. His discretion with regard to dissolution under Art. 68 was confirmed by the Constitutional Court as an important check on improvident action: "This provision permits dissolution only when three supreme constitutional organs of government – the Chancellor, the Parliament, and the President – have each made their own independent political decision." 62 BVerfGE at 35. See also id. at 50 (adding that the President was also obliged to determine – with appropriate deference to the Chancellor's decision – whether the conditions of Art. 68 itself were met).

[66] See text at note 52 supra; 62 BVerfGE at 37-38.

[67] See text at notes 195-98 infra.

[68] See 62 BVerfGE at 4-9.

The difficulty was that under Article 39(1) the next election date was two years away; the only practicable way to advance the schedule was to lose a vote of confidence under Article 68(1).[69] So the coalition decided to do just that – to ask its own adherents to deny it their support. Picking his way carefully through the constitutional thicket, the President approved the Chancellor's ensuing request to dissolve the assembly, and the case went to the Constitutional Court.[70]

Literally the requirement of Article 68(1) was satisfied: The Chancellor had lost a vote of confidence.[71] But that, the Court responded, was not enough. The unmistakable purpose of the provision was to make dissolution more difficult, in the interest of parliamentary stability. Although the immediate aim of Article 68(1) was to prevent the executive from dissolving the legislature without its consent, the four-year term prescribed by Article 39(1) was meant to be the rule rather than the exception. Thus even if the Chancellor, the Bundestag, and the President all agreed, Article 68(1) permitted dissolution only if the political situation in the Bundestag was such that the Chancellor's "ability to govern" was "no longer adequately assured."[72]

It might seem to follow, as two dissenting Justices argued, that the dissolution order was unconstitutional.[73] As a general matter

---

[69] A constitutional amendment would have required a two-thirds vote of both Bundestag and Bundesrat under Art. 79(2) and was subject to the objection that the constitution should not be lightly amended. The Social Democrats, who also wanted accelerated elections, argued that Kohl should resign in order to trigger the provision of Art. 63(4) permitting dissolution if Parliament was unable to agree on a new Chancellor; the coalition responded that this route would require delay as the members went through repeated ballots in an effort not to endorse his successor. See 62 BVerfGE at 11, 14-18.

[70] See id. at 9-19. Technically speaking, the case involved four interbranch controversies ("Organstreite") filed by members of the dissolved Parliament against the President, who had issued the order. See id. at 3, 31-33; Art. 93(1) cl. 1 GG.

[71] See 62 BVerfGE at 38 (arguing in effect that on its face "lack of confidence" meant only the unwillingness of a majority of the members to vote for the Chancellor or his program).

[72] Id. at 40-44. There is much in the legislative history, as reported in Justice Rinck's dissenting opinion, id. at 86-102, to support his conclusion that Art. 68(1) was designed for the case in which a majority of the Bundestag was opposed to the Chancellor but unable to agree on his successor. See, e.g., the official committee explanation to the Parliamentary Council (id. at 101): "The President's right of dissolution . . . under Article 68 of the Basic Law is – apart from the right of emergency legislation [discussed in note 164 infra] – the principal weapon of the Government against an obstructive and destructive parliamentary majority." The Court, which took a somewhat less exacting position, found the record less plain and added that in any event legislative history was not entitled to much weight. Id. at 44-47.

[73] See id. at 112-16 (Rottmann, J., dissenting) (adding that the coalition had agreed upon new elections before putting together its Government and that two days after the Chancellor had put the question of confidence the Bundestag had approved

there was obvious force in the President's protestation that there was no way to determine whether a legislator's vote was sincere,[74] but there was no doubt as to the members' motives in the actual case. No one arguing for dissolution had suggested any difference of opinion among the governing parties; both the Free Democrats and the Union had expressly proclaimed their intention to reinstitute after the election the Government they professed not to support.[75]

Nevertheless the Court managed to uphold the dissolution. Breach of the campaign promise of a liberal-social coalition, the majority conceded, did not (as one Justice argued)[76] justify the action; there could be no lack of democratic legitimacy in a government chosen by representatives exercising the discretion the constitution gave them.[77] Yet the "extraordinary situation" in the Bundestag in 1982 had given the Government a plausible basis for concluding that it could not be confident of a lasting majority. The decision to abandon the old coalition had created serious discord among the Free Democrats. Prominent members had resigned from the party, and it had suffered dramatic reverses in subsequent state elections. The coalition had been established for limited purposes and a limited time; by insisting on early elections, the Free Democrats had made clear that they were not prepared to support the Government until the end of the normal term.[78] Laying great stress on the deference due to the political branches in evaluating the realities of political power,[79] the Court concluded that their assessment was not clearly

---

his budget by the largest majority on any controversial issue in thirteen years): "The parliamentary stability of the Government was completely beyond question." See also id. at 108 (Rinck, J., dissenting).

[74] Id. at 18. Justice Rottmann suggested in dissent that the best evidence of a Government's lack of actual support would be its inability to obtain passage of substantive legislation. See id. at 110.

[75] See id. at 13 (Chancellor Kohl) ("The coalition parties . . . are basically prepared to work together again after the election"), 15 (FDP leader Genscher) ("The [Government's] mandate shall be renewed, but only after the voters have spoken"). The Chancellor proudly insisted that he had never made a secret of his motives; to have resigned in order to precipitate elections under Art. 63(4), as the opposition urged, would have been in his view "manipulative." See id. at 13-14.

[76] See id. at 67-69 (Zeidler, J., concurring) (arguing that there was no popular mandate for the present Government because the people had voted for Schmidt, not for Kohl). Justice Zeidler's opinion contains an interesting argument for changing constitutional interpretation in the light of changed circumstances. See also Herzog in 3 Maunz/Dürig, Art. 68, Rdnr. 76-77.

[77] 62 BVerfGE at 43.

[78] Id. at 51-62. For documentation of the view that none of the events recited by the majority had significantly affected the FDP's willingness or ability to continue the coalition see id. at 115-16 (Rottmann, J., dissenting).

[79] Id. at 50. See Schneider in 2 AK-GG, Art. 68, Rdnr. 6 (applauding this exercise of judicial restraint and finding in it the seeds of a political-question doctrine). See also 62 BVerfGE at 48-49 (finding it of significance that no one in authority had

erroneous; there was no basis for finding that they had acted without substantive justification in order simply to advance the election.[80]

The American observer may be reminded of occasions when our Supreme Court has spoken bravely while bowing to superior political force.[81] Strategic behavior of this nature may be more effective in the long run than charging the windmill; when Chancellor Kohl sought unsuccessfully to advance the date of elections following the East German accession in 1990, he rejected the dissolution option out of hand.

C. Supremacy

Article 20(3) of the Basic Law states the fundamental principle of statutory supremacy ("Gesetzesvorrang"): While the legislature itself is bound only by the constitutional order ("die verfassungsmäßige Ordnung"), the executive and the courts are bound by law ("Gesetz und Recht"). Just what is meant by "Recht" in this provision is unclear, as we shall see. What is generally understood is that the reference to "Gesetz" requires other branches of government to respect statutes constitutionally enacted.[82]

There is nothing surprising about this requirement. Indeed it would seem implicit in the grant of legislative power that statutes have the force of law. Despite the broader language of Justice Black's majestic opinion for the Court in our *Steel Seizure* case, for four of the six majority Justices all that had to be said was that the President was bound by law.[83] Statutory supremacy serves all the goals that led

---

raised constitutional objections when Chancellor Brandt had successfully pursued a similar strategy to accelerate the election in 1972).

[80] Id. at 62-63. See Herzog in 3 Maunz/Dürig, Art. 68, Rdnr. 78-84 (endorsing both the decision and the earlier suggestion of the Enquête-Kommission that the Basic Law be amended to permit the Bundestag to dissolve itself for any reason by a two-thirds vote). The Kommission was a panel of politicians and experts established by the Bundestag to consider possible constitutional amendments. For its recommendation see Schlußbericht der Enquête-Kommission, Teil 1, at 92, 102-07; for a dissenting view see Schneider in 2 AK-GG, Art. 68, Rdnr. 17. The Constitutional Commission, in 1993, concluded that the Basic Law should not be amended to give the Bundestag a right to dissolve itself, even by a two-thirds vote. See Bericht der VerfKomm at 86-88.

[81] See, e.g., Korematsu v. United States, 323 U.S. 214 (1944); Brown v. Board of Education (II), 349 U.S. 294 (1955); compare Watkins v. United States, 354 U.S. 178 (1957), with Barenblatt v. United States, 360 U.S. 109 (1959).

[82] See, e.g., Hans-Peter Schneider, Die Gesetzmäßigkeit der Recht-sprechung, 1975 DöV 443, 448.

[83] Youngstown Sheet & Tube Co. v. Sawyer, 343 U.S. 579 (1952) (opinions of Frankfurter, Jackson, Burton, and Clark). In the United States this conclusion is strengthened by Art. II, § 3, which requires the President to "take care that the laws

to the creation of a popularly elected legislative body in the first place: democratic self-government, representative deliberation, and the separation of powers.[84]

The principle of statutory supremacy was most severely tested in the famous *Soraya* decision of 1973.[85] Princess Soraya, former wife of the Shah of Iran, had brought an action for invasion of privacy, alleging that the defendants had written and published a fictitious interview in which she had purportedly revealed intimate details of her private life. The Civil Code expressly provided that damages for nonpecuniary injury could be awarded only in cases specified by statute.[86] No statute authorized such damages for invasion of privacy, but the Federal Court of Justice ("Bundesgerichtshof") held they could be awarded anyway. The defendants argued that the court had disobeyed its constitutional obligation to respect the limitations imposed by the Civil Code; the Constitutional Court held the court had acted within its powers.

To an outside observer the Court of Justice seems indeed to have contradicted the statute. The Civil Code did not merely fail to authorize damages for emotional harm; it flatly forbade them in the absence of statutory authority, which admittedly did not exist.[87] Indeed the Constitutional Court began its discussion with a startling passage that seemed to suggest that the courts were not always bound by statute after all. By altering the traditional formulation so that judges were no longer bound simply by "Gesetz" but by "Recht" as well, the Basic Law had deliberately abandoned "a narrow statutory positivism." "Recht" within the meaning of Article 20(3) was not coextensive with statutory law; under some circumstances it could include additional norms derived by judges from "the constitutional legal order as a whole" and functioning "as a corrective to the written law." It followed, said the Constitutional Court, that the judges could

---

be faithfully executed," and by Art. VI, which makes statutes the "supreme law of the land." See Currie, supra note 4, at 24.

[84] See id. at 21-23; Fritz Ossenbühl, Vorrang und Vorbehalt des Gesetzes, 3 Handbuch des Staatsrechts 315, Rdnr. 1-3 (tracing the German principle to democracy and the rule of law).

[85] 34 BVerfGE 269 (1973).

[86] See § 253 BGB: "Wegen eines Schadens, der nicht Vermögensschaden ist, kann Entschädigung in Geld nur in den durch das Gesetz bestimmten Fällen gefordert werden." Cases in which such damages are authorized are listed in § 847 BGB.

[87] For similar assessments by German commentators see Volker Krey, Rechtsfindung contra legem als Verfassungsproblem (I), 1978 Juristenzeitung [JZ] 361, 362 n. 14, and authorities cited; Reinhard Zimmermann, The Law of Obligations: Roman Foundations of the Civilian Tradition 1093-94 (1990): "It is hard to imagine a line of decisions more blatantly *contra legem* than this."

fill gaps in the statutes "according to common sense and 'general community concepts of justice.'"[88]

So far, so good; no Anglo-American observer would expect a court to hold that the supremacy of statutes deprived judges of the power to make interstitial common law. The problem was that there seemed to be no gap to fill. To get around this difficulty the Court proceeded to proclaim a most dynamic doctrine of statutory interpretation: As a codification grows older, the judge's "freedom to develop the law creatively" increases. "The interpretation of a statutory norm cannot always remain tied to the meaning it had at the time of its enactment"; as social conditions and attitudes change, so under certain circumstances does the content of the law. In such a situation the judge may not simply take refuge in the written text; he must deal freely with the statute if he is to meet his obligation to declare the law.[89]

This passage seems to come perilously close to saying that when a statute is perceived as outmoded a judge is under no obligation to follow it. Understandably, it has been severely criticized.[90] As the Court's rather cryptic opinion suggests, the root of the problem is the delphic reference to "Gesetz und Recht" in Article 20(3). Both terms can be translated as "law." "Gesetz" tends to be the narrower and more technical term; it is commonly, though not exclusively, used in connection with statutes.[91] "Recht" not only comprehends unwritten as well as written law; it often has the less positivist meaning of "justice."[92]

---

[88] 34 BVerfGE at 287.

[89] "Einem hiernach möglichen Konflikt der Norm mit den materiellen Gerechtigkeitsvorstellungen einer gewandelten Gesellschaft kann sich der Richter nicht mit dem Hinweis auf den unveränderten Gesetzeswortlaut entziehen; er ist zu freier Handhabung der Rechtsnormen gezwungen, wenn er nicht sein Aufgabe, 'Recht' zu sprechen, verfehlen will." Id. at 289.

[90] See, e.g., Krey, supra note 87 (Teil III), at 465; Schneider, supra note 82, at 445 ("most questionable extension of judicial decisionmaking authority," "devaluation of the obligation to follow the law," "first step toward 'unrestrained interpretation'"). But see Friedrich Kübler in 28 JZ 667, 667 (1973) (warning that a contrary decision would have turned every alleged misinterpretation of the BGB into a question for the Constitutional Court).

[91] See Fritz Ossenbühl, Gesetz und Recht – Die Rechtsquellen im demokratischen Rechtsstaat, 3 Handbuch des Staatsrechts 281, Rdnr. 4-13; Christian Starck, Der Gesetzesbegriff des Grundgesetzes 21-23, 37-39 (1970) (noting the familiar distinction between the formal and material senses of the term). "Gesetzgebung" (lawmaking) is the term the Basic Law employs to describe the legislative process. See, e.g., Art. 70-77. See also Art. 78 (describing the processes by which a statute ("Gesetz") passed by the Bundestag becomes law). On the other hand, the reference to "Gesetz" in the Art. 97 provision that judges are subject only to law ("nur dem Gesetze unterworfen") is widely understood to refer to the entire corpus of positive law. See Ossenbühl, supra, Rdnr. 15; Krey, supra note 87, at 465.

[92] The English version of the Basic Law published by the Press and Information Office of the German Federal Government confidently translates "Gesetz und

As the *Soraya* opinion suggests, one school of thought in Germany has been that the reference to "Recht" did more than broaden the categories of law that bound executive and judicial officers;[93] in reaction to the calamitous positivism of the Nazi era, it bound judges in cases of conflict to follow justice rather than law. At a minimum, on this theory Article 20(3) constitutionalizes natural law by requiring the judge to reject fundamentally unjust laws.[94] Some commentators have carried the argument further, as some language in *Soraya* seems to suggest: No law that is outmoded or misguided should stand in the way of a court's reaching the just result.[95]

The debates in the Parliamentary Council afford no evidence that the innocuous term "Recht" was intended to have any such sweeping consequences. As initially drafted, the provision would simply have bound executive and judicial officers to follow the law ("Gesetz").[96] The reference to "Recht" and the further provision binding the legislature to the constitutional order were added by what we would call the Committee on Style ("Redaktionsausschuß") in order better to express "the rule of law as the foundation of the Basic Law."[97] The defense of the original formulation was purely stylistic: Nothing had been said about "the constitutional order" because it went without saying that all organs of government were bound by the constitution. That the courts were also bound by law, the same speaker added, was equally obvious from the very nature of judicial activity: The judicia-

---

Recht" as "law and justice," thus glossing over the troublesome ambiguity of the original, as any translation would.

[93] Indeed it has been doubted whether the inclusion of "Recht" was meant to make judicial precedents binding at all. See Krey, supra note 87, at 464.

[94] See Krey, supra note 87, at 363-64, 465-66. Cf. Loan Ass'n v. Topeka, 87 U.S. 655 (1875). For the argument that fundamentally unjust laws that violate none of the other provisions of the Basic Law must be rare indeed see Herzog in 2 Maunz/Dürig, Art. 20, Abschnitt VI, Rdnr. 49-54. Ossenbühl, supra note 91, Rdnr. 18, views the reference to "Recht" as a reminder of past injustice ("Unrecht") directed essentially to the lawmakers.

[95] See the authorities cited in Krey, supra note 87, at 364. For other excursions by the Constitutional Court into the meadows of natural law see 1 BVerfGE 208, 233 (1952) (dictum) (asserting that the principle of equality before the law was so fundamental a part of the German constitutional order that it would be necessary to reach beyond positive law to find it if it had not been codified in Art. 3); 3 BVerfGE 225, 231-36 (1953) (also noted in chapter 4 infra) (suggesting that any provision of the Basic Law that offended fundamental higher law ("übergesetzliche") principles of justice ("jene äußersten Grenzen der Gerechtigkeit") would be invalid).

[96] See 1 JöR (n.F.) 195-99. After omission for stylistic reasons of references to the rule of law ("Herrschaft des . . . Gesetzes") and to the requirement (redundant in light of Art. 3) that the laws themselves be equal, the provision read: "Rechtsprechung und Verwaltung stehen unter dem Gesetz." Id. at 197.

[97] Id. at 200 (Delegate Dehler) ("zur besseren Kennzeichnung der Rechtsstaatlichkeit als der Grundlage des Grundgesetzes").

ry's sole task was "to apply and interpret the law."[98] To conclude that the ambiguous reference to "Recht" authorized judges (and presumably also administrators) to ignore constitutional statutes, it might be added, would contradict the plain command of the same sentence that they are bound by law ("Gesetz") – and all the fundamental policies of democracy, predictability, and separation of powers that underlie that provision as well.[99]

However difficult it may be to reconcile the result in the *Soraya* case with the principle of parliamentary supremacy, the fact remains that the Court was careful to couch its reasoning in terms of statutory interpretation, not of any right to defy the legislature. Its ultimate conclusion, however strained, was that there was indeed a gap in the legislation that the judges could properly fill by devising a new common law rule.[100] The new right to damages for intangible injuries attributable to the invasion of privacy, which served to promote the constitutionally protected interests in human dignity and the free development of personality, thus qualified as "Recht" within the meaning of Article 20(3) – "not in opposition to but in elaboration and extension of the written law."[101]

Later decisions have given no support to any suggestion in *Soraya* that courts might have power to disregard misguided but constitutional statutes. In 1978, for example, the Constitutional Court made clear that a court could not constitutionally "correct" a statute providing for damages for wrongful deprivation of personal liberty by restricting recovery to cases of intentional wrong: "It is not the business of a judge who is bound by the statute and laws to cut back claims for

---

[98] Id. (Delegate von Mangoldt) ("die Gesetze anzuwenden und auszulegen").

[99] For arguments on the latter basis see Krey, supra note 87, at 466-67. Such a conclusion would also create an irreconcilable conflict between Art. 20(3) and Art. 97(1), which says nothing about "Recht" and flatly declares the judges "subject to law." See note 91 supra; Krey, supra, at 465-66. See also Zimmermann, supra note 87, at 1094 n. 316: "Art. 97(1) GG makes it clear that this subjection of the judge to the law is inextricably linked with, and has to be regarded as a necessary prerequisite for, judicial independence."

[100] See 34 BVerfGE at 290: "Damit wurde eine Lücke im Blick auf die Sanktionen, die bei einer Verletzung dieses Persönlichkeitsrechts zu verhängen waren, sichtbar . . . ." See also 82 BVerfGE 6, 11-15 (1990) (applying the principles laid down in *Soraya* to uphold the extension by analogy to unmarried couples of one partner's right to assume the other's lease after death, although the governing statute spoke only of spouses).

[101] 34 BVerfGE at 281, 291. The Federal Court of Justice, whose decisions are summarized in id. at 273-75, had taken the arguably more candid approach of holding that Art. 1(1) and 2(1), which declare human dignity ("die Würde des Menschen") inviolable ("unantastbar") and guarantee the right to free development of the personality ("die freie Entfaltung [d]er Persönlichkeit"), *required* the state to provide redress for victims of invasions of privacy. For discussion of these provisions and of the interesting problem of affirmative state obligations to protect one citizen from another see chapter 6 infra.

liability that the statutes afford . . . ."[102] Whatever the authors of the earlier opinion had in mind, it seems clear today that both executive and judicial officers in Germany are bound by constitutional statutes, as Article 20(3) provides.[103]

D. Exclusivity

Less obvious perhaps than the principle that legislation binds other organs of government is a second and almost equally fundamental corollary of the grant of lawmaking power to the legislature: its exclusivity. It should come as no surprise that in Germany, as in the United States, no one but the legislature may enact statutes. What may not be so obvious is that in many cases it follows that the executive may not act without statutory authority.

In Germany, as in the United States, this is not generally true of the courts. The one noncontroversial conclusion of the *Soraya* opinion was that Article 20(3) did not preclude the courts from creating common law when the statutes were silent.[104] The authority to do so, the Court has persuasively argued, is implicit in the grant of jurisdiction to resolve disputes.[105]

---

[102] 49 BVerfGE 304, 320 (1978). See also 41 BVerfGE 231 (1976) (holding that a member of a local governing body could not constitutionally be barred from representing an individual charged with crime since the relevant disqualification statute applied only to claims against the government); 65 BVerfGE 182 (1983) (holding that by giving priority to wage claims in an insolvency proceeding the Federal Labor Court had exceeded the limits on judicial lawmaking imposed by Art. 20(3) since the bankruptcy statute left no room for additional priorities). The opinion just cited distinguished *Soraya* by noting that the judicially created rule in that case had "merely" afforded a remedy for a preexisting constitutional right and that it enjoyed widespread support among academic commentators. Id. at 194-95. Except to the extent that these passages may be taken to imply acceptance of the Court of Justice's argument that damages for invasion of privacy were compelled by the Basic Law itself, they seem typical of what courts tend to say when they deal with precedents for which they have no sympathy.

[103] Not every error in construing or applying a statute, however, is a violation of the judge's duty to follow the law; for if it were every question would be a constitutional question. See BVerfG, Judgment of Nov. 3, 1992, Case No. 1 BvR 1243/88 (not yet reported); cf. Arrowsmith v. Harmoning, 118 U.S. 194, 196 (1886) (reaching the same conclusion under the due process clause).

[104] German labor law, as the Court noted in *Soraya* (34 BVerfGE at 288), is mostly judge-made law. See 84 BVerfGE 212, 226-27 (1991) (upholding judicial authority to fashion rules respecting the legality of lockouts within the limits of Art. 9(3)).

[105] See 34 BVerfGE at 287; Ossenbühl, supra note 91, Rdnr. 35-41; Krey, supra note 87, at 466. The Supreme Court's decision in Erie R.R. v. Tompkins, 304 U.S. 64 (1938), constitutes a narrow and convincing exception to this general rule based on the limited purposes of federal jurisdiction over controversies between citizens of different states.

Various provisions of the Basic Law, however, preclude the courts as well as the executive from acting without statutory authority. Recognizing that even such fundamental values as freedom of expression and of movement must yield on occasion to overriding countervailing concerns, the framers of the Basic Law expressly provided that a number of the basic rights that document guaranteed could be limited – but in most cases only by or on the basis of statute.[106]

At first glance these provisions may appear to the American observer a shocking compromise of fundamental rights. A constitutional right to freedom of speech, it may be said, is of little value if it can be overridden by legislation. Any constitutional right worthy of the name would provide protection against the legislature as well.

Indeed the Basic Law *does* provide significant protection against legislative infringement of basic rights, even those which are explicitly subject to statutory limitation. A law limiting basic rights must expressly specify any right that is limited; it must be a general law that does not single out individuals for unfavorable treatment; and it may not impinge upon the essential content ("Wesensgehalt") of the right.[107] Perhaps most significantly, it must satisfy the stringent test of proportionality ("Verhältnismäßigkeit") that the Constitutional Court has found implicit in the rule of law and in the basic rights themselves: No limitation of a basic right is valid unless it is calculated to promote a legitimate governmental purpose, is the least restrictive means of attaining that goal, and imposes a reasonable burden.[108] It should be recalled that, although our rhetoric is different, our basic rights are not absolute either. The Supreme Court commonly engages in a similar balancing process to determine the extent of the constitutional guarantee itself – and often without requiring a showing that no less restrictive means are available.[109]

What then is the function of the German provisions permitting legislative limitation of basic rights? It is not merely to make explicit the unavoidable conclusion that even fundamental rights are not absolute, but also to protect the citizen by making clear that even when

---

[106] E.g., Art. 8(2) GG, which permits restriction of the right of outdoor assembly "durch Gesetz oder auf Grund eines Gesetzes." Similar provisions appear in connection with the right to life, personal liberty, and bodily integrity (Art. 2(2), reinforced by Art. 103(2), 104(1)), postal and telecommunications privacy (Art. 10(2)), freedom of movement (Art. 11(2)), occupational freedom (Art. 12(1)), and property (Art. 14(3)). The somewhat different provisions respecting expression (Art. 5(2)) and the right to free development of personality (Art. 2(1)) will be discussed in more detail below.

[107] Art. 19(1), (2) GG.

[108] See chapter 1 supra.

[109] E.g., Board of Trustees of SUNY v. Fox, 492 U.S. 469, 475-81 (1989) (commercial speech); Clark v. Community for Creative Non-Violence, 468 U.S. 288, 298-99 (1984) (time, place, and manner restrictions). See generally Alexander Aleinikoff, Constitutional Law in the Age of Balancing, 96 Yale L.J. 943 (1987).

competing interests predominate basic rights can be limited only with the consent of the people themselves as represented in Parliament, not by some appointed bureaucrat subject only to indirect political control.[110] The provisions requiring a legislative basis for limitation of basic rights ("Gesetzesvorbehalte") are therefore important elements both of democracy and of the separation of powers.[111] They have been vigorously enforced by the Constitutional Court.[112]

But the principle that the executive may act only on the basis of statute is by no means limited to actions impinging on those basic rights which the Constitution expressly provides may be limited only on the basis of legislation. The general freedom of action ("allgemeine Handlungsfreiheit") that the Constitutional Court has found in Article 2(1),[113] for example, finds its limits according to the text of the

---

[110] See Hesse, supra note 3, Rdnr. 314: "All reservation clauses empower only the legislature to limit basic rights . . . . A limitation of basic rights by executive or judicial authorities acting on their own is impermissible." For the 19th-century libertarian origins of these provisions see Dieter Grimm, Deutsche Verfassungsgeschichte 1776-1866, p. 117 (1988).

[111] Of all our Bill of Rights provisions, only the forgotten third amendment explicitly contains this important safeguard: "No soldier shall, in time of peace, be quartered in any house, without the consent of the owner, nor in time of war, but in a manner to be prescribed by law." Cf. U.S. Const., Art. I, § 9: "No money shall be drawn from the Treasury, but in consequence of appropriations made by law . . . ." Subject to limited exceptions, the latter principle is also laid down in Art. 110-12 GG. See Kisker, supra note 10, Rdnr. 40-47; 45 BVerfGE 1 (1977) (holding that the Finance Minister had exceeded his authority under Art. 112 to authorize nonbudgeted expenditures in cases of unforeseen and unavoidable necessity ("eines unvorhergesehenen und unabweisbaren Bedürfnisses")). For a summary of other explicit provisions of the Basic Law reserving particular powers to the legislature see Ossenbühl, supra note 84, Rdnr. 26-30.

[112] Some of the decisions are collected in chapter 6 infra. Most difficult to reconcile with the explicit requirement of a legislative basis for restriction of basic rights is once again the troublesome *Soraya* decision, where the Constitutional Court not only permitted the civil courts to invent a right to damages for invasion of privacy in the teeth of what appeared to be a plain legislative prohibition (see text at notes 85-101 supra) but went on to conclude without explanation (34 BVerfGE at 292) that this judicially made rule did not offend the Art. 5(2) requirement that restrictions on speech be based upon general laws ("allgemeine Gesetze") – although the purpose of this requirement, like that of the other provisions discussed in this section, seemed to be to reserve the power to limit basic rights to the democratic and representative parliament. See Ossenbühl, supra note 84, Rdnr. 13-14. The Court said only that § 823 of the BGB, which created a general right of action for torts, qualified as an "allgemeines Gesetz" within the meaning of Art. 5(2), and that the newly discovered right to damages for invasion of privacy did too (34 BVerfGE at 282, 292-93). Charitably viewed, the opinion may have meant that it was § 823, as construed in light of the constitutional guarantees of dignity and personality, that restricted speech in this case.

[113] Art. 2(1) on its face guarantees a right to the free development of personality ("die freie Entfaltung [d]er Persönlichkeit"). For its interpretation see 6 BVerfGE 32 (1957) (*Elfes*), discussed in chapter 6 infra.

Basic Law in "the rights of others, . . . the constitutional order, [and] the moral code" – a formulation that hardly seems restricted to acts of Parliament. Nevertheless the Constitutional Court has made clear that the requirement of legislative authorization applies to limitations of this freedom as well.

In a 1981 decision, for example, an administrative court had disqualified the law partner of a member of the local governing council from acting as counsel in a lawsuit against the local government, on grounds of possible conflict of interest. The relevant statute, however, disqualified only the members themselves. Because there was no legal basis for the court's action, said the Constitutional Court, it offended the basic principle of the rule of law embodied in Article 20(3). Thus it was not part of the "constitutional order," and thus not a legitimate limitation of the general freedom of action guaranteed by Article 2(1).[114]

Article 20(3) is the provision that binds both executive and judicial officers to follow the law. On its face it does not appear to embody the additional requirement that they act only on the basis of law, though as the Court remarked both can be characterized as aspects of the rule of law ("Rechtsstaatsprinzip"). The rule of law itself, while imposed on the constituent states by Article 28(1),[115] is not expressly made applicable to the central government; it is often said to be implicit in the basic structural provisions of Article 20, or in the Basic Law as a whole.[116] The subsidiary principle that liberty and property can be restricted only on the basis of legislation, which was created essentially out of whole cloth during the 19th century as a means of protection against the still autocratic executive, can perhaps best be

---

[114] 56 BVerfGE 99, 107-09 (1981) (adding that the further requirement of fair warning that has also been attributed to the rule of law had been offended as well). In the constitutional convention the influential Delegate Carlo Schmid had invoked "the rule of law postulate that every command and every prohibition must have a basis in law [Gesetz]"). See Sten. Ber. at 13. Cf. Richard Thoma in 2 Gerhard Anschütz & Richard Thoma (eds.), Handbuch des Deutschen Staatsrechts 227-31 (1930) (describing the doctrine as an unwritten component of the Rechtsstaat principle under earlier German constitutions); Carl Schmitt, Verfassungslehre 130 (1928): "Only a state in which . . . intrusions upon individual freedom are permitted solely on the basis of law [auf Grund eines Gesetzes] can be called a state under the rule of law." Later passages demonstrate that by "Gesetz" in this context Schmitt meant a law in both the material and the formal sense: a general norm adopted by the legislature. Id. at 149-51.

[115] "Die verfassungsmäßige Ordnung in den Ländern muß den Grundsätzen des republikanischen, demokratischen und sozialen Rechtsstaates im Sinne dieses Grundgesetzes entsprechen."

[116] See, e.g., Herzog in 2 Maunz/Dürig, Art. 20, Abschnitt VII, Rdnr. 30-35. For shrill criticism of the conventional learning see Richard Bäumlein & Helmut Ridder in 1 AK-GG, Art. 20, Abs. I-III, Rdnr. 33-77.

explained as implicit in Art. 20(2), which enunciates the general principle of separation of powers.[117]

Finding the legal basis for the general Gesetzesvorbehalt not in the basic rights alone but in the structural provisions of Article 20 made it only a matter of time until it was extended beyond its historical roots to require statutory authority not only for the invasion of individual rights but also for actions taken in dispensing government benefits. In upholding a statutory provision reducing payments to war victims living outside the Federal Republic, for example, the Constitutional Court was careful to insist that the legislature itself was required "to determine in essence" under what circumstances and to what extent the normal payments should be reduced.[118]

This is the basic principle of separation of powers on which Justice Hugo Black relied in concluding that President Truman could not seize the steel mills without statutory authorization.[119] It is the principle that Justice Jackson in the same case, contrasting the Article II requirement that the President take care that the laws be faithfully executed, convincingly traced to the due process clause: "One [clause] gives a governmental authority that reaches so far as there is law, the other gives a private right that authority shall go no further. These signify about all there is of the principle that ours is a government of laws and not of men."[120] It is also a fundamental and undisputed principle of German constitutional law.[121]

E. Nondelegability

In March 1933 the Nazi-dominated Reichstag enacted a statute ("Ermächtigungsgesetz") authorizing Adolf Hitler and his Cabinet to govern by decree.[122] Actions taken under this provision could be said literally to comply with any constitutional requirement that there be a

---

117 See Herzog in 2 Maunz/Dürig, Art. 20, Abschnitt VI, Rdnr. 59, 76-80. Art. 101 of the draft constitution prepared at Herrenchiemsee in anticipation of the Parliamentary Council provided explicitly that *every* exercise of public authority required a basis in law ("[j]ede Ausübung der Staatsgewalt bedarf der Grundlage im Gesetz"). See 2 Akten und Protokolle at 504, 600. The term "Gesetz" in this context was, as usual, ambiguous.

118 56 BVerfGE 1, 13 (1981). See also id. at 21, concluding that the legislature had fulfilled its duty.

119 Youngstown Sheet & Tube Co. v. Sawyer, 343 U.S. 579 (1952).

120 Id. at 643 (Jackson, J., concurring).

121 See Herzog in 2 Maunz/Dürig, Art. 20, Abschnitt VI, Rdnr. 55. As the Constitutional Court has emphasized, there are many areas (not least involving foreign affairs) in which the Basic Law itself vests important policymaking authority in the executive. What is reserved to the legislature is basically the formulation of law. See 1 BVerfGE 372, 394 (1952); 49 BVerf-GE 89, 124-27 (*Kalkar*).

122 "Reichsgesetze können außer in dem in der Reichsverfassung vorgesehenen Verfahren auch durch die Reichsregierung beschlossen werden." RGBl. 1933 I S. 141.

statutory basis for executive action; the legislature had authorized the Reichsregierung to pass whatever laws it liked. Yet such an unlimited transfer of legislative power to the executive could scarcely be found consistent with the purposes of any such requirement, or with provisions vesting lawmaking powers in the popularly elected Parliament. As our own Justice Black observed not so many years ago, "Congress [like any other parliamentary body] was created on the assumption that enactment of this free country's laws could be safely entrusted to the representatives of the people in Congress, and to no other official or government agency."[123]

Consequently, when the Germans turned to the task of drafting a new democratic constitution after the Second World War, they took care to prohibit the legislature from making any such sweeping transfer of authority in the future. In recognition of the obvious fact that legislators cannot be expected to regulate the details of every governmental program, Article 80(1) permits federal legislation to empower any federal minister, or the federal or state government as a whole, to promulgate regulations ("Rechtsverordnungen") having the force of law. It goes on to require, however, that the content, purpose, and extent ("Inhalt, Zweck und Ausmaß") of the authorization be specified by the statute itself.[124]

From a transatlantic perspective the Constitutional Court seems to have taken this provision very seriously. In its very first substantive decision, the Court struck down on the basis of Article 80(1) a provision authorizing the Minister of the Interior to adopt any regulations "necessary for the execution" of a statute respecting the rearrangement ("Neugliederung") of Länder in what is now Baden-Württemberg. In contrast to the practice of the Weimar period, said the Court,

> [t]he Basic Law in this as in other respects reflects a decision in favor of a stricter separation of powers. The Parliament may not escape its lawmaking responsibilities by transferring part of its legislative authority to the executive [Regierung] without considering and precisely determining the limits of the delegated authority. The

---

[123] Zemel v. Rusk, 381 U.S. 1, 22 (1965) (dissenting opinion).

[124] See Hesse, supra note 3, Rdnr. 526 (arguing that this delegation provision "frees the Parliament for its true task of carefully debating and deciding fundamental issues"). The list of potential delegates in Art. 80(2) is exclusive. See 11 BVerfGE 77, 83-88 (1960) (holding that federalism concerns reinforced the textual conclusion that the federal Parliament could not determine which state minister would have the responsibility of issuing regulations). Certain functions of the legislature, moreover, cannot be delegated at all. See, e.g., Art. 59(2) GG, which requires legislative approval of certain treaties "in the form of a federal statute [in der Form eines Bundesgesetzes]" as a check on the executive; 1 BVerfGE 372, 395-96 (1952). For limitations on the continued effectiveness of delegations made before the Basic Law took force see Art. 129(3) GG; 2 BVerfGE 307, 326-34 (1953) (finding in Art. 129(3) an exception to the usual rule (Art. 123(1)) that preexisting laws retained their validity only to the extent they were consistent with the Basic Law).

executive, on the other hand, may not step into the shoes of Parliament on the basis of indefinite provisions authorizing the promulgation of regulations.[125]

The authorization before them, the Justices concluded, was so indefinite that it was impossible to predict when and how it would be employed or what the resulting regulations might say. It therefore failed to specify the content, purpose, and extent of the authority conferred, as the Basic Law required.[126]

This decision by no means stands alone. In 1958, for example, the Court invalidated a delegation of power to adopt regulations "to compensate for the differential burdens imposed by the transfer tax" upon firms that were or were not vertically integrated ("einstufige und mehrstufige Unternehmen").[127] There were no generally accepted standards, said the Court, for determining whether a firm was vertically integrated; the statute left it to the executive to decide whether to achieve equalization by imposing a surtax on those firms the law favored or by reducing the tax on those it disadvantaged; indeed the statute did not even require the executive to exercise its authority at all.[128] The rule of law, the Court concluded, forbade the legislature to leave essential elements of the law ("das Wesentliche") to be determined by regulation. The authorization had to be specific enough that one could determine from the law itself what might be demanded of the citizen; the legislature "must have made some conscious decision."[129]

If this seems a rather strict application of the nondelegation principle,[130] other early decisions went even further. In 1962 the Constitutional Court struck down a grant of authority to prescribe average values ("Durchschnittswerte") for "specific articles or groups of articles" for purposes of a compensatory use tax on imported goods,

---

[125] 1 BVerfGE 14, 60 (1951).

[126] Id.

[127] 7 BVerfGE 282 (1958). Since the tax was assessed every time a product changed hands, firms that processed and marketed their own products from start to finish enjoyed a significant cost advantage. See id. at 291-92.

[128] Id. at 292-301.

[129] "Der Gesetzgeber . . . muß . . . selbst schon etwas gedacht und gewollt haben." Id. at 302, 304. Compare the requirement of a "primary standard" or "intelligible principle" formulated by our Supreme Court during the time when it too took seriously the provision vesting lawmaking powers in the legislature. See Buttfield v. Stranahan, 192 U.S. 470, 496 (1904); J.W. Hampton, Jr. & Co. v. United States, 276 U.S. 394, 409-11 (1928). For alternative formulations of the governing standard in Germany see Maunz in 3 Maunz/Dürig, Art. 80, Rdnr. 27-28.

[130] Contrast Field v. Clark, 143 U.S. 649 (1892), and J.W. Hampton Co. v. United States, supra note 129 (upholding delegations of authority to adjust tariffs to compensate for unreasonable foreign duties and for low foreign production costs respectively); Federal Energy Comm. v. Algonquin SNG, Inc., 426 U.S. 548 (1976) (upholding a delegation to the President of authority to "adjust . . . imports" in any way he deemed necessary to prevent them from endangering national security).

in lieu of determining the value of each individual item.[131] In 1964 it struck down an authorization to define the statutory term "ton-kilometer" for purposes of determining the amount of a tax on the transportation of freight.[132] In each of these cases one might have expected the Court to conclude that the lawmakers had left to the executive only the details of applying a policy that the legislature itself had determined.[133]

The Court has not always been so hostile to delegation. In a leading 1958 decision the Justices went out of their way to salvage a delegation of authority to promulgate regulations by which "prices, rents, fees, and other charges for goods and services of all kinds, with the exception of wages, are established or approved, or price levels are maintained."[134] Article 80(1) did not require, said the Court, that the content, purpose, and extent of the delegation appear expressly in the statutory text; resort could be had to such ordinary interpretive tools as purpose, context, and legislative history to illuminate the legislative will.[135] The purpose of the statute, as suggested by the last clause of the passage just quoted, was to preserve the general level of prices prevailing at the time of enactment. Intended as a temporary measure looking toward reestablishment of a free market economy, the statutory authority could be employed only to fend off "serious distortions with consequences for the price structure as a whole."[136] Nor was the statute too indeterminate in specifying the content of the delegated authority, for in light of long practice the general authorization to adopt measures other than those fixing prices was construed to embrace only associated accounting and reporting provisions and equalization charges assessed on one category of providers

---

[131] 15 BVerfGE 153 (1962). The statute, said the Court, "neither determined how far back in time one might go in determining the average value nor specified how long an average value remained in force once it had been established." Both the purposes and the articles for which average values were to be prescribed were left to executive discretion. Finally, the statute did not even say whether various articles grouped together had to be of approximately equal value, and thus the delegation enabled the executive "to introduce a different assessment principle . . . and thereby significantly to alter the basis" of the tax itself. Id. at 160-65.

[132] 18 BVerfGE 52 (1964). There were various ways of determining both weight and distance, the Court said, and the statute did not clearly choose among them. Id. at 63-64.

[133] "The legislature," said the Court in the case last mentioned, "must provide its delegate with a 'program.'" Id. at 62. In light of decisions such as those just noted, the Enquête-Kommission (see note 80 supra) recommended in 1976 that Art. 80(1) be amended to require only the purpose (not the content or extent) of a delegation to appear in the statute, in order to spare lawmakers the burden of prescribing details. See Schlußbericht der Enquête-Kommission, Teil 1, at 190-93.

[134] 8 BVerfGE 274, 278 (1958) (*Preisgesetz*).

[135] Id. at 307.

[136] Id. at 310, 312-13.

for the benefit of another.[137] Finally, the extent of the delegated authority was restricted by the limited purposes of the statute.[138]

This decision bears an uncanny resemblance to our own price-control case, *Yakus v. United States*,[139] which contrary to popular rumor was not inconsistent with meaningful limits on delegation of legislative power in the United States.[140] In each case the Court plausibly construed the statute in such a way that in administering it the executive was carrying out a legislative policy rather than imposing one of its own. In so doing the German court expressly invoked the principle, familiar in both countries but not always taken seriously in delegation cases, that whenever possible a statute should be interpreted so as to make it consistent with the Constitution.[141]

Later German decisions have tended to follow the price-control case rather than the less sympathetic decisions noted above.[142] The Constitutional Court has continued, however, to find delegations unconstitutionally broad.[143] Most strikingly, it has generally done so on the basis not of Article 80(1) itself but of other provisions that the Court has found to embody a similar nondelegation principle.

---

[137] Id. at 314-18.

[138] Id. at 318. It was not necessary, the Court added, that the delegation be "as specifically drafted as possible"; it must merely be "sufficiently specific." Id. at 312.

[139] 321 U.S. 414 (1944).

[140] See The Second Century at 300-01 (1990).

[141] See 8 BVerfGE at 324 (noting that the price-control law could be sustained *only* on the basis of this "verfassungskonforme[n] Auslegung"). For instances in which the respective tribunals seem to have tried less hard to find an acceptable narrowing construction see the German decisions cited in notes 131 and 132 supra, as well as Panama Refining Co. v. Ryan, 293 U.S. 388 (1935), and Justice Cardozo's more sympathetic dissent, id. at 437-38.

[142] See, e.g., 55 BVerfGE 207, 225-44 (1980) (exhaustively exploring history and tradition to find implicit limitations on a facially broad authorization to adopt regulations respecting moonlighting by public servants); 68 BVerfGE 319, 332-34 (1984) (upholding an authorization to set minimum and maximum fees for medical services because the statutory requirement that the regulations respect the legitimate interests of both doctors and patients required that fees be "neither too high . . . nor too low"); 76 BVerfGE 130, 142-43 (1987) (finding standards in the legislative history sufficient to save an otherwise unconfined grant of authority to determine the level of court costs payable by public institutions). See also Hesse, supra note 3, Rdnr. 528; Maunz in 3 Maunz/Dürig, Art. 80, Rdnr. 29-31 (arguing that the Court's tendency to merge the three constitutional requirements of content, purpose, and extent into a single quest for a legislative "program" has led to a certain loosening of the standard); Ulrich Ramsauer in 2 AK-GG, Art. 80, Rdnr. 46-56 (concluding (as suggested in 76 BVerfGE at 142-43) that the degree of specificity required has come to depend largely upon the degree of intrusiveness of the regulations authorized and on the complexity of the subject matter).

[143] More recent examples include 38 BVerfGE 373, 381-83 (1975) (striking down an authorization to specify the professional duties ("Berufspflichten") of pharmacists); 58 BVerfGE 257, 279 (1981) (invalidating an unconfined delegation of authority to determine which pupils should be expelled from school).

As recently as 1988, for example, the Court struck down a statute
making it a crime to violate any condition of a permit for the erection,
modification, or operation of broadcasting facilities.[144] Because of the
lack of meaningful statutory limitations on the authority to impose
the permit conditions themselves, the Court concluded, the statute
"leaves it to the postal authorities to determine the elements of an
offense by administrative action."[145] Since the statute contemplated
the issuance of permits rather than regulations, Article 80(1) did not
apply. However, under Articles 103(2) and 104(1) one may be
punished only for an offense previously defined by law ("gesetztlich
bestimmt") and imprisoned only on the basis of law in the formal
sense ("auf Grund eines förmlichen Gesetzes"). Like Article 80(1),
said the Court, these provisions required in principle
("grundsätzlich") that the legislature itself determine for what offenses one might be punished or imprisoned.[146]

If the requirement that offenses be "defined by law" seems to say
just what the Court said it meant, the requirement that imprisonment be "on the basis" of statute seems less clear. Article 12(1), for
example, permits occupational freedom to be limited "by or on the basis of statute"; as the Court has acknowledged, this disjunctive formulation demonstrates that some delegation of authority is allowed.[147] Moreover, the ubiquitous right to "free development of
personality" guaranteed by Article 2(1) is limited not by statutes but by
"the constitutional order," which on its face does not seem to require
that the legislature act at all. Nevertheless the Constitutional Court
has found that the nondelegation principle applies to measures limiting *any* of the fundamental rights protected by the Basic Law, even in
cases outside the scope of Article 80(1).

To begin with, Article 80(1) applies only to *federal* legislation. The
Court had little difficulty with this limitation; as a crucial ingredient
of democracy and the rule of law, both of which Article 28(1) requires
the constituent states to respect, the essence of Article 80(1) was applicable to the Länder as well.[148] More interestingly, although Article
80(1) applies only to the delegation of authority to adopt *regulations*,
the principle that it embodies has been held to apply to other delegations as well. For the doctrine that the legislature may not transfer
its functions is understood as a corollary of the principle that the

---

[144] 78 BVerfGE 374 (1988).

[145] Id. at 383-89.

[146] Id. at 381-83.

[147] See 33 BVerfGE 125, 155-56 (1972).

[148] 41 BVerfGE 251, 266 (1976). See Art. 28(1) GG: "Die verfassungsmäßige
Ordnung in den Ländern muß den Grundsätzen des republikanischen,
demokratischen und sozialen Rechtsstaates im Sinne dieses Grundgesetzes
entsprechen." Obviously this provision gives the Court a good deal of latitude in
determining which provisions applicable on their face only to the Bund are essential elements of republican democracy, the rule of law, and the social state. See
Herzog in 2 Maunz/Dürig, Art. 20, Abschnitt V, Rdnr. 122-25.

executive often may act only on the basis of legislation; both are aspects of a general reservation of legislative authority ("Gesetzesvorbehalt") said to be implicit in the separation of powers and in the rule of law.[149]

The groundbreaking case was the familiar *Price Control* decision. The governing statute authorized the executive to accomplish its purposes by issuing individual administrative orders ("Verfügungen") as well as regulations. That the provisions respecting individual orders did not fall within Art. 80(1), the Court declared, did not insulate them from constitutional limitations on delegation; here too the content, purpose, and extent of the delegated authority must be determined by statute. This conclusion was traced to three basic aspects of the rule of law: the principle (Art. 20(3)) that the administration is bound by law ("Gesetzmäßigkeit der Verwaltung"), the separation of powers (Art. 20(2)), and the requirement (Art. 19(4)) that administrative action be subject to judicial review.[150]

The first and third of these arguments appear unconvincing. To say that the executive is bound by law seems to mean it must obey legal limitations on its discretion, not that its discretion must be limited. Similarly, judicial review is not an end in itself but a means of enforcing limitations on executive authority; if there are no limitations there is nothing to review.[151] The separation of powers argument, however, is strong. "If the authority of the executive is not sufficiently restricted," said the Court, "then the executive is no

---

[149] See 49 BVerfGE 89, 126-27 (1978) (*Kalkar*); Maunz in 3 Maunz/-Dürig, Art. 80, Rdnr. 11; Ossenbühl, supra note 84, Rdnr. 10, 41. Indeed most of the decisions respecting the general Gesetzesvorbehalt deal with the delegation question. The requirement that there be *some* statutory basis for executive action follows a fortiori from the principle that even when it delegates authority the legislature must make the basic policy decisions.

[150] 8 BVerfGE at 325-26.

[151] The argument that there must be limits to delegation in order that the judges may have something to review was no more persuasive when made by Chief Justice Stone in the *Yakus* case, 321 U.S. at 426. In an introductory paragraph the German Court had hinted that the principle of fair warning might provide yet another basis for the specificity requirement, noting that the rule of law required that a delegation be definite enough to make administrative action predictable ("voraussehbar und berechenbar") by the affected citizen. 8 BVerfGE at 325. Fair warning is indeed an important element of the rule of law in Germany (see 56 BVerfGE 99, 109 (1981)), and the Constitutional Court recently confirmed that it was one of the purposes behind the specificity requirement for criminal statutes in Art. 103(2). 78 BVerfGE 374, 382 (1988). Fair warning could be provided by the adoption of administrative standards (see Kenneth Culp Davis, Administrative Law Treatise 207-08 (2d ed. 1978)), but that would not remove the basic objection to unbridled delegation of legislative authority.

longer executing the law . . . but making decisions in the legislature's place."[152]

In an important later decision the Court effectively traced the
nondelegation doctrine to the constitutional guarantee of democracy
as well.[153] By permitting restrictions of occupational freedom only by
or on the basis of statute, the Court added, Article 12(1) made it basically the responsibility of the legislature "to determine which public
interests are so weighty that the individual's right to liberty must
take second place":

> The democratic legislature may not abdicate this responsibility at its
> pleasure. In a governmental system in which the people exercise
> their sovereign power most directly through their elected Parlia-
> ment, it is rather the responsibility of this Parliament above all to re-
> solve the open issues of community life in the process of determining
> the public will by weighing the various and sometimes conflicting in-
> terests.[154]

Thus the implicit constitutional restrictions apply when authority is delegated not only to federal or state executive officers but also to
legislative committees,[155] to public corporations,[156] to local governments,[157] and to occupational associations.[158] In some of these
instances the standards applied are less stringent, in light of the fact
that the delegation may be said to promote self-government by those
most directly affected.[159] Moreover, the requisite specificity varies
with the degree to which the delegated authority impinges upon
fundamental rights. Thus while the crucial right to choose one's
occupation can basically be limited only by the legislature itself, the
power to regulate the conduct of those engaged in an occupation may
be delegated to a professional association.[160] Even in the latter case,

---

[152] 8 BVerfGE at 325. Since the terms of the delegation were the same as those of
the authority to adopt regulations, which the Court had found sufficiently confining,
they were upheld on the same reasoning. Id. at 326-227.

[153] 33 BVerfGE 125, 158 (1972) (*Fachärzte*).

[154] Id. at 159.

[155] 77 BVerfGE 1 (1987).

[156] 12 BVerfGE 319 (1961); 19 BVerfGE 253 (1965).

[157] 32 BVerfGE 346 (1972).

[158] 33 BVerfGE 125 (1972). See also Reinhold Hendler, Das Prinzip Selbstverwaltung, 4 Handbuch des Staatsrechts 1133, Rdnr. 58.

[159] See, e.g., 33 BVerfGE at 159; Ulrich Ramsauer in 2 AK-GG, Art. 80, Rdnr. 31-
32. Cf. United States v. Mazurie, 419 U.S. 544 (1975) (applying especially lenient
standards to a delegation of authority to an Indian tribe with governmental powers
of its own); City of Eastlake v. Forest City Enterprises, 426 U.S. 668 (1976) (holding
ordinary delegation standards inapplicable to a provision for referendum).

[160] 33 BVerfGE 125, 158, 160 (1972). For the same differentiation in the context of
Art. 80(1) itself see note 142 supra. Cf. Schneider v. State, 308 U.S. 147, 164 (1939)

however, the legislation must set forth those provisions which "essentially [wesentlich] characterize the image of the professional activity as a whole."[161]

The constitutional principle that emerged was neatly summed up in a major 1978 opinion upholding a grant of authority to license the construction and operation of a nuclear breeder reactor:

> Today it is firmly established by the decisions that – without regard to any requirement of an incursion [into individual freedom] – in basic normative areas, and especially when the exercise of basic rights is at stake, the legislature is required . . . to make all essential decisions itself [alle wesentlichen Entscheidungen selbst zu treffen] . . . . Articles 80(1) and 59(2) of the Basic Law, as well as the specific reservations of legislative power [in the catalog of fundamental rights] are particular instances of this general reservation [dieses allgemeinen Gesetzesvorbehalts].[162]

The decisions are numerous and not all easy to reconcile. They document the difficulty and uncertainty of administering a requirement that is necessarily a matter of degree.[163] Yet in reading them it is difficult to escape the conclusion that we have lost something significant that the Germans have worked hard to maintain. For over the years the Constitutional Court has devoted itself diligently to the task of assuring that major policy decisions respecting the content of the law are made by the representative and popularly elected legislature, as they should be in a republican democracy – a task

---

(invalidating a grant of discretionary authority to issue permits for the door-to-door distribution of handbills).

[161] 33 BVerfGE at 160. At stake in this case was an authorization of the medical profession itself to set standards for practice by medical specialists ("Fachärzte"). Concluding that the challenged rules impermissibly contracted occupational freedom on the merits, the Court did not have to decide whether the delegation itself was too broad. See id. at 165; see also chapter 6 infra.

[162] 49 BVerfGE 89, 126-27 (1978) (Kalkar). For a later statement of the same principle in the context of public education see 58 BVerfGE 257, 268-69 (1981); for a brief description of the radical changes wrought by the Constitutional Court in this field since 1970 see Ossenbühl, supra note 84, Rdnr. 43. Art. 59(2), to which the Court referred in the breeder case, requires legislative consent to any treaty affecting political relations or matters that are otherwise within legislative control. See note 207 infra. Such a treaty, however, need not specifically regulate everything that would be considered essential in the case of ordinary legislation; any such requirement, according to the Constitutional Court, would hamper the ability of the Federal Republic to deal with other nations. 77 BVerfGE 170, 231-32 (1987).

[163] Critical characterizations employing such terms as "bankruptcy" and "blind alley" are collected and gently dismissed in Ossenbühl, supra note 84, Rdnr. 44.

with which our Supreme Court has not seriously concerned itself
since 1936.[164]

II. EXECUTIVE POWER

The principal focus of 19th-century constitutionalism in Germany was on democratization of the legislative process. Even the visionary Frankfurt Constitution of 1849 ("Paulskirchenverfassung"),
which would have divided legislative authority between a council of
states ("Staatenhaus") and a popularly elected assembly, envisioned
as head of state a hereditary Kaiser who would exercise executive
powers through ministers of his own choosing.[165] Thus this first step

---

[164] For a comparison of the delegation decisions of the German and U.S. courts
see Georg Nolte, Ermächtigung der Exekutive zur Rechtsetzung, 118 AöR 378
(1993).

The Basic Law contains, however, a variety of provisions – most of them added
by constitutional amendment in 1968 – designed to preserve order in extraordinary
situations in which normal governmental processes are disrupted, and some of
them envision the possibility of lawmaking outside the Bundestag. In case of a
military emergency ("Verteidigungsfall") brought about by actual or threatened
external attack, federal legislative powers are not only expanded to include matters normally reserved to the Länder (Art. 115c(1) GG); they may also be exercised
by a joint committee made up of members of the Bundestag and Bundesrat
("Gemeinsamer Ausschuß," Art. 53a), if by a two-thirds vote the committee finds
that the Bundestag is unable to fulfill its duties (Art. 115e). In the less critical case
of a so-called legislative emergency ("Gesetzgebungsnotstand"), Art. 81 authorizes
the effective transfer of lawmaking powers from the Bundestag to the Bundesrat
(see Herzog in 3 Maunz/Dürig, Art. 81, Rdnr. 64-65) if after rejecting the Chancellor's request for a vote of confidence under Art. 68 the Bundestag is not dissolved.
For discussion of these and related provisions see Eckart Klein, Funktions-
störungen in der Staatsorganisation, 7 Handbuch des Staatsrechts 361; Eckart
Klein, Der innere Notstand, 7 Handbuch des Staatsrechts 387; Wolfgang Graf
Vitzthum, Der Spannungs- und Verteidigungsfall, 7 Handbuch des Staatsrechts
415. Defending emergency provisions in principle as preferable to
extraconstitutional action, former Justice Konrad Hesse has argued that the
various clauses concerning physical interruption of government are too
complicated and unconfined and that the whole idea of the legislative emergency is
misguided: "The only thing that can be achieved on the basis of Art. 81 GG is thus to
prolong the political crisis whose consequences it was designed to avoid." Hesse,
supra note 3, Rdnr. 719-71. Those inclined to be smug about the absence of
comparable provisions in the U.S. Constitution would be well advised to take
another look at the extent of implicit military authority acknowledged in cases of
true emergency by dicta in such brave and justly celebrated decisions as Ex parte
Milligan, 71 U.S. 2 (1866), and Duncan v. Kahanamoku, 327 U.S. 304 (1946).

[165] RV 1849, Abschnitte III-IV, § 101 gave the executive a suspensive veto that
could be overridden by passing the same bill in three consecutive sessions. § 73 del-
phically described the ministers appointed by the Kaiser as responsible
("verantwortlich"); the extent to which this term implied parliamentary control of
the executive was never clarified, since the constitution never took effect.

toward democracy, which was carried forward in Bismarck's 1871 constitution, brought with it a significant separation of powers: The people had an increasing say in the making of laws, but it was still the monarch who enforced them.[166]

The Weimar Constitution, adopted after the First World War, democratized the executive too but in so doing significantly diminished the separation of powers by making executive ministers dependent upon the popularly elected parliament.[167] At the same time, however, that constitution vested in an independently elected President ("Reichspräsident") extensive powers, not least the authority to take extraordinary measures whenever there was a serious threat to security or public order.[168] In fact this authorization enabled the President to rule much of the time without the interference of Parliament, which he freely dissolved under another express constitutional provision.[169]

In conscious response to the imperial tendencies of popularly elected Presidents during the Weimar period,[170] the present Basic Law opts for a parliamentary system without a strong independent executive,[171] thus further reducing the separation of powers.

A. The President, the Chancellor, and the Cabinet

The Federal Republic does have an independent President ("Bundespräsident"), but he is not elected by the people,[172] and he

---

[166] See RV 1871, Art. 5, 6, 11-20. At this point the German situation resembled that which Montesquieu had so admired in England, although at the time he wrote it had largely ceased to reflect reality. See Montesquieu, L'Esprit des Lois, bk. 11, ch. 6 (1748); Walter Bagehot, The English Constitution 69-72, 253-54, 303 (Dolphin ed.; first published 1872).

[167] Although ministers were chosen by the independent Reichspräsident, they also required the confidence of the Reichstag, which was given the express power to vote them out of office. Art. 53, 54 WRV.

[168] Art. 41, 48 WRV.

[169] Id., Art. 25. "Of the fourteen years of the Weimar Republic, more than nine were definitively shaped [bestimmt] by extraordinary measures under Art. 48." Ernst Rudolf Huber, 6 Deutsche Verfassungsgeschichte 689 (1981). See also Golo Mann, Deutsche Geschichte des 19. und 20. Jahrhunderts 756-58, 766-67 (1958) (14. Auflage der Sonderausgabe, printed 1979); Jürgen Jekewitz in 2 AK-GG, vor Art. 54, Rdnr. 5-10; n. 64 supra.

[170] See Sten. Ber. at 25 (Delegate Süsterhenn), 173 (Delegate Schmid). See also Klaus Schlaich, Die Funktionen des Bundespräsidenten im Verfassungsgefüge, 2 Handbuch des Staatsrechts 541, Rdnr. 88: "The debate in the Parliamentary Council [over the powers of the President] was shaped by the desire to depart from the principles of the Weimar Constitution."

[171] For comparison of the present provisions with those of the Weimar Constitution see Herzog in 3 Maunz/Dürig, Art. 54, Rdnr. 8-12.

[172] The President is elected by a special convention ("Bundesversammlung"). All members of the Bundestag are members of this convention; the state

performs a largely ceremonial role. Formally it is the President who represents the Federal Republic in its relations with other nations and concludes treaties,[173] who appoints cabinet ministers, judges, and other federal officials,[174] and who exercises the power to pardon offenders.[175] Most of his acts, however, require ministerial approval, which means that he cannot act on his own.[176] Moreover, in most cases the President has no discretion to *decline* to act either, but rather a duty to endorse whatever lawful course of action the political branches of government propose. In some instances this duty is made clear by the constitutional text;[177] in others it is said to be implicit in the decision to reject the Weimar model.[178]

---

legislatures choose an equal number of additional delegates "on the principle of proportional representation." Art. 54(1), (3) GG. For explanation of the reasons for this procedure see Herzog in 3 Maunz/Dürig, Art. 54, Rdnr. 10-12, 28. The President's term is five years, and he may be reelected only once (Art. 54(2)). On impeachment by a two-thirds vote of either the Bundestag or the Bundesrat, he may be removed from office if the Constitutional Court finds him guilty of deliberate violations of the Constitution or other federal law (Art. 61). Broad incompatibility provisions (Art. 55) promote the President's neutrality; immunities from arrest and prosecution (Art. 60(4)) protect him from harassment. See Herzog in 3 Maunz/-Dürig, Art. 55, Rdnr. 3 and Art. 60, Rdnr. 56.

[173] Art. 59(1) GG.

[174] Art. 60(1), 63(2), 64(1) GG. With respect to judges and nonministerial officials Art. 60(1) permits the appointment power to be vested elsewhere by law.

[175] Art. 60(2) GG. It is also said that certain unexpressed ceremonial prerogatives, such as the establishment of national symbols and the award of medals, are inherent in the office. See Herzog in 3 Maunz/Dürig, Art. 54, Rdnr. 69.

[176] With certain exceptions including the appointment and dismissal of the Chancellor, Art. 58 requires the countersignature ("Gegenzeichnung") of a responsible minister for presidential orders and decrees ("Anordnungen und Verfügungen"). This formulation, it is said, was meant to embrace all legally binding acts of the Bundespräsident, including pardons. See Schlaich, supra note 170, Rdnr. 68, 79; Herzog in 3 Maunz/Dürig, Art. 58, Rdnr. 21-44 (listing exceptions). The principal function of the approval requirement is to prevent the President from "pursuing an independent policy contrary to the wishes of the Government" or "interfering with the unified conduct of public affairs." Schlaich, supra, Rdnr. 64.

[177] E.g., Art. 63(2), which provides that the person chosen as Chancellor by the Bundestag shall be appointed by the Bundespräsident ("ist vom Bundespräsidenten zu ernennen"). Under Art. 63(1) it is the President who proposes the initial candidate, and in so doing he may exercise his own discretion, but the Bundestag is free to select someone else. See Art. 63(3) GG; Schlaich, supra note 170, Rdnr. 14. Somewhat less plain is Art. 64(1), which provides that the President shall appoint and dismiss other ministers upon proposal by the Chancellor ("auf Vorschlag des Bundeskanzlers"). Nevertheless it is understood that while the President has the right to argue over the merits of a ministerial nomination he must ultimately bow to the Chancellor's demand. See Schlaich, supra, Rdnr. 28 (acknowledging "an indefinable power to correct abuses"); Herzog in 3 Maunz/Dürig, Art. 54, Rdnr. 85 (finding the text clear).

[178] In the foreign affairs field, for example, it is said that the President has no

On the other hand, like other officials, the President is bound by the constitution and, except when participating in the legislative process, by other laws as well.[179] Accordingly it has been argued that he has both the power and the duty to refuse to endorse any governmental action contrary to law, and thus that he must review the legality of every executive or legislative act he is requested to approve.[180]

This issue has been extensively debated in the context of the Article 82(1) requirement that "laws enacted in accordance with the provisions of this Basic Law" be certified or authenticated ("ausgefertigt") by the President.[181] Central to the President's action is the largely technical certification that the published text corresponds to an actual legislative decision; it is clear that he has no right to veto a measure purely on policy grounds.[182] On the other hand, the language of the provision is generally understood to permit the President to refuse to certify a statute that has not been adopted in accordance with the procedural requirements of the Basic Law.[183] Whether he may also reject a statute on the ground that it offends *substantive* constitutional requirements is disputed, but Presidents have done so on rare occasions.[184]

---

policymaking authority whatever; even his speeches are cleared with the Foreign Ministry. See Schlaich, supra note 170, Rdnr. 50, 71. See also Herzog in 3 Maunz/Dürig, Art. 54, Rdnr. 86 (treaties), 87 (nonministerial appointments and general presumption against presidential discretion); Schlaich, supra, Rdnr. 29-30.

[179] See Art. 1(3), 20(3), 56, 61 GG.

[180] See Herzog in 3 Maunz/Dürig, Art. 54, Rdnr. 74-77. The President's refusal to sign is not an "order" or "decree" and thus according to most observers does not require ministerial approval under Art. 58. See id., Rdnr. 84; Herzog in id., Art. 58, Rdnr. 44 (adding that a countersignature requirement would defeat the purpose of providing a check on executive action).

[181] "Die nach den Vorschriften dieses Grundgesetzes zustande gekommenen Gesetze werden vom Bundespräsidenten nach Gegenzeichnung ausgefertigt und im Bundesgesetzblatte verkündigt."

[182] See Schlaich, supra note 170, Rdnr. 24-25.

[183] See id., Rdnr. 33.

[184] Schlaich, supra note 170, Rdnr. 31, found only five instances (as of 1987) in which a President had refused to certify laws on constitutional grounds, two of them for failure to comply with the procedural requirement of Bundesrat consent. For a more recent example see President von Weizsäcker's refusal to sign a law that would have transferred authority over air traffic controllers to a private corporation, on the substantive ground that Art. 33(4) permitted governmental functions to be carried out in most cases only by government officials. Die Zeit, Feb. 8, 1991, p. 5. "Der Staatsnotar bockt," says the headline – the notary refuses to sign. Art. 87d was amended in 1992 to remove the President's objection. See Gesetz zur Änderung des Grundgesetzes vom 14. Juli 1992, BGBl. I S. 1254 (authorizing Parliament to opt for organizing flight controllers under either public or private law).

The arguments are familiar from our own debates over the legitimacy of judicial review of federal legislation. Neither the President's obligation to obey the constitution nor his oath to uphold it[185] necessarily tells us what the constitution requires him to do; "in accordance with this Basic Law" might mean in conformity with its prescribed procedures.[186] In favor of the President's right to reject statutes on substantive constitutional grounds it has been argued with some force that such authority provides an additional check against infringement of the constitution; that it would undermine the legitimating function of the authentication provision to require the President to sign an unconstitutional law; and that it would be intolerable to insist that the President knowingly countenance an unconstitutional act.[187]

In a few instances, moreover, the President does exercise a discretion of his own. It is said, for example, that he does so in pardoning offenders, in establishing national symbols, and in calling the Bundestag into special session.[188] Most important in this connection, however, are the powers of the President in times in which the normal political process has broken down. If the Bundestag cannot muster a majority for the election of a Chancellor, the President decides whether to accept a minority candidate or to dissolve the Bundestag and precipitate new elections.[189] If the Chancellor upon losing a vote of confidence seeks to dissolve the Bundestag, it is the President who decides whether to do so.[190] If he decides not to order new elections in this situation, it is he (on application of the Cabinet with Bundesrat consent) who decides whether to declare a legislative

---

[185] Art. 56 GG ("das Grundgesetz und die Gesetze des Bundes wahren und verteidigen"). See Herzog in 3 Maunz/Dürig, Art. 56, Rdnr. 21 (arguing that the oath adds a moral obligation to the legal one imposed by Art. 20(3)).

[186] See Schlaich, supra note 170, Rdnr. 35-36; Ramsauer in 2 AK-GG, Art. 82, Rdnr. 11-16. Cf. Marbury v. Madison, 5 U.S. 137 (1803); The First Hundred Years at 72-73 For consideration of the analogous question whether executive officers in the United States are bound by unconstitutional laws see Frank Easterbrook, Presidential Review, 40 Case W. Res. L. Rev. 905 (1989-90).

[187] See Schlaich, supra note 170, Rdnr. 36, 37, 41. Accord von Mangoldt, supra note 24, at 442. The same dispute existed under a similar provision of the Weimar constitution. See Art. 70 WRV (requiring the Reichspräsident to certify constitutionally adopted laws ("die verfassungsmäßig zustande gekommenen Gesetze"); Anschütz, supra note 1, at 367-68 (arguing for substantive as well as procedural review). For arguments as to why the Art. 100(1) requirement that other judges who believe a statute unconstitutional certify the question to the Constitutional Court (see text at notes 324-26 infra) does not implicitly require the President to sign unconstitutional laws see Schlaich, supra, Rdnr. 38.

[188] See id., Rdnr. 6-11; Herzog in 3 Maunz/Dürig, Art. 54, Rdnr. 86 (stressing that Art. 39(3) requires the Bundestag to convene at the request of either "the President *or* the Chancellor").

[189] Art. 63(4) GG. In this case the normal countersignature requirement does not apply. See Art. 58 GG.

[190] Art. 68(1) GG.

emergency ("Gesetzgebungsnotstand") permitting the Cabinet and the Bundesrat to put a law into force without Bundestag action.[191] In all these instances the Basic Law employs the permissive word "may" ("kann") or its equivalent, and it is understood that the President exercises his own discretion in determining what action to take.[192]

Thus the Bundespräsident can exercise significant political power only in times of crisis in which the normal machinery of government does not function.[193] Ultimate federal executive authority rests with the Cabinet ("Bundesregierung") and the ministers of whom it is composed.[194]

Though formally appointed by the President, the Chancellor is elected by the Bundestag, and as a practical matter it is he who selects the other ministers.[195] Under Article 67 the Bundestag can remove the Chancellor – and with him his ministers[196] – at any time

---

[191] Art. 81(1), (2), (3). See note 164 supra.

[192] See Herzog in 3 Maunz/Dürig, Art. 54, Rdnr. 86. With respect to the vote of no confidence under Art. 68 the Constitutional Court confirmed the President's discretion, as well as his authority to determine whether the legal requirements for dissolution had been met, in its famous opinion respecting the dissolution of Parliament in 1983. See 62 BVerfGE 1, 35, 50 (1983); Schlaich, supra note 170, Rdnr. 15-21 (adding that as a practical matter the President's discretion in the case of a vote of no confidence has been severely limited by the Court's loose interpretation of the conditions justifying dissolution (see text at notes 65-80 supra) and by its insistence (62 BVerfGE at 50-51) that in assessing the political prospects for a viable Government the President is not to substitute his judgment for that of the Chancellor). See also Meinhard Schröder, Bildung, Bestand und parlamentarische Verantwortung der Bundesregierung, 2 Handbuch des Staatsrechts 603, Rdnr. 23 (arguing that the Bundespräsident is free to reject a minority Chancellor under Art. 63(4) only if he doubts the candidate's ability to form an effective government).

[193] See Sten. Ber. at 202 (Delegate Lehr) (describing the President as an "honest broker" in conflicts between Parliament and the executive); Schlaich, supra note 170, Rdnr. 58.

[194] See Art. 82 GG: "Die Bundesregierung besteht aus dem Bundeskanzler und aus den Bundesministern."

[195] Art. 63, 64 GG; see Herzog in 3 Maunz/Dürig, Art. 63, Rdnr. 1-6. In fact the choice of both Chancellor and Ministers is worked out by negotiation among the coalition parties in advance of the formal steps prescribed by the constitution. See Schröder, supra note 192, Rdnr. 1-2. Except for those ministries expressly named in the Basic Law (Defense, Finance, and Justice), the Chancellor determines which positions shall exist as an incident to his authority to fill them. See Herzog in 3 Maunz/Dürig, Art. 64, Rdnr. 3-5; Schröder, supra, Rdnr. 27-28 (arguing that the legislature is powerless to interfere). For early debates over this issue in the United States see David P. Currie, The Constitution in Congress: The First Congress, 1789-91 (forthcoming). That the Chancellor must nominate ministers and allot them significant areas of responsibility, however, is said to be established by the basic decision of Art. 62 in favor of a cabinet system. See Herzog in 3 Maunz/Dürig, Art. 62, Rdnr. 3.

[196] Art. 69(2) GG. Parliamentary removal of individual ministers, or of the Chancellor alone, is not permitted; the Cabinet stands or falls as a whole. See Herzog in 3 Maunz/Dürig, Art. 67, Rdnr. 10-11; id, Art. 69, Rdnr. 44. Some of the Län-

and for any reason, but only if it simultaneously names his successor.[197] The purpose of this provision is to guard against the risk of
an executive vacuum while ensuring ultimate parliamentary control.[198]

Thus in theory the Bundestag can determine the direction of executive policy through its power to select and replace the Chancellor,
and it has broad investigative powers to enable it better to perform its
oversight function.[199] In practice, it is often said, the situation tends
to be reversed: By virtue of its superior access to information and its
influence on the dominant political parties, the Cabinet effectively
determines *legislative* policy.[200] In any event, there is far less
structural separation between the legislature and top executive
officers in the Federal Republic than there is in the United States.[201]

---

der constitutions, in contrast, permit the Parliament to remove individual ministers. See Herdegen, supra note 7, Rdnr. 30.

[197] Thus when the Cabinet has lost the support of Parliament there are three
possibilities: The election of a new Chancellor under Art. 67 or (if the Chancellor
resigns) Art. 63, the dissolution of Parliament under Art. 68 (see text at notes 65-80
supra), and the continuation in office of a minority government. In the event of a
race between Parliament to replace the Chancellor and the Chancellor to seek the
dissolution of Parliament, Art. 68(1) gives the legislature a trump card by providing that the right to dissolution is extinguished as soon as a new Chancellor is chosen. See Herzog in 3 Maunz/Dürig, Art. 68, Rdnr. 63 (explaining that it would
make no sense to dissolve an assembly that was in a position to choose a viable cabinet).

[198] See Sten. Ber. at 28 (Delegate Menzel), 90 (Delegate Katz), 173 (Delegate
Schmid); Schröder, supra note 192, Rdnr. 33-35. But see Hesse, supra note 3, Rdnr.
635 (doubting whether a minority government kept in power by virtue of the Art. 67
requirement of a constructive vote of no confidence ("konstruktives Mißtrauensvo-
tum") is likely to be more effective than a caretaker government remaining in office in default of a successor, as under the Weimar Constitution); Herzog in 3
Maunz/Dürig, Art. 62, Rdnr. 80 and Art. 67, Rdnr. 16. For the argument that an attempt to force the Chancellor to resign by terminating his salary would amount to
an unconstitutional circumvention of Art. 67 see id., Rdnr. 44.

[199] Art. 44 GG. In accordance with this purpose, the implicit executive privilege
of withholding confidential or sensitive information is narrowly interpreted. See
67 BVerfGE 100, 127-46 (1984); Maunz in 3 Maunz/Dürig, Art. 44, Rdnr. 57. In fact,
since the Cabinet normally enjoys the support of a parliamentary majority, it is
more commonly the opposition that acts as a watchdog. To this end Art. 44(1) requires the Bundestag to conduct an investigation whenever requested by one fourth
of its members, and the Constitutional Court has held that the same quorum may
basically determine the agenda of the investigation – an important check in a system without strict structural separation of executive and legislative bodies. See 49
BVerfGE 70, 79-88 (1978); Herzog in 3 Maunz/Dürig, Art. 62, Rdnr. 105-06.

[200] See, e.g., Herzog in 2 Maunz/Dürig, Art. 20, Abschnitt II, Rdnr. 64 (noting
the clear predominance ("deutliches Übergewicht") of the Cabinet); id., Abschnitt
V, Rdnr. 54-55.

[201] Indeed, although the Chancellor and other ministers are forbidden to engage
in most other remunerative activities in order to minimize conflicts of interest,

Within the Cabinet, the Chancellor determines the general principles ("Richtlinien") of executive policy.[202] Within these principles, however, each minister conducts the affairs of his department autonomously and on his own responsibility ("selbständig und unter eigener Verantwortung").[203] Many significant powers, moreover, are given not to any individual minister but to the Cabinet as a whole.[204] Thus the executive power is not only less independent but also less centralized in Germany than it is in the United States, although the Chancellor can exercise ultimate control through his power to set guidelines and effectively to hire and fire other Cabinet members.[205]

---

they may serve simultaneously as members of Parliament, as is common in a parliamentary system. See Herzog in 3 Maunz/-Dürig, Art. 66, Rdnr. 2-4, 33-36 (explaining that historically a legislative seat does not qualify as a "salaried" office within the meaning of the incompatibility provision of Art. 66 GG, and that therefore (strange as it may seem) a federal minister is free to serve as a state legislator as well).

[202] Art. 65 GG. These principles or guidelines, which have been defined as "binding, abstract, normative instructions," have been compared to framework legislation (see chapter 2 supra) in that they must leave sufficient discretion to the individual ministers to work out the details. See Norbert Achterberg, Innere Ordnung der Bundesregierung, 2 Handbuch des Staatsrechts 629, Rdnr. 18-19; Herzog in 3 Maunz/Dürig, Art. 65, Rdnr. 5-10 (invoking the same analogy but concluding that the Chancellor is free to resolve particular controversies of significant political import so long as individual ministers retain a significant degree of overall discretion).

[203] Art. 65 GG. This means, for example, that it is the individual Minister who makes hiring and firing decisions and issues instructions to administrators within his department. See Herzog in 3 Maunz/Dürig, Art. 65, Rdnr. 59-61. Differences of opinion over matters concerning more than one Ministry are resolved by the Cabinet as a whole. Art. 65 GG; see Achterberg, supra note 202, Rdnr. 59. In normal times the Defense Minister is Commander in Chief of the armed forces (Art. 65a); in a military emergency (see note 164 supra), command passes to the Chancellor in the interest of unified policy (Art. 115b). Under Art. 112 expenditures not provided for in the budget may be made only with the Finance Minister's approval.

[204] See, e.g., Art. 76, 81 (proposals for legislation in normal times and after declaration of legislative emergency); Art. 84, 85, 86 (various devices for controlling officials engaged in actual administration of the laws); Art. 115a, 115f (application for declaration of a military emergency and extraordinary powers once such a declaration is made). The Basic Law's allocation of authority between the Cabinet and its various Ministers was consciously patterned after that of the Weimar Constitution. See Achterberg, supra note 202, Rdnr. 9-12. For a detailed breakdown of this allocation see Schröder, Aufgaben der Bundesregierung, 2 Handbuch des Staatsrechts 585, Rdnr. 17-24.

[205] Art. 64, 65 GG. See Achterberg, supra note 202, Rdnr. 54; Herzog in 3 Maunz/Dürig, Art. 64, Rdnr. 20 (finding the true basis of the Chancellor's preponderance in his power over the composition of the Cabinet). Contrast U.S. Const., Art. II, § 1: "The executive power shall be vested in a President of the United States."

In so doing, of course, the Chancellor himself is subject to the threat of replacement and thus to a measure of parliamentary control.

B. The Limits of Parliamentary Control

Despite the structural symbiosis inherent in the parliamentary system, the requirement of Article 20(2) that legislative and executive powers be exercised by distinct governmental bodies is not without significance. In the first place, at the functional level, there are limits to the methods by which the legislature may exercise control over executive actions.

At a minimum, Article 20(2) must mean that the Bundestag cannot itself execute the laws[206] or carry out those other functions – such as the conduct of foreign affairs – which the Basic Law fundamentally entrusts to the executive.[207] Nor, as a general rule, can the legislature tell the executive how to exercise its authority in a particular case;[208] the parliament controls policy at the wholesale rather than the retail level by passing laws and by replacing the Cabinet.

There is one important qualification of this principle that should strike a familiar chord for the observer from the United States. In the ubiquitous *Price Control* case the Constitutional Court expressly upheld a statutory provision empowering the Bundestag alone, without meeting the constitutional requirements for legislation, to veto regulations adopted by the executive setting prices for various goods and services.[209] Relying heavily on a long history of similar statutory provisions, the Court also justified its conclusion on the ground (asserted unsuccessfully by Justice White in his dissent from *INS v. Chadha*)[210] that the legislative veto compensated for the increase in

---

[206] See also Herzog in 2 Maunz/Dürig, Art. 20, Abschnitt V, Rdnr. 83, 111 (basing this conclusion on the requirement (partly codified in Art. 19(1)) that laws be of general applicability and on the general equality provision of Art. 3(1)).

[207] See 1 BVerfGE 372, 394-95 (1952). Art. 59(2), which requires parliamentary consent for the conclusion of treaties that "regulate the political relations of the Federation or relate to matters of federal legislation," serves to underline this general principle. See id. at 380-90 (holding that a commercial treaty with France did not fall within the first clause of this provision and that the second, in light of history and its purpose of protecting parliamentary prerogatives, applied only to treaties that could not be implemented without legislative action). As the text suggests, the Government perceives no need to obtain legislative consent to the *termination* of a treaty that falls within Art. 59(2), and the Constitutional Commission rejected the suggestion that it propose an amendment to alter the current practice. See Bericht der VerfKomm at 113-14. Cf. Goldwater v. Carter, 444 U.S. 996 (1979).

[208] See Wolfgang Loschelder, Weisungshierarchie und persönliche Verantwortung in der Exekutive, 3 Handbuch des Staatsrechts 521, Rdnr. 26, 41.

[209] 8 BVerfGE 274, 319-22 (1958).

[210] 462 U.S. 919 (1983).

executive power brought about by the delegation itself.[211] The context of the decision, however, was one of general rulemaking, not of individual executive action. Moreover, in any case the legislative veto is purely negative; it permits the Bundestag to prevent but not to compel executive action. The crudeness of the tools of legislative control thus affords the Cabinet considerable practical autonomy within the confines of the parliamentary system.

A variety of structural principles, moreover, further limit the degree of parliamentary control over the actual administration of the laws. As already indicated, the Bundestag can remove individual ministers only by removing the Chancellor, and it can do that only if it chooses his successor at the same time. In addition, there are significant limits to the authority of the Cabinet itself, and correspondingly to the indirect authority of Parliament, over the administration ("Verwaltung").

Even in those areas in which federal laws are administered by federal agencies directly responsible to one or another ministry,[212] some structural autonomy is provided by Article 33(2) and (5), which require that most public servants be selected without regard for their political inclinations and that the public service be conducted with due regard for the traditional principles of the professional civil service ("unter Berücksichtigung der hergebrachten Grundsätze des Berufsbeamtentums"). These principles embrace appropriate remuneration (including pensions and allowances for child support) and even titles, the right to a hearing before discharge, and above all (in most cases) protection against dismissal without cause.[213]

---

[211] For an approving view see Maunz in 2 Maunz/Dürig, Art. 80, Rdnr. 35, 60. As far as the U.S. Constitution is concerned, I have argued elsewhere that the Supreme Court was right: Once it is decided that the delegation is not too broad, the executive in acting under it is executing the law, and the legislature can interfere only by changing the law itself. The Second Century at 591-93. Indeed the German court acknowledged that a regulation approved by the Bundestag remained a regulation: The requirement of legislative approval did not make inapplicable the requirement of Art. 80(1) that the statute specify the content, purpose, and extent of the delegated authority. 8 BVerfGE at 322-23. See also 9 BVerfGE 268, 279-80 (1958) (holding in contrast to Buckley v. Valeo, 424 U.S. 1, 109-43 (1976), that the fact that one member of a board with power to arbitrate disputes over public employment was a legislator did not disqualify him). The arrangement was invalidated, however, on the distinct ground that the executive was entitled to control of fundamental matters affecting its own composition. See text at notes 226-29 infra.

[212] Such areas include defense, foreign affairs, some federal taxes, postal and telecommunications services, and some aspects of transportation. See Art. 32, 87(1), 87b, 87d, 108(1) GG; chapter 2 supra.

[213] See 7 BVerfGE 155 (1957); 8 BVerfGE 1, 22-28 (1958); 11 BVerfGE 203, 210-17 (1960); 43 BVerfGE 154, 165-77 (1976); 44 BVerfGE 249, 262-68 (1977); 62 BVerfGE 374, 382-91 (1982); 64 BVerfGE 323, 351-66 (1983). See also Helmut Lecheler, Der öffentliche Dienst, 3 Handbuch des Staatsrechts 717, Rdnr. 49-70; chapter 6 infra. Officers whose responsibilities involve the exercise of a discretion distinctively political, such as appointed mayors, may be discharged on political grounds. See 7

Because these provisions preserved the special privileges of public officers that Allied authorities had worked hard to eliminate, they were viewed as a victory for the civil servants' lobby.[214] As the Constitutional Court has emphasized, however, they also serve the broader and more important purpose of promoting the rule of law by limiting political influence on the execution of the laws.[215] Of course the politically responsible ministers exercise extensive control over the administration through their authority to appoint and instruct inferior officers.[216] In most cases, indeed, civil servants are expected to accept their superiors' decisions as to the legality of their orders. The official's ultimate responsibility, however, is to the nation, not to a particular government;[217] and in the extreme case he may even have a duty to resist illegitimate instructions.[218]

The question of autonomy in the civil service exposes a tension between basic constitutional values, for freedom from political influence means freedom from democratic control. This tension is exacerbated by the existence of certain executive or administrative bodies, at both federal and state levels, that are situated outside the normal hierarchy of direct ministerial control.

BVerfGE at 164-70; cf. Elrod v. Burns, 427 U.S. 347 (1976) (drawing a similar distinction for purposes of determining when patronage dismissals offend the guarantee of free expression in the United States). For complaints about the increasing incidence of patronage hiring in Germany in the teeth of the nondiscrimination provision of Art. 33(2) see Lecheler, supra, Rdnr. 20, 104, 107-09.

[214] See Wolfgang Benz, Von der Besatzungsherrschaft zur Bundesrepublik 113-16, 208-09 (1984).

[215] See 7 BVerfGE at 162-63, invoking the debates in the Parliamentary Council and emphasizing the virtues of stability, neutrality, and "a counterweight to the political forces" that determine public affairs; Schröder, Die Bereiche der Regierung und der Verwaltung, 3 Handbuch des Staatsrechts 499, Rdnr. 31.

[216] Technically all officers are appointed by the Bundespräsident under Art. 61(1) GG. Like most of his actions, however, appointments require the countersignature of the responsible minister, who makes the actual decision. See Art. 58 GG; Lecheler, supra note 213, Rdnr. 75. See also Walter Krebs, Verwaltungsorganisation, 3 Handbuch des Staatsrechts 567, Rdnr. 55 (arguing that constitutional provisions for direct federal administration imply a high degree of centralized control).

[217] See Lecheler, supra note 213, Rdnr. 91, 103. See also id., Rdnr. 51-53 (adding that objectivity on the part of the public servant is a constitutional command).

[218] See Loschelder, supra note 208, Rdnr. 92-102; Ulrich Battis, Der Verfassungsverstoß und seine Rechtsfolgen, 7 Handbuch des Staatsrechts 231, Rdnr. 47. The entire executive authority, of course, is bound by law ("Gesetz und Recht") under Art. 20(3). Like the Bundespräsident's oath to uphold the constitution (see text at note 185 supra), however, this provision does not tell us what the law requires the individual officer to do. See also Art. 20(4) GG, which codifies the right of revolution espoused by Locke and invoked in our Declaration of Independence: "All Germans shall have the right to resist any person or persons seeking to abolish th[e] constitutional order, should no other remedy be possible." See generally Rudolf Dolzer, Der Widerstandsfall, 7 Handbuch des Staatsrechts 455.

A few such organizations can trace their pedigree to the Basic Law itself. Most significant perhaps is the Bundesbank, a close cousin of our Federal Reserve Board, which is entrusted with the issuance of paper money and stabilization of the currency.[219] Article 88 says nothing about the structure of this bank, but the history of central banks in Germany leaves no doubt that an institution independent of the Cabinet was contemplated.[220] Accordingly, the statute expressly insulates the Bundesbank from Cabinet direction, requiring the Bank to support the overall economic policy of the Government only to the extent consistent with its own particular obligations ("unter Wahrung ihrer Aufgabe").[221] Similarly, Article 114 expressly envisions an even more independent auditing office ("Bundesrechnungshof") to supervise public accounts.[222] The former provision reflects the teaching of experience that politically responsible governments cannot be trusted to give monetary stability the priority it deserves,[223] the latter the conviction that public confidence in government requires auditing by a truly impartial outsider.[224]

Article 87 contemplates additional federal administrative bodies outside the normal hierarchy of direct ministerial supervision. Paragraph 2 of that Article requires that social-insurance agencies with responsibilities transcending state lines be conducted as public corporations; paragraph 3 permits the erection of additional public corporations and institutions ("bundesunmittelbare Körperschaften und Anstalten des öffentlichen Rechtes") in fields in which the Bund

---

[219] These powers are suggested by Art. 88 of the Basic Law itself, which speaks of a note-issuing and currency bank ("eine Währungs- und Notenbank"). To the end of controlling the money supply the Bundesbank has statutory authority among other things to fix interest and discount rates, to establish minimum reserve requirements for banks, and to make purchases and sales in the open market. See Maunz in 3 Maunz/Dürig, Art. 88, Rdnr. 29-40. Cf. 12 U.S.C. ch. 3 (Federal Reserve).

[220] See Maunz in 3 Maunz/Dürig, Art. 88, Rdnr. 16, 18-19 .

[221] See id., Rdnr. 17, 20.

[222] Art. 114 expressly requires that members of the Bundesrechnungshof enjoy "the independence of judges," which is discussed in the text at notes 253-307 infra. A similar institution had been created by statute during the Weimar period. See Friedrich Ernst Moritz Saemisch in 2 Anschütz & Thoma, supra note 114, at 447-48. See also Maunz in 4 Maunz/Dürig, Art. 114, Rdnr. 17-24; Kisker, supra note 10, Rdnr. 125 (complaining of excessive executive influence in the selection of members).

[223] See Maunz in 3 Maunz/Dürig, Art. 88, Rdnr. 16.

[224] In the field of higher education, the Art. 5(3) guarantee of academic freedom ("Wissenschaft, Forschung und Lehre") has been held to require a significant degree of self-government by faculties of public universities. E.g., 35 BVerfGE 79 (1973); see Krebs, supra note 216, Rdnr. 71. Cf. 12 BVerfGE 205 (1961) (holding that the guarantee of broadcasting freedom in Art. 5(1) forbade state interference with the management and program-ming of public television stations). See generally chapter 4 infra.

has legislative authority. The traditional concept of a public corporation or institution implies some degree of independence from ordinary ministerial control.[225]

As we move from modest civil service provisions to the more radical notion of autonomous administrative bodies, however, the tension between the desire for neutrality and the basic principles of parliamentary democracy becomes more acute. The difficulty was neatly illustrated by an important 1959 decision of the Constitutional Court.[226] A statute of the state of Bremen gave public officials and employees a say in decisions affecting staffing and conditions of employment. If the agency and the representatives of its personnel ("Personalrat") disagreed, the dispute was to be resolved by an arbitration panel on which the presiding officer of the state legislature held the balance of power.[227] Insofar as this measure applied to personnel decisions involving public officials ("Beamte"), the Court held it unconstitutional.

The fact that a member of the legislature was a member of the panel, the Court said, did not condemn the provision. The heart of the separation of powers requirement, made applicable to the states by Article 28(1) of the Basic Law, was to enable the various branches of government to act as checks on one another; a certain shifting of power in favor of the legislature was no cause for concern in a parliamentary democracy.[228]

What was wrong with the provision, in the Court's view, was that depriving the state Cabinet of power to make its own personnel decisions was inconsistent with the principle of responsible government implicit in the Article 28 prescription of democracy and the rule of law. "The autonomous authority of the Cabinet to make political decisions, its ability to carry out its constitutional duties, and its substantive responsibility to the people and to Parliament are obligatory requirements of the constitution of a democratic state characterized by the rule of law." Not every administrative function had necessarily to be subject to ministerial control.

> Yet there are some duties which, because of their political significance [wegen ihrer politischen Tragweite], may not be generally taken out of the area of Cabinet responsibility and transferred to agencies independent of both Cabinet and Parliament. If this were

---

[225] See Krebs, supra note 216, Rdnr. 55; Maunz in 3 Maunz/Dürig Art. 87, Rdnr. 66. The same provision also expressly authorizes the establishment of autonomous higher federal agencies ("selbständige Bundesoberbehörden") under the same conditions, but the term "autonomous" in this connection is understood to imply organizational distinctness rather than freedom from ministerial direction. See id., Rdnr. 83; Hans Peter Bull in 2 AK-GG, Art. 87, Rdnr. 28.

[226] 9 BVerfGE 268 (1958).

[227] The agency and the Personalrat each chose three other members of the panel. See id. at 269, 271-72.

[228] Id. at 279-80. See note 211 supra.

not so, it would be impossible for the Cabinet to bear the responsibility imposed upon it [by the Basic Law], since unsupervised agencies responsible to no one would be in a position to influence the administration.

Control over personnel decisions respecting public officers, the Court concluded, was an essential attribute of Cabinet authority, since the reliability and disinterestedness of the public service depended largely upon them: "The appointment of a poorly qualified official can impair or paralyze the work of an entire branch of the administration for years to come . . . ."[229]

Knowledgeable commentators disagree as to the scope of the doctrine enunciated in this decision.[230] As already noted, the Basic Law itself modifies the principle of responsible government by requiring an independent auditor and permitting an autonomous central bank. It is sometimes said that these explicit provisions are narrow exceptions to a general constitutional prohibition of "ministerialfreie Räume" – areas of administration immunized from ministerial control. The constitutional guarantee of parliamentary democracy, it is argued, normally requires a chain of authority reaching from the people by way of Parliament and Cabinet to those engaged in administering the laws.[231] The Court itself, however, has subsequently

---

[229] 9 BVerfGE at 281-84. For similar reasons the statute was held to offend the traditional civil service principles that Art. 33(5) requires both state and federal authorities to respect: The public official's responsibility to obey the laws and the lawful orders of his superiors was incompatible with his dependency on anyone else. Id. at 285-88. The Court added, however, that decisions as to "social" matters not directly affecting the duties of public officers, as well as even employment decisions affecting employees with lesser responsibilities ("Angestellte" and "Arbeiter"), might constitutionally be entrusted to the arbitration panels in question. Id. at 284-85.

[230] On the one hand it can be argued that the decision is a narrow one: Of course the Cabinet must be in a position to carry out its responsibilities, but the Basic Law does not say what those responsibilities are. See Art. 65 GG (empowering each minister to conduct "the affairs of his department" on his own responsibility); Wolfgang Müller, Ministerialfreie Räume, 25 JuS 497 (1985); Herzog in 3 Maunz/Dürig, Art. 65, Rdnr. 106 (stressing that the decision dealt only with administrative organization). On the other hand, one might respond that the framers of the Basic Law would hardly have bothered to ensure ministerial control of personnel decisions while permitting the entire subject being administered to be withdrawn from ministerial responsibility.

[231] See, e.g., Loschelder, supra note 208, Rdnr. 20-22, 37-40, 59; Erhard Denninger, Auswirkungen der Verfassungsrechtsprechung auf Verwaltung und Verwaltungsverfahren, 25 Der Staat 103, 107 (1986). See also 55 BVerfGE 144, 149 (1980) (finding that the relevant minister had sufficient authority over the setting of certain freight rates to satisfy the principle of ministerial responsibility ("das Prinzip der parlamentarischen Ministerverantwortlichkeit")); Sten. Ber. at 13 (Delegate Schmid): "Public officers must be appointed by ministers who themselves are confirmed and installed by a generally elected Parliament." The historical and functional test employed by the Constitutional Court in determining that a sub-

endorsed the establishment of independent committees or examiners to resolve disputes over individual tax assessments or to determine which publications are harmful to minors, on the ground that such decisions fall outside the policymaking realm ("dem Bereich der politischen Gestaltung") that the Basic Law reserves to the Cabinet.[232] Other observers point to the proliferation of more or less independent agencies and suggest that parliamentary control need not imply cabinet control. Even those unwilling to limit autonomous agencies to those specifically contemplated by the constitution, however, tend to conclude that there are narrow limits to the ability to remove important executive functions from political supervision entirely.[233] For as every student of government in the United States knows, the creation of independent agencies not only impairs democratic control of executive action; it also undermines the principle of unified executive policy implicit in constitutional provisions for parliamentary as well as presidential government.[234]

To the extent that federal agencies are free from ministerial direction, however, they are also relatively free from parliamentary interference. More significantly, additional structural separation be-

---

sidiary role in the supervision of banks was implicit in the conception of a "currency and note-issuing bank" under Art. 88 (14 BVerfGE 197, 215-19 (1962)), while serving in that case to delimit the boundary between federal and state powers, seems no less appropriate for determining the range of administrative activity that the same Article permits to be removed from ministerial control.

[232] 22 BVerfGE 106, 113 (1967); 83 BVerfGE 130, 150 (1990). Committee decisions in the first case were subject to review by the courts at the instance of the administration, but not by the administration itself.

[233] See, e.g., Krebs, supra note 216, Rdnr. 80-83; Müller, supra note 230, at 508; Herzog in 3 Maunz/Dürig, Art. 65, Rdnr. 103 (analogizing the relinquishment of parliamentary control over executive action to the delegation of rulemaking authority and suggesting a similar test of "essential" executive functions).

[234] Cf. Myers v. United States, 272 U.S. 52 (1926), a decision sadly eroded by later developments. See Humphrey's Executor v. United States, 295 U.S. 602 (1935); Morrison v. Olson, 487 U.S. 654 (1988). When executive authority is delegated to public bodies composed of those most immediately affected (e.g., disciplinary proceedings before professional associations), the democratic concern for parliamentary control is counterbalanced by the equally democratic argument of self-determination. See Hendler, supra note 158, Rdnr. 48-49, 56. The transfer of executive responsibilities to *private* organizations, on the other hand, is particularly problematic in light of theArt. 20(2) requirement that public authority be exercised by specified organs of government and the command of Art. 33(4) that governmental responsibilities be entrusted "as a rule" to civil servants. It was on this ground that the Bundespräsident recently refused to sign a law that would have privatized the business of air traffic control, which entails giving orders to pilots that have the force of law. See note 184 supra. See also Krebs, supra note 216, Rdnr. 10. For the impact of the organizational freedom guaranteed to workers by Art. 9(3) on the ability of workers and managers to set wages binding on nonparties see 34 BVerfGE 307, 315-20 (1973).

tween legislative and executive authority is provided by the Article 83 requirement that most federal laws be carried out by the Länder.

As I have explained elsewhere,[235] the Cabinet is given a variety of tools for ensuring that the Länder actually fulfill their enforcement duties. Outside those few areas in which the Länder enforce federal laws as agents of the Federation ("im Auftrag des Bundes"),[236] however, direct federal supervision is basically limited to ensuring the legality of administrative action rather than controlling the exercise of discretion in particular cases.[237] Moreover, the most effective of these tools can be employed only with the consent of the Bundesrat – that is, by a weighted vote of the states themselves.[238] Thus in Germany the vertical principle of federalism compensates to a significant extent for the lack of horizontal separation of powers that inheres in a parliamentary system.[239] Since Länder agencies are generally subject to direction by ministers reponsible to the state Parliament, it does so – in contrast to the creation of independent federal agencies – without impairing the important principle of democratic control.

In short, while there is less structural separation between the legislature and high executive officers in the Federal Republic than in the United States, those officers have less power over the administration than their counterparts in this country. Executive authority is divided among the Cabinet, the civil service, federal agencies and institutions outside the normal administrative hierarchy, and the Länder in such a way that the Bundestag has much less influence on those who actually enforce the law than one might expect in a parliamentary system.

III. JUDICIAL POWER

Unlike the executive, the German courts are entirely independent. Indeed in several respects their power to act as a check on

---

[235] See chapter 2 supra.

[236] Art. 85 GG. In these cases state agencies are subject to federal instructions respecting not only the legality ("Gesetzmäßigkeit") but also the appropriateness ("Zweckmäßigkeit") of their actions. See Art. 85(4), (5).

[237] See Art. 84(3): "The Federal Government [Bundesregierung] shall exercise supervision to ensure that the Länder execute federal laws in accordance with applicable law [dem geltenden Rechte gemäß]." See also Peter Lerche in 3 Maunz/Dürig, Art. 84, Rdnr. 152; Krebs, supra note 216, Rdnr. 41. Länder discretion may be limited by the issuance of general administrative rules ("Verwaltungsvorschriften") (Art. 84(2)) or (if the statute so provides) by regulations that also bind third parties ("Rechtsverordnungen") (Art. 80(1)). In either case the rule becomes part of the "law" that the state agency is required to apply in taking individual actions. See Lerche, supra, Rdnr. 157.

[238] See Art. 37, 80(2), 84(2), (4), (5) GG.

[239] See Otto Kimminich, Der Bundesstaat, 1 Handbuch des Staatsrechts 1113, Rdnr. 45; Herzog in 2 Maunz/Dürig, Art. 20, Abschnitt V, Rdnr. 28, 35.

abuses of authority by other organs of government is better protected than that of courts in the United States.

In contrast to most of their counterparts in this country, German courts are organized by subject matter. The Basic Law provides for a Federal Constitutional Court ("Bundesverfassungsgericht") and for a series of specialized federal supreme courts ("oberste Gerichtshöfe") in the fields of administrative law ("Bundesverwaltungsgericht"), taxation ("Bundesfinanzhof"), labor ("Bundesarbeitsgericht"), and social security ("Bundessozialgericht"), as well as a more general supreme court for other civil and criminal matters ("Bundesgerichtshof").[240] With few exceptions, moreover, there are no lower federal courts. Just as most federal laws are administered in the first instance by state executive officers, most lawsuits based on federal law are brought initially in state courts, which are likewise organized on subject matter lines.[241] In the United States such an arrangement would raise fears both of distracting litigation over jurisdictional boundaries and of inadequate enforcement of federal rights.[242] In Germany neither seems to have been a problem.[243]

In comparison with our Bill of Rights, the otherwise rather detailed Basic Law has surprisingly little to say about judicial procedure. Article 103 contains a ban on double jeopardy, a prohibition of

---

[240] See Art. 93-95 GG. As Walter Menzel explained in the Parliamentary Council in arguing for a separate labor court, no judge can be an expert in every field. Sten. Ber. at 31.

[241] See Art. 92 GG: "Judicial power . . . shall be exercised by the Federal Constitutional Court, by the federal courts provided for in this Basic Law, and by the courts of the Länder." Apart from the Constitutional Court and the supreme courts listed in Art. 95, the only federal courts provided for are for industrial property ("Angelegenheiten des gewerblichen Rechtsschutzes") and for disciplinary matters in the military and civil service. Art. 96(1), (2), (4).

[242] For a humble example justifying the former concern, consider the horrors that have arisen in attempting to distinguish the jurisdiction of our Court of Appeals for the Federal Circuit under 28 U.S.C. § 1295 from that of the ordinary Courts of Appeals under §§ 1291-92, as hinted at in David P. Currie, Federal Courts 601 (4th ed. 1990). For typical expressions of concern about the adequacy of appellate review to protect federal rights in the United States see Osborn v. Bank of the United States, 22 U.S. 738, 822-23 (1824); England v. Louisiana State Bd. of Medical Examiners, 375 U.S. 411, 416 (1964). The well-known benefits and costs of specialized courts in this country are discussed in hideous detail in David Currie & Frank Goodman, Judicial Review of Federal Administrative Action: Quest for the Optimum Forum, 75 Colum. L. Rev. 1 (1975).

[243] Art. 95 originally provided for creation of a separate tribunal to resolve differences of opinion among the various specialized judicial branches. So few conflicts arose, however, that no such court was ever established. The present Art. 95(3) substitutes a more practicable joint panel ("Gemeinsamer Senat") composed of members of the various Supreme Courts, as had been suggested in the Parliamentary Council. See Sten. Ber. at 185 (Delegate Dehler); Herzog in 4 Maunz/Dürig, Art. 95, Rdnr. 52-60. For discussion of the federalism aspects of this question see chapter 2 supra.

ex post facto punishments, and a requirement that offenses be specifically defined by statute;[244] Article 104 requires that persons taken into custody be brought before a judge by the end of the following day and prescribes in some detail the components of the preliminary hearing.[245] There is no explicit mention of the privilege against self-incrimination, the right to a speedy or public trial, the right to subpoena and confront witnesses, the right to counsel, or even the right to be informed of the nature and cause of the accusation.[246]

This is not to say that there are no such rights, or that they exist at legislative pleasure.[247] Article 103(1) guarantees every litigant (in civil as well as criminal matters) a hearing in accordance with law ("rechtliches Gehör"). In determining the contours of this hearing the Constitutional Court has begun to constitutionalize some of the elements of what we would consider a fair trial.

Central to the concept of a judicial hearing in Article 103 is the right to present one's case ("Äußerung") and have it considered ("Berücksichtigung").[248] To make this right meaningful, the Court has convincingly held that decisions may be based only on information that has been made available to the parties for possible rebuttal.[249] In addition, the Court has been quite aggressive in insisting that the right to be heard may not be forfeited by failure to file papers within the prescribed time period without some fault on the part of the party or of his attorney.[250]

---

[244] Art. 103(2), (3) GG.

[245] Art. 104(2)-(5) GG.

[246] Cf. U.S. Const., amend. V-VI.

[247] Under the first clause of Art. 74 the Federation has concurrent legislative authority over the procedures of state as well as federal courts – subject, of course, to limitations found elsewhere in the Basic Law. See chapter 2 supra.

[248] For general statements of these two requirements see, e.g., 64 BVerfGE 135, 143-44 (1983); Eberhard Schmidt-Aßmann in 4 Maunz/Dürig, Art. 103(1), Rdnr. 21, 66-67. Cf. the provisions of our Administrative Procedure Act, 5 U.S.C. § 553(b), (c), for so-called notice-and-comment rulemaking by administrative agencies. For particulars respecting the right to be heard see, e.g., 4 BVerfGE 190, 191-92 (1955) (adequate time to contest appeal of favorable decision); 5 BVerfGE 9, 11 (1956) (no constitutional right to oral argument); 60 BVerfGE 250, 252 (1982) (duty to hear all witnesses offered by the parties). Whether a judge has actually considered the submissions of the parties is obviously not always subject to proof, yet in a surprising number of cases the Constitutional Court has found that they were not considered. E.g., 11 BVerfGE 218, 219-20 (1960) (where it was admitted that the judges were unaware of the submission); 18 BVerfGE 380, 383-84 (1965) (where the submission had been erroneously rejected as untimely).

[249] E.g., 10 BVerfGE 177, 182-84 (1959); 12 BVerfGE 110, 112-113 (1961). Cf. Ohio Bell Tel. Co. v. Public Utilities Comm., 301 U.S. 292 (1937); Portland Cement Ass'n v. Ruckelshaus, 486 F.2d 375 393 (D.C. Cir. 1973).

[250] Thus late filings have regularly been excused on the ground that the defaulting party was on vacation when notice reached his home (25 BVerfGE 158, 166 (1969)), that mail delivery was unusually delayed (40 BVerfGE 42, 44-46 (1975)), that the party had relied on misleading official advice (40 BVerfGE 46, 50-51 (1975)),

Interestingly, the Court has not gone much beyond these elementary principles in interpreting Article 103(1). For unexplained reasons it has tended in declaring other procedural rights to find them implicit either in the rule of law or in particular substantive provisions of the Bill of Rights ("Grundrechtskatalog"). Thus, for example, both the right to an attorney and the right to a translator have been said to derive not from the explicit guarantee of a hearing but from the general principles of the rule of law,[251] while unreasonable procedural restrictions on a landlord's right to justify a rent increase have been held to offend the guarantee of property rights in Article 14.[252]

Taken all together, this case law has established an impressive battery of procedural rights of constitutional rank. The fact remains that the Constitutional Court has been much less preoccupied with procedural questions than has the Supreme Court of the United States.[253]

---

or that he was unable to understand the German language (40 BVerfGE 95, 99-100 (1975)). For the suggestion that the Court may have been overly generous in this regard see Schmidt-Aßmann in 4 Maunz/Dürig, Art. 103(1), Rdnr. 126. Contrast Wainwright v. Sykes, 433 U.S. 72 (1977) (permitting even constitutional rights in the context of a criminal proceeding to be lost for failure to raise them in time absent an affirmative showing of cause).

[251] The theory is that any interference with one's general freedom of action can be justified only by the constitutional order, the rights of others, or the moral code (Art. 2(1)); that any action inconsistent with the rule of law fails to satisfy these conditions; and that a fair trial is an element of the rule of law guaranteed by Art. 20(3). See 38 BVerfGE 105, 111-18 (1974) (attorney); 64 BVerfGE 135, 145-57 (1983) (translator). For criticism of these decisions see Schmidt-Aßmann in 4 Maunz/Dürig, Art. 103(1), Rdnr. 9, 103, 117-18 (arguing that the more specific provision of Art. 103(1) should take precedence and cogently noting that in many cases the right to a hearing is meaningless without the aid of an attorney or translator). Cf. Powell v. Alabama, 287 U.S. 45, 68-69 (1932).

[252] 53 BVerfGE 352, 358-61 (1980). See also 56 BVerfGE 37, 41-52 (1981) (tracing the privilege against self-incrimination to the provisions protecting human dignity (Art. 1(1)) and the right to development of personality (Art. 2(1))). For other examples see chapter 6 infra; Schmidt-Aßmann in 4 Maunz/Dürig, Art. 103(1), Rdnr. 8. This approach has the advantage of permitting the Court to find constitutional requirements for administrative as well as judicial procedure – unlike that based on Art. 103(1), which is expressly directed to the courts. Art. 19(4), which guarantees judicial review of administrative action (see text at notes 307-16 infra), is likewise understood to require procedures adequate to make such review effective. Its central focus, however, is on access to the courts; the quality of the judicial proceeding is governed principally by Art. 103(1). See Schmidt-Aßmann in 2 Maunz/Dürig, Art. 19, Rdnr. 19-26, and in 4 id., Art. 103(1), Rdnr. 7.

[253] Although it has been estimated that as many as forty-five percent of all constitutional complaints before the Court have concerned the right to a hearing under Art. 103(1), the vast bulk of these complaints present no new question of law, and the Court functions essentially to correct plain violations of the established rules. See Schmidt-Aßmann in 4 Maunz/Dürig, Art. 103(1), Rdnr. 157, 159.

A. Judicial Independence

With respect to the courts, the general separation of powers principle of Article 20(2) is reinforced by the flat statement in Article 92 that judicial authority is vested in judges of the various courts and by the unequivocal command of Article 97(1) that the judges be independent and subject only to law ("unabhängig und nur dem Gesetz unterworfen").[254] The requirement that judges follow the law forbids them to play favorites or to impose their own personal preferences. The requirement of independence protects them against outside influence, especially by other branches of government.[255]

Perhaps the most fundamental dimension of judicial independence is the organizational command of Article 20(2) that legislative, executive, and judicial functions be vested in distinct bodies ("besondere Organe").[256] This not only means that no legislative or executive agency may exercise judicial functions as such;[257] it also limits the ability of the same individual to serve simultaneously as both legislator or administrator and judge. Article 94(1) makes this incompatibility principle explicit as to members of the Constitutional Court;[258] as to other judges the Court has found its core implicit in

---

[254] In this context the term "Gesetz," despite its narrower alternative connotations, is understood to include all authoritative sources of positive law. See, e.g., Herzog in 4 Maunz/Dürig, Art. 97, Rdnr. 4-5; Günther Barbey, Der Status des Richters, 3 Handbuch des Staatsrechts 815, Rdnr. 32. For the disputed significance of the additional provision of Art. 20(3) binding the judiciary to "Recht" as well as "Gesetz" see text at notes 85-103 (discussing the *Soraya* case). For the argument that Art. 97(1) requires as a general rule that judges be trained in the law in order to be in a position to obey it see Herzog, supra, Art. 92, Rdnr. 77-84.

[255] See Wilhelm Karl Geck, Wahl und Status der Bundesverfassungsrichter, 2 Handbuch des Staatsrechts 697, Rdnr. 29-30, 49-51.

[256] See Herzog in 4 Maunz/Dürig, Art. 97, Rdnr. 10.

[257] See 14 BVerfGE 56, 67 (1962) (deriving from Art. 20(2) the requirement that the courts be "sufficiently separate from administrative agencies in the organizational sense"); Karl August Bettermann, Die rechtsprechende Gewalt, 3 Handbuch des Staatsrechts 775, Rdnr. 5, adding that the Basic Law itself makes two exceptions to this rule: Art. 84(4) makes it the responsibility of the Bundesrat in the first instance to determine whether one of the Länder has failed in its duty to enforce federal law, and Art. 10(2) authorizes the legislature to substitute agencies of its own for courts in passing upon the legality of electronic and postal surveillance in national security cases. Added in 1968, the latter provision was upheld with some difficulty over the objection that it contradicted fundamental principles of Art. 20, which Art. 79(3) protects even against constitutional amendment. See text at notes 354-55 infra. See also Art. 41(1) GG, noted in text at notes 60-61 supra, which in order to safeguard the independence of the Bundestag makes it basically the judge of the credentials of its own members.

[258] "They may not be members of the Bundestag, the Bundesrat, the Federal Government, or of any of the corresponding organs of a Land." The universal un-

the general requirement of separate judicial institutions in Article 20. Emphasizing the obvious inherent conflicts of interest, for example, the Court held in 1959 that mayors, municipal administrators, and members of municipal councils could not constitutionally act as judges in criminal matters that might also affect their other official duties.[259] Three years later, however, the Court gave notice that the incompatibility principle was not so absolute as one might have expected by permitting municipal officials to serve as judges in small claims controversies between private parties in which the local government itself had no interest.[260] Apart from the specific provision regarding the Constitutional Court, the constitutional incompatibility doctrine thus appears to be one largely of neutrality rather than of separation.[261]

---

derstanding that this is only an incompatibility and not an ineligibility provision is reflected in the statute establishing the Constitutional Court, which after repeating the language of Art. 94(1) adds that Justices cease to be members of the named governmental bodies upon their appointment to the Court. BVerfGG § 3(3). See also § 3(4) of the same statute, which extends the incompatibility principle further by barring the Justices from any professional activity except that of law professor at a German university.

[259] 10 BVerfGE 200, 216-18 (1959). See also 18 BVerfGE 241, 255-56 (1964) (holding for similar reasons that members of the executive or policymaking branches of a professional association could not serve as judges in cases involving complaints of unprofessional conduct).

[260] 14 BVerfGE 56, 68-69 (1962). Thus in the result the incompatibility doctrine the Constitutional Court has derived from the separation of powers is somewhat reminiscent of the limitations our Supreme Court has found in the due process clause in such cases as Tumey v. Ohio, 273 U.S. 510 (1927).

[261] But see Herzog in 2 Maunz/Dürig, Art. 20, Abschnitt V, Rdnr. 47, 49 (arguing that Art. 20(2) also forbids members of the Bundestag or of the Cabinet to serve simultaneously as judges). See also Deutsches Richtergesetz vom 8. Sept. 1961, BGBl I S. 1665 [hereafter cited as DRiG], § 4, which subjects judges to a broad statutory incompatibility rule.

On the related question of the extent to which judges may be entrusted with non-judicial functions the Constitutional Court has been somewhat equivocal. In 1971 it held that an authorization to examine witnesses in conjunction with an administrative investigation did not compromise judicial independence precisely because in so doing the judge was *not* engaged in adjudication. 31 BVerfGE 43, 45-46. See also Rudolf Wassermann in 2 AK-GG, Art. 92, Rdnr. 39 (concluding that the Basic Law does not forbid giving judges nonjudicial duties). Subsequent decisions, however, have upheld the grant of such arguably extracurricular functions as the correction of land registers only after concluding that they were closely related to some traditional judicial function. 76 BVerfGE 100, 106 (1987); see also 64 BVerfGE 175, 179-80 (1983) (computations incident to financial arrangements on divorce). For American analogies contrast Hayburn's Case, 2 U.S. 409, 410-14 n. (a) (1792), where five Justices on circuit convincingly concluded that federal judges as such could not exercise nonjudicial functions, with the troublesome decision in Mistretta v. United States, 488 U.S. 361 (1989) (permitting judges to serve as members of a sentencing commission with substantive rulemaking powers).

No less obvious is the conclusion that Article 97(1) affords the judges what the Germans call substantive ("sachliche") independence: They are subject to no one else's orders.[262] Article 101(1) contains two further provisions designed to preclude either the legislature or the executive from affecting judicial decisions by determining which judges will hear a particular case. Ad hoc courts ("Ausnahmegerichte") are flatly prohibited,[263] and no one may be removed from the jurisdiction of his lawful judge ("seinem gesetzlichen Richter entzogen werden"). The latter provision, though hardly self-explanatory, requires among other things that both jurisdiction and the assignment of judges within a multimember tribunal be fixed in advance as nearly as practicable – all in the interest of reducing the risk of outside influence on judicial decisions.[264]

To make the guarantee of substantive independence a reality, however, the judges must be personally independent as well.[265] Other provisions of the Basic Law help to specify just what this means.

Not surprisingly, the judges are not free from political influence with respect to their appointment. In a country in which all power emanates from the people, the judges like other public servants require democratic legitimation.[266] In recognition of the political

---

[262] See 3 BVerfGE 213, 224 (1953); Herzog in 4 Maunz/Dürig, Art. 97, Rdnr. 9, 22-24; Geck, supra note 255, Rdnr. 49.

[263] As Art. 101(2) acknowledges, this provision does not preclude the creation of specialized courts for such subjects as labor law; Art. 95 expressly contemplates them. What Art. 101 requires is that their jurisdiction be specified by statute, in general terms, and in advance. See 3 BVerfGE 213, 223 (1953); Christoph Degenhart, Gerichtsorganisation, 3 Handbuch des Staatsrechts 859, Rdnr. 27.

[264] See 4 BVerfGE 412, 416 (adding that the prohibition of extraordinary courts was designed to prevent evasion of this provision); 17 BVerfGE 294, 298-302 (1964); Degenhart, supra note 263, Rdnr. 17-24; Eduard Kern in 2 Anschütz & Thoma, supra note 114, at 491-95 (discussing a comparable Weimar provision). Art. 101(1) serves also as the procedural tool enabling individual litigants to challenge the status of those who pass upon their cases; for a judge who does not satisfy all the constitutional requirements for the exercise of judicial authority cannot be the "lawful judge" to whom every litigant is entitled. See 10 BVerfGE 200, 213 (1959); Barbey, supra note 254, Rdnr. 62.

[265] See Herzog in 4 Maunz/Dürig, Art. 97, Rdnr. 11, 47; Geck, supra note 255, Rdnr. 50; Wassermann in 2 AK-GG, Art. 97, Rdnr. 15: "The guarantee of freedom from instructions would be ineffective if the judge had to fear dismissal or transfer in the event of an unpleasing decision."

[266] See Art. 20(1) GG; Geck, supra note 255, Rdnr. 6; Wassermann in 2 AK-GG, Art. 92, Rdnr. 13a-14. Thus the Constitutional Court has held that Art. 92, which vests judicial power in courts of the Bund and of the Länder, permits municipalities or public corporations to exercise such power only if the state itself has a decisive say in selecting the judges. See 10 BVerfGE 200, 214-15 (1959) (holding that municipal courts were Länder courts within the meaning of Art. 92); 18 BVerfGE 241, 253-54 (1964) (rejecting objections in principle to the exercise of judicial powers by a

significance of the Constitutional Court's decisions, half of its members are chosen by the Bundestag and half by the Bundesrat, which represents the state governments.[267] Judges of the five supreme courts are selected by the federal minister with responsibility over the subject matter in conjunction with a committee ("Richterwahlausschuß") on which the respective state ministers and the Bundestag have an equal voice.[268] The appointment of state-court judges is regulated by the Länder, subject to more or less general principles that may be laid down in federal framework legislation ("Rahmenvorschriften")[269] and to the Article 28 requirement that they respect the principles of "republican, democratic, and social government based on the rule of law."

Once appointed, however, the judges enjoy a significant measure of job security. In contrast to federal judges in the United States, who can be removed under extraordinary but unreviewable circumstances by the Senate,[270] most German judges can be removed, suspended, transferred, or retired during their term of office only pursuant to the decision of other judges.[271] By confining this pro-

---

medical association organized as a corporation under public law but invalidating a provision for judicial selection by members of that body).

[267] Art. 94(1) GG. The implementing statute provides for indirect election of those members chosen by the Bundestag, evidently in the interest of efficiency. The constitutionality of this departure has been questioned on the ground that election by the Bundestag itself would provide a greater measure of democratic legitimacy. The statute also requires a two-thirds vote for approval of each appointment, in the interest of assuring broad popular support for the institution. Any implication that Justices were appointed to further the policies of a particular political majority, it is argued, could impair the public confidence on which the Court's effectiveness depends. In practice the two major parties (SPD and CDU/CSU) have agreed to divide the seats equally, reserving one of those assigned to whichever party happens to be in the Cabinet for its inevitable coalition partner, the FDP. One of the consequences has been that most of the Justices have been either members of the major parties or very close to them – a situation which has also been called detrimental to the image of a disinterested Court. See Geck, supra note 255, Rdnr. 7-20. For a peek into the politics of judicial selection and thumbnail sketches of early Justices see Donald P. Kommers, Judicial Politics in West Germany: A Study of the Federal Constitutional Court 120-44 (1976).

[268] Art. 95(2) GG. Both the federal minister and the committee must agree on the choice. See Maunz in 4 Maunz/Dürig, Art. 95, Rdnr. 63.

[269] Art. 98(3) GG. See Herzog in 4 Maunz/Dürig, Art. 98, Rdnr. 1-2, 13-14, 34-40 (also noting the tradition of ministerial appointment of Länder judges and the explicit provision in Art. 98(4) permitting participation by a committee such as those that help to select most federal judges). The concept of framework legislation is discussed in chapter 2 supra.

[270] U.S. Const., Art. I, §§ 2, 3; Art. II, § 4. See Nixon v. United States, 113 S. Ct. 732 (1993).

[271] Art. 97(2) GG ("nur kraft richterlicher Entscheidung"). Thus even as it held that municipal officials could constitutionally sit as judges in cases involving small claims between private parties (see text at notes 259-60 supra), the Consti-

tection to judges with full-time regular appointments ("die haupt-amtlich und planmäßig endgültig angestellten Richter"), however, Article 97(2) implies that not all judges enjoy this protection. Indeed the perceived need for training positions, for nonlegal expertise, and for community participation has generated a longstanding assortment of probationary, part-time, and lay judges who fall outside the express limitations on premature removal.[272] Acutely aware that abuse of this practice might undermine the more comprehensive requirement of substantive independence set forth in Article 97(1), the Constitutional Court has insisted that the use of nontenured judges be kept to a minimum and that absent extraordinary circumstances not more than one probationary judge at a time pass judgment on any particular case.[273]

---

tutional Court found it contrary to Art. 97(2) to provide that they lost their position as judges when they left the local government, because this arrangement effectively enabled the municipality to fire the judge. 14 BVerfGE 56, 71-72 (1962). Further provisions for removal on the basis of criminal conviction or after a formal disciplinary proceeding were upheld since in both cases removal depended upon judicial decision. Id. at 71. See also 17 BVerfGE 252, 259-62 (1964) (holding Art. 97(2) offended by a selective assignment of cases that left a judge with essentially nothing to do even though he had not been formally transferred, retired, suspended, or removed). The further provision of Art. 97(2) permitting transfer or discharge of judges upon restructuring of the court system itself ("Veränderung der Gerichte oder ihrer Bezirke") has an obvious practical explanation but has been criticized as a potentially significant gap in the guarantee of an independent judiciary. See Herzog in 4 Maunz/Dürig, Art. 97, Rdnr. 53-54 (insisting that courts may not be abolished or otherwise altered in order to get rid of individual judges or influence a particular case). Cf. the Jeffersonian Judiciary Act of 1802, 2 Stat. 132, which is widely understood to have abolished the Circuit Courts created just a year before in order to put their Federalist judges out of a job; Stuart v. Laird, 5 U.S. 299 (1803), where the Supreme Court ducked the troublesome constitutional question; The First Hundred Years at 74-75.

[272] See Barbey, supra note 254, Rdnr. 41-48; Herzog in 4 Maunz/Dürig, Art. 97, Rdnr. 49-52 (terming the lack of any requirement that judges be given regular appointments one of the "open flanks" of the independent judiciary). Lay judges in administrative and criminal proceedings (called "Schöffen" in the latter case) serve a purpose somewhat analogous to that of the Anglo-American jury. Cf. Gerhard Casper, The Judiciary Act of 1789 and Judicial Independence, in Maeva Marcus (ed.), Origins of the Federal Judiciary 281 (1992).

[273] See 14 BVerfGE 56, 70 (1962); 14 BVerfGE 156, 161-73 (1962) (invoking both Art. 97(2) and Art. 92). See Barbey, supra note 254, Rdnr. 53-55; Herzog in 4 Maunz/Dürig, Art. 97, Rdnr. 62, 67-69. In conformity with the Constitutional Court's conclusion that most part-time and lay judges must partake of the protections that Art. 97(2) expressly affords their regular colleagues, the statute defining the status of judges (§ 44(2) DRiG) provides that (unlike probationary judges under § 22) they can be removed only pursuant to judicial decision. See also § 29 of the same statute, which makes the Court's presumption against multiple probationary judges an absolute rule; Wassermann in 2 AK-GG, Art. 97, Rdnr. 68 (branding the

With respect to the grounds on which judges may be removed or retired, the German constitution is plainly less protective. The permissible grounds are not specified in the Basic Law itself. Article 97(2) requires that they be determined by statute, but they may also be altered by statute – subject once again, one assumes, to the fundamental requirement that they not be such as to impair the independence of the judge.[274]

Somewhat less satisfactory in terms of judicial independence are the provisions respecting the term of office itself. Unlike Article III of our Constitution,[275] the Basic Law does not prescribe life tenure expressly, and the explicit provision of Article 97(2) authorizing the legislature to fix a retirement age for those judges who are appointed for life forbids the conclusion that it does so by implication.[276] The current statute provides that members of the Constitutional Court – unlike most federal judges, who serve until they reach the age of sixty-five[277] – be appointed for a term of twelve years, with no possibility of reappointment.[278] The abbreviated term is designed (at some cost in terms of lost experience) to avoid too great a gap between

---

whole idea of judges who are less than fully independent questionable ("fragwürdig")).

[274] Art. 97(2) GG ("nur aus Gründen und unter den Formen, welche die Gesetze bestimmen"). The statutes provide for retirement or removal on the basis of incapacity as well as misconduct. §§ 21, 24, 34 DRiG; § 105 BVerfGG. See Geck, supra note 255, Rdnr. 24 (adding that the statutory procedure is so structured as to pose no threat to judicial independence and that (as of 1987) no member of the Constitutional Court had ever been subjected to these provisions); Herzog in 4 Maunz/Dürig, Art. 97, Rdnr. 58, 61 (concluding that the Constitutional Court has established a general principle of personal independence going beyond the specific terms of Art. 97(2)). Art. 98(2) additionally authorizes the Constitutional Court, on application of the Bundestag and by a two-thirds vote, to remove any federal judge for infringement of the Basic Law or "the constitutional order of a Land." See Gerd Roellecke, Aufgabe und Stellung des Bundesverfassungsgerichts in der Gerichtsbarkeit, 2 Handbuch des Staatsrechts 683, Rdnr. 13 (assimilating this provision to others designed to protect against subversion of the basic constitutional system and adding that it had never yet been invoked).

[275] "The judges, both of the supreme and inferior courts, shall hold their offices during good behavior." U.S. Const., Art. III, § 1.

[276] See 3 BVerfGE 213, 224 (1953); Herzog in 4 Maunz/Dürig, Art. 97, Rdnr. 55-56.

[277] See § 48 DRiG (as amended Dec. 12, 1985, BGBl. I S. 2226). Länder judges are subject to similar provisions. See Herzog in 4 Maunz/Dürig, Art. 97, Rdnr. 59. The mandatory retirement provision seems well designed to avoid the embarrassment of members who have passed their peak without posing any serious threat to judicial independence. For examples of difficulties experienced by our Supreme Court for want of a similar requirement see The First Hundred Years at 320 n. 250; The Second Century at 3.

[278] § 4(1), (2) BVerfGG. Paragraph (3) of the same section adds that Justices must retire at age sixty-eight even if their twelve years have not expired.

the Court and the country,[279] the ban on a second appointment to
eliminate the incentive to curry popular favor.[280] If these prescrip-
tions were written into the constitution, they might be entirely adequate; there is more than one way to achieve judicial autonomy. Yet
the legislature may revise the criteria at any time, and it has done so
more than once. To shorten the terms much further, or to permit
reappointment, as was done at one time,[281] might significantly
impair the independence of the judges.[282]

Nor does the Basic Law expressly regulate either the number of
judges or the amount of their compensation. Hamilton's basic insight that "a power over a man's subsistence amounts to a power over
his will" persuaded our Framers to forbid diminution of judicial
salaries;[283] Franklin Roosevelt's attempt to pack the Supreme Court
with Justices of his own persuasion graphically exposed the dangers
of their failure to fix their number.[284] The Basic Law gives the
legislatures authority over both the composition of the courts and the
legal status of their judges.[285]

Like our own Congress, the German legislature has from time to
time altered the number of Justices, presumably on neutral
grounds.[286] Decisions of the Constitutional Court, however, have
made clear that the general guarantee of judicial independence
places strict limits on legislative power to tamper with judicial
salaries. Compensation may not be left to executive discretion, lest it
be manipulated to influence judicial decisions.[287] Most significantly,

---

[279] Cf. the New Deal crisis of the 1930s in the United States, The Second Century,
ch. 7.

[280] For exposition and criticism of this reasoning see Geck, supra note 255,
Rdnr. 21-22 (noting that the age limit of sixty-eight years provides significant
protection against obsolescence and arguing that decisions may be influenced by
the desire to obtain alternative employment at the end of the twelve-year term).

[281] Originally those Justices appointed from the various Supreme Courts served
for life, other Justices for eight years subject to reappointment. See Franz Klein in
Maunz/ Schmidt-Bleibtreu, § 4, Rdnr. 1.

[282] See id., Rdnr. 3; 14 BVerfGE 56, 70-71 (1962) and 18 BVerfGE 241, 255 (1964)
(finding terms of six and four years respectively "not so short as seriously to
impair the personal independence"of judges not covered by the specific provisions
of Art. 97(2)); Herzog in 4 Maunz/Dürig, Art. 97, Rdnr. 66 (arguing that for professional judges eight years should be the constitutional minimum).

[283] U.S. Const., Art. III, § 1; see The Federalist, No. 79.

[284] See The Second Century at 235-36.

[285] For the composition of ordinary federal and state courts see Art. 74 cl. 1 GG;
for that of the Constitutional Court see Art. 94(2). Art. 98(1) authorizes federal
regulation of the status of federal judges, Art. 98(3) state regulation of that of state
judges subject to federal framework legislation and to the concurrent federal legislative authority over salaries granted by Art. 74a.

[286] See Geck, supra note 255, Rdnr. 4.

[287] See 12 BVerfGE 81, 88 (1961) (basing this conclusion on the general requirement in Art. 33(5) of respect for traditional principles of public service); 26

the judge's salary must be adequate to assure an appropriate standard of living,[288] though reductions are not per se prohibited.[289] These decisions seem to afford a sound basis for predicting that the Court would be equally vigilant to invoke the general guarantee of Article 97 against any effort to undermine judicial independence by such devices as altering the term or number of Justices or the grounds for their removal.

Finally, judicial autonomy cannot be sidestepped in Germany by the creation of "legislative courts" or quasi-judicial administrative agencies, which our Supreme Court has so startlingly allowed in the teeth of Article III.[290] The basic German provision (Art. 92) is similar on its face: "The judicial power shall be vested in the judges."[291] It is common ground that, in light of its unmistakable purpose of assuring an independent arbiter, this provision means that judicial power may be exercised *only* by judges.[292] Just what the judicial power in this context means, however, is disputed.

At a minimum, Article 92 has been described as reaffirming that specific provisions such as Article 104(2), which requires that a "judge" pass upon the legality and length of incarceration, mean exactly what they say.[293] The Constitutional Court, however, has held that Article 92 has an independent scope of its own. In an important 1967 decision the Court concluded that this provision reserved to the courts alone the decision of "at least the core of those duties traditionally entrusted" to their jurisdiction – specifically including the imposition of criminal fines ("Geldstrafen"), which fell outside the command of Article 104(2).[294]

BVerfGE 79, 93-94 (1969) (explaining and following the earlier decision as an interpretation of the guarantee of judicial independence in Art. 97(1)).

[288] See 12 BVerfGE 81, 88 (1961) (attributing to the traditional public-service principles recognized by Art. 33(5) the requirement of a fixed and appropriate salary (eine "angemessene – feste – Besoldung")); 26 BVerfGE 141, 157-58 (1969) (finding challenged judicial salaries consistent with Art. 97 because they were not so plainly insufficient as to threaten judicial independence). Indeed the Court has gone so far as to hold that traditional principles under Art. 33(5) require that judges be given a suitably dignified *title* as well. 38 BVerfGE 1, 12-14 (1974).

[289] See 55 BVerfGE 372, 393 (1981).

[290] See generally David Currie, Bankruptcy Courts and the Independent Judiciary, 16 Creighton L. Rev. 441 (1983). Recent decisions upholding such tribunals include Thomas v. Union Carbide Agric. Prods. Co., 473 U.S. 568 (1985), and Commodity Futures Trading Comm. v. Schor, 478 U.S. 833 (1986).

[291] Cf. U.S. Const., Art. III, § 1: "The judicial power of the United States shall be vested in one Supreme Court, and in such inferior courts as the Congress may from time to time ordain and establish."

[292] See, e.g., 22 BVerfGE 49, 73-75 (1967); Bettermann, supra note 257, Rdnr. 4; Herzog in 4 Maunz/Dürig, Art. 92, Rdnr. 42.

[293] E.g., id., Rdnr. 43-46. See also 22 BVerfGE 49, 76-77 (1967).

[294] Id. at 77-81.

At the same time, however, the Court made clear that not everything the courts did was an exercise of "judicial power" reserved by Article 92 to the judges alone.[295] What made criminal fines such a serious matter as to require that they be entrusted from the start to independent judges was above all the stigma of moral blameworthiness ("ethischer Schuldvorwurf") attached to them; once the criminal label was removed, administrative agencies could be empowered to impose money penalties ("Geldbußen") for traffic violations and other civil offenses ("Ordnungswidrigkeiten") not generally perceived to involve moral turpitude,[296] and similarly to suspend driving privileges temporarily in order to bring home to particular offenders the importance of future compliance with the law.[297]

Thus, like our Supreme Court, the Constitutional Court has divided the business of the courts into that which is inherently judicial and that which may be entrusted either to judges or to administrators at legislative discretion.[298] Whatever may be the case in this country,[299] however, the inalienable core of judicial power in the Federal Republic is not limited to serious criminal cases. Not only does it embrace a wide panoply of matters specifically assigned to the courts by other provisions of the Basic Law;[300] the Court has twice flatly stated in dictum that it also includes the entire field of civil law ("die bürgerliche Rechtspflege").[301]

Moreover, even in those cases that may be decided by an administrative agency in the first instance, the litigant has a constitutional

---

[295] See id. at 78.

[296] 27 BVerfGE 18, 28-32 (1969).

[297] 27 BVerfGE 36, 40-44 (1969). For criticism of these criteria as too lenient see Bettermann, supra note 257, Rdnr. 20-22, as too strict see Herzog in 4 Maunz/Dürig, Art. 92, Rdnr. 42-50 (finding it perverse to hold that only a judge could impose a trifling fine on a professional driver while permitting a bureaucrat to suspend his license and thus to "annihilate his civil existence").

[298] Cf. Murray's Lessee v. Hoboken Land & Improv. Co., 59 U.S. 272 (1856); Ex parte Bakelite Corp., 279 U.S. 438 (1929).

[299] See note 290 supra.

[300] See 22 BVerfGE at 76-77.

[301] 27 BVerfGE at 28. In support of this conclusion see Bettermann, supra note 257, Rdnr. 30-46 (arguing that applying the law to particular facts is an executive function only in matters to which the government is itself a party, and that therefore only a neutral judge can resolve disputes between private parties). Cf. the "public right" distinction embraced by the Supreme Court in Ex parte Bakelite Corp., supra note 298, and watered down by Crowell v. Benson, 285 U.S. 22 (1932), and later decisions cited in note 290 supra. This is not to deny that in Germany, as elsewhere, private parties may agree to resolve disputes by arbitration or that private associations may discipline their own members. The best explanation for such instances of private adjudication seems to be consent, cf. Commodity Futures Trading Comm. v. Schor, 478 U.S. 833 (1986), and even in such cases the Basic Law is said to require judicial review at least to prevent gross abuses ("Mißbrauchskontrolle") if not also to ensure the legality ("Rechtmäßigkeit") of the decision. See Herzog in 4 Munz/Dürig, Art. 92, Rdnr. 145-69; Bettermann, supra, Rdnr. 77-79.

right to unrestricted judicial review. "Should any person's rights be violated by public authority," says Article 19(4), "recourse to the courts shall be open to him."[302] The Constitutional Court has made clear both that this provision guarantees access to judges who satisfy all the criteria of judicial independence prescribed by the Basic Law[303] and that the reviewing court is free to take new evidence and to reexamine de novo any administrative conclusions of fact or of law.[304] Under these circumstances the requirement of initial resort to the administration is not likely seriously to impair the right to an ultimate decision by an independent judge.[305] Thus in this respect too the Basic Law is more protective of the right to an independent adjudication than is the U.S. Constitution as interpreted by the Supreme Court.[306]

In short, although the Basic Law is not as explicit as one might wish with respect to the number and terms of the Justices, their compensation, or the grounds for their premature removal, the unequivocal guarantee that judicial power be wielded by independent judges and the express provision that they can be displaced only by other judges may be construed to afford more comprehensive protection against attacks by other branches of government than the Constitution of the United States.

B. Judicial Review

The Basic Law does not leave judicial review to implication. As already noted, Article 19(4) guarantees judicial review of administrative action to anyone whose rights are infringed by public authority.[307] In contrast, despite Chief Justice Marshall's famous dictum

---

[302] "Wird jemand durch die öffentliche Gewalt in seinen Rechten verletzt, so steht ihm der Rechtsweg offen."

[303] E.g., 22 BVerfGE at 77; see Bettermann, supra note 257, Rdnr. 61.

[304] See, e.g., 27 BVerfGE 18, 33-34 (1969); 27 BVerfGE 36, 43 (1967); Bettermann, supra note 257, Rdnr. 50; Herzog in 4 Maunz/Dürig, Art. 92, Rdnr. 67, 70.

[305] Cf. United States v. Raddatz, 447 U.S. 667 (1980).

[306] See, e.g., Crowell v. Benson, 285 U.S. 22 (1932) (permitting limited judicial review of most factual matters decided by an administrative agency in workers' compensation cases).

[307] As the constitutional term "rights" suggests, it is necessary but not sufficient that the complainant be adversely affected by the action of which he complains; he must also be within a class of persons the law he invokes was designed to protect. See Schmidt-Aßmann in 2 Maunz/Dürig, Art. 19(4), Rdnr. 118-20, 136-42. Cf. Association of Data Processing Organizations v. Camp, 397 U.S. 150 (1970). The text of Art. 19(4) also requires a present rather than a future invasion of right, but in some cases a threat of future action constitutes a present injury. See Schmidt-Aßmann, supra, Rdnr. 164, 278-79. Cf. the treatment of this question in the context of the constitutional complaint, note 319 infra. See also 46 BVerfGE 166, 177-80 (1977) (holding that Art. 19(4) also requires the courts to grant preliminary relief to prevent irreparable harm).

about the importance of the right to redress,[308] the Supreme Court has never held that our Constitution requires judicial review of administrative action as a general matter.[309] Moreover, it follows from the language and purpose of Article 19(4) that the reviewing court must determine both the law and the facts de novo; for otherwise it could not determine whether the complainant's rights had been denied.[310]

Indeed, in suggesting on several early occasions that the courts must also exercise independent judgment in applying the law to the facts[311] the Constitutional Court may have gone further in this direction than the Basic Law warranted. For the use of imprecise statutory language ("unbestimmte Rechtsbegriffe") may indicate a legislative desire to leave the details of regulatory policy to administrative discretion,[312] and Article 19(4) seems to say nothing about the breadth of discretion that may be conferred on an executive agency.[313] In providing a remedy for infringement of legal rights it helps to effectuate the command of Article 20(3) that the administration follow the law, and the law ends where discretion begins.[314]

---

[308] "The very essence of civil liberty certainly consists in the right of every individual to claim the protection of the laws, whenever he receives an injury." Marbury v. Madison, 5 U.S. 137, 163 (1803).

[309] On occasion the Court has held that in particular contexts due process requires judicial process, e.g., Ng Fung Ho v. White, 259 U.S. 276 (1922); Ohio Valley Water Co. v. Ben Avon Borough, 253 U.S. 287 (1920); St. Joseph Stock Yards Co. v. United States, 298 U.S. 38 (1936), and it once held that Art. III required de novo review of jurisdictional facts decided by an administrative agency in a workers' compensation case. Crowell v. Benson, 285 U.S. 22 (1932). Beyond this, *Crowell* implied that Art. III required review of questions of law decided by quasi-judicial agencies and of the reasonableness – not the correctness – of their factual findings. See generally Louis Jaffe, Judicial Control of Administrative Action 381-89 (1965).

[310] E.g., 15 BVerfGE 275, 282 (1963); 61 BVerfGE 82, 111 (1982) (quoted in note 315 infra). Contrast the limited judicial review of fact findings typically afforded in the United States by the formula "supported by substantial evidence on the record as a whole." E.g., Administrative Procedure Act, § 10(e), 5 U.S.C. § 706(2)(E). In support of the constitutionality of this limited review in most cases see *Crowell v. Benson*, note 309 supra.

[311] E.g., 8 BVerfGE 274, 326 (1958) (*Preisgesetz*): "Der durch [Art. 19 Abs. 4 GG] erteilte Rechtsschutzauftrag kann nur dann verwirklicht werden, wenn die Anwendung der Norm durch die . . . Exekutive von den Gerichten nachprüfbar ist." See also 11 BVerfGE 168, 192 (1960) (suggesting that a statutory provision attempting to limit judicial review of such questions by placing them within agency discretion would raise a serious constitutional issue).

[312] See Roman Herzog, Verfassung und Verwaltungsgerichte – zurück zu mehr Kontrolldichte?, 1992 NJW 2601, 2604. Cf. Chevron, USA, Inc. v. Natural Resources Defense Council, 467 U.S. 837 (1984).

[313] For limits on the delegation of lawmaking authority see text at notes 121-64 supra (discussing Art. 80(1) GG and related doctrines).

[314] See Bettermann, Die Rechtsweggarantie des Art. 19 Abs. 4 GG in der Rechtsprechung des BVerfG, 96 AöR 528, 543 (1971): Art. 19(4) "says nothing about the existence, content, or extent of the rights against whose infringement it

More recent statements by the Court appear to acknowledge this limitation.[315]

Despite its apparently all-encompassing reference to persons whose rights are infringed by public authority ("die öffentliche Gewalt"), Article 19(4) has been held to provide redress essentially only to victims of *executive* action.[316] Ever since the beginning, however, the statutes have authorized anyone whose constitutional rights are invaded by *any* branch of public authority to file a constitutional complaint ("Verfassungsbeschwerde") with the Constitutional Court,[317] and since 1969 this remedy has been anchored in the Basic Law itself (Art. 93(1) cl. 4a).[318] Though the language of this provision

---

promises judicial protection. It does not afford them; it assumes them." See also Schmidt-Aßmann in 2 Maunz/Dürig, Art. 19(4), Rdnr. 78; Fritz Scharpf, Die politischen Kosten des Rechtsstaats 38-52 (1970) (criticizing the intrusiveness of German review in this regard in light of practice in the United States).

[315] See, e.g., 61 BVerfGE 82, 111 (1982) (reaffirming that Art. 19(4) "basically precludes binding the judiciary to accept findings of fact or conclusions of law made by other branches of government" but "[w]ithout prejudice to areas of [administrative] latitude for the exercise of creativity, discretion, or judgment conferred by law [unbeschadet normativ eröffneter Gestaltungs-, Ermessens- und Beurteilungsspielräume]"); BVerfG, Judgment of Dec. 16, 1992, Case No. 1 BvR 167/87 (not yet reported), slip op. at 21-22. The highest administrative court ("Bundesverwaltungsgericht") has been even more explicit: "If two or more lawful decisions are possible, Art. 19(4) does not require that the choice among them be made on the ultimate responsibility of the court." 39 BVerwGE 197, 205 (1971). See also Schmidt-Aßmann in 2 Maunz/Dürig, Art. 19(4), Rdnr. 184-85.

[316] See 15 BVerfGE 275, 280 (1963) ("Art. 19(4) provides protection *by* the judges, not *against* the judges"); 24 BVerfGE 33, 49-51 (1968) (arguing among other things that the authors of the Basic Law would have used more explicit language if they had meant to overturn the traditional rule against direct challenges to legislation); Sten. Ber. at 30 (Delegate Menzel) (arguing for a general right of recourse to the administrative courts in order to ensure that administrators followed the law). As originally proposed, the provision was expressly limited to administrative action. See Herrenchiemsee Bericht, in 2 Akten und Protokolle 504, 612. *Administration* of the legislature or the courts, however, is subject to Art. 19(4); and the exclusion of statutes from that provision remains disputed. See Schmidt-Aßmann in 2 Maunz/Dürig, Art. 19(4), Rdnr. 91, 93, 102; Wassermann in 1 AK-GG, Art. 19, Abs. 4, Rdnr. 37.

[317] See §§ 90 ff. BVerfGG. For comprehensive essays on all aspects of the Constitutional Court's jurisdiction see Christian Starck (ed.), 1 Bundesverfassungsgericht und Grundgesetz (1976).

[318] As the Basic Law contemplates, the implementing statute requires in most cases that ordinary legal remedies be exhausted before a constitutional complaint is filed (§ 90(2) BVerfGG). Moreover, the statute permits the Court (or a screening panel ("Kammer") of three Justices) to decline jurisdiction over complaints that reveal neither a constitutional question in need of clarification nor serious harm to the complainant. Id., §§ 93b, 93c. Contrast 54 BVerfGE 277, 293-95 (1980), where the Court, sitting en banc, surprisingly concluded that Art. 3(1) precluded reading a statute that authorized state supreme courts ("Oberlandesgerichte") to decline juris-

is no broader than that of Article 19(4), it was plainly intended to provide a remedy for unconstitutional legislative and judicial as well as administrative action, and it has consistently been so applied.[319]

Although the constitutional complaint lies only to vindicate certain specified rights (most particularly those contained in the catalog of fundamental rights in Part I of the Basic Law), those rights include the right to free development of personality (Art. 2(1)), which the Constitutional Court has interpreted to include anything the individual might wish to do and which may be restricted only by a law satisfying all substantive and procedural requirements of the constitution.[320] Thus "every burden imposed on the citizen by the state has become the invasion of a fundamental right,"[321] and thus the affected

---

diction when the matter was without general significance ("wenn die Rechtssache keine grundsätzliche Bedeutung hat") to mean what it said: To allow the pressures of an overburdened docket to dictate which cases to decide would create such a risk of unequal treatment that the rule itself could only be characterized as arbitrary. How the practice disapproved in this case differs from that of the Constitutional Court as described above the Court has yet to explain. For discussion of a proposed amendment to the statute that would give the Court somewhat greater though still not unrestricted discretion see Eckart Klein, Konzentration durch Entlastung?, 33 NJW 2073 (1993).

[319] See, e.g., 1 BVerfGE 97, 100-04 (1951) (complaint attacking statute); 7 BVerfGE 198, 203-12 (complaint attacking judicial decision); Maunz/Schmidt-Bleibtreu, § 90, Rdnr. 68. Because a complaint is permissible only if the complainant is presently affected by the official action of which he complains, however, ordinarily no complaint may be filed directly against a statute whose impact on the complainant depends upon some further administrative act; in such a case no right is infringed until that act is taken. 1 BVerfGE at 102-03. Appropriately, however, the Court has recognized that it would be intolerable to require that one violate a criminal statute in order to test its validity; in such a case the enactment of the law itself is held to violate the complainant's rights. See 13 BVerfGE 225, 227 (1961) (entertaining a pharmacist's complaint against a statute that limited his hours of operation); 46 BVerfGE 246, 255-56 (1977) (entertaining a complaint by producers and sellers of margarine against a law regulating the composition of their product: "Under these circumstances the complainants cannot be expected to take the risk of violating the law"). Cf. Steffel v. Thompson, 415 U.S. 452, 468 n. 18 (1974): "The court, in effect, by refusing an injunction, informs the prospective victim that the only way to determine whether the suspect is a mushroom or a toadstool, is to eat it." At the other end of the time scale the Constitutional Court, like the Supreme Court, is willing to relax ordinary mootness principles in order to assure judicial review of measures whose effect on any individual is normally so fleeting that most cases would otherwise be mooted before a decision could be reached. See, e.g., 49 BVerfGE 24, 52 (1978) (entertaining a complaint against the temporary isolation of imprisoned terrorists after the challenged order had expired); 81 BVerfGE 138, 140-41 (1989). Cf. Roe v. Wade, 410 U.S. 113 (1973).

[320] See 6 BVerfGE 32, 41 (1957) (*Elfes*); chapter 6 infra.

[321] See Klaus Schlaich, Das Bundesverfassungsgericht 107 (1985).

citizen may invoke the interests of third parties[322] and may raise
questions of federalism and separation of powers as well.[323]

There is no comparable provision in the U.S. Constitution. Even
the incidental power of judicial review announced in *Marbury v.
Madison*[324] ensures only that the courts may not be used to help carry
out unconstitutional laws; it provides no guarantee of judicial
intervention to protect the citizen from unconstitutional actions taken
outside the courts. Incidental review of the constitutionality of
statutes sought to be applied in ordinary litigation in Germany
("konkrete Normenkontrolle") is assured by Article 100(1), which requires that other tribunals refer such questions to the Constitutional
Court if they believe a statute invalid.[325] The Constitutional Court's
monopoly of the power to declare statutes unconstitutional expresses
respect for the dignity of the legislature and adds legitimacy to the
judicial determination; it also serves to promote uniformity and to
reduce the risk of an erroneous or uninformed decision.[326]

---

[322] See 85 BVerfGE 191, 205-06 (1992) (permitting an employer to argue that a ban
on nocturnal employment discriminated against female employees). This
conclusion was a departure from the Court's earlier decisions. See, e.g., 77 BVerf-
GE 84, 101 (1987).

[323] See, e.g., 26 BVerfGE 246, 253-58 (1969) (lack of federal authority); 20
BVerfGE 257, 268-71 (1966) (excessive delegation); Schlaich, supra note 321, at 10-11,
107-08; Wolfgang Löwer, Zuständigkeiten und Verfahren des Bundesverfassungsgerichts, 2 Handbuch des Staatsrechts 737, Rdnr. 153. Nor is standing invariably restricted to those directly regulated by the challenged action, as it may
also infringe the rights of others. Thus customers have been permitted to argue that
a law limiting the hours when stores could be open denied them their constitutional
right to make purchases (13 BVerfGE 230, 233 (1961)), and businesses to raise equal-
protection objections to tax preferences granted their competitors (18 BVerfGE 1, 11-
14 (1964)).

[324] 5 U.S. 137 (1803).

[325] Incidental judicial review had been found implicit in the Weimar Constitution on grounds reminiscent of *Marbury v. Madison*. 111 RGZ 320 (1925). See
chapter 1 supra.

[326] See Sten. Ber. at 31 (Delegate Menzel) (complaining that under the Weimar
Constitution "every municipal court [Amtsgericht] presumed to pass upon statutes
enacted by the Reichstag"); Löwer, supra note 323, Rdnr. 66; Schlaich, supra note
321, at 73-74; 1 BVerfGE 184, 197-201 (1952) (stressing the duty of every court to
examine the constitutionality of each norm it is asked to apply). Cf. the once
general requirement in 28 U.S.C. §§ 1253, 2281, 2282 (1948 ed.) (present truncated
version in id., §§ 1253 and 2284 (1988)) of a three-judge district court, subject to direct and mandatory Supreme Court review, to pass upon the validity of state or federal statutes; David Currie, The Three-Judge District Court in Constitutional Litigation, 32 U. Chi. L. Rev. 1 (1964). From the first of these justifications for the Constitutional Court's exclusive jurisdiction it follows that other courts may strike
down statutes adopted before promulgation of the Basic Law or state laws that conflict with later federal statutes, for in neither case does the decision imply that the
legislature has violated its constitutional duties. See 2 BVerfGE 124, 128-35 (1953);
10 BVerfGE 124, 127-28 (1959); Maunz in 4 Maunz/Dürig, Art. 100, Rdnr. 12-13.

The constitutional provisions for constitutional and administrative complaints, as noted, go further. Moreover, they are subject to no implicit limitations based on sovereign immunity, which would contradict their assurance of a remedy in whole or in part.[327] On the contrary, Article 34 goes so far as to guarantee that the courts will be open even to claims for money damages against the state itself for injuries caused by violations of official duties[328] – a type of claim that lies at the core of sovereign immunity in this country and that the Supreme Court has never allowed in the absence of statute.[329]

An even sharper contrast between the German and American systems of judicial review, however, is provided by a series of provisions in Article 93(1) of the Basic Law authorizing a variety of proceedings between governmental bodies that would not meet prevailing standards for a justiciable "case" or "controversy" in the United States. These proceedings include contests between various branches of the federal government ("Organstreite"), between the Federation and the individual states ("Bund-Länder Streitigkeiten"), and between two or more states ("föderalistische Streitigkeiten") over the limits of their respective powers.[330] These provisions reflect the entirely plausible conviction that a governmental body itself is the most

---

[327] Contrast U.S. Const., amend. XI; Hans v. Louisiana, 134 U.S. 1 (1890); Edelman v. Jordan, 315 U.S. 651 (1974). The Administrative Procedure Act's recent waiver of immunity in nondamage actions challenging federal administrative action (5 U.S.C. § 702) rests on legislative grace alone (see United States v. Lee, 106 U.S. 196 (1882)), and it does not apply to suits against individual states. For some of the complex distinctions our Supreme Court has drawn in this unfortunate area see David Currie, Sovereign Immunity in Suits against Officers, 1984 Sup. Ct. Rev. 149; The Second Century at 568-80.

[328] See Hans-Jürgen Papier in 2 Maunz/Dürig, Art. 34, Rdnr. 12-13 (noting that Art. 34 not only requires the state to pay whenever the offending official is liable under private law but also contains "an institutional guarantee of government liability" as an important element of the rule of law); Helmut Rittstieg in 2 AK-GG, Art. 34, Rdnr. 7-8.

[329] See, e.g., *Edelman v. Jordan*, supra note 327; Jaffe, Suits Against Governments and Officers: Sovereign Immunity, 77 Harv. L. Rev. 1, 39 (1963).

[330] Art. 93(1) Nr. 1, 3, 4 GG. There was precedent for most of these powers in earlier constitutions. See chapter 1 supra; Helmut Steinberger, Bemerkungen zu einer Synthese des Einflusses ausländischer Verfassungsideen auf die Entstehung des Grundgesetzes mit deutscher verfassungsrechtlichen Traditionen, in Klaus Stern (ed.), 40 Jahre Grundgesetz: Entstehung, Bewährung und internationale Ausstrahlung 41, 65-66 (1990) (finding roots in the old Holy Roman Empire). In a bold but not unprecedented decision involving an analogous state constitutional provision the Constitutional Court concluded that political parties, because of their central role in the electoral process as recognized by Art. 21 of the Basic Law, were entitled to initiate Organstreit proceedings in certain cases. 1 BVerfGE 208, 223-28 (1952); cf. Ernst Friesenhahn in 2 Anschütz & Thoma, supra note 114, at 537 (describing the practice under the Weimar Constitution). See also 60 BVerfGE 53, 61-62 (1982); Art. 93(1) cl. 1 GG (extending the Organstreit proceeding to controversies over the rights and duties not only of supreme federal organs but also of "other parties who have been vested with rights of their own by this Basic Law").

appropriate party to argue against any encroachment on its authority;[331] they squarely repudiate the peculiar limitations on government standing erected by the Supreme Court in such cases as *Massachusetts v. Mellon.*[332]

Most foreign to the United States experience is the provision in
the second clause of Article 93(1) for what is familiarly known as abstract judicial review ("abstrakte Normenkontrolle"), by which the
Constitutional Court is authorized to resolve "differences of opinion
or doubts" respecting the constitutionality of federal or state legislation. As the term itself suggests, abstract judicial review is not based
upon the concrete facts of a particular case;[333] the Constitutional
Court determines the validity of a challenged statute on its face. Nor,
strictly speaking, is there any requirement of adverse parties.[334] The
implementing statute does provide that jurisdiction lies only if one
governmental body (or one third of the members of the Bundestag)
believes a statute enacted by another invalid, and other bodies likely to
disagree with the complainant's position have a right to be heard;[335]
the likelihood that both sides of the question will be presented is
therefore great.[336] Moreover, the text of the Basic Law makes clear
that only laws actually adopted can be subjected to abstract review;
the Court cannot determine whether a mere proposal for legislation
would be constitutional if enacted.[337] Once an abstract review
proceeding is begun, however, it is not necessarily mooted either by
withdrawal of the complaint[338] or by expiration of the challenged law

---

[331] See Löwer, supra note 323, Rdnr. 11. See also id., Rdnr. 27-28 (arguing that as
a substitute for the use of force the judicial remedy must be comprehensive).

[332] 262 U.S. 447 (1923) (holding the state without standing to argue that a federal
statute invaded powers reserved to the states).

[333] See Maunz/Schmidt-Bleibtreu, § 76 Rdnr. 1; Löwer, supra note 323, Rdnr. 63.

[334] See 1 BVerfGE 208, 220 (1952): "Thus there is no defendant in this proceeding."

[335] BVerfGG §§ 76, 77. For widespread reservations as to the constitutionality of
the former provision in light of the fact that Art. 93 empowers the Court to resolve
"doubts" as well as "differences of opinion" see Maunz/ Schmidt-Bleibtreu, § 76,
Rdnr. 50-52.

[336] See Löwer, supra note 323, Rdnr. 63.

[337] 1 BVerfGE 396, 400-10 (1952). See Löwer, supra note 323, Rdnr. 59. In its
original form, § 97(2) of the statute establishing the Constitutional Court (BVerfGG)
also provided for advisory opinions ("Gutachten") at the request of certain officials
or public bodies, but it was repealed in 1956 after the Court characterized such opinions as "basically foreign to the judicial function." 2 BVerfGE 79, 86 (1952). See
also 1 BVerfGE 76 (1951) (giving an advisory opinion to the Bundespräsident with
regard to the necessity of Bundesrat consent to a bill passed by the Bundestag); 3
BVerfGE 407 (1954) (advising the Bundestag and Bundesrat as to the constitutionality of a proposed federal building code); Kommers, supra note 38, at 12. Some of
the Länder provide for abstract review of proposed legislation, sometimes at the instance of any citizen. See Herdegen, supra note 7, Rdnr. 49.

[338] See 1 BVerfGE at 414 (insisting that the subject of the Court's inquiry was not
the complaint but the constitutionality of the law).

– at least when, to use the terminology of our Supreme Court, the issue is one capable of repetition but otherwise evading review.[339] Moreover, in contrast to the various intergovernmental controversies noted above, the entity attacking a law need not be asserting an infringement of its own constitutional rights or powers;[340] often its contention is that the law invades individual rights.[341]

Indeed a large percentage of the abstract judicial review proceedings have been filed by members of the opposition in the Bundestag, as Article 93 expressly permits; the party that loses in the legislative process commonly pursues the controversy before the Constitutional Court.[342] The same thing often occurs in Organstreit proceedings between branches of the central government, since a parliamentary caucus ("Fraktion") is entitled to assert the rights of the Parliament itself.[343] Accordingly the provisions for intergovernmental controversies, and especially the provision for abstract judicial review, have been criticized as casting the Court into the heart of the political process.[344] Yet the questions the Court must decide are inherently of political significance, and it can be argued that it is only appropriate that it be given full authority to decide them. Abstract judicial review can thus be defended as assuring the airtight ("lückenlose") system of judicial review that the rule of law is said to demand;[345] perhaps more than any other avenue of relief it epitomizes the role of the Constitutional Court as guardian of the Constitution ("Hüter der Verfassung").[346]

---

[339] 79 BVerfGE 311, 327-28 (1989); cf. *Roe v. Wade,* supra note 319.

[340] See 1 BVerfGE at 407; 52 BVerfGE 63, 80 (1979) (upholding the right of a Land government to challenge the constitutionality of a federal law limiting the deductibility of political contributions). Contrast BVerfGG §§ 64(1), 69; 2 BVerfGE 143, 149-59 (1953).

[341] The famous 1975 abortion case, for example, in which the Constitutional Court held the state had a duty to protect the unborn by making abortion generally a crime, was an abstract review proceeding brought by state governments and by the minority of the Bundestag. 39 BVerfGE 1 (1975).

[342] See Löwer, supra note 323, Rdnr. 54; Schlaich, supra note 321, at 68.

[343] See BVerfGG § 64(1); 1 BVerfGE 351, 359 (1952); Schlaich, supra note 321, at 49: "By virtue of the standing of party caucuses, the Organstreit has also become an instrument of control by the parliamentary opposition."

[344] See, e.g., Alfred Rinken in 2 AK-GG, vor Art. 93/94, Rdnr. 105. Other critical sources are cited in Kommers, supra note 38, at 65 n. 132 (1989).

[345] See 8 BVerfGE 274, 326 (1958) (*Preisgesetz*) (discussing Art. 19(4) GG).

[346] See 1 BVerfGE 184, 195 (1952). Decisions in abstract and concrete norm control proceedings, as well as those invalidating or upholding statutes on the basis of constitutional complaints, are declared by statute to have the force of law ("Gesetzeskraft"). § 31 BVerfGG. This means that they not only bind the parties but constitute, as our Supreme Court said in Cooper v. Aaron, 358 U.S. 1 (1958), "the law of the land." See Herzog in 4 Maunz/Dürig, Art. 94, Rdnr. 19-32. In the United States this conclusion was highly controversial in light of the fact that the judicial power extends only to the resolution of particular cases and controversies (U.S. Const., Art. III, § 2). In Germany it is expressly contemplated by the constitution

In accordance with this point of view, it is commonly said that German law knows no equivalent of our political question doctrine: All constitutional questions presented must be decided by the Constitutional Court.[347] Whether the law is otherwise in this country may be a matter more of semantics than of substance. It is entirely consistent with a judicial duty to say what the law is to conclude that the law commits a particular issue to the discretion or determination of another branch of government.[348] The German court has done so a number of times,[349] and it is not clear that our political question doc-

---

(Art. 94(2) GG: "Federal law . . . shall specify in which cases [the Court's] decisions shall have the force of law"). This does not mean that the Court itself is bound by its own decisions (see 4 BVerfGE 31, 38 (1954)), but for reasons familiar to any Anglo-American lawyer there is said to be a presumption in favor of following precedent. See Martin Kriele, Grundrechte und demokratischer Gestaltungsspielraum, 5 Handbuch des Staatsrechts 101, Rdnr. 29-36. Overruling is in fact not very common. For a recent example see 85 BVerfGE 264, 285-95 (1992) (public financing of political parties), discussed in chapter 4 infra.

[347] See, e.g., Rinken in 2 AK-GG, vor Art. 93/94, Rdnr. 85: "Within its jurisdiction the Constitutional Court has a duty to decide." See also Wasserman in 1 id., Art. 19, Abs. 4, Rdnr. 29; Schneider, supra note 82, 1975 DöV at 451.

[348] See Gerald Gunther, Judicial Hegemony and Legislative Autonomy: The Nixon Case and the Impeachment Process, 22 UCLA L. Rev. 30, 34 (1974). This seems to be all that Chief Justice Marshall had in mind when he disclaimed judicial authority to interfere with "questions, in their nature political, or which are, by the constitution and laws, submitted to the executive." Marbury v. Madison, 5 U.S. 137, 170 (1803); see The First Hundred Years at 67 n. 19.

[349] E.g., 2 BVerfGE 213, 224-25 (1953) (holding that the question whether there was a need for the exercise of concurrent federal legislative power under Art. 72(2) was "a question for the faithful exercise of legislative discretion that is by its nature nonjusticiable and therefore basically not subject to review by the Constitutional Court"); 4 BVerfGE 157, 174 (1955) (holding that whether a treaty with France respecting the Saarland impeded the integration of that territory into the Federal Republic and thus offended Art. 23 was "a question of political judgment not susceptible of determination as a matter of constitutional law"); 25 BVerfGE 353, 361-63 (1969) (concluding 4-4, for want of the majority vote necessary to find the challenged action unconstitutional, that provisions vesting the pardon power in the executive implicitly excepted its exercise from judicial review and adding that there were no judicially manageable standards ("greifbare Maßstäbe") to apply); 66 BVerfGE 39, 60-62 (1983) (refusing to decide whether the decision to station additional nuclear weapons on German soil increased the danger of war because there were no justicially manageable standards for resolving the question ("es fehlt hierfür an rechtlich maßgebenden Kriterien") and because the evaluation was committed to other branches of government ("Einschätzungen dieser Art obliegen den für die Außen- und Verteidigungspolitik der Bundesrepublik Deutschland zuständigen Bundesorganen"). See also the decisions interpreting the Sozialstaat clause, discussed in chapter 1 supra; Schneider in 2 AK-GG, Art. 68, Rdnr. 6 (finding the seeds of a political-question doctrine in the Court's deference to the political branches in determining the constitutionality of a dissolution of the Bundestag under Art. 68 (note 79 supra and accompanying text)); Friedrich Klein, Bundesverfassungsgericht und richterliche Beurteilung politischer Fragen 10

trine means anything more.[350] In one important respect, however, the German approach is quite convincing: A refusal to decide "political" questions that the constitution does *not* commit to other branches would indeed be difficult to reconcile with the basic principle of judicial review.

Finally, whatever other indirect weapons other branches may have at their disposal for counteracting decisions of the Constitutional Court,[351] it is clear that they cannot undermine judicial review by enacting statutes that limit the Court's jurisdiction. In the United States scholars determined to assure a meaningful check on unconstitutional legislation have struggled for decades to prove that the provisions of Article III giving Congress authority to define federal jurisdiction mean less than they plainly say;[352] in Germany every avenue of judicial review mentioned above is expressly guaranteed by the constitution.[353]

It is true that the Basic Law can be amended by a process significantly less demanding than that prescribed in the Constitution of the United States.[354] Indeed in the aftermath of the radical activities of the late 1960s Article 10 of the Basic Law was amended to permit the preclusion of judicial review of the legality of postal and electronic surveillance measures in certain national security cases. The Constitutional Court in a controversial split decision managed to uphold this amendment against the argument that it offended Article 79(3) by impairing fundamental principles of human dignity, the separation of powers, and the rule of law, but only after insisting that the

(1966): "'Political questions are those for whose decision there are no legal norms.'"

[350] See Henkin, Is There a "Political Question" Doctrine?, 85 Yale L.J. 597 (1976).

[351] See text at notes 253-307 supra.

[352] For citations to the extensive literature see The First Hundred Years at 27.

[353] Art. 93(2) explicitly empowers the legislature to add to the jurisdiction conferred by the Basic Law itself, but not to take it away. See 24 BVerfGE 33, 48 (1968) (construing a statute to preclude only constitutional complaints (which at that time were authorized only by statute) and not the abstract or concrete norm control authorized by the Basic Law, in order to preserve its constitutionality: "The legislature cannot by ordinary statute preclude acccess to a Constitutional Court procedure authorized by the Basic Law itself."). See also Roellecke, supra note 274, Rdnr. 2. For implicit limits on the power to *add* to the Court's jurisdiction see Maunz in 4 Maunz/-Dürig, Art. 93, Rdnr. 3.

[354] Compare U.S. Const., Art. V (proposal by two-thirds vote of each House of Congress and ratification by three-quarters of the individual states) with Art. 79(2) GG (two-thirds vote of the Bundestag and of the states as represented in the Bundesrat). A single extraordinary majority in the Bundesrat may well be easier to obtain than simple majorities in thirty-eight separate assemblies. The proposed constitution drafted by the experts at Herrenchiemsee had contained a provision requiring that constitutional amendments also be approved by referendum; it was dropped by the Parliamentary Council. See 1 JöR (n.F.) at 574-79.

case was exceptional and that the alternative tribunal to which the reviewing function was entrusted be as independent as the courts themselves.[355]

In short, the Federal Republic is fully committed to independent judicial review of both executive and legislative action as an indispensable means of assuring that other branches of government not exceed the limits of their authority. Judicial review in both aspects is more extensive and in important respects more securely guaranteed by the Basic Law than by the Constitution of the United States.

IV. CONCLUSION

Separation of powers has dramatically different contours in the Federal Republic and in the United States. A parliamentary system, which Germany shares with most other successful democracies, necessarily entails a sacrifice of separation to better coordination of official policy and more effective safeguards against the abuse of executive authority. Fundamental choices of this nature tend to reflect the varying crises that preceded adoption of a particular constitution. The United States opted for a strong and independent executive after a period of dissatisfaction with the excesses and inadequacies of populist legislatures; the Federal Republic strengthened legislative prerogatives after an era of executive tyranny.

Consistent with this historical development, the Germans have been more vigilant than we to enforce the principle that basic decisions as to the content of the law must be made by the democratic and representative Parliament. Not only must the executive obey statutes once they have been enacted; there are great fields in which it may not act without statutory authorization, and there are meaningful limitations on the delegation of legislative power. Thus the three categories of executive action that Justice Jackson so carefully distinguished in our *Steel Seizure* case[356] have been conflated in Germany

---

[355] 30 BVerfGE 1, 23-29 (1970) (over three vigorous dissents). The decision is criticized by Wassermann in 1 AK-GG, Art. 19, Abs. 4, Rdnr. 62. See also Schmidt-Aßmann in 2 Maunz/Dürig, Art. 19(4), Rdnr. 30: "Judicial protection of individual rights against acts of public authority basically cannot be excluded even by constitutional amendment"; Hesse, supra note 3, Rdnr. 377 (arguing that in upholding the exclusion of judicial review the decision "sacrifices a fundamental principle of the rule of law"). For German views as to the importance of judicial review in assuring obedience to law see Sten. Ber. at 31-32 (Delegate Menzel) (arguing that without a constitutional court the legislature would be its own judge); Hesse, supra, Rdnr. 202; Maunz in Maunz/Dürig, Art. 100(1), Rdnr. 3. A judicially enforceable Bill of Rights had been a condition of Allied approval of the Basic Law. See 2 Quellen zum Staatsrecht at 209. But see Roellecke, supra note 274, Rdnr. 30 (arguing that an amendment significantly contracting the Constitutional Court's jurisdiction might be consistent with Art. 79(3)).

[356] Youngstown Sheet & Tube Co. v. Sawyer, 343 U.S. 579, 637 (1952).

to a significant degree in accordance with a single guiding principle: The legislature, not the executive, shall make the law.[357]

Safeguards against the abuse of executive authority in Germany include not only parliamentary control and strict limits on executive lawmaking but division of executive power itself – among the Cabinet, the administration, autonomous entities like the Bundesbank, and most significantly the constituent states. Federalism thus compensates in substantial measure for the lack of structural separation between the central legislative and executive powers, since freedom from the Cabinet means freedom from the Bundestag as well. At the same time, however, significant agencies as independent of centralized democratic control as our Federal Trade Commission are essentially limited to two special cases mentioned in the Basic Law itself; the Constitutional Court has been far more alert to prevent incoherence and unresponsiveness in executive policy than our Supreme Court.

Finally, in establishing an independent judiciary crowned by a Constitutional Court with broad powers of judicial review and in anchoring in the constitution itself a guarantee of judicial relief for every victim of illegal administrative action, the Federal Republic has gone even beyond the United States to ensure actual observance of the constitution and to promote the rule of law.

---

[357] See Hesse, supra note 3, Rdnr. 508, 524.

4

Freedom of Expression

Like most modern constitutions, the Basic Law contains a Bill of Rights (Grundrechtskatalog). Not surprisingly, among its provisions are several relating to freedom of expression; and those provisions are the subject of this chapter.

With characteristic brevity, our Bill of Rights speaks simply of freedom of speech and press and of the right "peaceably to assemble, and to petition the Government for a redress of grievances."[1] Typically, the German provisions are more detailed. Article 5(1) guarantees to "everyone" the right not only "to express and disseminate his opinion by speech, writing, and pictures" but also "to inform himself from generally accessible sources,"[2] assures freedom of the press and of "reporting by means of broadcasts and films," and outlaws censorship. Article 5(3) provides that "art and science [Wissenschaft], research, and teaching shall be free." Articles 8(1), 9(1), and 17 protect freedom of assembly, association, and petition;[3]

---

[1] U.S. Const., amend. I.

[2] "Only the informed citizen is in a position to form his own opinions and to participate in the democratic process as envisioned by the Basic Law." Konrad Hesse, Grundzüge des Verfassungsrechts der Bundesrepublik Deutschland (18th ed. 1991), Rdnr. 393. Adopted in response to Nazi restrictions on access to independent sources such as foreign radio, this provision forbids Government interference with access to a willing informant; it does not require the Government to make information available. See Hermann von Mangoldt, Das Bonner Grundgesetz 62 (1953); Michael Kloepfer, Öffentliche Meinung, Massenmedien, 2 Handbuch des Staatsrechts 171, Rdnr. 54 ("the right to ask, but no right to an answer"). Contrast Verfassung des Landes Brandenburg vom 20. August 1992, GV. BB. S. 298, Art. 21(4), which confers a general right of access to government files in the absence of "overriding public or private interests." For what is meant by "generally available sources" in light of the background of Art. 5(1) see note 237 infra; for limitations imposed on the government's *power* to disclose personal information by the right to free development of personality in Art. 2(1) see chapter 6 infra. The ticklish interplay between the right of one person to seek information and the right of another to keep it secret is considered in Hans-Ullrich Gallwas, Der allgemeine Konflikt zwischen dem Recht auf informationelle Selbstbestimmung und der Informationsfreiheit, 1992 NJW 2785.

[3] The right to petition, the Constitutional Court has held, implies a corresponding obligation of the state to accept the petition, to consider it, and to inform the petitioner of its decision – but (in order to avoid undue burdens) not to give reasons. 2

Article 21(1) provides that political parties "may be freely established"; Article 3(3) forbids preference or prejudice on grounds of "political opinions." Our Supreme Court has managed to find most if not all of these guarantees implicit in the spare terms of the first amendment; the framers of the Basic Law chose not to leave them to the vagaries of interpretation.

For in the Federal Republic, as in the United States, freedom of expression and those cognate rights which make it effective occupy a central place in the scale of constitutional values. In words reminiscent of Justice Brandeis's famous declaration in *Whitney v. California*,[4] the Constitutional Court in its first major discussion of these provisions made clear that freedom of expression was of cardinal importance both as an end and as a means:

> As the most immediate manifestation of the human personality in society, the basic right to free expression of opinion is one of the noblest of all human rights . . . . To a free democratic constitutional order it is absolutely basic [schlechthin konstituierend], for it alone makes possible the continuing intellectual controversy, the contest of opinions that forms the lifeblood of such an order. In a certain sense it is the basis of all freedom whatever, "the matrix, the indispensable condition of nearly every other form of freedom" (Cardozo).[5]

In light of this focus on the central role of free expression in the functioning of democracy, it is understandable that the German court, like its counterpart in the United States, has emphasized that political speech lies at the heart of the constitutional provisions.[6] At the same time, however, in light of the equally important relation between expression and the free development of personality, the Constitutional Court like the Supreme Court has applied the general lan-

---

BVerfGE 225, 230 (1953). Otherwise, the Court reasoned, the right would be without practical value (ein "Scheinrecht"). Id. See also Günter Dürig in 2 Maunz/Dürig, Art. 17, Rdnr. 4-9; Joachim Burmeister, Das Petitionsrecht, 2 Handbuch des Staatsrechts 73, Rdnr. 14; Ekkehart Stein in 1 AK-GG, Art. 17, Rdnr. 29 (the last two arguing for a duty to give reasons for the rejection of a petition). Cf. Administrative Procedure Act, 5 U.S.C. § 553 (requiring agencies in notice-and-comment rulemaking proceedings to consider the materials submitted).

[4] 274 U.S. 357, 375 (1927) (concurring opinion): "Those who won our independence . . . valued liberty both as an end and as a means . . . ."

[5] 7 BVerfGE 198, 208 (1958) (*Lüth*). The Cardozo quotation, in English, is from Palko v. Connecticut, 302 U.S. 319, 327 (1937). See also Roman Herzog in 1 Maunz/Dürig, Art. 5, Abs. I, II, Rdnr. 2-10.

[6] E.g., 42 BVerfGE 163, 170 (1976); 61 BVerfGE 1, 11-12 (1982). For a general discussion of the political dimension of such rights as those of expression, assembly, and association see Walter Schmitt Glaeser, Die grundrechtliche Freiheit des Bürgers zur Mitwirkung an der Willensbildung, 2 Handbuch des Staatsrechts 49, Rdnr. 3-20.

guage of Article 5(1) to other types of expression too.[7] Freedom of the press, the Court concluded in 1967, embraced the right to publish not only opinions but news as well; and advertisements – specifically those seeking applicants for jobs outside the Federal Republic – were a form of news entitled to constitutional protection.[8]

Yet attempts to insulate purely commercial speech from legislative restriction on free expression grounds have met with less success in Germany than in the recent history of the United States. A ban on inappropriate and ostentatious ("unangemessene und marktschreierische") advertising by pharmacists was upheld in 1980 with the curt observation that it suppressed no opinions as such but only certain abuses ("Auswüchse")[9] – evidently a reminder that in Germany, as in the United States, a neutral law limiting only the time,

---

[7] See Herzog in 1 Maunz/Dürig, Art. 5, Abs. I, II, Rdnr. 55a, 126-28 (concluding in light of this relation that the speech and press guarantees extend to communications on any subject whatever). Commentators differ as to whether the same is true of the right to assembly guaranteed by Art. 8. Compare Hesse, supra note 2, Rdnr. 404-05, and Wolfgang Hoffman-Riem in 1 AK-GG, Art. 8, Rdnr. 12-13 (both viewing assembly solely as a means of promoting the formation of public opinion), with Michael Kloepfer, Versammlungsfreiheit, 6 Handbuch des Staatsrechts 739, Rdnr. 16-24, and Herzog in 1 Maunz/Dürig, Art. 8, Rdnr. 13-15, 47-51 (arguing that Art. 8 extends to gatherings of two or more persons for any lawful purpose because being with others is "one of the most vital of all human needs"). Cf. Gerhard Anschütz, Die Verfassung des Deutschen Reichs 566 (4th ed. 1933) (construing a comparable provision of the Weimar Constitution to protect assembly for the purpose of demonstration and discussion). Art. 9 of the Basic Law, which expressly mentions labor organizations, is plainly not limited to political associations. See Hesse, supra, Rdnr. 410; Alfred Rinken in 1 AK-GG, Art. 9, Abs. 1, Rdnr. 35-39; Detlef Merten, Vereinsfreiheit, 6 Handbuch des Staatsrechts 775, Rdnr. 3-11. Similarly, neither the artistic nor the academic freedom protected by Art. 5(3) is restricted to political matters. See Erhard Denninger, Freiheit der Kunst, 6 Handbuch des Staatsrechts 847, Rdnr. 3-17; Thomas Oppermann, Freiheit von Forschung und Lehre, 6 Handbuch des Staatsrechts 809, Rdnr. 10-12.

[8] 21 BVerfGE 271, 278-80 (1967). The Court went on to hold that a prohibition of such advertisements infringed not only freedom of the press but also the citizen's right to "inform himself from generally available sources," on the ground that it applied only to the domestic press and thus did not qualify as a "general law," which alone (under these circumstances) might permissibly limit the constitutional freedoms. Id. at 280, 291. Cf. Virginia State Bd. of Pharmacy v. Virginia Consumer Council, 425 U.S. 748, 764-65 (1976). Reaffirming in 1983 that advertisements enjoyed constitutional protection, the Court added that the importance of advertising revenues to the viability of the press lent further strength to this conclusion. 64 BVerfGE 108, 114 (1983). Still later, however, the Court made clear that what mattered in this regard was the overall financial position of the affected medium, not advertising as a particular source of revenue. 74 BVerfGE 297, 342 (1987). See also 84 BVerfGE 372 (1991) and 85 BVerfGE 97 (1991) (striking down limitations on advertising by an association of tax consulting firms and by tax consultants themselves as infringements of the associational and occupational freedoms guaranteed by Art. 9(1) and 12(1) respectively).

[9] 53 BVerfGE 96, 99 (1980).

place, and manner of a message is understandably easier to sustain than one prohibiting its dissemination entirely.[10] Suggestions of a more sweeping limitation, however, seemed to lurk in the same opinion's insistence, in rejecting a parallel objection based on occupational freedom, on the incompatibility of the "commercial" character of a "drugstore" (apparently in the American sense) with the pharmacist's principal obligation to supply the medicinal needs of the public.[11] The seed thus planted bore fruit in 1985, when once again with little discussion the Court upheld a virtually absolute ban on advertising by doctors: Even assuming that medical advertisements qualified as "opinion" within the meaning of Article 5(1), the prohibition was justified by the need to protect susceptible patients from undue influence and to preserve public confidence that physicians would not propose treatment for reasons of personal gain.[12]

For no more in Germany than in the United States does freedom of expression entail the right to say whatever one pleases – much less to say it at any time or place or in any manner. Unlike the U.S. Constitution, the Basic Law to some extent makes this conclusion explicit. Article 8(2) provides that open-air assemblies may be restricted "by or pursuant to a law [Gesetz]"; Articles 9(2) and 21(2) go so far as

---

[10] See, e.g., 7 BVerfGE 230 (1958) (upholding a judgment forbidding an apartment dweller to make known his opinions by tacking political posters on the outside wall of the building without the landlord's consent): "The great importance of the basic right to free expression of political opinions in a liberal democracy . . . does not lead to the conclusion that one may express his opinion in every form and by every means." Id. at 234. See also 47 BVerfGE 198, 233 (1978) ("Art. 5(1) poses less of an obstacle to the application of [a statute forbidding calumny against the Government] when the expression in question offends the provision only because of its form"); 42 BVerfGE 143, 149-50 (1976). Cf. Cox v. New Hampshire, 312 U.S. 569, 575 (1941) (neutral requirement of parade permit); Kovacs v. Cooper, 336 U.S. 77 (1949) ("loud and raucous" soundtrucks).

[11] 53 BVerfGE at 98.

[12] 71 BVerfGE 162, 174, 176 (1985). The Court went on to hold, however, that the prohibition could not constitutionally be applied to an autobiographical book simply because it contained passages praising the controversial treatment the doctor had elsewhere advertised – thus illustrating the difficulty of distinguishing mere commercial speech from that warranting more extensive constitutional protection. Id. at 178-83. See also 85 BVerfGE 248, 263-64 (1992) (striking down sanctions against a doctor for cooperating with a reporter in the preparation of magazine articles praising his work); 74 BVerfGE 297, 341-44 (1987) (upholding a ban on advertising in connection with local and regional telecasts over public channels after finding that the lost revenue was not essential to the viability of the enterprise, without even discussing whether the message itself might be constitutionally protected); 80 BVerfGE 124 (1989) (upholding postal rates that discriminated against advertising circulars). Publications "in which information and expression of opinion are subordinated to extraneous business purposes," the Court declared in this last case, "are not primarily designed as contributions to the formation of public opinion. Like the rest of the press, such publications do enjoy freedom from governmental direction, but they do not necessarily have the same claim to governmental support." Id. at 135.

to outlaw associations or political parties designed to subvert the constitutional order; Article 5(2) declares that the rights guaranteed by
the preceding section (expression of opinion, access to information,
and reporting) find their limits in "the provisions of the general laws,
the provisions of law for the protection of youth, and the right to inviolability of personal honor."[13] The artistic and academic freedoms
recognized by Article 5(3) are not expressly limited, but the Court has
held that they are implicitly restricted when they come into conflict
with other constitutional values.[14]

On its face the provision subjecting freedom of speech and press
to "the provisions of the general laws" might appear to place those
freedoms essentially at the mercy of the legislature – subject only to
the provision of Article 19(2) that no law may impair the essential
content ("Wesensgehalt") of a basic right.[15] The Constitutional Court
made clear at the outset, however, that the requirement of "general
laws" was more than a mere protection against executive or judicial
action unauthorized by statute ("Gesetzesvorbehalt")[16] and more than
a reiteration of the prohibition in Article 19(1) of legislation governing
"an individual case." The fundamental position of freedom of
expression in the constitutional scheme, said the Court in the
germinal *Lüth* decision in 1958, precluded the conclusion that the
Basic Law had left its scope entirely to legislative discretion. The concept of "general laws" was itself limited by the guarantee it purported
to restrict:

> The mutual relationship between basic rights and "general laws" is
> not to be understood as a unilateral limitation on the applicability of
> the basic right . . . . There is rather a reciprocal effect
> [Wechselwirkung] . . . . To be sure, as the text makes clear, the
> "general laws" set limits to the basic right; but they themselves must
> be interpreted in recognition of the value-setting significance of this
> right in a free democratic state, and thus their limiting effect on the
> basic right must itself be restricted.[17]

---

[13] Although the ban on prior censorship also appears in Art. 5(1), it is understood
not to be limited by Art. 5(2); rather it is interpreted as a limit on the limitations
("Schrankenschranke") that may be imposed by general laws or for the protection
of youth or personal honor. See, e.g., Herzog in 1 Maunz/Dürig, Art. 5, Abs. I, II,
Rdnr. 302; Edzard Schmidt-Jortzig, Meinungs- und Informationsfreiheit, 6
Handbuch des Staatsrechts 635, Rdnr. 44.

[14] 30 BVerfGE 173, 193-95 (1971) (*Mephisto*); see text at notes 77-78 infra. The
facially unrestricted right to petition (Art. 17 GG) is similarly limited by other
constitutional provisions. See BVerfG, Judgment of Dec. 12, 1990, Case No. 1 BvR
839/90, 1991 NJW 1475.

[15] In light of the developments about to be recounted, this provision has played
little part in the decisions. See Maunz in 2 Maunz/Dürig, Art. 19, Abs. II, Rdnr. 16.
For the remarkable variety of views as to what it means see id., Rdnr. 1-15.

[16] See chapter 3 supra.

[17] 7 BVerfGE 198, 208-09 (1958).

Even under the Weimar Constitution of 1919, the opinion continued, "general laws" in this context had been understood to include only those designed not to suppress the expression of opinion as such but to protect some neutral and overriding interest.[18] Article 5(2), the Court concluded, accordingly required a balancing of interests ("Güterabwägung"): "The right to free expression of opinion must yield when its exercise would infringe superior interests of others that are deserving of protection."[19]

Whether the Weimar experience truly supported the Court's conclusions could certainly be questioned. Some commentators of that period argued that the requirement that laws limiting expression be "general" was the result of a clerical error and should therefore be ignored. Others contended that, however the term had found its way into the constitution, it had to be dealt with; but they disagreed vigorously over just what it might mean. One prominent position was that a general law was one that, like the comprehensive ban on unethical intentional injury in *Lüth*, did not apply to expression alone; another applied the term more broadly to any law not directed against expression of a particular (e.g., Communist, Fascist, or atheistic) opinion. Sometimes, as the Court said, a general law was described as one serving some interest unrelated to the suppression of free expression, such as the protection of life or bodily integrity,[20] but the notion that it implied any balancing of interests seems to have been a decidedly minority position. So long as the law was not directed against speech itself, the present President of the Constitutional Court has written, the dominant view during the Weimar period was that free expression had to give way before "*any* other legal interest, however insignificant."[21]

---

[18] Id. at 209-10. Though the requirement that the law not be directed at the suppression of opinion may remind the reader of the principle of content neutrality central to first amendment jurisprudence in the United States, the two are not identical. As applied to the boycott invitation in *Lüth*, the Civil Code provision banning the intentional infliction of injury in a manner contrary to good morals was a restriction based on the content of speech; but because the law applied to *all* such injuries whether or not they were caused by speech it was "general" in that it was not aimed at expression alone and certainly not at any particular opinion. See id. at 214.

[19] Id. at 210.

[20] Cf. United States v. O'Brien, 391 U.S. 367 (1968).

[21] See Herzog in 1 Maunz/Dürig, Art. 5, Abs. I, II, Rdnr. 250-57. See also Anschütz, supra note 7, at 551-56; Kurt Häntzschel in 2 Gerhard Anschütz & Richard Thoma, Handbuch des Deutschen Staaatsrechts 657-64 (1930) (criticizing the balancing approach advocated by Rudolf Smend in 4 Veröffentlichungen der Vereinigung der Deutschen Staatsrechtslehrer 44, 51-53 (1928)); 1 von Mangoldt/Klein/Starck, Art. 5, Abs. 1, 2, Rdnr. 120-23. In the constitutional convention the Committee on Style ("Redaktionsausschuß"), referring to the Weimar practice, had explained that "general laws" were those not directed against a particular opinion but had said nothing about balancing interests. See 1 JöR (n.F.) at 87. In the

Thus, on the basis of sheer disbelief aided by a little debatable history, the Constitutional Court managed to hold that freedom of expression enjoyed a good deal more protection than the text of Article 5 appeared to afford.[22] If the mystical terminology of "reciprocal effect" sounds peculiar to American ears,[23] the bottom line of interest balancing does not.[24] Later decisions, while parroting the original language of reciprocal effect, have tended in performing the actual balancing to apply the more orthodox proportionality principle the Court has developed for testing limitations on other fundamental rights: A "general law" restricting expression is valid only if it is adapted ("geeignet") to the attainment of a legitimate purpose, if it is

---

first edition of his commentary on the Basic Law, published only four years after its adoption, Professor von Mangoldt, who had been a member of the Parliamentary Council, took an identical view of the term "general laws" in Art. 5(2) on the basis of the Weimar experience: "General laws are therefore all laws intended to protect a particular interest [Rechtsgut] generally, without reference to any particular opinion." Von Mangoldt, supra note 2, at 67. See also Herzog, supra, Rdnr. 261-62 (arguing that interest balancing was thus supported not by history but by the provision of Art. 19(2) immunizing the essence of all fundamental rights from legislative assault). Accord Schmidt-Jortzig, supra note 13, Rdnr. 41-43.

[22] One might add that the express command of Art. 1(3) that the Bill of Rights bind the legislature as well as the executive and the courts would be deprived of much of its effect if every statutory restriction of general applicability qualified as a "general law" under a provision like Art. 5(2). See Christian Starck, Die Verfassungsauslegung, 7 Handbuch des Staatsrechts 189, Rdnr. 39 (justifying the proportionality principle on this basis); Carl Schmitt in 2 Anschütz & Thoma, supra note 21, at 592 (arguing, even in the absence of a provision like that of Art. 1(3) in the Weimar Constitution, that no authorization to limit a basic right should be interpreted to permit its elimination). Cf. Henry Hart's famous argument that the power of Congress to make "exceptions" to the Supreme Court's appellate jurisdiction not be taken literally lest it "destroy the essential role of the Supreme Court in the constitutional plan." See Paul Bator, Daniel Meltzer, Paul Mishkin, & David Shapiro, Hart & Wechsler's The Federal Courts and the Federal System 394 (3d ed. 1988). Contrast the unwillingness of both the Supreme Court and the Philadelphia Convention to accept a similar argument respecting the facially sweeping authority to amend the Constitution and the Articles of Confederation, respectively. See National Prohibition Cases, 253 U.S. 350, 386-87 (1920); Leser v. Garnett, 258 U.S. 130, 136 (1922); Max Farrand (ed.), 1 Records of the Federal Convention of 1787, at 249, 262 (rev. ed. 1937).

[23] See Herzog in 1 Maunz/Dürig, Art. 5, Abs. I, II, Rdnr. 263-64 (explaining the Court's approach as an example of the familiar practice of interpreting statutes in such a way as to avoid having to hold them unconstitutional ("verfassungskonforme Auslegung")).

[24] See generally Alexander Aleinikoff, Constitutional Law in the Age of Balancing, 96 Yale L.J. 943 (1987). Examples in the speech field include Barenblatt v. United States, 360 U.S. 109 (1959); Simon & Schuster, Inc. v. New York State Crime Victims Board, 112 S. Ct. 501 (1991).

necessary ("erforderlich") to that end, and if the burden it imposes is not excessive ("unzumutbar") in light of the benefits to be achieved.[25]

In short, despite constitutional provisions that differ significantly on their face, both the Constitutional Court and the Supreme Court have adopted a similar approach to defining the limits of free expression. Particular decisions, however, reveal interesting divergences, some of which are of major significance.

I. BALANCING

A balancing test is no more protective of expression than the judges who administer it; only an examination of actual decisions can give us an insight into the degree of freedom that prevails in Germany.

Cases concerning political parties, subversion, broadcasting, and higher education have produced specialized bodies of law of particular interest that are considered in detail below. We begin with a series of more traditional cases pitting political or artistic expression against such countervailing interests as economic freedom, reputation, and privacy.

Three distinct stages can be discerned in the Court's developing approach to conflicts of this kind. The earliest decisions, which evinced a fierce attachment to the values of free expression, were followed by a period in which the Court permitted or even required the state to afford greater protection to interests such as reputation and privacy than one would expect from our Supreme Court. More recent decisions, on the other hand, have tended to come down on the side of expression.[26]

A. Boycotts

The story begins with the groundbreaking *Lüth* opinion of 1958, which as noted above established the basic principle of reciprocal effect ("Wechselwirkung") requiring a balance of competing interests

---

[25] For a general statement of the proportionality principle see 78 BVerfGE 232, 245-47 (1988); see also chapters 1 supra and 6 infra. Applications in the field of expression include 71 BVerfGE 162, 180-83 (1985) (finding the benefits of applying a ban on medical advertising to an autobiographical book outweighed by the burden on expression of opinion); 74 BVerfGE 297, 341-44 (1987) (finding a ban on advertising in conjunction with local and regional programming of public television stations an appropriate, necessary, and not overly burdensome means of protecting the revenues of private broadcasters and of the press).

[26] Many of the cases discussed in this section have been carefully and independently analyzed from a similar perpective, often in greater detail, in Peter Quint, Free Speech and Private Law in German Constitutional Theory, 48 Md. L. Rev. 247 (1989).

when freedom of expression is sought to be limited, as Article 5(2) envisions, by "general laws."[27] As a result of public pronouncements pointing out that a well-known motion-picture director had been largely responsible for a notorious anti-Semitic film during the Nazi period, the President of the Hamburg Press Club (who was also press secretary for the Hamburg state government) had been enjoined from further entreating theater owners and members of the public to boycott the director's new films.[28] The Constitutional Court held the injunction impermissibly abridged the right of free expression guaranteed by Article 5(1).

To the observer from the United States the Court seemed to have surprising difficulty with the threshold question whether Article 5 had any impact at all upon rules of private tort law.

Like our own Bill of Rights, most of the fundamental freedoms enumerated in the German Basic Law appear to limit only the state. "The following basic rights," says Article 1(3), "shall bind the legislature, the executive and the judiciary as directly enforceable law."[29] Nevertheless the Federal Labor Court had concluded in 1954 that a private employer would offend both freedom of expression and the ban on political discrimination in Article 3(3) if it discharged a worker on political grounds:

> Not all, but a number of significant basic constitutional rights are meant not only as guarantees of freedom vis-à-vis state authority but also as organizing principles [Ordnungsgrundsätze] for the entire society, which to an extent to be determined from the nature of each right have immediate significance for the legal relations of citizens with one another. . . . The basic right to free expression of opinion . . . would be rendered [largely] ineffective . . . if . . . individuals and others with economic and social power . . . were in a position by virtue of that power to restrict this right at will . . . .[30]

----

[27] 7 BVerfGE 198 (1958). See text at notes 14-19 supra.

[28] Id. at 199-202.

[29] See Ernst Forsthoff, Rechtsstaat im Wandel 139 (2d ed. 1976). This conclusion seems only to be strengthened by the fact that occasional provisions expressly limit private action as well. Thus Art. 9(3) outlaws private yellow-dog contracts ("Agreements which restrict or seek to impair this right [to form labor unions] shall be null and void"), Art. 48(1) requires that private employees be given leave to campaign for the Bundestag, and Art. 48(2) forbids private interference (including dismissal) with the right to serve in that body. See also Art. 21(2) and 9(2) (discussed in text at notes 169-214 infra) (outlawing political parties and other organizations designed to subvert the constitutional order), and Art. 6(2) (providing that "the care and upbringing of children are a natural right of, and a duty primarily incumbent upon, the parents"). Cf. U.S. Const., amend. XIII, § 1: "Neither slavery nor involuntary servitude . . . shall exist within the United States"; U.S. Const., amend. XVIII (since repealed) (forbidding "the manufacture, sale, or transportation of intoxicating liquors . . . for beverage purposes").

[30] 1 BArbGE 185, 192-94 (1954). Thus the Federal Labor Court concluded that the guarantee of free expression had what has come to be known as "unmittelbare

This interpretation was not dependent solely on the wishful argument that one needed protection from private as well as public oppression, or on the fact that the corresponding article of the Weimar Constitution had expressly forbidden *anyone* to interfere with freedom of speech[31] – a fact that arguably cuts in the opposite direction.[32] The records of the constitutional convention contain powerful evidence that the right to human dignity recognized by Article 1(1) was meant to bind individuals as well as the state,[33] and the entire Bill of Rights was meant to protect human dignity.[34] Nevertheless the decisions of the Labor Court provoked vehement disagreement, not least on the ground that to hold individuals bound by the Bill of Rights would deny them the freedom of action essential to human dignity and guaranteed by the fundamental rights themselves.[35]

Drittwirkung" – an immediate limiting impact on the actions of private parties. See also the further explanations by the Chief Justice of that court, Hans Nipperdey, Die Würde des Menschen, in 2 Franz Neumann et al., Die Grundrechte 1, 18-21, 35-46 (1954), and Hans Nipperdey, Grundrechte und Privatrecht, in Festschrift für Erich Molitor 17 (1962), passim.

[31] See Art. 118 WRV, cited in id. at 25: "No employment relationship may hinder him in this right, and no one may disadvantage him" for its exercise. Several postwar Länder constitutions contain similar provisions. See, e.g., Verfassung des Freistaates Bayern vom 2. Dezember 1946, BayRS 100-1-S, Art. 110(1); Verfassung des Landes Hessen vom 1. Dezember 1946, GVBl. S. 229, Art. 11.

[32] See 1 BArbGE at 192 (defensively noting that the omission of this language from the Basic Law was unexplained); von Mangoldt, supra note 2, at 62-63 (arguing that the omission was immaterial). The fact that two provisions of the Weimar Constitution expressly limited private action was often the basis of an argument that other provisions of the same document had no such application. See Wolfgang Rüfner, Grundrechtsadressaten, 5 Handbuch des Staatsrechts 525, Rdnr. 55, and authorities cited.

[33] Citing the example of slavery, the report of the conference that drafted the Basic Law flatly declared that "Article 1 is meant to bind private persons too," although even at the time that article included a clause requiring "public authority in all its aspects" to respect and protect human dignity. See Herrenchiemsee Bericht, in 2 Akten und Protokolle at 513, 580. In the convention itself Theodor Heuss (soon to become first President of the Federal Republic) objected to the addition of words making clear that it was the duty of "all public authorities as well as of every individual" to respect human dignity on the ground that this principle was already implicit in the provision (as it then stood) that "human dignity stands under the protection of the public order [im Schutze der staatlichen Ordnung]," while the influential Christian Democrat Adolf Süsterhenn explained without contradiction that the terminology ultimately adopted ("The dignity of man is inviolable. To respect and protect it shall be the duty of all state authority") was "an absolute declaration, directed toward everyone, toward state authorities as well as toward every individual and toward every institution." 1 JöR (n.F.) at 50, 51.

[34] See 36 BVerfGE 174, 188 (1973); Dürig in 1 Maunz/Dürig, Art. 1, Rdnr. 10, 55.

[35] See, e.g., Günter Dürig, Grundrechte und Zivilrechtsprechung, in Theodor Maunz, ed., Vom Bonner Grundgesetz zur gesamtdeutschen Verfassung: Fest-

Without taking a definitive position on the question whether the guarantee of free expression bound private parties directly, the Constitutional Court concluded that it did bind the civil court in *Lüth*. "The primary purpose of the Basic Rights," said the Court, "was doubtless to protect the liberties of the individual against invasion by public authority. They are defensive rights [Abwehrrechte] of the citizen against the state." That was not, however, their sole function. The Bill of Rights also embodied an objective order of values ("eine objektive Wertordnung") that pervaded all areas of law, private as well as public – especially in those cases in which the law prescribed binding rules that displaced the will of the parties.[36]

From this side of the ocean the result seems easy enough to sustain without resort to the mystical notion of an objective order of values – which, as we shall see, has had consequences far transcending the humble question whether rules of private law embody state action for purposes of the Bill of Rights.[37] As the Supreme Court said in *New York Times Co. v. Sullivan*, it was the state that had made the policy decision to declare the offending expression unlawful; whether

---

schrift für Hans Nawiasky 157, 158-59, 163-64 (1956) (adding (at 170) that for this reason the Weimar provision for private interference with speech had been narrowly construed). See also Dürig in 1 Maunz/Dürig, Art. 1, Abs. III, Rdnr. 129-30 (arguing that direct application of the Bill of Rights to private actions "strikes at the root of private autonomy"). Defenders of the Labor Court's view responded that considerable autonomy would remain after balancing the conflicting rights of the parties. See Nipperdey, Grundrechte und Privatrecht, supra note 30, at 26-28.

[36] 7 BVerfGE at 203-07. See also id. at 220 (adding that the Constitution could not be construed to impose restrictions upon private actors as stringent as those imposed on the state since in private disputes both parties possessed basic rights that had to be balanced against each other). Oddly, the Court has never completely laid to rest the question whether freedom of expression imposes any limits on private parties; its emphasis in later cases on a duty of the state to *protect* as well as to respect the Basic Rights (see Art. 1(1), which makes this duty explicit as to human dignity) seems to have pushed the more radical theory that private parties are directly bound into relative oblivion. See Dürig in 1 Maunz/Dürig, Art. 1, Abs. III, Rdnr. 130-32; Erhard Denninger in 1 AK-GG, Art. 1, Abs. 2-3, Rdnr. 32; Hesse, supra note 2, Rdnr. 349-57 (concluding (at 355) that "as a general rule the Basic Rights cannot directly bind private parties"). For a recent restatement of the opposing view see Hoffmann-Riem in 1 AK-GG, Art. 5, Abs. 1, 2, Rdnr. 37.

[37] These additional consequences include affirmative duties of state support and protection against third parties, procedural guarantees, and organizational requirements for such institutions as broadcasting and higher education. See Dieter Grimm, Die Zukunft der Verfassung 221 (1991) (arguing, id. at 224-27, that the original thrust of basic rights in Europe, as contrasted with the United States, was objective). See also the dissenting opinion in the *Gruppenuniversität* case, text at note 290 infra, where two Justices protested that the "objective order of values" concept ought to be confined to the private law context in which it originated; Denninger in 1 AK-GG, vor Art. 1, Rdnr. 29-30.

the sanctions it attached to the prohibition were sought by the state itself or by private parties should be immaterial.[38]

The injunction had been based upon a provision of the Civil Code ("Bürgerliches Gesetzbuch" or "BGB"), and there was a time in German history when Bill of Rights provisions did not apply to legislation. Parliamentary democracy was originally conceived as a cure for oppression, not as another source of it.[39] Thus even under the Weimar Constitution it was possible to read many fundamental rights provisions as limitations only on executive and judicial action; in its pathbreaking opinion establishing the principle of judicial review of legislation under that constitution, the Reichsgericht expressly left open the question whether a guarantee of equality before the law ("vor dem Gesetze") restricted legislative as well as executive and judicial acts.[40]

The Basic Law removed all doubts on this score by specifying that the Bill of Rights limited legislative, executive, and judicial powers.[41] Some scholars nevertheless argued that even this terminology did not embrace everything the state might do. In the first place, it was said, there was no reason to subject the state to special rules when it acted, like any individual, in what we would call a proprietary capacity.[42]

---

[38] 376 U.S. 254, 265 (1964). See also Quint, supra note 26, 48 Md. L. Rev. at 268-69.

[39] See Herrenchiemsee Bericht, in 2 Akten und Protokolle at 512: "Since the people's representatives participated in the lawmaking process, legislation was seen as the true guarantee of freedom, and it was thought necessary only to require the administration to follow the law." See also Carl Schmitt, Verfassungslehre 130 (1928); Herzog in 2 Maunz/Dürig, Art. 20, Abschnitt VII, Rdnr. 12.

[40] 111 RGZ 320 (1925). Cf., e.g., Art. 111, 115 WRV (permitting freedom of movement and the inviolability of the home to be restricted only on the basis of legislation), 118 (declaring the right to express one's opinions "within the limits of the general laws"). See also Denninger in 1 AK-GG, Art. 1, Abs. 2, 3, Rdnr. 17.

[41] See text at note 29 supra.

[42] See, e.g., Dürig, supra note 35, at 184-90. It had been widely understood that proprietary activities were not restricted by fundamental rights during the Weimar period. See, e.g., Walter Jellinek, Verwaltungsrecht 25 (3d ed. 1931). Even before adoption of the Basic Law, however, doubts were raised as to the desirability of such an exemption. "What happens," Ernst Forsthoff inquired in the improbable year of 1938, "if the state turns the individual's dependence upon it into a tool for domination?" Forsthoff, Die Verwaltung als Leistungsträger 15 (1938). Surely, the same author added in 1950, "the public administration cannot be permitted to avoid its specific responsibilities simply by changing the form in which it acts." 1 Forsthoff, Lehrbuch des Verwaltungsrechts 61 (1950). Quoting this latter passage, even supporters of a proprietary exemption tended to concede that the test was substantive rather than formal: The state was bound by the Bill of Rights whenever it fulfilled a "public function," even if it did so through a corporation or other organization established under private law. See Dürig, supra, at 186. Others went further: Because of the threat to individual freedom, the Bill of Rights applied whenever the state appeared as "provider of essential services" or possessed "a legal or factual monopoly." See Otto Bachof, Der Rechtsschutz im öffentlichen Recht: gelöste und ungelöste Probleme, 6 DöV 417, 423 (1953). Still others have argued for complete abolition of the proprietary exemption on both textual and

This qualification, which still enjoys considerable support,[43] has vestigial counterparts (however controversial) in our own jurisprudence.[44] Beyond this, it was argued, the fact that judicial power was state power did not mean the courts offended the Bill of Rights whenever they enforced a contract that the state itself was forbidden to make; for such a conclusion would put an end to private autonomy.[45]

This concern is a real one, and it lies at the heart of the widespread criticism of our Supreme Court's decision in *Shelley v. Kraemer*.[46] Any such concern seems to have been misplaced in *Lüth*, however, since the rule against unethical behavior had been prescribed by the state itself and not by the parties – as the Constitutional Court appeared to acknowledge in distinguishing between prescriptive rules and those that merely enforced private decisions.[47]

---

teleological grounds. See, e.g., Rüfner, supra note 32, Rdnr. 39-46; Denninger in 1 AK-GG, Art. 1, Abs. 2, 3, Rdnr. 30; Hesse, supra note 2, Rdnr. 346-48: "All public authorities are always bound by the Constitution." The Constitutional Court has never resolved the question, but its flat rejection of a similar traditional exception for prisoners and others in "special relationships" with the state augurs ill for the future of the proprietary rule. See 33 BVerfGE 1, 11 (1972) (finding the notion that prisoners' rights could be restricted at will inconsistent with the comprehensive terms of Art. 1(3)); note 107 infra.

[43] See, e.g., Dürig in 1 Maunz/Dürig, Art. 1, Abs. III, Rdnr. 134-38; Michael Ronellenfitsch, Wirtschaftliche Betätigung des Staates, 3 Handbuch des Staatsrechts 1171, Rdnr. 45-49 (dealing with the textual difficulty by arguing that in buying coal or brewing beer the state is not exercising official *power* ("Gewalt")).

[44] Justice Holmes's obtuse refusal to perceive a threat to civil liberties in the selective award of privileges (There is "no constitutional right to be a policeman," McAuliffe v. Mayor of New Bedford, 155 Mass. 216, 200, 29 N.E. 517 (1892)), has long since been rectified. E.g., Speiser v. Randall, 357 U.S. 513 (1958). But see the questionable proprietary exception from the implicit Art. I prohibition of state measures unduly burdening or discriminating against interstate commerce, Reeves, Inc. v. Stake, 447 U.S. 429 (1980). Cf. the less objectionable decisions denying the states such benefits as immunity from taxation, regulation, or suit when they act in a proprietary capacity. E.g., South Carolina v. United States, 199 U.S. 437 (1905); United Transportation Union v. Long Island R.R., 455 U.S. 678 (1982); Parden v. Terminal Ry., 377 U.S. 184 (1964).

[45] See, e.g., Dürig in 1 Maunz/Dürig, Art. 1, Abs. III, Rdnr. 121; Merten, supra note 7, Rdnr. 19: "If citizens are not bound by the Basic Rights directly, the fact that they submit their disputes for resolution by courts that are so bound does not make them so."

[46] 334 U.S. 1 (1948). See The Second Century at 358-59.

[47] See text at note 36 supra. Commentators nevertheless continue to call for application of the "objective values" of the Bill of Rights in the enforcement of private contracts as well, especially when one party can be said to possess monopoly power. E.g., Denninger in 1 AK-GG, vor Art. 1, Rdnr. 31-32; Hesse, supra note 2, Rdnr. 357. For a recent judicial example outside the sphere of free expression see BVerfG, Decision of Oct. 19, 1993, Case No. 1 BvR 567/89 (not yet reported), where the Court held the guarantee of private autonomy implicit in Art. 2(1) forbade enforcement of

In support of a broader distinction between public and private law it might plausibly be argued that the danger of state oppression is at its height when the state is itself a party to the controversy; when it seeks merely to resolve conflicts between private interests there may be less need for constitutional protection.[48]

Precisely this distinction cropped up in the United States not long ago in a major effort to explain the troublesome distinction between regulation and taking under the fifth amendment.[49] As a generalization about the relative danger of various types of state action it cannot be dismissed as wholly without weight. As a justification for excluding private law from constitutional scrutiny entirely, however, it seems to fall short. The same balance of interests may often underlie provisions of both public and private law; public regulation may resolve conflicts between private interests, and private enforcement may serve public purposes. As the Supreme Court observed in the *Sullivan* case, a private action for seditious libel would have much the same effect on speech as a public prosecution; to hold the former exempt from constitutional restraints would give the state a means of suppressing expression it was the particular purpose of the first amendment to protect.[50]

Thus it was entirely understandable for the Constitutional Court to conclude that the guarantee of free expression was implicated by the injunction in *Lüth*, even if one assumes, as the Basic Law seems to say, that Article 5 limits only state action. In order to reach that conclusion, however, the Court embraced a far broader principle of objective constitutional values that has had sweeping consequences in later cases.

With this threshold question out of the way, the Constitutional Court proceeded to balance the competing interests in order to assess the validity of the injunction. On the one hand lay the interest of the offending director, who stood to suffer a serious loss of professional opportunity by virtue of a boycott invitation that the civil courts had characterized as unethical ("gegen die guten Sitten").[51] On the other lay the speaker's interest, protected by Article 5(1), in participating in the formation of public opinion. The call to boycott had been motivated by no crass considerations of personal profit; the speaker was not a competitor in the movie market. The question of Germany's

---

an unconscionable surety agreement between parties of unequal bargaining power.

[48] For a more theoretical justification in terms of the traditional German understanding of the nature of private law see Quint, supra note 26, at 254-57.

[49] See Joseph Sax, Takings and the Police Power, 74 Yale L.J. 36 (1964); Sax, Takings, Private Property and Public Rights, 81 Yale L.J. 149 (1971).

[50] 376 U.S. 254, 277-78 (1964).

[51] The full provision, § 826 BGB, provides that anyone who "intentionally causes harm to another in a manner offensive to good morals" shall be liable for compensatory damages.

reputation in the outside world was of great public importance; the speaker had concluded in good faith that general acceptance of motion pictures directed by a former purveyor of anti-Semitic propaganda might induce people to think that nothing had changed since the fall of the Nazis. The boycott invitation, inseparable from the expression of opinion, was already implicit in the assertion that the director was not a fit representative of the German film industry.[52] The peroration was a ringing defense of freedom of expression: "When the formation of public opinion on a question important to the general welfare is at stake, private and particularly economic interests of individuals must basically take second place."[53] The remedy for harmful speech in this context, the Court concluded in terms familiar to the U.S. reader, was not suppression but more speech.[54]

The limits of this decision were revealed in the *Blinkfüer* case in 1969, where the Constitutional Court reversed a decision upholding the right of powerful newspaper publishers to threaten to withhold their products from news dealers who continued to sell program guides to East German radio and television broadcasts.[55] Even those with significant economic power, the Court acknowledged, were entitled to request others, as in *Lüth*, to participate in a boycott on political grounds – for in such a case those against whom the boycott was directed could defend themselves by counterarguments of their own. But it was quite another thing for powerful publishers to compel others to participate by the threat of boycotting *them* if they did not comply – for the application of such economic force deprived the news dealers of power to make their own decision and thus gave those calling for the boycott an unfair advantage in the struggle to influence public opinion.[56]

Up to this point the results of the German boycott cases should strike a responsive chord in those acquainted with the decisions of the U.S. Supreme Court. For while publication of facts and opinions respecting a dispute of significant public interest is protected by the first amendment despite its inherent tendency to dissuade third parties from dealing with the other party to the dispute,[57] secondary boycotts are not protected in this country either, even if based on polit-

---

[52] 7 BVerfGE at 214-21.

[53] Id. at 219.

[54] See id.: "Wer sich durch die öffentliche Äußerung eines anderen verletzt fühlt, kann ebenfalls vor der Öffentlichkeit erwidern." Cf. Whitney v. California, 274 U.S. 357, 377 (1927) (Brandeis, J., concurring).

[55] 25 BVerfGE 256 (1969).

[56] Id. at 264-67. Cf. 62 BVerfGE 230 (1982).

[57] Thornhill v. Alabama, 310 U.S. 88 (1940).

ical rather than economic grounds[58] – except, of course, for those conducted by the NAACP.[59]

Here, however, the parallel between the German and American decisions comes to a screeching halt. Unwilling to rest on the conclusion that Article 5(1) did not forbid the courts to award damages against publishers who had coerced dealers into refusing to deal, the Court held the same Article actually *required* them to do so. Publication of East German program guides was itself an exercise of freedom of the press; "the purpose of [the press provision] to facilitate and promote the uninhibited formation of public opinion requires that the press be protected against attempts to short-circuit the market place of ideas by coercive economic means."[60] By denying a remedy against private interference with dissemination of these guides, the civil court had infringed their publishers' freedom of the press.

On this momentous question the *Blinkfüer* opinion was conspicuously short of reasons. At two points the Court even appeared to embrace the far more radical position that the purely private act of threatening a boycott was itself a violation of Article 5.[61] In light of a number of analogous decisions, however, it seems likely that the language quoted above more accurately reflects the *Blinkfüer* holding: Like numerous other Bill of Rights provisions, Article 5(1)'s free press guarantee imposes an affirmative duty on the state to protect the press against third parties, not merely to leave it alone.[62]

---

[58] International Longshoremen's Ass'n v. Allied International, Inc., 456 U.S. 212 (1982).

[59] NAACP v. Claiborne Hardware Co., 458 U.S. 886 (1982). See The Second Century at 506 n. 4.

[60] 25 BVerfGE at 268.

[61] "The boycott . . . infringed this constitutionally guaranteed [press] freedom. . . . In violation of the freedom of reporting, the conduct of the defendants was designed to suppress information by predominantly economic means." Id. at 268-69. For discussion of this issue see text at notes 28-35 supra.

[62] See the general discussion of positive constitutional rights in chapter 1 supra. Cf. the famous abortion cases, 39 BVerfGE 1 (1975) and 88 BVerfGE 203 (1993) and other decisions discussed in chapter 6, as well as those finding in similar provisions an affirmative state duty to remove technical, financial, and organizational obstacles to the exercise of broadcasting and academic freedoms, text at notes 252-59, 285-86 infra. Even dogged opponents of the theory that provisions like Art. 5(1) directly bind private parties tend to accept the "more restrained" principle – which leads to the same practical result in many cases – of an indirect effect ("mittelbare Drittwirkung") derived from the state's obligation to prevent private interference with interests protected by the Bill of Rights. E.g., Dürig in 1 Maunz/Dürig, Art. 1, Abs. III, Rdnr. 102, 131; Herzog in 1 Maunz/Dürig, Art. 5, Abs. I, II, Rdnr. 28-29. See also Denninger in 1 AK-GG, vor Art. 1, Rdnr. 33 (finding the state's duty to protect against private actions a logical outgrowth of the "objective order of values" principle announced in *Lüth*); 36 BVerfGE 321, 331-33 (1974) and 81 BVerfGE 108, 115-17 (1989) (concluding that the state has an affirmative duty under Art. 5(3) to promote art but no duty to refrain from taxing it); Rupert Scholz in 1 Maunz/Dürig, Art. 5, Abs. III, Rdnr. 40 (adding that there is no obliga-

B. Early Defamation Cases

The *Lüth* decision had given impressive scope to freedom of expression as against significant economic interests. The well-known
Schmid-Spiegel decision of 1961 applied the principles laid down in
Lüth to give the same guarantee a similarly broad scope in the face of
a countervailing interest in reputation.[63]

Responding to an article in the newsmagazine "Der Spiegel" intimating that he was little better than a Communist, Schmid had
gone beyond merely denying its assertions to compare the periodical
itself to a purveyor of pornography, concerned less with the truth
than with increasing its own circulation.[64] In punishing these an-
imadversions as a criminal libel against the magazine's editors, said
the Constitutional Court, the courts below had failed to give adequate
consideration to Article 5(1). Striking a theme that has featured
prominently in its later decisions, the Court began by pointing out
that Schmid had not attacked "Der Spiegel" gratuitously; he had reacted to the magazine's own attack against him.[65] Nor was the
matter one simply of defending the speaker's personal honor; since
Schmid was a judge of the highest court of one of the Länder, his fitness for that office was, like the reputation of the German film industry in *Lüth*, a subject of significant public interest. Finally, the Court
concluded, Schmid's response was not excessive under the circumstances: An attack on the periodical's general reputation for veracity
was a more powerful defense than denial of its particular allegations
standing alone, and "Der Spiegel" had opened itself up to such
charges by its unreliable treatment of the facts in this case.[66]

---

tion to subsidize particular artists). For limitations on *selective* art subsidies see
text at notes 295-309 infra.

[63] 12 BVerfGE 113 (1961).

[64] Id. at 114-18.

[65] See also 24 BVerfGE 278, 286 (1968), where in setting aside an injunction
against suggesting that the imposition of fees for tape recording copyrighted works
might bring about East German conditions ("östliche Verhältnisse") the Court extended the counterpunch doctrine to embrace responses not only to personal attacks
but to political positions as well); 54 BVerfGE 129, 138 (1980); Herzog in 1
Maunz/Dürig, Art. 5, Abs. I, II, Rdnr. 278. There may be a darker side to the ap-
pealing principle that one has greater latitude in responding to an attack; it suggests that constitutional protections may not be so great, even in matters of significant public interest, for those who cast the first stone.

[66] 12 BVerfGE at 128-32. Along the way (id. at 126-27) the Court adverted to the
question whether an attack on the magazine could fairly be said to impugn the reputation of its editors at all but found it unnecessary to resolve that question. Cf. New
York Times v. Sullivan, 376 U.S. 254, 286-88 (1964). See also BVerfG, Judgment of
Mar. 5, 1992, Case No. 1 BvR 1770/91, 1992 NJW 2815, 2816 (observing that little

As the Court would soon emphasize, injury to reputation brings into play not only a variety of "general laws" restricting expression but also the provision of Article 5(2) that the freedoms enumerated in Article 5(1) encounter additional limits in the right to inviolability of personal honor ("in dem Recht der persönlichen Ehre").[67] Although it seemed to treat the case as if it concerned only the reciprocal effect of free expression on general laws purporting to restrict that liberty,[68] the *Schmid-Spiegel* decision necessarily implied that the same balancing process applied to the independent personal honor limitation – as the Court expressly confirmed a few years later.[69]

Any suspicion that this conclusion might portend the general demise of defamation laws, however, was dispelled by a summary 1965 decision.[70] In the context of a controversy over the management of an apartment house, the defendant had accused two members of

---

weight should be given to "indirect" harm to individual reputation caused by criticism of public conduct).

[67] See 19 BVerfGE 73, 74 (1965). This limitation was added, as Theodor Heuss explained to the constitutional convention, "because defamation and false reporting about an individual's private and public life ought not to be allowed." 1 JöR (n.F.) at 80. The Convention may well have been influenced in reaching this conclusion by the devastating effect of systematic defamation during the Nazi period. See David Riesman, Democracy and Defamation: Control of Group Libel, 42 Colum. L. Rev. 727, 728 (1942) ("In the rise of the Nazis to power in Germany, defamation was a major weapon."); Riesman, Democracy and Defamation: Fair Game and Fair Comment I, 42 Colum. L. Rev. 1085 (1942) (describing the Nazi strategy). Special mention of personal honor and of the protection of youth – the third limitation on expressive freedoms enumerated in Art. 5(2) – was necessary, it has been said, to permit those interests to be promoted by laws that were not "general" but were directed against the expression itself. See 1 von Mangoldt/Klein/Starck, Art. 5, Abs. 1, 2, Rdnr. 131; Schmidt-Jortzig, supra note 13, Rdnr. 47-48.

[68] See 12 BVerfGE at 124-25.

[69] 42 BVerfGE 143, 150 (1976). Balancing also applies to the third limitation on the rights conferred by Art. 5(1), namely "the provisions of law for the protection of youth." See 30 BVerfGE 336, 347-48, 353 (1971) (upholding a prohibition on mailorder distribution of publications harmful to minors but finding it unreasonable to apply it to all nudist colony propaganda). For the view that by listing personal honor and the protection of youth specifically in Art. 5(2) the framers meant for these values almost always to prevail against speech see Herzog in 1 Maunz/Dürig, Art 5, Abs. I, II, Rdnr. 268.

The Constitutional Court has so far been spared the disagreeable task of determining the limits of permissible regulation of obscene publications in the case of adults. See § 184 of the Strafgesetzbuch (StGB) (criminal code); Scholz in 1 Maunz/Dürig, Art. 5, Abs. III, Rdnr. 77 (arguing that obscenity can qualify as art within Art. 5(3) and that it may be forbidden only in particularly gross cases involving such subjects as violence, child abuse, or bestiality); Karl-Heinz Ladeur in 1 AK-GG, Art. 5, Abs. 3, Abschnitt II, Rdnr. 14-17 (documenting a liberalization in the decisions of the civil courts).

[70] 19 BVerfGE 73 (1965).

its governing body of self-enrichment, fraud, denunciation, dishonesty, and untrustworthiness ("Bereicherung, Betrug, Denunziation, Unehrlichkeit und Unglaubwürdigkeit"). Without bothering to distinguish the *Schmid-Spiegel* decision, the Court upheld a preliminary injunction against further dissemination of these accusations. The defamation law served to protect personal honor, which in turn restricted freedom of expression; the defendant had exhibited his intention to inflict reputational harm and forfeited any defense of protecting his own concerns by circulating his defamatory accusations far beyond the circle of persons with any legitimate interest in the controversy. Finally, the opinion added, the injunction did not prevent the offending speaker from bringing suspected grievances concerning building management, "in suitable form," to the attention of management or of public authority.[71]

To have invalidated defamation laws entirely would have read the personal-honor clause out of the Constitution, but that provision did not compel the Court to reach the result it did. The case could have been distinguished from *Schmid-Spiegel* on the basis of the earlier opinion: There was no reason to think that a dispute over management of an apartment building was of significant public interest and no suggestion that the defendant was responding to an attack by those whom he disparaged.

Significantly, however, the Court never addressed the question whether the allegations of fraud, dishonesty, and the like that it permitted to be enjoined were true or false. The criminal code generally makes truth a justification for dissemination of specific facts injurious to reputation, but not of defamatory conclusions.[72] Taken together with these provisions, the Court's reminder that the injunction left the speaker free to phrase his message in suitable form seemed to suggest that in the absence of special circumstances – such as the necessity to reply to previous allegations respecting a matter of public importance – even a truthful speaker could be required to confine himself to specific facts and to refrain from uttering defamatory conclusions.

C. *Mephisto*

The cases just discussed set the stage for the controversial *Mephisto* decision of 1971, in which the Constitutional Court by an unsatisfying 3-3 vote upheld an injunction against publication of a novel on defamation grounds.[73]

---

[71] Id. at 74-75.

[72] Contrast §§ 186 StGB ("üble Nachrede"), 185 ("Beleidigung"). See Eduard Dreher & Herbert Tröndle, Strafgesetzbuch und Nebengesetze, § 186, Rdnr. 1-3.

[73] 30 BVerfGE 173 (1971). In 1971, as today, each panel of the Court consisted of eight Justices. Why Justices Haager and Simon did not take part in the decision the report does not reveal.

The novel was *Mephisto*, by Klaus Mann. Its central figure was an actor called Hendrik Höfgen, who was said to have made his name by portraying the devil in Goethe's *Faust,* and who as the Court put it "betrayed his own political convictions and cast off all ethical and humanitarian restraints to further his career by making a pact with the possessors of power in Nazi Germany." It was admitted that Höfgen had been based upon the real-life actor Gustaf Gründgens, who had likewise built his career around the Mephisto role and achieved great success under the Nazi regime.

Mann made no claim that he was presenting an accurate portrait of Gründgens. As he explained elsewhere and repeated in a preface to the edition that was enjoined, Höfgen was meant to symbolize a type, not an individual; his thoughts and actions were in large part the product of the author's imagination. Despite these disclaimers, the civil courts seized upon discrepancies between the fictitious Höfgen and the real Gründgens to conclude that the novel defamed the memory of the deceased actor by making him appear more disreputable than he had actually been.[74] In enjoining such an injurious distortion of the facts, three Justices concluded, the civil courts had not offended Article 5.

The novel itself, the Court conceded, was a work of art.[75] Even if it also contained expressions of opinion, it was therefore to be judged by the guarantee of artistic freedom rather than by that of freedom of expression; for in this context the former was the more specific provision.[76] This conclusion seemed only to make the injunction more difficult to sustain. For while the freedom to express opinions, like freedom of broadcasting and of the press, is expressly made subject to "the general laws, the provisions of law for the protection of youth, and the right to inviolability of personal honor," artistic freedom, as the Court confirmed, is not: Article 5(3) provides flatly that "art and science, research, and teaching, shall be free."[77]

That did not mean, said the Court, that there were no limits on artistic (or academic) freedom. Article 5(3) must be read in conjunc-

---

[74] Id. at 174-81.

[75] Id. at 189-90. For a glimpse into the formidable difficulties of defining art for purposes of Art. 5(3) see Denninger, supra note 7, Rdnr. 1-17.

[76] 30 BVerfGE at 200. For other examples of the prevalent *lex specialis* principle in German constitutional law see chapter 2 supra, and chapter 5 infra. In the United States one would be inclined to say a work embodying both artistic and political expression would have to surmount both hurdles before it could be upheld.

[77] 30 BVerfGE at 191-92. Expression, press, and broadcasting appear in the first paragraph of Art. 5; the second paragraph enumerates the limitations on these rights ("diese Rechte") quoted in the text; the third provides separately for artistic and academic freedom, with the sole qualification that "freedom of teaching shall not absolve from loyalty to the constitution." See also 30 BVerfGE at 192-93 (adding for similar textual reasons that the reference in Art. 2(1) to "the rights of others, the constitutional order, and the moral code" restricted only the right to development of personality guaranteed by that provision, not the more specific freedoms listed in Art. 5).

tion with other constitutional provisions such as the guarantee of human dignity (Art. 1(1)) and the right to free development of personality (Art. 2(1)). Since Gründgens was dead, the latter provision did not apply; for (said the Court without giving any reasons) the right of personality "presumes the existence of a person at least potentially capable of taking action in the future." But it would be inconsistent with human dignity to permit an individual to be freely disparaged after death. Since neither dignity nor artistic freedom was automatically entitled to precedence in case of conflict, it was the duty of the courts to balance the artist's interest in freedom against his subject's interest in dignity under the circumstances of each particular case.[78]

The reader steeped in the U.S. Constitution may have difficulty perceiving any such conflict. Even in Germany, as we have seen, most constitutional provisions appear to apply only to the state,[79] and it was Klaus Mann, not the government, who had allegedly offended Gründgens's dignity. For those who have followed the exposition in this chapter, however, the explanation should come as no surprise. For as the Court said in paraphrasing the language of the Basic Law itself, Article 1(1) expressly imposes an affirmative obligation upon

---

[78] Id. at 193-96. Examples commonly cited to show that an absolute right could never have been intended include the midnight trumpeter and the authentic stage murder, see Ladeur in 1 AK-GG, Art. 5, Abs. 3, pt. II, Rdnr. 11; Denninger, supra note 7, Rdnr. 38. See also 33 BVerfGE 52, 65-71 (1972), text at note 238 infra (upholding a restriction on importation of artistic films on the basis of the constitutional obligation to protect national security); BVerfG, Judgment of March 19, 1984, Case No. 2 BvR 1/84, 1984 NJW 1293, 1294 (Sprayer von Zürich) (finding no barrier to extradition of a talented graffiti artist both because Art. 5(3) in itself conferred no right to the use of the property of others and because of the countervailing constitutional right to property); Scholz in 1 Maunz/Dürig, Art. 5, Abs. III, Rdnr. 51-78 (summarizing the limits of artistic freedom). The records of the constitutional convention reveal no discussion one way or the other respecting the limiting effect of other constitutional provisions on the freedoms guaranteed by Art. 5(3). See 1 JöR (n.F.) at 89-92. At least one prominent commentator, however, finding it impossible to believe that a similarly worded provision of the Weimar Constitution had been intended to be absolute, had read it as if, like the expression and religion clauses of the same document, it had expressly permitted artistic freedom to be limited by "general laws." See Anschütz, supra note 7, at 658-61. For criticism of the Court's position that only other constitutional provisions can limit rights not subject to an express reservation of legislative authority see Martin Kriele, Grundrechte und demokratischer Gestaltungsspielraum, 5 Handbuch des Staatsrechts 101, Rdnr. 69-75 (doubting that all legitimate limits on artistic freedom can fairly be traced to the Basic Law itself and citing (at 74) the counterexample of the right to choose one's occupation (see chapter 6 infra), which Art. 12(1) guarantees without reservation but which the Court has held subject to legislative restriction on the basis of a balance of interests).

[79] See text at notes 29-35 supra; Denninger, supra note 7, Rdnr. 26 (confirming that this is true of the artistic freedom guaranteed by Art. 5(3)).

the state to protect human dignity, not merely to refrain from abusing it by its own actions.[80]

For the three Justices who believed the injunction valid, the conclusion followed swiftly from these premises. It was for the civil courts to make the constitutional commands concrete by balancing the opposing interests in the particular case, and the Constitutional Court's reviewing authority was narrowly limited:

> It is not enough to infringe the losing party's basic rights that in performing the balancing process entrusted to him the judge has reached a questionable result by giving too much or too little weight to the interests on one or the other side. Unlike an ordinary appellate tribunal, the Constitutional Court is not empowered to substitute its own evaluation of the particular case for that of the duly authorized judge. It may find an infringement of the losing party's basic rights in such cases only if that judge has either failed to recognize his obligation to balance competing constitutional rights or bases his decision on a fundamentally erroneous conception of the meaning of one or the other of the rights in question.[81]

In determining that *Mephisto* impermissibly defamed Gründgens's memory, these Justices concluded, the civil courts had neither misunderstood the meaning of the relevant provisions, nor failed to perceive the necessity for balancing the competing interests, nor weighed them arbitrarily within the meaning of Article 3. Finally, the opinion added, there was no need to decide whether the result was consistent with the principle of proportionality ("Verhältnismäßigkeit"), which limited incursions by public authority into the realm of individual freedom; for that principle, the Justices declared without giving any reasons, did not apply in passing upon judicial resolution of private interests – a conclusion in obvious tension with the purposes of the proportionality requirement and with the *Lüth* decision as well.[82]

Three Justices took issue with these conclusions, and two wrote powerful dissenting opinions.[83] Thus the Court was equally divided;

---

[80] 30 BVerfGE at 194. See Art. 1(1) GG: "Die Würde des Menschen ist unantastbar. Sie zu achten *und zu schützen* ist Verpflichtung aller staatlichen Gewalt." (emphasis added). Cf. the *Blinkfüer* decision, text at notes 54-62 supra. See also Art. 4 of the Constitution of Rheinland-Pfalz (Verfassung für Rheinland-Pfalz vom 18. Mai 1947, VBl. S. 209), which expressly provides that personal honor is entitled to state protection ("Die Ehre des Menschen steht unter dem Schutz des Staates") and requires prosecution of group libel.

[81] 30 BVerfGE at 197.

[82] Id. at 199-200. For the proportionality principle see chapter 1 supra; for *Lüth* see text at notes 35-36 supra.

[83] 30 BVerfGE at 200-27 (opinions of Stein and Rupp-von Brünneck, JJ.). The third dissenter was not identified.

and since a majority was necessary to establish a violation of the constitution, the injunction could not be set aside.[84]

Both dissenting opinions disagreed vehemently with the prevailing Justices' narrow view of the Constitutional Court's function. As the dissenters pointed out, this conception seemed contrary to long-standing precedent: Ever since the *Lüth* decision the Court had balanced competing interests for itself in determining whether the regular courts had correctly applied the constitutional standard.[85] Moreover, as Justice Stein suggested, it seemed difficult to reconcile the prevailing opinion's hands-off attitude with the provision authorizing constitutional complaints whenever basic rights had been infringed; for almost by definition a court that has given too much weight to countervailing interests has denied the asserted right.[86]

On the merits the central objection of both dissenting opinions was that the civil courts had given too little weight to the fact that *Mephisto* was not a biography but a novel. Justice Stein emphasized among other things that art could not fulfill its function without drawing on sources from the real world;[87] Justice Rupp-von Brünneck argued there was little risk that anyone would think the author was making factual assertions about Gründgens and suggested that the framers' decision to state artistic freedom in unqualified terms might imply that they had doubted a work of fiction could ever be defamatory.[88] The latter Justice closed with the observation that extraordinary latitude for polemic should be afforded to those who, like

---

[84] Id. at 196. See § 15(3) BVerfGG.

[85] 30 BVerfGE at 200-02 (Stein, J.), 219-21 (Rupp-von Brünneck, J.). Suggestions of the narrow standard enunciated in *Mephisto* had appeared in two then recent decisions not involving art or expression, which not surprisingly were relied upon by the prevailing opinion. See id. at 196-97, citing 18 BVerfGE 85, 92-93 (1964) and 22 BVerfGE 93, 97 (1967). For the dissenters' less restrictive interpretation of the former opinion (on which the later decision had relied) see 30 BVerfGE at 219-20.

[86] See Art. 93(1) cl. 4a GG ("Verfassungsbeschwerden, die von jedermann mit der Behauptung erhoben werden können, durch die öffentliche Gewalt in einem seiner Grundrechte . . . verletzt zu sein"); 30 BVerfGE at 201-02 (arguing that with a narrow review standard the Court "could not fulfill its role as guardian of basic rights"). Of course it is conceivable that Bill of Rights provisions themselves might require only a good-faith balancing by the regular courts, not a decision that gives proper weight to constitutional values. Cf. The First Century at 73 (discussing *Marbury v. Madison*). But that is hardly the reading most compelling in light of either the text or its purpose. Cf. the broad standard of review the Court has consistently held required by Art. 19(4), which ensures a judicial remedy whenever the executive infringes a legal right. See chapter 3 supra.

[87] 30 BVerfGE at 206-10. See also id. at 217 (applying the proportionality principle the prevailing opinion found inapplicable).

[88] Id. at 223-24. See also id. at 221-22 (accusing the prevailing Justices of having subjected artistic freedom in effect, despite their protestations, to the inapplicable limitations of Art. 5(2)); Ladeur in 1 AK-GG, Art. 5, Abs. 3, pt. II, Rdnr. 19 (noting that Thomas Mann's classic novel *Buddenbrooks* had also been accused of falsifying the portraits of actual citizens).

Klaus Mann in *Mephisto*, were attempting to respond to an attack on their position in a matter of great public interest – and for this conclusion she cited not only the *Schmid-Spiegel* decision but also *New York Times v. Sullivan*.[89]

The analogy was apt. The *Sullivan* opinion had broken new ground in the United States by requiring the traditional interest in reputation to yield to freedom of expression, absent essentially deliberate falsehood, whenever the person injured was a public official (or, later decisions added, some other public figure). It had also made clear beyond peradventure that the Court itself must determine de novo not only the meaning of the constitution but also its application to the facts.[90] On the one hand, Gustaf Gründgens would surely qualify as a public figure for purposes of the Supreme Court's test.[91] On the other hand, the author of *Mephisto* plainly knew his fictitious character did not correspond in every significant respect with the real Gründgens; he did not intend it to. Thus in one sense his falsification of the actor was deliberate; but would the Supreme Court have considered it a falsification at all?

The more recent decision in *Hustler Magazine v. Falwell*[92] suggests a negative answer. For in that case the Supreme Court sensibly concluded that there could be no cause of action when a caricature was so ludicrous that no one could possibly believe it had been intended as a statement of fact.[93] The Supreme Court has not had the occasion to apply its calculus to a more conventional work of fiction, and anyone who takes the protection of reputation seriously must be concerned – as the dissenters in *Mephisto* conceded – not to permit the libel laws to be evaded by simply affixing to defamatory assertions the figleaf of a fictitious name.[94] Nevertheless one might expect the Supreme Court after *Sullivan* to give more weight to the interest in uninhibited discourse on matters of public concern than the Constitutional Court gave it in *Mephisto*. In the light of *Lüth* and *Schmid-*

---

[89] 30 BVerfGE at 225-26 (citing 12 BVerfGE 113 (1961), text at notes 62-69 supra, and New York Times Co. v. Sullivan, 376 U.S. 254 (1964)).

[90] 376 U.S. at 284-85. See also Bose Corp. v. Consumers Union, 466 U.S. 485 (1984) (reaffirming this conclusion with particular repect to the question of actual malice); Quint, supra note 26, at 311 (observing that the prevailing opinion in *Mephisto* exhibited an "extraordinary lack of concern about the decision in the individual case (from an American point of view)").

[91] Cf. Curtis Publishing Co. v. Butts, 388 U.S. 130 (1967) (holding a prominent football coach a public figure).

[92] 485 U.S. 46 (1988).

[93] A generation later, in setting aside a damage award based upon the satirical designation of a public figure as a "born murderer," the Constitutional Court recognized the essence of the *Falwell* principle: "This [recognizably nonserious] satire must be stripped of its verbal and pictorial disguise in order that one may appreciate its real content." 86 BVerfGE 1, 12 (1992). Five years earlier, however, in a case more closely resembling *Falwell* on its facts, the Court had held the utterance unprotected. See text at note 128 infra.

[94] See 30 BVerfGE at 210-12, 224.

Spiegel one might have expected as much from the Constitutional
Court as well.

D. Other Restrictive Decisions

In the years immediately following *Mephisto* the Constitutional
Court rendered a series of decisions reaffirming the respect afforded
by the prevailing opinion in that case to such interests as reputation
and privacy as limits on freedom of expression.

In the famous *Soraya* decision in 1973, the Court applied the balancing test laid down in *Lüth* to uphold an award of damages for
publication of a fictitious interview with the former wife of the Shah
of Iran: "An *imaginary* interview adds nothing to the formation of
real public opinion. As against press utterances of this sort, the protection of privacy takes unconditional priority."[95] Later the same

---

[95] 34 BVerfGE 269, 283-84 (1973). Cf. 54 BVerfGE 208 (1980) (*Böll*) (holding for
similar reasons that false quotations were not protected by Art. 5). "The degree of
care that must be expended to avoid dissemination of an *imaginary* interview," the
Court declared in *Soraya*, "is never too much to expect." 34 BVerfGE at 286. Contrast
Masson v. New Yorker, 111 S.Ct. 2419 (1991) (unexpectedly concluding that even
deliberate falsification of quotations did not necessarily demonstrate the knowledge of falsity required by *New York Times v. Sullivan*).

More troubling than the substantive issue of balancing in *Soraya* was an important question of separation of powers. Art. 5(2) seems to say that, apart from matters
of personal honor and the protection of youth, the expressive freedoms protected by
Art. 5(1) may be limited only by legislation ("Vorschriften der allgemeinen
Gesetze"). See Hesse, supra note 2, Rdnr. 314. No statute purported to authorize an
award of damages for emotional harm resulting from invasion of privacy. § 823 of
the Civil Code did provide generally for compensatory relief in cases of negligent
or intentional infringement of another's rights. § 253 of the same Code, however,
appeared on its face to *forbid* damages in a case like *Soraya*. It was only by placing
great weight on the use of the conjunctive term "Gesetz und Recht" (sometimes
translated as "law and justice") in Art. 20(3) that the Court was able to avoid the
conclusion that the civil courts had violated their obligation to respect the law (see
chapter 3 supra), and Art. 5(2) contains no such terminology.

The Court in *Soraya* said only that § 823 qualified as an "allgemeines Gesetz"
within the meaning of Art. 5(2), and that the newly discovered right to damages for
invasion of privacy did too (34 BVerfGE at 282, 292). Charitably viewed, the opinion
may have meant that it was § 823, as construed in light of the constitutional guarantees of dignity and personality, that restricted speech in this case; to permit limitations based solely on judge-made law would seem to compromise an important
constitutional safeguard.

Similarly disturbing was the interpretation the Court had given, just a few years
before *Soraya*, to the related proviso of Art. 19(1) that "insofar as a basic right may
be restricted by law," the right must be explicitly mentioned in the statute. This requirement, the Court concluded, did not apply to "general laws" limiting expression under Art. 5(2), since such laws merely determined the content of the right itself. 28 BVerfGE 36, 46-47 (1970); 28 BVerfGE 282, 289 (1970). Cf. 10 BVerfGE 89, 99
(1959); 24 BVerfGE 367, 396-97 (1968); 64 BVerfGE 72, 79-81 (1983) (reaching the

year, in an opinion remarkably similar to one rendered by the California Supreme Court about the same time, it concluded that privacy and the interest in rehabilitation outweighed any public interest in publicizing an individual's role in a crime for which he had already paid the penalty.[96] In sustaining an order forbidding the defendant to stigmatize the plaintiff's newspaper as an inflammatory screed of the radical right ("ein rechtsradikales Hetzblatt") in 1976, the Court even seemed to narrow the protection afforded by *Schmid-Spiegel*: The right of counterattack basically extended only to the content and not to the form of expression; although special restraint was called for in imposing retrospective sanctions even for an offensive choice of words, no such reluctance was necessary in the case of a simple injunction.[97]

In the United States, of course, the distinction runs the other way: An injunction is considered a prior restraint and thus subjected to particularly strict scrutiny.[98]

The Constitutional Court's reasoning will be familiar to those who have considered the intricacies of our own prior restraint doctrine: Criminal and compensatory sanctions apply retrospectively,

---

same conclusion, for similar reasons, with respect to free development of personality (Art. 2(1)), the content, limits, and condemnation of property (Art. 14(1), (3)), and occupational freedom (Art. 12(1)), respectively). With all respect, this conclusion seems difficult to square either with the language of Art. 19(1) or with its purpose to assure that basic rights not be limited without a deliberate legislative decision, and it seems to leave little scope for operation of the citation provision. Accord Herzog in 2 Maunz/Dürig, Art. 19, Abs. I, Rdnr. 48-58; Denninger in 1 AK-GG, Art. 19, Abs. 1, Rdnr. 16-18. The same language, it should be noted, applies to the requirement of the same paragraph that laws restricting basic rights be general rather than limited to a particular case.

[96] 35 BVerfGE 202 (1973) (*Lebach*). Cf. Briscoe v. Reader's Digest, 93 Cal. 866, 483 P.2d 34 (1971). Later cases suggest the U.S. Supreme Court might now reach a different result. E.g., Time, Inc. v. Hill, 385 U.S. 374 (1967); Cox Broadcasting Corp. v. Cohn, 420 U.S. 469 (1975). As in *Mephisto*, the remedy in *Lebach* was an injunction; as in *Blinkfüer*, the Court held the constitution *required* a remedy – this time to protect the right to free development of personality guaranteed by Art. 2(1) in conjunction with the right to human dignity, which under Art. 1(1) the state has an explicit affirmative obligation to protect.

[97] 42 BVerfGE 143, 153 (1976). Two Justices dissented, one of them insisting that the danger of injury to reputation was relatively slight because the disparaging characterization had been directed toward the publication itself rather than to those responsible for its publication. Id. at 157 (opinion of Rupp-von Brünneck, J.). Cf. the Supreme Court's conclusion in New York Times v. Sullivan, 376 U.S. 254, 288-89 (1964), that criticism of the Birmingham police could not be taken to defame the police commissioner.

[98] Near v. Minnesota, 283 U.S. 697 (1931). Professor Kommers has suggested that the difference in approach may be attributable to the "high value attached to the personality and dignity clauses of the Basic Law." See Donald Kommers, The Jurisprudence of Free Speech in the United States and in the Federal Republic of Germany, 53 So. Cal. L. Rev. 657, 692 (1980).

subjecting the speaker to a risk of unanticipated loss that may deter even protected conduct for fear of a wrong guess; an injunction inflicts no punishment but merely makes the limits of permissible speech plain for the future.[99]

We have dealt with the retrospectivity problem by providing anticipatory remedies that make it possible to determine the constitutionality of criminal sanctions without incurring them;[100] the Germans too are sensitive to this concern.[101] But the argument that has persuaded our Supreme Court that injunctions pose a particular danger to freedom of expression is that an erroneous order precludes even constitutionally protected conduct until it is finally set aside on appeal. The German Basic Law flatly forbids prior censorship for similar reasons.[102] Whether an injunction has this effect, however, depends upon the collateral bar rule, which in this country generally requires that even an illegal order be obeyed until it is formally reversed.[103] This rule has a strong basis in the respect required for orderly functioning of the courts, but it seems not to be followed in Germany.[104]

---

[99] 42 BVerfGE at 151 (adding that in the case before the Court the author had already disseminated his message and had merely been enjoined from repeating it). See also 54 BVerfGE 129, 136 (1980) (stressing the deterrent effect of a damage award).

[100] See Steffel v. Thompson, 415 U.S. 452, 468 & n. 18 (1974).

[101] See chapter 3 supra.

[102] See Art. 5(1) GG: "Eine Zensur findet nicht statt." This provision means that no expression can be made "dependent upon prior governmental authorization." See Herzog in 1 Maunz/Dürig, Art. 5, Abs. I, II, Rdnr. 78, 298-99; 87 BVerfGE 209, 230-33 (1992) (holding that impoundment of an allegedly violent film as the result of a proceeding to determine whether it was suitable for children offended the censorship ban). Despite its placement in Art. 5(1), the prohibition is said also to apply to the academic (and artistic) freedoms guaranteed without express restriction by Art. 5(3) on the basis of the maxim "a minore ad maius." See Oppermann, supra note 7, Rdnr. 26.

[103] United States v. United Mine Workers, 330 U.S. 258 (1947).

[104] § 890 of the Code of Civil Procedure ("Zivilprozeßordnung") [hereafter cited as ZPO] authorizes fines and incarceration for violation of an injunction ("Unterlassungsurteil"), and the validity of the injunction itself may not be attacked in the enforcement proceeding. See § 767 ZPO (authorizing collateral attack on a judgment only in a separate proceeding and only on grounds arising after the original hearing); Wilhelm Pastor, Die Unterlassungsvollstreckung nach § 890 ZPO (3d ed. 1981), at 255: "The general principle that substantive issues have no place in an execution proceeding also prevails without qualification in the context of a negative injunction." See also 80 BVerfGE 244 (1989) (upholding the imposition of criminal sanctions for violation of an administrative order outlawing a neo-Nazi organization pursuant to Art. 9(2) despite the fact that the order was still subject to appeal).

If the injunction has already been set aside, however, no sanction may be imposed even for a violation committed while the order was still in effect. See Pastor, supra, at 70, 74-75; Bernhard Wieczorek et al., 4 Zivilprozeßordnung und Nebengesetze, § 890, at 349-50 (2d ed. 1981); Adolf Baumbach et al., Zivilprozeßordnung 1865

Indeed a 1992 decision of the Constitutional Court seems to suggest that the collateral bar rule *cannot* constitutionally be followed. The case involved a constitutional complaint against the imposition of money penalties for violation of a police order dispersing an open-air assembly on the ground that it posed an immediate threat to public order and safety. The police could employ immediate force to enforce such an order, the Court conceded, because otherwise public safety could not be assured. No penalties could be imposed, however, unless the dispersal order was valid; for there was no comparable need to compound what in retrospect might be found an unlawful infringement of the freedom to assemble.[105]

This reasoning seems equally applicable to injunctions and to other communicative freedoms, and thus it adds strength to the conclusion that German courts will not ultimately impose sanctions for violation of an order that is set aside on appeal. If this is true, then the Constitutional Court's more tolerant attitude toward injunctions limiting expression can be explained on the ground that a German injunction does not operate as a prior restraint, as a similar order in the United States would.

Quite apart from the prior restraint question, the *Hetzblatt* decision seemed surprisingly tolerant of restrictions on expression respecting a matter of great public interest. Even allowing for the particular connotation of such an accusation in the context of post-Nazi Germany,[106] it is difficult to imagine the U.S. Supreme Court sustaining any sanctions at all against characterizing a periodical as an inflammatory screed of the radical right.[107]

(50th ed. 1992); Richard Zöller et al., Zivilprozeßordnung (16th ed. 1990), § 890, Rdnr. 8-9. If the injunction is reversed after sanctions have been imposed, the contempt judgment is to be set aside as well. See id., Rdnr. 23, citing §§ 775, 776 ZPO;Wieczorek, supra, § 890, at 350. Any fines already paid are then to be refunded ("öffentlich-rechtliche Ersatzleistung") by analogy to the unjust enrichment provision of § 812 BGB (see Baumbach, supra, at 1866 (citing BGH RR 88, 153); 1989 OLGZ 471 (OLG Hamm 1989)), and the other party is liable for other losses attributable to the erroneous injunction under §§ 717 and 945 ZPO. See Zöller, supra, § 890, Rdnr. 23.

[105] 87 BVerfGE 399, 406-13 (1992).

[106] See Quint, supra note 26, at 319 n. 222 (noting that the words "carried rather clear overtones of persecution by the Nazis").

[107] A series of decisions rendered during this period reflect a similarly grudging attitude toward the right of expression by members of the armed forces and intelligence services. The Court seemed sensitive enough to speech concerns in sustaining a soldier's prerogative to write a letter to the editor taking issue with the political views of his superior (28 BVerfGE 55 (1970)), and it would be hard to disagree with its holding that a soldier had no constitutional right to exhort his comrades to disobey orders (28 BVerfGE 51 (1970)). There was also something to be said for the Court's conclusion that an official of the Office for Defense of the Constitution ("Verfassungsschutz") could generally be required to take complaints of illegal wiretapping to his superiors before revealing official secrets to the public (28

E. The Trend Toward Greater Protection

Even as it rendered the restrictive decisions just noted, the Constitutional Court began to lay the groundwork for an approach more protective of expression.

In concluding that the Basic Law did not protect the right to disclose prior crimes, for example, the Court had flatly stated that ordinary proportionality principles applied in assessing the impact of Article 5 on private law and proceeded to balance the competing interests for itself without perceptible deference to the views of the civil courts – all in apparent contradiction to the prevailing opinion in

---

BVerfGE 191 (1970)), and for the later decision that neither Art. 5 nor Art. 8 gave members of the armed services any right to attend political functions in uniform. Any restriction of the right to free development of personality (Art. 2(1)), the Court added in the latter case, was justified by the need to avoid entangling the military in politics. 57 BVerfGE 29, 35-36 (1981). More debatable was the conclusion that a soldier had no right to distribute among his fellows handbills urging them to become conscientious objectors (28 BVerfGE 282 (1970)). Most restrictive of all, however, was the language the Court employed in upholding punishment of a petty officer for venting his spleen before a group of subordinates: By asserting that in the Federal Republic one could not say what one pleased, the officer had "defamed the free democratic order." 28 BVerfGE 36, 50 (1970). In reaching this result, one commentator acidly contended, the Court "confirmed the correctness" of the offending assertion. See Helmut Ridder, Vorbemerkungen zur Begrifflichkeit, Herkunft und Funktion des "Verfassungsschutzes," 2 AK-GG 1409 (1984), Rdnr. 24.

Art. 17a, added in 1956, authorizes statutory restrictions of the speech, assembly, and petition rights of military personnel that go beyond those permitted in the case of civilians – in the interest, as the Court put it, of the effectiveness of the armed forces. See 28 BVerfGE 282, 291 (1970). In none of the above cases did the Court find it necessary to rely on this additional authority; the regulations upheld were all found to qualify as "general laws" within the meaning of Art. 5(2).

For decisions respecting the rights of prisoners to send and receive mail see 33 BVerfGE 1 (1972); 34 BVerfGE 384 (1973); 35 BVerfGE 35 (1973); 40 BVerfGE 276 (1975); 42 BVerfGE 234 (1976). Although the results of these decisions seem unsurprising from across the Atlantic, the first of them – applying the conventional requirement that restrictions of freedom be based upon legislation – created a significant stir. Previously it had often been assumed that fundamental rights basically had no application to "special relationships" such as those of prisoners, soldiers, and pupils in public schools; since then it has been recognized that the normal balancing process applies, although the special governmental interests inherent in such situations often justify greater restrictions of basic rights than would otherwise be allowed. See 33 BVerfGE at 10-11; Wolfgang Loschelder, Grundrechte im Sonderstatus, 5 Handbuch des Staatsrechts 805, Rdnr. 2, 7, 31, 33, 38. To the extent that the state limits the ability of persons in such special status to provide for themselves, however, it may be under a correspondingly enhanced duty to protect and support them. See id., Rdnr. 45-46; see also chapter 5 infra (discussing religious services in the military and in prison).

Mephisto. In the *Hetzblatt* case, moreover, the Court expressly qualified the hands-off approach taken in the *Mephisto* opinion. The degree of scrutiny demanded, the Court now explained, increased with the severity of the restriction. When all that was at stake was a particular form of words, as in the case before it, the Court would be as deferential as it had been in *Mephisto*. But when a particular opinion was suppressed entirely, as in *Lüth* and *Schmid-Spiegel*, the Court would balance the interests de novo.[108]

A companion case decided the same day as *Hetzblatt* demonstrated that the Constitutional Court meant just what it said. The deference practiced in *Mephisto* was out of place, the Court held, when a court had enjoined not only literal repetition of the charge that the Deutschland-Stiftung was a nationalist organization in democratic clothing ("ein nationalistisches Unternehmen mit einem demokratischen Deckmantel") but also dissemination of the same idea in different terms.[109] The civil courts had erred, the Court added, in holding that derogatory value judgments respecting matters of great public interest could not be uttered without providing facts to back them up: "The basic right to free expression of opinion is intended not merely to promote the search for truth but also to assure that every individual may freely say what he thinks, even when he does not or cannot provide an examinable basis for his conclusion."[110] Indeed value judgments, the Court concluded not long afterward, lay at the heart of the right to express one's opinion protected by Article 5(1); unlike statements of fact, they could not be prohibited on the ground that they were false.[111]

---

[108] 42 BVerfGE at 148-50. See also Justice Rupp-von Brünneck's dissent, id. at 154-62 (insisting, as she had in *Mephisto*, on more intensive review).

[109] 42 BVerfGE 163, 168-71 (1976) (*Echternach*) (also applying the same reasoning to the assertion that the Deutschland-Stiftung was misusing the name of former Chancellor Adenauer for right-wing purposes).

[110] Id. at 170-71.

[111] 61 BVerfGE 1, 7-8 (1982) (setting aside an injunction against calling the main-line Christian Social Union (CSU) "the NPD of Europe," an allusion to a domestic party of the radical right). At least for utterances in the political sphere, this decision appeared to reverse the priorities established in the apartment-management case, which had seemed to express particular disfavor toward epithets as contrasted with specific fact allegations. See text at notes 70-72 supra. In terms familiar to readers in the United States, the Court added that the CSU had little basis for complaint since it had voluntarily thrust itself into public view and little need for judicial relief since it had ready access to the media for purposes of self-defense. 61 BVerfGE at 13; cf. Gertz v. Robert Welch, Inc., 418 U.S. 323, 342-45 (1974).

Even the speaker's choice of words was generally protected, the Court later added, despite the distinction drawn in the *Hetzblatt* case. 54 BVerfGE 129, 138-39 (1980) (*Kunstkritik*) (setting aside an award of damages for a critical response to a disgruntled sculptor's attack on the contemporary art establishment); 60 BVerfGE 234, 241 (1982) (setting aside an injunction against use of the term credit sharks ("Kredithaie") for failure to balance the interests of credit brokers against the sub-

Further decisions confirmed the new protective attitude. Criminal sanctions against expression were subject to heightened scrutiny because of their severity,[112] damages for pain and suffering ("Schmerzensgeld") because of their deterrent effect.[113] Even in injunctive cases, if the subject was a matter of significant public interest, there was a presumption in favor of free speech.[114] A work of art had to be evaluated as a whole; it was impermissible to find a display representing the Bavarian leader Franz Josef Strauß in the presence of prominent Nazis defamatory without considering the context in which it appeared.[115]

Even fact findings, moreover, could be scrutinized in criminal cases, especially when they depended solely upon interpretation of written documents in the record.[116] Thus the Court found no adequate justification for interpreting the assertion that the much-maligned Mr. Strauß gave cover to Fascists ("Strauß deckt Faschisten") to mean that he was a Fascist himself,[117] or a reference to the German longing for a strongman ("Sehnsucht nach dem starken Mann") in yet another anti-Strauß diatribe to brand him an adherent of the Nazi cult of the Führer.[118]

Furthermore, the Court added in the opinion just cited, even if the last statement had meant what the lower court thought, it would have been wrong to exclude it entirely from the ambit of Article 5(1) on the ground that it was a mere personal attack ("Schmähkritik"); like the accompanying accusation that Strauß was a democrat only by compulsion ("Zwangsdemokrat"), even calling him a Nazi in this context would have been incidental to discussion of a general threat

---

stantial public interest in information concerning abuses in the credit industry). Cf. Cohen v. California, 403 U.S. 115 (1971).

[112] 43 BVerfGE 130, 135-36 (1976); 67 BVerfGE 213, 223 (1984) (*Straßentheater*); 75 BVerfGE 369, 376 (1987).

[113] 54 BVerfGE 129, 135-36 (1980). Such damages, as the Court pointed out, are awarded only when the defendant is seriously at fault ("wenn den Schädiger der Vorwurf schwerer Schuld trifft") or when the plaintiff has suffered a substantial infringement of reputation or privacy ("eine erheblich ins Gewicht fallende Beeinträchtigung des Persönlichkeitsrechts"). Id. at 135.

[114] 68 BVerfGE 226, 232 (1984).

[115] 67 BVerfGE at 228-29. Like the novel in *Mephisto*, the street-theater production involved in this case was treated as an exercise of artistic freedom rather than as an expression of opinion, notwithstanding its political content.

[116] 43 BVerfGE 130, 136-38 (1976) (rejecting arguments of the court below for interpreting a handbill to accuse a former Nazi of complicity in the death of Polish citizens).

[117] 82 BVerfGE 43, 52 (1990).

[118] 82 BVerfGE 272, 283 (1990). See also 85 BVerfGE 1, 17-23 (1991) (concluding that assertions that the Bayer concern had spied upon and applied pressure to its critics while supporting complaisant right-wing politicians were not fact statements subject to suppression for mere falsity but value judgments entitled to presumptive protection).

to the democratic order. "Within the framework of an argument about the issues," the Court concluded, "even a democratic politician must put up with the reproach inherent in the epithet 'democrat by compulsion.'"[119]

In most of these decisions the Constitutional Court stopped short of the ultimate conclusion that the utterance in question was itself protected by the constitution.[120] Both the methodology and the results of the recent opinions, however, suggest that the Court has substantially altered its position since the days of the *Mephisto* and *Hetzblatt* decisions.[121] By strict scrutiny of both the legal and factual bases of the opinions of the regular tribunals, the Constitutional Court managed in each of the cited cases to come down on the side of free expression – and in several instances to reject the most plausible bases for restricting the utterance in so doing. In numerous cases, moreover, the Court explicitly acknowledged that it was employing a degree of scrutiny far more intrusive than that practiced by the prevailing opinion in *Mephisto*.

A major 1985 opinion in which the Court first considered in detail the right of assembly guaranteed by Article 8 reflects a similarly protective approach.[122] Setting aside an order enjoining a demonstration against construction of a nuclear power plant on procedural grounds, the Court eloquently explained the importance of demonstrations as an element of democracy,[123] approved a requirement that the authorities generally be notified in advance so that they could make necessary preparations,[124] emphasized that violent acts by a minority of demonstrators would not justify suppressing the assembly as a whole, and added that the remedy for violence *against* demonstrators was to restrain the offenders, not the victims[125] – a decided improvement on the position once apparently embraced by the Supreme Court in *Feiner v. New York*.[126]

---

[119] 82 BVerfGE at 283-84.

[120] Even the opinion just quoted reversed on the ground that the court below had applied an erroneous legal standard and closed with the traditional suggestion that it might reach a different result on remand, id. at 285. But see 68 BVerfGE 226, 232 (1984) (omitting this formula after flatly declaring that a publisher could not be enjoined from disseminating a postcard critically depicting a private security guard).

[121] As evidence of the change in climate, *Mephisto* itself is back in the bookstores and has been made into a highly acclaimed motion picture as well.

[122] 69 BVerfGE 315 (1985) (*Brokdorf*).

[123] Id. at 344-47; cf. Edwards v. South Carolina, 372 U.S. 229, 237-38 (1963).

[124] 69 BVerfGE at 348-51; cf. Cox v. New Hampshire, 312 U.S. 569, 576 (1941).

[125] 69 BVerfGE at 360-61.

[126] 340 U.S. 315, 320-21 (1951). Later developments casting doubt on the vitality of the *Feiner* opinion in the United States include Edwards v. South Carolina, 372 U.S. 229 (1963), and Gregory v. Chicago, 394 U.S. 111 (1969). In two later decisions, while sensibly acknowledging that freedom of assembly did not justify blockading either a military installation or an airport, the German court divided 4-4 over whether the acts in question could be found sufficiently reprehensible ("verwerflich") to justify

Occasional restrictive decisions are still to be found. In 1985 the
Court relied on the defendant's right to privacy as well as to an unbi-
ased trial in upholding a ban on premature publication of the transcript of a preliminary examination in a criminal case.[127] Two years
later the Justices unanimously held that a political caricature had
"far overstepped the boundary" of political debate in portraying Mr.
Strauß as a copulating pig;[128] most recently they concluded that
denial of the Holocaust could be punished as a mendacious affront to
surviving Jews.[129]

The overall trend, nevertheless, has been toward greater protection of speech, especially in matters of public concern. Despite earlier
decisions that appeared to embrace a more restrictive philosophy, it
thus seems fair to say that, while the Constitutional Court continues
to give the constitutionally protected interest in personal honor more
weight than do analogous decisions of the Supreme Court, the gap
has narrowed considerably. In most cases the German court seems
inclined today to afford political and artistic expression a degree of
protection comparable to that afforded by the Supreme Court.

Indeed two very recent decisions graphically illustrate the extent
to which Article 5 has been interpreted to provide *greater* protection
to the exchange of information than does the first amendment. One
plaintiff sought to compel a private landlord to permit installation of
an antenna for regional television broadcasts, the other to compel a

---

punishment for the serious crime of forcible duress ("Nötigung mit Gewalt") (73
BVerfGE 206 (1986)) and whether an organizer who had literally abjured violence
in urging his followers to close the Frankfurt airport could nevertheless be held
responsible for their violent acts (82 BVerfGE 236 (1990)). In each case the
prevailing opinion invoked a narrow standard of review reminiscent of that which
had prevailed in *Mephisto*.

[127] 71 BVerfGE 206, 216-19 (1985) (*Stern*). In this country dignity and privacy
seem unlikely to be given such protection after Hustler Magazine v. Falwell, 485
U.S. 46 (1988), and Cox Broadcasting Corp. v. Cohn, 420 U.S. 469 (1975), while the
standard remedy for prejudicial pretrial publicity is not suppression but reversal of
the conviction. See Nebraska Press Ass'n v. Stuart, 427 U.S. 539, 551-54 (1976).

[128] 75 BVerfGE 369 (1987). For exploration of the striking contrast between this
decision and *Falwell*, supra note 127, see Georg Nolte, Falwell vs. Strauß: Die
rechtlichen Grenzen politischer Satire in den USA und der Bundesrepublik, 15 Eu-
GRZ 253 (1988) (gently wondering whether it was really appropriate to employ the
"heavy artillery" of Art. 1 against an attack by an "insignificant caricaturist" in a
paper of limited circulation and adding that it was "scarcely imaginable that a
prominent politician like Bavarian Prime Minister Strauß suffered serious psy-
chological harm or loss of respect" as a result).

[129] BVerfG, Judgment of June 9, 1992, Case No. 1 BvR 824/90, 1993 NJW 916. Cf.
Beauharnais v. Illinois, 343 U.S. 250 (1950) (group defamation). See also BVerfG,
Judgment of Dec. 12, 1990, Case No. 1 BvR 839/90, 1991 NJW 1475 (holding
allegations of "petty crimes" and "drug dealing" in connection with a flea market
unprotected because false statements of fact); 86 BVerfGE 1, 13-14 (1992) (upholding
an award of damages for the demeaning epithet "cripple").

private employer to offer him a job. In each case the Constitutional Court held the civil tribunals had offended Article 5 by denying a remedy.[130]

The applicability of the Basic Law to these purely private disputes was taken for granted. In one case the Court said only that under *Lüth* Article 5 influenced the interpretation and application of private law;[131] in the other it said nothing at all. Thus the "objective value" thesis enunciated in *Lüth* was reaffirmed in its most extreme application. Not only does Article 5 limit the rules of private law the state itself may prescribe, as in *Lüth* itself; not only may it also limit the ability of the courts to enforce private decisions limiting speech pursuant to neutral laws, in cases more analogous to *Shelley v. Kraemer*;[132] it also, as the Court had established as early as *Blinkfüer*, may require the state to give affirmative relief against wholly private action.

In such a context judicial restraint – not merely the deference to civil courts emphasized once again in both opinions[133] – makes eminent sense if private autonomy is to have any meaning at all.

II. POLITICAL PARTIES

"Political parties," says Article 21(1), "shall participate in shaping the political will [die politische Willensbildung] of the people. They may be freely established." Our Constitution ignores political parties, which prominent patriots tended to view with distaste;[134] the Basic Law institutionalizes them as essential instruments of democracy.

Article 21 does not expand much on this basic guarantee. Recognizing the enormous influence of political parties, it does require that their internal organization "conform to democratic principles."[135]

---

[130] BVerfG, Judgment of Oct. 15, 1991, Case No. 1 BvR 976/89, 1992 NJW 493 (holding free access to information denied because the landlord offered no satisfactory reason for refusal to permit the antenna); 86 BVerfGE 122, 130-32 (1992) (holding freedom of expression infringed because the job applicant's article applauding a violent demonstration against nuclear power could not properly be interpreted to advocate violence in the workplace).

[131] See 86 BVerfGE at 128-29.

[132] See Rüfner, supra note 32, Rdnr. 63 (equating this with the preceding example).

[133] See 86 BVerfGE at 129; 1992 NJW at 494.

[134] See The Federalist, No. 10 (Madison); Washington's Farewell Address of Sept. 17, 1796, in James Richardson, 1 Messages and Papers of the Presidents 213, 218-19 (1900). Earlier German constitutions were silent on the subject as well. See Dieter Grimm, Die Politischen Parteien, in Ernst Benda, Werner Maihofer, & Hans-Jochen Vogel (eds.), 1 Handbuch des Verfassungsrechts 317, 318-19 (1983).

[135] See Philip Kunig, Parteien, 2 Handbuch des Staatsrechts 103, Rdnr. 27: "Only a democratic internal structure makes it possible [for parties] to fulfill their task of participation in the formation of the political will." For an introductory ex-

Moreover, weighing the value of public information more heavily
than the deterrent effect of disclosure, it requires parties to "account
publicly for the sources and uses of their funds."[136] A striking provision considered in detail below goes so far as to declare certain subversive parties unconstitutional. Other questions about the rights and
duties of political parties, however, are left to interpretation or to ordinary laws.[137]

Prominent among the issues not explicitly resolved by Article 21
(apart from the matter of disclosure) is the question of campaign financing, which has posed difficult problems of policy and law in the
Federal Republic as it has in the United States. Repeated legislative
efforts to deal with the subject have given birth to an intricate series
of decisions that contrast in interesting ways with opinions of the
Supreme Court.

From the institutional guarantee of political parties in conjunction with the provision for equal elections in Article 38(1) and the
general principle of equality expressed in Article 3(1), the Constitutional Court has inferred a doctrine of equal electoral opportunity
("Chancengleichheit"), which basically forbids the state to take sides
in election campaigns. This understandable principle has obvious
implications for state support of political parties. Thus, for example,
the government may not distribute political propaganda for the parties to which its members belong,[138] exclude disfavored parties from

---

position of what internal democracy means see Maunz in 2 Maunz/Dürig, Art. 21,
Rdnr. 52-77; for consideration of the possible impact of this provision on a party's
right to choose its own members see Grimm, supra note 134, at 342-43.

[136] For the dangers of disclosure see NAACP v. Alabama, 357 U.S. 449, 460-63
(1958). Later cases upholding disclosure requirements in this country include
Buckley v. Valeo, 424 U.S. 1, 64, 70 (1976); Brown v. Socialist Workers '74 Campaign Comm., 459 U.S. 87 (1982). These dangers have not gone unnoticed in the
German literature. See Maunz in 2 Maunz/Dürig, Art. 21, Rdnr. 81 (suggesting a
tension between Art. 21(1) and the guarantee of secret elections in Art. 38). The
leading decision interpreting the disclosure provision struck down a statute exempting donations of less than 40,000 DM ($25,000): Art. 21(1) was designed to en-
sure public knowledge of all contributions large enough to have a significant influence on party policy, and any minimum higher than 20,000 DM was therefore
unacceptable. 85 BVerfGE 264, 323 (1992). For criticism of the 20,000 DM minimum
prescribed by earlier law (which the Court upheld in 24 BVerfGE 300, 356-57 (1968))
see Gerhard Casper, Williams v. Rhodes and Public Financing of Political Parties under the German and American Constitutions, 1969 Sup. Ct. Rev. 271, 287-88.
See also Grimm, supra note 134, at 349 (complaining that most contributions were
reported in the name of the associations that collected them; "the real contributors
remain[ed] anonymous").

[137] See Art. 21(3) GG: "Details shall be regulated by federal law."

[138] 44 BVerfGE 125, 144-46, 155-66 (1977).

the free use of public broadcast media that others enjoy,[139] or pick
and choose which parties to subsidize directly or indirectly.[140]

More surprising to the outside observer was a 1958 decision concluding that the principle of equal opportunity was offended by a
statute permitting deduction of political contributions in determining
taxable income.[141] Because the tax rates were progressive, taxpayers
with higher incomes benefited most from this provision; and thus,
the Court concluded, the law impermissibly favored those parties
most likely to obtain contributions from those who were well-to-do.[142]
The factual analysis was unimpeachable, but the law was neutral on
its face; despite its disclaimers,[143] the opinion seems to embrace a
theory of de facto equality[144] basically foreign to the decisions of our
Supreme Court.[145]

---

[139] 14 BVerfGE 121, 131-37 (1962).

[140] 20 BVerfGE 119, 133 (1966); 6 BVerfGE 273, 279-81 (1957). See also chapter 6
infra. This does not mean, however, that the Government must distort competition
by giving small parties as much assistance as large ones or squander funds in
support of splinter parties with no chance of success. See 20 BVerfGE 56, 117-19
(1966). In this context, it has been said, "state neutrality can only mean noninter-
ference with inequality." Grimm, supra note 134, at 344. Accord Buckley v. Valeo,
424 U.S. 1, 85-109 (1976).

[141] 8 BVerfGE 51 (1958).

[142] Id. at 65-67. The Court went on to hold, for similar reasons, that the provision
also infringed the right of the individual voter to equal treatment under Art. 3(1) of
the Basic Law. Id. at 68-69. Reaffirming over thirty years later that deductibility of
contributions exceeding the capacity of the average taxpayer offended the rights of
both parties and individuals, the Court added that corporations and other
associations could not be permitted to deduct political contributions at all: Deductibility of institutional donations would effectively double the deduction available to corporate shareholders and members of other associations, in violation of
the equality principle of Art. 3(1). 85 BVerfGE 264, 312-18 (1992).

[143] See 8 BVerfGE at 66-67: "Of course the legislature is not required to compensate for differences in competitive opportunities attributable to the varying social structure of the parties."

[144] See also the dictum, id. at 68-69, that equality *demanded* progressive (i.e,.
formally unequal) taxation. As the Court noted, Art. 134 of the Weimar Constitution had expressly required citizens to contribute to public revenues in proportion to
their means, but the Basic Law contains no such provision.

[145] Hints of such an interpretation have appeared in such decisions as Griffin v.
Illinois, 351 U.S. 12 (1956), and Harper v. Virginia Bd. of Elections, 383 U.S. 663
(1966), but the Supreme Court's basic approach is best illustrated by Washington v.
Davis, 426 U.S. 229 (1976), which flatly took the contrary position. See generally
David P. Currie, Positive and Negative Constitutional Rights, 53 U. Chi. L. Rev.
864, 882-84 (1986). One might expect the U.S. court to conclude that the deduction provision benefited the wealthy only to the extent the tax law otherwise discriminated
against them. See also 1 BVerfGE 97, 107 (1951) (denying that Art. 3(1) GG required
the state to take affirmative action to compensate for de facto inequalities not of its
own making); Maunz in 2 Maunz/Dürig, Art. 21, Rdnr. 82-84 (suggesting that the
concept of equality employed in the tax-deduction decision was foreign to German
jurisprudence as well).

Most interesting of all, however, was the Constitutional Court's 1966 conclusion that, even if all concerns for equality were satisfied, unrestricted state subsidies infringed the autonomy of political parties and thus were forbidden by Article 21(1).[146]

Though long, the opinion contains little more than an unexplained conclusion. At one point the reader is treated to the unappetizing prospect of parties dependent upon the state;[147] the suggestion seemed to be that he who paid the piper might well end up calling the tune. Anyone connected with an institution of higher learning in the United States has ample reason to appreciate this danger,[148] but one might expect it to be met – as the Court seemed later to acknowledge – by limiting the conditions that could be imposed upon grants rather than by outlawing the grants themselves.[149] Subsidies without strings are commonly thought to promote rather than to impede the exercise of fundamental rights, as our Supreme Court concluded in upholding federal financing of Presidential campaigns.[150] Indeed the party-financing decision contrasts most starkly with other equally bold decisions of the Constitutional Court suggesting or even holding that the Basic Law *requires* the state in some circumstances to subsidize the assertion of a constitutional right.[151]

In the abstract there is something to be said for both arguments. On the one hand, state subsidies can pose a significant threat to freedom; on the other, they may be necessary to make freedom a reality. But it can hardly be that the Basic Law both prohibits and requires

---

[146] 20 BVerfGE 56, 111-12 (1966).

[147] See id. at 102: "To be sure, a partial public financing of the parties through yearly or monthly payments for their entire political activity would not incorporate the parties into the state's organizational sphere, but it would entangle them in it [mit diesem Bereich verschränken] and render the parties dependent upon state support." See also id. at 107-11, explaining Art. 21 as a reaction to the unwholesome symbiotic relationship that had existed between the Nazi party and the state during the Hitler period; Maunz in 2 Maunz/Dürig, Art. 21, Rdnr. 85.

[148] See also South Dakota v. Dole, 483 U.S. 203 (1987). The German court's sensitivity to this problem in the field of conditional grants to state and local governments was manifested in two important decisions concerning urban renewal. 39 BVerfGE 96 (1975); 41 BVerfGE 291 (1976); see chapter 2 supra.

[149] See 85 BVerfGE 264, 287: "Einer Gefahr mittelbarer Einflußnahme durch finanzielle Leistungen ist allerdings durch die Art und Weise zu begegnen, in der der Staat solche Leistungen an die Parteien erbringt."

[150] Buckley v. Valeo, 424 U.S. 1, 85-109 (1976). As Justice Geiger noted in a dissenting opinion not published until many years after the party-financing decision, members of the Bundestag are entitled to remuneration from the state precisely in order to assure their independence. See Art. 48(3) GG, noted in chapter 3 supra; Willi Geiger, Abweichende Meinungen zu Entscheidungen des Bundesverfassungsgerichts 142, 158 (1989).

[151] E.g., 33 BVerfGE 303 (1972) (*Numerus Clausus*); 75 BVerfGE 40 (1987) (private schools) (both discussed in chapter 6 infra). Cf. the first *Television* case, text at notes 252-59 infra; *Gruppenuniversität* case, text at notes 282-87 infra. See also Currie, supra note 145, at 870-72.

the same subsidy; the question must be why political parties are different in this regard from private schools, which the Court has held constitutionally entitled to state support.[152]

An alternative ground of the party-financing decision may help to explain the distinction. State subsidies for political parties, the Court concluded, not only abridged the freedom of the parties themselves under Article 21(1); they also offended the provision of Article 20(2) that "all state authority emanates from the people."[153] Political parties, the Court seemed to be saying, were the indispensable instrument through which the people asserted their prerogative to determine the actions of public authority;[154] Government assistance, by weakening the parties' dependence on the people, thus impaired the people's right to exercise their sovereign powers.[155]

Whether these risks were sufficient to justify the Court's conclusion is plainly a matter on whch reasonable minds may differ.[156] In any case, the constitutional ban on state assistance to political parties is by no means absolute. In its earlier decision striking down unrestricted tax deductions for private contributions on grounds of inequality, the Constitutional Court had expressly rejected the contention that the Basic Law forbade all public support of political parties. "Since the holding of elections is a public function and the parties have a decisive role to play" in the electoral process under the constituion, "it must be permissible for the state to make financial

---

[152] 75 BVerfGE 40, 61-66 (1987).

[153] 20 BVerfGE at 111-12.

[154] See id. at 97-99.

[155] This argument, at best implied in the 1966 opinion, was made explicit when the Court reexamined the question in 1992:

> The freedom of parties from the state posited by the Basic Law requires not only that parties be independent of the state itself but also that they retain their identity as freely constituted associations rooted in the social and political sphere. The parties must remain dependent upon citizen approval and support not only politically but economically and organizationally as well. Public funds thus may not be permitted to liberate individual parties from the risk of failure of their efforts to obtain sufficient support from the voters.

85 BVerfGE 264, 287 (1992). It is not obvious why the Court in this later opinion chose to tie this argument to Art. 21(1), which guarantees freedom from state influence, rather than to the Art. 20(2) principle of popular control. Perhaps the best explanation is that the Court interpreted Art. 21(1) to require that parties be free not merely from state interference but from *entanglement* with the state, so that they could fulfill their constitutional role as servants of the people. Cf. U.S. Const., amend. I (forbidding establishment as well as abridgement of religion).

[156] The people of course had other ways of controlling political parties, not least by expressing their displeasure at the ballot box – a strategy that would strike the unresponsive party in the pocketbook as well since the subsidies at issue in the 1966 case were proportioned to electoral strength. See 20 BVerfGE at 57-59.

means available not only for the elections themselves but also for the political parties that sustain them."[157]

In striking down unrestricted grants to the parties a few years afterwards, the Justices attempted to explain and narrow this language rather than disavow it completely. What the earlier decision meant was that the state could provide financial support to the parties in order to cover the necessary costs of an appropriate electoral campaign ("die notwendigen Kosten eines angemessenen Wahlkampfes") – not to subsidize the activities of the parties in their entirety.[158]

Since campaign costs are such a substantial part of any party's budget, this neat division of the baby took much of the sting out of the party financing decision.[159] Moreover, the distinction the Court drew seemed less than wholly convincing. That elections are indubitably public functions seems not to diminish the risk either of dependence on government or of lack of accountability to the voters that led the Court to conclude that support of nonelectoral activities was impermissible.[160]

Acknowledging these difficulties, the Court modified its position in an important 1992 decision. There was no basis for distinguishing between elections and other party activities; what mattered was the total amount of the subsidy, its relation to resources raised from other sources, and their distribution among the various parties. The bottom line – in an opinion resembling in its prescriptive detail the celebrated "legislative" pronouncements in *Miranda v. Arizona* and *Roe v. Wade* – was that the total subsidy for all parties was not to exceed the mean sum that had been granted during the preceding three years; that no party was to receive more from the state than it raised on its own; and that each party's share must be based in part upon its relative success in attracting private contributions.[161]

One of the arguments in favor of public financing of political parties in Germany, as in the United States, was that it would limit the influence of large private contributors. The Court's response was

---

[157] 8 BVerfGE at 63.

[158] 20 BVerfGE at 97. See also id. at 113-119.

[159] See, e.g., 24 BVerfGE 300 (1968) (upholding a distribution to the parties of 38,000,000 marks to cover expenses of the 1965 election); Ulrich K. Preuß in 2 AK-GG, Art. 21, Abs. 1, 3, Rdnr. 77.

[160] See id., Rdnr. 79; Kunig, supra note 135, Rdnr. 75; Grimm, supra note 134, at 351-52; Casper, supra note 136, 1969 Sup. Ct. Rev. at 296: "Reading the opinion one is left with the very strong impression that doctrinal purity was sacrificed on the altar of judicial compromise."

[161] 85 BVerfGE 264, 285-95 (1992) (striking down a subsidy provision on the ground that its amount was essentially independent of the electoral or financial appeal of the recipient party). In applying the standard of financial appeal, the opinion added, only those contributions should be considered which the average citizen could afford; otherwise the subsidy, like unlimited tax deductions for private contributions, would impermissibly favor well-to-do voters and the parties they found congenial. Id. at 293; cf. text at notes 140-45 supra.

that the Basic Law forbade only state influence[162] – which was true enough but hardly seemed conclusive.[163] Legislative efforts to combat excessive private influence by limiting private contributions directly, as in the statute the Supreme Court considered in *Buckley v. Valeo*,[164] would pose very different but equally difficult questions. Despite notorious and relatively recent scandals over corruption in connection with private contributions in Germany,[165] the Constitutional Court has yet to pass on any such limitation.[166]

Finally, one brief passage in its most recent opinion on the subject of public financing raises the possibility that the Court may yet attempt to have it both ways. "It is unnecessary to decide," the Court took pains to observe, "whether, in light of the indispensability of parties to the process of formation of the political will in a democratic society, the state could withhold all financial support whatever if adequate financing by the parties themselves should prove impossible under the conditions of modern democracy."[167] In its earlier opinion the Court had flatly denied that the Basic Law imposed any obligation to subsidize political parties.[168] By going out of its way to imply that the issue was nevertheless unsettled, the Court seemed to invite speculation that it may yet find itself drawing lines between those political subsidies the constitution forbids and those the constitution requires.

III. SUBVERSION

Among the more startling aspects of the Basic Law to an observer from the other side of the Atlantic is a set of provisions that appear to embody Milton's view that the enemies of freedom are not entitled to its blessings.[169] The central provision is found in Article 21(2):

---

[162] 20 BVerfGE at 105-06.

[163] Elsewhere in the opinion the Court had said the test was whether there were particular legitimating grounds to justify the constitutionality of a measure, not whether it was *required* by the constitution. Id. at 99.

[164] 424 U.S. 1, 12-59 (1976).

[165] See 67 BVerfGE 100 (1984) (*Flick*).

[166] See 85 BVerfGE 264, 315 (1992): "Contributions to political parties, including those of corporations and other associations, are permissible under German law without regard to their amount." For the unusual argument that limits on private spending are not only permissible but implicit in the Basic Law itself see Preuß in 2 AK-GG, Art. 21, Abs. 1, 3, Rdnr. 71: "The dependency of a party upon one contributor or a small number of contributors [would be] inconsistent with the first and third sentences" of Art. 21(1). For the view that a blanket prohibition of private contributions would offend Art. 21(1) see Kunig, supra note 135, Rdnr. 32.

[167] 85 BVerfGE 264, 288 (1992).

[168] 20 BVerfGE at 102-03.

[169] John Milton, Areopagitica, in 4 The Works of John Milton 349 (Frank Allen Patterson et al., eds. 1931). See Kommers, supra note 98, at 680-81.

Parties which, by reason of their aims or the behavior of their adherents, seek to impair or abolish the free democratic order or to endanger the existence of the Federal Republic of Germany, are unconstitutional.

Article 9(2) makes similar provision for other associations; Article 5(3) declares that academic freedom "shall not absolve from loyalty to the constitution";[170] Article 18 provides for forfeiture of certain basic rights, including freedom of expression, by persons who "abuse" them "in order to combat the free democratic basic order."[171]

Collectively characterized by the concept of militant democracy ("streitbare" or "wehrhafte Demokratie"),[172] these provisions reflect

---

[170] Too many professors, said the Social Democratic delegate Ludwig Bergsträßer in the constitutional convention, had abused their position to undermine the Weimar Republic. The new provision, Carlo Schmid added, did not forbid professors to criticize the government; it did mean they should not make it appear contemptible ("verächtlich"). See 1 JöR (n.F.) at 89, 92. See generally Scholz in 1 Maunz/Dürig, Art. 5, Abs. III, Rdnr. 197-204.

[171] The only two proceedings brought under this extraordinary provision prior to 1993 were dismissed, the first on the ground that the individual whose rights were sought to be declared forfeit had ceased his allegedly subversive activities after the party to which he belonged was proscribed under Art. 21(2) (11 BVerfGE 282 (1960)), the second on the ground that there was no showing that the accused anti-Semitic publisher posed any threat to the free democratic order (38 BVerfGE 23 (1974)). The interpretation in the latter opinion, which is hardly suggested by the constitutional text, is reminiscent of the famous "clear and present danger" test of Schenck v. United States, 249 U.S. 47, 51 (1919).

Art. 139, inspired in part by § 3 of our fourteenth amendment, provides that "the legislation enacted for Liberation of the German People from National Socialism and Militarism [die zur 'Befreiung des deutschen Volkes vom Nationalsozialismus und Militarismus' erlassenen Rechtsvorschriften] shall not be affected by the provisions of this Basic Law." The purpose of this provision was to preserve the effectiveness of denazification laws enacted during the Allied occupation following World War II, some of whose sanctions (e.g., disqualification from office and disfranchisement of former Nazis) were recognized as contrary to various fundamental rights contained in the new Basic Law. See 1 BVerfGE 5, 7 (1951) (dismissing a challenge to one of these laws on the basis of Art. 139). In light of the use of quotation marks and of the past participle ("erlassenen") in this provision, its placement among transitional provisions ("Übergangsbestimmungen"), its explicit legislative history (the words "and to be enacted" ("und zu ergehenden") were omitted in order to avoid blanket approval of future laws), and the interesting argument that because of this conflict Art. 139 was itself unconstitutional (see also text at notes 199-204 infra), it was understood from the first to apply only to laws already in force, the last of which expired in 1953. Art. 139 thus has no remaining effect except perhaps to suggest that political discrimination in such matters as the civil service is impermissible in the absence of an explicit constitutional exception. See 1 JöR (n.F.) 897-99; von Mangoldt, supra note 2, at 658; Herzog in 4 Maunz/Dürig, Art. 139, Rdnr. 1-4; Ladeur in 2 AK-GG, Art. 139, Rdnr. 1-3.

[172] See 5 BVerfGE 85, 139 (1956).

the bitter experience of the Weimar Republic, in which antidemocratic forces took advantage of political freedoms to subvert the constitution itself. If the constitutional system is to be overthrown again, the argument runs, it can only be done by force; the tools of democracy may not be used to destroy the very values they were designed to preserve.[173] We like to think we are more tolerant in this country. Our Constitution contains no comparable provisions; we are wont to proclaim the inappropriateness of combatting totalitarianism with totalitarian methods.[174] But the fact is that in periods of real or imagined danger we have tended to adopt measures strikingly similar in effect to those expressly countenanced by the Basic Law, and the Supreme Court has tended to uphold them – in the teeth of an ostensibly absolute constitutional protection.[175]

A. Unconstitutional Parties

Article 21(2) makes it the responsibility of the Constitutional Court to determine whether a political party offends its provisions. In the 1950s the Court was twice asked to declare a party unconstitutional, and on both occasions it did. Its opinions in these early cases bear a close family resemblance to that of the Supreme Court in *Dennis v. United States*.[176]

---

[173] See Sten. Ber. at 13-14 (1948) (Delegate Schmid); 2 BVerfGE 1, 11 (1952); 5 BVerfGE 85, 138-39 (1956); Dürig in 2 Maunz/Dürig, Art. 18, Rdnr. 1-14 ("'Demokratie als Selbstmord'"); Maunz in 2 Maunz/Dürig, Art. 21, Rdnr. 101; Jürgen Becker, Die wehrhafte Demokratie des Grundgesetzes, 7 Handbuch des Staatsrechts 309, passim. For a dissenting view of the relevant history see Ridder, supra note 107, Rdnr. 28-29.

[174] See also id., Rdnr. 7 (terming it contradictory "to secure democracy by suspending democratic freedoms"); Grimm, supra note 134, at 338 (observing that with increasing distance from the Weimar experience "the plausibility" of Art. 21(2) "has diminished").

[175] See, e.g., Act of July 14, 1798, ch. 74, 1 Stat. 596 (Sedition Act); Schenck v. United States, 249 U.S. 47 (1919) (Espionage Act); Gitlow v. New York, 268 U.S. 652 (1925) and Whitney v. California, 274 U.S. 357 (1927) (state syndicalism laws); Dennis v. United States, 341 U.S. 494 (1951) (Smith Act); Communist Party v. Subversive Activities Control Board, 367 U.S. 1 (1961) (Subversive Activities Control Act). See also, inter alia, Adler v. Board of Education, 342 U.S. 485 (1952); Lerner v. Casey, 357 U.S. 468 (1957); Barenblatt v. United States, 360 U.S. 109 (1959); Walter F. Murphy, Excluding Political Parties: Problems for Democratic and Constitutional Theory, in Paul Kirchhof & Donald P. Kommers (eds.), Germany and Its Basic Law 173, 182 (1993). More tolerant decisions of the later Warren Court (e.g., Gibson v. Florida Legislative Investigation Comm., 372 U.S. 539 (1963); Elfbrandt v. Russell, 384 U.S. 11 (1966); Brandenburg v. Ohio, 395 U.S. 444 (1969)) came after the scare had passed (see The Second Century at 434-38); it is easy to be brave when the wolf is home in bed.

[176] 341 U.S. 494 (1951).

The first case, decided in 1952, involved the Sozialistische Reichspartei (SRP), a neo-Nazi organization.[177] Article 21(2), the Court
emphasized, was an exception to the general democratic principle
permitting the development of parties of whatever political orientation; it was not to be used as a means of silencing legitimate dissent.[178] Not every party seeking to alter particular constitutional
provisions or even institutions could be stigmatized as endeavoring to
subvert "the free democratic basic order," but only those striving to
undermine the most fundamental principles of a free democratic
constitutional state ("oberste Grundwerte des freiheitlichen
demokratischen Verfassungsstaates") – such as human rights, popular sovereignty, the separation of powers, the independence of the
courts, and the multiparty system.[179] Nor was it enough that a
party's internal organization failed to conform with "democratic
principles," as Article 21(1) independently required – although an
authoritarian internal structure might give rise to the presumption
that a party wished to impose a similar authoritarian structure on
the state itself.[180] An exhaustive review of the facts led the Court to
conclude that the leadership of the SRP was composed largely of former Nazis selected because of their past activities,[181] that the party
itself was organized on dictatorial lines,[182] and that its program
entailed nothing less than the overthrow of the free democratic order.[183] The SRP was accordingly dissolved, its assets confiscated, and
its elected representatives deprived of their seats in Parliament – for
otherwise, said the Court, they would be in a position to continue
working to effectuate the party's nefarious goals.[184]

Given the existence of Article 21(2), the banning of the Sozialistische Reichspartei was surely no surprise. As the Court emphasized,
there was no doubt that the old Nazi party, whose misdeeds had provoked the adoption of the constitutional provision, would have fallen
within its proscription; and the SRP looked and acted very much like
the Nazis.[185] It would have been asking a lot to expect the new Republic to put up with continued Nazi political activity so soon after the
Nazis had destroyed its predecessor, even if one might entertain
doubts as to the efficacy as well as the philosophy of suppression.

Yet several aspects of the *SRP* opinion seem disquieting even if
one accepts the correctness of the basic decision. Of course the Court
was right that a party acts only through individuals and therefore, as
Article 21(2) recognizes, its nature can be discerned only through the

---

[177] 2 BVerfGE 1 (1952).
[178] Id. at 10-12.
[179] Id. at 12-13.
[180] Id. at 14.
[181] Id. at 23-40.
[182] Id. at 40-47.
[183] Id. at 47-68.
[184] Id. at 71-79.
[185] Id. at 70.

behavior of its adherents.[186] Nevertheless the opinion's emphasis on collective responsibility for the actions of "all who engage themselves on behalf of the SRP," whether or not members,[187] conjures up uncomfortable recollections of efforts in this country to impute guilt by association[188] – even though, to be sure, the upshot was to dissolve the association itself rather than to impose sanctions on individual members. Moreover, many of the statements adduced to demonstrate the anticonstitutional bearing of the SRP seemed more than anything else to illustrate the difficulty of distinguishing subversive rhetoric from legitimate political oratory. Contemptuous characterizations of contemporary political leaders as architects of the Weimar failure are condemned as having "nothing to do with the constitutionally guaranteed freedom of expression" but rather as displaying a tendency "to shake the foundations of public confidence in those who represent the Federal Republic" and thereby to discredit the free democratic order.[189] References to orthodox parties as "eunuch parties," "monopoly parties," and tools of the occupying powers are interpreted as efforts to undermine the multiparty system as a whole and to pave the way for dictatorship.[190] Expressions of sympathy with Hitler, assertions that the German defeat in 1945 was attributable to yet another stab in the back ("Dolchstoß"), and disparaging comments about the "yellow" or "mustard" color of the flag[191] are all taken as further evidence of the party's unconstitutional aims. Beyond this, the Court's presumption that an authoritarian party structure implies a design to impose a similar structure on the state seems strained; and the severity of the remedial measures ordered in consequence of the finding of unconstitutionality is uncomfortably reminiscent of the disproportionate sanctions inflicted upon the Mormon Church in this country after it was justifiably found to have unlawfully promoted polygamy.[192]

---

[186] Id. at 21-22. See Art. 21(2) GG: "Parties that by reason of their aims or the behavior of their adherents . . . ."

[187] 2 BVerfGE at 22.

[188] See, e.g., Whitney v. California, 274 U.S. 357 (1927).

[189] 2 BVerfGE at 57-59.

[190] Id. at 61-62.

[191] Id. at 50-57, 62. Cf. Art. 22 GG: "The federal flag shall be black, red, and gold."

[192] Compare Reynolds v. United States, 98 U.S. 145 (1879) (holding polygamy prosecution consistent with the free-exercise clause of the first amendment), with Davis v. Beason, 133 U.S. 333, 346-47 (1890) (upholding disenfranchisement of members of the Mormon Church), and Mormon Church v. United States, 136 U.S. 1, 44-48 (1890) (upholding revocation of the Church's charter and confiscation of its property). See The First Hundred Years at 439-42 ; The Second Century at 56 n. 8. For the extreme view that the only legitimate sanction against an unconstitutional party in Germany is loss of the party's official status and ability to take part in elections see Helmut Ridder in 2 AK-GG, Art. 21, Abs. 2, Rdnr. 18-24.

The second decision, in the famous *Communist Party* case, was not rendered until 1956.[193] By that time the Constitutional Court had had time for reflection on the obvious tension between militant democracy and the basic values it was designed to protect.[194] Like the SRP, the Communist Party (KPD) was found unconstitutional;[195] but this time the opinion displayed somewhat greater sensitivity to the risks that proceedings of this nature posed to freedom of association and expression.

The *SRP* opinion consumed nearly eighty pages, the *Communist Party* opinion over 300. The bulk of it, as in the earlier case, was devoted to the facts. This time there was little need to rely on statements by isolated party adherents;[196] the public platform of the KPD made abundantly plain that its goals were revolution and the dictatorship of the proletariat, which the Court understandably concluded meant an end to both fundamental rights and the democratic state.[197] This part of the opinion bears a close resemblance to the corresponding exposition in *Dennis v. United States*, which had been decided just five years before.[198]

Of greater interest was the Court's exposition of the meaning of Article 21(2), which brought it into close accord with the law of the United States as expounded by Chief Justice Vinson for four Justices in *Dennis*. This section of the opinion begins startlingly enough for the external observer with the question whether Article 21(2) is contrary to "a fundamental principle of the Constitution" – namely freedom of expression – and thus unconstitutional.[199] This was not the first time the Court had suggested the possibility that a provision of the Constitution might itself be invalid.[200] Indeed, although the reader may be tempted to retort that what is in the Constitution is by definition constitutional, one can readily imagine a constitution that explicitly or implicitly contains a hierarchy of provisions in which

---

[193] 5 BVerfGE 85 (1956). Like the *SRP* case, this proceeding had been instituted in 1951. Id. at 102. For an effort to explain the delay in decision see Donald P. Kommers, The Constitutional Jurisprudence of the Federal Republic of Germany 227-28 (1989).

[194] See 5 BVerfGE at 134 ("eine gewisse Spannung zwischen der Vorschrift des Art. 21 Abs. 2 GG und der politischen Meinungsfreiheit").

[195] Id. at 391-93.

[196] Indeed this time the Court went out of its way to warn of the dangers of drawing conclusions about the party itself from isolated conduct of individuals who might be engaged in what we might call frolics ("Entgleisungen") of their own. Id. at 143.

[197] Id. at 147-390.

[198] 341 U.S. 494 , 497-502 (1951).

[199] 5 BVerfGE at 137.

[200] See 1 BVerfGE 14, 32-33 (1951) (*Southwest State*); 3 BVerfGE 225, 230-36 (1953). See also note 171 supra (discussing Art. 139).

those of subordinate rank must be tested for conformity to its more basic principles.[201]

As in earlier cases, however, the Court found no conflict between the challenged provision and allegedly higher constitutional values: Article 21(2) reflected the deliberate decision of the framers that the fundamental principles of constitutional democracy could be preserved only by limiting the freedom of those who would destroy them.[202] Other liberal states had reacted differently to the same problem, the Court added, but none gave free rein to the political activity of its enemies.[203] Indeed, the opinion rather defensively concluded, the unusually explicit German provision accorded *greater* protection against suppression of legitimate opposition than did the constitutions of other countries, for it alone gave exclusive authority to determine which parties were subversive to an independent constitutional court.[204]

---

[201] This is how the Court put the question in the Communist Party case, and this is how it had been put in the first decision on the subject (1 BVerfGE 14, 32-33 (1951) (upholding Art. 118 GG against the argument that it offended basic principles of democracy and federalism by allowing Baden to be forced into the reorganized state of Baden-Württemberg against its will)). In between, however, the Court had enunciated a standard that appeared significantly different in theory, though similar in practical effect. Since the constitution was a unit, it was basically inconceivable ("grundsätzlich undenkbar") that one of its norms might be struck down because it conflicted with a higher ranking provision of the constitution itself: "It is in the nature of the pouvoir constituant that it may make exceptions to its own basic principles . . . ." To conclude that there were no limits to what might be put into a constitution, however, would be to revert to a value-free positivism long repudiated both in scholarship and in practice. In the improbable event that a provision of the Basic Law exceeded the outer limits of the higher-law ("übergesetzliche") principle of justice ("die äußersten Grenzen der Gerechtigkeit"), it would be the Court's duty to strike it down. 3 BVerfGE 225, 231-36 (concluding that judicial enforcement of the ban on gender discrimination in Art. 3(2) offended neither the rule of law ("Rechtsstaatsprinzip") nor the separation of powers). See also Peter Badura, Arten der Verfassungsrechtssätze, 7 Handbuch des Staatsrechts 33, Rdnr. 7 (arguing that, apart from the limitations on constitutional amendment imposed by Art. 79(3), the notion of an unconstitutional constitutional provision is essentially only of theoretical concern).

[202] 5 BVerfGE at 137-39.

[203] Id. at 136.

[204] Id. at 139-40. The extent and effect of the Constitutional Court's decisional monopoly have given rise to a number of difficult line-drawing problems. See, e.g., 9 BVerfGE 162, 164-66 (1959) (holding that determination of the unconstitutionality of a party was not a prerequisite to prosecuting one of its adherents for activities preparatory to treason); 10 BVerfGE 118, 123-24 (1959) (holding that a state law authorizing the government to ban from editorial responsibilities persons who had abused their positions for subversive purposes infringed the parallel provision of Art. 18 giving the Constitutional Court exclusive jurisdiction to declare the forfeiture of fundamental rights); 12 BVerfGE 296, 306-07 (1961) (holding that Art. 21(2) forbade prosecution, even after the Court found a party unconstitutional, for otherwise lawful activities in its behalf undertaken before that decision); 13 BVerf-

With this threshold question behind it, the Court proceeded to a
further narrowing of the definition of parties that "seek to impair or
abolish the free democratic basic order." It was not enough that, as
the *SRP* decision had required, a party rejected the most fundamental principles of democracy or freedom.

> The party must in addition take an actively belligerent, aggressive
> attitude toward the existing order; it must plan as well as desire to
> impair the operation of this order and eventually to set it aside en-
> tirely. That is to say, the free democratic state does not take out after
> parties with inimical aims on its own initiative. Rather it behaves de-
> fensively; it merely wards off assaults upon its basic order.[205]

Similar language appears in *Dennis v. United States*.[206]
That did not mean, the Court added, that the plan must have proceeded beyond mere intention to concrete actions that would be punishable under ordinary criminal law: "Intervention against a party
on the basis of Art. 21(2) is by its nature a preventive measure, a pre-
caution for the future."[207] Nor was it necessary that there be any

---

GE 174, 176-77 (1961) (permitting a state interior ministry to find an association
other than a political party unconstitutional under Art. 9(2), which contains no
monopoly provision); 16 BVerfGE 4 (1963) (permitting election authorities to determine that a political organization was a successor to the forbidden Communist
Party without initiating a second proceeding before the Constitutional Court); 25
BVerfGE 88 (1969) (holding that Art. 18 did not preclude a criminal court from prohibiting future editorial activity as a sanction for violation of the Constitutional
Court's order banning the Communist Party); 40 BVerfGE 287, 292-94 (1975)
(holding Art. 21(2) did not forbid inclusion of an unbanned party on a published list
of "subversive" organizations); 47 BVerfGE 198, 227-29 (1978) (holding that Art.
21(2) forbade a public broadcaster to reject political advertisements on the ground
that they sought to undermine the constitutional order). See also Dürig in 2
Maunz/Dürig, Art. 18, Rdnr. 88-97 (arguing that the monopoly should be interpreted to extend to all orders banning future activity protected by the enumerated
rights but not to punishment for past actions); Ridder in 2 AK-GG, Art. 18, Rdnr. 18-
19 (suggesting that Art. 18 forbids the imposition of *any* extraneous sanctions for
endangering the free democratic order).

205 5 BVerfGE at 141. See also id. at 145-46.

206 [The petitioners attack] the statute on the grounds that by its terms it
      prohibits academic discussion of the merits of Marxism-Leninism,
      that it stifles ideas and is contrary to all concepts of a free speech and
      free press. . . . [But t]he very language of the Smith Act
      [demonstrates that i]t is directed at advocacy, not discussion. Thus,
      the trial judge properly charged the jury that they could not convict if
      they found that petitioners did "no more than pursue peaceful studies
      and discussions or teaching and advocacy in the realm of ideas."

341 U.S. at 501-02 (opinion of Vinson, C.J., for four Justices).
207 5 BVerfGE at 141-42.

reasonable prospect that the party might be in a position to effectuate its plan in the foreseeable future, or even that it intend to try: "If the anticonstitutional purpose can be demonstrated, there is no need to wait and see whether the political situation changes and the party actually undertakes to realize its unconstitutional goals."[208] This formulation was plainly difficult to square with Justice Brandeis's brave insistence that suppression was impermissible while time for discussion remained;[209] but so was the strikingly parallel language in the *Dennis* case.[210]

In the thirty-five years that succeeded the *Communist Party* decision, no further proceedings have been instituted under Article 21(2). The Communist Party itself, after an initial successor organization was found to fall afoul of the original decree,[211] changed the order of its initials (from KPD to DKP) and was allowed to operate unmolested.[212] As the totalitarian past receded and confidence in the solidity of the Republic increased, it no longer appeared necessary or desirable to invoke the prohibition of antidemocratic parties.[213]

In late 1992, however, as a rash of violent attacks on foreigners reached alarming proportions, the Government resorted once again to the parallel provision of Article 9(2) permitting it to proscribe other associations seeking to subvert the constitutional order, and there was talk of invoking the Article 18 provision respecting forfeiture of individual rights as well.[214] Those who believe in constitutional liberties will continue to differ as to whether such measures are appropriate means of protecting them.

B. The Civil Service

The desuetude of Article 21(2) has not prevented the state from taking antisubversive measures under other provisions that raise

---

[208] Id. at 143. See also id. at 143-44 (adding that Art. 21(2) did not distinguish between immediate and long-term goals).

[209] Whitney v. California, 274 U.S. 357, 376-77 (1927) (concurring opinion).

[210] See 341 U.S. at 509:

Obviously the words [clear and present danger] cannot mean that before the Government may act, it must wait until the *putsch* is about to be executed . . . . If Government is aware that a group aiming at its overthrow is attempting to indoctrinate its members and to commit them to a course whereby they will strike when the leaders feel the circumstances permit, action by the Government is required.

[211] 16 BVerfGE 4 (1963).

[212] See Kommers, supra note 193, at 231.

[213] See id. (citing Dan Gordon, Limits on Extremist Political Parties: A Comparison of Israeli Jurisprudence with that of the U.S. and the Federal Republic of Germany, 10 Hastings Int'l & Comp. L. Rev. 347, 376 (1987)).

[214] See, e.g., New York Times, Dec. 10, 1992, p. A6.

similar issues of the tension between national security and freedom of expression or association. Most notably, in 1972, following an extended period of radical unrest, both federal and state governments issued "loyalty" guidelines designed to exclude enemies of democracy from the civil service, and the Constitutional Court upheld them in a major 1975 opinion.[215]

Loyalty to the state and to the Constitution, the Court began, was among the "traditional principles" of public service given constitutional sanction by Article 33(5).[216] Loyalty did not preclude criticism, but it did require that public officials "take a positive attitude toward the state and the existing constitutional order" and be prepared to "actively stand up for them."[217] In light of Article 21(2) and other provisions reflecting the principle of militant democracy, the duty of loyalty must be interpreted to exclude from public service those "who reject and oppose the free democratic order, the rule of law, and the social state. . . . The free democratic state governed by the rule of law cannot and must not hand itself over to those who would destroy it."[218]

Like the Supreme Court in *American Communications Association v. Douds*, the Constitutional Court concluded that the question was not whether the individual had committed subversive acts for which he could be punished criminally; a public officer was uniquely positioned to injure the state, and exclusion from office was a less severe sanction.[219] At the same time, like the Supreme Court in *Douds*, the German Justices were fully aware of the dampening effect of such exclusion upon the exercise of constitutionally protected freedoms.[220] What was required was to reach an accommodation ("Ausgleich") of competing constitutional values. Rules implementing the Article 3(5) duty of loyalty were thus to be treated as "general laws" within the meaning of Article 5(2), as that concept had been explained in the *Lüth* decision: Expression was protected only if con-

---

[215] 39 BVerfGE 334 (1975).

[216] Id. at 346-47. See Art. 33(5) GG: "The law of the public service shall be regulated with due regard to the traditional principles of the professional civil service." See also Art. 33(4) GG, cited in 39 BVerfGE at 347, which requires that public authority be exercised as a rule by "members of the public service who occupy a position of service and loyalty defined by public law." The purpose of this provision is to ensure that only public officials ("Beamte") exercise public authority; their duty of loyalty is defined by traditional principles under Art. 33(5).

[217] 39 BVerfGE at 347-49. This formulation had been anticipated during the constitutional convention. See Sten. Ber. at 28 (Delegate Menzel).

[218] 39 BVerfGE at 349.

[219] Id. at 357-59. See also id. at 372-75 (holding it inconsistent with the occupational freedom guaranteed by Art. 12(1) to exclude from mandatory training for private professions all those who failed to meet the strict standard of loyalty demanded of public servants). Cf. *Douds*, 339 U.S. 382 (1950); The Second Century at 355-57.

[220] See also the general discussion of what we would call unconstitutional conditions in text at notes 295-309 infra.

sistent with the public servant's duty, but that duty was to be interpreted in light of the basic right on which it was a limitation.[221] Everything would turn, in other words, on how the competing interests were balanced in particular cases. On that subject the *Civil Service* opinion was excruciatingly vague.[222] Membership in a political party pursuing goals inimical to the constitution, the Court did say, might be a significant factor ("ein Stück des Verhaltens, das . . . erheblich sein kann") in evaluating fitness for public office.[223] A few pages earlier, however, the Court had gone out of its way to warn against the adoption of laws making "particular concrete forms of behavior" conclusive proof of disloyalty,[224] and a few pages later it quoted extensively from an opinion flatly stating what the Constitutional Court described as the "dominant view" that membership alone had not been enough to justify disciplinary action for disloyalty during the Weimar period.[225] Two Justices wrote separately to insist that mere membership did not suffice to disqualify an applicant under the Basic Law either,[226] a third to respond that it created a rebuttable presumption against him.[227] Later decisions have added little to the debate.[228] Thus even today the German court has not yet

---

[221] 39 BVerfGE at 366-67 (adding that the same principles governed the scope of the freedoms of assembly and association guaranteed by Art. 8 and 9, even though neither contained an explicit reference to limitations found in "general laws").

[222] The question presented by the referring court (in a concrete norm-control proceeding under Art. 100(1) GG) was the general one whether the Land of Schleswig-Holstein could limit practical training positions ("Referendarstellen") to those aspiring attorneys who were prepared "to stand up at all times for the free democratic basic order." Id. at 339.

[223] Id. at 359.

[224] Id. at 354-55.

[225] Id. at 362-64.

[226] Id. at 376 (Seuffert, J.), 380 (Rupp, J.) (concluding that mere membership should not even be considered). See also Grimm, supra note 134, at 339 (arguing that to make membership in a subversive but unbanned party a ground for denial of public employment would infringe the Constitutional Court's monopoly under Art. 21(2)).

[227] 39 BVerfGE at 389-90 (Wand, J.).

[228] Several years after the *Civil Service* decision, emphasizing that the civil service principles of Art. 33(5) were inapplicable to private professionals and without discussing freedom of expression or association, the Court held that an applicant could not constitutionally be excluded from the Bar for affiliation with a subversive but unbanned political party falling short of acts that were criminally punishable, on the ground that there was no statutory authority for such a limitation of occupational freedom, as Art. 12(1) required. 63 BVerfGE 266 (1983). See also id. at 298-312 (Simon, J.) (branding the exclusion also, among other things, a substantively disproportionate restriction of occupational freedom and an infringement of the neglected ban in Art. 3(3) on discrimination based on "political opinions"); Ekkehart Stein in 1 AK-GG, Art. 3, Rdnr. 96 (arguing that the state offends Art. 3(3) whenever it "treats some people better or worse than others on the basis of their polit-

resolved the question – answered in favor of freedom by our Supreme Court as early as *Wieman v. Updegraff* in 1952[229] – whether innocent membership in a party with a subversive program is enough to disqualify a citizen from public employment.

C. Other Measures

As in the United States, outlawry of subversive organizations and exclusion of subversive individuals from public service do not exhaust the measures that have from time to time been taken and sustained in Germany to protect the state from its enemies. In other cases too the Constitutional Court has grappled with the tension between national security and the values of free expression and association.

The first of these decisions was anything but reassuring in this regard. In 1953 the Government refused to renew the passport of one of its noisy critics. The lower courts found this action justified on the ground of the applicant's past participation in a number of meetings abroad, including a conference sponsored by an organization called Peoples for Peace.[230] At the end of an important opinion largely devoted to other issues,[231] the Constitutional Court gave short shrift to an objection based on the guarantee of free expression in Article 5(1):

> To be sure, this constitutional provision embraces the right to express one's opinion both at home and abroad. But when the right to leave the country is restricted in order to effectuate some superior concern – here that of security and essential interests [wesentlicher Belange] of the state – then the complainant may not rely upon Article 5 of the Basic Law simply in order to be able to make his views known in the outside world.[232]

The opinion said nothing about what had transpired at the meetings in question or the organizations under whose auspices they were held, much less about the nature of the complainant's participation

---

ical convictions," except in cases falling within the militant-democracy provisions of Art. 9(2), 18, and 21(2)).

[229] 344 U.S. 183 (1952); see also Elfbrandt v. Russell, 384 U.S. 11 (1966); Keyishian v. Board of Regents, 385 U.S. 589 (1967); United States v. Robel, 389 U.S. 258 (1967). Intervening decisions were not always so clear on this point. E.g., Adler v. Board of Education, 342 U.S. 485 (1952); Lerner v. Casey, 357 U.S. 468 (1957).

[230] 6 BVerfGE 32, 33 (1957) (*Elfes*).

[231] The decision is best known for its expansive interpretation of the right to free development of personality (Art. 2(1)), which also proved of no help to the complainant. Id. at 36-44; see chapter 6 infra.

[232] 6 BVerfGE at 44.

in them. In discussing the right to travel, the Court noted that the facts were essentially undisputed and that there was no basis for upsetting the conclusion of the ordinary courts that renewal of the passport would seriously endanger important interests of the state, but it neither identified those interests nor explained why it was appropriate to find them endangered.[233]

Similarly, in 1959 the Constitutional Court upheld a prosecution for publication of articles respecting the Communist Party program for German reunification on the abstract ground that the statute punishing preparation of treasonable enterprises ("Vorbereitung eines hochverräterischen Unternehmens") was a general law designed to protect the constitutional order, without so much as bothering to explain what the offending articles had said.[234] A significant step forward was taken, however, in 1967, when in rejecting freedom of expression objections to a conviction for unauthorized publication of military plans the Court took pains to point out the necessity for balancing the public interest in information against the need for secrecy in each particular case.[235]

Two subsequent cases respecting the exclusion of Communist propaganda from East Germany induced the Court to take a middle ground. The impoundment of East German newspapers, the Court concluded in 1969, offended no constitutional right of the sender, since the court below had found them to give direct support to the outlawed Communist Party.[236] At the same time, however, the opinion added that the trial court had erred in failing to balance the dangers of such material against the recipient's right under Article 5(1) to inform himself from generally available sources and suggested that periodicals prepared for circulation in East Germany itself could hardly be found to present a serious threat.[237] In 1972 the Court over

---

[233] Contrast Aptheker v. Secretary of State, 378 U.S. 500 (1964) (holding that revocation of a passport on the ground of mere membership in the Communist Party infringed the constitutional right to travel).

[234] 9 BVerfGE 162, 166 (1959). In the famous *Spiegel* case, 20 BVerfGE 162, 178-81 (1966), four Justices argued that Art. 5(1) forbade application of the so-called mosaic theory to justify prosecution of a publisher who had assembled publicly available materials in such a way as to afford meaningful insights into military secrets. The other four Justices, who concluded that the mosaic theory had not been employed, did not reach the question. See id. at 186.

[235] 21 BVerfGE 239, 243-44 (1967). Cf. Near v. Minnesota, 283 U.S. 697, 716 (1931) (dictum) (listing disclosure of the sailing dates of troopships as a rare example in which even a prior restraint of speech might be justified); New York Times Co. v. United States, 403 U.S. 713 (1971) (finding inadequate proof of danger to justify enjoining publication of the so-called Pentagon Papers).

[236] 27 BVerfGE 71, 78-79 (1969) (adding that it was also permissible to base the impoundment on calumny ("Verunglimpfung") against the Government: "Notwithstanding the breadth of permissible asperity in public debate, the manner in which an attack is phrased can bring about intolerable consequences").

[237] Id. at 79-88. Whether a source is "generally available" for purposes of this provision is determined principally by the desires of its owner, not by government

two dissents upheld a law excluding films that served as "a means of propaganda against the free democratic basic order," but only after interpreting the statute to apply only to films presenting an actual and intended threat to the democratic system and insisting on a showing that the danger was direct and immediate ("unmittelbar und gegenwärtig") in the case of any film that qualified as a work of art within the meaning of Article 5(3).[238]

In 1975 the Court rejected as frivolous the argument that publication of a report listing the National Democratic Party (NPD) as a subversive party of the radical right infringed the freedom of party organization guaranteed by Article 21(1).[239] The report, the Court insisted, left the NPD legally free to participate in the political process; it was simply an exercise of the Government's right to compete for the support of the electorate, a "part of the continuous intellectual debate that is the very basis of the free democratic system."[240] Three years later, however, the Court concluded that public broadcasters had no right to reject political advertisements on the ground that they were designed to undermine the constitution: The grant of exclusive jurisdiction to the Constitutional Court in Article 21(2) meant that all unbanned parties were entitled to participate in the political process without hindrance so long as they did not offend generally applicable criminal laws.[241]

---

regulation; for otherwise the provision would be a dead letter. See Schmidt-Jortzig, supra note 13, Rdnr. 31-33. More troubling was a companion decision, 27 BVerfGE 88 (1969), that upheld the power of postal authorities to detain suspicious items pending determination whether they met the standard for impoundment. As the opinion argued (id. at 99-100), temporary detention interfered less with freedom of information than did the ultimate suppression the Court had already approved. Like any prior restraint, however, the detention provision also had the vice of delaying access to material that could not constitutionally be suppressed. Cf. Times Film Corp. v. City of Chicago, 365 U.S. 43 (1961), where the Supreme Court fell into the same trap in upholding prior censorship of all motion pictures because there was no right to exhibit obscene films. The argument that detention before proof of violation constituted censorship expressly forbidden by another sentence of Art. 5(1) ("Eine Zensur findet nicht statt") was rejected on the less than obvious ground that by its nature the censorship provision protected only the sender and not the recipient of information. 27 BVerfGE at 102. For a contrary view see Schmidt-Jortzig, supra, Rdnr. 45.

[238] 33 BVerfGE 52, 65-71 (1972).

[239] 40 BVerfGE 287 (1975).

[240] Id. at 292-94. An earlier decision had reached the same conclusion with respect to an Interior Minister's assertion, in answer to a parliamentary inquiry, that the complaining party was a Communist-front organization. 13 BVerfGE 123, 125-26 (1961). Cf. the unresolved controversy over publication of the notorious Attorney General's List of allegedly subversive organizations in the United States, to which various Justices raised both substantive and procedural objections in Joint Anti-Fascist Refugee Comm. v. McGrath, 341 U.S. 123 (1951).

[241] 47 BVerfGE 198, 227-29 (1978).

The succeeding years have witnessed little development in this field. Actions directed toward perceived subversion appeared until the disorders of 1992 to have dwindled.[242] Recent decisions in the more trivial but related area of disrespect for the flag and other national symbols seem to exhibit an increased sensitivity to the values expressed in Article 5.[243] The more militant earlier decisions, however, have never been repudiated; the jurisprudence of the Constitutional Court with respect to the delicate balance between free expression and national security remains less protective of individual freedom than that of the later Warren Court.

IV. THE MEDIA

Insofar as the printed word is concerned, the German law respecting the institutional press is devoid of major surprises.[244] State subsidies for the press are neither forbidden nor required; subsidized postal rates must be viewpoint neutral but may exclude publications that serve the individual interests of the sender without contributing significantly to the formation of public opinion.[245] Since the publisher must be free to determine editorial policy, the state may not deprive him of the right to base employment decisions on compatibility of views; but the obligation to inform a workers' council ("Betriebsrat") of the reasons for discharging an editor does not impair this right.[246]

---

[242] See 47 BVerfGE 130, 131-32, 143 (1978) (upholding a prosecution for publications disparaging the Army ("Bundeswehr") as a "parasitical, destructive instrument directed against the people" and inciting soldiers to resist being trained "to murder other peoples"); 57 BVerfGE 250, 270-71 (1981) (upholding a conviction for serving as secret agent for a foreign power against the Federal Republic); 77 BVerfGE 240, 250-51 (1987) (remanding for reexamination in light of artistic freedom convictions for employing the symbols of a prohibited organization in advertising for a dramatic production).

[243] See 81 BVerfGE 278, 294-98 (1990) and 81 BVerfGE 298, 306-08 (1990) (remanding convictions for disparaging the flag and the national anthem, respectively, for reconsideration in light of the conclusion that the point of the challenged depictions was not to attack the symbols themselves but to protest departures from the values for which they stood). See Peter Quint, The Comparative Law of Flag Desecration: The United States and the Federal Republic of Germany, 15 Hast. Int'l & Comp. L. Rev. 613 (1992) (stressing (at 631-34) that the German court in the flag case, unlike even the dissenters from comparable decisions in the United States, acknowledged the legitimacy of the state's interest in preventing attacks on the constitutional order).

[244] The specific guarantee of press freedom protects the press as an institution. Opinions expressed in print are governed by the general provision of Art. 5(1) respecting freedom to express one's opinion. See 85 BVerfGE 1, 11-13 (1991).

[245] 80 BVerfGE124 (1989).

[246] 52 BVerfGE 283 (1979). Cf. Associated Press v. NLRB, 301 U.S. 103, 132-33 (1937) (holding the press not immune from generally applicable labor laws). See also Herzog in 1 Maunz/Dürig, Art. 5, Abs. I, II, Rdnr. 168-77 (arguing despite the

Freedom of the press extends not only to publication but also to the acquisition of information, including the right to attend judicial proceedings that are open to the general public.[247] Though confidentiality both of outside informants and of editorial deliberations is recognized as essential to the operation of a free press,[248] the press enjoys no blanket immunity either from questioning[249] or from searches and seizures[250] – any more than it does in the United States.[251]

Constitutional Court's decision that the democratic principle of Art. 20(1) might require that individual journalists enjoy a certain degree of independence from their employers).

[247] 50 BVerfGE 234, 239-43 (1979) (holding it impermissible to exclude a reporter from court because of an unfavorable article about the judge). Cf. Richmond Newspapers, Inc. v. Virginia, 448 U.S. 555 (1980). See also BVerfGE, Judgment of Nov. 11, 1992, Case No. 1 BvR 1595/92, 1992 NJW 3288 (granting a preliminary injunction to permit a television camera in the courtroom before the anticipated trial of former East German leader Eric Honecker). As in the United States, however, despite occasional hints in the opinions (e.g., 20 BVerfGE 162, 176 (1966)), freedom of the press is generally said to imply no duty on the part of the government to make information available. See Herzog in 1 Maunz/Dürig, Art. 5, Abs. I, II, Rdnr. 136-38; Kloepfer, supra note 2, Rdnr. 62.

[248] 20 BVerfGE 162, 176 (1966) (informants); 66 BVerfGE 116, 133-35 (1984) (holding that the civil courts had given too little weight to the need for confidentiality in allowing publication of a transcript of an editorial conference that a private individual had obtained by deceit). See also Martin Bullinger, Freiheit von Presse, Rundfunk, Film, 6 Handbuch des Staatsrechts 667, Rdnr. 32-33.

[249] 25 BVerfGE 296 (1969) (no right to refuse to testify or produce records respecting bribes allegedly given to government officials in exchange for access to information); 64 BVerfGE 108 (1983) (no right to withhold name and address of tax consulting firm that placed unlawful anonymous advertisement). Cf. 77 BVerfGE 65 (1987) (no right to withhold television films showing commission of violent crimes). After the Court first suggested that Art. 5(1) might place limits on the ability to obtain confidential information from the press, the legislature extended a preexisting statutory privilege to embrace both the identity of outside sources of information and the content of their communications, §§ 53(1) cl. 5, 97(5) StPO. As the Court observed, two of the cases cited in this note involved disclosure neither of information from outside informants nor of their identity, while the third concerned a commercial circular entitled to diminished constitutional protection. Indeed, the Court added in the most recent of these cases, both the right to fair trial and the duty to punish crime set limits to the state's *ability* to immunize the press from giving evidence. 77 BVerfGE at 75-77 (dictum). Cf. Davis v. Alaska, 415 U.S. 308 (1974) (confrontation clause limits privilege of confidentiality with respect to juvenile offenders); In re Farber, 78 N.J. 259, 394 A.2d 330 (1978) (comparable state provision precludes broad privilege against disclosure of news sources).

[250] In the controversial *Spiegel* case, decided in 1966, the Government had responded to an article critical of Germany's military preparedness by filing charges of betraying state secrets. A resulting search of the periodical's offices, which lasted nearly a year, was upheld by an equally divided Court applying the familiar test of proportionality in light of the special respect due to the press by virtue of Art. 5(1): "It can hardly be in the spirit of the Basic Law that freedom of the

Broadcasting, however, is another story. One of the most interesting and important of all decisions of the German Constitutional Court was the great *Television* case of 1961.[252]

The subject of controversy was an effort by the central government to set up a new broadcasting network. As I have explained elsewhere, the effort failed in part because the Court held that the Bund had invaded powers reserved to the individual states.[253] But the opinion went on to find a violation of the guarantee of broadcasting freedom in Article 5(1) as well.

The critical flaw in this respect was that the new network was controlled by the state: "Article 5 precludes the state from governing, directly or indirectly, an institution or organization engaged in broadcasting."[254] That is not the most obvious interpretation of the constitutional provision; to American eyes the mandate that "freedom of broadcasting" be afforded looks like a guarantee against government interference with private broadcasting, not a ban on broadcasting by the government. But the Court made clear that it viewed the broadcasting provision as going beyond the traditional right to be left alone by the state:

Article 5 of the Basic Law contains more than the citizen's individual basic right to a sphere of freedom within which he can express his opinion without state interference. . . . Article 5 requires in any event that this modern instrument of public opinion not be placed in the hands either of the state or of any particular social group. Broadcasting institutions must therefore be organized in such a way that all relevant interests have the opportunity to exert influence on their governing bodies and to express themselves in the overall program.[255]

In other words, the guarantee of broadcast freedom imposed a duty on the state to see to it that broadcasting facilities were controlled by a

---

press . . . should be employed to frustrate the investigation of serious offenses against national security." 20 BVerfGE 162, 209-22 (1966). See also 56 BVerfGE 247 (1981) (rejecting as frivolous a constitutional challenge to a search for and seizure of pictures taken by newspaper photographers showing the identity of the perpetrators of violent crime).

[251] See Branzburg v. Hayes, 408 U.S. 665 (1972); Zurcher v. Stanford Daily, 436 U.S. 547 (1978).

[252] 12 BVerfGE 205 (1961).

[253] See chapter 2 supra.

[254] 12 BVerfGE at 263 (distinguishing, as it had in determining the boundaries between federal and state authority, between matters respecting programming and those concerned solely with the "neutral" question of transmitting signals).

[255] Id. at 259-60, 262-63, adding that programming guidelines must assure "a minimum of balance, objectivity, and mutual respect" and that all these principles must be made binding by statute.

broad spectrum of interests and provided a forum for a broad spectrum of opinion.[256]

I have noted elsewhere the tendency of the German court to find affirmative government obligations in provisions that on their face seem only to limit state power.[257] As the first decision to exhibit this tendency, the *Television* case is of particular historical significance. The Court made no effort to establish a general principle of positive constitutional rights, nor did it rely on textual handholds that might have lent support to its conclusion.[258] Rather it relied upon peculiarities of the broadcast medium to demonstrate that without active state intervention the freedom to broadcast would be a hollow shell:

> To be sure, it is not true that newspapers, publishers, and printing houses can be established and maintained in unlimited numbers. The distinction between the press and the broadcast media, however, lies in the fact that a relatively large number of autonomous publications reflecting a broad spectrum of political and ideological views exists in the German press, while in the realm of broadcasting the number of stations must remain relatively small both for technical reasons and because of the extraordinarily high cost of broadcasting. This unique situation in the broadcasting field renders it necessary that special precautions be taken to preserve the broadcasting freedom guaranteed by Article 5 and to make it a reality.[259]

Similar arguments have been employed in the United States to justify government restrictions on broadcasters that could not be ap-

---

[256] Even supporters of this model concede that it has not worked out precisely as they had hoped, complaining among other things about the dominance of political parties in determining network policy. E.g., Hoffmann-Riem in 1 AK-GG, Art. 5, Abs. 1-2, Rdnr. 177, 182-83. For more sweeping doubts see Herzog in 1 Maunz/Dürig, Art. 5, Abs. I, II, Rdnr. 219; Bullinger, supra note 248, Rdnr. 92; for more on the influence of political parties see Grimm, supra note 134, at 365-69.

[257] See chapter 1 supra; text at notes 59-62, 78-80 supra; chapter 6 infra.

[258] Art. 5(1) provides not that the state shall not abridge broadcasting freedom but that freedom of broadcasting shall be afforded ("gewährleistet") (see Hoffmann-Riem in 1 AK-GG, Art. 5, Abs. 1-2, Rdnr. 137); Art. 1(1) directs the state not only to respect ("achten") but also to protect ("schützen") human dignity, which the entire Bill of Rights is designed to secure. See Schmidt-Jortzig, supra note 13, Rdnr. 11: "The second sentence of Art. 1(1) expressly requires the state to protect . . . the human rights content" of communicative freedoms. The same language, however, applies to freedom of the (printing) press, which the opinion carefully distinguished for reasons to be noted.

[259] 12 BVerfGE at 261. See Hoffmann-Riem in 1 AK-GG , Art. 5, Abs. 1-2, Rdnr. 168-69 (endorsing this reasoning with respect to broadcasting and suggesting that the competitive model may also be deficient in the case of the press); Bullinger, supra note 248, Rdnr. 51, 145-48 (arguing for extension of the private model to broadcasting).

plied to publishers,[260] but never yet to *require* them. The standard objection to any such argument in this country would be that the first amendment limits only state action, not that of a private broadcaster,[261] and that it imposes no affirmative duties on the state.

Even in this country, however, a respectable argument can be made for adopting the German position. The fifth amendment is not generally understood to require the state to feed its citizens. Yet if the state puts an individual in jail, it incapacitates him from providing for his own needs; to incarcerate him without food is thus to deprive him of life.[262] The same reasoning might arguably be applied to broadcasting: By limiting the number of licenses without requiring licensees to provide public access to their facilities, the state prevents most people from making use of the broadcast medium, and this the Constitution forbids.[263]

Like subsequent decisions concluding or suggesting that the state is required to provide affirmative support for constitutional rights, the *Television* opinion contrasts sharply with the almost contemporaneous holding that the constitution *forbids* subsidies for political parties.[264] Moreover, the Court did not stop to explain, and it was not obvious, why its reasoning required that the state not operate its second network. The Länder already provided a network that the Court found to satisfy the requirements of public access and influence;[265] the existence of federal competition that did not meet this standard in no way reduced the opportunities this network provided.

Not surprisingly, the *Television* decision proved to be the first in a series; the discovery of a constitutional duty to assure well-balanced broadcasting facilities generated a need for continuing supervision to ensure that new arrangements conformed to the requirements laid down by the Court.

In 1971, with Article 5 obligations in the background, the Court held that the user fees by which public television was largely financed could not be subjected to a federal sales tax, since they could

---

[260] Contrast Red Lion Broadcasting Co. v. FCC, 395 U.S. 367 (1969) (upholding a provision requiring broadcasters to afford those they criticized a right of reply), with Miami Herald Publishing Co. v. Tornillo, 418 U.S. 241 (1974) (striking down a similar provision applicable to publishers).

[261] See Columbia Broadcasting System v. Democratic National Committee, 412 U.S. 94 , 114-21 (1973) (opinion of Burger, C.J.).

[262] Cf. Cruz v. Beto, 405 U.S. 319, 322 (1972) (religion); Estelle v. Gamble, 429 U.S. 97 (1976) (medical needs).

[263] See *Columbia Broadcasting System*, 412 U.S. at 170-204 (Brennan, J., dissenting).

[264] See text at notes 145-67 supra. Indeed, without questioning the first *Television* decision itself, three Justices argued in a later case that Art. 5 forbade state subsidies for broadcasters just as Art. 20 forbade them for political parties. 31 BVerfGE 314, 344-45 (Geiger, Rinck, and Wand, JJ., dissenting). For less categorical reservations on this score see Hoffmann-Riem in 1 AK-GG, Art. 5, Abs. 1-2, Rdnr. 181.

[265] 12 BVerfGE at 261-62.

not be classified as compensation for goods or services.[266] In 1981 it struck down a Saarland statute respecting private broadcasting on the grounds that it gave the executive too much discretion in awarding licenses and failed to assure popular control of programming decisions.[267] Later the same year, and again in 1983, it held that the principle of popular control required that a broadcasting station's governing body have the authority to discharge employees having a significant impact upon programming.[268] Lengthy and detailed opinions in additional cases decided in 1986, 1987, and 1991 uncovered a variety of flaws in broadcasting laws adopted by Lower Saxony,[269] Baden-Württemberg,[270] and North Rhine-Westphalia.[271]

The details of these intricate decisions need not detain us here.[272] In announcing them, however, the Court made at least two general pronouncements of wider significance. Although the scarcity of broadcasting frequencies had been the central basis for the initial conclusion that Article 5(1) required the state to provide a framework

---

[266] 31 BVerfGE 314 (1971) (over three dissents). This conclusion made it unnecessary to decide whether, as the state argued, federal taxation was an unacceptable interference with the broadcasting freedom guaranteed by Art. 5(1). See id. at 318-19, 333. Cf. 36 BVerfGE 321 (1974) (denying that either freedom of expression or artistic freedom conferred any exemption from ordinary taxes and upholding a sales tax that was higher for records and tapes than for books because of the financial strength of the recording industry); Grosjean v. American Press Co., 297 U.S. 233 (1936).

[267] 57 BVerfGE 295 (1981).

[268] 59 BVerfGE 231 (1982); 64 BVerfGE 256 (1983). Cf. Myers v. United States, 272 U.S. 52 (1926) (reaching a similar conclusion, for similarly persuasive reasons, with respect to the President of the United States).

[269] 73 BVerfGE 118 (1986).

[270] 74 BVerfGE 297 (1987).

[271] 83 BVerfGE 238 (1991).

[272] A few of the principal conclusions may interest the curious. Private stations alone cannot provide the variety that Art. 5(1) requires, because among other things the advertisers on whom private broadcasting depends cannot be expected to pay for expensive cultural programs that do not appeal to a mass audience (73 BVerfGE at 155-56). Correspondingly, private broadcasters need not be subject to the strict requirements that apply to public facilities, but they may not be permitted to afford any single person or group undue influence on the formation of public opinion (id. at 158-60). To protect the viability of private broadcasters, the state may forbid advertising on public stations (74 BVerfGE at 341-44), but it need not do so, except to the extent necessary to prevent undue susceptibility to advertisers' desires (83 BVerfGE at 310-12); and it may not forbid public stations to carry local or regional programs (74 BVerfGE at 331-40). Public broadcasters may be authorized to engage in such ancillary activities as the creation and sale of radio or television programs and the publication of program guides (83 BVerfGE at 303-05, 312-15). See also 87 BVerfGE 181, 197-206 (1992) (upholding a total ban on advertising on public television after finding that the complaining network had adequate alternative sources of revenue); BVerfG, Decision of Oct. 5, 1993, Case No. 1 BvL 35/91 (not yet reported) (concluding that placing a public broadcasting organization in bankruptcy would be inconsistent with Art. 5(1)).

to assure balanced programming, the 1981 opinion flatly declared that the duty would persist even if technical advances eliminated the shortage; for there would still be no guarantee that the market would produce a balance adequate to meet the demands of Article 5.[273] Furthermore, in concluding that the existence of one public network meeting the criteria of Article 5(1) did not obviate the necessity for balance in licensing private competitors, the same opinion explained why the Bund had been denied permission to operate a second network in 1961: Additional stations in the hands of a single interest gave it an unfair advantage and thus contradicted the equal access principle.[274]

But perhaps the greatest significance of the later broadcasting decisions lies in their very existence: The basic conclusion that Article 5(1) requires the state affirmatively to guarantee a balanced offering of radio and television programming has thrust the Constitutional Court to a very significant degree into supervision of the broadcasting industry.

V. ACADEMIC FREEDOM

Broadcasting is not the only activity subject to intensive judicial oversight by virtue of broad interpretation of the Bill of Rights. Higher education is subject to equally intrusive examination.

I have elsewhere adumbrated the degree of judicial control of university admissions policy the Constitutional Court has derived from the guarantee of occupational freedom in Article 12(1) in connection with the equality provision of Article 3(1) — with strong intimations that here too the state may be under an affirmative duty to see to it that adequate facilities are available.[275] A comparable degree of judicial control over other aspects of university governance has been deduced from the guarantee of academic freedom ("Wissenschaft, Forschung und Lehre") in Article 5(3).[276]

---

[273] 57 BVerfGE at 322-23. See also 73 BVerfGE at 154-55. For criticism of both the technical and the economic arguments see Herzog in 1 Maunz/Dürig, Art. 5, Abs. I, II, Rdnr. 221-27.

[274] 57 BVerfGE at 324.

[275] See chapter 6 infra (citing, e.g., 33 BVerfGE 303 (1972) (*Numerus Clausus*)). Cf. 75 BVerfGE 40 (1987), also discussed in chapter 6 infra (holding that Art. 7(4) requires a subsidy of private schools).

[276] Wissenschaft (science or scholarship) is said be an umbrella concept that includes both Forschung (research) and Lehre (teaching). See Oppermann, supra note 7, Rdnr. 37; Denninger in 1 AK-GG, Art. 5, Abs. III, pt. I, Rdnr. 13. For a modest effort to distinguish scholarship from politics (Marxism?) on the one hand and superstition (astrology?) on the other without imposing any notion of "correct" or "incorrect" science see id., Rdnr. 14-19.

Like broadcasting, higher education has been largely a public function in Germany.[277] In both areas the freedom of autonomous public institutions from extraneous influence has been one of the hallmarks of the Constitutional Court's jurisprudence; but it was slower to develop in the educational field.[278]

The first decision interpreting the guarantee of academic freedom was not especially encouraging in this regard.[279] Concluding that Hesse's Ministry of Culture had acted lawfully in appointing a medical professor without a formal request by the academy to which he was appointed, the Court softened the blow by pointing out that the institution was not a full-fledged university and that it had effectively manifested its approval.[280] The opinion added, however, that there was no reason to think the Basic Law was meant to give universities for the first time an absolute right to select their own professors and even described it as an open question whether Article 5(3) gave any rights at all to universities as such or only to individual scholars.[281]

The breakthrough came in a major opinion in 1973.[282] Among the reforms instituted in the wake of student unrest in the late 1960s was the so-called "Gruppenuniversität," in which senior academics ("Hochschullehrer"), who had traditionally dominated university governance, were required to share their authority with junior faculty members, students, and even employees, all of whom were considered also to have a legitimate stake in the institution.[283] In striking down several aspects of this new system, the Court undertook a major exposition of the meaning of academic freedom.

One obvious function of that freedom, the Court explained, was – within the limits of Article 5(3)'s loyalty proviso, which is an element of the "militant democracy" already discussed[284] – to protect the individual scholar or scientist from government interference with either research or teaching.[285] Beyond this, however, Article 5(3) – like

---

[277] See Scholz in 1 Maunz/Dürig, Art. 5, Abs. III, Rdnr. 142. The right to establish private universities, subject to appropriate state standards, is guaranteed by Art. 5(3). See id., Rdnr. 147.

[278] For brief sketches of academic freedom under earlier constitutions see id., Rdnr. 1-11; Oppermann, supra note 7, Rdnr. 2-8.

[279] 15 BVerfGE 256 (1963).

[280] Id. at 265-67.

[281] Id. at 263-65. See Oppermann, supra note 7, Rdnr. 35-36 (citing p. 262 of the same opinion for the proposition that universities do have rights under Art. 5(3)); Scholz in 1 Maunz/Dürig, Art. 5, Abs. III, Rdnr. 123-25 (arguing in effect that although the University has standing to assert academic freedom the substantive rights are those of individual scholars).

[282] 35 BVerfGE 79 (1973).

[283] For a brief summary of this background see id. at 109-112. The statutory provisions considered in the case appear in id. at 82-89.

[284] Art. 5(3) GG: "Freedom of teaching shall not absolve from loyalty to the constitution." See note 170 supra and accompanying text.

[285] 35 BVerfGE at 112-14.

Article 5(1) in the field of broadcasting – embodied an endorsement of academic freedom as an "objective value" and thus imposed an obligation on the state to take affirmative action to make that freedom a reality. Given the state's "practical monopoly" of the financial and other means necessary for the pursuit of scholarship (especially in the natural sciences), this meant that the state must actively promote research and teaching by providing the necessary financial, organizational, and human resources; and that meant that it was the state's duty under Article 5(3) to make available functioning institutions in which scholarship might be freely pursued ("funktionsfähige Institutionen für einen freien Wissenschaftsbetrieb zur Verfügung zu stellen"). Without such affirmative state sustenance, the Court concluded, freedom of scholarship – like freedom of broadcasting – could never be achieved.[286]

None of this, the Court hastened to add, meant that the Basic Law had frozen the concept of the German university in its traditional form. As far as purely administrative matters were concerned, Article 5(3) had nothing to say about who ran the university. Decisions directly affecting research and teaching, however, including those in curricular and appointment matters and the allocation of research funds, had to be left ultimately to the scholars themselves.[287]

Application of these principles has led the Court far into the details of academic organization; twelve additional decisions over the past twenty years have helped to make them concrete.[288] As in the case of broadcasting, we need not follow the Court into the particu-

---

[286] "Eine Ausübung der Grundfreiheiten aus Art. 5 Abs. 3 GG ist hier notwendig mit einer Teilhabe an staatlichen Leistungen verbunden." See id. at 114-16. Whether this means that the individual scholar has a justiciable claim to adequate financial support is disputed; the Federal Administrative Court ("Bundesverwaltungsgericht") has said he does not. See 52 BVerwGE 339 (1977); Oppermann, supra note 7, Rdnr. 22.

[287] 35 BVerfGE at 116-24. See also id. at 130: "Es muß aber verhindert werden, daß wissenschaftlicher Sachverstand bei der Entscheidung von Fragen der Forschung und Lehre in den Beschlußorganen der Wissenschaftsverwaltung überspielt wird."

[288] 39 BVerfGE 247 (1975); 43 BVerfGE 242 (1977); 47 BVerfGE 327 (1978); 51 BVerfGE 369 (1979); 54 BVerfGE 363 (1980); 55 BVerfGE 37 (1980); 56 BVerfGE 192 (1981); 57 BVerfGE 70 (1981); 61 BVerfGE 210 (1982); 66 BVerfGE 270 (1984); 67 BVerfGE 202 (1984); BVerfG, Judgment of March 3, 1993, Case No. 1 BvR 757/88 (not yet reported). Less common are decisions dealing with traditional issues of the legitimacy of measures impinging directly on the freedom of individual members of the academic community. See 47 BVerfGE 327 (1978) (holding that researchers can be required to take account of and to disclose dangers to the public); 67 BVerfGE 1 (1984) (upholding a reduction in the retirement age for professors from 68 to 65 years). Like artistic freedom, academic freedom is not expressly subject to any limitation; like artistic freedom, it is understood to be restricted when it comes into conflict with other constitutional values. See Oppermann, supra note 7, Rdnr. 27-29: "A professor may not incite to the commission of crimes in the classroom in reliance on academic freedom."

lars. Suffice it to say that teaching assistants may be given more of a
say in curricular than in research and appointment matters, in
which senior professors must be able as a group to have their way,
and that nonacademic employees may take no part in decision making in any of these fields.[289]

In the United States, it is said, the judges run the prisons and the
public schools; in Germany it can be said with equal justice that they
run the universities and the mass media. Whether this represents
an appropriate use of judicial resources can be debated. Two dissenters from the *Gruppenuniversität* decision argued vigorously that
the Court had usurped the legislative function;[290] the majority saw
no other way to make academic freedom a reality.[291]

In the United States we like to think the best guarantee of academic freedom lies in a broad spectrum of private educational institutions. Despite our best efforts to insulate them, public universities
proved alarmingly vulnerable to political influence during the
lamentable McCarthy period. Private institutions were not wholly
immune to such pressures, but their ability to appeal for financial
support to private benefactors of all ideological colorations – critically
encouraged by generous and neutral tax benefits for educational contributions – enabled many of them to function as safe harbors in the
eye of the storm.

The autonomy of private universities in the United States has
been sadly compromised by increasing dependence upon government
subsidies, with their apparently inevitable strings – for reasons fully
appreciated by the German Constitutional Court in its decisions limiting state support of local government[292] and of political parties.[293]
Nevertheless private universities remain one of America's most
prized resources, and their excellence is in no small measure
attributable to their relative freedom from government control.

---

[289] 35 BVerfGE at 124-46. Cf. the Court's similar resolution, not long afterward,
of the related controversy over statutory provisions giving industrial workers a
right to codetermination ("Mitbestimmung") of company policy in light of the
occupational freedom and property rights guaranteed the owner by Art. 12(1) and
14(1) GG. 50 BVerfGE 290 (1979); see chapter 6 infra. For the view that the Court did
not go far enough in the *Gruppenuniversität* case to protect the prerogatives of senior
professors see Scholz in 1 Maunz/Dürig, Art. 5, Abs. III, Rdnr. 158.

[290] 35 BVerfGE at 148-70 (Simon and Rupp-von Brünneck, JJ.).

[291] Even after this decision it has been said that public universities cannot
generally make appointments without ministerial approval, see Scholz in 1
Maunz/Dürig, Art. 5, Abs. III, Rdnr. 168. To an outsider it seems difficult to reconcile such a degree of state influence with the Court's general principle of academic
autonomy, but it has been defended by a thoughtful advocate of academic freedom as
a safeguard against political appointments *by the university*. See Denninger in 1
AK-GG, Art. 5, Abs. 3, pt. I, Rdnr. 23. Public universities, it need hardly be said,
are also dependent upon the state for financing. See Scholz, supra, Rdnr. 169.

[292] See the urban renewal cases discussed in chapter 2 supra.

[293] See text at notes 145-67 supra.

It may seem surprising at first glance that the Germans, despite their black history of state interference with academic freedom during the Nazi period and their acute awareness of the risk of subservience implicit in state support, did not opt for widespread private higher education after World War II. But a mature and self-sufficient system of private universities can scarcely be established overnight. Progressive taxation and soaring costs have reduced the number of individual Rockefellers affluent enough to bankroll entire institutions; traditions of private giving must be carefully cultivated. The Constitutional Court may well have been right in its assessment that only the state was in a position to provide adequate facilities for higher education in Germany; let us do our best to see to it that it remains otherwise in the United States.

VI. CONCLUSION

Examination of the German law of free expression reminds one once again how easily two well-intentioned societies, starting from substantially identical premises, can arrive at significantly different results. Expression is a cardinal value both in Germany and in the United States, both as an end in itself and as an indispensable tool of democracy. In both countries it must yield on occasion to competing values, and there is room for honest disagreement as to where to draw the line.

By means of the imaginative doctrine of reciprocal effect ("Wechselwirkung") developed in the *Lüth* case, the Constitutional Court has smoothed over one of the principal differences suggested by the text of the two constitutions, affording expressive freedoms considerably more protection than the language of Article 5(1) and (2) would appear to give them. Yet other equally creative doctrines of the Constitutional Court have brought about differences of first importance with respect to such subjects as political parties, broadcasting, and higher education.

In some respects the German law of free expression is less thoroughly developed than that of the United States. The Constitutional Court has had few occasions to elaborate on such issues as obscenity, symbolic speech, time, place, or manner restrictions, or the public forum.[294] Such glimpses as the Court has afforded suggest that its

---

[294] The Federal Administrative Court, without adverting to the special problems that arise when the citizen claims the right to express opinions on public property, has applied the conventional balancing process to strike down a law requiring a permit for the distribution of handbills on the streets. 56 BVerwGE 24, 26-30 (1978). Cf. Schneider v. State, 308 U.S. 147 (1939). On the question whether communicative use of public property is a negative ("Abwehr-") or positive right ("Teilhaberecht") see Dietrich Murswiek, Grundrechte als Teilhaberechte, soziale Grundrechte, 5 Handbuch des Staatsrechts 243, Rdnr. 66-67, 82; Currie, supra note 145, 53 U. Chi. L. Rev. at 878-80.

approach to many of these problems may not differ substantially from our own.

Until very recently one might have been tempted to add that the problem of unconstitutional conditions, which has played such a crucial role in free speech cases in the United States, was also largely undeveloped in Germany. The term itself is foreign to the opinions of the Constitutional Court,[295] and there have been fewer opportunities to work out the details; but a series of recent decisions has cast considerable light upon this previously murky area and suggested that here too the German law is strikingly similar to that of the United States.[296]

Development of an unconstitutional conditions doctrine in Germany was retarded in the past by the traditional understanding that basic rights had no application either to the "special relationships" between the state and its employees, students, or prisoners or to actions taken by the government in a proprietary capacity. The dangers posed to fundamental freedoms by such an approach were pointed out as early as 1938, and the restrictive learning has essentially been repudiated. The Court held in 1972 that the basic rights did apply to prisoners; it has long been established that if there is a proprietary exception it does not extend to the provision of social benefits; and commentators increasingly conclude that the basic rights apply to everything the state chooses to do.[297]

Insofar as discrimination on religious or political grounds is concerned, Article 3(3) appears to erect an absolute bar: "No one shall be disadvantaged or favored because of . . . his faith or his religious or political opinions." As we shall see, this paragraph was given an unnaturally narrow interpretation in the *Civil Service* case and essentially disappeared from view; but it seems to have been resurrected by a recent "clarification" of earlier opinions and should play a significant role in conditional benefit cases in the future.[298] Quite apart from the equality provisions, moreover, the Court has frequently held that conditional benefits that discriminate against the exercise of a fundamental right infringe the substantive right itself.

To begin with, the Constitutional Court never accepted Justice Holmes's regrettable position that the power to withhold a benefit included the power to grant it on whatever condition the state saw fit.[299]

---

[295] The term "unconstitutional conditions" has been criticized in the United States as unnecessary and distracting from the real issue of burdens and justifications. See Cass Sunstein, Why the Unconstitutional Conditions Doctrine Is an Anachronism, 70 B.U.L. Rev. 593 (1990). I find it a useful way to identify a pervasive and often poorly understood type of problem.

[296] My thinking on this subject has been stimulated by an excellent paper by Clemens Ladenburger, Unconstitutional Conditions in the United States and in Germany (on file with the author).

[297] See notes 41-44 and accompanying text and note 107 supra.

[298] See 39 BVerfGE 334, 367-69 (1975); 85 BVerfGE 191, 206 (1992); chapter 6 infra.

[299] McAuliffe v. City of New Bedford, 155 Mass. 216, 220, 29 N.E. 517, 517 (1892).

Despite the existence of the Sozialstaat clauses, for example, the Court has never held that the state is obliged to provide welfare benefits to orphans. Without resolving that question, however, the Court held in 1970 that if such benefits were provided at all they could not be denied to orphans who were married; for the constitutional protection of marriage and family in Article 6(1) implied a "strict prohibition of differentiation respecting government benefits according to family status alone."[300] Thus from the beginning the Court recognized that it was possible for the state to violate constitutional rights without actually forbidding their exercise; a 1957 decision had already established that to impose higher income taxes on two individuals because they were married placed an unacceptable penalty on the constitutional right to marry.[301]

In other contexts too the Constitutional Court has long made clear that the constitution can be offended by conditions attached to benefits the state had no obligation to grant. The state, as we have seen, was held to have no duty to subsidize political parties; yet in a series of decisions the Court held that the state had infringed the Article 21(1) guarantee of the right to establish such parties by unjustifiably discriminating among them in handing out various forms of economic support.[302] In the field of federalism, where our Supreme Court gave up on this problem years ago, the *Urban Renewal* decisions reflect a similar philosophy.[303] A 1988 opinion striking down application of an oath requirement for members of a local council squarely rejected Holmes's argument: Neither the fact that the councilman had voluntarily chosen to seek election nor the fact that the sanction for refusal to take the oath was mere exclusion from office made the requirement any less an invasion of his religious freedom.[304]

---

[300] 28 BVerfGE 324, 356 (1970); see also id. at 347. Similarly, while concluding that separation of powers and competing priorities precluded it from holding that the state was obliged to build a new university, the Court had no hesitation in holding that the equality provision of Art. 3(1), in conjunction with the social state principle and the right to select one's place of professional training under Art. 12(1), forbade invidious discrimination in allotting existing educational capacity. See 33 BVerfGE 303, 332-36, 351-56 (1972); 37 BVerfGE 342, 352-60 (1974).

[301] 6 BVerfGE 55, 70-84 (1957). This decision and those cited in the preceding note are also noted in chapter 6 infra.

[302] See 8 BVerfGE 51, 62-67 (1958) (deductibility of contributions); 14 BVerfGE 121, 133 (1962) (free broadcast time). See also 44 BVerfGE 125, 146 (1977) (propaganda issued by the government itself). See generally text at notes 138-45 supra.

[303] See chapter 2 supra.

[304] 79 BVerfGE 69, 76 (1988). Even the arguably insensitive *Civil Service* opinion, which upheld the exclusion of political extremists from public employment on security grounds, acknowledged that denial of a government job had constitutionally significant effects on freedoms of expression, association, and assembly; the Court stressed the need to balance those effects against the countervailing interest in loyal administration embodied in Art. 33(5) and found them outweighed. See

Two recent decisions of the Constitutional Court should remove any lingering doubts on this score. The first came in a 1989 case in which publishers of advertising circulars challenged their exclusion from a postal subsidy that was afforded to other publications. Finding ample justification for the distinction, the Court emphasized that any discrimination in the grant of government benefits to the press must be subjected to scrutiny under Article 5:

> The second sentence of Article 5(1) does not simply protect against governmental restrictions of freedom of the press but also has an impact upon benefits afforded to the press by the state. The freedom of the press that Article 5(1)(2) is meant to secure can be endangered no less by state assistance than by governmental intrusions and limitations. This is especially true of selective support measures that do not benefit all publications protected by Article 5(1)(2).[305]

Acknowledging that the state had no obligation to subsidize the press at all, the Court made clear that if it chose to do so there were strict limits on its authority to play favorites. In such a case, said the Court,

> Article 5(1)(2) requires that any influence on the content and form of individual publications, as well as any overall distortion of competition in the written word, be avoided. State support may neither favor nor disfavor particular opinions or points of view. Rather Article 5(1)(2) establishes for the state a duty of viewpoint neutrality that forbids any distinctions on the basis of the content of an opinion.[306]

The second decision, already noted in connection with the state's affirmative duty to protect against invasions of basic rights by private parties, was rendered in 1992. The complainant had been denied a job on the basis of an article he had written expressing sympathy with violent demonstrations against the development of nuclear power. In denying him a remedy against his prospective employer, the Consti-

---

text at notes 215-29 supra. See also 84 BVerfGE 9, 18 (1991) (rejecting the argument that the parties had consented to application of a rule prescribing the husband's name as family name in default of a choice because they were under no obligation to marry. The record affirmatively showed that they had not consented; the price of avoiding the regulation by remaining single was unacceptably high; and even in enacting noncoercive provisions the legislature was bound to respect basic rights).

[305] 80 BVerfGE 124, 131 (1989). See also 82 BVerfGE 209, 223-24 (1990) (employing similar reasoning in scrutinizing the effect of selective subsidies on occupational freedom).

[306] 80 BVerfGE at 133-34. The discrimination against commercial publications was upheld as viewpoint neutral and reasonable. Id. at 134-36; see also text at notes 244-45 supra.

tutional Court concluded, the lower courts had offended the complainant's freedom to express his opinions:

> It is true that the complainant remains free to continue expressing and disseminating his opinion of the incidents at Brokdorf without alteration. But freedom of expression is affected not only when conduct protected by the basic rights is itself restricted or prohibited. It is enough that disadvantageous legal consequences are attached to such conduct. That is what has happened here.[307]

In short, recent decisions suggest that, though never given a comparable title, the doctrine of unconstitutional conditions is alive and well in Germany. Like the Supreme Court, the Constitutional Court has conceded that the state may have more leeway when a denial of benefits rather than an outright prohibition is involved.[308] For the intrusion may be less severe and the government's interest greater – e.g., its right to set priorities in expending its own funds or the special dangers of placing the machinery of the democratic state in the hands of its enemies. But the more significant fact is the Constitutional Court's clear recognition that denial of a government benefit on the ground of opinion impinges upon the freedom of expression guaranteed by Article 5(1); like any other limitation of that right, it can be justified only under the conditions specified in Article 5(2), which under the *Lüth* decision include a governmental interest that outweighs the burden imposed.[309]

Unconstitutional conditions aside, German jurisprudence is notable for the heavy emphasis the Constitutional Court has placed on protection of reputation and privacy, which on a number of occasions – though less frequently in recent years – has led to restrictions on artistic or political expression that the Supreme Court would not have accepted. This emphasis was perhaps inevitable in light of the specific provision of Article 5 that expression is limited by "personal honor," which in turn may be traceable – like so many provisions of the Basic Law – to specific evils perpetrated in the none too distant past.

The same may be said of the Constitutional Court's decisions respecting subversion, which have given the interest in national security a weight more reminiscent of the decisions of the early Warren Court than of those of its successor. Given the framers' explicit decision in favor of "militant democracy," again in response to the disas-

---

[307] 86 BVerfGE 122, 128 (1992).

[308] See 80 BVerfGE at 134; 36 BVerfGE 321, 332-33 (1974) (upholding the exclusion of phonograph records from a tax break afforded to other media of expression less financially secure); Rüfner, supra note 32, Rdnr. 32-34, 45-46; Scholz in 1 Maunz/Dürig, Art. 5, Abs. III, Rdnr. 40 (arguing that in deciding which artists to support the state may make artistic but not political distinctions). Cf. American Communications Ass'n v. Douds, 339 U.S. 382 (1950).

[309] See 86 BVerfGE at 129-30.

trous experience of Weimar, the outlawing of the Sozialistische
Reichspartei and the Communist Party was a foregone conclusion,
and the exclusion of perceived subversives from positions of power
was entirely understandable despite its dangers. Lest one be too hasty
in criticism of this line of cases, it would be well to recall once again
that our Supreme Court has sustained similar measures in times of
real or imagined crisis, and that it has done so with the concurrence
of such thoughtful and respected jurists as Felix Frankfurter and
Robert Jackson.

Indeed much of what distinguishes German decisions in the
field of expression from those of the recent Supreme Court is an attitude of judicial restraint that may remind the U.S. reader of Justice
Frankfurter in yet another respect. Determined at any cost to avoid
the judicial suppression of the popular will that had characterized
the *Lochner* period, Frankfurter bent over backward not to substitute
his judgment for that of the legislature, even when the result was to
tolerate what others found a shocking invasion of civil liberties.[310] In
such cases as *Mephisto* the Constitutional Court developed an
analogous principle of deference not to the legislature but to other
courts, refusing to substitute its judgment for theirs on the ultimate
question whether freedom of expression had actually been infringed.

More recently the German court has receded somewhat from this
deferential position. In developing this attitude of restraint, however,
the Justices seem to have been influenced by that feature of its fundamental rights jurisprudence that most strikingly contrasts with
that of the Supreme Court: its tendency to find in Bill of Rights provisions more than a simple right to be free from official interference.
Building upon the text of Article 1(1), which affirmatively requires
the state to protect human dignity, and upon the argument that certain fundamental rights would be worthless without affirmative government support, the Court has developed the notion of an "objective
order of values" that permeates the entire legal system and that has
significant consequences even for the relations between one citizen
and another. Thus in the *Blinkfüer* case the courts were not only
permitted but required to protect publishers against a secondary boycott; thus in the first *Television* case the state was required to assure
that a broad spectrum of views were disseminated; thus in the *Gruppenuniversität* case the state was required to guarantee the existence
of adequate facilities for higher education and research. Thus too, as
in *Mephisto*, every private controversy involves a conflict between
competing constitutional values. In such a context judicial restraint
becomes a necessity if the Constitutional Court is not to supplant the
civil courts entirely – and the legislative discretion implicit in popular sovereignty as well.

In all this there is much food for thought as to the proper role of a
constitutional court as well as the proper scope of free expression and

---

[310] See, e.g., West Virginia State Bd. of Education v. Barnette, 319 U.S. 624, 648-
49 (1943) (dissenting opinion); The Second Century at 319-20.

of those cognate rights that help to make it a reality. And that, in addition to the more modest but equally worthy goal of better understanding, is what comparative law is all about.

5

Church and State

The Basic Law has a great deal to say about the relation between church and state. In comparison with the Supreme Court, however, the Constitutional Court has decided relatively few cases involving religion.

The central provision is found in Article 4(1): "Freedom of faith and of conscience, and freedom to profess a religion or a particular philosophy, are inviolable."[1] Paragraph (2) of the same Article adds that "the undisturbed practice of religion is guaranteed [wird gewährleistet]," Paragraph (3) that "no one may be compelled against his conscience to render military service involving the use of arms [Kriegsdienst mit der Waffe]." Article 140 complicates matters by incorporating by reference five articles of the Weimar Constitution providing, among other things, that "there shall be no state church"[2] and that religious organizations shall enjoy the right to "regulate and administer [their] own affairs . . . within the limits of the laws that apply to everyone."[3] Article 3(3), overlapping yet another incorporated Weimar provision, adds that "no one may be prejudiced or favored because of . . . his faith or his religious . . . opinions."[4]

---

[1] "Die Freiheit des Glaubens, des Gewissens und die Freiheit des religiösen und weltanschaulichen Bekenntnisses sind unverletzlich." Freedom of conscience ("Freiheit . . . des Gewissens") is not merely another name for religious freedom; it protects "every sincere ethical [sittliche] decision," i.e., every decision "made with reference to the categories of 'good' and 'evil.'" See Herbert Bethge, Gewissensfreiheit, 6 Handbuch des Staatsrechts 435, Rdnr. 4, 10 (1989).

[2] Art. 137(1) WRV.

[3] Art. 137(3) WRV. Among other things, other incorporated provisions protect against compulsion to "disclose [one's] religious convictions" (Art. 136(3) WRV) or to "perform any religious act or ceremony" (Art. 136(4) WRV), and guarantee "the freedom . . . to form religious bodies" (Art. 137(2) WRV). Several of the Weimar provisions, like the basic guarantees of Art. 4(1) and (2), can be traced back to the abortive but influential Paulskirche constitution of 1849. See RV 1849, §§ 144-51.

[4] See also Art. 33(3) GG and Art. 136(1), (2) WRV, both of which further particularize the principle against religious discrimination. Addition of the Weimar provisions as a separate appendix was an untidy compromise between delegates unable to agree on the inclusion of institutional guarantees in the Bill of Rights itself. See 1 JöR (n.F.) at 75-76, 78-79, 899-907 (collecting the legislative history); Axel

In short, to reduce the matter to essentials familiar to the reader versed in the U.S. Constitution, the Basic Law both protects the free exercise of religion and forbids the establishment of an official church.[5] In addition, the detailed provisions of the Basic Law expressly resolve many of the specific questions that our Supreme Court has had to determine as a matter of interpreting the generalities of the first amendment. Interpretive problems have also arisen, of course, under the German provisions. To facilitate comparison I shall discuss both the provisions themselves and the decisions applying them according to the familiar categories of establishment and free exercise.

I. Establishment of Religion

We begin with the declaration of Article 137(1) of the Weimar Constitution, incorporated by Article 140 of the Basic Law, that "there shall be no state church." Reminiscent on its face of the first amendment's command that Congress shall make "no law respecting an establishment of religion," it means a good deal less in practice; the Constitutional Court has not taken it to imply nearly so complete a separation between church and state as that currently required by the Supreme Court.

Several questions as to the permissibility of particular state actions arguably supporting religion in Germany are expressly resolved by other constitutional provisions. Article 4(3) eliminates any argument of special religious preferences by extending the exemption from armed service to everyone with conscientious objections.[6] Article 137(4) of the Weimar Constitution (also preserved by Art. 140 of the Basic Law) forecloses Madison's perhaps overly fastidious doubts about the issuance of corporate charters to religious bodies[7] by

---

Freiherr von Campenhausen, Religionsfreiheit, 6 Handbuch des Staatsrechts 369, Rdnr. 34-35.

[5] See Alexander Hollerbach, Grundlagen des Staatskirchenrechts, 6 Handbuch des Staatsrechts 471, Rdnr. 88-89 (arguing that the guarantees of freedom of belief and free exercise in Art. 4(1) and (2) GG, together with the ban on an official church and the right of ecclesiastical self-government in Art. 137(1), (3) WRV, constitute a core of religious provisions so intimately connected with inviolable human rights in the sense of Art. 1(2) that under Art. 79(3) they are protected even against constitutional amendment); Roman Herzog in 1 Maunz/Dürig, Art. 4, Rdnr. 11-12 (arguing that at least freedom to believe and to express one's beliefs are unamendable elements of human dignity).

[6] Cf. United States v. Seeger, 380 U.S. 163 (1965), and Welsh v. United States, 398 U.S. 333 (1970) (plurality opinion) (construing a statutory exemption for conscientious objectors broadly so as to avoid a serious establishment question in the United States).

[7] See 22 Annals of Congress 982-85 (1811). Insofar as he may have implied that religious bodies be denied benefits available to others similarly situated, Madis-

providing that "religious bodies shall acquire legal capacity according to the general provisions of civil law."[8] Article 139 of the same document avoids the serious controversy that surrounded the validity of Sunday laws in this country by providing specifically that "Sunday and public holidays recognized by the state shall remain under legal protection as days of rest from work and of spiritual edification."[9] Most interestingly, Weimar Article 137(6) provides that "religious bodies that are corporations under public law shall be entitled to levy taxes in accordance with state law." To put it in plain English, religious organizations are given the power to impose taxes for religious purposes, and state machinery is employed to collect them.[10]

Needless to say, nothing of the kind is permissible in the United States. Any such arrangement would very likely offend all three branches of the familiar *Lemon* test laid down by the Supreme Court: The purpose and primary effect of the tax are to promote religion, and its collection appears to entangle the state in church affairs.[11] Taxation for religious ends was the precise target of Madison's famous Memorial and Remonstrance of 1785, which the Supreme Court has taken as the foundation of establishment clause jurisprudence since 1947;[12] and giving governmental authority of any kind to

---

on's position raised a serious question under the free exercise clause. See The Second Century at 341-42 (discussing Everson v. Board of Education, 330 U.S. 1 (1947)). Cf. 83 BVerf-GE 341 (1991) (holding in light of the religious freedoms guaranteed by Art. 4(1) and (2) GG and Art. 137(2) WRV that the hierarchical structure of the Baha'i religion did not justify denying its local governing councils the right to register as unincorporated associations under Art. 137(4) WRV).

[8] See also Art. 137(5) WRV (providing for recognition of religious organizations meeting certain criteria as "corporate bodies under public law").

[9] See Alexander Hollerbach, Freiheit kirchlichen Wirkens, 6 Handbuch des Staatsrechts 595, Rdnr. 61-62 (arguing that this provision reflects both secular and religious interests and demonstrates that the separation of church and state in Germany is less than complete); 87 BVerfGE 363, 393 (1992) (upholding a statutory ban on Sunday baking on the basis of the obligation imposed by Art. 139 WRV). Cf. McGowan v. Maryland, 366 U.S. 420 (1961) (upholding Sunday laws in the United States by refusing to look behind a legitimate secular purpose for a religious one).

[10] In principle the Basic Law leaves collection of religious taxes to the churches themselves, but in practice, in most of the Länder, the state collects the tax as agent of the churches. See Hollerbach, Der verfassungsrechtliche Schutz kirchlicher Organisation, 6 Handbuch des Staatsrechts 557, Rdnr. 55.

[11] See Lemon v. Kurtzman, 403 U.S. 602, 612-13 (1971).

[12] See Everson v. Board of Education, 330 U.S. 1, 11-13 (1947). *Lemon* itself, of course, struck down the use of tax moneys to support even *secular* activities of religious organizations. See 403 U.S. at 614-22. In contrast, a three-judge panel of the Constitutional Court recently dismissed as frivolous a complaint asserting conscientious objections to the payment of taxes for defense purposes on the ground that the tax revenues were not earmarked: Whether the money would be spent on defense depended upon a further decision of Parliament, and the taxpayer's freedom of con-

religious organizations raises a particular red flag.[13] In these as in other respects, as we shall see, the Germans are less hostile to public support of religion.[14]

Yet there are significant limits to the power of German religious bodies to invoke state authority for the collection of revenue, and they obviate some of Madison's most serious objections. As the Constitutional Court has made clear, the general principle of official neutrality embodied in other constitutional provisions precludes any interpretation of Article 137(6) that would permit religious institutions to exercise governmental authority over anyone other than their own members.[15] Thus a religious organization has no right to assess taxes against corporations or other associations,[16] against the spouses of its members,[17] or against individuals who have withdrawn from the congregation.[18] Consequently it is more difficult to argue in Germany that taxation for religious purposes requires citizens to support causes with which they disagree; state enforcement in such cases comes closer to enforcement of an ordinary contract or of the rules of any voluntary association, and thus to an exercise of

---

science was thus unaffected. BVerfG, Judgment of Aug. 26, 1992, Case No. 2 BvR 478/92, 1993 NJW 455, 455-56.

[13] See Larkin v. Grendel's Den, Inc., 459 U.S. 116 (1982), where a modest provision giving churches the right to veto nearby liquor licenses was condemned as allowing them in effect to govern.

[14] See Hollerbach, supra note 10, Rdnr. 50: "The state lends a hand to the church [under the taxing provisions] . . . by virtue of its fundamental decision in favor of the furtherance of churches and religious communities." Similarly, although Art. 138(1) WRV provides for the abolition ("Ablösung") of state subsidies ("Staatsleistungen") guaranteed to religious bodies under prior agreements and laws, it is said to require adequate compensation for their loss; and they account for a sizeable percentage of church income even today. See Hollerbach, supra, Rdnr. 56-61; Maunz in 4 Maunz/Dürig, Art. 140 (Art. 138 WRV), Rdnr. 1-9.

[15] See 19 BVerfGE 206, 216 (1965): "Aus dieser Pflicht zur religiösen und konfessionellen Neutralität folgt, daß der Staat einer Religionsgesellschaft keine Hoheitsbefugnisse gegenüber Personen verleihen darf, die ihr nicht angehören." See also von Campenhausen, supra note 4, Rdnr. 46 (justifying this conclusion on the basis of the religious freedom guaranteed by Art. 4).

[16] 19 BVerfGE at 215-26.

[17] 19 BVerfGE 226, 235-42 (1965). See also 19 BVerfGE 268, 273-74 (1965) (adding that the amount of a church member's obligation may not be increased to reflect the earnings of a nonmember spouse).

[18] 44 BVerfGE 37, 49-58 (1977) (basing this conclusion flatly on Art. 4). See also 30 BVerfGE 415, 423-27 (1971) (holding that baptism sufficed to subject an individual to church taxes until he affirmatively resigned); 44 BVerfGE 59 (1977) (permitting a brief interval between resignation and termination of liability on administrability grounds). See also 19 BVerfGE 248, 251-53 (1965) (enforcing the requirement of Art. 137(6) WRV that church taxes be authorized by state law); 19 BVerfGE 253, 257-67 (1965) (finding a sufficient legal basis in longstanding practice despite the absence of express statutory authorization).

the right of self-government guaranteed by Article 137(3) of the
Weimar Constitution, than to permitting churches to exercise governmental authority over the public as a whole.[19]

Almost as foreign to prevailing conceptions of church-state relations in the United States as the provision for religious taxation is the
German law with respect to religion in the public schools.

Not the least startling to American eyes is the express provision
of Article 7(3) that "religious instruction shall form part of the standard curriculum [ist . . . ordentliches Lehrfach] in public schools."
There is an exception for secular ("bekenntnisfreie") schools,[20] and
neither pupil nor teacher can be forced to take part in religious instruction against his will;[21] but the fact remains that Article 7(3) puts
the state squarely in the business of providing religious education.[22]

This specific provision eliminates any contention that religious
education in public schools offends the ban on establishment of any
"state church," as it would in the United States.[23] The exception for
secular public schools and the further provision permitting the establishment of private schools of an interdenominational, confessional,
or ideological nature in the absence of a comparable public institution
(Art. 7(5)), make clear that there may also be public schools whose religious quality goes beyond providing separate religious courses.[24]
The decisions in this field are accordingly confined to the distinct
question whether in establishing *only* schools in which the entire

---

[19] See Herzog in 1 Maunz/Dürig, Art. 4, Rdnr. 29-31 (arguing that the privileges
given to religious organizations by the institutional provisions of the Weimar
Constitution are comparable to those afforded to other voluntary associations and
political parties by Art. 9(1) and 21(1)). As the Constitutional Court has emphasized,
however, church taxes remain distinguishable from ordinary assessments upon
members because of the state's duty to provide administrative machinery for their
collection. 19 BVerfGE 206, 217 (1965).

[20] Art. 7(3) GG.

[21] Art. 7(2), (3) GG; Art. 136(4) WRV. Art. 141 GG (familiarly known as the
"Bremen clause") contains a further exception for any Land in which religious
instruction was not given in public schools at the time the Basic Law was adopted.

[22] Art. 7(3) declares that religious instruction shall be provided "in accordance
with the tenets of the religious communities," and at least in some Länder it has
been imparted by the religious organizations themselves. See, e.g., the Baden
school laws considered by the Constitutional Court in 41 BVerfGE 29, 35 (1975). In
such a case the German practice somewhat resembles the "shared time" system of
religious instruction on public premises struck down by a divided Supreme Court
in Grand Rapids School District v. Ball, 473 U.S. 373 (1985) – with the symbiosis
that led that Court to perceive a forbidden state endorsement of religion compounded
by the explicit constitutional command that religious instruction is part of the basic
public education. See also Hollerbach, supra note 9, Rdnr. 42-43 (justifying public
religious instruction on grounds both of religious freedom and of the state's own
interest in the development of "morally responsible citizens").

[23] See, in addition to the *Grand Rapids* decision cited in the preceding note, the
school prayer cases cited in note 27 infra.

[24] See 41 BVerfGE at 46.

curriculum was tinged with a homogenized form of Christianity characterized by the Court as more cultural than confessional the Länder infringed the religious freedoms of those who thought there was either too much religion or too little.[25]

Controversies involving school prayers and state identification with the symbols of religion have likewise been resolved not on establishment but on free exercise grounds in the Federal Republic. Thus in 1979, when the Constitutional Court was asked to pass upon the constitutionality of voluntary prayers led by teachers in public schools, it measured them solely against the religious and parental rights protected by Articles 4, 6, and 7 of the Basic Law;[26] the express prohibition of a "state church" was not even mentioned. Any notion that such prayers might offend some principle analogous to that which led our Supreme Court to condemn similar exercises as an establishment of religion[27] was rejected with the curt observation that any general separation principle inferred from institutional provisions respecting the relation between church and state was trumped by the more specific provisions of Article 7, which plainly envisioned some state sponsorship of religion in schools.[28] Similarly, when the Court held the placement of a large crucifix on a courtroom bench unconstitutional in 1973, it did so on the ground that a dissenting attorney's religious freedom had been infringed; any argument based upon broader principles requiring separation of church and state the Court found it unnecessary to consider.[29]

The debates of the Parliamentary Council shed no light on the meaning of the prohibition of an official church.[30] When this provision was proposed in the Weimar assembly in 1919, its sponsor explained it as the expression of a "principle of separation" designed to put an end to the "special close relationship" then existing between the Evangelical Church and some of the Länder – a relationship in which the state was said to have governed the Church either directly or by appointing its officials. In light of this history the leading commentator of the period concluded that Article 137(1) was directed against "administration of internal church affairs by any governmental body or by any entity within the church erected or staffed by

---

[25] See id. at 63-64 and 41 BVerfGE 65 (1975) (both holding there was not too much religion); 41 BVerfGE 88 (1975) (holding there was not too little). Cf. von Campenhausen, supra note 4, Rdnr. 65-67 (arguing that freedom of religion *requires* that religious bodies determine questions relating to appointments, curriculum, and research in public theological schools).

[26] 52 BVerfGE 223, 235 (1979).

[27] Engel v. Vitale, 370 U.S. 421 (1962); Abingdon School District v. Schempp, 374 U.S. 203 (1963).

[28] 52 BVerfGE at 236-37. For other examples of the application of the principle that the more specific of two constitutional provisions governs see chapter 2 supra.

[29] 35 BVerfGE 366 (1973).

[30] See 1 JöR (n.F.) at 899-907.

the state" – i.e., "against any institutional connection between church and state."[31]

Given the paucity of judicial authority on the subject, the commentators take a variety of positions with respect to the current meaning of the prohibition. One observer declares categorically that it forbids "all institutional connections between church and state except those provided for by the Constitution" itself.[32] Another, enumerating the many intimate connections still existing between government and religion, describes the governing principle as one of cooperation rather than separation.[33] A third occupies an intermediate and somewhat fuzzier position. Taken with other provisions guaranteeing various aspects of religious freedom, Article 137(1) commits the state to secularity, neutrality, and above all parity in the sense of equality among religions. It also means that "church and state are separate from one another in principle [prinzipiell]," but not entirely.[34] How much separation is enough, to paraphrase the old saying, is beyond the scope of this commentary.

In any event, the explicit ban on establishment of an official church has a much narrower meaning in the Basic Law than the establishment clause has in the United States, and it has played no significant role in the decisions.

II. RELIGIOUS FREEDOMS

Article 4 explicitly protects what our Supreme Court has described as the two dimensions of religious freedom: the right to believe ("die Freiheit des Glaubens," Art. 4(1)) and the right to practice one's religion ("die ungestörte Religionsausübung," Art. 4(2)).[35] As in the case of establishment, specific provisions of the Basic Law help define the contours of these freedoms. Conscientious objectors, whether religious or not, are entitled to exemption from armed military service (Art. 4(3))[36] but may be required to perform alternative

---

[31] See Gerhard Anschütz, Die Verfassung des Deutschen Reichs 631 (4th ed. 1933). The prohibition was understood not to be self-executing; disestablishment was accomplished in Prussia by statute. Id. at 632.

[32] See Ulrich K. Preuß in 2 AK-GG, Art. 140, Rdnr. 41.

[33] See Maunz in 4 Maunz/Dürig, Art. 140 (Art. 137 WRV), Rdnr. 3-6.

[34] See Hollerbach, supra note 5, Rdnr. 111-13.

[35] Cf. Cantwell v. Connecticut, 310 U.S. 296, 303-04 (1940). Ever since Weimar, the Constitutional Court has said, the right to free exercise has been implicit in the right to believe; the specific reference to free exercise in Art. 4(2) was a reaffirmation in the wake of Nazi interference and serves to make clear that religious freedom extends not only to individuals but to religious bodies as well. 24 BVerfGE 236, 245-46 (1968). For a different view (admittedly without practical consequences) see Herzog in 1 Maunz/Dürig, Art. 4, Rdnr. 99.

[36] This provision has given rise to considerable litigation. Although two Justices recently argued to the contrary (see 69 BVerfGE 1, 77-86 (1985) (Mahrenholz and

service ("Ersatzdienst") for an equivalent period (Art. 12a(2)).[37] No one may be compelled to take part in religious ceremonies, to take a religious oath, or to disclose his religious convictions,[38] and no teacher may be required to give religious instruction.[39] Discrimination on religious grounds is repeatedly proscribed.[40] Religious insti-

---

Böckenförde, JJ., dissenting)), the Constitutional Court concluded as early as 1960 that only those opposed to war in principle, not merely to a particular war, qualified as conscientious objectors under Art. 4(3). 12 BVerfGE 45 (1960). Cf. Gillette v. United States, 401 U.S. 437 (1971). For criticism of this conclusion see Otto-Ernst Kempen in 1 AK-GG, Art. 4(3), Rdnr. 6-6a. One who becomes a conscientious objector after induction into the military is entitled to exemption but must serve until his application has been ruled upon (28 BVerfGE 243 (1970), criticized by Kempen, supra, Rdnr. 12), and even after his status has been recognized he may be punished for a prior refusal to serve (32 BVerfGE 40 (1971) (over three dissents)); but once a conscientious objector has been punished for refusing to perform alternative service he may not be called up a second time (78 BVerfGE 391 (1988)). The most interesting decision respecting conscientious objection went off on grounds of inequality: The state could not dispense altogether with an inquiry into the sincerity of a claim of conscientious objection, for that would mean in effect that only the law-abiding had a duty to serve. 48 BVerfGE 127 (1978) (also noted in chapter 6 infra).

[37] See 19 BVerfGE 135, 138 (1965) (rejecting the argument that alternative service offended the freedom of conscience guaranteed by Art. 4(1) on the basis of this explicit provision, which was added in 1956, and of the narrow exemption from armed service in Art. 4(3)); 23 BVerfGE 127, 132 (1968) (same). See also Bethge, supra note 1, Rdnr. 45, 60, and Herzog in 1 Maunz/Dürig, Art. 4, Rdnr. 203-06 (both arguing that alternative service for conscientious objectors is *required* by the constitutional principle of equality of burdens).

Although Art. 12a unambiguously provides that the duration ("Dauer") of such service not exceed that of ordinary military service, a divided Court in 1985, with more respect for the spirit of this requirement than for its language, upheld a statute providing for 15 months of regular and 20 months of alternative service in light of the more onerous nature of the former. 69 BVerfGE 1 (1985). See also id. at 66-77 (Mahrenholz and Böckenförde, JJ., dissenting); Kempen in 1 AK-GG, Art. 4(3), Rdnr. 29 (anticipating the dissent); 80 BVerfGE 354 (1989) (holding that neither Art. 4(3) nor Art. 12a was offended by denominating alternative service as a form of military service ("Wehrdienst")).

[38] Art. 136(3), (4) WRV. The latter paragraph contains an explicit exception permitting inquiry into religious affiliation in cases (such as those involving church taxes, see text at notes 9-19 supra) in which it is determinative of legal rights and duties, and for statistical purposes prescribed by law. See 46 BVerfGE 266 (1977) (permitting a medical patient to be asked about his religion but stressing that he was under no duty to reply); 49 BVerfGE 375 (1978) (holding it permissible to note a taxpayer's religion in his withholding tax file); 65 BVerfGE 1 (1983) (upholding census inquiries into religious affiliation). See also von Campenhausen, supra note 4, Rdnr. 56 (explaining that one may sometimes be required to disclose membership in a religious body but not the content of one's beliefs).

[39] Art. 7(3) GG.

[40] Art. 3(3), 33(3) GG; Art. 136(1), (2) WRV. The overlap between Art. 33(3) GG and Art. 136(2) WRV, it has been said, is so substantial as to leave the latter without

tutions may be freely established and are entitled to administer their own affairs "within the limits of generally applicable laws."[41] Their right of access to military personnel for pastoral and liturgical purposes is expressly guaranteed.[42]

These provisions, of course, have not eliminated controversy over the extent of religious freedom protected by the Basic Law. The decisions are relatively sparse but of considerable interest.

A. Conflicting Constitutional Rights

Unlike the various expressive freedoms guaranteed by Article 5(1), the religious liberties recognized by Article 4 are not expressly made subject to limitations on the basis of personal honor, the protection of youth, or the "general laws."[43] Nevertheless neither freedom of conscience nor freedom to exercise one's religion has been interpreted in Germany, any more than in the United States, as absolute. In the first place, like the equally unrestricted artistic and academic liberties recognized by Article 5(3),[44] religious freedoms have been held to be implicitly qualified by other provisions of the Basic Law.

---

independent significance. Hollerbach, supra note 5, Rdnr. 20. These various equality provisions should make it unnecessary to decide whether denial of public benefits on religious grounds is also an infringement of religious freedom under Art. 4. See Herzog in 1 Maunz/Dürig, Art. 4, Rdnr. 71; Ekkehart Stein in 1 AK-GG, Art. 3, Rdnr. 95 (arguing that Art. 3(3) commits the state to strict neutrality in matters of religion). But see 1 von Mangoldt/Klein/Starck, Art. 4 Abs. 1, 2, Rdnr. 84: "A forbidden discrimination under Art. 3(3) or Art. 33(3) is at the same time a forbidden invasion of the basic right protected by Art. 4." Despite the panoply of provisions directed specifically against religious discrimination, however, it was to avoid offending the general provision of Art. 3(1) that "all persons are equal before the law," not the more explicit prohibition in Art. 3(3), that the Constitutional Court construed a statutory provision exempting "churches" from the payment of certain fees to apply not only to three traditional denominations that had enjoyed special privileges under Prussian law. 19 BVerfGE 1 (1965). See also 19 BVerfGE 129, 133-35 (1965) (rejecting claims that restricting a sales tax exemption to those religious organizations incorporated under public law offended either Art. 3(1) or the guarantee of religious freedom, essentially on the ground that there was nothing to prevent the complainant from becoming such a corporation).

[41] Art. 137(2), (3) WRV. See also Art. 138(2) WRV (protecting the property rights of religious organizations). Secular societies dedicated to promoting a particular philosophy of life ("Weltanschauung") are given the same protected status by Art. 137(7).

[42] Art. 141 WRV.

[43] See 33 BVerfGE 23, 29 (1972). For interpretation of the provision to this effect in Art. 5(2) see chapter 4 supra. Art. 135 of the Weimar Constitution, which was not incorporated by Art. 140 of the Basic Law, contained a similar provision: "The general laws are unaffected [by religious freedom]." See text at notes 63-64 infra.

[44] See the discussion of the *Mephisto* case, 30 BVerfGE 173 (1971), in chapter 4 supra.

The leading authority for this principle is the so-called *Tobacco Atheist* case, decided in 1960.[45] The complainant was a convict whose parole application had been denied on the ground that he had attempted to bribe fellow inmates by offering them tobacco to forswear their religion. The Constitutional Court held that the denial of parole did not infringe his religious freedom. Article 4 protected the right to proselytize for or against religion only to the extent consistent with the dignity of others. To exploit the constraints of prison life by offering such inducements was morally reprehensible ("sittlich verwerflich"), an abuse ("Mißbrauch") of religious freedom, and thus not protected by Article 4.[46]

Here too, as in analogous decisions respecting artistic freedom, the Court found in the Article 1(1) guarantee of human dignity a limitation not only on state action but also on the rights of other individuals.[47] In so doing the opinion relied expressly on the thesis, developed in the *Lüth* case with respect to freedom of expression not long before, that the Bill of Rights established an objective order of values (eine "allgemeine Wertordnung") that influenced decision making by all organs of government, even in controversies between private parties.[48]

Similarly, in the later decisions respecting school prayers and interdenominational public schools the claims of dissenting children to be free from state-sponsored exposure to religion were subordinated to the rights of religious children and their parents, based upon Article 4, to free exercise of their religion.[49]

The complaining parents' desire to keep their children's education free from religious influence, said the Court in the first interdenominational school case, conflicted with the wishes of other parents to provide their children with a Christian upbringing. To eliminate all traces of religious thinking from the schoolroom would not be neutral with respect to religion; it would disadvantage those parents who preferred a religious education.[50] Resolution of competing claims to religious liberty, the Court concluded, was basically entrusted to the democratic process; so long as public schools did not become "missionary schools" or attempt to preach the infallibility of Christian beliefs, a curricular affirmation of Christianity more cultural than confessional infringed no one's religious freedom.[51]

The constitutionality of school prayers might appear at first glance to follow a fortiori from that of public religious instruction and

---

[45] 12 BVerfGE 1 (1960).

[46] Id. at 4-5.

[47] Cf. chapter 4 supra (discussing *Mephisto*).

[48] 12 BVerfGE at 4. See also chapter 4 supra (discussing *Lüth*).

[49] 41 BVerfGE 29 (1975); 52 BVerfGE 223 (1979). The parents' right to bring up their children (Art. 6(2) GG) also figured in these decisions. See 41 BVerfGE at 44-48; 52 BVerfGE at 235-36; see also chapter 6 infra.

[50] 41 BVerfGE at 49-50.

[51] Id. at 50-52, 64.

of interdenominational public schools. But the Court did not view the matter this way, and with good reason. For religious instruction was conducted in separate courses that dissenters did not attend, while the Court had reduced the "Christian" content of other subjects in interdenominational schools essentially to the cultural rather than the religious. Since it was clear from these precedents that mere state sponsorship of religious exercises was not enough to condemn them, the question was whether the burden of publicly excusing oneself from the common classroom while the concededly religious prayer was recited was too much to impose on the pupil who did not wish to participate.[52]

The U.S. Supreme Court has never faced this question squarely in the context of ordinary classroom prayers, but it seems likely it would resolve it the other way. Given its firm decision that the establishment clause forbade the state to sponsor such prayers at all, it was unnecessary for the Court to decide whether the free exercise clause was infringed as well.[53] More recently, however, when it struck down "voluntary" prayers at public high school graduations in 1992, the Supreme Court relied exclusively on the coercive nature of the exercise: "[T]o say a teenage student has a real choice not to attend her high school graduation is formalistic in the extreme."[54] This conclusion was strongly influenced by the peculiar significance of the graduation ceremony itself,[55] but in reaching it the Court invoked the earlier prayer cases and argued that graduation was "analogous to the classroom setting, where we have said the risk of compulsion is especially high."[56]

---

[52] See 52 BVerfGE at 238: "Even this generalized prayer remains an act of religious faith, namely the invocation of God on the basis of Christian belief." See also id. at 240 (distinguishing the "Christian" aspect of interdenominational schools on this ground).

[53] See Engel v. Vitale, 370 U.S. 421 (1962); Abingdon School District v. Schempp, 374 U.S. 203 (1963). Justice Black did suggest in passing in *Engel* that there was a coercive tendency to all government endorsement of religion. See 370 U.S. at 431: "When the power, prestige and financial support of government is placed behind a particular religious belief, the indirect coercive pressure upon religious minorities to conform to the officially approved religion is plain."

[54] Lee v. Weisman, 112 S. Ct. 2649, 2659 (1992). This emphasis on coercion provoked two anguished concurrences pointing out that the Court's opinion seemed to be ignoring the original state-sponsorship basis of the earlier decisions. Id. at 2661-78 (opinions of Blackmun and Souter, JJ., both joined by Stevens and O'Connor, JJ.).

[55] For a student to absent herself from the graduation ceremony, wrote Justice Kennedy, "would require forfeiture of those intangible benefits which have motivated the student through youth and all her high school years." Id at 2659.

[56] Id. at 2660. See also id. at 2658 (arguing that the *Engel* and *Schempp* decisions "recognize, among other things, that prayer exercises in public schools carry a particular risk of indirect coercion").

The German court did not dismiss the risk of coercion out of hand;[57] rather it held that the state could reasonably find any such risk outweighed by the constitutional right of other pupils to pray.[58] Article 4 guaranteed the freedom not only to believe but also to express one's belief in public; in authorizing school prayers the state was merely giving religious pupils the opportunity to do so.[59] When balanced against this competing interest, the Court concluded, the risk of embarrassment to a pupil who wished to excuse himself was not excessive.[60]

Justice Stewart made a similar argument in his dissent in *Engel v. Vitale*,[61] and Justice Clark dismissed it curtly the following year: The free exercise clause "has never meant that a majority could use the machinery of the State to practice its beliefs."[62] Clark's response seems compelling enough under a constitution that forbids not only compulsion but also state sponsorship of religion; it is less so in Germany, where coercion is the only question. In that context it may make little difference whether the teacher leads the pupils in prayer or merely observes while they collectively pray on their own. The more serious question is whether they might not be expected to pray silently and individually to avoid offending the sensibilities of others; but that, as the Constitutional Court emphasized, would entail a limitation of their own freedom. While Article 4 did not require the state to favor the interests of those who wished to pray aloud in the classroom, it permitted it to do so; and thus a measure of judicial restraint helped the Justices to reach their conclusion.[63]

B. Exemptions from General Laws

Article 135 of the Weimar Constitution provided flatly that neither freedom of belief nor freedom to exercise one's religion had any effect

---

[57] See 52 BVerfGE at 248-49 (conceding that the position of a young child in the schoolroom was much more difficult in this regard than that of a dissenting adult).

[58] See id. at 248-53.

[59] Id. at 240-41.

[60] Id. at 248-53 (stressing the teacher's obligation to instill an attitude of tolerance and reserving the possibility that coercion might be found in exceptional cases). For a ringing defense of the decision on these grounds see von Campenhausen, supra note 4, Rdnr. 97-102. Accord Herzog in 1 Maunz/Dürig, Art. 4, Rdnr. 61, 121.

[61] See *Engel*, 370 U.S. at 445.

[62] *Schempp*, 374 U.S. at 226.

[63] See 52 BVerfGE at 241-42: "How the state strikes this balance . . . is basically left to its own decision." Cf. the deference given to the civil courts in balancing competing artistic and reputational interests in the *Mephisto* case, chapter 4 supra. On the other hand, the Court added, once the state had decided to make prayers a part of the school routine, it could not abandon them in a particular school without examining the facts of the individual case. 52 BVerfGE at 255.

upon the provisions of generally applicable laws: "Die allgemeinen Staatsgesetze bleiben hiervon unberührt." This proviso, according to the leading treatise of the time, merely made plain what would have been implicit in any case:

> Religious freedom, in all its particular manifestations, finds its limits in the laws of the state. . . . That which the laws forbid as dangerous to public order and safety, contrary to public morals, or for other reasons does not become permissible simply because it is done on the basis of religious conviction.[64]

A substantially identical provision was stricken from the religion provisions of the Basic Law as they made their way through the Parliamentary Council. The omission was deliberate: The sponsor of the amendment explained that he was afraid that subjecting the exercise of religion to general laws would enable the legislature to destroy the right entirely. Elimination of the proviso, he hastened to add, would not mean that religious liberty was absolute; for Article 2(1) made clear that personal freedoms were limited by the rights of others, the constitutional order, and the moral law.[65]

In view of this concession, it is not at all clear what elimination of the reference to "general laws" was meant to accomplish. The sponsor's paraphrase of that provision as a general authorization of legislation restricting religious freedom ("einen allgemeinen Gesetzesvorbehalt") suggests he may have misunderstood it, since under the Weimar Constitution "general laws" in this context had been widely interpreted to mean those not directed against a particular point of view.[66] Even so it is not obvious why he thought the multiple limitations of Article 2(1) posed less of a threat to religious liberty than the express provision they were thought implicitly to replace.

For reasons that seem abundantly persuasive, the Constitutional Court has rejected the argument that the restrictions in Article 2(1) apply to rights recognized by other articles of the Basic Law.[67] The legislative history just summarized makes plain, however, that elimination of the "general laws" provision was not meant to transform religious freedom into a general excuse for doing what the law forbade. Nor was there any indication in the debates that limits on free exercise of religion were to be found only in other provisions of the Basic Law itself; examples specifically mentioned by the sponsor of

---

[64] Anschütz, supra note 31, at 621.

[65] See 1 JöR (n.F.) at 74-75 (Delegate Süsterhenn).

[66] See Anschütz, supra note 31, at 622 (equating this language with the similar terms of Art. 118 WRV respecting freedom of expression, discussed in chapter 4 supra).

[67] See chapter 4 supra (discussing *Mephisto*). This point was made to no avail in opposition to omitting the "general laws" language in the Parliamentary Council. See 1 JöR (n.F.) at 75 (Delegate von Mangoldt).

the amendment included building codes and laws designed to limit the spread of communicable disease.[68]

This confused state of affairs led Professor von Mangoldt, who as a delegate in the Parliamentary Council had opposed elimination of the qualifying reference to "general laws," to argue in his 1953 treatise that the omission had no effect at all: It was an inherent limitation on religious freedom that it gave no license to disobey generally applicable laws.[69] Others have argued that the same result should follow from the Parliamentary Council's decision to incorporate Article 136(1) of the Weimar Constitution, which declares that "[c]ivil and political rights and duties shall be neither conditioned upon nor restricted [weder bedingt noch beschränkt] by the exercise of freedom of religion."[70] The Constitutional Court has given this provision the back of its hand: In light of the significantly greater protection afforded to religious freedom under the Basic Law, which civil duties may be enforced under Art. 136(1) can be determined "only in accordance with the value system established by Art. 4(1)."[71]

Article 136 was added without explanation to a package of Weimar provisions incorporated in the Basic Law in order to regulate the institutional relations between church and state, at the suggestion of the Committee on Style ("Redaktionsausschuß").[72] Under these circumstances the Constitutional Court seems right: It hardly appears likely that adoption of Article 136(1) was intended to reverse the convention's deliberate rejection of a provision that would expressly have subjected the exercise of religion to provisions of the general laws.

Even apart from the limitations implicit in other constitutional provisions, the Constitutional Court has nevertheless made clear that, as in the United States, the religious and conscientious freedoms of the Basic Law confer no absolute exemption from generally applicable laws. In 1965, for example, the Court concluded that nothing in Article 4 exempted a religious institution from the obligation of paying taxes on the sale of meals and lodging to its members in connection with a religious assembly – for even in that context the sale of food and lodging was not itself an exercise of religion.[73] In 1992 the

---

[68] See id. (Delegate Süsterhenn).

[69] See Hermann von Mangoldt, Das Bonner Grundgesetz 57 (1953) (giving as examples polygamy and vaccination laws).

[70] See von Campenhausen, supra note 4, Rdnr. 82; 1 von Mangoldt/Klein/Starck, Art. 4 Abs. 1, 2, Rdnr. 46 (both suggesting a balancing test similar to that undertaken under Art. 5(2)); Preuß in 1 AK-GG, Art. 4(1), (2), Rdnr. 30 (arguing that Art. 136(1) subjects church bells to general noise regulations). See also Anschütz, supra note 31, at 623 (equating the second half of this provision with the "general laws" proviso of Art. 135(1)).

[71] 33 BVerfGE 23, 31 (1972).

[72] See 1 JöR (n.F.) at 899-907.

[73] 19 BVerfGE 129, 133 (1965) (distinguishing the Supreme Court decision in Murdock v. Pennsylvania, 319 U.S. 105 (1943), which had involved the sale of reli-

Court dismissed as frivolous a complaint asserting conscientious objections to the payment of that portion of taxes expended for defense purposes on the ground that, since the funds collected were not earmarked, the taxpayer's conscience was not affected.[74]

On the other hand, the decisions make clear that when religious rights are really at stake Article 4 is more than a mere right to be free from discrimination on religious grounds, which Article 3(3) independently guarantees. Rather the opinions plainly establish that in some instances religious individuals and institutions are entitled to special privileges, as the Supreme Court for a brief period acknowledged before flatly holding to the contrary in the controversial peyote case in 1990.[75]

In part such privileges seem to be explicitly recognized by the Basic Law itself. Article 137(6) of the Weimar Constitution, as noted, gives certain religious bodies taxing powers not shared by arguably analogous secular institutions.[76] Such express examples are rare. But the decisions recognize additional privileges.

1. Article 4(1) and (2). In the so-called *Rumpelkammer* case in 1968, a Catholic youth organization had been enjoined from exhorting parishioners from the pulpit to contribute rags, old clothes, and used paper to raise funds for the relief of hunger and want in underdeveloped nations on the remarkable ground that the church's moral influence over its members gave it an unfair advantage over commercial rag dealers and thus rendered the exhortation a form of unethical competition ("Wettbewerbshandlung gegen die guten Sitten").[77] Finding the collection drive and its attendant publicity an exercise of

---

gious tracts, on this ground). Cf. Jimmy Swaggart Ministries v. Board of Equalization, 493 U.S. 378 (1990) (holding that the first amendment did not require a tax exemption even for the sale of religious materials). See also 19 BVerfGE at 132 (expressly holding that a religious organization itself enjoyed rights under Art. 4). Contrast 44 BVerfGE 103 (1977) (rejecting an employer's objection to the obligation to withhold church taxes on the ground that nonreligious associations had no religious freedom). See Art. 19((3) GG: "The basic rights apply also to domestic juristic persons to the extent that the nature of such rights permits."

[74] BVerfG, Judgment of Aug. 26, 1992, Case No. 2 BvR 478/92, 1993 NJW 455, 455-56. See also Bethge, supra note 1, Rdnr. 13-14, 32 (arguing that although freedom of conscience extends to actions as well as to thoughts, it cannot be understood as a general license to disobey the laws); Herzog in 1 Maunz/Dürig, Art. 4, Rdnr. 153-57. For a more radical view see Preuß in 1 AK-GG, Art. 4(1), (2), Rdnr. 45-46.

[75] Employment Division v. Smith, 494 U.S. 872 (1990).

[76] The privilege is limited to those religious bodies incorporated under public law, and other associations so incorporated may have similar powers. See chapter 4 supra (discussing the user fees assessed to support public broadcasting). But not all private associations enjoy the privilege of incorporating under public law, which is given to certain religious bodies by Art. 137(5) WRV.

[77] 24 BVerfGE 236, 236-39 (1968).

religion, the Constitutional Court set the injunction aside: In issuing it the civil court had misconceived the scope of religious freedom.

The bulk of the opinion is devoted to what we might consider the easy question whether under the circumstances collecting old clothes was a religious exercise at all.[78] Once the Court concluded that it was, the finding of unconstitutionality seemed to follow almost as a matter of course. Commercial rag dealers had no constitutional freedom from competition; religious exercises enjoyed special protection ("besonderen Schutz") under Article 4(2); it was unnecessary to decide whether similar collections by nonreligious organizations would likewise be protected by the general freedom of action guaranteed by Article 2(1).[79]

Thus the Court held the charitable collection in the *Rumpel-kammer* case constitutionally protected not because religious activities had been singled out for discriminatory treatment – as they arguably had been[80] – but because Article 4(2) afforded "special protection" to religious exercises – whether or not otherwise identical activities not motivated by religion could validly have been prohibited. In other words, the Constitutional Court did what the Supreme Court refused to do in the flag-salute case of *Minersville School District v. Gobitis*:[81] it carved out on the basis of religious freedom an exception from a generally applicable law assumed to be valid on its face.[82]

This emphasis on the special protection afforded to religious freedom was even more evident three years later, when the Court set aside the conviction of a husband who on religious grounds had refused to urge his dying wife to submit to a blood transfusion.[83] This was not the case, so familiar in the United States, of a parent's interposing religious objections to prevent medical care that might save the life of a minor child.[84] In such a case one might expect the German court too to find the parent's religious freedom outweighed

---

[78] Id. at 245-51. See Preuß in 1 AK-GG, Art. 4(1), (2), Rdnr. 24-26 (arguing that the "exercise of religion" should have been limited to religious services and symbols, prayers, and other "communicative" manifestations of religious faith).

[79] 24 BVerfGE at 251-52.

[80] It was the special moral authority exerted by a religious body over its members that had led the civil court to find the request for contributions unethical. See text at note 77 supra. Arguably, however, this reasoning represented not a special rule for religious organizations but application of a general principle embracing all cases of undue influence. Cf. the condemnation of the use of economic power to drive program guides to East German television from the market in the *Blinkfüer* case, discussed in chapter 4 supra.

[81] 310 U.S. 586 (1940).

[82] For examples of other exceptions recognized by lower courts (including an unemployment insurance case analogous to Sherbert v. Verner, 374 U.S. 398 (1963)) see von Campenhausen, supra note 4, Rdnr. 53-54.

[83] 32 BVerfGE 98 (1971) (*Gesundbeter*).

[84] See, e.g., People ex rel. Wallace v. Labrenz, 411 Ill. 618, 104 N.E.2d 769, 773-74 (1952).

by the child's right to life, which is guaranteed by Article 2(2).[85] In the actual case the wife was not only an adult *sui juris*; she had retained consciousness and the ability to make her own decision until the very end.[86] Under these circumstances one could argue with considerable force for the religiously neutral conclusion, analogous to that of the Supreme Court in the second flag salute case, that the constitutional guarantees of human dignity and free development of personality forbade the state to require *anyone* to accept medical treatment against her will or to punish anyone else for refusing to interfere with her decision.[87]

This was not the approach taken by the Constitutional Court. The freedom to act upon one's religious convictions, said the Court, was – like the artistic freedom guaranteed by Article 5(3) – limited only by other constitutional provisions, not – like the expressive freedoms protected by Article 5(1) – by provisions of the general laws.[88] For this reason it was impermissible to subject religiously motivated conduct without more to official sanctions provided for similar acts in general:[89]

> In light of the duty of all public authorities to afford sincere religious convictions the greatest respect . . . , the criminal law must give way whenever the concrete conflict between a legal duty recognized by prevailing mores and a command of faith places the actor in such spiritual distress that criminal punishment . . . would amount to an

---

[85] See 32 BVerfGE at 111 (noting that in light of the affirmative duties imposed upon a parent by Art. 6(2) the result would obviously ("selbstverständlich") have been different if the defendant "on the pretext of his own religious convictions" had chosen to allow his wife to die and thus to deprive his children of a mother; in this case he had believed prayer the most effective means of saving her life. Cf. the *Tobacco Atheist* case and the decisions respecting religion in public schools, text at notes 44-63 supra).

[86] See 32 BVerfGE at 102, 110.

[87] See 32 BVerfGE at 110: "In deciding to what extent one spouse is obliged to intervene in the other's sphere of free determination for the latter's own good, one must bear in mind that within the marriage there are two autonomous personalities, each with the right to free development." See generally chapter 6 infra. Cf. West Virginia State Board of Education v. Barnette, 319 U.S. 624 (1943) (holding that no one could be forced to salute the flag without infringing the universal freedom not to speak). See generally Philip B. Kurland, Religion and the Law of Church and State and the Supreme Court 41-47 (1962). The Court had expressly left open the question whether a similar argument would protect the rights of secular charitable solicitors in the *Rumpelkammer* case. See text at note 79 supra.

[88] 32 BVerfGE at 107-08 (citing the *Mephisto* decision, discussed in chapter 4 supra).

[89] "Diese Gründe schließen es aus, Betätigungen und Verhaltensweisen, die aus einer bestimmten Glaubenshaltung fließen, ohne weiteres den Sanktionen zu unterwerfen, die der Staat für ein solches Verhalten – unabhängig von seiner glaubensmäßigen Motivierung – vorsieht." 32 BVerfGE at 108.

excessive reaction on the part of society and thus an infringement of his dignity as a human being.[90]

This passage may fall short of a declaration that criminal laws must *always* take second place to religious convictions; but it unmistakably affirms that in at least some cases religious liberty requires exceptions from generally applicable laws.[91]

The same philosophy underlies the Constitutional Court's subsequent decisions respecting the oaths demanded of witnesses or public officials and the presence of a crucifix in the courtroom. Most people may be compelled to swear to tell the truth or to uphold the Constitution, so long as no religious affirmation is required; those with religious scruples against oaths are constitutionally exempt from the requirement.[92] Similarly, the Court was willing to assume that nothing in the Basic Law forbade the state endorsement of religion implicit in placing a symbol of the Christian faith on a judge's desk; yet attorneys who found its presence offensive to their religious or philosophical convictions were nevertheless entitled to have it removed when they appeared in court.[93]

The 1972 opinion respecting the witness's oath is most explicit on this point. Not content merely to restate the passage quoted above from the transfusion decision, the Court expressly upheld the validity of the oath requirement in the normal case and flatly declared that Article 4(1) required an exception ("Ausnahme") for those with religious objections.[94] Dissenters and members of unorthodox sects, the

---

[90] Id. at 109.

[91] Application of this principle to the case was accomplished by a bare conclusion: "In cases of the present sort the criminal law may not require that two individuals of the same religious faith attempt to persuade one another of the dangers of a decision in accord with their convictions." Id. at 110. See also von Campenhausen, supra note 4, Rdnr. 58 (agreeing on nonconstitutional grounds that the complainant ought not to have been convicted but taking issue with the Court's reasoning): To recognize religious belief as a justification for what would otherwise be a crime would pose a serious threat to the criminal law itself and thus to "one of the great achievements of the rule of law for the protection of freedom." Accord 1 von Mangoldt/Klein/Starck, Art. 4 Abs. 1, 2, Rdnr. 25, 52 (warning against generalization of the decision and arguing that maintenance of the public peace precludes conscientious exceptions from criminal laws).

[92] See 33 BVerfGE 23 (1972) (judicial witness); 79 BVerfGE 69 (1988) (public official). Art. 136(4) of the Weimar Constitution, incorporated by Art. 140 of the Basic Law, provides that no one may be compelled to take a *religious* oath. But see Maunz in 4 Maunz/Dürig, Art. 140 (Art. 136 WRV), Rdnr. 5 (arguing that Art. 136(1) WRV, by providing that neither rights nor duties may be conditioned on religion, should have been read to preclude religious exemptions from oath requirements).

[93] 35 BVerfGE 366, 374-76 (1973). For criticism of this decision see von Campenhausen, supra note 4, Rdnr. 94-95 (arguing that Art. 4 gives no right to be protected from other people's expressions of religious faith).

[94] 33 BVerfGE at 26-32. Justice von Schlabrendorff dissented (id. at 35-42) on the astounding ground that the complainant had misunderstood the Sermon on the

Court now summarized, must be allowed freely to develop their personalities in accord with their own subjective convictions so long as they did not come into conflict with other values protected by the constitution itself and thus bring about perceptible injury to the community or to the fundamental rights of others.[95]

In its 1972 opinion the Court distinguished the witness's oath from that expressly required of the President and Cabinet ministers by Articles 56 and 64(2) on two grounds: Like any public official, these officers had voluntarily chosen to seek office, and such a position presupposed the incumbent's complete identification with the values laid down in the Constitution.[96] In one sense the distinction was much easier than that: What the Constitution itself prescribes cannot readily be found unconstitutional.[97] To the extent that the explicit oath provisions might be taken to imply that nonreligious oaths in general were consistent with the Basic Law, the Court's distinctions seem to suggest an approach to the pervasive problem of unconstitutional conditions reminiscent of the balancing test adopted by the Supreme Court in *American Communications Ass'n v. Douds*:[98] The public official's oath did less harm to religious freedom because the dissenter did not have to seek office, and the government's interest was greater because of the official's access to the machinery of the state.[99]

Mount. In Germany too, one would have thought, it was up to the individual, within the limits of sincerity, to say what his own religion required. See id. at 30 (opinion of the Court) (noting that the complainant's position had a plausible basis in Biblical text and adding that the state was forbidden to determine whether a citizen's beliefs were true or false); Maunz in 4 Maunz/Dürig, Art. 140 (Art. 136 WRV), Rdnr. 6 (branding the dissenting argument "dangerous").

[95] 33 BVerfGE at 29. See also id. at 32-34 (concluding that exempting religious objectors from the oath requirement would not significantly impair the constitutionally entrenched interest in a functioning judicial system (citing Art. 92 GG, which somewhat distantly provides that judicial power shall be entrusted to judges, and noting grandly that "all adjudication serves in the end to protect fundamental rights"), since an alternative form of enforceable promise to tell the truth could and must [!] be devised without employing the "historically freighted" term "oath" ("Eid")).

[96] 33 BVerfGE at 31.

[97] But see the discussion of this general question in connection with the so-called "militant democracy" provisions of the Basic Law in chapter 4 supra.

[98] 339 U.S. 382 (1950); see The Second Century at 355-57. For recent advocacy of a similar test in Germany see Wolfang Rüfner, Grundrechtsadressaten, 5 Handbuch des Staatsrechts 525, Rdnr. 32-34, 45-46; see also the general discussion of unconstitutional conditions in chapter 4 supra.

[99] By emphasizing the state's interest as well as the voluntary nature of the office the Court seemed to reject Justice Holmes's simplistic and since repudiated position that there was no constitutional problem at all in such cases because there was "no constitutional right to be a policeman." McAuliffe v. Mayor of New Bedford, 155 Mass. 216, 220, 29 N.E. 517, 517 (1892). Nevertheless the Court's distinction was

In 1988, however, the Court significantly modified this calculus in holding in effect that a county councillor could not be required against his convictions to take an oath of office either, even though he had the alternative of resigning his position.[100] The state had no compelling need to require such an oath of such an officer, since a simple affirmation would equally serve to assure faithful performance of official duties; a mere county functionary did not share the attributes that had led the Court in its earlier decision to justify the more exacting requirements imposed by the Basic Law itself on the President and Cabinet ministers.[101] Thus the Court seemed to establish that only a compelling interest could support making an oath a condition of exercising a position that the religious objector was under no obligation to seek; and once again it interpreted Article 4(1) to require an exception to a law assumed to be otherwise valid for the benefit of those with religious objections.

2. *The right of self-government.* The principle that religious freedom can require exemptions from generally applicable laws was confirmed, finally, by several decisions involving the right of self-government guaranteed to religious bodies by Article 137(3) of the Weimar Constitution, which Article 140 makes a part of the Basic Law.[102] Ironically, of all the religion clauses in the German constitution this provision appears most clearly to say precisely the opposite: Self-government is guaranteed only within the limits of laws that apply to everyone ("innerhalb der Schranken des für alle geltenden Gesetzes"). Similar clauses limiting both freedom of expression and the guarantee of local government in Article 28(2), however, had already been construed to mean less than they appeared to say.[103] The commentators all agreed, the Court declared, that the reference to general laws in Article 137(3) was not to be taken literally either; not even a generally applicable law could validly interfere with a religious body's regulation of its own truly internal affairs, and a merely "indirect" effect on the outside world did not remove the matter from the internal sphere.[104] "Laws applicable to everyone,"

---

severely criticized: "That one can avoid the officer's oath by declining the office is not a sufficient argument." Von Campenhausen, supra note 4, Rdnr. 57.

[100] 79 BVerfGE 69, 76 (1988). Properly speaking, the Court held only that a preliminary injunction should issue to permit the complaining councillor to occupy his position pending final resolution of the controversy; but in so holding the Justices left little doubt how that controversy would ultimately be resolved.

[101] Id. at 76-77.

[102] See also Hollerbach, supra note 5, Rdnr. 114 (describing the self-government provision as the focal point ("Drehpunkt") of most recent religion decisions).

[103] See chapters 2 and 4 supra.

[104] See 42 BVerfGE 312, 333-34 (1976) (adding that the unique relationship between church and state forbade simply equating the reference to general laws in Art. 137(3) with those in Art. 5(2) and 28(2)).

the Court concluded, meant "those which had the same significance for the church as for everyone else"; any regulation that had a more profound effect on religious bodies than on others could not constitutionally be applied.[105]

Following these principles, the Court held in 1976 that the Evangelical Church in Bremen could lawfully suspend a minister's pastoral rights and duties during the time he served as a representative in the state or federal legislature.[106] Strictly speaking, the Court's conclusion that the relation between a church and its clergy was beyond the reach of generally applicable legislation seems to have been unnecessary to the decision, since the Justices construed the provisions invoked against suspension not to apply.[107] The implication, however, was plain: A neutral law forbidding suspension of employees' rights and duties during legislative service, even if constitutional on its face, could not be applied to ministers of the gospel.[108]

It was also on the basis of the right of self-government protected by Article 137(3) that the Constitutional Court held in 1980 that a variety of neutral statutory provisions regulating the decision-making

---

In reaching its conclusion the Court drew heavily upon its earlier decision, 18 BVerfGE 385, 386-88 (1965), that the Constitutional Court had no jurisdiction to determine a dispute over the division of an evangelical parish. This result seemed obvious from the explicit provision that a constitutional complaint lay only to correct the abuse of public authority ("öffentliche Gewalt"), which religious bodies exercised only in levying taxes (see 19 BVerfGE 206, 215 (1965)). Yet the Court went on to justify the limitation by reference to the guarantee of self-government in Art. 137(3): The state had no power to intervene in the church's internal affairs.

[105] 42 BVerfGE at 334. This criterion appeared to establish a standard of de facto inequality under Art. 137(3) that has found occasional expression elsewhere in German constitutional law. Cf. the decisions respecting deductibility of tax contributions (8 BVerfGE 51, 63-69 (1958); 85 BVerfGE 264, 312-18 (1992)) noted in chapter 4 supra and in chapter 6 infra.

[106] 42 BVerfGE 312 (1976). The decision applied to certain high officers of the Church as well. See id. at 342-44.

[107] The principal argument was that suspension of pastoral duties offended Art. 48(2), which forbids anyone to obstruct a member of the Bundestag in accepting or exercising his office. For the Court's reply see 42 BVerfGE at 326-30 (giving other examples of factual obstacles not inconsistent with Art. 48(2)). See also 57 BVerfGE 220, 245-49 (1981) (finding no basis in law ("Gesetz") for the requirement that church-related institutions permit non-employees to solicit for membership in a labor union).

[108] Id. at 335-38 (adding in dictum (at 335) that for similar reasons the testimonial privilege for matters revealed during confession could not constitutionally be abolished despite its impact on the acertainment of facts at trial). In reaching its conclusion that the church's incompatibility rule was an internal matter the Court argued both that its effect on secular affairs was indirect and that state regulation would affect the church differently from anyone else, and it appeared to balance competing interests in arguing that the rule helped to assure that ministers devoted full time to their duties while having only a limited impact upon their ability to hold legislative office.

structure of hospitals could not constitutionally be applied to those
operated by religious institutions.[109] Once again the Court emphasized that Article 137(3) in some cases required exemption of religious bodies from generally applicable laws.[110] For determining
which those cases were, however, the Justices enunciated a new but
no less familiar standard. Conspicuously missing were the slippery
inquiries that had characterized the previous opinion's test for identi-
fying "internal affairs": whether the challenged measure had the
same practical effect on the religious organization as on everyone
else and whether the impact of the religious practice on the outside
world was "indirect." Rather the Court proclaimed a test taken almost verbatim but without attribution from decisions interpreting the
Article 5(2) provision that various expressive freedoms find their
limits, inter alia, in "the provisions of the general laws."

Even outside "the inviolable core of the church's right of self-determination," said the Court, regulation could not be justified simply
on the ground that religious activities had effects outside the organization itself. By guaranteeing self-government within the limits of
generally applicable laws, Article 137(3) served to assure both autonomous administration of the church's own affairs and state protection of other significant interests of the community. Thus the right
of self-government had a reciprocal effect ("Wechselwirkung") on the
clause permitting its own restriction, and the constitutionality of a
neutral limitation on that right was to be determined – you guessed
it! – by yet another balancing of competing interests ("Güterabwägung").[111]

Assuring the optimal provision of hospital services, the Court
conceded, was an important legislative goal ("ein wichtiges Anliegen
des Gesetzgebers"). Thus, at the outer boundary ("im Randbereich")
of the realm of self-government, state regulation might be
permissible to the extent that this goal would otherwise be unattainable ("nicht erreichbar"). But the challenged regulations went far beyond what was indispensable to assure the best possible care and
treatment of the sick, requiring a complete restructuring of hospital
organization without regard to the peculiar religious needs of the
church; and for this intrusion into the right of self-government the

---

[109] 53 BVerfGE 366 (1980).

[110] Id. at 402.

[111] 53 BVerfGE at 400-01, 404. A leading commentator had suggested this
analysis some years before the decision. See Maunz in 4 Maunz/Dürig, Art. 140
(Art. 137 WRV), Rdnr. 20. Cf. 7 BVerfGE 198 (1958) (*Lüth*), discussed in chapter 4
supra (applying the same analysis to the free-expression provisions of Art. 5(1) and
(2)). Only four years before, in the case of the preacher in Parliament, the Court had
gone out of its way to deny the analogy between Art. 137(3) and Art. 5(2). See note 104
supra.

state had shown no compelling or imperative ("zwingend" or "dringend") need.[112]

Finally, in 1985 the Court over a single dissent concluded on the basis of the same calculus that a general law protecting employees against arbitrary dismissal could not be applied to prevent a Catholic hospital from firing a doctor for taking a public stand in favor of abortion.[113] "The credibility of the Church," wrote the Justices, "may depend upon whether those of its members whom it employs respect the Church's rules [die kirchliche Ordnung]"; the Church had a right to expect that they observe at least the basic principles of its teaching.[114]

Religious freedoms in Germany, in short, commonly require religious exemptions from generally applicable laws.[115]

---

[112] 53 BVerfGE at 401-07. Justice Rottmann dissented both from the Court's new test and from its conclusion that the challenged provisions could not constitutionally be applied. See id. at 408-20. For an approving view of the majority's new standard see Hollerbach, supra note 5, Rdnr. 117-19; for criticism of the result in the hospital case, of the balancing principle it enunciated, and of the internal-affairs test it replaced see Preuß in 2 AK-GG, Art. 140, Rdnr. 25-32. See also 66 BVerfGE 1, 19-25 (1983) (concluding on the basis of a similar balancing analysis that generally applicable bankruptcy laws could not be applied to churches incorporated under public law and repeating (at 20) the earlier definition of "laws that apply to everyone" as those having the same effect on religious bodies as on anyone else).

[113] 70 BVerfGE 138, 162-72 (1985). See also id. at 172 (reaching the same result, over two dissents, with respect to the discharge of a bookkeeper for a Catholic youth home who had left the Church).

[114] Id. at 166. Cases concerning relations between a religious organization and its employees can pose a severe test to the acceptability of a theory of strict neutrality: To require such an organization to entrust pastoral responsibilities to persons with dissenting convictions would arguably strike at the very core of the collective exercise of religious freedom. See NLRB v. Catholic Bishop of Chicago, 440 U.S. 490, 504-07 (1979) (construing the Labor-Management Relations Act not to apply to teachers in parochial schools in order to avoid a serious question under the free exercise clause).

[115] The state is said to be under no general obligation affirmatively to support religion. See von Campenhausen, supra note 4, Rdnr. 40; 1 von Mangoldt/Klein/Starck, Art. 4 Abs. 1, 2, Rdnr. 10. In special situations such as imprisonment and military service, however, the state, having limited the individual's access to religious services, may be under an obligation to see that they are made available. See id., Rdnr. 38; Hollerbach, supra note 9, Rdnr. 13-15, 18-19. Cf. Cruz v. Beto, 405 U.S. 319, 322 (1972); see David Currie, Positive and Negative Constitutional Rights, 53 U. Chi. L. Rev. 864, 874 (1986). But see von Mangoldt/Klein/Starck, supra, Rdnr. 10 (arguing that the Basic Law requires only that religious organizations be given the access to such institutions guaranteed by Art. 141 WRV); Preuß in 2 AK-GG, Art. 140, Rdnr. 71 (taking the position that the appointment of military or prison chaplains offends the prohibition of an official church).

III. CONCLUSION

As the Constitutional Court has made clear, church and state are far more separate in Germany today than they were in earlier centuries.[116] This chapter should make equally plain, however, that they are still nowhere near as separate in that country as they are in the United States under the first amendment as currently interpreted by the Supreme Court.[117]

No more in Germany than in the United States may the state establish an official church; but that does not mean, as it has come to mean here, that there may be no state endorsement or promotion of religion. Some state sponsorship of religion in public schools is expressly authorized by Article 7, and religious bodies are given explicit authority to tax their own members, with the aid of the state. So long as the state does not give official or preferential status to a particular religion, the sole question under the Basic Law has been free exercise, not establishment; the prohibition of a state church in Article 137(1) of the Weimar Constitution means no more than the establishment clause seems to say and may have meant to its framers.

Nor, according to the Constitutional Court, does freedom of religion in Germany require only the neutrality toward religion demanded by recent decisions of the Supreme Court. Article 4 is subject to no clause permitting restriction on the basis of generally applicable laws and thus has been held to be limited only by other provisions of the Basic Law itself. The right of ecclesiastical self-government in Article 137(3) of the Weimar Constitution, which is subject to such a clause, may nevertheless be restricted only to the extent indispensable to effectuation of a compelling governmental interest. Both Article 4 and Article 137(3), unlike the first amendment in recent years, have been squarely held to require religious exemptions from neutral and otherwise valid laws.

Once our establishment clause was interpreted to forbid state action designed to promote religion, it was easy enough to read the two clauses of the first amendment together to require strict governmental neutrality; for the free exercise clause cannot very well be construed to require what the establishment clause forbids.[118] Since the Basic Law does not forbid the state to promote religion, this argument against interpreting religious freedom to require special exemptions

---

[116] See 42 BVerfGE 312, 330-31 (1976). See also von Campenhausen, supra note 4, Rdnr. 6-32 (noting (at Rdnr. 6) that in earlier times "the churches as a rule were both privileged and governed by the state").

[117] See also Donald Kommers, West German Constitutionalism and Church-State Relations, 19 German Politics and Society 1, 10-11 (1990).

[118] See, e.g, Texas Monthly, Inc. v. Bullock, 489 U.S. 1 (1989) (striking down a tax exemption for the sale of religious periodicals). If one had begun at the other end, of course, the same approach would have produced the opposite result: If the free exercise clause required religious exemptions, the establishment clause could not be held to forbid them.

is unavailable in Germany. Even under the Basic Law, however, it can be argued that to exempt those with religious objections from burdens borne by everyone else discriminates against the non-religious in violation of Articles 3(3), 33(3), and the equality provisions of the Weimar Constitution[119] and denies them the freedom of conscience guaranteed by Article 4(1) and (2); for the Constitutional Court has made clear that freedom of conscience includes the right *not* to believe.[120] More powerfully still, it can be argued that religious exemptions from general laws squarely contradict the further provision of Article 3(3) that no one may be *favored* ("bevorzugt") because of his religion.[121]

The Constitutional Court has not seen it that way. As the Court has acknowledged, there has been growing support in the literature for a general principle of "nonidentification" of the state with religion – in other words, for a more complete separation akin to that in the United States.[122] So far, however, the nonidentification principle has not taken root in constitutional soil, and the explicit ban on favoritism on religious grounds has been ignored.[123] The Court itself has described the relationship between church and state as a "partnership" characterized by partial or limping ("hinkende") separation[124] – a separation more closely resembling that practiced in the

---

[119] See 53 BVerfGE 366, 419 (1980) (Rottmann, J., dissenting); Preuß in 2 AK-GG, Art. 140, Rdnr. 37-38 (relying on Art. 136(1) and (2) WRV, both incorporated by Art. 140 GG: "Civil and political rights and duties shall be neither conditioned on nor restricted by the exercise of freedom of religion. The enjoyment of civil and political rights . . . shall be independent of religious creed").

[120] See 24 BVerfGE 236, 245 (1968); 33 BVerfGE 23, 28 (1972); von Campenhausen, supra note 4, Rdnr. 44.

[121] Professor Dürig (1 Maunz/Dürig, Art. 3(3), Rdnr. 99) perceives an apparent conflict between Art. 4, which "permits all distinctions based upon religious faith," and Art. 3(3), which forbids them. For his attempt to resolve the conflict see id., Rdnr. 106 et seq.

[122] See 35 BVerfGE 366, 375 (1973).

[123] As we shall see in the next chapter, the development of Art. 3(3) has been stunted by a narrow conception of the requisite connection between the forbidden criterion and the challenged provision. Now that the Constitutional Court has cleared away this obstacle, the apparent tension between Art. 3(3) and the religious exemptions required by the Court under Art. 4(1) and (2) and 137(3) WRV should come into sharper focus.

[124] See 42 BVerfGE 312, 331 (1976). The first quotation comes from the late Chancellor Willy Brandt, the second from Ulrich Stutz, Das Studium des Kirchenrechts an den deutschen Universitäten, in 6 Deutsche Akademische Rundschau 2 (1924). See also Hollerbach, supra note 5, Rdnr. 81-85 (taking the explicit mention of God in the Preamble to negate any notion of a wholly areligious state); von Campenhausen, supra note 4, Rdnr. 4: "Religious freedom and complete separation of church and state are in a certain sense mutually exclusive"; Maunz in 4 Maunz/Dürig, Art. 140, Rdnr. 43-54.

United States before the *Everson* case[125] than that which has since developed under the guidance of the Supreme Court.[126]

---

[125] 330 U.S. 1 (1947).

[126] The Constitutional Commission decided not to recommend amendment of the church and state provisions of the Weimar Constitution as incorporated by Art. 140 of the Basic Law. See Bericht der VerfKomm at 106-08.

6

Other Fundamental Rights

[T]here exists some strange misconception of the scope of this [due process] provision . . . . [I]t would seem, from the character of many of the cases before us, and the arguments made in them, that the clause . . . is looked upon as a means of bringing to the test of the decision of this court the abstract opinions of every unsuccessful litigant . . . of the justice of the decision against him, and of the merits of the legislation on which such a decision may be founded.[1]

As Justice Miller's famous lament suggests, wishful thinkers have sought since the beginning to find a way of making the United States Supreme Court ultimate censor of the reasonableness of all governmental action.[2] For a time, following the notorious decision in *Lochner v. New York*,[3] it was. Essentially throttled during the New Deal Revolution of the late 1930s, general reasonableness review began a cautious comeback in the days of Chief Justice Warren – sometimes without much attention to the textual basis of the decision[4] or behind such smokescreens as cruel and unusual punishment[5] and the "penumbras" of actual constitutional provisions.[6] Substantive due process itself was finally trotted back out of the closet in *Roe v. Wade*,[7] while serious enforcement of the equality principle was extended beyond race to other more or less "suspect" classifica-

---

[1] Davidson v. New Orleans, 96 U.S. 97, 104 (1878) (Miller, J.).

[2] Justice Chase thought he had discovered the magic wand in natural law (see Calder v. Bull, 3 U.S. 386, 387 (1798) (separate opinion)), Justice Bradley in the privileges or immunities clause (see Slaughter-House Cases, 83 U.S. 36, 116-24 (1873) (dissenting opinion)), Justice Goldberg in the ninth amendment (see Griswold v. Connecticut, 381 U.S. 479, 486-493 (1965) (concurring opinion)). Miller himself had lent significant support to the enemy with his freewheeling opinion in Loan Association v. Topeka, 87 U.S. 655 (1875).

[3] 198 U.S. 45 (1905).

[4] E.g., Slochower v. Board of Higher Education, 350 U.S. 551, 558-59 (1956). See also the earlier decision in Wieman v. Updegraff, 344 U.S. 183, 190-92 (1952).

[5] Robinson v. California, 370 U.S. 660, 666-68 (1962).

[6] Griswold v. Connecticut, 381 U.S. 479, 484-86 (1965).

[7] 410 U.S. 113, 152-56 (1973).

tions like sex, alienage, and illegitimacy[8] and to those affecting such "fundamental" interests as voting, free expression, and interstate travel.[9]

So far, in this country, the genie has been kept partly in the bottle by the Court's relative restraint in defining what is suspect or fundamental; and Justice White seemed to sound a call for retreat with his reminder that "the Court is most vulnerable and comes nearest to illegitimacy when it deals with judge-made constitutional law having little or no cognizable roots in the language or design of the Constitution."[10] In Germany, on the other hand, the Constitutional Court has reviewed the reasonableness of governmental action in general almost from the start.

To begin with, the Bill of Rights in the Basic Law is far more detailed than that in the U.S. Constitution. In addition to familiar articles guaranteeing the expressive and religious liberties discussed in the preceding chapters and the sanctity of the home (Art. 13),[11] there

---

[8] Craig v. Boren, 429 U.S. 190 (1976); Graham v. Richardson, 403 U.S. 365 (1971); Levy v. Louisiana, 391 U.S. 68 (1968).

[9] Reynolds v. Sims, 377 U.S. 533 (1964); Carey v. Brown, 447 U.S. 455 (1980); Shapiro v. Thompson, 394 U.S. 618 (1969).

[10] Bowers v. Hardwick, 478 U.S. 186, 194 (1986). Nevertheless the controversial abortion decision was reaffirmed by the narrowest of majorities in 1992. Planned Parenthood v. Casey, 112 S. Ct. 2791 (1992).

[11] Art. 13(1) declares the home inviolable ("Die Wohnung ist unverletzlich"); Art. 13(2) requires a judicial search warrant unless there is danger in delay ("Gefahr im Verzuge"); Art. 13(3) limits the purposes for which other invasions may be permitted. In contrast to the search and seizure provision of our fourth amendment, Art. 13 has not figured prominently in the decisions of the Constitutional Court. In light of history and the maxim "in dubio per libertate," the ostensibly restrictive term "home" ("Wohnung") has been construed to include business premises (32 BVerfGE 54, 68-72 (1971); see also 1 JöR (n.F.) at 139 (remarks of Delegate Zinn)); but necessity and long practice led the Court to conclude that mere entry and visual inspection of such premises did not constitute either a search or an "invasion" subject to the restrictions of Art. 13 (32 BVerfGE at 73-77 (laying down conditions for the acceptability of such inspections within the framework of Art. 2(1))). Contrast 75 BVerfGE 318 (1987) (requiring a hearing before the state could enter a private dwelling to take sound measurements, although no "search" was involved). In light of its wording, purpose, and legislative history the warrant requirement extends to all searches, not merely to those undertaken in the enforcement of criminal laws (51 BVerfGE 97, 105-10 (1979)), and the rights secured by Art. 13 may be asserted by associations as well as individuals (42 BVerfGE 212, 219 (1976)). Moreover, although Art. 13 mentions neither the specificity nor the reasonableness requirement of our fourth amendment, the Court has enforced the former as an element of the general proportionality principle (see 42 BVerfGE at 219-21 (invalidating a warrant for failure adequately to describe the alleged offense and the objects to be seized)), and substantive reasonableness is an element of proportionality as well. See text at notes 234-51 infra. See also BVerfG, Judgment of May 26, 1993, No. 1 BvR 208/93, 1993 NJW 2035, 2037, where the Court held Art. 13(1) afforded no protection against eviction: What is protected is privacy, not possession. For detailed consideration of the problem of excluding illegally obtained evidence

are specific clauses codifying a number of other substantive rights, some but not all of which our Supreme Court has protected under more open-ended provisions. Article 6 protects marriage and the family,[12] Article 7(4) the right to establish private schools.[13] Article 9(3), which guarantees the right to form labor unions and employer organizations "to safeguard and improve economic and working conditions" and outlaws private contracts that purport to limit this right, has been interpreted to protect not only the right of collective bargaining but also the right to resort to such economic weapons as strikes and lockouts, within the limits of proportionality.[14] Article 10 extends the right of privacy to embrace postal and telecommunications services;[15] Article 11 protects the right to travel and thus to establish a new home anywhere in the Federal Republic.[16] Article 12(1) guarantees the right to choose and to pursue

---

in Germany see Craig Bradley, The Exclusionary Rule in Germany, 96 Harv. L. Rev. 1032 (1983).

[12] Cf. Loving v. Virginia, 388 U.S. 1 (1967); Moore v. City of East Cleveland, 431 U.S. 494 (1977).

[13] Cf. Pierce v. Society of Sisters, 268 U.S. 510 (1925).

[14] See 84 BVerfGE 212 (1991) (holding a lockout of 130,000 workers a disproportionate response to a strike by 4,300 and therefore unprotected). See generally Rupert Scholz, Koalitionsfreiheit, 6 Handbuch des Staatsrechts 1115.

[15] Cf. Katz v. United States, 389 U.S. 347 (1967) (finding similar protection in the search and seizure provision of the fourth amendment). Limitations on this right require a statutory basis (see 85 BVerfGE 386 (1992) (condemning a practice of registering the identity of anonymous callers for want of legislative authority but leaving it in place pending fulfillment of the lawmakers' affirmative duty (!) to protect subscribers against unwanted calls)) and are subject to review for reasonableness under the proportionality principle (see 27 BVerfGE 88, 102-03 (1969) (finding a provision authorizing inspection of newspapers and other items mailed from East Germany necessary to protect national security and not an impairment of the "essential content" of Art. 10)). The most significant decision respecting Art. 10 upheld a controversial amendment of its provisions against the argument that by providing a substitute for judicial review of certain invasions it significantly derogated from the principles of Art. 1 and 20, which Art. 79(3) protects even against constitutional amendment. See chapter 3 supra.

[16] Freedom of travel is guaranteed only to Germans and only within the Republic ("im ganzen Bundesgebiet"). Thus freedom to *leave* Germany is governed not by Art. 11 but by the guarantee of free development of personality in Art. 2(1). See 6 BVerfGE 32, 34-36 (1957) (*Elfes*) (criticized by Dürig in 1 Maunz/Dürig, Art. 11, Rdnr. 104-06, and by Konrad Hesse, Grundzüge des Verfassungsrechts der Bundesrepublik Deutschland (18th ed. 1991), Rdnr. 371); see also text at notes 290-91 infra. Legislative history respecting the decision to extend the right of travel to East Germans, however, was held to demonstrate that Art. 11 did establish their right to *enter* the Republic. 2 BVerfGE 266, 272-73 (1953). On the right to change residence see id. at 273; 1 JöR (n.F.) at 129 (remarks of Dr. von Mangoldt); Kay Hailbronner, Freizügigkeit, 6 Handbuch des Staatsrechts 137, Rdnr. 22-27.

The right to travel is expressly made subject to statutory limitation in cases of epidemic, disaster, or imminent danger to the free democratic order, as well as to

one's occupation.[17] Article 16(1) provides that German citizenship may not be taken away ("entzogen") and permits its involuntary loss ("Verlust") only when statelessness does not result.[18] Article 16(2) not only flatly forbids extradition of German citizens to any foreign country[19] but – in a generous humanitarian reaction to the plight of German citizens who were driven away by the Nazis and had nowhere to go[20] – in its original form afforded a right of asylum to any person "persecuted on political grounds" anywhere in the world.[21] As in the case of the expressive and religious freedoms

---

prevent crime and to avoid "special burdens to the community" when "an adequate basis of existence is lacking." In 1953 the Constitutional Court held that this last clause could not be interpreted to justify categorical exclusion of East Germans from the Federal Republic in view of the deliberate decision to extend the right to "all Germans." 2 BVerfGE 266, 274-78 (1953). See also Art. 17a(2) GG, added in 1956, which permits further statutory limitations in the interest of military or civil defense. For discussion of the various limitation provisions see Hailbronner, supra, Rdnr. 46-59.

[17] Cf. New State Ice Co. v. Liebmann, 285 U.S. 262 (1932). Art. 12(2) and (3) prohibit compulsory labor except for traditional forms of community service (e.g., firefighting, see 13 BVerfGE 167, 170-71 (1961)) and obligations imposed upon persons convicted of crime. See Rupert Scholz in 1 Maunz/Dürig, Art. 12, Rdnr. 476-95. Art. 12a makes a further exception by authorizing a military draft for men having attained the age of eighteen. For consideration of provisions respecting conscientious objectors see chapter 5 supra.

[18] This provision was attacked as self-contradictory when proposed, but it is not; citizenship may be lost under some circumstances as the result of deliberate actions such as the acquisition of foreign citizenship, but it may not otherwise be revoked. See 1 JöR (n.F.) at 164 (remarks of Delegates von Mangoldt and Zinn); Albrecht Randelzhofer in 2 Maunz/Dürig, Art. 16(1), Rdnr. 49. Cf. Afroyim v. Rusk, 387 U.S. 253 (1967) (finding in the fourteenth amendment's provision for the *acquisition* of U.S. citizenship a prohibition of its involuntary loss). Art. 16(1) prescribes no criteria for obtaining German citizenship; the statutes base citizenship by birth on blood rather than soil and make naturalization difficult. See Randelzhofer, supra, Rdnr. 65-66. See also Art. 116 GG (making special provision for certain refugees of German origin and for persons deprived of their citizenship by the Nazis).

[19] See Randelzhofer in 2 Maunz/Dürig, Art. 16, Abs. 2, Satz 1, Rdnr. 2 (explaining this provision as based on considerations of sovereignty and fear of possible injustice). For discussion of the meaning of "foreign country" ("Ausland") in this connection see chapter 2 supra.

[20] See Albrecht Randelzhofer, Asylrecht, 6 Handbuch des Staatsrechts 185, Rdnr. 4; Erich Maria Remarque, Arc de Triomphe (1946), passim.

[21] Religious or racial persecution qualifies for historical reasons as "political" for purposes of this provision (see 54 BVerfGE 341, 357-58 (1980); 76 BVerfGE 143, 156-59 (1987)), and private persecution may suffice if the state from which asylum is sought is unwilling to provide protection (83 BVerfGE 216, 235-36 (1991)). Not every instance of discrimination, however, amounts to persecution; the consequences must be inconsistent with human dignity (76 BVerfGE 143, 158-60 (1987)).

considered in the preceding chapters, the application of these provisions commonly involves a balancing test; I shall discuss some of them at the outset of this chapter.

More interesting from the jurisprudential standpoint are decisions of the Constitutional Court doing what the Supreme Court did in *Lochner*: protecting additional substantive rights on the basis of general provisions that correspond roughly to our due process and equal protection clauses.

There are several such provisions. Article 2(2) contains a general guarantee of life, limb, and (physical) liberty.[22] Article 14 not only imposes familiar limits on condemnation but also includes a general guarantee of property. Article 3 provides both general and specific assurances of equality. Article 1(1), which is commonly described as the central provision of the entire constitution[23] and the heart of which is explicitly protected from amendment,[24] declares human dignity inviolable ("die Würde des Menschen ist unantastbar"). Most interesting for present purposes is Article 2(1)'s enigmatically phrased right to free development of personality ("die freie Entfaltung [der] Persönlichkeit"), which has been interpreted to embrace the freedom to do everything not dealt with more specifically elsewhere.

From these open-ended provisions, in conjunction with even more general conceptions derived from other articles of the Basic Law – in particular the social state ("Sozialstaat") and what may be literally but incompletely translated as a state governed by the rule of

---

Art. 16(2) was massively abused in recent years by many thousands of individuals seeking not asylum but economic opportunity. Although their applications were ultimately denied, the process of hearing and judicial review could consume years, during which the applicants had to be supported at state expense. See 56 BVerfGE 216, 242-44 (1981) (forbidding expulsion before final rejection of an application). Despite responsible protests against throwing out the baby with the bath (see, e.g., Manfred Zuleeg in 1 AK-GG, Art. 16, Abs. 2, Rdnr. 10, 63), the asylum provision (now in a new Art. 16a) was amended in 1993, with the support of all major political parties, so as not merely to expedite the process but significantly to contract the right itself. Among other things, anyone entering Germany from a "safe" country in which the rights of refugees are respected will now be turned back at the border, and all countries bordering Germany have been designated as "safe." See Gesetz zur Änderung des Grundgesetzes vom 28. Juni 1993, BGBl I, 1002, 44 Sammelblatt für Rechtsvorschriften des Bundes und der Länder 2181 (1993); Gesetz zur Änderung asylverfahrens-, ausländer- und staatsangehörigkeitsrechtlicher Vorschriften vom 30. Juni 1993, § 26a & Anlage I, BGBl I, 1062, 44 id. at 2182, 2184, 2190.

[22] Specific procedural protections for those taken into custody or accused of crime are provided in Art. 103 and 104.

[23] See, e.g., 6 BVerfGE 32, 41 (1957); Peter Häberle, Die Menschenwürde als Grundlage der Staatlichen Gemeinschaft, 1 Handbuch des Staatsrechts 815, Rdnr. 98-100.

[24] Art. 79(3) GG.

law ("Rechtsstaat")[25] – the Constitutional Court has fashioned a set of tools that make it what, notwithstanding Justice Miller's warning, our Supreme Court was for the first third of the twentieth century: ultimate censor of the reasonableness of governmental action.

I. MARRIAGE, THE FAMILY, AND PRIVATE SCHOOLS

"Marriage and the family," says Article 6(1), "enjoy the special protection of the state." The paragraphs that follow contain specific provisions for parents and children, motherhood, and persons born out of wedlock, while Article 7(4) guarantees "the right to establish private schools." Thus Articles 6 and 7 provide explicit protection for several of the interests our Supreme Court has accorded the benefits of heightened scrutiny under the fourteenth amendment.[26]

The draft of the Basic Law prepared by the conference of experts at Herrenchiemsee contained no such provisions. Most of them are traceable to a package of amendments offered by Christian Democrats in the Parliamentary Council in an effort to strengthen traditional religious and family values.[27]

Articles 6 and 7 look very different from most other paragraphs of the Bill of Rights. They contain an eclectic assortment of provisions ranging from conventional defensive rights and unconventional positive claims to grants of authority and affirmative obligations imposed on the state and even on private parties. These peculiarities led the Parliamentary Council's Committee on Style ("Redaktionsausschuß") to complain at one point that most of Article 6 would be merely programmatic and unenforceable – as a leading commentator had said of similar provisions of the Weimar Constitution, from which most of the language of Articles 6 and 7 was taken.[28] Yet in practice both articles have proved to mean much more than the Committee expected; in fact the decisions interpreting Articles 6 and 7 present in microcosm many of the important issues respecting fundamental rights that have arisen under the Basic Law.

---

[25] See Art. 20, 28(1) GG.

[26] See, e.g., Zablocki v. Redhail, 434 U.S. 374 (1977); Moore v. City of East Cleveland, 431 U.S. 494 (1978); Levy v. Louisiana, 391 U.S. 68 (1968); Pierce v. Society of Sisters, 268 U.S. 510 (1925).

[27] See 1 JöR (n.F.) at 93-94, 99, 103. The entire package was hotly contested. Delegates from the Center Party ("Zentrum"), a once powerful group responsive to Roman Catholic concerns, wound up voting against adoption of the Basic Law because it did not do enough to protect parental rights. See Sten. Ber. at 240 (Delegate Wessel). The private school provisions, on the other hand, were proposed by a Free Democratic delegate in order to prevent a state monopoly. See 1 JöR (n.F.) at 111-12 (Delegate Heuss).

[28] See 1 JöR (n.F.) at 97-98, 100; Art. 119-122, 143-49 WRV; Gerhard Anschütz, Die Verfassung des Deutschen Reichs 560 (4th ed. 1933).

A. Defensive Rights

Several provisions of the family and school articles function in traditional fashion to protect the individual from unjustified interference by the state. Some of the relevant clauses unmistakably invite such application. Article 6(2) emphasizes both the "right" and the "duty" of parents to bring up their children.[29] Article 7(2) particularizes this guarantee (and the religious freedoms guaranteed by Article 4(1) and (2)) by specifying the parents' right "to decide whether the child shall attend religion classes";[30] Article 6(3) reinforces it by restricting state authority to separate children from their families.[31] Article 7(4), already mentioned, guarantees "the right to establish private schools."

Most of these rights are expressly limited by the Basic Law. The state is directed to watch over the process of childrearing; statutes may and do authorize removal of children from parental custody in cases of severe neglect or breach of duty.[32] Article 7(1) places the entire educational system "under the supervision of the state," and Art. 7(4) imposes additional requirements on the licensing of private schools that provide an alternative rather than a supplement to public education.[33] In the interest of reducing class distinctions and establishing a common culture, Article 7(5) permits private *elementary* schools only when they serve "a special pedagogical interest" or fill an otherwise unsatisfied need for education along particular religious or philosophical lines.[34]

Not surprisingly, the Constitutional Court has struck down several statutory provisions as unwarranted intrusions upon the parental rights protected by Article 6(2). As early as 1958, for example, the Court concluded that publications promoting nudism were

---

[29] Other examples of private duties imposed by the Basic Law and (in greater number) by the Weimar Constitution are noted in chapter 1 supra.

[30] See also Art. 7(3), which among other things provides that "[n]o teacher may be obliged against his will to give religious instruction." See generally chapter 5 supra.

[31] See 1 JöR (n.F.) at 100 (Delegates Heuss and Schmid) (seeing in this provision a reaction to conscription of children into such organizations as the Hitlerjugend).

[32] Art. 7(2), (3) GG. See §§ 1666, 1666a BGB, which expressly make separation from the parents a last resort available only when the danger to the child's welfare "cannot be avoided by other means."

[33] No such school may be licensed if it is inferior in quality to public schools, if it would contribute to the economic segregation of pupils, or if "the economic and legal position of the teaching staff is not sufficiently assured."

[34] For discussion of what constitutes a "special pedagogical interest" within this provision see 88 BVerfGE 40 (1992). Art. 7(6) takes the unusual step of abolishing "Vorschulen," which were not as the term seems to imply the equivalent of our kindergartens but rather what we would call preparatory schools, see Anschütz, supra note 28, at 676, 684-85; presumably they too were thought to contribute to an undesirable segregation of the elite.

not so intrinsically harmful to minors as to justify a blanket provision punishing third parties who provided them to children even with parental consent; the statute restricted the rights of the parents more than was necessary to accomplish the state's legitimate goal.[35] Similarly, insisting upon a particular ("besondere") justification for such a significant limitation of parental rights and finding none, the Court later held that the state could not forbid parents who were divorced or had never been married to opt for joint custody of their children.[36] Other decisions, while acknowledging the broad discretion afforded by the Article 7(1) provision that "the entire educational system shall be under the supervision of the state," have read Article 6(2) to ensure parents a significant role in determining which school their children attend and what course of study they pursue[37] as well as the affirmative right of access to information about their educational performance.[38]

Article 6(1), which provides simply that marriage and the family "enjoy the special protection of the state," is not so unequivocal in this regard. Nevertheless the Constitutional Court has squarely held that, among other things, this provision establishes an individual right to marry that may be limited only for convincing reasons ("einleuchtende Sachgründe");[39] neither the bride's earlier German divorce (though treated as a bar by the law of the husband's domicile)[40] nor the bridegroom's previous sexual relationship with the bride's mother[41] is a sufficient justification. Nor, according to the Court, may the state impose unreasonable burdens on the marriage relationship once it has been established; Article 6(1) has accordingly been held to require that a wife be given a reasonable opportunity to visit her husband in jail.[42]

---

[35] 7 BVerfGE 320, 322-26 (1958). See also 30 BVerfGE 336, 352-55 (1971) (noted in chapter 4 supra) (finding a flat ban of youth access to pictorial nudist propaganda an unjustified restriction of free expression even in the absence of parental consent).

[36] 61 BVerfGE 358, 371-82 (1982); 84 BVerfGE 168, 178-86 (1991) (also relying, in the alternative, on the protection for illegitimates afforded by Art. 6(5)).

[37] 34 BVerfGE 165, 182-92, 196-99 (1972) (*Förderstufe*) (upholding a comprehensive restructuring of grades 5 and 6 but striking down a prohibition on attending public schools outside the district and adding (at 198) that application of the same ban to private schools offended Art. 7(4)).

[38] 59 BVerfGE 360, 381-82 (1982). A more sweeping proposal to guarantee parents a say in determining the religious or philosophical orientation of the public schools was repeatedly rejected in the Parliamentary Council. See 1 JöR (n.F.) at 105, 107, 110-11; 41 BVerfGE 29, 44-46 (1975) (confirming, on the basis of this legislative history, that no such right exists).

[39] See 36 BVerfGE 146, 163 (1973); Helmut Lecheler, Schutz von Ehe und Familie, 6 Handbuch des Staatsrechts 211, Rdnr. 71-72.

[40] 31 BVerfGE 58, 80-87 (1971) (*Spanish Marriage* case). This decision also resolved important issues as to the territorial scope of the basic rights and the constitutional limits on application of foreign law. See chapter 1 supra.

[41] 36 BVerfGE 146, 161-69 (1973).

[42] 42 BVerfGE 95, 100-103 (1976).

B. Nondiscrimination

Various provisions of Articles 6 and 7 are also commonly applied in conjunction with the general equality provision of Article 3(1) to assure intensive examination of classifications disfavoring marriage, the family, or private schools.[43] Sometimes, indeed, Article 6(1) is applied independently to strike down discrimination against the classes it protects, as a more specific equality provision. Thus married couples may not be assessed higher income taxes than if they were single;[44] orphans may not be denied welfare benefits simply because they are married;[45] a broker who helps a prospective renter find an apartment may not be denied a fee because she is married to the landlord's manager.[46] These decisions reflect the Court's recognition that it is possible to infringe a right without denying it altogether: All too often the state effectively discourages some fundamental right by attaching onerous consequences to its exercise.[47]

The case of children born out of wedlock deserves special mention in this connection. On its face Article 6(5) appears to place the obligation of protecting illegitimates entirely upon the lawmakers: "Illegitimate children shall be provided *by legislation* with the same opportunities for their physical and mental development and for their place in society as are enjoyed by legitimate children." This phrasing, moreover, was no accident. Throughout the debates in the Parliamentary Council, various Social Democratic and Free Democratic delegates proposed language that would have forbidden discrimination against illegitimates outright.[48] At every turn these proposals

---

[43] See, e.g., 75 BVerfGE 40, 69-78 (1987) (finding provisions for private school subsidies contrary to Art. 7(4) in conjunction with Art. 3(1) because they discriminated against adult education and in favor of religious schools). See also the marriage and family decisions discussed in notes 393-94 infra and accompanying text.

[44] 6 BVerfGE 55, 70-84 (1957).

[45] 28 BVerfGE 324, 347-61 (1970). See id. at 356 (finding in Art. 6(1) a "strict prohibition of differentiation respecting government benefits according to family status alone").

[46] 76 BVerfGE 126, 128-30 (1987). See id. at 128: "Article 6(1) forbids [the state] to disadvantage married persons simply because they are married." See also Lecheler, supra note 39, Rdnr. 68 (describing the prohibition of discrimination as the heart of Art. 6(1)'s protection of marriage and the family).

[47] See the general discussion of the problem of unconstitutional conditions in chapter 4 supra.

[48] The various proposals included making family status ("Familienstand") a forbidden basis of discrimination under Art. 3(3) (see 1 JöR (n.F.) at 94 (Delegate Eberhard)), declaring legitimate and illegitimate children "equal in their rights" (id. at 95 (Delegate Heuss)), and simply declaring that "[i]llegitimate and legiti-

were rejected. Opponents agreed that something should be done to improve the plight of children born out of wedlock, but they attacked the notion of equal rights as both impracticable and inconsistent with the basic decision in Article 6(1) to promote marriage and the family.[49] Instead they proposed what was described as "an appeal to the legislature": "Illegitimate children have the same right as legitimate children to the support [Förderung] of the community."[50] It was with the express intention to accomplish the aims of this suggestion that the actual language of Article 6(5) – lifted almost verbatim from Article 121 of the Weimar Constitution, which the leading treatise of the time had flatly described as a mere guideline ("Richtlinie") without derogatory effect on existing laws[51] – was put forward and approved.[52]

From the beginning, however, the Constitutional Court gave Article 6(5) more than mere programmatic effect.[53] To begin with, the Court construed Article 6(5) to impose a constitutional obligation on the legislature[54] – an interpretation certainly consistent with if not compelled by the text of the provision. Neither text nor the debates in the Parliamentary Council, however, lent support to the Court's contemporaneous conclusion that Article 6(5) also embodied an objective principle of equality that bound the administration and the courts in their interpretation and application of existing laws.[55] Thus, for example, in 1958 the Court took what the Justices acknowledged to be significant liberties with a statute in order to bring it into conformity with what they viewed as the constitutional command that illegitimate children be afforded the opportunity to obtain a judicial determination of paternity.[56] There was academic support for a similar interpretation of the marriage and family provisions of the Weimar Constitution, which had been said not to be directly enforceable either;[57] the Court itself had taken a similar view of the social state provisions of Articles 20(1) and 28(1);[58] and the objective-value thesis

---

mate children are equal" (id. at 98 (the SPD contingent in the Principal Committee (Hauptausschuß))).

[49] See id. at 93-94, 96 (Delegates Süsterhenn and Wessel). See also Sten. Ber. at 223-24, 226 (1949) (Delegates Weber and Wessel) (invoking respect for the family and interests of the unwed mother).

[50] See 1 JöR (n.F.) at 96, 97 (Delegate Süsterhenn).

[51] See Anschütz, supra note 28, at 563.

[52] See 1 JöR (n.F.) at 97 (Delegate Seebohm).

[53] See, e.g., 25 BVerfGE 167, 172 (1969): "It is generally agreed that Article 6(5) of the Basic Law is more than a mere programmatic declaration such as the almost identically phrased provision of Article 121 of the Weimar Constitution."

[54] 8 BVerfGE 210, 216 (1958).

[55] Id. at 210, 217.

[56] Id. at 217-21.

[57] See Anschütz, supra note 28, at 560.

[58] See chapter 1 supra.

had been enunciated just a few months before in an opinion involving freedom of expression under Article 5(1).[59] Nevertheless the practical effect came perilously close to holding that Article 6(5) provided a basis for determining the constitutionality of legislation – and that seemed to be precisely what in selecting the language of the provision the Parliamentary Council had attempted to avoid.

Moreover, it was not long before the Court concluded that it actually had power to review the adequacy of laws enacted in pursuance of the duty imposed by Article 6(5).[60] Thus, for example, once the legislature got around to extending to illegitimates the right to inherit property from their fathers, the Court held it permissible to limit the right to children born after the Basic Law took effect[61] but not to those whose paternity had been established (or made the subject of a pending complaint) while their fathers were still alive.[62] While this position too lacked support in either the language or the history of the provision, it was at least arguably implicit. Various provisions of Art. 93(1), after all, gave the Court jurisdiction to determine the constitutionality of legislative action or inaction; the only question was whether the peculiar terms and origins of Article 6(5) required an exception from the general principle of judicial review.[63]

In 1969 the Court dropped the final shoe. Twenty years had passed, and the legislature had done virtually nothing to comply with its mandate to ensure "equal conditions for [the] . . . development" of illegitimate children. Understandably exasperated, the Court threatened to enforce Article 6(5) itself if the legislature did not act by the end of its current session. The framers could not have intended, said the Court, to permit the legislature to defeat the purpose of the provision by failing to do its duty. Judicial review of existing laws that discriminated against illegitimate children might be an inadequate method of achieving the framers' goals, but it was better than nothing; as the Court had said in upholding a temporary arrangement for governing the Saarland that did not conform in all respects with the Basic Law, it would move matters in the direction of greater compliance with the constitution.[64] Continuing discrimination against illegitimate children, the Court added, could not in the long run be reconciled with the constitutional commands of equality and free development of personality. Thus Article 6(5) should be viewed as analogous to Article 117(1), which had postponed the effective date of Article 3's sex discrimination provisions in order to give the legislature time to enact a nondiscriminatory new code. The gender provisions

---

[59] See chapter 4 supra (discussing the *Lüth* decision).

[60] See 17 BVerfGE 148, 155 (1963); 25 BVerfGE 167, 173 (1969).

[61] 44 BVerfGE 1, 31-33 (1976).

[62] 74 BVerfGE 33, 38-43 (1986). Cf. the line of cases beginning with Levy v. Louisiana, 391 U.S. 68 (1968).

[63] Cf. Pacific States Tel. & Tel. Co. v. Oregon, 223 U.S. 118 (1912); Nixon v. United States, 113 Sup. Ct. 732 (1993).

[64] Cf. 4 BVerfGE 157 (1955), discussed in chapter 2 supra.

had been held judicially enforceable after the grace period expired, and the requirement of equality for illegitimates provided no less manageable a standard.[65]

The outside observer may find this decision a remarkable exercise in judicial creativity. Article 3 contained a normal self-executing equality clause whose applicability Article 117 had postponed; Article 6(5) was a direction to the legislature adopted in conscious preference to such a provision. The legislative history that stood in the way of the Court's conclusion was ignored.

The legislature finally complied with Article 6(5) shortly after this decision, thus freeing the Court from the necessity of determining the constitutionality of preexisting laws.[66]

C. The Institutional Guarantee of Marriage

Several provisions of Articles 6 and 7 conspicuously go beyond the conventional defensive function of protecting against discrimination or other state infringement of private rights. Article 6(1), for example, was explained in the Parliamentary Council as guaranteeing the continued existence of marriage as an institution: Any law abolishing marriage would be unconstitutional.[67]

There is no doubt that, as the Constitutional Court later confirmed, the term "marriage" was understood in its traditional sense. The formulation initially proposed in the Parliamentary Council, which explicitly defined marriage as "the lawful form of lasting domestic partnership [Lebensgemeinschaft] between man and woman," was abandoned by the Committee on Style on the ground that the definition was self-evident.[68]

---

[65] 25 BVerfGE 167, 173-84 (1969), citing 3 BVerfGE 225 (1953), also noted in chapter 4 supra. Since in its view the deadline for legislative action had not yet arrived, the Court went on to interpret the statute before it in light of the objective principle of equality laid down in Art. 6(5), concluding that because a legitimate child would receive both an inheritance and an orphan's pension, an illegitimate child's pension could not be set off against his statutory right to support from his father's heirs. Id. at 191-94.

[66] See BGBl. II, pt. I, S. 1243 (1969); Hans F. Zacher, Elternrecht, 6 Handbuch des Staatsrechts 265, Rdnr. 120.

[67] See 1 JöR (n.F.) at 94 (Delegates Maier and Süsterhenn).

[68] Id. at 97. See also 10 BVerfGE 59, 66 (1959) (dictum): "'Marriage' within the meaning of the Basic Law is the union of a man and a woman in a basically indissoluble domestic partnership, and 'family' is the comprehensive relationship between parents and children." See also 36 BVerfGE 146, 165 (1973) (dictum) (denying, as had Delegate von Mangoldt in the Parliamentary Council (1 JöR (n.F.) at 94), that concubinage ("das Konkubinat"), of whatever duration, was entitled to a constitutional guarantee of permanency). For an even narrower definition of family see Lecheler, supra note 39, Rdnr. 42-47 (excluding even the widowed single parent and leaving illegitimate children to the special provisions of Art. 6(5)). Before it was streamlined by the Committee on Style, the provision that be-

Despite this history, and despite warnings in the Parliamentary Council that equal rights for illegitimates would be inconsistent with Article 6(1),[69] the institutional guarantee of marriage has never been understood to freeze all the details of preexisting marriage law or to exclude unmarried persons from the enjoyment of all privileges once reserved exclusively to husbands and wives.[70] Thus although Article 6(1) helps to justify a statutory requirement that husband and wife bear a common name, it does not compel the legislature to so provide.[71] Nor does Article 6(1) forbid the award of joint custody to unwed parents,[72] preclude extending to the surviving member of an unmarried couple the right to succeed to a deceased partner's apartment lease,[73] or require that concubinage (concededly not protected by Article 6 itself)[74] be made a crime – for as the Court said in the case of the departed lessee the right to free development of personality protected by Article 2(1) now includes the right to live in what used to be called sin.[75]

On the other hand, the explicit declaration that marriage shall enjoy particular state protection certainly appears to put a damper on any argument that discrimination against persons not formally married is constitutionally *barred*.[76] Moreover, like its Weimar an-

---

came Art. 6(1) protected marriage and its concomitant family ("die mit ihr gegebene Familie"). See 1 JöR (n.F.) at 95. The Court has made clear, however, that the parental rights protected by Art. 6(2) include those of the parents of illegitimate children. See 84 BVerfGE 168, 179 (1991); text at note 36 supra.

[69] See note 49 supra and accompanying text. Professor Anschütz had made the same argument in discussing the similar Weimar provisions. See Anschütz, supra note 28, at 559-60.

[70] Even Professor Anschütz, who took quite a restrictive view of the analogous Art. 119 of the Weimar Constitution, conceded it did not forbid all changes in preexisting law. See id. at 559.

[71] See 78 BVerfGE 38, 49 (1988); 84 BVerfGE 9, 19 (1991).

[72] 84 BVerfGE 168, 184 (1991). Indeed the Court held that Art. 6(2) and (5) *required* the legislature to permit joint custody in the case before it. See text at note 36 supra.

[73] 82 BVerfGE 6, 15 (1990).

[74] See note 68 supra. See also Lecheler, supra note 39, Rdnr. 91 (arguing that to treat as a marriage a relationship between individuals who chose not to marry would contradict not only Art. 6(1) but also the intentions of the parties).

[75] See 82 BVerfGE at 16. See also Verfassung des Landes Brandenburg vom 20. August 1992, GV BB 298, Art. 26(2), which expressly affirms that lasting relationships outside of marriage are also deserving of state protection: "Die Schutzbedürftigkeit anderer, auf Dauer angelegter Lebensgemeinschaften wird anerkannt." The suggestion that a corresponding provision be added to Art. 6(1) of the Basic Law was rejected by the Constitutional Commission in 1993. See Bericht der VerfKomm at 54, 56-58.

[76] Not long ago, in a case in which a German woman had gone through a religious marriage ceremony with an Englishman in Germany, the Court held it offended Art. 6(1) to deny her widows' benefits on the ground that German law required a civil wedding. 62 BVerfGE 323, 329-33 (1982) (*Hinkende Ehe*). This deci-

tecedent,[77] Article 6(1) arguably does forbid changes in the law that would alter the fundamental nature of the institution. A statute authorizing polygamy, for example, would appear difficult to reconcile with the assumptions that underlay adoption of Article 6(1), and the same can be said of marriages between members of the same sex.[78]

For similar reasons, the implicit definition of marriage as a lasting partnership would also appear to place serious limitations on the power to authorize divorce. Indeed it had been said before the Basic Law was adopted that the analogous provision of the Weimar Constitution, which contained no definition, forbade the legislature to abandon the principle that marriage was a lifetime commitment,[79] and in one of its earliest opinions the Constitutional Court solemnly affirmed that "marriage" in the sense of Article 6(1) was a "basically indissoluble partnership."[80] Not long afterward, however, the Court emphasized that marriage was required to be permanent only in principle; far from forbidding divorce generally, Article 6(1) gave those who had been divorced a constitutional right to remarry.[81]

Emboldened by this decision, the legislature revised the Civil Code to abandon the fault principle that had previously dominated divorce law. The pious declaration that marriage was a lifetime commitment ("auf Lebenszeit geschlossen") was retained. One separate section, however, provided that divorce was permissible whenever a marriage had broken down ("wenn sie gescheitert ist"), another that when husband and wife had lived apart for three years (or for one year if both spouses agreed to the divorce) a breakdown was conclusively presumed.[82]

The Constitutional Court managed to uphold these provisions in yet another remarkable opinion. It was true, the opinion acknowledged, that Article 6(1) required marriage to be indissoluble in principle; divorce had to remain the exception, not the rule. But the fault principle had proved uncertain in application as well as inequitable, destructive, and demeaning to the parties; marriages could fall

---

sion is reminiscent of the nonconstitutional doctrine of putative marriage long recognized under community property laws in the United States; it is a far cry from holding that similar benefits must be extended to those who choose not to marry or are forbidden to do so.

[77] See Anschütz, supra note 28, at 559 (arguing, for example, that the state could not dispense altogether with the requirement of a marriage ceremony). For a contrary conclusion on the question of formalities see Lecheler, supra note 39, Rdnr. 21.

[78] See id., Rdnr. 19.

[79] See Art. 119 WRV; Anschütz, supra note 28, at 559 ("Grundsatz der Lebenslänglichkeit der Ehe").

[80] See note 68 supra.

[81] 31 BVerfGE 58, 82-83 (1971); see text at notes 40-41 supra.

[82] §§ 1353, 1565-66 BGB, as amended by the Act of June 14, 1976, BGBl. I S. 1421 ("Zerrüttungsprinzip").

apart without fault on the part of either spouse, and no law could effectively keep them intact. What mattered was that the parties enter into marriage with the intention and commitment to make it a lasting partnership, not that they succeed. Marriage was after all a relationship based on consent; Article 6(1) did not require the state to preserve it as an involuntary partnership ("Zwangsgemeinschaft") over the enduring objection of one of the parties. Continuing needs of one spouse for the other's support, four Justices added in rejecting the argument that the constitution at least required a broader hardship exception than the statute provided, could be satisfied without taking the draconian step of denying the supporting party the right to form a new and more satisfactory union.[83]

One commentator has mildly observed that the provisions upheld in this case went to the limit of what Article 6(1) allowed.[84] One might add that however sound it may be in policy, divorce on the basis of mere separation was hardly what the framers of the Basic Law had in mind. Perhaps what really explains the decision is the Court's insistence that Article 6(1) guarantees marriage not in the abstract but in the form prescribed by law in accordance with prevailing mores ("wie sie den herrschenden, in der gesetzlichen Regelung maßgebend zum Ausdruck gelangten Anschauungen entspricht").[85] In other words, the Court seems – without saying why – to have adopted the view that the meaning of the marriage guarantee may change over time, as our Supreme Court has said of the prohibition of cruel and unusual punishment.[86]

No-fault divorce is still a far cry from either multiple or homosexual marriage. But the Court's dynamic understanding of the marriage provision suggests that if the legislature ever enacts more radical departures from tradition the Court may not reject them simply on the ground that they do not conform with the framers' conception of marriage.

---

[83] 53 BVerfGE 224, 245-51 (1980). Four Justices dissented from this last conclusion (id. at 251-52), two from the basic decision that breakdown of the marriage could be made a sufficient ground for divorce: Not even a failed marriage could be placed entirely at the disposition of the parties. Id. at 252-53. Later the same year, confronted with psychiatric evidence suggesting that a divorce might bring about a nervous breakdown and even lead to suicide, the entire panel agreed that Art. 6(1) sometimes forbade immediate divorce even after the five years' separation that under the statute put an end to the judge's power to preserve the legal bond of marriage. 55 BVerfGE 134, 1237-38, 141-44 (1980). See also 57 BVerfGE 361 (1981) (holding that Art. 6(1) did not require that the duty of support after divorce be based on fault either).

[84] See Lecheler, supra note 39, Rdnr. 84.

[85] 53 BVerfGE at 245.

[86] See Furman v. Georgia, 408 U.S. 238 (1972).

D. Affirmative Duties and Positive Rights

The family and school articles also contain several provisions that expressly or implicitly impose affirmative duties on the state and may even give private parties a positive right to state support. In so doing Articles 6 and 7 go far beyond the Bill of Rights of the U.S. Constitution as it has generally been interpreted by the Supreme Court.

Once again several provisions are explicit in this respect. Articles 6(2) and 7(1) do not simply authorize the state to watch over parental child care and the entire educational system; they require it to do so.[87] Article 7(2) does not merely permit religious instruction in public schools; it prescribes it in most cases as an obligatory component of the curriculum.[88] Article 6(4) provides that mothers are entitled to the support of the community. Article 6(5), discussed in detail above, directs the legislature to take affirmative steps to assure equality of opportunity for illegitimate children. Most of these provisions were taken directly from the Weimar Constitution, which bristled with affirmative duties and positive rights.[89] Interestingly, the one affirmative Weimar provision that had widespread counterparts in the United States was omitted: The duty of the state to provide public schooling was assumed rather than expressed.[90]

Under the Weimar Constitution, it is said, nothing much came of these affirmative obligations.[91] Under the Basic Law they have had a much more significant effect. We have seen how, lacking authority to order the legislature to act, the Constitutional Court prodded it to take action on behalf of illegitimate children by threatening to do the job on its own.[92] Once it was held to permit judicial review of new legislation and to control interpretation of existing laws, moreover,

---

[87] See Joseph Isensee, Das Grundrecht als Abwehrrecht und staatliche Schutzpflicht, 5 Handbuch des Staatsrechts 143, Rdnr. 14-17 (citing the Art. 6(2) provision for state supervision of child care ("über ihre Betätigung wacht die staatliche Gemeinschaft") as a paradigmatic affirmative duty).

[88] Neither pupils nor teachers, as noted above, may be compelled to participate; but the state must see to it that religious instruction is provided.

[89] See chapter 1 supra. Social Democrats in the Parliamentary Council opposed the entire Art. 6 on the ground that its inclusion was inconsistent with the decision to omit other affirmative social or economic rights (such as the right to employment or social security) that had been guaranteed by the Weimar Constitution. See 1 JöR (n.F.) at 94 (Delegates Menzel and Bergsträßer).

[90] See Art. 143 WRV: "Für die Bildung der Jugend ist durch öffentliche Anstalten zu sorgen." Cf., e.g., Ill. Const., Art. X, § 1 (1970). The state's duty to ensure that children are educated ("Erziehungsauftrag"), the Constitutional Court has said, is implicit in the Art. 7(1) provision that the educational system "shall be under the supervision of the state." 52 BVerfGE 223, 236 (1979). It is explicit in several Länder constitutions. See, e.g., Landesverfassung der Freien Hansestadt Bremen vom 21. Oktober 1947, SaBremR 100-a-1, Art. 27.

[91] See Dietrich Murswiek, Grundrechte als Teilhaberechte, soziale Grundrechte, 5 Handbuch des Staatsrechts 243, Rdnr. 44, and authorities cited.

[92] See text at notes 63-65 supra.

Article 6(5) was understandably read not only to limit outright discrimination against illegitimates[93] but also to justify[94] and even to require[95] special privileges to compensate for the disadvantages with which illegitimates were saddled; for otherwise they could not enjoy the actual equality of opportunity to which they were entitled.

Similarly, the Constitutional Court has directly enforced the affirmative requirement of Article 6(4) that "[e]very mother is entitled to the protection and care of the community." An analogous Weimar provision referring impersonally to motherhood ("die Mutterschaft") had been said to be only a direction to the legislature without effect on existing laws.[96] The Parliamentary Council, however, substituted the term "every mother" in a conscious effort to ensure that Article 6(4) would give rise to immediately enforceable claims.[97] Citing this history, the Court made clear in 1972 that the new wording not only imposed a legal obligation on the legislature but also expressed a constitutional value judgment ("eine verfassungsrechtliche Wertentscheidung") with binding force throughout the field of public and private law.[98]

In conformity with the spirit of this provision, the discharge of both public and private employees during or within four months after pregnancy had been forbidden by statute even before adoption of the Basic Law.[99] In 1972 the Court held this protection did not have to be extended to an employee who had negligently failed to give her employer the requisite notice of her condition.[100] Seven years later, however, the Court held that Article 6(4) forbade the state to make excusable failure to meet the notice requirement a ground for denying the statutory immunity from loss of private employment.[101] In 1991, flatly declaring that women who were pregnant or had recently given birth could not be left without legal protection against losing their jobs, the Court went even further: Article 6(4) forbade the state to dismiss an expectant or recent mother even when in light of the

---

[93] See text at notes 61-62 supra; 44 BVerfGE 1, 18 (1976); 74 BVerfGE 33, 38 (1986) (insisting that Art. 6(5) must be understood as a particular expression of the general equality provision of Art. 3(1)).

[94] See 17 BVerfGE 280, 283-86 (1964) (longer period of child support from father).

[95] See 8 BVerfGE 210, 214-21 (1958) (judicial proceeding to establish paternity); BVerfG, Decision of Jan. 18, 1988, 1 BvR 1589/87, 1988 NJW 3010 (right to know father's identity); Michael Sachs, Besondere Gleichheitsgarantien, 5 Handbuch des Staatsrechts 1017, Rdnr. 149-51. See also Sten. Ber. at 226 (Delegate Wessel) (noting that under Art. 6(5) both "state and society will have to do more for the illegitimate child than they do for the legitimate" one).

[96] See Art. 119 WRV; Anschütz, supra note 28, at 560.

[97] See 1 JöR (n.F.) at 95 (Delegate Greve).

[98] See 32 BVerfGE 273, 277 (1972).

[99] See 52 BVerfGE 357, 359-60 (1979).

[100] 32 BVerfGE at 277-78.

[101] 52 BVerfGE at 365-68.

abolition of many offices of the former East German government her services were no longer required.[102]

As its terminology suggests ("marriage and the family shall enjoy the special protection of the state"), Article 6(1) is said to impose an affirmative duty on the state actively to promote marriage and the family, but it is also said to give the legislature wide discretion in determining how to do so.[103] Article 119 of the Weimar Constitution had expressly provided that families with numerous children had a claim to state assistance to equalize their burdens ("Anspruch auf ausgleichende Fürsorge"), but this provision was said to create no directly enforceable rights,[104] and it was not included in the Basic Law. Nevertheless the Court has in effect required state subsidies for children by holding that Article 6(1) in conjunction with traditional civil service principles (Art. 33(5)) and the general equality provision (Art. 3(1)) demanded that public officers with children receive additional compensation and that child care expenses be deductible from taxable income, respectively.[105]

Unlike the provisions just considered, Article 7(4) says nothing about affirmative duties. Literally it guarantees only the traditional defensive right to be free from state interference in establishing a private school.[106] Yet in a landmark 1987 opinion the Constitutional Court held that Article 7(4) in connection with the Sozialstaat principle also required the state in certain circumstances to *subsidize* private schools. Otherwise, said the Court, the explicit right to establish such schools would be hollow; for the requirement of the same paragraph that private institutions not promote "segregation of pupils according to the means of the parents" made it impossible for them to survive without public support.[107]

---

[102] 84 BVerfGE 133, 155-56 (1991); see also 85 BVerfGE 360 (1992). Art. 6(4) is understood to apply only to the period of pregnancy, birth, and nursing; thereafter the relation is governed by the more general clauses respecting parental rights and duties and the family. See Zacher, supra note 66, Rdnr. 15.

[103] See Lecheler, supra note 39, Rdnr. 50.

[104] See Anschütz, supra note 28, at 560.

[105] See 44 BVerfGE 249, 262-68 (1977); 61 BVerfGE 319 (1982); 82 BVerfGE 60 (1990). See also text at notes 222, 394 infra.

[106] Cf. Pierce v. Society of Sisters, 268 U.S. 510 (1925) (finding such a right protected by the due process clause). See 34 BVerfGE 165, 197-98 (1972) (also cited in note 37 supra) (striking down a measure that forbade certain public school pupils to transfer to private schools). As noted above, Art. 7(4) has also been held to require intensive scrutiny under Art. 3(1) of measures that discriminate among private schools. See note 43 supra.

[107] 75 BVerfGE 40, 61-66 (1987). "Private schools," said the Court, "must be generally accessible – not in the sense that like public schools they must accept every pupil who satisfies generally applicable criteria, but in the sense that pupils can attend them essentially without regard to their economic situation." Id. at 64. This limitation, and consequently also the right to state support, apply only to those private schools which are approved as substitutes for public institutions ("Ersatzschulen"). See id. at 62. See also Erhard Denninger, Staatliche Hilfe zur Grund-

As of this writing, this is the only decision of the Constitutional
Court to hold squarely that any provision of the Basic Law imposed
an affirmative duty, untinged with considerations of equality, to provide an outright state subsidy.[108] This conclusion was made more
remarkable by the fact that, like the decision that Article 6(5)'s command of equality for illegitimates was judicially enforceable, it was
reached in the teeth of contrary legislative history. This time, however, that history was not simply ignored; what was most striking
was that it informed the entire first half of the opinion.

The first proposal in the Parliamentary Council to guarantee the
right to establish private schools had included an explicit right to a
subsidy reflecting the money the state saved by not having to educate
those pupils who elected to attend a private institution. This proposal
was rejected out of hand. A second proposal was then made along the
lines of the provision ultimately adopted as Article 7(4). Not only did
this second proposal say nothing about subsidies; its sponsor carefully dissociated himself from the original proposal and explained
that no subsidy was intended.[109] All of this was faithfully reported in

---

rechtsausübung durch Verfahren, Organisation und Finanzierung, 5 Handbuch
des Staatsrechts 291, Rdnr. 44-46. Contrast the Court's conclusion, 20 BVerfGE 56,
96-112 (1966) (discussed in chapter 4 supra and qualified by later decisions), that
general subsidies for political parties were inconsistent with the guarantee of party
autonomy in Art. 21(1). There is some truth in the arguments that underlie both the
private school and political party decisions, but there is a certain tension between
the conclusions that subsidies are constitutionally forbidden and that they are constitutionally required.

[108] Indeed the Court's reliance on the fact that other language in Art. 7 severely
restricted the ability of substitute schools to survive on their own weakens the value
even of this decision as a precedent for construing other basic rights provisions to
impose similar affirmative duties. Since the prohibition on charging fees that
would segregate pupils according to wealth was contained in the Basic Law itself,
the decision cannot be paraphrased as holding that by imposing it the state had
unconstitutionally invaded the right to establish private schools. Nevertheless
there is a family resemblance between this situation and others in which the state is
required to provide affirmative support because it has prevented individuals from
exercising their rights on their own. See chapters 4 and 5 supra (discussing the
First Television case and the arguable obligation of the state to provide religious
services to prisoners). See also 75 BVerfGE at 66: "The state must also protect educational pluralism from the state itself by providing state support to neutralize the
damage done . . . by its own actions." The Court also carefully refrained from saying that any particular private school had a positive right to receive any particular
subsidy. Indeed, as in other cases involving affirmative obligations, it stressed the
broad discretion afforded the political branches in determining how best to satisfy
their duty in light of competing demands for limited funds. Id. at 66-69.

[109] See 1 JöR (n.F.) at 111-13.

the Court's opinion, and it led the Justices to the ineluctable conclusion that Article 7(4) was not meant to provide a subsidy.[110]

Separated by a cultural gap as well as an ocean, the reader may find it surprising that the opinion did not end right there. Without batting an eye the Court went on, as indicated, to hold that Article 7(4) did what it was intended not to do – it required a subsidy for private schools.

No explanation was offered for this course of action. Plainly the Court did not mean to say that the proceedings of the Parliamentary Council were irrelevant to the meaning of the Basic Law. If that had been the Justices' position, they would hardly have taken the trouble of painstakingly recounting the debates. Moreover, only a few years had passed since the Court had flatly reaffirmed the significance of legislative history in constitutional interpretation.[111]

The explanation may be the same as that hazarded above in connection with the decision upholding no-fault divorce. The original meaning of any constitutional provision is determined in part by its history. But the meaning of Article 7(4), like that of Article 6(1), may not be fixed for all time. No one initially believed the Basic Law required subsidies for private schools. Changing circumstances later made it apparent to the Court, however, that without state assistance private schools could no longer survive.[112] Under those conditions a subsidy was necessary if Article 7(4) was to serve its purpose, and thus a subsidy was now required.[113]

In any event, Articles 6 and 7 are among those provisions of the Basic Law that have been held to create not merely traditional defensive rights against government intrusion ("Abwehrrechte") but positive governmental duties to protect or support the individual ("Schutzpflichten") as well.[114] Additional examples will be noted as

---

[110] 75 BVerfGE at 58-61. See id. at 61: "Einen Subventionsanspruch, dessen Aufnahme in die Verfassung ausdrücklich abgelehnt worden war, sollte die verfassungsrechtliche Garantie der Privatschulfreiheit nicht einschließen."

[111] See 62 BVerfGE 1, 45-47 (1983) (*Parliamentary Dissolution* case), discussed in chapter 2 supra.

[112] See 75 BVerfGE at 63: "In the face of present high costs, the owners of private schools are no longer in a position today to satisfy all the conditions laid down in the third and fourth sentences of Article 7(4) simultaneously in the long run on the basis of their own resources." Whether similar conditions existing at the time the Basic Law was adopted would have led the Court even then to prefer the general purpose of Art. 7(4) over the specific intentions of its framers it was unnecessary to decide.

[113] Cf. the converse suggestion in the *First Television* case, discussed in chapter 4 supra, that the duty imposed by Art. 5(2) to take affirmative steps to assure diversity in broadcasting might disappear once technical advances eliminated the scarcity of frequencies that had led the Court to its conclusion.

[114] See Lecheler, supra note 39, Rdnr. 104; Zacher, supra note 66, Rdnr. 99-100, 118-19; Thomas Oppermann, Schule und berufliche Ausbildung, 6 Handbuch des Staatsrechts 329, Rdnr. 83. See also the general discussion of affirmative rights and duties in chapter 1 and other examples noted in chapter 4 supra.

we proceed, but suffice it for now to remind the reader once again of the striking contrast between these decisions and the prevailing understanding of the U.S. Constitution.[115] What is equally significant for present purposes is that Articles 6 and 7 explicitly codify some of the rights our Supreme Court has found to be "fundamental" for due process and equal protection purposes and thus add legitimacy to judicial review of governmental action affecting private education and the family.

II. PROPERTY

"Property and inheritance," says Article 14(1), "are guaranteed." Their "content and limits" are determined by statute ("Gesetz") (id.). Property imposes duties ("Eigentum verpflichtet"), and its use shall also serve the public weal ("[s]ein Gebrauch soll zugleich dem Wohl der Allgemeinheit dienen") (Art. 14(2)). Condemnation is permitted only for the public good and pursuant to statutes providing just compensation (Art. 14(3)).

The right to property occupies a prominent position in German constitutional law. The Constitutional Court put the point most plainly in a major 1968 opinion:[116]

> Property is an elementary constitutional right that is closely connected to the guarantee of personal liberty. Within the general system of constitutional rights its function is to secure its holder a sphere of liberty in the economic field and thereby enable him to lead a self-governing life. . . . The guarantee of property is not primarily a material but rather a personal guarantee.

Thus property rights are by no means relegated to an inferior position in Germany, as they have been in the United States.[117] Economic independence is understood to be essential to every other freedom,[118] and property rights are taken very seriously. The explicit

---

[115] Contrast DeShaney v. Winnebago County Department of Social Services, 489 U.S. 189 (1989); Harris v. McRae, 448 U.S. 297 (1980). See generally David Currie, Positive and Negative Constitutional Rights, 53 U. Chi. L. Rev. 864 (1986).

[116] 24 BVerfGE 367, 389, 400 (1968) (*Hamburg Flood Control* case).

[117] Contrast Murdock v. Pennsylvania, 319 U.S. 105, 115 (1943) ("preferred position" for first amendment rights); Kovacs v. Cooper, 336 U.S. 77, 95-96 (1949) (Frankfurter, J., concurring) ("those liberties of the individual which history has attested as the indispensable conditions of an open as against a closed society come to this Court with a momentum for respect lacking when appeal is made to liberties which derive merely from shifting economic arrangements"). This is not to deny that even in Germany there are subtle differences in the levels of judicial scrutiny according to how intimately the right in question is bound up with the development of personality. See Denninger in 1 AK-GG, vor Art. 1, Rdnr. 11, 14, and cases cited.

[118] Cf. Friedrich von Hayek, The Road to Serfdom 103-04 (1944).

constitutional references to the social obligations of property have been held to permit considerable regulation. Article 14 has nevertheless been applied not only to prevent unjustified takings in the narrow sense but also to prevent unreasonable limitations of property rights that fall short of a traditional taking. Moreover, like the marriage provision of Article 6(1), Article 14(1) is understood to guarantee the existence of private property as an institution.[119]

A. Takings

The Constitutional Court has made clear that takings cannot be justified simply by providing adequate compensation. Article 14 is basically a guarantee of property itself, not of its equivalent in money.[120] Consequently the Court has scrutinized attempted takings carefully to ensure that constitutional limitations other than the compensation provision have been observed.

The requirement that condemnation be authorized by statute ("Gesetzesvorbehalt") reflects a fundamental principle that we have encountered before and shall encounter again in the course of this chapter: Individual rights may be restricted, if at all, only in accordance with laws made by the popularly elected legislature. This principle is by no means unknown to Anglo-American law. It informed Justice Black's monumental opinion for the Supreme Court in *Youngstown Sheet & Tube Co. v. Sawyer*,[121] and it represents an early and often neglected aspect of the due process clauses.[122] In Germany it is explicit in a number of Bill of Rights provisions, and it has been found implicit as a general principle in the rule of law.[123]

---

[119] See 24 BVerfGE at 389; Hans-Jürgen Papier in 2 Maunz/Dürig, Art. 14, Rdnr. 11-17. The same is true of the guarantee of inheritance in the same clause, see id., Rdnr. 243-48; it was also true (with an important explicit qualification in the case of inheritance) of the comparable provisions (Art. 153(1), 154) of the Weimar Constitution. See Anschütz, supra note 28, at 706, 721.

[120] See 24 BVerfGE 367, 400 (1968). See also 84 BVerfGE 90 (1991) (upholding a constitutional amendment providing that property expropriated during the Soviet occupation of East Germany need not be restored in specie because the Federal Republic was not responsible for acts committed by foreign powers outside its territory and before its adoption, but reserving the question whether an appropriate compensation might nevertheless lie in the unalterable heart of the Sozialstaat principle of Art. 20(1) within the meaning of Art. 79(3)).

[121] 343 U.S. 579, 582-89 (1951).

[122] See id. at 646 (Jackson, J., concurring) (arguing that the President's duty to take care that the laws be faithfully executed and the due process clause "signify about all there is of the principle that ours is a government of laws, not of men": "One [clause] gives a governmental authority that reaches so far as there is law, the other gives a private right that authority shall go no farther"); Corwin, The Doctrine of Due Process of Law Before the Civil War, 24 Harv. L. Rev 366 (1911).

[123] See 49 BVerfGE 89, 126 (1978): "The general principle that lawmaking authority is reserved to the legislature [Gesetzesvorbehalt] requires a statutory basis

When takings have been attempted without adequate statutory authority, they have been struck down.[124]

There have been few decisions of the Constitutional Court on the question of what constitutes the public weal ("Wohl der Allgemeinheit") for which private property may be taken. On its face the term seems broader than the "public use" formulation that courts in the United States have so generously construed.[125] The Constitutional Court had no difficulty in upholding takings for the purpose of refugee settlement[126] or the transmission of private power to serve the general public.[127] More interesting challenges were posed by cases involving a private cable car for recreational purposes[128] and a test track for a private automaker.[129] The first provoked a strongly worded separate opinion deploring years of inattention to the public weal requirement;[130] approval in the second might seriously have eroded the distinction between private and public interests.[131] Both cases, however, went off on the ground of lack of statutory authority; the limiting case has yet to be decided.[132]

The Constitutional Court has also had little to say on the question of what constitutes just compensation. Article 14 provides that compensation is to be determined by "an equitable balance" between pub-

---

for executive acts fundamentally [wesentlich] affecting the freedom and equality of the citizen." See the general discussion of this issue in chapter 3 supra.

[124] 56 BVerfGE 249, 261-66 (1981) (cable car); 74 BVerfGE 264, 284-97 (1987) (automobile test track). On the other hand, neither condemnation nor the definition of the "content and limits" of property is considered a "restriction" of the basic right so as to require that the statute explicitly mention Art. 14(1). 24 BVerfGE at 396-97; see the discussion of Art. 19(1) in chapter 4 supra.

[125] See, e.g., Berman v. Parker, 348 U.S. 26 (1954); Hawaii Housing Authority v. Midkiff, 467 U.S. 229 (1984).

[126] 46 BVerfGE 268, 288-89 (1977).

[127] 66 BVerfGE 248, 257-59 (1984) (explaining (id. at 257) that condemnation on behalf of a private enterprise was permissible at least "when the enterprise [was] subject to a statutory obligation promoting the general welfare and . . . conducted for the benefit of the public").

[128] 56 BVerfGE 249 (1981).

[129] 74 BVerfGE 264 (1987).

[130] 56 BVerfGE at 266, 269-95 (separate opinion of Böhmer, J.) (concluding (id. at 287) that the condemnation in question was "for the benefit of a private undertaking designed solely for private profit"). For Justice Böhmer's narrow view of the permissible scope of condemnation for private companies see id. at 293.

[131] The argument was that the test track (for Daimler-Benz) would create jobs and stimulate the economy. Cf. Charles Wilson's legendary observation that "what's good for General Motors is good for the country." "Condemnation for the benefit of private persons . . . that serves the public weal only indirectly and presents an enhanced danger of abuse to the detriment of the weak," the Court observed, "poses particular constitutional problems." 74 BVerfGE at 287.

[132] See generally Papier in 2 Maunz/Dürig, Art. 14, Rdnr. 495-509.

lic and private interests;[133] not surprisingly, the Court has taken this to mean that full market value is not necessarily required.[134] More strikingly, the requirement that the statute itself provide for compensation has led the Constitutional Court to reject the familiar American doctrine of inverse condemnation entirely. If government action has the effect of taking property without compensation, the remedy is disallowance, not damages; for otherwise the state would have to pay compensation the legislature had not authorized, contrary to the constitutional allocation of powers.[135] The Constitutional Court therefore tests laws regulating property not under the taking provisions but for their consistency with the general guarantee of property;[136] and nonconfiscatory taxes are generally held not to be limitations on property at all.[137]

Even when the explicit requirements of statutory authority, public weal, and just compensation appear to be met, the Constitutional Court has made clear that condemnation is an exceptional remedy that may be employed only as a last resort. Property may not be taken until efforts to buy it on the open market have failed;[138] property that has been condemned reverts to its former owner when it is no longer

---

[133] See Art. 14(3) GG: "Die Entschädigung ist unter gerechter Abwägung der Interessen der Allgemeinheit und der Beteiligten zu bestimmen."

[134] See 24 BVerfGE 367, 420-22 (1968). For criticism of this conclusion see Walter Leisner, Eigentum, 6 Handbuch des Staatsrechts 1023, Rdnr. 180-83 (1989). For an introduction to the extensive jurisprudence of the civil courts on the question of the level of compensation see Papier in 2 Maunz/Dürig, Art. 14, Rdnr. 510-60.

[135] See 4 BVerfGE 219, 230-37 (1955); 58 BVerfGE 300, 322-24 (1981). For discussion of the impact of the latter decision upon the civil courts' practice of awarding common-law or statutory compensation for wrongful takings see Papier in 2 Maunz/Dürig, Art. 14, Rdnr. 597-638; for criticism of the Constitutional Court's position see Leisner, supra note 134, Rdnr. 173-79.

[136] The civil and administrative courts, on the other hand, have developed an extensive jurisprudence for determining when regulation amounts to a taking; the problem has proved as refractory in Germany as it has in the United States. See Papier in 2 Maunz/Dürig, Art. 14, Rdnr. 291-450, (arguing (Rdnr. 449) for a test based upon the severity of the restriction (cf. Pennsylvania Coal Co. v. Mahon, 260 U.S. 393 (1922))); Leisner, supra note 134, Rdnr. 148-52 (arguing that such a test should be complemented by a special concern for those made to bear an undue share of the total burden ("Sonderopfertheorie")).

[137] See, e.g., 4 BVerfGE 7, 17 (1954) (upholding a special assessment for relief of the troubled iron, steel, and coal industries). Compare the dictum that the state of Hesse could demand free copies of all books published there in the interest of improving its library – so long as the burden of doing so was not disproportionate to the profitability of the publication. 58 BVerfGE 137, 144-52 (1981). See id. at 144 (explaining that, like a tax, the law imposed no duty to convey a *particular* piece of property to the government). See also Hesse, supra note 16, Rdnr. 447 (arguing that taxation is the "open flank" of the property guarantee). An income tax that does not leave the taxpayer enough resources to cover minimal living expenses, however, offends the right to free development of personality guaranteed by Art. 2(1). BVerfG, Judgment of Sept. 25, 1992, Case No. 2 BvL 5/91, 1992 NJW 3153.

[138] 45 BVerfGE 297, 335 (1977).

needed.[139] Property thus may be condemned only when and to the
extent necessary. The Court justified this conclusion in the latter
case by a narrow interpretation of the explicit term "public weal,"[140]
in the former by application of the more general principles of
proportionality and least burdensome means which – as we have
seen[141] – the Court has found implicit in the rule of law.[142]

B. Limitations

Less familiar to those versed in U.S. law than the restrictions on
actual takings imposed by Article 14(3) are the limitations on regulation imposed by the assurance in Article 14(1) that "property . . . [is]
guaranteed." The provision acknowledging the lawmakers' authority
to determine the "content and limits" of property has not been taken to
place property rights wholly at legislative disposal; the property
guarantee is more than a mere Gesetzesvorbehalt. On the other
hand, the further provisions that "property imposes duties" and that
"[i]ts use shall also serve the public weal" make clear that property
rights are by no means absolute.[143] Not surprisingly in light of the

---

[139] 38 BVerfGE 175, 179-85 (1974).

[140] See id. at 180-81; Leisner, supra note 134, Rdnr. 170.

[141] See the general discussion in chapter 1 supra.

[142] See 45 BVerfGE at 335; Papier in 2 Maunz/Dürig, Art. 14, Rdnr. 507-09. See
also Art. 15 GG, which authorizes nationalization of land, natural resources, and
means of production by statute, subject to compensation in accordance with Art.
14(3). Art. 15 neither requires socialization nor impedes privatization of existing
public enterprises (see 12 BVerfGE 354, 363-64 (1961) (upholding the sale of a majority of shares in the Volkswagen firm)); whether "means of production" includes
such service industries as insurance and banking is disputed (see Helmut
Rittstieg in 1 AK-GG, Art. 14-15, Rdnr. 241 (giving an affirmative answer); Maunz
in 2 Maunz/-Dürig, Art. 15, Rdnr. 15 (contra)). Although authority to acquire
private property for purposes of government enterprise seems implicit in the condemnation provisions of Art. 14 (see id., Rdnr. 2), a separate provision was thought
desirable because socialization represented a "structural change in the economic
constitution." See 1 JöR (n.F.) at 154-55, 156 (remarks of Delegate Schmid); Maunz,
supra, Rdnr. 5; Rittstieg, supra, Rdnr. 229 (arguing that Art. 15 frees the
lawmakers from any implication that Art. 14 requires perpetuation of a free-
enterprise economy). With the exception of insignificant efforts under a socialist
constitution in force in Hesse when the Basic Law was adopted, no use has ever been
made of this provision. See id., Rdnr. 226.

[143] These clauses are viewed as concrete applications of the general Sozialstaat
principle of Art. 20(1) and 28(1). They were derived from more intrusive limitations in Art. 153-155 of the Weimar Constitution of 1919, in which social provisions were far more prominent. See Hans Schneider, Die Reichsverfassung vom
11. August 1919, in 1 Handbuch des Staatsrechts 85, Rdnr. 37-38 (1987). Whether
they create directly enforceable obligations or merely reinforce the legislature's
ability to define and limit property rights remains disputed, but they have played a
significant role in the interpretation of ordinary law. See Hasso Hoffmann,

competing public and private interests recognized by the Basic Law itself, the Constitutional Court has applied a balancing test in determining the permissible scope of limitations on property: Like condemnation measures, definitions and limitations of property must conform with the proportionality principle.[144]

As in the United States, the ownership of property does not include the right to cause a public nuisance; the state may prevent mining companies from depleting groundwater supplies[145] and destroy dogs suspected of rabies.[146] But the social duties of property in Germany, like various public interests in this country, justify limitations that go far beyond the simple case of preventing affirmative harm to others. Renters may be protected from unusual or sudden rent increases[147] as well as against eviction[148] and the diversion of rental property to other uses.[149] Farm and forest lands may be protected against sales that appear detrimental to the interests of agriculture or forestry.[150] For the well-being of the wine industry, the legislature may forbid the growing of grapes on unsuitable soil.[151] To promote recreation it may establish associations to administer private fishing rights and distribute the profits to their former owners.[152] To assure a safe and adequate public water supply it may go so far as to abolish private rights to the use of groundwater, so long as landowners are given a grace period in which to phase out existing uses.[153] To promote industrial peace and democracy it may give workers the right to participate in management decisions (codetermination)[154] – but so far, at least, only because the owners

---

Grundpflichten und Grundrechte , 5 Handbuch des Staatsrechts 321, Rdnr. 18, 42-43.

[144] See, e.g., 21 BVerfGE 150, 154-55 (1967).

[145] 10 BVerfGE 89, 112-14 (1959).

[146] 20 BVerfGE 351, 355-62 (1966). See also 25 BVerfGE 112, 117-21 (1969) (upholding a prohibition of construction on dike lands). Cf. Mugler v. Kansas, 123 U.S. 623, 661-72 (1887); Miller v. Schoene, 276 U.S. 272 (1928). On the issue of floodplain zoning in this country see Joseph Sax, Takings, Private Property and Public Rights, 81 Yale L.J. 149 (1971).

[147] 37 BVerfGE 132, 139-43 (1974); 71 BVerfGE 230, 246-51 (1985). Cf. Block v. Hirsch, 256 U.S. 135 (1921).

[148] 68 BVerfGE 361, 367-71 (1985).

[149] 38 BVerfGE 348, 370-71 (1975).

[150] 21 BVerfGE 73, 82-85 (1967); 21 BVerfGE 87, 90-91 (1967); 21 BVerfGE 102, 104-05 (1967).

[151] 21 BVerfGE 150, 154-60 (1967).

[152] 70 BVerfGE 191, 199-213 (1985).

[153] 58 BVerfGE 300, 338-53 (1981). Cf. Goldblatt v. Town of Hempstead, 369 U.S. 590 (1962).

[154] 50 BVerfGE 290, 339-52 (1979) (stressing the social function and the impersonal nature of shareholder interests in industrial facilities). Several Länder constitutions specifically guarantee workers the right of codetermination. E.g., Verfassung des Landes Hessen vom 1. Dezember 1946, GVBl. S. 229, Art. 37; Ver-

retain ultimate control.[155] It may even redefine the balance of public
and private interests in copyrighted material retroactively, by
shortening the statutory period of protection of already copyrighted
works from 50 to 25 years.[156]

At the same time, however, the Constitutional Court has found in
the general property guarantee substantive limits on regulation reminiscent of those imposed by our Supreme Court during the *Lochner*
era. The public interest in protection of renters cannot justify generally depriving owners of the right to terminate garden leases[157] or to
recapture rented premises for their own residential use.[158] The
public interest in preserving a viable agricultural economy cannot
justify prohibiting the purchase of agricultural land for investment
purposes,[159] the breakup of large holdings as such,[160] or the use of
trademarked place names on wine bottles.[161]

Of particular interest are decisions concluding, despite initial
holdings to the contrary,[162] that government benefits may constitute
property for purposes of Article 14.[163] This conclusion is reminiscent
of our Supreme Court's position, in the line of cases beginning with
Goldberg v. Kelly,[164] that certain "entitlements" to state assistance
are protected by the due process clauses. The test for determining
which benefits qualify as property mirrors the Supreme Court's
insistence that the law give the claimant a right rather than leaving

---

fassung für das Land Nordrhein-Westfalen vom 28. Juni 1950, GS NW 100 S. 3,
Art. 26.

[155] 50 BVerfGE at 351. See Papier in 2 Maunz/Dürig, Art. 14, Rdnr. 430 (arguing
that the power to decide how property is to be used is central to Art. 14 and thus that
the owners must retain the last word). Cf. Trustees of Dartmouth College v.
Woodward, 17 U.S. 518 (1819).

[156] 31 BVerfGE 275, 284-85, 291-92 (1971). Retroactive redefinition of the date on
which the period of protection began to run, however, was held impermissible. Id. at
292-95.

[157] 52 BVerfGE 1, 29-40 (1979). See also 87 BVerfGE 114, 135-51 (1992) (permitting
such a limitation in the case of gardens designated in an official land use plan but
finding the accompanying rent limitation too restrictive).

[158] 68 BVerfGE 361, 374-75 (1985).

[159] 21 BVerfGE 73, 85-86 (1967).

[160] 26 BVerfGE 215, 221-28 (1969).

[161] 51 BVerfGE 193, 216-21 (1979).

[162] E.g., 2 BVerfGE 380, 399-403 (1953) (compensation for victims of Nazi
wrongs). Property, said the Court, did not include "claims that the state affords its
citizens by statute in fulfillment of its duty to provide for their welfare," for if it did
welfare laws could never be repealed. Id. at 402.

[163] E.g., 16 BVerfGE 94, 111-18 (1963) (retirement benefits); 53 BVerfGE 257, 289-
94 (1980) (same); 69 BVerfGE 272, 298-306 (1985) (health insurance). For justification of this development see Hesse, supra note 16, Rdnr. 443-45.

[164] 397 U.S. 254 (1970).

the matter to official discretion,[165] but the German cases are more restrictive; the benefits must also be based upon the claimant's own contributions and designed to provide minimum conditions for survival.[166]

The German decisions, however, do not merely insist upon a fair hearing before individuals are deprived of benefits that qualify as property. It is true that the Constitutional Court has found a requirement of fair procedure implicit in the substantive property guarantee.[167] But the decisions sometimes protect welfare rights against unreasonable legislative impairment as well. In one case, for example, the Court held that a new rule doubling the waiting period required to qualify for unemployment benefits could not constitutionally be applied to persons who had already satisfied the original requirement.[168] This is a step our Court has been unwilling to take, although we have had difficulty explaining why. Perhaps the answer is that the legislature meant to limit only administrative and not leg-

---

[165] E.g., 63 BVerfGE 152, 174 (1983). Cf. Board of Regents v. Roth, 408 U.S. 564 (1972).

[166] See 69 BVerfGE 272, 300 (1985). See id. at 305-06 and 72 BVerfGE 9, 18-21 (1986) (respectively applying this test to conclude that rights to medical and unemployment insurance constituted property). Cf. Sniadach v. Family Finance Corp., 395 U.S. 337, 341-42 (1969) (limiting pretrial wage garnishment on due process grounds because garnishment of wages may "drive a wage-earning family to the wall").

[167] See, e.g., 46 BVerfGE 325, 333-37 (1977) (holding that transfer of property pursuant to judicial sale must be postponed to permit judicial inquiry into adequacy of the price); 53 BVerfGE 352, 358-61 (1980) (striking down an unreasonable burden imposed upon the landlord in showing that increased rent did not exceed the prevailing rate). Cf. 35 BVerfGE 348, 361-63 (1973) (finding a requirement of adequate opportunity for judicial review, including the provision of counsel in cases of poverty, implicit in the property provision). This approach is by no means restricted to the property field. See, e.g., note 218 infra (occupational freedom); Denninger, supra note 107, passim. Cf. Mapp v. Ohio, 367 U.S. 643 (1961), and Bivens v. Six Unknown Named Agents of the Federal Bureau of Narcotics, 403 U.S. 388 (1971) (both suggesting that judicial remedies may be implicit in substantive constitutional provisions).

[168] 72 BVerfGE 9, 22-25 (1986). As in the case of conventional property, limitations on existing rights are not forbidden outright. See, e.g., 53 BVerfGE 257, 308-11 (1980) (permitting application of a new provision for division of retirement benefits on divorce to persons married under the old scheme, subject to an extended hardship clause); 69 BVerfGE 272, 304-07 (1985) (upholding an increase in the cost of medical insurance for those already insured). Yet the Court has gone so far as to suggest that the property guarantee may require the state actually to increase benefits to counteract inflation, which reduces their real value. See 64 BVerfGE 87, 97-103 (1983) (holding that such adjustments need not be made annually). Contrast the Legal Tender Cases, 79 U.S. 457 (1871) (rejecting a due process challenge to the inflationary issue of paper money); Atkins v. United States, 556 F.2d 1028 (Ct. Cls. 1977) (concluding that the ban on reducing judicial salaries in Article III did not require cost of living increases).

islative withdrawal of benefits; the legislature is after all still free
under the U.S. cases to define the substantive scope of the right.[169]

Most interesting from the United States point of view is the 1971
decision of the Constitutional Court striking down a statute that authorized schools to use copyrighted material free of charge.[170] This
decision was not based upon impairment of preexisting rights conferred by statute or common law. Rather the Court seems to have
found the right to profit from the fruits of one's labors secured by the
Constitution itself: "In accord with the property guarantee the author
has in principle the right to claim compensation for the economic
value of his work . . . ."[171] In the United States the Constitution does
not create property; the due process and taking clauses protect only
against infringement of property rights created by other laws.[172] The
copyright decision seems to suggest that, like "liberty" in our due
process clauses,[173] property in the Basic Law has a dimension
independent of ordinary law. Article 14, the Court seems to be saying,
constitutionalizes the Lockean principle of *Pierson v. Post*.[174]

The text of the Basic Law lends support to this interpretation:
Property is not merely protected against "deprivation" or "taking," it
is "guaranteed." So does the constitutional purpose, as expounded by
the Court, of affording the individual a sphere of economic security in
order to reduce dependence on the state.[175] Of course the creator of
economic values does not have an unlimited right to exploit them.
The copyright decision itself, invoking the explicit legislative authority to determine the content and limits of property, acknowledged that
the author's interests would prevail only "insofar as the interests of
the general public do not take priority."[176] Indeed the same opinion
held that the public interest justified permitting schools to use copyrighted material without the author's consent so long as adequate

---

[169] For doubts as to whether an American legislature could bind itself not to
revoke a welfare program see Crenshaw v. United States, 134 U.S. 99, 104-08 (1890)
(permitting Congress to repeal a law providing tenure for federal employees);
Stone v. Mississippi, 101 U.S. 814, 815-20 (1880) (permitting modification of a
twenty-five-year charter to conduct a lottery on the ground that the state had no
power to promise not to exercise its police power).

[170] 31 BVerfGE 229 (1971).

[171] Id. at 243. See also id. at 240-41 (defining "the essential elements of copyright
as property within the meaning of the Constitution"); Rittstieg in 1 AK-GG, Art.
14/15, Rdnr. 110a. The Constitution of the Land of Hesse is explicit in this regard:
"The rights of authors, inventors, and artists shall enjoy the protection of the state."
Verfassung des Landes Hessen vom 1. Dezember 1946, GVBl. S. 229, Art. 46.

[172] See Board of Regents v. Roth, 408 U.S. 564, 577 (1972).

[173] See Ingraham v. Wright, 430 U.S. 651, 672-74 (1977) (right to bodily integrity).

[174] 3 Cai. R. 175 (N.Y. Sup. Ct. 1805); see John Locke, Second Treatise of Government 15 (Barnes & Noble ed. 1966).

[175] See text at note 116 supra. See also text at note 119 supra (noting the institutional aspect of the property guarantee).

[176] 31 BVerfGE at 243.

royalties were paid.[177] A later decision limited the applicability of Lockean theory by upholding a statute providing for state ownership of certain archeological discoveries,[178] and the Court in so holding seemed to say that the Constitution did not create property rights after all.[179] Whatever its current status or justification, however, the copyright case indicates one of several ways in which the German Constitutional Court has gone beyond current Supreme Court practice in the constitutional protection of property.[180]

III. OCCUPATIONAL FREEDOM

Article 12(1) codifies the occupational freedom once recognized by the Supreme Court in such cases as *Lochner*:

> All Germans have the right freely to choose their trade, occupation, or profession, their place of work, and their place of training. The practice of trades, occupations, and professions may be regulated by or pursuant to statute.

Like the right to property, occupational freedom is taken very seriously in Germany as an element of individual autonomy and an essential basis of other freedoms.[181] The right extends to preparation

---

[177] Id. at 242.

[178] 78 BVerfGE 205, 211-12 (1988). Cf. the English common law of treasure trove, noted in James Casner & W. Barton Leach, Cases and Text on Property 35 (3d ed. 1984).

[179] 78 BVerfGE at 211 (citing earlier cases): Art. 14(1) "guarantees only those rights which the owner already has." In the next breath, however, the Court acknowledged that the case was a special one: The mere opportunity to acquire an object by the largely fortuitous means of finding it was not a property right entitled to constitutional protection. Id. at 211-12.

[180] See generally Rittstieg in 1 AK-GG, Art. 14/15, Rdnr. 37 (concluding that the judges have become more protective of property interests since the early 1970s); Leisner, supra note 134, Rdnr. 102-17, 133-42 (arguing that the Court has done too little to protect property).

[181] See, e.g., 7 BVerfGE 377, 397 (1958):

> [Art. 12(1)] guarantees the individual more than just the freedom to engage independently in a trade. To be sure, the basic right aims at the protection of economically meaningful work, but it views work as a "vocation." Work in this sense is seen in terms of its relationship to the human personality as a whole: It is a relationship that shapes and completes the individual over a lifetime of devoted activity; it is the foundation of a person's existence through which that person simultaneously contributes to the total social product.

Cf. text at note 116 supra, discussing property.

for as well as exercise of an occupation.[182] Like property, it may be
limited basically only in accordance with statute.[183] Even statutory
limitations, moreover, have been subjected to sometimes demanding
scrutiny under the pervasive proportionality principle, and quite a
number of them have been struck down.

The leading case remains the germinal 1958 *Pharmacy* decision,[184] which established varying degrees of judicial review
("Stufentheorie") according to the severity of the intrusion. To begin
with, regulation of how a profession is practiced is easier to justify
than limitation of entry into the profession itself:

> The practice of an occupation may be restricted by reasonable
> regulations predicated on considerations of the common good. The
> freedom to choose an occupation, however, may be restricted only in-
> sofar as an especially important public interest compellingly
> requires . . . – [and] only to the extent that protection cannot be
> accomplished by a lesser restriction on freedom of choice.[185]

Moreover, "subjective" entry limitations such as educational requirements designed to protect the public from unqualified practitioners are easier to justify than "objective" ones irrelevant to individual ability; and the desire to protect existing practitioners from com-

---

In recent years our Supreme Court has not seen it that way. See, e.g.,
Williamson v. Lee Optical Co., 348 U.S. 483 (1955). Serious due process protection of
the right to a livelihood in the United States has been limited to instances in which
the individual's very existence was threatened, and then to a guarantee of fair
hearing. Sniadach v. Family Finance Corp., 395 U.S. 337 (1969).

[182] See, e.g., 33 BVerfGE 303 (1972) (striking down limits on admission to public
universities), discussed in the text at notes 211-18 infra.

[183] For decisions invalidating limitations on occupational freedom not adequately authorized by statute see, e.g., 22 BVerfGE 114, 119-23 (1967) (disqualification of attorney); 38 BVerfGE 373, 380-85 (1975) (ban on deposit boxes for prescrip-
tions in outlying areas); 41 BVerfGE 251, 259-66 (1976) (expulsion from vocational
school); 43 BVerfGE 79, 89-92 (1976) (ban on representation of codefendants by
members of same law firm); 54 BVerfGE 224, 232-36 (1980) (ban on doctor's discussing disciplinary proceedings with patients); 63 BVerfGE 266, 288-97 (1983)
(exclusion of Communist from bar); 65 BVerfGE 248, 258-64 (1983) (requirement
that price be marked on goods offered for sale). The Court has also made clear,
however, that limitations may be based upon customary law existing before the
adoption of the Basic Law in 1949. 15 BVerfGE 226, 233 (1962). See also Scholz in 1
Maunz/Dürig, Art. 12, Rdnr. 315-16. Moreover, the Art. 19(1) requirement that any
statute that restricts a basic right must name it has been held inapplicable to most
cases of occupational freedom on the less than overwhelming ground that Art. 12(1)
authorizes the practice of professions to be regulated ("geregelt") rather than restricted ("eingeschränkt"). 64 BVerfGE 72, 79-81 (1983); see the discussion of Art.
19(1) in chapter 4 supra.

[184] 7 BVerfGE 377 (1958).

[185] Id. at 405.

petition, the Court said, could "never" justify an entry restriction.[186] On the basis of this calculus the Constitutional Court has achieved results reminscent of those reached by the Supreme Court during the *Lochner* period.[187]

As under the reign of *Lochner*, a great many limitations of occupational freedom have been upheld – some of them rather intrusive. Compulsory retirement ages may be set for chimney sweeps[188] and midwives.[189] The sale of headache remedies may be restricted to pharmacists,[190] and the latter may be forbidden to own more than one store.[191] Shops may be required to close on Saturday afternoons, Sundays, holidays, and in the evening;[192] nocturnal baking may be prohibited.[193] The legislature may outlaw the erection or expansion of flour mills[194] and limit the amount of flour produced.[195] The state may monopolize building insurance[196] and employment agencies.[197] It may require employers to hire the handicapped,[198] limit the

---

[186] Id. at 406-08. The language of Art.12(1) might be taken to suggest that the mere exercise of a profession was subject to unlimited legislative regulation, the choice of profession to none at all. Citing the difficulty of drawing clear lines between choice and exercise, the explicit authorization to regulate access to certain professions in Art. 74 cl. 19, and the debates of the constitutional convention, the Court found that choice and exercise of an occupation constituted poles of a continuum: Art. 12(1) guaranteed a unitary freedom of occupational activity that was subject at any point to reasonable regulation, but what was reasonable varied according to the severity of the limitation. See id. at 400-03. For approval of this "realistic" approach see Rüdiger Breuer, Freiheit des Berufs, 6 Handbuch des Staatsrechts 877, Rdnr. 32-33; for the argument that it should be extended to other basic rights (such as artistic and academic freedoms) guaranteed without express allowance for legislative restriction see Martin Kriele, Grundrechte und demokratischer Gestaltungsspielraum, 5 Handbuch des Staatsrechts 101, Rdnr. 69-75.

[187] See The Second Century, chs. 2, 4, 5. The German decisions are considered in detail in Fritz Ossenbühl, Economic and Occupational Rights, in Paul Kirchhof & Donald P. Kommers (eds.), Germany and its Basic Law 251 (1993).

[188] 1 BVerfGE 264, 274-75 (1952).

[189] 9 BVerfGE 338, 344-48 (1959).

[190] 9 BVerfGE 73, 77-81 (1959).

[191] 17 BVerfGE 232, 238-46 (1964).

[192] 13 BVerfGE 237, 239-42 (1961).

[193] 23 BVerfGE 50, 56-60 (1968); 87 BVerfGE 363, 382-89 (1992).

[194] 25 BVerfGE 1, 10-23 (1968) (stressing that these limitations were a temporary response to a serious glut on the flour market).

[195] 39 BVerfGE 210, 225-37 (1975).

[196] 41 BVerfGE 205, 217-28 (1976) (inferring from the limitation of federal legislative competence to "private" insurance in Art. 74 cl. 11 GG that provisions respecting public insurance were not to be measured against Art. 12(1)). For criticism of this decision see Breuer, Die staatliche Berufsregelung und Wirtschaftslenkung, 6 Handbuch des Staatsrechts 957, Rdnr. 65.

[197] 21 BVerfGE 245, 249-60 (1967).

[198] 57 BVerfGE 139, 158-65 (1981).

number of notaries,[199] and require them to serve welfare applicants without charge.[200]

At the same time, throughout its history the Constitutional Court has struck down as unwarranted infringments on occupational freedom an impressive array of restrictions that would pass muster without question in the United States today. The state may not limit the number of drugstores on the ground that there are already enough of them[201] or license taxicabs only in cases of special need.[202] It may not require vending machines to be shut down after stores are closed[203] or require barbers who close on Saturday afternoon to shut down on Monday morning too.[204] It may ban neither door-to-door sales of veterinary medicines[205] nor C.O.D. shipments of live animals.[206] It may not require that retailers be competent to practice their trade,[207] forbid doctors ever to specialize in more than one field or to perform services outside their specialties,[208] or ban the collection of dead birds for scientific purposes.[209] Finally, in perfect contrast to the decision that sealed the death of economic due process in the United States, it may not forbid the manufacture and sale of healthful food products on the ground that they might be confused with chocolate.[210]

---

[199] 17 BVerfGE 371, 376-81 (1964) (stressing the public functions that notaries performed).

[200] 69 BVerfGE 373, 378-81 (1985) (finding the burden trivial).

[201] 7 BVerfGE 377, 413-44 (1958). See also 86 BVerfGE 28, 41-44 (1992) (alternative holding) (similarly concluding that the state could not limit the number of persons certified to render expert opinions ("Sachverständigen"), even though certification was not a prerequisite for employment).

[202] 11 BVerfGE 168, 183-90 (1960). Cf. New State Ice Co. v. Liebmann, 285 U.S. 262 (1932).

[203] 14 BVerfGE 19, 22-25 (1962).

[204] 59 BVerfGE 336, 355-59 (1982).

[205] 17 BVerfGE 269, 274-80 (1964).

[206] 36 BVerfGE 47, 56-65 (1973).

[207] 19 BVerfGE 330, 336-42 (1965).

[208] 33 BVerfGE 125, 165-71 (1972).

[209] 61 BVerfGE 291, 317-19 (1982).

[210] 53 BVerfGE 135, 145-47 (1980). Cf. Carolene Products Co. v. United States, 323 U.S. 18 (1944). The German court conceded that more stringent measures respecting margarine might be permissible to preserve the viability of the crucial dairy industry (53 BVerfGE at 146), but the second *Carolene Products* decision was based on the danger of confusion alone (323 U.S. at 27-31).

The chocolate decision and others noted above demonstrate that, despite the suggestion of Scholz in 1 Maunz/Dürig, Art. 12, Rdnr. 322 that judicial review under Art. 12(1) has become less intensive than it was in the days of the drugstore case, it has by no means lost its bite. As recently as November 1992, for example, the Constitutional Court held that Art. 12(1) was infringed when licenses to practice law were denied or revoked on the ground that simultaneous employment in menial or commercial jobs was inconsistent with the integrity or image of the legal profession. 87 BVerfGE 287, 325-30 (1992). See also 75 BVerfGE 284 (1987) (striking down a

Here too, as in connection with familial rights and private schools, there are strong indications that the Basic Law may impose affirmative duties on government. The most notable decision is that in the so-called *Numerus Clausus* case,[211] where, despite insisting it was not deciding whether Article 12(1) required the state to set up institutions of higher learning, the Constitutional Court flatly declared that the right to obtain a professional education was worthless if the state did not provide one, and therefore that access to public education was not a matter of legislative grace. "In the field of education," said the Court, "the constitutional protection of basic rights is not limited to the function of protection from governmental intervention traditionally ascribed to basic liberty rights."[212]

While recognizing that financial constraints limit any constitutional duty to expand educational facilities and acknowledging the breadth of legislative discretion in this regard,[213] the Court has applied Article 12(1) in conjunction with the general equality provision of Article 3(1) and the Sozialstaat principle[214] to scrutinize with great care any restrictions on access by qualified applicants to

---

limitation on the issuance of licenses to insurance advisers). None of this is to say that there is actually more occupational freedom in West Germany than in the United States. Notwithstanding the lack of judicial interest in the area, legislators in this country seem less inclined to inhibit such freedom than their German counterparts, as Americans seem more mistrustful of government in general. In Chicago, for example, it is possible to buy groceries after two p.m. on Saturday; it is basically illegal in Germany.

[211] 33 BVerfGE 303 (1972).

[212] Id. at 330-32. "The more involved a modern state becomes in assuring the social security and cultural advancement of its citizens," the opinion added, "the more the complementary demand that participation in governmental services assume the character of a basic right will augment the initial postulate of safeguarding liberty from state intervention. This development is particularly important in the field of education." Id. See Scholz in 1 Maunz/Dürig, Art. 12, Rdnr. 63 (explaining that where the state has a practical monopoly (as it has of higher education in West Germany), exclusion comes close in practical effect to prohibition). For more critical views see Breuer, supra note 186, Rdnr. 76-79; Christian Starck, Die Verfassungsauslegung, 7 Handbuch des Staatsrechts 189, Rdnr. 28: "Whether all demands for opportunities for higher education should be met is a question the constitution does not answer." Unlike Art. 163(2) of the Weimar Constitution, Art. 12(1) is understood not to require the state to assure everyone employment. See Breuer, supra, Rdnr. 6-7, 73 (noting that the Weimar provision was treated as merely hortatory and never enforced).

[213] See 33 BVerfGE at 332-36.

[214] See id. at 331. It is common practice for the Constitutional Court to base a decision on the combined effect of two or more provisions. See also Denninger in AK-GG, vor Art. 1, Rdnr. 23-25 (explaining that, although the Sozialstaat principle is not generally directly enforceable by private suit, it places upon the state "shared responsibility for the creation and maintenance of the factual conditions necessary for the exercise of freedoms guaranteed by the Bill of Rights"), and the general discussion of the Sozialstaat principle in chapter 1 supra.

existing facilities. A university in one state is forbidden to discriminate against residents of another.[215] Even relatively poor grades are
no excuse for excluding applicants who satisfy minimum standards
when there is unused capacity,[216] and the Court has gone so far as to
review the adequacy of teaching loads in order to determine whether
there is room for additional students.[217] Thus the judges exercise a
substantial degree of supervision over university administration in
the interest of equal access to professional education.[218]

Closely related to the occupational freedom guaranteed by Article
12(1) is the requirement of Article 33(5) that public employment be
regulated "with due regard to the traditional principles of the professional civil service." A major victory of the powerful civil servants'
lobby over Allied efforts at reform, this provision preserves to a significant extent the privileged position of the German civil servant. It has
also been defended as helping to ensure the competence and impar-
tiality of the public service.[219]

Article 33(5) requires only due regard ("Berücksichtigung") for
traditional principles, not unswerving adherence to them;[220] but they
have been given considerable weight in practice. One of these basic
principles is "suitable compensation" for public service, which has
led to invalidation of insufficient provisions for retirement benefits[221]
and to a requirement of extra pay for civil servants with children.[222]
The Court has also employed Article 33(5) to reinforce the conclusion
that other branches may not be given discretion to limit judicial

---

[215] See 33 BVerfGE at 351-56.

[216] 39 BVerfGE 258, 269-74 (1975).

[217] 54 BVerfGE 173, 191-207 (1980); 66 BVerfGE 155, 177-90 (1984). See also 85
BVerfGE 36 (1991).

[218] "At the cost of harsh public criticism, the Constitutional Court has transformed itself into a veritable ministry of education." Donald P. Kommers, The
Constitutional Jurisprudence of the Federal Republic of Germany 303 (1989). Cf. the
intensive control exercised by the Constitutional Court over other aspects of university administration in the interest of the academic freedom guaranteed by Art. 5(3),
chapter 4 supra. Like other substantive provisions, Art. 12(1) has also been read to
guarantee adequate procedures to assure vindication of the right itself. See, e.g., 39
BVerfGE 276, 294-301 (1975) (right to file a complaint protesting the rejection of an
application for university admission); 52 BVerfGE 380, 388-91 (1979) (right to warning as to the importance of answering questions during bar examination); 84
BVerfGE 34 (1991) (right to examine and challenge bar examination results).

[219] See Wolfgang Benz, Von der Besatzungsherrschaft zur Bundesrepublik 113-
16, 208-09 (1984); see also the discussion in chapter 3 supra.

[220] 3 BVerfGE 58, 137 (1953) (noting that an earlier draft of the provision would
have made traditional principles determinative ("maßgebend"). For criticism of
this conclusion see Maunz in 2 Maunz/Dürig, Art. 33, Rdnr. 58.

[221] 8 BVerfGE 1, 22-28 (1958); 11 BVerfGE 203, 210-17 (1960).

[222] 44 BVerfGE 249, 267-68, 279 (1977); 81 BVerfGE 363, 375-83 (1990) (both invoking Art. 33(5) in conjunction with Art. 6(1) and the Sozialstaat principle).

salaries[223] and to protect traditional prerogatives we might be inclined to think less significant: the right of judges, teachers, and professors to titles befitting their dignified positions.[224]

Not long ago all of this (with the exception of matters affecting judges, whose independence is guaranteed by Article III) would have been a matter of legislative grace in the United States under the privilege doctrine.[225] Even today it is difficult to see how a court in the United States could have reached any of the results just noted, since none of the provisions struck down by the German court involved indirect limitations on protected interests such as expression or religion.[226] Thus while Article 12(1) of the Basic Law specifically guarantees the freedom from state interference with private occupations that our Supreme Court once protected under the rubric of substantive due process, Article 33(5) goes beyond anything the Supreme Court ever did by affording significant substantive protections to public employees as well.

IV. LIFE, LIBERTY, AND PERSONALITY

A. Life and Liberty

Article 2(2) contains a general guarantee of life, bodily integrity, and personal liberty:

> Everyone has the right to life and to inviolability of the person [körperliche Unversehrtheit]. Personal liberty [die Freiheit der Person] shall be inviolable. These rights may be impinged upon only pursuant to statute [auf Grund eines Gesetzes].

The liberty protected by Article 2(2) is freedom from bodily restraint;[227] other liberties are protected by other provisions.

The last sentence of Article 2(2) should by now be familiar; only the legislature may authorize incursions on interests protected by this provision.[228] However, not every law suffices to justify physical

---

[223] 26 BVerfGE 79, 91-94 (1969) (also invoking the guarantee of judicial independence in Article 97(1)). See generally chapter 3 supra.

[224] 38 BVerfGE 1, 11-17 (1974) (judges); 62 BVerfGE 374, 382-91 (1982) (teachers); 64 BVerfGE 323, 351-66 (1983) (professors). See also 43 BVerfGE 154, 165-77 (1976) (holding that Article 33(5) required a hearing before dismissal even of probationary public workers).

[225] Cf. Holmes's famous comment in McAuliffe v. New Bedford, 155 Mass. 216, 220, 29 N.E. 517, 517 (1892), that "there is no constitutional right to be a policeman."

[226] Contrast Perry v. Sindermann, 408 U.S. 593 (1972).

[227] See Dürig in 1 Maunz/Dürig, Art. 2(2), Rdnr. 1, 49; Eberhard Grabitz, Freiheit der Person, 6 Handbuch des Staatsrechts 109, Rdnr. 4-6; 1 JöR (n.F.) at 63.

[228] See Dieter Lorenz, Recht auf Leben und körperliche Unversehrtheit, 6 Handbuch des Staatsrechts 3, Rdnr. 36; Grabitz, supra note 227, Rdnr. 17.

restraint or invasion of bodily integrity. Article 104 specifies a number of limitations on arrest and imprisonment.[229] Article 103 requires courts to afford a hearing, permits punishment only on the basis of preexisting statutes that afford fair warning, and forbids double jeopardy.[230] Article 102 abolishes the death penalty.[231] Article 19(2) draws the outer boundary of legislative restriction of any basic right: "In no case may the essential content of a basic right be encroached upon."

Despite early expectations, this last provision has played little part in the decisions.[232] It did form the principal basis of the Court's 1967 conclusion that a person could not be committed to a mental hospital for mere improvement ("Besserung"):

---

[229] Among other things, any person arrested or otherwise taken into custody is entitled to a preliminary judicial hearing before the end of the following day (Art. 104(2), (3)). Physical or mental mistreatment of persons in custody is prohibited by Art. 104(1). See generally Grabitz, supra note 227, Rdnr. 20-30.

[230] For the dimensions of the hearing requirement see chapter 3 supra. The most interesting decisions respecting double jeopardy have involved the difficult question whether a continuing refusal to perform military or alternative service constitutes one offense or several for purposes of Art. 103(3). In 1968 the Second Senate of the Constitutional Court concluded that an acknowledged conscientious objector could be punished only once for disobeying repeated orders to report for nonmilitary duties, since he had made a single decision not to satisfy his single obligation to render 18 months of service. 23 BVerfGE 191, 202-06 (1968). Two years later the First Senate held that a soldier whose claim to conscientious-objector status had not yet been resolved could be disciplined separately under military law each time he defied an order to perform a particular task. 28 BVerfGE 264 (1970). Not content to point out that the explicit double-jeopardy ban applied only to punishments under the general criminal laws ("die allgemeinen Strafgesetze") and that the rule of law did not require so strict a standard (id. at 276-79), the Court also attempted to distinguish the two cases on the facts: The soldier's single decision to disobey orders could not be considered because at the time of his refusal it had not yet been determined to be genuine, and he had declined to participate in several distinct exercises. Id. at 279-80. See also id. at 279 (pointedly observing that the other panel's decision had been contrary to the overwhelming weight of academic opinion when rendered); 78 BVerfGE 391, 396 (1988), where a later generation of Second Senate Justices adhered to the result reached by their predecessors without reaching the double-jeopardy question.

[231] See the response of Delegate Wagner in the Parliamentary Council to the suggestion that this provision be omitted from the Basic Law:

Human life is something sacred. . . . Capital punishments have been imposed and carried out among us to such a terrible extent that no other people has such cause to make a clear decision against the death penalty.

Sten. Ber. at 187-88. For the suggestion that adoption of this provision implied an equal obligation to protect unborn life see id. at 214 (Delegate Wessel).

[232] For the expectations see Dürig in 1 Maunz/Dürig, Art. 2(1), Rdnr. 31-32, 62-63; for the results see Klaus Stern, Idee und Elemente eines Systems der Grundrechte, 5 Handbuch des Staatsrechts 45, Rdnr. 85-86.

It is not among the tasks of the state to "improve" its citizens. The state therefore has no right to deprive them of freedom simply to "improve" them, when they pose no danger to themselves or to others . . . . Since the purpose of improving an adult cannot constitute a sufficient ground for the deprivation of personal liberty, [the statute] encroaches upon the essential content of the basic right . . . .[233]

The same opinion went on, however, to state an alternative ground that, because of its greater stringency, has made it unnecessary in most cases to inquire whether a restriction invades the "essential content" of a basic right. Quite apart from the limitation imposed by Article 19(2), the institutionalization of an individual who endangered neither himself nor others offended "the principle of proportionality [Verhältnismäßigkeit], which is rooted in the rule of law."[234]

We have encountered the proportionality principle before. The time has come to explore it in greater detail.[235]

The idea is a venerable one, suggested in Magna Carta and more generally by Blackstone.[236] It was developed further by thinkers of the German Enlightenment, most notably by Carl Gottlieb Svarez, principal draftsman of the Allgemeines Landrecht der Preußischen Staaten, a monumental codification of Prussian law that took effect in 1794. In a series of lectures delivered two years earlier, Svarez had plainly stated two distinct proportionality requirements. First, the state was justified in restricting the liberty of the individual "only to the extent necessary for the liberty and security of others"; second, the evil to be prevented must be substantially greater than the attendant harm to individual liberty.[237] Thus Svarez insisted on proportionality both between ends and means and between costs and benefits; both aspects of the principle are reflected in the jurisprudence of the Constitutional Court.

---

[233] 22 BVerfGE 180, 218-20 (1967).

[234] Id. at 220.

[235] For insights into the origins of the proportionality principle I am indebted to a splendid paper by George Frumkin, A Survey of the Sources of the Principle of Proportionality in German Law (copy in author's file). See also Klaus Stern, Zur Entstehung und Ableitung des Übermaßverbots, in Peter Badura & Rupert Scholz (eds.), Wege und Verfahren des Verfassungslebens: Festschrift für Peter Lerche 165, 168-69 (1993).

[236] See Magna Carta 19 (G. R. C. Davis (ed.) 1963) (requiring that criminal punishment be proportional to the offense); 1 Blackstone, Commentaries *125 (stating as a political principle that civil liberty consisted in "natural liberty so far restrained by human laws (and no farther) as is necessary and expedient for the general advantage of the public"). For suggestions of Roman origins see Stern, supra note 235, at 167-68, and authorities cited.

[237] See Carl Gottlieb Svarez, Vorträge über Recht und Staat 486-87 (Hermann Conrad & Gerd Kleinheyer (eds.) 1960).

Not surprisingly, the first of these principles found its way into the Allgemeines Landrecht, which made it the duty of the administration (Polizei) to take *necessary* measures ("[d]ie nöthigen Anstalten") to preserve the public peace, order, and security.[238] Decisions of the Prussian Oberverwaltungsgericht (Supreme Administrative Court) invalidating administrative actions under this provision were legion. In 1882, for example, that court struck down a prohibition on obstructing the view of a national monument on the ground that it served none of the purposes listed in the statute;[239] four years later it found the closing of a general store an unnecessarily intrusive sanction for illegally serving alcohol on the premises.[240]

Even before adoption of the Basic Law, courts and commentators displayed a tendency to extend the necessity requirement beyond the confines of the statute that codified it, treating it in substance as a general principle of administrative law.[241] Necessity does not seem to have been viewed as a constitutional requirement, however, until after the Second World War.[242] At that point it began to appear in Länder constitutions as a limitation on legislation; and Länder decisions applying these provisions came to interpret them as incorporating Svarez's second principle too. It was not enough that the means the legislature had selected were necessary in order to attain its legitimate goal; the burdens the statute imposed had also to be proportional to the benefits it was designed to achieve.[243]

---

[238] Allgemeines Landrecht für die Preußischen Staaten, pt. II, tit. 17, § 10 (1794). § 79 of the 1787 draft of the same statute had stated the principle as a limitation on legislature and administration alike: "State statutes and orders [may] restrict the rights and liberties of the citizen no further than their purpose requires." The statute itself, however, was subject to legislative repeal. See Dieter Grimm, Deutsche Verfassungsgeschichte 1776-1866, pp. 51-52 (1988).

[239] 9 PrOVG 353 (1882).

[240] 13 PrOVG 424 (1886).

[241] See Stern, supra note 235, at 168-69.

[242] See Anschütz, supra note 28, at 700-01 (dismissing Art. 151(2) WRV, which provided that legal compulsion could be employed only in order to protect the rights of others or to achieve overriding public interests ("im Dienst überrangender Forderungen des Gemeinwohls") as a merely programmatic provision whose effectuation was entrusted to the legislature).

[243] The Bavarian Constitution, for example, expressly permits fundamental rights to be limited only when public safety, morals, health, or welfare imperatively require ("zwingend erfordern"). See Verfassung des Freistaates Bayern vom 2. Dezember 1946, BayRS 100-1-S, Art. 98; Stern, supra note 235, at 171-72, and cases cited. Similar provisions appear in the constitutions of Bremen and Rheinland-Pfalz. See Landesverfassung der Freien Hansestadt Bremen vom 21. Oktober 1947, SaBremR 100-a-1, Art. 3; Verfassung für Rheinland-Pfalz vom 18. Mai 1947, VBl. S. 209, Art. 1. The newly adopted constitutions of Brandenburg and Saxony-Anhalt, in contrast, speak not of necessity but of proportionality ("Verhältnismäßigkeit"). See Verfassung des Landes Brandenburg vom 20. August 1992, GV BB 298, Art. 5(2); Verfassung des Landes Sachsen-Anhalt vom 16. Juli 1992, GVBl S. 600, Art. 20(2). For careful documentation of the expansion of the

Unlike these state constitutions, the Basic Law nowhere mentions a general proportionality principle.[244] From the very first, however, the Constitutional Court appeared to assume its existence at the constitutional level. The first decisions did so in a very offhand way, without any attempt to explain where the principle was to be found in the Basic Law.[245] Some later decisions seemed to find it implicit in the basic rights themselves, or in the provisions permitting legislatures to limit them.[246] One prominent commentator attributed it to the guarantee of "essential content" in Article 19(2).[247] As the quotation above suggests, proportionality is now commonly understood to be one aspect of the Rechtsstaat principle implicit in the various provisions of Article 20 and made explicit as to the Länder in Article 28(1).[248] Just what proportionality has to do with the rule of law the Court has never explained; as a leading student of the subject noted some years ago, one can distill the one from the other only if one first pours it in.[249]

As explained in chapter 1, the proportionality principle requires today that limitations of fundamental rights, even when specifically authorized by the Basic Law, meet three criteria, all of which were explicit or implicit in Svarez's lectures of 1791-92: They must be adapted ("geeignet") to the attainment of a legitimate purpose, neces-

---

term "proportionality" (formerly virtually a synonym for necessity) to include a balance of costs and benefits after World War II see Lothar Hirschberg, Der Grundsatz der Verhältnismäßigkeit 2-19 (1981).

244 Art. 21(4) of the original draft prepared for the Parliamentary Council at Herrenchiemsee would expressly have codified the necessity requirement: "Restriction of the basic rights is permissible only by statute and only on condition that the public safety, morals, or health imperatively so requires." See Herrenchiemsee Bericht, in 2 Akten und Protokolle at 504, 582.

245 See, e.g., 2 BVerfGE 266, 280-81 (1953); 3 BVerfGE 383, 399 (1954); 7 BVerfGE 377, 407 (1958).

246 See, e.g., 17 BVerfGE 108, 117 (1963): "Respect for the basic right of bodily integrity demands respect across the board for the principle of proportionality in passing upon the validity of incursions into this right." For defense of this position see Philip Kunig, Das Rechtsstaatsprinzip 350-62 (1986); Starck, supra note 212, Rdnr. 39 (stressing that under Art. 1(3) it is of the essence of the basic rights that they also limit legislation).

247 See Dürig in 1 Maunz/Dürig, Art. 2(1), Rdnr. 31-32, 62-63.

248 See also 30 BVerfGE 1, 20 (1970); Hermann Hill, Verfassungsrechtliche Gewährleistungen gegenüber der staatlichen Strafgewalt, 6 Handbuch des Staatsrechts 1305, Rdnr. 21; Stern, supra note 235, at 165, 173-74 (explaining that proportionality is an element of justice ("Gerechtigkeit"), which in turn is an element of the rule of law). Proportionality is said to have attained constitutional rank in Austria and Switzerland too on the basis of similar arguments. See id. at 169 and authorities cited.

249 See Peter Lerche, Übermaß und Verfassungsrecht 32 (1961). See also id. at 29-53 (criticizing other conventional efforts to find an anchor for proportionality in the Basic Law).

sary ("erforderlich") to that end, and not excessive ("unzumutbar") in comparison to the benefits to be achieved.[250] Necessity is narrowly defined: As in certain instances of strict scrutiny in the United States, the legislature must select the least burdensome means of achieving its goal.[251]

Applying these requirements, the Constitutional Court has afforded intensive scrutiny to the reasonableness of measures impinging upon the interests protected by Article 2(2). Pretrial incarceration is permitted only when necessary to investigate the case[252] or when there is a grave risk of recurrence,[253] and it may not last too long.[254] Persons accused of crime may be institutionalized to determine their mental competency[255] and subjected to an electroencephalogram[256] but not to a spinal tap in connection with a relatively minor offense.[257] One may not be punished for another's wrongs,[258] put on trial when dangerously ill,[259] or evicted when suffering from depression.[260]

Article 2(2) has also been the most prolific source of decisions recognizing the affirmative duty of the state to protect the individual from harm inflicted by third parties. The critical case was the famous 1975 abortion decision, which produced a result the polar opposite of that our Supreme Court had reached two years earlier in *Roe v. Wade*: Far from giving the woman a right to terminate her pregnancy, the Basic Law demanded in principle that abortion be made a crime; the German constitution required what our Constitution forbade.[261]

---

[250] See, e.g., 78 BVerfGE 232, 245-47 (1988); see also chapter 1 supra.

[251] See 78 BVerfGE at 245. Cf. Shelton v. Tucker, 364 U.S. 479, 488 (1960); Dean Milk Co. v. Madison, 340 U.S. 349, 354 (1951). This general formulation does not exclude varying levels of scrutiny according to the seriousness and intimacy of the intrusion. See Denninger in 1 AK-GG, vor Art. (1), Rdnr. 14; text at notes 184-86 supra, discussing the *Pharmacy* case.

[252] 19 BVerfGE 342, 347-53 (1965).

[253] 35 BVerfGE 185, 190-92 (1973).

[254] 20 BVerfGE 45, 49-51 (1966).

[255] 2 BVerfGE 121, 122-23 (1953).

[256] 17 BVerfGE 108, 114-15 (1963).

[257] 16 BVerfGE 194, 198-203 (1963). See also 17 BVerfGE 108, 117-20 (1963).

[258] Cf. 20 BVerfGE 323, 330-36 (1966) (finding a violation of the general freedom of action guaranteed by Art. 2(1) in the punishment of a faultless association, which had no rights protected by Art. 2(2)).

[259] 51 BVerfGE 324, 343-50 (1979). This decision was based not on fair trial considerations but on the danger to the defendant's health.

[260] 52 BVerfGE 214, 219-22 (1979).

[261] See 39 BVerfGE 1 (1975); Roe v. Wade, 410 U.S. 113 (1973). See also Donald Kommers, Liberty and Community in Constitutional Law: The Abortion Cases in Comparative Perspective, 1985 B.Y.U. L. Rev. 371; Winfried Brugger, A Constitutional Duty to Outlaw Abortion? A Comparative Analysis of the American and German Abortion Decisions, 36 JöR (n.F.) 49 (1987).

Two conclusions at variance with the prevailing American understanding inform the German decision. The first is that life begins before birth,[262] the second that fundamental rights are not simply a guarantee against governmental intrusion.[263] Article 1(1) makes the latter point clear with regard to the right of human dignity, which the state is expressly directed to "respect and protect."[264] Article 1(1) was invoked along with Article 2(2) in the abortion case,[265] and since the more specific Bill of Rights provisions are commonly viewed at least in part as concrete aspects of human dignity,[266] the "protect and respect" clause – along with the "objective value" thesis first developed in determining the effect of the free-speech guarantee on private law, which the Court expressly mentioned – very likely influenced the interpretation of Article 2(2) as well.[267]

---

[262] See 39 BVerfGE at 37-42. In reaching this conclusion the Court relied heavily on the records of the constitutional convention, which despite some contrary evidence included a committee report expressly declaring that an explicit provision protecting unborn children had been rejected only because of the prevailing understanding that the right to "life" already included them. The opinion said only that life began no later than fourteen days after conception, 39 BVerfGE at 37; for an argument that it begins at conception see Lorenz, supra note 228, Rdnr. 11-14.

[263] 39 BVerfGE at 42-51. Contrast DeShaney v. Winnebago County Department of Social Services, 489 U.S. 189, 195-96 (1989): "[N]othing in the language [or history] of the Due Process Clause . . . requires the State to protect the life, liberty, and property of its citizens against invasion by private actors." See also chapter 1 supra.

[264] In one of its very first opinions, while taking a narrow view of the protective duty imposed by Art. 1(1), the Constitutional Court expressly acknowledged it: "The second sentence [of Art. 1(1) . . . obliges the state indeed to the positive act of 'protection,' but that means protection against attacks on human dignity by other people, such as humiliation, stigmatization, persecution, ostracism, and the like – not protection from material want." 1 BVerfGE 97, 104 (1951) (conceding that the social-state principle of Art. 20(1) required the legislature to assure "tolerable living conditions" for the needy but insisting that "only the legislature can do what is essential to make the social state a reality" (id. at 105)). Later decisions respecting the government's obligation under more specific Bill of Rights provisions to support or provide education (see text at notes 105-13, 211-18 supra) have cast doubt upon this narrow interpretation. See generally Denninger in 1 AK-GG, vor Art. 1, Rdnr. 23-28.

[265] 39 BVerfGE at 41, 51.

[266] See Art. 1(2) GG, declaring that the German people acknowledge human rights *because of* the inviolability of human dignity; Dürig in 1 Maunz/Dürig Art. 1, Rdnr. 10, 55; Lorenz, supra note 228, Rdnr. 4-5.

[267] See Dürig in 1 Maunz/Dürig Art. 1, Rdnr. 102; 39 BVerfGE at 41-42 (invoking the "objective value" principle in explaining why it was unnecessary to decide whether an unborn child had enforceable rights of its own). See also chapter 4 supra (discussing the *Lüth* decision); Grabitz, supra note 227, Rdnr. 14-15 (explaining the state's affirmative duty to protect life on the basis of objective values). The connection between Art. 2(2) and the express duty to protect human dignity was emphasized when the Court unanimously reaffirmed the duty to protect unborn life in 1993. See 88 BVerfGE 203, 251 (1993).

There were dissents in the abortion case, but the dissenting Justices conceded the state's duty to protect fetal life, arguing only that criminal penalties were not an indispensable means to this end.[268] Subsequent decisions have affirmed the state's constitutional duty to protect against the hazards of nuclear power plants,[269] aircraft noise,[270] terrorism,[271] and chemical weapons.[272] Acutely aware of the danger of constitutionalizing ordinary tort law as well as other matters basically committed to other branches, the Court has afforded legislative and executive organs great leeway in determining how to fulfill their protective duties; in none of these cases did it find government action insufficient to protect life and limb.[273] Moreover, even the abortion decision permitted destruction of the fetus for medical, eugenic, ethical, and social reasons,[274] and there is reason to think that in practice the "social" exception may largely have swallowed the rule.[275]

---

[268] See 39 BVerfGE at 68-95 (Rupp-von Brünneck and Simon, JJ., dissenting). See also Denninger in 1 AK-GG, vor Art. 1, Rdnr. 33-34.

[269] 49 BVerfGE 89, 140-44 (1978) (*Kalkar*); 53 BVerfGE 30, 57-69 (1979) (*Mülheim-Kärlich*).

[270] 56 BVerfGE 54, 73-86 (1981).

[271] 46 BVerfGE 160, 164-65 (1977) (*Schleyer*). Cf. 55 BVerfGE 349, 364-68 (1980) (involving the adequacy of German efforts to secure the release of the aged Nazi leader Rudolf Hess from Allied imprisonment).

[272] 77 BVerfGE 170, 214-16, 222-30 (1987). See also the Court's dictum, in the course of finding a ban on night work that applied only to women a violation of the gender equality provision of Art. 3(3), that Art. 2(2) in connection with the social-state principle of Art. 20(1) required the state to take appropriate action to protect all workers against the dangers of nocturnal employment. 85 BVerfGE 191, 213 (1992). The earlier decisions are collected in Eckart Klein, Grundrechtliche Schutzpflicht des Staates, 1989 NJW 1633, 1634-35.

[273] For the general principle of deference see Lorenz, supra note 228, Rdnr. 45. See also 66 BVerfGE 39, 60-61 (1983) (rejecting an attack on the stationing of nuclear missiles in West Germany on the ground that, to whatever extent German officials were responsible for the decision, the question how best to defend the country was committed to the discretion of the political branches). In the environmental field the Constitutional Commission in 1993 proposed a new Article 20a that would commit the state to protect the conditions necessary for continued existence ("die natürlichen Lebensgrundlagen") but explained that, like the Sozialstaat clauses of Art. 20 and 28, the new provision would merely declare an objective goal of state policy (ein "objektiv-rechtliches Staatsziel"), not create enforceable private rights. See Bericht der VerfKomm at 65-68. On the other hand, on several occasions the Court has held that other tribunals offended the Basic Law by denying remedies for private interference with such constitutionally protected values as human dignity and free expression. See, e.g., the *Lebach* and *Blinkfüer* cases discussed in chapter 4 supra.

[274] See 39 BVerfGE at 49-50.

[275] See Isensee, supra note 87, Rdnr. 166 (arguing that the authorities had failed to enforce the limitations laid down by the Court); Brugger, supra note 261, 36 JöR (n.F.) at 63: "Obviously it is not very difficult [in Germany] to find a physician and a counselor who will approve the pregnant woman's choice."

In the summer of 1992, following reunification, the Bundestag with Bundesrat approval adopted a new abortion statute liberalizing the law along lines similar to those found wanting in 1975. Once again, over three partial dissents, the statute was struck down. Apart from exceptional instances in which the burdens of pregnancy and motherhood would be as serious as those in cases of rape or incest, fetal deformity, or danger to the health of the mother, the Court reaffirmed, abortion could not be made lawful. In one significant respect, however, the Court modified its position: Article 2(2) did not require that either a woman or her doctor be punished criminally for an abortion during the first twelve weeks of pregnancy if she adhered to her decision after counseling designed to change her mind.[276] Thus the Court took back in practice much of what it proclaimed in theory, and thus at the practical level the abortion situation in the two countries looks more and more the same: In both the woman who wants an early abortion can effectively get one if she can afford it; in neither has she a constitutional right to have the state foot the bill.[277]

At the theoretical level, however, the latest abortion decision is a ringing and unanimous reaffirmation of the state's positive constitutional duty to protect the individual against harm from third parties.[278] Notwithstanding their strikingly contrasting outcomes, both *Roe v. Wade* and its German counterparts are prime examples of

---

[276] See 88 BVerfGE 203 (1993). The Court's theory was essentially that of the dissenters in the 1975 case: The state's duty to protect the fetus could be fulfilled better by attempting to persuade the mother than by threatening her with criminal penalties. Justices Mahrenholz and Sommer dissented from the conclusion that abortions not meeting the majority's stringent hardship criteria could not be made lawful and from the further conclusion that insurers could not pay for them, Justice Böckenförde from the latter holding alone. The conclusion that no sanctions are necessary to enforce the constitutional command that most abortions be made unlawful seems to sit uneasily beside the Court's earlier decisions (noted in chapter 5 supra and in note 409 infra) that the elimination of withholding or reporting with respect to investment income and of hearings on claims of conscientious objection offended the equality clause of Art. 3(1) by effectively requiring only the law-abiding to pay taxes or to perform military service.

[277] On the other hand, while insurance payments for illegal abortions are forbidden by the latest German decision, social assistance payments for the poor are not; for otherwise a woman without means would be discouraged from seeking medical help, with adverse consequences in terms not only of her own health but also of the additional arguments against abortion that the doctor is required to provide. See 88 BVerfGE at 321-22. For an early critical response to the 1993 decision see Georg Hermes & Susanne Walther, Schwangerschaftsabbruch zwischen Recht und Unrecht, 1993 NJW 2337.

[278] See 88 BVerfGE at 339 (Mahrenholz and Sommer, JJ., dissenting): "For us too, as for the Court, the state's constitutional obligation to protect unborn human life from its inception is beyond question."

intrusive judicial review based on open-ended constitutional provisions.[279]

B. Human Dignity

Article 2(2) is indeterminate as to the limits of legislative intervention, but not as to the nature of the rights it protects. Articles 1(1) and 2(1) are indeterminate in both respects.

Article 1(1) provides that "human dignity [die Würde des Menschen] is inviolable." Obviously this language leaves a great deal of latitude for interpretation. The Constitutional Court attempted to define its essence in a major 1977 opinion:

> It is contrary to human dignity to make the individual the mere tool [bloßes Objekt] of the state. The principle that "each person must always be an end in himself" applies unreservedly to all areas of the law; the intrinsic dignity of the person consists in acknowledging him as an independent personality.[280]

If this helps, well and good. Concrete examples may help too.

Earlier cases, the opinion continued, had established that it was inconsistent with human dignity to impose punishment without fault[281] or to inflict cruel or disproportionate penalties.[282] Life imprisonment, the Court concluded, was permissible only on condition that the possibility of release was never foreclosed: "[T]he state strikes at the very heart of human dignity if [it] treats the prisoner without regard to the development of his personality and strips him of all hope of ever regaining his freedom."[283] On other occasions the

---

[279] See Mary Ann Glendon, Abortion and Divorce in Western Law 33 (1987); Brugger, supra note 261, 36 JöR (n.F.) at 66: "Both Courts have assumed too much power."

[280] 45 BVerfGE 187, 228 (1977) (*Life Imprisonment* case). For more detail along the same lines see Dürig in 1 Maunz/Dürig Art. 1(1), Rdnr. 28.

[281] 45 BVerfGE at 228 (citing 20 BVerfGE 323, 331 (1966), which had based this conclusion on Art. 2(1) in conjunction with the Rechtsstaat principle).

[282] 45 BVerfGE at 228 (citing 1 BVerfGE 332, 348 (1952), and 25 BVerfGE 269, 285-86 (1969)).

[283] 45 BVerfGE at 245; see also id. at 228-29. For further refinement of the requirements applicable to life imprisonment see 86 BVerfGE 288 (1992). As the quotation suggests, these decisions were not based entirely on Art. 1(1). See 45 BVerfGE at 223 (noting the obvious involvement of the right to personal liberty under Art. 2(2)); id. at 239 (concluding that the "interest in rehabilitation flows from Article 2(1) in tandem with Article 1"). In early days doubts had been expressed whether Art. 1(1) was directly enforceable at all, partly because Art. 1(3) made only the "following" basic rights binding on government organs as "directly enforceable law." See, e.g., Dürig in 1 Maunz/Dürig, Art. 1(1), Rdnr. 4, 7 (adding, at Rdnr. 13, 16, that it hardly mattered since the dignity principle had to be employed as a standard in interpreting other constitutional provisions as well as

Court has invoked the dignity clause in conjunction with other Bill of Rights provisions to protect informational privacy[284] and the right to have birth records reflect the results of a sex-change operation. "Human dignity and the constitutional right to the free development of personality," said the Court in the latter case, "require that one's civil status be classified according to the sex with which he is psychologically and physically identified."[285]

Commentators agree that human dignity also forbids such atrocities as torture, slavery, and involuntary human experiments; not surprisingly, they differ as to such matters as the death penalty (which at present Article 102 expressly forbids), artificial insemination, and suicide.[286] The open-endedness of the dignity provision is compounded by the Court's explicit conclusion that the meaning of human dignity may change over time:

> The history of criminal law shows clearly that milder punishments have replaced those more cruel in character and that the wave of the future is toward more humane and differentiated forms of punishment. Thus any decision defining human dignity in concrete terms must be based on our present understanding of it and not on any claim to a conception of timeless validity.[287]

In short, human dignity is a pretty flexible concept.

In the cases so far discussed, Article 1(1) was invoked in traditional fashion to protect the citizen against government intrusion. In the well-known *Mephisto* decision, in contrast, the dignity clause provided the principal justification for *permitting* government limitation of the artistic freedom guaranteed by Article 5(3) – an injunction against publication of a novel impugning the memory of a deceased actor.[288] The later *Lebach* case took this reasoning a giant step fur-

---

the ordinary law). For the contrary view see Adalbert Podlech in 1 AK-GG, Art. 1(1), Rdnr. 61. To this date the Constitutional Court has never invalidated government action on the basis of Art. 1(1) alone.

[284] See, e.g., 27 BVerfGE 1, 6 (1969) (*Microcensus*): "It would be inconsistent with the principle of human dignity to require a person to record and register all aspects of his personality, even though such an effort is carried out in the form of a statistical survey; [the state] may not treat a person as an object subject to an inventory of any kind." The census questions in issue, which pertained to vacation habits, were held permissible.

[285] 49 BVerfGE 286, 298 (1978).

[286] Compare Dürig in 1 Maunz/Dürig Art. 1(1), Rdnr. 30-41, with Podlech in 1 AK-GG, Art. 1(1), Rdnr. 43-55. See also the suggestion in Häberle, supra note 23, Rdnr. 93-95, that human dignity should be interpreted to impose strict limits on the imprisonment of mothers of small children.

[287] 45 BVerfGE 187, 229 (1977). Cf. the discussion of changing standards of cruel and unusual punishment in Furman v. Georgia, 408 U.S. 238 (1972).

[288] 30 BVerfGE 173 (1971), discussed in chapter 4 supra. See id. at 195: "[T]he values embodied in Article 1(1) influence the guarantee [of artistic freedom]." All

ther: As the first abortion case would soon reaffirm,[289] Article 1(1) directed the state not only to respect human dignity but affirmatively to protect it against third parties; it followed that the constitution not only permitted but required an injunction against publication of information respecting the plaintiff's past crimes.[290]

C. The Development of Personality

We come now to Article 2(1), which epitomizes substantive due process in the Federal Republic:

Everyone has the right to the free development of his personality insofar as he does not violate the rights of others or offend against the constitutional order or the moral code.

Free development of personality ("die freie Entfaltung der Persönlichkeit") is no more self-defining in German than it is in English. Literally it seems to suggest something akin to a right of privacy, an intimate sphere of autonomy into which the state is forbidden to intrude. Various aspects of privacy are indeed embraced within Article 2(1), but any such limiting construction was firmly rejected in the groundbreaking *Elfes* decision in 1957. The free development of personality, the Court argued, could not be limited to "that central area of personality that essentially defines a human person as a spiritual and moral being, for it is inconceivable how development within this core area could offend the moral code, the rights of others, or even the constitutional order . . . ." Rather the Court construed the provision to guarantee a general right of freedom of action ("eine allgemeine Handlungsfreiheit") – citing the debates of the constitutional convention for the conclusion that "linguistic rather than legal considerations prompted the framers to substitute the current language for the original proposal" that – within essentially the same limits that found their way into the final version – "[e]very person is free to do or not to do what he wishes."[291] Casting Article 2(1) loose from its re-

---

Justices agreed on the general principle that in such a case the interest in artistic freedom had to be balanced against the interest in reputation; the injunction itself was affirmed by an equally divided Court.

[289] See 39 BVerfGE 1, 41, 51 (1975); text at notes 260-79 supra.

[290] 35 BVerfGE 202, 238-45 (1973) (relying on Art. 1(1) in conjunction with Art. 2(1)). See also chapter 4 supra.

[291] 6 BVerfGE 32, 36-37 (1957) (citing the explanation given by Dr. von Mangoldt at the constitutional convention (Parlamentarischer Rat, Verhandlungen des Hauptausschusses 533 (1949))). Cf. Art. 4 of the French Declaration of Rights (1789): "La liberté consiste à pouvoir faire tout ce que ne nuit pas à autrui." Similarly express provisions had found their way into several Länder constitutions before the Parliamentary Council began its deliberations. See Verfassung des Freistaates

strictive terminology – like the freeing of "liberty" in the fourteenth amendment from its history in *Allgeyer v. Louisiana*[292] – opened the door to judicial review of all restrictive governmental action.[293]

What this review would produce in practice depended upon interpretation of the three limits Article 2(1) places upon freedom of action: "the rights of others, . . . the constitutional order, [and] the moral code." The first and last are easy enough to understand, if not always to apply: The rights of others justify banning such activities as arson and trespass; the moral code has been held, as in the United States, to authorize punishment for sodomy.[294] More difficult to determine was the meaning of the second limitation, which leaves unprotected those activities which offend against the constitutional order ("die verfassungsmäßige Ordnung").

This term or something very like it appears in several other articles in connection with constitutional limitations on subversive activities.[295] In those articles, in order not unduly to encroach upon legitimate political opposition, it has been given a restrictive meaning.[296] In the quite different context of Article 2(1) the "constitutional order" has been interpreted more broadly. The general right to freedom of action, the Court stated in *Elfes*, was limited both by the

---

Bayern vom 2. Dezember 1946, BayRS 100-1-S, Art. 101; Landesverfassung der Freien Hansestadt Bremen vom 21. Oktober 1947, SaBremR 100-a-1, Art. 3; Verfassung des Landes Hessen vom 1. Dezember 1946, GVBl. S. 229, Art. 2. The Constitutional Court's interpretation has nevertheless met with some criticism from the commentators, e.g., Hesse, supra note 16, Rdnr. 425-28, and Justice Grimm attacked it vigorously in a recent dissenting opinion, 80 BVerfGE 137, 164-70. See id. at 170: "The development of an individual's personality does not depend upon his ability to ride horseback in the woods." For a more approving view see Dürig in 1 Maunz/Dürig, Art. 2, Rdnr. 3, 10, 11.

[292] 165 U.S. 578 (1897).

[293] See Klaus Schlaich, Das Bundesverfassungsgericht 107 (1985): "[E]very burden imposed on the citizen has become the invasion of a fundamental right." For the argument that such indirect harms as those caused by construction of a military base or subsidization of a competitor do not constitute invasions of the right guaranteed by Art. 2(1) see Hans-Uwe Erichsen, Allgemeine Handlungsfreiheit, 6 Handbuch des Staatsrechts 1185, Rdnr. 75-84.

[294] See 6 BVerfGE 389, 432-37 (1957); 36 BVerfGE 41, 45-46 (1973). Cf. Bowers v. Hardwick, 478 U.S. 186 (1986). For criticism of the German decisions see Podlech in AK-GG, Art. 2(1), Rdnr. 64. Contrast the later decision in 49 BVerfGE 286, 298-301 (1979) (upholding the right to have birth records corrected to reflect a sex-change operation: "[T]he sexual change secured by the complainant cannot be considered immoral").

[295] See Art. 9(2), 18, 21(2) GG, all discussed in chapter 4 supra.

[296] See, e.g., 5 BVerfGE 85 (1956) (*Communist Party* case). See also Art. 20(3), which in using similar language requires the legislature to follow only the constitution itself. See 6 BVerfGE at 38.

Basic Law itself and "by every legal norm that conforms procedurally
and substantively with the constitution."[297]

This interpretation, like the decision that the privileges or immunities clause of our fourteenth amendment forbade impairment
only of rights already protected by other federal laws,[298] provoked the
question whether Article 2(1) added anything at all. At a minimum,
as the cases have shown, it provided affected individuals with
standing to attack laws passed without legislative authority[299] or
delegating excessive rulemaking power to the executive.[300] Equally
important and more interesting was the reminder in *Elfes* that a law
qualified as part of the constitutional order only if it conformed with
"the principles of the rule of law and the social welfare state."[301]

While the Sozialstaat principle standing alone has never yet been
held to invalidate governmental action or inaction, the rule of law
has given Article 2(1) much of its bite. As we have seen, even in the
absence of express provisions such as those applicable to bodily restraint, condemnation, and occupational freedom, the Rechtsstaat
principle has been held to permit restrictions of liberty only in accordance with statute,[302] and limitations on general freedom of action
lacking a sufficient legal basis have been struck down.[303] As noted in
earlier chapters, the Rechtsstaat principle also restricts both retroactivity and the delegation of legislative power as well as requiring both
fair warning and fair procedure.[304] Most important, as we have also
seen, the German conception of the rule of law embodies the

---

[297] 6 BVerfGE 32, 38 (1957). See also id. at 38-40 (invoking legislative history);
Hermann von Mangoldt, Das Bonner Grundgesetz 47 (1953). For an argument in
favor of a narrower interpretation see Dürig in 1 Maunz/-Dürig, Art. 2(1), Rdnr.
18-25.

[298] Slaughter-House Cases, 83 U.S. 36 (1873).

[299] E.g., 26 BVerfGE 246, 253-58 (1969) (striking down a statute for want of
federal competence to regulate use of the title of Engineer). See the discussion of
standing in chapter 3 supra.

[300] E.g., 20 BVerfGE 257, 268-71 (1966) (invalidating a provision for fees in
antitrust proceedings for violation of the delegation limits of Art. 80(1)). For the argument that the injured party may nevertheless complain only of the violation of
those norms which directly or indirectly serve to promote individual freedom see
Erichsen, supra note 293, Rdnr. 43-46.

[301] 6 BVerfGE 32, 41 (1957).

[302] See chapter 3 and text at notes 120-24 supra.

[303] E.g., 56 BVerfGE 99, 106-09 (1981) (reversing a decision that forbade a lawyer
to appear as counsel against a municipality if his partner was a member of the
municipal council for want of "a legal basis in the governing provisions of ordinary law"). See also Erichsen, supra note 293, Rdnr. 35. On the other hand, the
requirement of Art. 19(1) that the legislature expressly refer to a constitutional
right in order to restrict it has been held inapplicable to Art. 2(1) on the ground that
those statutes which belong to "the constitutional order" serve merely to define the
scope of the right itself. See 10 BVerfGE 89, 99 (1959) and the discussion of Art. 19(1)
in chapter 4 supra.

[304] See chapters 1 and 3 supra.

pervasive principle of proportionality.[305] It is this principle, in connection with the broad interpretation of "personality" in *Elfes*, that has enabled the German court to act as censor of the reasonableness of all governmental action.

As in the United States during the *Lochner* era, most measures challenged on this basis have passed muster. National security was held to justify the law limiting issuance of passports in *Elfes*;[306] price regulations were upheld because they were reasonable.[307] At the same time, a number of restrictions on the general freedom of action have been struck down for want of proportionality. The state may not prohibit intermediaries from seeking to match willing drivers with people who are looking for rides.[308] A person in pretrial custody may not be denied a typewriter.[309] As noted in connection with the human dignity provision, persons who have undergone sex change operations are entitled to have birth records corrected to reflect their new gender.[310] Parents may not be given unlimited power to bind minor children by contract;[311] the filing of criminal charges in good faith may not be treated as a tort.[312] In one of the best known cases of this nature the Constitutional Court found it unreasonable to require those who sought to hunt with falcons to demonstrate competence in the use of firearms. Not only did the required skills have "no connection either with the care of falcons or with the practice of falconry"; any hunter who discharged a weapon during the chase would frighten away his own falcon.[313]

---

[305] See especially text at notes 234-51 supra.

[306] 6 BVerfGE 32, 41-44 (1957). All that the disappointed traveler had done, apparently, was to speak critically of West German defense and reunification policy on prior journeys behind the Iron Curtain. See Hailbronner, supra note 16, Rdnr. 66-68 (criticizing the decision and adding that subsequent decisions of the administrative courts have applied a stricter constitutional standard). For the Court's rejection of the equally plausible free-expression argument see chapter 4 supra.

[307] 8 BVerfGE 274, 327-29 (1958).

[308] 17 BVerfGE 306, 313-18 (1964).

[309] 35 BVerfGE 5, 9-11 (1973). A television set, however, is not required. 35 BVerfGE 307, 309-10 (1973) (rejecting a claim based upon the freedom to inform oneself from generally available sources, Art. 5(1)).

[310] 49 BVerfGE 286, 298-301 (1979).

[311] 72 BVerfGE 155, 170-73 (1986) (giving a corresponding interpretation to the provision respecting parental rights and duties in Art. 6(2) in order to ensure that the child not be saddled with overwhelming obligations upon reaching maturity).

[312] 74 BVerfGE 257, 259-63 (1987) (making the Lockean argument that the citizen, having surrendered his natural right to self-help, is entitled to seek state protection).

[313] 55 BVerfGE 159, 165-69 (1980). See also 82 BVerfGE 6, 16 (1990), where in rejecting constitutional challenges to a judicial decision extending to unmarried couples the right of one spouse to assume the other's apartment lease after the latter's death the Court declared flatly that Art. 2(1) guaranteed the right to establish a domestic partnership without marriage; 87 BVerfGE 153, 169-77 (1992) (striking down

Article 2(1) and the proportionality principle have also been employed on a number of occasions to secure a general right of informational self-determination ("informationelle Selbstbestimmung"), or freedom from unwarranted investigation and revelation of one's private affairs. The reasoning that underlies these decisions was most convincingly explained in a 1973 opinion respecting disclosure of the complainant's past crimes. Such revelations, said the Court, could inhibit the free development of personality by diminishing the complainant's reputation and thus frustrating his reintegration into society.[314] Similarly, other disclosures might well impair that development either by discouraging constitutionally protected activity[315] or by causing direct injury to personality through embarrassment or shame.[316]

First elaborated in the *Microcensus* case in 1969,[317] the right to informational self-determination has been held to limit divulgence of divorce files,[318] medical records,[319] and private recordings of conversations.[320] More recently it has led the Court to require greater

---

a tax provision that did not exempt enough income to satisfy minimal living expenses). One lower court has gone so far as to conclude that the criminalization of marijuana offended Art. 2(1): "Intoxication, like food, drink, and sex, is a fundamental human need." See Die Zeit, Mar. 6, 1992, p. 16. In refusing to stay a criminal judgment in a similar case, however, the Constitutional Court later branded the argument as frivolous. See BVerfG, Decision of Dec. 22, 1993, Case No. 2 BvR 2031/92 (not yet reported). In general it has been observed that, in applying Art. 2(1) as well as other Bill of Rights provisions, the Court tends to scrutinize most strictly those limitations affecting rights that are "fundamental" either in the sense that they are personal or that they are crucial to the functioning of democracy. See Kriele, supra note 186, Rdnr. 44-50. Cf. the discussion of Art. 5 in chapter 4 and of Art. 12(1) in text at notes 184-86 supra.

[314] See 35 BVerfGE 202, 226, 235-38 (1973) (*Lebach*); cf. Briscoe v. Reader's Digest, 93 Cal. 866, 483 P.2d 34 (1971).

[315] See NAACP v. Alabama, 357 U.S. 449 (1958).

[316] Thus the decisions on informational privacy confirm that, as the Court has recognized in numerous other contexts, it is not only by outright prohibition of protected activity that constitutional rights can effectively be denied. See also the general discussion of unconstitutional conditions in chapter 4 supra. In recent years an explicit right of informational privacy has begun to make its way into the constitutions of individual Länder. See, e.g., Verfassung für das Land Nordrhein-Westfalen vom 28. Juni 1950, GS. NW. 100 S. 3, geändert durch Gesetz vom 19.3.1985, GVBl. S. 255, Art. 4(2); Verfassung des Saarlandes vom 15. Dezember 1947, BS Saar 100-1, in der Fassung des Gesetzes Nr. 1183 vom 25.1.1985, ABl. S. 106, Art. 2.

[317] 27 BVerfGE 1, 6-8 (1969) (finding adequate justification for requiring a cross section of inhabitants to answer questions pertaining to their vacation habits).

[318] 27 BVerfGE 344, 350-55 (1970).

[319] 32 BVerfGE 373, 378-86 (1972).

[320] 34 BVerfGE 238, 245-51 (1973).

restraint and confidentiality in connection with both the census[321] and legislative investigations[322] and even to forbid general dissemination of the names of individuals who have been stripped of contracting authority as spendthrifts[323] – although one might have thought publicity essential to protection of those with whom the spendthrift might deal.[324] In this as in so many other respects the German court has gone beyond its American counterpart; while the first, fourth, and fifth amendments afford freedom from certain disclosures in this country as well,[325] we have as yet no general right to informational privacy – much less a governmental duty to prevent *private* revelations of past crimes, such as the German court established in the *Lebach* case.[326]

Article 2(1), in conjunction with the proportionality principle, is thus the ultimate guarantor of substantive due process in Germany.

---

[321] 65 BVerfGE 1, 41-70 (1983).

[322] 77 BVerfGE 1, 38-63 (1987) (*Neue Heimat*).

[323] 78 BVerfGE 77, 84-87 (1988).

[324] In 1989 the Court divided 4-4 on the question whether it was consistent with Art. 2(1) to use the diary of a defendant charged with murder to demonstrate his compulsion to employ violence against women. 80 BVerfGE 367 (1989). The Constitutional Commission, reexamining the adequacy of the Basic Law in 1993, decided not to recommend codification of the judicially recognized right to informational self-determination. See Bericht der VerfKomm at 60-63.

[325] See U.S. Const., amend. IV ("The right of the people to be secure . . . against unreasonable searches and seizures shall not be violated"), V ("nor shall any person . . . be compelled in any criminal case to be a witness against himself"); NAACP v. Alabama, 357 U.S. 449 (1957).

[326] 35 BVerfGE 202, 218-44 (1973), also noted at notes 288-90 and in chapter 4 supra. Cf. Briscoe v. Reader's Digest, 93 Cal. 866, 483 P.2d 34 (1971) (permitting but not requiring damages for a strikingly similar disclosure on strikingly similar grounds). For a recent example of the effect of Art. 2(1) on the enforcement of private contracts see BVerfG, Decision of Oct. 19, 1993, Case No. 1 BvR 567/89 (not yet reported) (concluding that Art. 2(1) forbade enforcement of an unconscionable surety agreement between parties of unequal bargaining power). For consideration of the relationship between the right of informational self-determination and the right of others to acquire information under Art. 5(1) see Hans-Ullrich Gallwas, Der allgemeine Konflikt zwischen dem Recht auf informationelle Selbstbestimmung und der Informationsfreiheit, 1992 NJW 2785. As in the case of occupational freedom, however, it would be dangerous to conclude from the more extensive constitutional protection of informational privacy in the Federal Republic that Germans are in fact freer than Americans in this regard. Citizens of the Federal Republic are required both to carry identity cards and to register their place of residence; a legislator who voted for either measure in this country might well find herself out of a job. See Gesetz über Personalausweise vom 21 April 1986, BGBl. I, S. 548; Melderechtsrahmengesetz vom 16 August 1980, BGBl. I, S. 1429, in 1 Sartorius, Verfassungs- und Verwaltungsgesetze der Bundesrepublik Deutschland, Nr. 255-56.

V. EQUALITY

"All persons," says Article 3(1), "shall be equal before the law." Relying on the statement in Article 1(3) that the Bill of Rights binds legislative as well as executive and judicial authorities, the Constitutional Court made clear at the outset that – in contrast to a similarly worded clause in the 1850 Prussian Constitution – Article 3(1) forbade not only unequal administration of the laws but unequal legislation too.[327]

It could hardly have been the intention of those who wrote this provision to forbid all distinctions between persons – to require that murderers go unpunished or blind children be allowed to practice brain surgery. Taking a cue from decisions interpreting predecessor provisions, the Court in its very first substantive decision concluded that Article 3(1) required equal treatment only when inequality would be arbitrary ("willkürlich").[328] Thus, as in the United States, the equality provision forbids only those classifications which are without adequate justification; but the Constitutional Court has taken the need for such justification very seriously.

A. Classifications Expressly Prohibited

Article 3(3) gives specific content to the general equality requirement by listing a number of bases of classification that basically cannot be justified: "No one may be prejudiced or favored because of sex, ancestry [Abstammung], race, homeland and origin [Heimat und Herkunft], faith, or religious or political opinions."[329] A number of

---

[327] 1 BVerfGE 14, 52 (1951) (*Southwest Reorganization* case). Cf. Constitution for the Prussian State (1850), Art. 4. See also the 1925 decision of the Reichsgericht (111 RGZ 320, 322-23) (recounting the earlier understanding and leaving open the question whether the comparable provision in Art. 109 of the Weimar Constitution should be more broadly construed); Ekkehart Stein in 1 AK-GG, Art. 3, Rdnr. 5-6.

[328] 1 BVerfGE 14, 52 (1951). See also 111 RGZ 320, 329 (1925) (reaching the same conclusion under the analogous clause of the Weimar Constitution); von Mangoldt, supra note 297, at 51. For the suggestion that the inspiration for this interpretation came from Switzerland and from the United States see Stein in 1 AK-GG, Art. 3, Rdnr. 6.

[329] Like other basic rights, the nondiscrimination provisions of Art. 3(3) are expressly made binding on all organs of federal state, and local government by Art. 1(3). Like other basic rights, however, they may also have an indirect effect on relations between private parties ("mittelbare Drittwirkung"). See Dürig in 1 Maunz/Dürig, Art. 1, Abs. III, Rdnr. 133 (arguing that by virtue of Art. 3(3) a contract not to rent apartments to Jews would have to be struck down as contrary to good morals ("sittenwidrig") under the Civil Code); see also chapter 4 supra. But see 1 von Mangoldt/Klein/Starck, Art. 3, Abs. 3, Rdnr. 261 (warning that any application of the nondiscrimination provisions to private actions is narrowly limited by other articles guaranteeing private autonomy): "The freedom afforded by the Basic

other provisions contain additional specific guarantees of equality. Article 6(5), discussed earlier in this chapter, requires that affirmative steps be taken to assure illegitimate children the same opportunities as those born in wedlock.[330] Article 33(1) echoes our privileges and immunities clause by assuring every German "the same rights and duties of citizenship in every Land";[331] Article 33(2) guarantees equal eligibility for public office according to ability;[332] Articles 28(1) and 38(1) provide for "equal" and "general" elections for state and federal legislators respectively,[333] while Article 19(1) requires that any law restricting basic rights "apply generally and not solely to an individual case."

The characteristics listed in Article 3(3) are not all self-explanatory. Interpretation of the similar terms ancestry, homeland, and origin ("Abstammung, Heimat und Herkunft") has given rise to particular difficulty. In rejecting an Article 3(3) challenge to a provision limiting pensions for Spanish Civil War veterans to those living in the Federal Republic, however, the Constitutional Court concluded that "Heimat" meant geographical origin and "Herkunft" social class.[334] Commentators have suggested that the inclusion of "Abstammung" forbids nepotism, among other things[335] – an interesting contrast to the Supreme Court's 1947 decision that a system under which only "relatives and friends" of established pilots were accepted as apprentices was consistent with the fourteenth amendment.[336]

Rights normally permits the individual to make distinctions on the basis of the criteria listed in Art. 3(3)."

[330] See text at notes 47-66 supra.

[331] Cf. U.S. Const., Art. IV, § 2. This provision, however, has played no significant part in the decisions; it was not even mentioned when the Court struck down a preference for local applicants ("Landeskinder") for university admission as a violation of the general equality provision of Art. 3(1) in conjunction with the guarantee of occupational freedom in Art. 12(1). 33 BVerfGE 303, 351-56 (1972) (*Numerus Clausus*). See text at note 215 supra; Sachs, supra note 95, Rdnr.113.

[332] See id., Rdnr. 139-48.

[333] See chapter 3 supra. For discussion of Art. 33(3) and Art. 140 in connection with Art. 136(1) and (2) of the Weimar Constitution, all of which reinforce the Art. 3(3) ban on religious discrimination, see chapter 5 supra. The meaning of the additional provision in Art. 3(2) that "[m]en and women shall have equal rights" is considered in the text at notes 368-70 below.

[334] 48 BVerfGE 281, 287-88 (1978). See also 5 BVerfGE 17, 22 (1956); 1 JöR (n.F.) at 69 (Delegate Dehler); Dürig in 1 Maunz/Dürig Art. 3(3), Rdnr. 75, 87 (confirming that the "Heimat" provision was designed to protect refugees and that "Herkunft" refers to social class).

[335] See id., Rdnr. 45-46; 1 von Mangoldt/Klein/Starck, Art. 3, Abs. 3, Rdnr. 268.

[336] Kotch v. Pilot Commissioners, 330 U.S. 552 (1947).

Thus the list of suspect classifications is significantly longer in Germany than it is in the United States.[337] Discrimination on grounds of alienage, however, is not among them. As in the United States, political rights need not be extended to aliens.[338] Indeed the Constitutional Court held in 1990 that the right to vote *could* not be, since Article 20(2) provided that all state authority was derived from "the people," and that meant citizens of the Federal Republic.[339] Moreover, the fact that a number of additional rights including occupational freedom (Art. 12(1)) are expressly limited to Germans seems to exclude the possibility of finding a violation of the equality provisions in such measures as exclusion of aliens from the practice of law, as our Supreme Court did in *In re Griffiths* in 1973.[340]

The requirements of equal elections, as we have seen, have been strictly enforced.[341] In contrast to the United States, however, where race decisions have formed the heart of equal protection jurisprudence, the sex discrimination provision is the only one of the specific prohibitions in Article 3(3) that has played a significant role in the German cases.

One reason for the relative quiescence of Article 3(3) is that until very recently the Constitutional Court gave it a surprisingly narrow interpretation. The story begins in 1953, when the Court summarily rejected the contention that a statute restricting the right of travel by residents of the Soviet occupation zone worked a forbidden discrimination on grounds of homeland ("Heimat"). Not every distinction in terms of this criterion, the Court said, was a distinction *because of* ("wegen") homeland. Article 3(3) applied only when there was a causal relationship between the forbidden criterion and the disadvantage the law imposed. The rights of East Germans had been curtailed not because of any animus against East Germans as such, but be-

---

[337] See also Verfassung des Landes Brandenburg vom 20. August 1992, GV. BB. 298, Art. 12(2), which adds to the list both disability ("Behinderung") and sexual identity ("sexuelle Identität") – which if it is not merely to repeat the immediately preceding reference to gender ("Geschlecht") can only mean what in this country has come to be known as sexual orientation. Despite this example, the Constitutional Commission in 1993 declined to recommend the addition of either disability or sexual orientation to the list of prohibited bases of classification in Art. 3(3) of the Basic Law. See Bericht der VerfKomm at 52-54.

[338] Cf. Foley v. Connelie, 435 U.S. 291, 297 (1978).

[339] 83 BVerfGE 37, 50-59 (1990). In 1992, however, Art. 28(1) was amended to permit citizens of other countries within the European Community to vote and to run for office in local elections in accordance with Community law. See BGBl. I (1992), S. 2086; 44 Sammelblatt für Rechtsvorschriften des Bundes und der Länder 309 (1993).

[340] 413 U.S. 717 (1973). See Wolfgang Rüfner, Grundrechtsträger, 5 Handbuch des Staatsrechts 485, Rdnr. 8. This is not to say that discrimination against aliens can *never* offend Art. 3(1). See 51 BVerfGE 1, 22-29 (1979) (finding it arbitrary ("willkürlich") to deny social insurance benefits to foreigners living abroad without returning their contributions).

[341] See chapter 3 supra; see also note 399 infra.

cause of the social and economic difficulties presented by the flood of refugees from East Germany; the explicit mention of residents of the Soviet zone in the statute was merely a shorthand way of expressing the true legislative goal.[342]

Equal protection law in the United States knows the converse of this proposition: A classification nominally in race-neutral terms will be treated as race discrimination if no other plausible explanation can be found.[343] If this were not so, the prohibition could be readily evaded. But in this country the search for an underlying purpose may be used only to enlarge, not to contract the field of suspect classifications. To employ race or some other disfavored criterion as a surrogate for some other characteristic with which it overlaps or coincides is to engage in the very sort of stereotyping the fourteenth amendment was meant to preclude; any classification in racial terms is subject to heightened scrutiny. This is not to deny that there may be compelling justifications for suspect classifications in particular cases, but that is a far cry from saying that some explicit racial distinctions are not to be treated as racially based at all.[344]

In 1957 the Court brushed aside the contention that Article 3(3) forbade a city council to discharge a mayor before the end of his term with the offhand observation that when political differences between an agent and his employer lead to a critical lack of confidence politics "must necessarily play a decisive role."[345] Standing alone, the quoted passage might plausibly be interpreted to suggest that under such circumstances there was a compelling reason for political discrimination, as our Supreme Court has indicated in cases involving officials exercising significant political discretion.[346] In light of the earlier opinion concerning the right of travel, however, the preceding sentence seemed to suggest that the Court thought the mayor had been discharged not "because of" his political views but rather to avoid a crisis of confidence: "The prohibition of distinctions on the ba-

---

[342] 2 BVerfGE 266, 286 (1953). See also 1 von Mangoldt/Klein/Starck, Art. 3, Abs. 3, Rdnr. 264; 5 BVerfGE 17, 21-22 (1956) (permitting reference to East German law to determine the age of majority for East Germans: The reason for the distinction was neither homeland nor social class but the fact that East Germans were subject to different legal rules). Cf. Conner v. Elliott, 59 U.S. 591 (1856). Contrast 23 BVerfGE 98, 107 (1968), where the Court said that it would offend Art. 3(3) to recognize the Nazis' denaturalization of the Jews.

[343] E.g., Neal v. Delaware, 103 U.S. 370 (1880) (all-white jury); Guinn v. United States, 238 U.S. 347 (1915) (grandfather clause); Gomillion v. Lightfoot, 364 U.S. 339 (1960) (city boundary that excluded most blacks).

[344] See, e.g., Korematsu v. United States, 323 U.S. 214 (1944), where the Court upheld a shockingly overbroad exclusion of Japanese-Americans from the West Coast for reasons of national security but insisted that it was applying strict scrutiny because the classification was after all on racial grounds; Cooper v. Aaron, 358 U.S. 1, 16 (1958) (holding the risk of violence no excuse for continued segregation of public school pupils by race); Palmore v. Sidoti, 466 U.S 429 (1984).

[345] 7 BVerfGE 155, 170-71 (1957).

[346] See Elrod v. Burns, 427 U.S. 347 (1976); Branti v. Finkel, 445 U.S. 507 (1980).

sis of political convictions" provided "no measuring rod for the facts before us" at all.[347]

The famous *Civil Service* decision of 1975, in concluding that the exclusion of suspected subversives from public office did not offend the ban on political discrimination, picked up this narrow interpretation and added two or three more. It would be absurd, the Court argued, to find in Article 3(3) an absolute prohibition of distinctions in terms of the enumerated criteria – to hold, for example, that religion could not be taken into account in selecting a teacher for a denominational school, or gender in appointing the principal of a school for girls. There were at least two ways, the Court said, to explain the conclusion that normally suspect characteristics might be considered in such cases. The first was to hold (in accord with the earlier decisions) that Article 3(3) forbade only purposive ("bezweckte") discriminations, not those that were the mere consequence ("Folge") of a rule having a completely different purpose. The second was to take refuge in the nature of the case ("die Natur der Sache") – an interpretive tool reminiscent of Chief Justice Marshall's pet argument that the framers of the Constitution could not have intended to lay down unreasonable rules.[348]

Moreover, the Court continued, Article 3(3) could not be read in isolation from other constitutional provisions. In light of the various explicit articles of the Basic Law setting up a militant democracy ("eine streitbare, wehrhafte Demokratie"), there was no way one could interpret the ban on political discrimination to require the Federal Republic to hand itself over to its enemies.[349] Finally, Article 3(3) forbade the state to disadvantage anyone only for *holding* political opinions, not for expressing or acting upon them; for political speech and behavior were governed by other constitutional provisions (citing Articles 2, 4, 5, 8, and 9 of the Basic Law), and the limits on these rights would mean nothing if they could be trumped by invocation of the antidiscrimination provision.[350]

It was not long after this decision that Justice Helmut Simon was to lament in a notable concurring opinion that the explicit ban on political discrimination in Article 3(3) had essentially been read out of the Basic Law. It made no sense, he argued, to restrict the provision to discrimination on the ground of merely holding an opinion. Until an opinion was expressed or acted upon, there was no way it could be made the basis for discrimination; and therefore the Court's interpretation left the provision with no effect whatever. Even other constitutional provisions, he added, could limit the prohibition only to the extent necessary to accomplish their purposes, in accordance with

---

[347] 7 BVerfGE at 171.

[348] 39 BVerfGE 334, 368 (1975). Cf. Marbury v. Madison, 5 U.S. 137, 178-79 (1803); Cohens v. Virginia, 19 U.S. 264, 377 (1821).

[349] 39 BVerfGE at 368-69. See the discussion of Art. 5(3), 9(2), and 21(2) in chapter 4 supra.

[350] 39 BVerfGE at 368.

the proportionality principle; and the only constitutional limits on political speech were found in Articles 18 and 21 (providing for forfeiture of rights and prohibiting political parties in certain extreme
cases) and in general laws within the meaning of Article 5(2).[351]

Despite Justice Simon's attack, the Court restated its familiar
causality test in an important 1987 decision respecting discrepancies
in public financing of religious and secular private schools.[352] In
1992, however, under the guise of "clarifying" the 1987 opinion, the
Constitutional Court quietly abandoned this crippling interpretation.
The case involved sex discrimination, the one category of Article 3(3)
that had proved significant in earlier cases, and in that field the
Court had never made much of the vaunted distinction between burdens imposed "because of" and merely in terms of the forbidden criterion.[353] Now, however, the Court enunciated a new standard applicable not only to gender discrimination but to all Article 3(3) criteria across the board:

Sex, like the other characteristics enumerated in paragraph 3, basically may not be used as a determining factor ("Anknüpfungs-
punkt") for differential treatment under law. This is true even when
the regulation is not intended to produce a discrimination forbidden
by Article 3(3) but primarily promotes some other goal.[354]

Rejection of the causal test will not compel the Constitutional
Court to strike down political or other distinctions that can be justi-

---

[351] 63 BVerfGE 266, 302-04 (1983) (Simon, J., concurring). The case concerned
exclusion of an alleged subversive from the practice of law; the majority found an
infringement of occupational freedom not authorized by statute, as Art. 12(1)
requires. See also 1 von Mangoldt/Klein/Starck, Art. 3, Abs. 3, Rdnr. 286: "This
characteristic relates to political opinions that are *expressed*" (emphasis added).

[352] 75 BVerfGE 40 (1987). Religious schools received a larger subsidy, the Court
concluded, not because of their point of view but, among other things, to protect
legitimate expectations based upon prior practice in compensation for the closing of
denominational public schools. These reasons were ultimately found insufficient
to satisfy the general equality requirement of Art. 3(1) in conjunction with Art. 7(4)
(see note 43 supra), but in the Court's view they did not make the state guilty of discrimination "because of" religion. Id. at 69-71.

[353] See, e.g., 43 BVerfGE 213, 225 (1977) (paraphrasing the parallel provision of
Art. 3(2) guaranteeing equal rights for men and women as outlawing rules that
attach legal consequences to gender ("rechtliche Regelungen, die allein an den
Unterschied der Geschlechter anknüpfen"); Sachs, supra note 95, Rdnr. 83. Many
of the laws tested under the sex-discrimination provisions served purposes other
than discrimination for its own sake and thus did not meet the causality standard
laid down in other Art. 3(3) decisions. See text at notes 356-88 infra. The discrep-
ancy may be traceable to the fact that until the 1992 decision sex discrimination
cases tended to be decided under Art. 3(2), which does not contain the term "wegen"
(because of), which had encouraged narrow interpretation of Art. 3(3).

[354] 85 BVerfGE 191, 206 (1992) (invalidating a ban on nocturnal employment
applicable only to women).

fied by some compelling interest, as in the case of the dissenting
mayor. The Court itself showed the way with its references to militant democracy and to the nature of the case in the *Civil Service* opinion: Like such other facially absolute rights as artistic and religious
freedom,[355] Article 3(3) finds its limits in other constitutional provisions, and arguably in common sense as well. But this
"clarification" of the Court's position has finally cleared the way for
Article 3(3) to serve the purpose for which it was apparently designed, and which in the field of sex discrimination it has actually
fulfilled – namely to require intensive scrutiny when special benefits
or burdens are allotted in terms of a variety of characteristics rightly
perceived as suspect in the light of bitter experience.[356]

B. Sex Discrimination

There have been many sex discrimination decisions, and they
long antedate our Supreme Court's first forays into the field.[357]
Article 117(1) gave legislatures until 1953 to eliminate gender distinctions from the civil code and other laws, but in that year the Constitutional Court affirmed its authority to strike down nonconforming
provisions as soon as the grace period expired.[358]

The Court has made clear from the beginning that the specific
requirement of sex equality demands heightened scrutiny of classifications based on gender. Merely rational grounds that might suffice
under the general equality provision cannot justify sex discrimination; a "compelling" reason is required.[359] Compelling reasons for
this purpose have been specifically defined: "Differential treatment of
men and women . . . is permissible only if sex-linked biological or
functional differences so decisively characterize the matter to be regulated that common elements can no longer be recognized or at least
fade completely into the background."[360]

---

[355] See chapters 4, 5 supra.

[356] See Sachs, supra note 95, Rdnr. 40, 65-74. See also id., Rdnr. 78 (urging
employment of Art. 3(3) to combat "the massive constitutional violations" attributable to political patronage).

[357] The Supreme Court first invalidated sex discrimination in Reed v. Reed, 404
U.S. 71 (1971) (striking down a preference for males to administer decedents'
estates).

[358] 3 BVerfGE 225, 237-48 (1953) (rejecting objections, which look strange to
American eyes, that judicial enforcement of the constitutional prohibition might
offend higher-law principles of predictability and separation of powers). For development of the interesting notion of unconstitutional constitutional provisions in
Germany see 1 BVerfGE 14, 32-33 (1951); 3 BVerfGE at 230-36; 5 BVerfGE 85, 137
(1956) (all discussed in chapter 4 supra).

[359] See, e.g., 15 BVerfGE 337, 343-44 (1963); 48 BVerfGE 327, 337 (1978); 85
BVerfGE 191, 207 (1992).

[360] 39 BVerfGE 169, 185-86 (1975).

The reference to biological differences is readily understandable and would justify sex distinctions for such purposes as procreation and marriage.[361] Recognition of the legitimacy of "functional" distinctions, on the other hand, seemed to create the risk of perpetuating stereotypes based on traditional male and female roles.[362]

In fact some early decisions applying the gender provision were not auspicious in this regard. The Court permitted the state to limit the work done by women in the interest of protecting their health,[363] to place the primary duty of financial support of illegitimate children on fathers,[364] and to require widowers but not widows to prove dependency in order to obtain benefits upon the death of a spouse.[365] In accordance with explicit language now found in Article 12a,[366] the Court upheld a military draft of men only.[367] Most strikingly, in 1957 the Justices went so far as to uphold a law that punished homosexual activity only between men – on the armchair sociological ground that female homosexuals tended to be quiet about it and thus posed less of a threat to society.[368]

From a very early date, however, the Court also began to strike down gender classifications, and the trend has intensified with the passage of time. As early as 1959 the Justices invoked Article 3(3) in conjunction with the familial rights guaranteed by Article 6 to invalidate a law giving fathers the last word on childrearing;[369] four years later they gave legislators two years to do away with a preference for men in the inheritance of farms.[370] Later decisions have established

---

[361] See Dürig in 1 Maunz/Dürig, Art. 3(2), Rdnr. 13; Ekkehart Stein in 1 AK-GG, Art. 3, Rdnr. 81.

[362] See Dürig's criticism of the "functional" criterion in 1 Maunz/-Dürig, Art. 3(2), Rdnr. 18.

[363] 5 BVerfGE 9, 11-12 (1956) (finding differential treatment justified by "the objective biological and functional differences between men and women").

[364] 11 BVerfGE 277, 281 (1960).

[365] 17 BVerfGE 1, 17-26 (1963). Contrast Frontiero v. Richardson, 411 U.S. 677 (1973) (striking down a similar provision in the United States several years later).

[366] "Men who have attained the age of eighteen years . . . ."

[367] 12 BVerfGE 45, 52-53 (1960) (invoking Art. 12(3) and 73 cl. 1, which then contained the limitation later placed in Art. 12a). Cf. Rostker v. Goldberg, 453 U.S. 57 (1981) (upholding a similarly selective draft registration requirement without benefit of such an explicit constitutional provision). For doubts whether the statutory exclusion of women from *voluntary* military service would survive constitutional scrutiny see Sachs, supra note 95, Rndr. 104.

[368] 6 BVerfGE 389, 420-32 (1957). The Court adhered to this decision as late as 1973. See 36 BVerfGE 41, 45-46 (1973) (upholding a ban on homosexual acts between men and boys). Apparently it did not occur to anyone to argue that it was unequal to permit men to have sexual relations with women but not with other men; the distinct contention that the prohibition infringed the right to free development of personality guaranteed by Art. 2(1) was rejected on the ground that "homosexual activity unmistakably offends the moral code." 6 BVerfGE at 434. See text at note 294 supra.

[369] 10 BVerfGE 72-89 (1959).

[370] 15 BVerfGE 337, 342-46, 352 (1963).

that mothers must sometimes share the cost of child care,[371] that a father's citizenship cannot determine that of his child,[372] that married couples may select the wife's maiden name,[373] and that a "housework day" for single workers may not be prescribed for women only.[374] In 1967 the Court struck down a dependency requirement for widowers' benefits in the civil service, distinguishing its earlier decision on the ground that here, in contrast to the private sector, pensions were generally based upon services rendered rather than need.[375] In 1975 it added that changing patterns of women's employment would soon require a similar conclusion in the case of other pensions as well;[376] in 1992 it found no justification for limiting a prohibition of nocturnal employment to women.[377]

Gender classifications continue to be upheld in some cases. A 1976 decision permitted men for the time being to receive greater retirement benefits than women because their wages were higher.[378] Mothers may still be given preferential custody of children born out of wedlock.[379] Most recently, invoking the Sozialstaat principle, the Court for the first time expressly endorsed a variant of affirmative action in this field: Women may be given special benefits to compensate for disadvantages having a biological basis.[380] Upholding a provision permitting women to opt for retirement earlier than men against an Article 3(3) challenge on the ground that the traditionally disfavored position of women in the workplace was attributable in part to anticipated and actual interruptions during pregnancy, birth, and childrearing, the Court went so far as to raise

---

[371] 26 BVerfGE 265, 273-77 (1969). The Court specifically reaffirmed its earlier decision (see note 364 supra) that fathers could generally be required to support illegitimate children as a counterweight to the mother's duty to rear them, but it saw no reason to distinguish between parents when the child lived with neither one.

[372] 37 BVerfGE 217, 244-59 (1974). Nor may the husband's citizenship determine the law governing marital property (63 BVerfGE 181, 194-96 (1983)) or divorce (68 BVerfGE 384, 390 (1985)).

[373] 48 BVerfGE 327, 337-40 (1978). In 1991 the Court went further, striking down a law that prescribed the husband's name when the parties were unable to agree. 84 BVerfGE 9 (1991). In so doing the Court cast doubt on the entire notion that "functional" differences between men and women might justify distinctions in legal treatment: There was no need to decide to what extent functional differences might ever still be invoked to justify disadvantageous treatment of women, because the relative scarcity of women in high professional positions was itself in part the result of unlawful discrimination. Id. at 18-19.

[374] 52 BVerfGE 369, 373-79 (1979).

[375] 21 BVerfGE 329, 340-54 (1967).

[376] 39 BVerfGE 169, 185-95 (1975).

[377] 85 BVerfGE 191, 206-10 (1992). "Night work," said the Court, "is basically harmful to everyone." Id. at 208.

[378] 43 BVerfGE 213, 225-230 (1977). For the limits of this holding see 57 BVerfGE 335, 342-46 (1981).

[379] 56 BVerfGE 363, 387-90 (1981).

[380] 74 BVerfGE 163 (1987).

the question whether such a measure might even be constitutionally *required*.[381]

The opinion did not say where in the Basic Law such a requirement might be found. Article 6(5) explicitly obliges the legislature to take positive steps to assure equality of opportunity for illegitimate children,[382] but no such language appears in Article 3(3). One possibility might be to interpret the latter provision to impose a standard of de facto rather than de jure inequality, which the U.S. Supreme Court has refused to find in the fourteenth amendment.[383] There are suggestions of such an approach in occasional equality opinions in other contexts,[384] and an analogy in the Constitutional Court's consistent view that such negatively phrased rights as those to life and bodily integrity impose a duty to protect one individual from injury by another.[385] An even more recent opinion, however, provides a more solid basis for the suggestion that the state may have an obligation to make up for disadvantages suffered by women: the additional provision of Article 3(2) that "Männer und Frauen sind gleichberechtigt" – men and women shall have equal rights.

At first glance this provision appears to be redundant, and it was long treated accordingly: The Constitutional Court repeatedly declared that it merely reinforced the Article 3(3) prohibition of discrimination based on sex.[386] In striking down a gender-based prohibition of night work as a violation of Article 3(3) in 1992, however, the Court announced a change of heart: Like Article 6(5) in the field of illegitimacy, Article 3(2) went beyond mere discrimination to impose on the state an affirmative responsibility to assure that men and women actually enjoyed equal opportunity.[387]

---

[381] Id. at 178-81.

[382] See text at notes 47-66 supra.

[383] See Washington v. Davis, 426 U.S. 229 (1976); Currie, supra note 115, 53 U. Chi. L. Rev. at 880-86.

[384] See text at notes 425-26 infra (discussing progressive taxes and the deductibility of political contributions).

[385] See text at notes 260-79 supra.

[386] E.g., 3 BVerfGE 225, 240-41 (1953); 43 BVerfGE 213, 225 (1977). Accord von Mangoldt, supra note 297, at 52; Sachs, supra note 95, Rdnr. 79-80; Dürig in 1 Maunz/Dürig Art. 3(3), Rdnr. 4 (explaining the origins of the two provisions). The bulk of the debate in the Parliamentary Council, as Dürig says, supports the unexpected conclusion that both provisions were meant to serve the same purpose. Near the end of the discussion, however, Carlo Schmid explained that in the opinion of the principal committee ("Hauptausschuß") the clause respecting equal rights for women embraced the principle of equal pay for equal work – a principle whose effectuation in the private sphere would require affirmative legislative action rather than mere avoidance of state-imposed discrimination. See 1 JöR (n.F.) at 69-72.

[387] 85 BVerfGE 191, 206-07 (1992). No reasons were stated in support of this conclusion. The Constitutional Commission proposed in 1993 to make this affirmatiive duty explicit: "The state shall promote the de facto realization [die tatsächliche Durchsetzung] of equal rights for men and women and shall take steps to

Thus there remain cases in which sex may be taken into account, and there may even be cases in which it must be. As in the United States, however, gender is treated as a relatively suspect classification in Germany – along with race, religion, and the other bases of distinction enumerated in Article 3(3).[388]

C. The General Equality Provision

The list of forbidden bases of classification in Article 3(3) is not exhaustive. Despite its initial definition of forbidden distinctions as those that were arbitrary[389] and repeated professions of judicial restraint,[390] the Constitutional Court has applied the general equality clause of Article 3(1) to strike down an impressive variety of measures.[391]

To begin with, the Court has scrutinized with especial care those classifications affecting interests specifically protected by other provisions of the Basic Law. Often it has done so on the basis of the other provisions themselves.[392] On other occasions the substantive provisions have been drawn upon to give content to the general prohibition of Article 3(1). Thus the Court has been quick to condemn discrimination against married persons[393] or families with children[394] under Article 3(1) in conjunction with the applicable paragraphs of Article 6. It has done the same in cases respecting inequalities

---

eliminate existing disadvantages." See Bericht der VerfKomm at 49-51 (making clear that, like the Sozialstaat provisions, this language would not give rise to judicially enforceable private rights).

[388] For the conclusion that German and American sex discrimination decisions reveal striking similarities in both structure and result see Hartwin Bungert, Gleichberechtigung von Mann und Frau im amerikanischen und deutschen Verfassungsrecht, 89 Zeitschrift für Vergleichende Rechtswissenschaft 441, 463-65 (1990).

[389] See text at note 328 supra.

[390] E.g., 12 BVerfGE 326, 337-38 (1961).

[391] For a thorough taxonomic compilation of the decisions see Michael Sachs, Die Auswirkungen des allgemeinen Gleichheitssatzes auf die Teilrechtsordnungen, 5 Handbuch des Staatsrechts 1085 (passim).

[392] See, e.g., the marriage and family decisions discussed at notes 42-66 supra.

[393] E.g., 13 BVerfGE 290, 295-318 (1962) (deductibility of salary paid to owner's spouse); 67 BVerfGE 186, 195-99 (1984) (unemployment compensation when both spouses are out of work).

[394] See 61 BVerfGE 319, 343-44, 351-54 (1982) (requiring the cost of child care to be considered in determining taxable income); 82 BVerfGE 60 (1990). The discrimination involved in these cases was arguably de facto rather than de jure. See text at notes 423-26 infra.

affecting the academic[395] and occupational[396] freedoms guaranteed by Articles 5(3) and 12(1), the traditional rights of civil servants under Article 33(5),[397] the right to operate private schools under Article 7(4),[398] and above all the right to participate in elections.[399] In several of these cases,[400] as in those passing upon classifications made suspect by Article 3(3), the Court explicitly required an unusually strong justification for discrimination. In 1986 it expressly generalized the principle: "If the rule to be tested under Article 3(1) affects other interests protected by the Bill of Rights, the legislature's freedom of action is more narrowly circumscribed."[401] These decisions closely resemble those reached under the fundamental rights strand of equal protection analysis in the United States.[402]

As in the United States, there is some tendency to extend this heightened scrutiny to classifications affecting other interests deemed fundamental – such as the right to have birth records altered to reflect a sex-change operation – which are not specifically enumerated in the Basic Law.[403] Indeed it has often been said that classifications made in tax laws require special justification because

---

[395] E.g., 56 BVerfGE 192, 208-16 (1981).

[396] E.g., 37 BVerfGE 342, 352-60 (1974). See also the cases discussed at notes 213-18 supra.

[397] 56 BVerfGE 146, 161-69 (1981).

[398] 75 BVerfGE 40, 71-78 (1987).

[399] E.g., 1 BVerfGE 208, 241-60 (1952) (exclusion of party receiving less than 7.5 percent of vote from proportional representation in legislature); 3 BVerfGE 19, 23-29 (1953) (requirement of 500 petition signatures for Bundestag candidate of party not already represented); 6 BVerfGE 273, 279-82 (1957) (nondeductibility of contributions to unrepresented parties); 7 BVerfGE 99, 107-08 (1957) (denial of public television time to unrepresented party); 16 BVerfGE 130, 138-44 (1963) (unequal population of election districts); 41 BVerfGE 399, 412-23 (1976) (exclusion of independent candidate from reimbursement of election expenses); 44 BVerfGE 125, 138-66 (1977) (government propaganda for parties in ruling coalition). See also Sachs, supra note 95, Rdnr. 137-38. Some of these decisions were based in part upon the explicit guarantee of "equal" Bundestag elections in Art. 38(1) or on the guarantee of the rights of political parties in Art. 21(1), discussed in chapters 3 and 4 supra; others add references to the guarantee of democracy in Art. 20(2) and 28(1). Cf. Justice Stone's suggestion – which has been followed – of heightened scrutiny of measures impairing the integrity of the democratic process. United States v. Carolene Products Co., 304 U.S. 144, 152-53 n. 4 (1938).

[400] E.g., 1 BVerfGE 208, 249, 255, 256 (1952) (elections); 37 BVerfGE 342, 352-54 (1974) (occupational freedom); 67 BVerfGE 186, 195-96 (1984) (marriage).

[401] 74 BVerfGE 9, 24 (1986).

[402] See, e.g., Carey v. Brown, 447 U.S. 455, 461-62 (1980) (freedom of speech); Niemotko v. Maryland, 340 U.S. 268 (1951) (free exercise of religion).

[403] 60 BVerfGE 123, 133-35 (1982) (striking down a provision limiting this right to persons at least 25 years old). Cf. Reynolds v. Sims, 377 U.S. 533, 561-62 (1964) (subjecting limitations on the value of votes to strict scrutiny although the right to vote was nowhere generally guaranteed).

of the severity of their impact.[404] A surprising number of such distinctions have actually been found wanting: discriminatory taxation of chain stores,[405] preferential treatment of vertically integrated firms under the value-added tax,[406] nondeductibility of partners' salaries[407] and of child-care expenses,[408] to name only a few.[409] These decisions stand in sharp contrast to modern decisions in the United States; our Supreme Court has not scrutinized classifications in tax laws with any care since the New Deal revolution.[410]

Moreover, although the Constitutional Court has sometimes said that legislatures have particularly broad discretion in determining how to spend public funds,[411] one dissenting Justice, in language reminiscent of that of Justice Thurgood Marshall, has argued for heightened scrutiny of discriminatory welfare provisions under the influence of Article 20(1)'s social state principle.[412] Indeed, in contrast to the American cases, the German decisions lend her consid-

---

[404] See, e.g., 21 BVerfGE 12, 27 (1966); 35 BVerfGE 324, 335 (1973). For a rare protest against the notion of strict scrutiny in tax cases see 15 BVerfGE 313, 318 (1963).

[405] 19 BVerfGE 101, 111-18 (1965). But see 29 BVerfGE 327, 335-36 (1970) (permitting discriminatory taxation of multiply owned saloons).

[406] 21 BVerfGE 12, 26-42 (1966).

[407] 13 BVerfGE 331, 338-55 (1962).

[408] 68 BVerfGE 143, 152-55 (1984).

[409] Note also the intensive scrutiny practiced in an early decision striking down an exaction for support of the fire department that was imposed only upon men between the ages of 18 and 60 who had not served as firemen, 9 BVerfGE 291, 302 (1959): "[A]s a special assessment [the exaction] would have to be limited to those who derived special benefits from the fire department; as a substitute for service it could reach only those under a duty to serve; as a general tax it could not be imposed only on men between 18 and 60 years of age." A revised exaction limited to those who were eligible for fire duty but had not served was later upheld, 13 BVerfGE 167 (1961).

A 1991 decision warning the legislature that it could not continue to tax interest income without requiring the payor either to withhold the tax or to report the transaction added an interesting twist to this line of cases. By failing to assure effective collection of the tax, the Court argued, the legislature in effect taxed only the honest: "The equality clause does not permit a statutory rule that releases a person from his legal obligation whenever he declares his unwillingness to meet it." 84 BVerfGE 239, 273 (1991). The same reasoning had been employed some years earlier to strike down a law dispensing with any effort to probe the sincerity of a claim of conscientious objection. 48 BVerfGE 127, 168-69 (1978).

[410] See, e.g, Lehnhausen v. Lake Shore Auto Parts Co., 410 U.S. 356 (1973) (upholding a personal property tax imposed on property not owned by individuals, without a serious effort to justify the distinction). See generally Gerald Gunther, Foreword: A Model for a Newer Equal Protection, 86 Harv. L. Rev. 1, 8 (1972). For a rare exception to this pattern see Allegheny Pittsburgh Coal Co. v. Webster County, 488 U.S. 336 (1989).

[411] E.g., 17 BVerfGE 210, 216 (1964).

[412] See 36 BVerfGE 237, 248-50 (Rupp-von Brünneck, J., dissenting). Cf. Dandridge v. Williams, 397 U.S. 471, 520-23 (1970) (Marshall, J., dissenting).

erable support. Among other things, the Constitutional Court has found fault with the exclusion of unemployment benefits for students[413] and for persons formerly employed by their parents,[414] limitations on aid for the blind[415] or disabled,[416] and the denial of retirement benefits to persons living abroad.[417] Some of these decisions may be explainable on the ground that the classification impinged upon some other fundamental right; but the overall impression is that the Constitutional Court is rather strict in scrutinizing classifications in the distribution of welfare benefits as such.

Indeed, without regard to the various categories of heightened scrutiny already discussed, more recent opinions have exhibited a marked tendency to replace the deferential arbitrariness standard originally enunciated with the apparently more aggressive search for a reason "sufficient to justify" the challenged distinction.[418] Decisions in the past few years suggest that, whatever formulation is employed, review under the general equality provision is never as toothless as it has become in economic cases in the United States. In striking down limitations on the assessment and award of agency or court costs[419] without intimating that the distinctions either embodied suspect classifications or impinged upon fundamental rights, for example, the Constitutional Court conjured up memories of the vigorous way in which the equal protection clause was enforced in economic cases during the *Lochner* era in this country.[420]

Furthermore, in more recent decisions the notion of arbitrariness has tended to come loose from its moorings and to enjoy an independent life of its own. Originally a test for the legitimacy of legal distinctions, arbitrariness began to appear, despite cogent warnings

---

[413] 74 BVerfGE 9, 24-28 (1986).

[414] 18 BVerfGE 366, 372-80 (1965) (noting the severity of the exclusion and the impact of the Sozialstaat principle).

[415] 37 BVerfGE 154, 164-66 (1974).

[416] 39 BVerfGE 148, 152-56 (1975) (finding such a limitation not yet unconstitutional but warning that it soon might be).

[417] 51 BVerfGE 1, 23-29 (1979) (holding that they must at least be given their contributions back).

[418] See, e.g., 74 BVerfGE 9, 29-30 (1986) (dissenting opinion) (pointing out the general and unannounced change in the governing standard).

[419] 50 BVerfGE 217, 225-33 (1979); 74 BVerfGE 78, 94-96 (1986). See also 54 BVerfGE 277, 293-97 (1980) (holding in contrast to our certiorari practice that state appellate courts could not decline jurisdiction of meritorious cases simply because of their overloaded dockets).

[420] Cf., e.g., Gulf, C. & S.F. Ry. v. Ellis, 165 U.S. 150 (1897) (striking down a provision that imposed attorneys' fees in actions for livestock losses only if the defendant was a railroad). See generally The Second Century, chs. 2, 5, 7. Most recently, however, the Constitutional Court has reaffirmed the existence of varying levels of scrutiny under Art 3(1), stressing in particular that the legislature has more freedom to draw distinctions on the basis of conduct than on the basis of personal characteristics over which the individual has no control. BVerfG, Judgment of June 8, 1993, Case No. 1 BvL 20/85 (not yet reported), slip op. at 11-12.

in dissent,[421] as a ground for condemning official action – especially
judicial action – without mention of inequality at all.[422] Thus the
equality clause of Article 3(1) bade fair to become a guarantee of
substantive and procedural due process as well – though there
seemed no need for another such provision in view of the broad interpretation already given the right to free development of personality
under Article 2(1).

Finally, although the Constitutional Court has sometimes said
that Article 3 imposes no duty to rectify inequalities existing apart
from governmental action,[423] other opinions have more than hinted
that it may outlaw de facto inequality under some circumstances.
The first was an opinion, reminiscent of *Griffin v. Illinois*, relying on
Article 3(1) to require the assignment of counsel to an indigent party
at state expense[424] – one of the very few areas in which our Supreme
Court has come close to recognizing positive rights to government
support. Most arresting in this connection was the decision that
allowing taxpayers unrestricted deductions for political contributions
gave an unfair advantage to wealthy contributors and the parties they
tended to support[425] – with an explicit dictum to the effect that
progressive taxation was constitutionally required.[426] This decision

---

[421] See 42 BVerfGE 64, 79-83 (1976) (Geiger, J., dissenting).

[422] E.g., 57 BVerfGE 39, 41-42 (1981); 58 BVerfGE 163, 167-68 (1981); 62 BVerfGE
189, 191-94 (1982); 62 BVerfGE 338, 343 (1982); 71 BVerfGE 202, 204-05 (1985). A
plausible explanation may be that to deviate from the law in a particular case is to
apply it unequally. See 54 BVerfGE 117, 124-26 (1980); Dürig in 1 Maunz/Dürig,
Art. 3(1), Rdnr. 52.

[423] See, e.g., 1 BVerfGE 97, 107 (1951).

[424] 2 BVerfGE 336, 339-41 (1953). Cf. *Griffin*, 351 U.S. 12 (1956). See also 1
BVerfGE 109, 111 (1952) (finding assignment of counsel required by the more general requirements of democracy and the social state); 54 BVerfGE 251, 266-73 (1980)
(requiring a state-assigned guardian for an impecunious ward).

[425] 8 BVerfGE 51, 63-69 (1958). See also 85 BVerfGE 264, 312-18 (1992) (striking
down a revised law that permitted deductions of contributions up to 60,000 DM on
similar grounds). These decisions are also noted in chapter 4 supra.

[426] 8 BVerfGE at 68-69: "[I]n the tax field a formally equal treatment of rich and
poor by application of the same tax rate would contradict the equality provision.
Here justice requires that in the interest of proportional equality a person who can
afford more pay a higher percentage of his income in taxes than one with less economic power." This principle may also help to explain the constitutionally required deductibility of child-care expenses, note 394 supra. See also 82 BVerfGE 322,
339-42, 348-51 (1990) (also noted in chapter 3 supra) (holding it unconstitutional to
exclude East German parties from the first Bundestag elected after reunification on
the formally equal ground of inability to attract five percent of the nationwide vote);
text at notes 95, 387 supra (discussing the affirmative duties imposed by Art. 6(5)
and 3(2) to assure actual equality of opportunity for illegitimate children and for
women, respectively). The Constitution of Bremen appears to generalize this last
principle: "All persons . . . have the right to equal opportunities for economic and
cultural development." Landesverfassung der Freien Hansestadt Bremen vom 21.
Oktober 1947, SaBremR 100-a-1 (as amended Sept. 8, 1987, GBl. S. 233), Art. 2.

is but one more example of the ways in which the equality clauses, like other provisions of the Basic Law, have been employed to make the Constitutional Court ultimate censor of the reasonableness of all governmental action.

VI. CONCLUSION

What is one to make of all this? What one will; my aims are descriptive and comparative. For better or worse, the German Constitutional Court is in the business of determining the reasonableness of governmental action – and, to a significant degree, of inaction as well. In exercising this authority the Court has delved repeatedly into details of the organization and practices of higher education[427] and broadcasting,[428] passed upon such minutiae as the appropriate titles of teachers and judges, and joined our Supreme Court in composing a detailed (though strikingly different) abortion code. Moreover, while the German court has so far generally been deferential to other branches of government in determining how and how far to protect citizens against third parties and against want, the abortion and private-school subsidy cases demonstrate the potential for constitutionalizing vast additional areas of tort, criminal, and welfare law. The general tendency of the German decisions has been progressive rather than reactionary, and the notion of affirmative duties of government protection is largely foreign to our jurisprudence; but the basic principle of freewheeling judicial review is reminiscent of that which gave us *Scott v. Sandford, Lochner v. New York,* and *Roe v. Wade.*

Whether the German judges were justified in finding that the Basic Law conferred such sweeping judicial authority I leave to those brought up in the system. I have explained at some length elsewhere why I believe our Constitution does not,[429] but both the language and the history of the two documents differ significantly. That familial and occupational rights are entitled to some constitutional protection in Germany, for example, is obvious from the text; so is the disfavored position of discrimination on grounds of sex. Only to a limited

---

[427] In addition to the cases on university admissions noted above, see the line of decisions discussed in chapter 4 supra, beginning with 35 BVerfGE 79 (1973), invoking Art. 5(3)'s guarantee of academic freedom to assure faculty control of basic questions relating to curriculum and research.

[428] The seminal decision on broadcasting was 12 BVerfGE 205 (1961), where the Court interpreted the Art. 5(1) provision that "freedom of reporting by means of broadcasts . . . [is] guaranteed" to require the state to regulate broadcasting in such a way that various social and political interests had the opportunity to utilize the medium and to participate in its governance. For later decisions applying and refining these requirements see, e.g., 57 BVerfGE 295 (1981); 73 BVerfGE 118 (1986). These decisions too are discussed in chapter 4 supra.

[429] See The First Hundred Years and The Second Century, passim.

extent, therefore, are the German decisions directly relevant to the interpretation of our Constitution.

More important for us is what the German decisions have to say about the desirability of empowering politically insulated judges to make open-ended judgments regarding the reasonableness of government action. Some may find in the German experience confirmation of the dangers of unchecked judicial intervention, others proof of the need for broad judicial review. Unlike their American counterparts during the *Lochner* years, the German judges do not seem often to have blocked desirable or even fairly debatable reforms; they do seem to have spared their compatriots a flock of unjustified restrictions on liberty and property. Whether this record affords a basis for confidence that either American or German judges would exercise such a power wisely in the long run is another matter; so is the question whether so broad a power, however wisely exercised, is consistent with one's conception of democracy.[430]

---

[430] See Philip B. Kurland, Politics, the Constitution, and the Warren Court 204 (1970): "Essentially because [the Supreme Court's] most important function is anti-majoritarian, it ought not to intervene to frustrate the will of the majority except where it is essential to its functions as guardian of interests that would otherwise be unrepresented in the government of the country."

Epilogue

The Basic Law has been a resounding success. Drafted and adopted by a people only recently emerged from the depths of darkness, it not only embodies all the elements of a classic liberal constitution on paper; it has been translated into practice too. Forty-five years under the Basic Law has meant forty-five years of democracy, freedom, and the rule of law. As President von Weizsäcker said in commemorating its fortieth anniversary in 1989, the Basic Law laid the cornerstone for a German state that stands for democracy, peace, and human rights and has earned respect throughout the world.[1]

In making the noble phrases of the Basic Law a reality the Constitutional Court has played a central role. In case after case it has vindicated basic rights. Unlike our Supreme Court, it has given up neither on federalism nor on the separation of powers.[2] And since its inception the Constitutional Court has unhesitatingly been obeyed.

In interpreting the Basic Law the Constitutional Court has employed familiar tools: text, context, structure, history, purpose, and plain common sense.[3] But interpretation, as former Justice Konrad

---

[1] See Frankfurter Allgemeine Zeitung, May 26, 1989, p. 12.

[2] Contrast Wickard v. Filburn, 317 U.S. 111 (1942); Federal Energy Administration v. Algonquin SNG, 426 U.S. 548 (1976); Humphrey's Executor v. United States, 295 U.S. 602 (1935); Crowell v. Benson, 285 U.S. 22 (1932). See generally David Currie, The Distribution of Powers after *Bowsher*, 1986 Sup. Ct. Rev. 19. To an outside observer the most questionable German decisions in this regard are 2 BVerfGE 213, 224 (1953) (holding nonjusticiable the question whether there was a need for the exercise of concurrent federal legislative power under Art. 72(2)) and 30 BVerfGE 1, 23-29 (1970) (upholding a constitutional amendment that precluded judicial review of eavesdropping orders). See chapters 2 and 3 supra.

[3] See, e.g. 12 BVerfGE 205, 226-37 (1961) (first *Television* case) (discussed in chapter 4), where the first five of these instruments were successively employed; 39 BVerfGE 334, 368 (1975), where in concluding that Art. 3(3) did not forbid every classification in terms of the criteria it enumerated the Court echoed John Marshall's argument that the framers could not have intended an absurd result. See also Winfried Brugger, Legal Interpretation, Schools of Jurisprudence, and Anthropology: Some Remarks from a German Point of View (forthcoming in Am. J. Comp. L.) (finding a "common methodological ground" in the pragmatic use of textual, structural, historical, and teleological arguments in both Germany and the United States).

Hesse has written, is not simply a quest for answers supplied by the constitution itself; often it is a process of making abstract principles concrete in applying them to cases the framers did not attempt to resolve.[4]

The Constitutional Court has been most creative in its interpretation. Indeed many of the central concepts in German constitutional jurisprudence have no visible roots in the text or legislative history of the Basic Law: proportionality, reciprocal effect, the impact of fundamental rights on private conduct, the requirement of fidelity to the federal system. As in the United States, there has been a tendency away from rules and toward a balancing of competing interests. Among the consequences are an enhancement of judicial discretion and a reduction in the certainty of law.[5]

The substantive results have often been commendable. Freedom of expression, for example, has been given far more protection against legislative encroachment than the text of the Basic Law would have led one to expect. Developments of this nature, however, inevitably raise questions as to the boundary between legitimate interpretation and judicial amendment of the constitution. Moreover, the authority of any court rests ultimately on public acceptance, and

---

In one of its earliest opinions the Court went out of its way to disparage the value of legislative history as an aid to statutory construction (see 1 BVerfGE 299, 312 (1952)), but later opinions have not hesitated to give significant weight to the proceedings of the Parliamentary Council. See, e.g., 12 BVerfGE at 236-37 (first *Television* case); 6 BVerfGE 32, 36-37 (1957) (*Elfes*) (also discussed in chapter 4) (relying heavily on the debates in reaching the controversial conclusion that Art. 2(1) conferred a general right of freedom of action); 62 BVerfGE 1, 45-47 (1983) (where the Court spent two pages exploring the debates on the provision of Art. 68 respecting dissolution of the Bundestag after stressing that although such materials would normally not be decisive they could not be completely ignored). Most interesting in this regard is 75 BVerfGE 40, 58-61 (1987) (discussed in chapter 6), where after concluding that legislative history conclusively showed that Art. 7(4) was not meant to require subsidies for private schools the Court held they were required anyway – a course of action that seems to affirm the legitimacy both of dynamic interpretation and of legislative history as a guide to original meaning. See also 45 BVerfGE 187, 227 (1977), where the Court explicitly affirmed the mutability of human dignity and the rule of law in light of new understanding both of the effects of life imprisonment and of the nature of the basic rights themselves; Christian Starck, Die Verfassungsauslegung, 7 Handbuch des Staatsrechts 189, Rdnr. 57 (arguing that in most cases involving the allocation of authority legislative history has played a decisive role).

[4] See Konrad Hesse, Grundzüge des Verfassungsrechts der Bundesrepublik Deutschland (18th ed. 1991), Rdnr. 60.

[5] See Erhard Denninger, Verfassungsrechtliche Schlüsselbegriffe, in Festschrift für Rudolf Wassermann 279 (1985).

its judgments are most likely to command respect when they can readily be traced to the orders of the people.[6]

On the other hand, the acceptability of decisions – and the standing of the document itself – can also be threatened if the constitution does not keep pace with the times. The Basic Law, writes Justice Dieter Grimm of the Constitutional Court, has admirably fulfilled its original task of protecting the individual from oppressive governmental action, and that is no mean achievement. But the greatest dangers, he argues, no longer emanate from the state; any constitution that confines itself to its conventional defensive function risks increasing irrelevance to the needs of modern society.[7]

This argument brings us back to what from the transatlantic perspective may be the most interesting and novel provisions of the entire Basic Law: Articles 20(1) and 28(1), which commit both Bund and Länder to the principle of the social state. Though for a number of reasons not directly enforceable, these clauses have supplied a powerful impetus for the Constitutional Court's imaginative jurisprudence of affirmative state obligations and have had a profound impact on the interpretation of existing laws.

So far the Court, while bold in enunciating affirmative duties, has been notably reticent in enforcing them. The jury is still out on the question whether it would be wise, or consistent with democracy, or even feasible, to go further. When one contemplates the intimidating problems attendant on the reunification of East and West Germany, or the state of the inner cities in the United States, Justice Grimm's question becomes urgent: Can and should the constitution be made more responsive to the needs of the twenty-first century? Or is a constitution inherently ill-suited, as Peter Badura has argued, to serve as a medium for resolving issues of social and economic policy?[8]

Reunification has provided a pressing occasion for confronting these questions. The Constitutional Commission, set up by the Bundestag and Bundesrat pursuant to a recommendation in the Unifica-

---

[6] See The Federalist, No. 78 (Hamilton); Bowers v. Hardwick, 478 U.S. 186, 194 (1986).

[7] See Dieter Grimm, Die Zukunft der Verfassung 7, 62-64, 152-53, 166-68, 325-26(1991).

[8] See Peter Badura, Die Verfassung des Bundesstaates Deutschland in Europa 31 (1993) (adding, id. at 25, that the Basic Law has been successful precisely because it has not promised more than it can deliver); Cass Sunstein, Against Positive Rights, 2 East European Constitutional Review 35, 38 (1993): "A constitution that purports to guarantee a decent society may, in the process, guarantee nothing at all." See generally David Currie, Written Constitutions and Social Rights, in Vivien Hart & Shannon C. Stimson (eds.), Writing a National Identity: Political, Economic, and Cultural Perspectives on the Written Constitution 41 (1993).

tion Treaty itself,[9] has proposed a number of amendments to the Basic Law while expressing satisfaction with that document as a whole. At the same time the ambitious Maastricht Treaty has raised important new questions about the future relation between Germany and an increasingly powerful European Union.

Thus the next few years promise to be a time of constitutional ferment in Germany. We have already learned a great deal from the German experience under the Basic Law, and the continuing debate should add significantly to our understanding of the role of a written constitution two centuries after the adoption of our own. As Konrad Adenauer said in closing the Parliamentary Council that drafted the Basic Law in 1949, "May the will and the spirit embodied in its provisions live forever in the hearts of the German people."[10]

---

[9] Vertrag zwischen der Bundesrepublik Deutschland und der Deutschen Demokratischen Republik über die Herstellung der Einheit Deutschlands, approved Sept. 23, 1990, BGBl. II S. 885, Art. 5.

[10] Sten. Ber. at 273 .

Appendix

BASIC LAW FOR THE FEDERAL REPUBLIC OF GERMANY

of May 23, 1949
as amended to December 1, 1993

PREAMBLE[1]

Conscious of their responsibility before God and men,

Animated by the resolve to serve world peace as an equal partner in a united Europe, the German people have adopted, by virtue of their constituent power, this Basic Law.

The Germans in the Länder of Baden-Württemberg, Bavaria, Berlin, Brandenburg, Bremen, Hamburg, Hesse, Lower Saxony, Mecklenburg-Western Pomerania, North Rhine-Westphalia, Rhineland-Palatinate, Saarland, Saxony, Saxony-Anhalt, Schleswig-Holstein, and Thuringia have achieved the unity and freedom of Germany in free self-determination. This Basic Law is thus valid for the entire German People.

I. BASIC RIGHTS

Article 1 (Protection of human dignity)

(1) Human dignity is inviolable. To respect and protect it is the duty of all state authority.

(2) The German people therefore acknowledge inviolable and inalienable human rights as the basis of every community, of peace and of justice in the world.

---

[1] As amended by the Unification Treaty of August 31, 1990, and federal statute of September 23, 1990 (BGBl. II S. 885).

(3)[2] The following basic rights shall bind the legislature, the executive, and the judiciary as directly enforceable law.

Article 2 (Rights of liberty)

(1) Everyone has the right to the free development of his personality insofar as he does not violate the rights of others or offend against the constitutional order or the moral law.

(2) Everyone has the right to life and to physical integrity. The liberty of the individual is inviolable. Intrusion on these rights may be made only pursuant to statute.

Article 3 (Equality before the law)

(1) All persons are equal before the law.

(2) Men and women shall have equal rights.

(3) No one may be disadvantaged or favored because of his sex, his parentage, his race, his language, his homeland and origin, his faith, or his religious or political opinions.

Article 4 (Freedom of faith, of conscience, and of creed)

(1) Freedom of faith and of conscience, and freedom to profess a religion or a particular philosophy [Weltanschauung], are inviolable.

(2) The undisturbed practice of religion is guaranteed.

(3) No one may be compelled against his conscience to render military service involving the use of arms. Details shall be regulated by federal statute.

Article 5 (Freedom of expression)

(1) Everyone has the right freely to express and disseminate his opinion in speech, writing, and pictures and freely to inform himself from generally accessible sources. Freedom of the press and freedom of reporting by means of broadcasts and films are guaranteed. There shall be no censorship.

(2) These rights find their limits in the provisions of general statutes, in statutory provisions for the protection of youth, and in the right to respect for personal honor.

(3) Art and science, research, and teaching shall be free. Freedom of teaching shall not release anyone from his allegiance to the constitution.

---

[2] As amended by federal statute of March 19, 1956 (BGBl. I S. 111).

Article 6 (Marriage and the family; illegitimate children)

(1) Marriage and family enjoy the special protection of the state.

(2) The care and upbringing of children is a natural right of and a duty primarily incumbent upon the parents. The state shall watch over their endeavors in this respect.

(3) Children may not be separated from their families against the will of the persons entitled to bring them up, except, pursuant to statute, when those so entitled fail in their duties or the children are otherwise threatened with serious neglect.

(4) Every mother is entitled to the protection and care of the community.

(5) Illegitimate children shall be provided by legislation with the same opportunities for their physical and mental development and for their place in society as are enjoyed by legitimate children.

Article 7 (Education)

(1) The entire educational system shall be under the supervision of the state.

(2) The persons entitled to bring up a child have the right to decide whether the child shall attend religion classes.

(3) Religion classes shall form part of the ordinary curriculum in public schools, except in secular [bekenntnisfreien] schools. Without prejudice to the state's right of supervision, religious instruction shall be given in accordance with the tenets of the religious communities. No teacher may be obliged against his will to give religious instruction.

(4) The right to establish private schools is guaranteed. Private schools, as a substitute for public schools, shall require the approval of the state and shall be subject to the statutes of the Länder. Such approval shall be given when private schools are not inferior to the public schools in their educational aims, their facilities, and the professional training of their teaching staff, and when segregation of pupils according to the means of the parents is not encouraged thereby. Approval shall be withheld if the economic and legal position of the teaching staff is not sufficiently assured.

(5) A private elementary school shall be permitted only if the education authority finds that it serves a special pedagogic interest, or if, on the application of persons entitled to bring up children, it is to be established as an interdenominational school or as a denominational school or as a school based on a particular philosophical persuasion [Weltanschauungsschule] and a public elementary school of this type does not exist in the community.

(6) Preliminary schools [Vorschulen] shall remain abolished.

Article 8 (Freedom of assembly)

(1) All Germans have the right to assemble peaceably and unarmed without prior notification or permission.

(2) With regard to open-air meetings, this right may be restricted by or pursuant to statute.

Article 9 (Freedom of association)

(1) All Germans shall have the right to form associations and corporations.

(2) Associations whose purposes or activities conflict with criminal statutes or that are directed against the constitutional order or the concept of international understanding are prohibited.

(3) The right to form associations to safeguard and improve working and economic conditions is guaranteed to everyone and to all occupations. Agreements that restrict or seek to impair this right are null and void; measures directed to this end are illegal. Measures taken pursuant to Article 12a, to paragraphs (2) and (3) of Article 35, to paragraph (4) of Article 87a, or to Article 91 may not be directed against any industrial conflicts engaged in by associations within the meaning of the first sentence of this paragraph in order to safeguard and improve working and economic conditions. [3]

Article 10[4] (Privacy of letters, posts, and telecommunications)

(1) Privacy of letters, posts, and telecommunications is inviolable.

(2) Restrictions may be ordered only pursuant to statute. When a restriction serves to protect the free democratic basic order or the existence or security of the Federation, the statute may stipulate that the person affected shall not be informed of such restriction and that recourse to the courts shall be replaced by a review of the case by bodies and auxiliary bodies appointed by Parliament.

Article 11 (Freedom of movement)

(1) All Germans shall enjoy freedom of movement throughout the federal territory.

---

[3] Last sentence inserted by federal statute of June 24, 1968 (BGBl. I S. 709).

[4] As amended by federal statute of June 24, 1968 (BGBl. I S. 709).

(2)[5] This right may be restricted only by or pursuant to statute, and only in cases in which an adequate basis for personal existence is lacking and special burdens would result therefrom for the community, or in which such restriction is necessary to avert an imminent danger to the existence or the free democratic basic order of the Federation or a Land, to combat the danger of epidemics, to deal with natural disasters or particularly grave accidents, to protect young people from neglect, or to prevent crime.

Article 12[6] (Right to choose an occupation; prohibition of forced labor)

(1) All Germans have the right freely to choose their trade, occupation, or profession, their place of work, and their place of training. The practice of trades, occupations, and professions may be regulated by or pursuant to statute.

(2) No person may be forced to perform work of a particular kind except within the framework of a traditional compulsory community service that applies generally and equally to all.

(3) Forced labor may be imposed only on persons deprived of their liberty by court sentence.

Article 12a[7] (Liability to military and other service)

(1) Men who have attained the age of eighteen years may be required to serve in the Armed Forces, in the Federal Border Guard, or in a civil defense organization.

(2) A person who refuses, on grounds of conscience, to render military service involving the use of arms may be required to render substitute service. The duration of such substitute service shall not exceed the duration of military service. Details shall be regulated by statute, which shall not interfere with the freedom to make a decision based on conscience and shall also provide for the possibility of substitute service not connected with units of the Armed Forces or of the Federal Border Guard.

(3) Persons liable to military service who are not required to render service pursuant to paragraph (1) or (2) of this Article may, during a state of defense [Verteidigungsfall], be assigned by or pursuant to statute to an employment involving civilian services for defense purposes, including the protection of

---

[5] As amended by federal statute of June 24, 1968 (BGBl. I S. 709).

[6] As amended by federal statutes of March 19, 1956 (BGBl. I S. 111) and June 24, 1968 (BGBl. I S. 709).

[7] Inserted by federal statute of June 24, 1968 (BGBl. I S. 710).

the civilian population. However, it shall not be permissible to assign persons to an employment subject to public law except for the purpose of discharging police functions or such other functions of public administration as can only be discharged by persons employed under public law. Persons may be assigned to an employment – as referred to in the first sentence of this paragraph – with the Armed Forces, including the supplying and servicing of the latter, or with public administrative authorities. Assignments to employment connected with supplying and servicing the civilian population shall not be permissible except in order to meet their vital requirements or to guarantee their safety.

(4) If, during a state of defense, civilian service requirements in the civilian health system or in the stationary military hospital organization cannot be met on a voluntary basis, women between eighteen and fifty-five years of age may be assigned to such services by or pursuant to statute. They may on no account render service involving the use of arms.

(5) Prior to the existence of a state of defense, assignments under paragraph (3) of this Article may be made only if the requirements of paragraph (1) of Article 80a are satisfied. It shall be permissible to require persons by or pursuant to statute to attend training courses in order to prepare them for the performance of such services in accordance with paragraph (3) of this Article as require special knowledge or skills. To this extent, the first sentence of this paragraph shall not apply.

(6) If, during a state of defense, staffing requirements for the purposes referred to in the second sentence of paragraph (3) of this Article cannot be met on a voluntary basis, the right of a German to terminate the pursuit of his occupation or quit his place of work may be restricted by or pursuant to statute in order to meet these requirements. The first sentence of paragraph (5) of this Article shall apply prior to the existence of a state of defense.

Article 13 (Inviolability of the home)

(1) The home is inviolable.

(2) Searches may be ordered only by a judge or, in the event of danger resulting in any delay in taking action, by other organs as provided by statute and may be carried out only in the form prescribed by law.

(3) Intrusions and restrictions may otherwise be made only to avert a public danger or a mortal danger to individuals, or, pursuant to statute, to prevent substantial danger to public safety and order, in particular to relieve a housing shortage, to combat the danger of epidemics, or to protect juveniles who are exposed to a moral danger.

Article 14 (Property; right of inheritance; taking of property)

(1) Property and right of inheritance are guaranteed. Their content and limits shall be determined by statute.

(2) Property imposes duties. Its use should also serve the public weal.

(3) The taking of property is permissible only for the public weal. It may be effected only by or pursuant to a statute regulating the nature and extent of compensation. Such compensation shall be determined by establishing an equitable balance between the public interest and the interests of those affected. In case of dispute regarding the amount of compensation, recourse may be had to the courts of ordinary jurisdiction.

Article 15 (Socialization)

Land, natural resources, and means of production may for the purpose of socialization be transferred to public ownership or other forms of collective enterprise for the public benefit by a statute regulating the nature and extent of compensation. In respect of such compensation the third and fourth sentences of paragraph (3) of Article 14 shall apply.

Article 16 (Deprivation of citizenship; extradition)

(1) No one may be deprived of his German citizenship. Citizenship may be lost only pursuant to statute, and it may be lost against the will of the person affected only where such person does not become stateless as a result thereof.

(2)[8] No German may be extradited to a foreign country.

Article 16a[9] (Right of asylum)

(1) Persons persecuted on political grounds shall enjoy the right of asylum.

(2) Paragraph (1) cannot be invoked by a person who enters from a member country of the European Communities or from another third country in which application of the Agreement Concerning the Status of Refugees and of the Convention for the Protection of Human Rights and Fundamental Freedoms is guaranteed. The states outside the European Communities to which the criteria of the first sentence of this paragraph apply shall be specified by a statute requiring the consent of the Bundesrat. In the cases specified in the first sentence of this paragraph, measures to terminate an applicant's stay may be taken without regard to any legal action commenced against such measures.

---

[8] As amended by federal statute of June 28, 1993 (BGBl. I S. 1002).

[9] Inserted by federal statute of June 28, 1993 (BGBl. I S. 1002).

(3) By a statute requiring the consent of the Bundesrat, nations may be specified in which, on the basis of their legal situation, enforcement of law, and general political conditions, it seems assured that neither political persecution nor cruel or demeaning punishment or treatment exists. It will be presumed that a foreigner from such a state is not persecuted, so long as he does not present evidence justifying a claim that, contrary to this presumption, he is persecuted on political grounds.

(4) In the cases specified by paragraph (3) and in other cases which are apparently unfounded or deemed apparently unfounded, the execution of measures to terminate an applicant's stay may be suspended by a court only if serious doubts exist as to the legality of the measures; the extent of the investigation may be limited, and evidence tardily presented may be disregarded. Further details shall be determined by statute.

(5) Paragraphs (1) through (4) shall not interfere with international treaties of member countries of the European Communities among each other or with nonmember countries which, while respecting those obligations arising from the Agreement Concerning the Status of Refugees and the Convention for the Protection of Human Rights and Fundamental Freedoms whose enforcement must be guaranteed in the contracting states, establish rules respecting competency to determine requests for asylum, including the reciprocal recognition of decisions regarding refugees.

Article 17 (Right of petition)

Everyone has the right individually or jointly with others to address written requests or complaints to the competent agencies and to parliaments.

Article 17a[10] (Restriction of individual basic rights by legislation enacted for defense purposes and concerning substitute service)

(1) Statutes concerning military service and substitute service may, by provisions applying to members of the Armed Forces and of the substitute services during their period of military or substitute service, restrict the basic right freely to express and to disseminate opinions in speech, writing, and pictures (first half-sentence of paragraph (1) of Article 5), the basic right of assembly (Article 8), and the right of petition (Article 17) insofar as this right permits the submission of requests or complaints jointly with others.

(2) Statutes serving defense purposes including protection of the civilian population may provide for the restriction of the basic rights of freedom of movement (Article 11) and inviolability of the home (Article 13).

---

[10] Inserted by federal statute of March 19, 1956 (BGBl. I S. 111).

Article 18[11] (Forfeiture of basic rights)

Whoever abuses freedom of expression of opinion, in particular freedom of the press (paragraph (1) of Article 5), freedom of teaching (paragraph (3) of Article 5), freedom of assembly (Article 8), freedom of association (Article 9), privacy of letters, posts, and telecommunication (Article 10), property (Article 14), or the right of asylum (Article 16a) in order to combat the free democratic basic order shall forfeit these basic rights. Such forfeiture and the extent thereof shall be determined by the Federal Constitutional Court.

Article 19 (Restriction of basic rights)

(1) Insofar as a basic right may, under this Basic Law, be restricted by or pursuant to statute, such statute shall apply generally and not solely to an individual case. Furthermore, such statute shall name the basic right, indicating the Article concerned.

(2) In no case may the essence of a basic right be encroached upon.

(3) The basic rights shall apply also to domestic juristic persons to the extent that the nature of such rights permits.

(4) Should any person's rights be violated by public authority, recourse to the court shall be open to him. Insofar as no other jurisdiction has been established, recourse shall be to the courts of ordinary jurisdiction. The second sentence of paragraph (2) of Article 10 shall not be affected by the provisions of this paragraph.[12]

II. THE FEDERATION AND THE STATES [LÄNDER]

Article 20 (Basic principles of state order; right to resist)

(1) The Federal Republic of Germany is a democratic and social federal state.

(2) All state authority emanates from the people. It shall be exercised by the people through elections and voting and by specific legislative, executive, and judicial organs.

(3) Legislation is subject to the constitutional order; the executive and the judiciary are bound by law and justice.

---

[11] As amended by federal statute of June 24, 1968 (BGBl. I S. 710).

[12] Last sentence inserted by federal statute of June 24, 1968 (BGBl. I S. 710).

(4)[13] All Germans have the right to resist any person or persons seeking to abolish this constitutional order, should no other remedy be possible.

Article 21[14] (Political parties)

(1) The political parties shall participate in the formation of the political will of the people. They may be freely established. Their internal organization shall conform to democratic principles. They shall publicly account for the sources and use of their funds and for their assets.

(2) Parties that, by reason of their aims or the behavior of their adherents, seek to impair or abolish the free democratic basic order or to endanger the existence of the Federal Republic of Germany are unconstitutional. The Federal Constitutional Court shall decide on the question of unconstitutionality.

(3) Details shall be regulated by federal statute.

Article 22 (Federal flag)

The Federal flag shall be black, red, and gold.

Article 23[15] (European Union)

(1) In the interest of the realization of a united Europe, the Federal Republic of Germany shall participate in the development of a European Union that is committed to democratic, social, and federal principles, to the rule of law, and to the principle of subsidiarity, and that guarantees a level of protection of basic rights essentially comparable to that of this Basic Law. To this end the Federation may transfer sovereign powers by statute with the consent of the Bundesrat. For the establishment of the European Union, as well as for changes in its treaty foundations and for comparable regulations by which this Basic Law is amended or supplemented in its content, or by which such amendments or supplements are made possible, paragraphs (2) and (3) of Article 79 shall apply.

(2) The Bundestag and the Länder, through the Bundesrat, shall participate in the affairs of the European Union. The Federal Government shall keep the Bundestag and the Bundesrat informed, comprehensively and at the earliest possible time.

---

[13] Inserted by federal statute of June 24, 1968 (BGBl. I S. 710).

[14] As amended by federal statute of December 21, 1983 (BGBl. I S. 1461).

[15] Original Article 23 repealed by the Unification Treaty of August 31, 1990, and federal statute of September 23, 1990 (BGBl. II S. 885); new Article 23 inserted by federal statute of December 21, 1992 (BGBl. I S. 2086).

(3) Before participating in lawmaking activities of the European Union, the Federal Government shall provide the Bundestag with an opportunity to state its position. The Federal Government shall take the position of the Bundestag into consideration during the negotiations. Further details shall be regulated by statute.

(4) The Bundesrat shall participate in the decision-making of the Federation insofar as it would have been competent to do so in a comparable internal action, or insofar as the Länder would have been competent to do so internally.

(5) Insofar as, in a matter within the exclusive competence of the Federation, interests of the Länder are affected, and in other matters, insofar as the Federation has legislative power, the Federal Government shall take into consideration the position of the Bundesrat. Whenever the legislative powers of the Länder, the structure of Land agencies, or Land administrative procedures are primarily affected, to that extent the position of the Bundesrat shall be the decisive consideration in determining the Federation's position; at the same time the responsibility of the Federation for the nation as a whole shall be respected. In matters that may lead to increased expenditures or reduced revenues for the Federation, the consent of the Federal Government is required.

(6) When legislative powers exclusive to the Länder are primarily affected, the exercise of the rights belonging to the Federal Republic of Germany as a member nation of the European Union shall be transferred to a representative of the Länder to be appointed by the Bundesrat. These rights shall be exercised with the participation and agreement of the Federal Government; in their exercise the responsibility of the Federation for the nation as a whole shall be respected.

(7) Details pertaining to paragraphs (4) through (6) shall be regulated by statute requiring the consent of the Bundesrat.

Article 24 (Entry into a collective security system)

(1) The Federation may by legislation transfer sovereign powers to intergovernmental institutions.

(1a)[16] Insofar as the Länder are competent to exercise governmental powers and to perform governmental functions, they may, with the consent of the Federal Government, transfer sovereign powers to institutions that transcend national boundaries.

(2) For the maintenance of peace, the Federation may enter a system of mutual collective security; in doing so it shall consent to such limitations upon

---

[16] Inserted by federal statute of December 21, 1992 (BGBl. I S. 2086).

its rights of sovereignty as will bring about and secure a peaceful and lasting order in Europe and among the nations of the world.

(3) For the settlement of disputes between states, the Federation shall accede to agreements concerning international arbitration of a general, comprehensive, and obligatory nature.

Article 25 (Public international law and federal law)

The general rules of public international law are an integral part of federal law. They take precedence over statutes and directly create rights and duties for the inhabitants of the federal territory.

Article 26 (Ban on preparation for war of aggression)

(1) Acts tending to and undertaken with intent to disturb the peaceful relations between nations, especially to prepare for a war of aggression, are unconstitutional. They shall be made a criminal offense.

(2) Weapons designed for warfare may not be manufactured, transported, or marketed except with the permission of the Federal Government. Details shall be regulated by federal statute.

Article 27 (Merchant fleet)

All German merchant vessels shall form one merchant fleet.

Article 28 (Federal guarantee of Länder constitutions; guarantee of self-government for local authorities)

(1) The constitutional order in the Länder must conform to the principles of republican, democratic and social government under the rule of law, within the meaning of this Basic Law. In each of the Länder, counties [Kreise], and communities [Gemeinden], the people shall be represented by a body chosen in general, direct, free, equal, and secret elections. In county and community elections, persons who possess citizenship in any member state of the European Communities are also eligible to vote and to be elected in accord with European Community law.[17] In the communities the communal assembly may take the place of an elected body.

(2) Communities must be guaranteed the right to regulate all the affairs of the local community on their own responsibility, within the limits set by statute. Within the framework of their statutory functions, associations of communities [Gemeindeverbände] shall also have such rights of self-government as may be provided by statute.

---

[17] Third sentence inserted by federal statute of December 21, 1992 (BGBl. I S. 2086).

(3) The Federation shall ensure that the constitutional order of the Länder conforms to the basic rights and to the provisions of paragraphs (1) and (2) of this Article.

Article 29 [18] (New delimitation of Länder boundaries)

(1) A new delimitation of federal territory may be made to ensure that the Länder by their size and capacity are able effectively to fulfil the functions incumbent upon them. Due regard shall be given to regional, historical, and cultural ties, economic expediency, and the requirements of local and regional planning.

(2) Measures for a new delimitation of federal territory shall be effected by federal statutes which shall require confirmation by referendum. The affected Länder shall be given an opportunity to be heard.

(3) A referendum shall be held in the Länder from whose territories or partial territories a new Land or a Land with redefined boundaries is to be formed (affected Länder). The referendum shall be held on the question whether the affected Länder are to remain within their existing boundaries or whether the new Land or Land with redefined boundaries should be formed. The referendum shall be deemed to be in favor of the formation of a new Land or of a Land with redefined boundaries when approval is given to the change by a majority in the future territory of such Land and by a majority in all the territories or partial territories of an affected Land whose assignment to a Land is to be changed in the same sense. The referendum shall be deemed not to be in favor when in the territory of one of the affected Länder a majority reject the change; such rejection shall, however, be of no consequence where in one part of the territory whose assignment to the affected Land is to be changed a majority of two-thirds approve the change, unless in the entire territory of the affected Land a majority of two-thirds reject the change.

(4) When in a clearly definable area of interconnected population and economic settlement, the parts of which lie in several Länder and which has a population of at least one million, one tenth of those of its population entitled to vote in Bundestag elections petition by popular initiative for the assignment of that area to one Land, provision shall be made within two years in a federal statute determining whether the delimitation of the affected Länder shall be changed pursuant to paragraph (2) of this Article or determining that a plebiscite shall be held in the affected Länder.

(5) The plebiscite shall establish whether approval is given to a change of Länder delimitation to be proposed in the statute. The statute may put forward different proposals, not exceeding two in number, for the plebiscite.

---

[18]As amended by federal statutes of August 19, 1969 (BGBl. I S. 1241), and of August 23, 1976 (BGBl. I S. 2381).

When approval is given by a majority to a proposed change of Länder delimitation, provision shall be made within two years in a federal statute determining whether the delimitation of the Länder concerned shall be changed pursuant to paragraph (2) of this Article. When approval is given, in accordance with the third and fourth sentences of paragraph (3) of this Article, to a proposal put forward for the plebiscite, a federal statute providing for the formation of the proposed Land shall be enacted within two years of the plebiscite and shall no longer require confirmation by referendum.

(6) A majority in a referendum or in a plebiscite shall consist of a majority of the votes cast, provided that they amount to at least one quarter of the population entitled to vote in the Bundestag elections. Other detailed provisions concerning referendums, popular petitions, and plebiscites [Volksentscheide, Volksbegehren, Volksbefragungen] shall be made by federal statute; such statute may also provide that popular petitions may not be repeated within a period of five years.

(7) Other changes concerning the territory of the Länder may be effected by state agreements between the Länder concerned or by federal statute with the approval of the Bundesrat, if the territory which is to be the subject of a new delimitation does not have more than 10,000 inhabitants. Detailed provision shall be made by federal statute requiring the approval of the Bundesrat and the majority of the members of the Bundestag. It shall make provision for the affected communities and counties to be heard.

Article 30 (Distribution of competence between the Federation and the Länder)

Except as otherwise provided or permitted by this Basic Law, the exercise of governmental powers and the discharge of governmental functions is a matter for the Länder.

Article 31 (Supremacy of federal law)

Federal law takes precedence over Land law.

Article 32 (Foreign relations)

(1) Relations with foreign states shall be conducted by the Federation.

(2) Before the conclusion of a treaty affecting the special circumstances of a Land, that Land shall be consulted in sufficient time.

(3) Insofar as the Länder have power to legislate, they may, with the consent of the Federal Government, conclude treaties with foreign states.

Article 33 (Equal political status of all Germans; professional civil service)

(1) Every German shall have in every Land the same rights and duties of citizenship.

(2) Every German shall be equally eligible for any public office according to his aptitude, qualifications, and professional achievements.

(3) Enjoyment of civil and political rights, eligibility for public office, and rights acquired in the public service shall be independent of religious denomination. No one may suffer any disadvantage by reason of his adherence or nonadherence to a denomination or to a philosophical persuasion.

(4) The exercise of state authority as a permanent function shall, as a rule, be entrusted to members of the public service whose status, service, and loyalty are governed by public law.

(5) The law of the public service shall be regulated with due regard to the traditional principles of the professional civil service.

Article 34 (Liability in the event of a breach of official duty)

If any person, in the exercise of a public office entrusted to him, violates his official obligations to a third party, liability shall rest in principle on the state or public body that employs him. In the event of willful intent or gross negligence, the right of recourse against the holder of a public office shall be reserved. In respect to the claim for compensation or the right of recourse, the jurisdiction of the ordinary courts shall not be excluded.

Article 35[19] (Legal and administrative assistance; assistance during disasters)

(1) All federal and Land authorities shall render each other legal and administrative assistance.

(2) In order to maintain or to restore public security or order, a Land may, in cases of particular importance, call upon forces and facilities of the Federal Border Guard to assist its police when without this assistance the police could not, or only with considerable difficulty, fulfill a task. In order to deal with a natural disaster or an especially grave accident, a Land may request the assistance of the police forces of other Länder or of forces and facilities of other administrative authorities or of the Federal Border Guard or the Armed Forces.

---

[19] As amended by federal statute of June 24, 1968 (BGBl. I S. 710), and by federal statute of July 28, 1972 (BGBl. I S. 1305).

(3) If the natural disaster or accident endangers a region larger than a single Land, the Federal Government may, insofar as necessary to deal effectively with such danger, instruct the Land governments to place their police forces at the disposal of other Länder, and may use units of the Federal Border Guard or the Armed Forces to support the police forces. Measures taken by the Federal Government pursuant to the first sentence of this paragraph shall be revoked at any time at the demand of the Bundesrat, and otherwise immediately upon removal of the danger.

Article 36 (Personnel of the federal authorities)

(1) Civil servants employed in the highest federal authorities shall be drawn from all Länder in appropriate proportion. Persons employed in other federal authorities shall, as a rule, be drawn from the Land in which they serve.

(2)[20] Military laws shall, inter alia, take into account both the division of the Federation into Länder and the regional ties of their populations.

Article 37 (Federal coercion)

(1) If a Land fails to comply with its obligations of a federal character imposed by this Basic Law or another federal statute, the Federal Government may, with the consent of the Bundesrat, take the necessary measures to enforce such compliance by the Land by way of federal coercion.

(2) For the purpose of exercising such federal coercion, the Federal Government or its commissioner shall have the right to give instructions to all Länder and their authorities.

III. THE FEDERAL PARLIAMENT [BUNDESTAG]

Article 38 (Elections)

(1) The deputies to the German Bundestag shall be elected in general, direct, free, equal, and secret elections. They shall be representatives of the whole people, not bound by orders or instructions, and shall be subject only to their conscience.

(2)[21] Anyone who has attained the age of eighteen years is entitled to vote; anyone who has attained majority is eligible for election.

(3) Details shall be regulated by federal statute.

---

[20] Inserted by federal statute of March 19, 1956 (BGBl. I S. 111).

[21] As amended by federal statute of July 31, 1970 (BGBl. I S. 1161).

Article 39 (Assembly and legislative term)

(1)[22] The Bundestag shall be elected for a four-year term. Its legislative term shall end with the assembly of a new Bundestag. The new election shall be held forty-five months at the earliest, and forty-seven months at the latest after the beginning of the legislative term. If the Bundestag is dissolved, the new election shall be held within sixty days.

(2)[23] The Bundestag shall assemble, at the latest, on the thirtieth day after the election.

(3) The Bundestag shall determine the termination and resumption of its meetings. The President of the Bundestag may convene it at an earlier date. He shall do so where one third of its members or the Federal President or the Federal Chancellor so demand.

Article 40 (President; rules of procedure)

(1) The Bundestag shall elect its President, vice presidents, and secretaries. It shall draw up its rules of procedure.

(2) The President shall exercise proprietary and police powers in the Bundestag building. No search or seizure may take place on the premises of the Bundestag without his permission.

Article 41 (Scrutiny of elections)

(1) The scrutiny of elections shall be the responsibility of the Bundestag. It shall also decide whether a deputy has lost his seat in the Bundestag.

(2) Complaints against such decisions of the Bundestag may be lodged with the Federal Constitutional Court.

(3) Details shall be regulated by federal statute.

Article 42 (Proceedings; voting)

(1) The meetings of the Bundestag shall be public. Upon a motion of one tenth of its members, or upon a motion of the Federal Government, the public may be excluded by a two-thirds majority. The decision on the motion shall be taken at a meeting not open to the public.

---

[22] As amended by federal statute of August 23, 1976 (BGBl. I S. 2381).

[23] As amended by federal statute of August 23, 1976 (BGBl. I S. 2381).

(2) Decisions of the Bundestag require a majority of the votes cast unless this Basic Law provides otherwise. The rules of procedure may provide for exceptions with respect to elections to be conducted by the Bundestag.

(3) True and accurate reports on the public meetings of the Bundestag and of its committees shall not give rise to any liability.

Article 43 (Presence of members of the Federal Government and of the Bundesrat)

(1) The Bundestag and its committees may demand the presence of any member of the Federal Government.

(2) The members of the Bundesrat and of the Federal Government as well as persons commissioned by them shall have access to all meetings of the Bundestag and its committees. They shall have the right to be heard at any time.

Article 44 (Committees of investigation)

(1) The Bundestag has the right, and upon the motion of one quarter of its members the duty, to set up a committee of investigation, which shall take the requisite evidence at public hearings. The public may be excluded.

(2) The rules of criminal procedure shall apply mutatis mutandis to the taking of evidence. The privacy of letters, posts, and telecommunications is unaffected.

(3) Courts and administrative authorities are bound to render legal and administrative assistance.

(4) The decisions of committees of investigation are not subject to judicial review. The courts shall be free to evaluate and judge the facts on which the investigation is based.

Article 45 [24] (Committee on European Union)

The Bundestag shall appoint a Committee on the Affairs of the European Union. It may authorize the committee to exercise the rights of the Bundestag vis-à-vis the Federal Government in accordance with Article 23.

---

[24] Original Article 45 repealed by federal statute of August 23, 1976 (BGBl. I S. 2381; new Article 45 inserted by federal statute of December 21, 1992 (BGBl. I S. 2086).

Article 45a[25] (Committees on Foreign Affairs and Defense)

(1)[26] The Bundestag shall appoint a Committee on Foreign Affairs and a Committee on Defense.

(2) The Committee on Defense shall also have the rights of a committee of investigation. Upon the motion of one quarter of its members it shall have the duty to make a specific matter the subject of investigation.

(3) Paragraph (1) of Article 44 shall not apply to defense matters.

Article 45b[27] (Defense Commissioner of the Bundestag)

A Defense Commissioner of the Bundestag shall be appointed to safeguard the basic rights and to assist the Bundestag in exercising parliamentary control. Details shall be regulated by federal statute.

Article 45c[28] (Petitions Committee)

(1) The Bundestag shall appoint a Petitions Committee to deal with requests and complaints addressed to the Bundestag pursuant to Article 17.

(2) The powers of the Committee to consider complaints shall be regulated by federal statute.

Article 46 (Indemnity and immunity of deputies)

(1) A deputy may not at any time be subjected to court proceedings or disciplinary action or otherwise called to account outside the Bundestag for a vote cast or a statement made by him in the Bundestag or in any of its committees. This provision does not apply to defamatory insults.

(2) A deputy may not be called to account or arrested for a punishable offense without permission of the Bundestag, unless he is apprehended during commission of the offence or in the course of the following day.

(3) The permission of the Bundestag shall also be necessary for any other restriction of the personal liberty of a deputy or for the initiation of proceedings against a deputy under Article 18.

---

[25] Inserted by federal statute of March 19, 1956 (BGBl. I S. 111).

[26] Second sentence deleted by federal statute of August 23, 1976 (BGBl. I S. 2381).

[27] Inserted by federal statute of July 15, 1975 (BGBl. I S. 1901).

[28] Inserted by federal statute of July 15, 1975 (BGBl. I S. 1901).

(4) Any criminal proceedings or any proceedings under Article 18 against a deputy, any detention, or any other restriction of his personal liberty shall be suspended at the demand of the Bundestag.

Article 47 (Right of deputies to refuse to give evidence)

Deputies may refuse to give evidence concerning persons who have confided facts to them in their capacity as deputies, or to whom they have confided facts in such capacity, as well as evidence concerning these facts themselves. To the extent that this right of refusal to give evidence exists, no seizure of documents shall be permissible.

Article 48 (Entitlements of deputies)

(1) Every candidate for election to the Bundestag shall be entitled to the leave necessary for his election campaign.

(2) No one may be prevented from accepting and exercising the office of deputy. No one may be given notice of dismissal nor dismissed from employment on this ground.

(3) Deputies are entitled to remuneration adequate to ensure their independence. They are entitled to the free use of all state-owned means of transport. Details shall be regulated by federal statute.

Article 49[29] (Repealed)

IV. THE COUNCIL OF STATES [BUNDESRAT]

Article 50[30] (Functions)

The Länder shall participate through the Bundesrat in the legislation and administration of the Federation and in affairs of the European Union.

Article 51 (Composition)

(1) The Bundesrat shall consist of members of the Land governments, which appoint and recall them. Other members of such governments may act as substitutes.

---

[29]Amended by federal statute of March 19, 1956 (BGBl. I S. 111); repealed by federal statute of August 23, 1976 (BGBl. I S. 2381).

[30] As amended by federal statute of December 21, 1992 (BGBl. I S. 2086).

(2)[31] Each Land shall have at least three votes; Länder with more than two million inhabitants shall have four, Länder with more than six million inhabitants five, and Länder with more than seven million inhabitants six votes.

(3) Each Land may appoint as many members as it has votes. The votes of each Land may be cast only as a block vote and only by members present or their substitutes.

Article 52 (President; rules of procedure)

(1) The Bundesrat shall elect its President for one year.

(2) The President shall convene the Bundesrat. He shall convene the Bundesrat when delegates from at least two Länder or the Federal Government so demand.

(3) Decisions of the Bundesrat require the votes of at least a majority of its members. It shall draw up its rules of procedure. Its meetings shall be public. The public may be excluded.

(3a)[32] For affairs of the European Union the Bundesrat may establish a European Chamber whose decisions shall be considered decisions of the Bundesrat; paragraph (2) and the second sentence of paragraph (3) of Article 51 shall apply.

(4) Other members of or persons commissioned by Land governments may serve on the committees of the Bundesrat.

Article 53 (Presence of members of the Federal Government)

The members of the Federal Government shall have the right, and on demand the duty, to attend the meetings of the Bundesrat and of its committees. They shall have the right to be heard at any time. The Bundesrat shall be kept informed by the Federal Government as regards the conduct of affairs.

---

[31] As amended by the Unification Treaty of August 31, 1990, and federal statute of September 23, 1990 (BGBl. II S. 885).

[32] Inserted by federal statute of December 21, 1992 (BGBl. I S. 2086).

IVa.[33] THE JOINT COMMITTEE

Article 53a (Composition; rules of procedure; right to information)

(1) Two thirds of the members of the Joint Committee shall be deputies of the Bundestag and one third shall be members of the Bundesrat. The Bundestag shall delegate its deputies in proportion to the relative strength of its parliamentary groups; deputies shall not be members of the Federal Government. Each Land shall be represented by a Bundesrat member of its choice; these members shall not be bound by instructions. The establishment of the Joint Committee and its procedures shall be regulated by rules of procedure to be adopted by the Bundestag and requiring the consent of the Bundesrat.

(2) The Federal Government shall inform the Joint Committee about its plans for a state of defense. The rights of the Bundestag and its committees under paragraph (1) of Article 43 are unaffected by the provision of this paragraph.

V. THE FEDERAL PRESIDENT

Article 54 (Election)

(1) The Federal President shall be elected, without debate, by the Federal Convention [Bundesversammlung]. Every German who is entitled to vote for Bundestag candidates and has attained the age of forty years is eligible for election.

(2) The term of office of the Federal President shall last five years. Reelection for a consecutive term shall be permitted only once.

(3) The Federal Convention shall consist of the members of the Bundestag and an equal number of members elected by the parliaments of the Länder according to the principles of proportional representation.

(4) The Federal Convention shall meet not later than thirty days before the expiration of the term of office of the Federal President or, in the case of premature termination, not later than thirty days after that date. It shall be convened by the President of the Bundestag.

(5) After the expiration of a legislative term, the period specified in the first sentence of paragraph (4) of this Article shall begin with the first meeting of the Bundestag.

(6) The person receiving the votes of the majority of the members of the Federal Convention shall be elected. If after two ballots no candidate has ob-

---

[33] Inserted by federal statute of June 24, 1968 (BGBl. I S. 710).

tained such a majority, the candidate who receives the largest number of votes on the next ballot shall be elected.

(7) Details shall be regulated by federal statute.

Article 55 (Incompatibilities)

(1) The Federal President may not be a member of the government nor of a legislative body of the Federation or of a Land.

(2) The Federal President may not hold any other salaried office, nor engage in an occupation, nor belong to the management or the board of directors of an enterprise carried on for profit.

Article 56 (Oath of office)

On assuming his office, the Federal President shall take the following oath before the assembled members of the Bundestag and the Bundesrat:

"I swear that I will dedicate my efforts to the well-being of the German people, enhance their benefits, avert harm from them, uphold and defend the Basic Law and the statutes of the Federation, fulfill my duties conscientiously, and do justice to all. So help me God."

The oath may also be taken without religious affirmation.

Article 57 (Representation)

When the Federal President is prevented from acting, or when his office falls prematurely vacant, his powers shall be exercised by the President of the Bundesrat.

Article 58 (Countersignature)

Orders and directions of the Federal President require for their validity the countersignature of the Federal Chancellor or the appropriate Federal Minister. This provision does not apply to the appointment and dismissal of the Federal Chancellor, the dissolution of the Bundestag under Article 63, or a request made under paragraph (3) of Article 69.

Article 59 (Authority to represent the Federation in its international relations)

(1) The Federal President shall represent the Federation in its international relations. He shall conclude treaties with foreign states on behalf of the Federation. He shall accredit and receive envoys.

(2) Treaties that regulate the political relations of the Federation or relate to subjects of federal legislation require the consent or participation, in the form of federal statute, of the bodies competent in any specific case for such federal

legislation. In the case of administrative agreements the provisions concerning the federal administration shall apply.

Article 59a [34] (Repealed)

Article 60 (Appointment and dismissal of federal judges, federal civil servants, and soldiers; right of pardon)

(1)[35] The Federal President shall appoint and dismiss federal judges, federal civil servants, officers, and noncommissioned officers, except as may otherwise be provided by statute.

(2) He shall exercise the right of pardon in individual cases on behalf of the Federation.

(3) He may delegate these powers to other authorities.

(4) Paragraphs (2) to (4) of Article 46 apply to the Federal President.

Article 61 (Impeachment before the Federal Constitutional Court)

(1) The Bundestag or the Bundesrat may impeach the Federal President before the Federal Constitutional Court for willful violation of this Basic Law or of any other federal statute. The motion of impeachment must be supported by at least one quarter of the members of the Bundestag or one quarter of the votes of the Bundesrat. A decision to impeach requires a majority of two thirds of the members of the Bundestag or of two thirds of the votes of the Bundesrat. The impeachment shall be pleaded by a person commissioned by the impeaching body.
(2) If the Federal Constitutional Court finds the Federal President guilty of a willful violation of this Basic Law or of another federal statute, it may declare him to have forfeited his office. After impeachment it may issue an interim order preventing the Federal President from exercising his functions.

VI. THE FEDERAL GOVERNMENT [BUNDESREGIERUNG]

Article 62 (Composition)

The Federal Government shall consist of the Federal Chancellor and the Federal Ministers.

---

[34] Inserted by federal statute of March 19, 1956 (BGBl. I S. 111), and repealed by federal statute of June 24, 1968 (BGBl. I S. 711).

[35] As amended by federal statute of March 19, 1956 (BGBl. I S. 111).

Article 63 (Election and appointment of the Federal Chancellor)

(1) The Federal Chancellor shall be elected, without debate, by the Bundestag upon the proposal of the Federal President.

(2) The person obtaining the votes of the majority of the members of the Bundestag shall be elected. The person elected shall be appointed by the Federal President.

(3) If the person proposed is not elected, the Bundestag may elect a Federal Chancellor within fourteen days after the ballot by the vote of more than one half of its members.

(4) If no candidate has been elected within this period, a new ballot shall take place without delay, on which the person obtaining the largest number of votes shall be elected. If the person elected has obtained the votes of the majority of the members of the Bundestag, the Federal President shall appoint him within seven days of the election. If the person elected did not obtain such a majority, the Federal President shall, within seven days, either appoint him or dissolve the Bundestag.

Article 64 (Appointment of Federal Ministers)

(1) The Federal Ministers shall be appointed and dismissed by the Federal President upon the proposal of the Federal Chancellor.

(2) The Federal Chancellor and the Federal Ministers, on assuming office, shall take before the Bundestag the oath provided for in Article 56.

Article 65 (Powers within the Federal Government)

The Federal Chancellor shall determine and be responsible for the general policy guidelines. Within the limits set by these guidelines, each Federal Minister shall conduct the affairs of his department autonomously and on his own responsibility. The Federal Government shall resolve differences of opinion between Federal Ministers. The Federal Chancellor shall conduct the affairs of the Federal Government in accordance with rules of procedure adopted by it and approved by the Federal President.

Article 65a [36] (Power of command over the Armed Forces)

Power of command in respect to the Armed Forces shall be vested in the Federal Minister of Defense.

---

[36] Inserted by federal statute of March 19, 1956 (BGBl. I S. 111), and amended by federal statute of June 24, 1968 (BGBl. I S. 711).

Article 66 (Incompatibilities)

The Federal Chancellor and the Federal Ministers may not hold any other salaried office, or engage in an occupation, or belong to the management or, without the consent of the Bundestag, to the board of directors of an enterprise carried on for profit.

Article 67 (Constructive vote of no confidence)

(1) The Bundestag may express its lack of confidence in the Federal Chancellor only by electing a successor by a vote of the majority of its members and by requesting the Federal President to dismiss the Federal Chancellor. The Federal President shall comply with the request and appoint the person elected.

(2) Forty-eight hours shall elapse between the motion and the election.

Article 68 (Vote of confidence; dissolution of the Bundestag)

(1) If a motion of the Federal Chancellor for a vote of confidence is not supported by the majority of the members of the Bundestag, the Federal President may, upon the proposal of the Federal Chancellor, dissolve the Bundestag within twenty-one days. The right of dissolution shall lapse as soon as the Bundestag elects another Federal Chancellor by the vote of a majority of its members.

(2) Forty-eight hours shall elapse between the motion and the vote thereon.

Article 69 (Deputy Federal Chancellor; tenure of office of members of the Federal Government)

(1) The Federal Chancellor shall appoint a Federal Minister as his deputy.

(2) The tenure of office of the Federal Chancellor or a Federal Minister shall end in any event on the assembly of a new Bundestag; the tenure of office of a Federal Minister shall also end on any other termination of the Federal Chancellor's tenure of office.

(3) At the request of the Federal President the Federal Chancellor, or at the request of the Federal Chancellor or of the Federal President a Federal Minister, shall be bound to continue to manage the affairs of his office until the appointment of a successor.

VII. LEGISLATIVE POWERS OF THE FEDERATION [BUND]

Article 70 (Legislation of the Federation and the Länder)

(1) The Länder shall have the right to legislate insofar as this Basic Law does not confer legislative power on the Federation.

(2) The division of authority between the Federation and the Länder is determined by the provisions of this Basic Law respecting exclusive and concurrent legislative powers.

Article 71 (Exclusive legislative power of the Federation: definition)

In matters within the exclusive legislative power of the Federation, the Länder shall have power to legislate only when and to the extent that they are given such explicit authorization by federal statute.

Article 72 (Concurrent legislative power of the Federation: definition)

(1) In matters within the concurrent legislative power, the Länder shall have power to legislate so long as and to the extent that the Federation does not exercise its right to legislate.

(2) The Federation has the right to legislate in these matters to the extent that a need for regulation by federal legislation exists because:

1. a matter cannot be effectively regulated by the legislation of individual Länder, or

2. the regulation of a matter by a Land statute might prejudice the interests of other Länder or of the people as a whole, or

3. the maintenance of legal or economic unity, especially the maintenance of uniformity of living conditions beyond the territory of any one Land, necessitates such regulation.

Article 73 (Exclusive legislative power: catalogue)

The Federation has exclusive power to legislate in the following matters:

1.[37] foreign affairs and defense, including protection of the civilian population;

2. citizenship in the Federation;

3. freedom of movement, passport matters, immigration, emigration, and extradition;

4. currency, money, and coinage, weights and measures, as well as the determination of standards of time;

---

[37] As amended by federal statutes of March 26, 1954 (BGBl. I S. 45), and June 24, 1968 (BGBl. I S. 711).

5. the unity of the customs and trading area, treaties respecting commerce and navigation, freedom of movement of goods, and the exchange of goods and payments with foreign countries, including customs and other frontier protection;

6. federal railroads and air transport;

7. postal and telecommunication services;

8. the legal status of persons employed by the Federation and by federal corporate bodies under public law;

9. industrial property rights, copyrights, and publishing law;

10.[38] cooperation between the Federation and the Länder concerning

(a) criminal police,

(b) protection of the free democratic basic order, of the existence and the security of the Federation or of a Land (protection of the constitution), and

(c) protection against activities in the federal territory which, by the use of force or actions in preparation for the use of force, endanger the foreign interests of the Federal Republic of Germany,

as well as the establishment of a Federal Criminal Police Office and the international control of crime;

11. statistics for federal purposes.

Article 74 (Concurrent legislation: catalogue)

Concurrent legislative powers extend to the following subjects:

1. civil law, criminal law, and execution of sentences, the organization and procedure of courts, the legal profession, notaries, and legal advice [Rechtsberatung];

2. registration of births, deaths, and marriages;

3. the law of association and assembly;

4. the law relating to residence and settlement of aliens;

---

[38] As amended by federal statute of July 28, 1972 (BGBl. I S. 1305).

4a.[39] the law relating to weapons and explosives;

5. the protection of German cultural assets against migration abroad;

6. refugee and expellee matters;

7. public welfare;

8. citizenship in the Länder;

9. war damage and reparations;

10.[40] benefits to war-disabled persons and to dependents of those killed in the war as well as assistance to former prisoners of war;

10a.[41] war graves of soldiers, graves of other victims of war and of victims of despotism;

11. the law relating to economic matters (mining, industry, supply of power, crafts, trades, commerce, banking, stock exchanges, and private insurance);

11a.[42] the production and utilization of nuclear energy for peaceful purposes, the construction and operation of installations serving such purposes, protection against hazards arising from the release of nuclear energy or from ionizing radiation, and the disposal of radioactive substances;

12. labor law, including the legal organization of enterprises, protection of workers, employment exchanges and agencies, as well as social insurance, including unemployment insurance;

13.[43] the regulation of educational and training grants and the promotion of scientific research;

14. the law regarding expropriation, to the extent that matters enumerated in Articles 73 and 74 are concerned;

---

[39] Inserted by federal statute of July 28, 1972 (BGBl. I S. 1305), and amended by federal statute of August 23, 1976 (BGBl. I S. 2383).

[40] As amended by federal statute of June 16, 1965 (BGBl. I S. 513).

[41] Inserted by federal statute of June 16, 1965 (BGBl. I S. 513).

[42] Inserted by federal statute of December 23, 1959 (BGBl. I S. 813).

[43] As amended by federal statute of May 12, 1969 (BGBl. I S. 363).

15. transfer of land, natural resources, and means of production to public ownership or other forms of collective enterprise for the public benefit;

16. prevention of the abuse of economic power;

17. promotion of agricultural production and forestry, securing the supply of food, the importation and exportation of agricultural and forestry products, deep-sea and coastal fishing, and preservation of the coasts;

18. real estate transactions, land law, and matters concerning agricultural leases, as well as housing, settlement, and homestead matters;

19. measures against human and animal diseases that are communicable or otherwise endanger public health, admission to the medical profession and to other medical occupations or practices, as well as trade in medicines, curatives, narcotics, and poisons;

19a.[44] the economic viability of hospitals and the regulation of hospitalization fees;

20.[45] protection regarding the marketing of food, drink, and tobacco, of necessities of life, fodder, agricultural and forest seeds and seedlings, and protection of plants against diseases and pests, as well as the protection of animals;

21. ocean and coastal shipping, as well as navigational markers, inland navigation, meteorological services, sea routes, and inland waterways used for general traffic;

22.[46] road traffic, motor transport, construction and maintenance of long-distance highways, as well as the collection of charges for the use of public highways by vehicles and the allocation of revenue therefrom;

23. non-federal railroads, except mountain railroads;

24.[47] waste disposal, air pollution control, and noise abatement.

---

[44] Inserted by federal statute of May 12, 1969 (BGBl. I S. 363).

[45] As amended by federal statute of March 18, 1971 (BGBl. I S. 207).

[46] As amended by federal statute of May 12, 1969 (BGBl. I S. 363).

[47] As amended by federal statute of April 12, 1972 (BGBl. I S. 593).

Article 74a[48] **(Concurrent legislative power of the Federation: remuneration and pensions of members of the public service)**

(1) Concurrent legislative power further extends to the remuneration and pensions of members of the public service whose service and loyalty are governed by public law, insofar as the Federation does not have exclusive power to legislate pursuant to item 8 of Article 73.

(2) Federal statutes enacted pursuant to paragraph (1) of this Article require the consent of the Bundesrat.

(3) Federal statutes enacted pursuant to item 8 of Article 73 likewise require the consent of the Bundesrat, insofar as they contemplate standards for the structure or assessment of remuneration or pensions (including the rating of positions), or minimum or maximum rates, other than those provided for in federal statutes enacted pursuant to paragraph (1) of this Article.

(4) Paragraphs (1) and (2) of this Article shall also apply to the remuneration and pensions of judges in the Länder. Paragraph (3) of this Article shall also apply to statutes enacted pursuant to paragraph (1) of Article 98.

Article 75[49] **(Power of the Federation to pass framework legislation; catalogue)**

Subject to the conditions laid down in Article 72, the Federation has the right to enact framework legislation concerning:

1.[50] the legal status of persons in the public service of the Länder, communities, or other corporate bodies under public law, insofar as Article 74a does not otherwise provide;

1a.[51] general principles governing higher education;

2. the general legal status of the press and the film industry;

3. hunting, nature conservation, and landscape management;

4. land distribution, regional planning, and the management of water resources;

---

[48] Inserted by federal statute of March 18, 1971 (BGBl. I S. 206).

[49] As amended by federal statute of May 12, 1969 (BGBl. I S. 363).

[50] As amended by federal statute of March 18, 1971 (BGBl. I S. 206).

[51] Inserted by federal statute of May 12, 1969 (BGBl. I S. 363).

5. matters relating to the registration of residence or domicile [Meldewesen] and to identity cards.

Article 76 (Bills)

(1) Bills may be introduced in the Bundestag by the Federal Government or by members of the Bundestag or by the Bundesrat.

(2)[52] Bills of the Federal Government shall first be submitted to the Bundesrat. The Bundesrat is entitled to state its position on such bills within six weeks. If upon submitting a bill to the Bundesrat the Federal Government specifically designates it as particularly urgent, it may submit the bill to the Bundestag three weeks later, even if it has not yet received the statement of the Bundesrat's position; upon receipt, such statement shall be transmitted to the Bundestag by the Federal Government without delay.

(3)[53] Bills of the Bundesrat shall be submitted to the Bundestag by the Federal Government within three months. In submitting them the Federal Government shall state its own view.

Article 77 (Legislative procedure)

(1) Federal statutes are enacted by the Bundestag. Once they are adopted, the President of the Bundestag shall transmit them to the Bundesrat without delay.

(2)[54] Within three weeks after receipt of an adopted bill, the Bundesrat may demand that a committee for joint consideration of bills, composed of members of the Bundestag and members of the Bundesrat, be convened. The composition and procedure of this committee shall be regulated by rules of procedure to be adopted by the Bundestag and requiring the consent of the Bundesrat. The members of the Bundesrat on this committee are not bound by instructions. When the consent of the Bundesrat is required for a bill to become law, the Bundestag and the Federal Government may also demand that such a committee be convened. Should the committee propose any amendment to the adopted bill, the Bundestag shall vote on the bill again.

(3)[55] Insofar as the consent of the Bundesrat is not required for a bill to become law, the Bundesrat may, once proceedings under paragraph (2) of this

---

[52] As amended by federal statute of November 15, 1968 (BGBl. I S. 1177).

[53] As amended by federal statute of July 17, 1969 (BGBl. I S. 817).

[54] As amended by federal statute of November 15, 1968 (BGBl. I S. 1177).

[55] As amended by federal statute of November 15, 1968 (BGBl. I S. 1177).

Article are completed, enter an objection within two weeks against a bill adopted by the Bundestag. The period for entering an objection shall begin, in the case of the last sentence of paragraph (2) of this Article, upon receipt of the bill as readopted by the Bundestag, and in all other cases upon receipt of a communication from the chairman of the committee provided for in paragraph (2) of this Article to the effect that the committee's proceedings have been concluded.

(4) If the objection was adopted by the majority of the votes of the Bundesrat, it can be rejected by a decision of the majority of the members of the Bundestag. If the Bundesrat adopted the objection by a majority of at least two thirds of its votes, its rejection by the Bundestag requires a majority of two thirds, including at least the majority of the members of the Bundestag.

Article 78 (Passage of federal statutes)

A bill adopted by the Bundestag shall become law if the Bundesrat consents to it, or fails to make a demand pursuant to paragraph (2) of Article 77, or fails to enter an objection within the period stipulated in paragraph (3) of Article 77, or withdraws such objection, or if the objection is overridden by the Bundestag.

Article 79 (Amendment of the Basic Law)

(1) This Basic Law can be amended only by statutes that expressly amend or supplement its text. In the case of an international treaty respecting a peace settlement, the preparation of a peace settlement, or the phasing out of an occupation regime, or designed to promote the defense of the Federal Republic, it shall be sufficient, for the purpose of clarifying that the provisions of this Basic law do not preclude the conclusion and entry into force of such a treaty, to add language to the Basic Law confined to such clarification.[56]

(2) Any such statute shall require the consent of two thirds of the members of the Bundestag and two thirds of the votes of the Bundesrat.

(3) Amendments of this Basic Law affecting the division of the Federation into Länder, the participation in principle of the Länder in legislation, or the basic principles laid down in Articles 1 and 20 shall be inadmissible.

Article 80 (Issuance of regulations)

(1) The Federal Government, a Federal Minister, or the Land governments may be authorized by statute to issue regulations [Rechtsverordnungen]. The content, purpose, and scope of the authorization so conferred shall be specified in the statute. Each regulation shall contain a statement of its legal ba-

---

[56] Second sentence inserted by federal statute of March 26, 1954 (BGBl. I S. 45).

sis. If a statute provides that such authorization may be delegated, such sub-delegation shall require another regulation.

(2) The consent of the Bundesrat shall be required, unless otherwise provided by federal legislation, for regulations issued by the Federal Government or a Federal Minister concerning fees or basic rules for the use of facilities of the federal railroads and of postal and telecommunication services or the construction and operation of railroads, as well as for regulations issued pursuant to federal statutes that require the consent of the Bundesrat or that are executed by the Länder as agents of the Federation or as matters of their own concern.

Article 80a[57] (Application of legal provisions in a state of emergency)

(1) If the Basic law or a federal statute respecting defense, including protection of the civilian population, stipulates that legal provisions may be applied only in accordance with this Article, their application shall, except when a state of defense exists, be permissible only after the Bundestag has determined that a state of emergency [Spannungsfall] exists or where it has specifically approved such application. With respect to the cases mentioned in the first sentence of paragraph (5) and the second sentence of paragraph (6) of Article 12a, such determination of a state of emergency and such specific approval shall require a two-thirds majority of the votes cast.

(2) Any measures taken by virtue of legal provisions enacted under paragraph (1) of this Article shall be revoked whenever the Bundestag so demands.

(3) Notwithstanding paragraph (1) of this Article, the application of such legal provisions shall also be permissible by virtue of and in accordance with a decision made with the consent of the Federal Government by an international body within the framework of a treaty of alliance. Any measures taken pursuant to this paragraph shall be revoked whenever the Bundestag, by a vote of the majority of its members, so demands.

Article 81 (State of legislative emergency)

(1) If, in the circumstances of Article 68, the Bundestag is not dissolved, the Federal President, at the request of the Federal Government and with the consent of the Bundesrat, may declare a state of legislative emergency with respect to a bill, if the Bundestag rejects the bill although the Federal Government has declared it to be urgent. The same shall apply if a bill has been rejected although the Federal Chancellor had combined with it the motion under Article 68.

---

[57] Inserted by federal statute of June 24, 1968 (BGBl. I S. 711).

(2) If, after a state of legislative emergency has been declared, the Bundestag again rejects the bill or adopts it in a version stated to be unacceptable to the Federal Government, the bill shall be deemed to have become law to the extent that the Bundesrat consents to it. The same shall apply where the bill is not passed by the Bundestag within four weeks of its reintroduction.

(3) During the term of office of a Federal Chancellor, any other bill rejected by the Bundestag may become law in accordance with paragraphs (1) and (2) of this Article within a period of six months after the first declaration of a state of legislative emergency. After the expiration of this period, a further declaration of a state of legislative emergency shall be inadmissible during the term of office of the same Federal Chancellor.

(4) This Basic Law may not be amended nor repealed nor suspended in whole or in part by a statute enacted pursuant to paragraph (2) of this Article.

Article 82 (Promulgation and effective date of legal provisions)

(1) Statutes enacted in accordance with the provisions of this Basic Law shall, after countersignature, be certified by the Federal President and promulgated in the Federal Law Gazette [Bundesgesetzblatt]. Regulations shall be certified by the agency that issues them and, unless otherwise provided by statute, shall be promulgated in the Federal Law Gazette.

(2) Every statute or regulation shall specify its effective date. In the absence of such a provision, it shall take effect on the fourteenth day after the end of the day on which the Federal Law Gazette containing it was published.

VIII. THE EXECUTION OF FEDERAL STATUTES AND THE FEDERAL ADMINISTRATION

Article 83 (Distribution of competence between the Federation and the Länder)The Länder shall execute federal statutes as matters of their own concern insofar as this Basic Law does not otherwise provide or permit.

Article 84 (Land execution and Federal Government supervision)

(1) When the Länder execute federal statutes as matters of their own concern, they shall provide for the establishment of the requisite agencies and the regulation of administrative procedures insofar as federal statutes enacted with the consent of the Bundesrat do not otherwise provide.

(2) The Federal Government may, with the consent of the Bundesrat, issue general administrative rules.

(3) The Federal Government shall exercise supervision to ensure that the Länder execute federal statutes in accordance with applicable law. For this purpose the Federal Government may send commissioners to the highest

Land authorities and, with their consent or, where such consent is refused, with the consent of the Bundesrat, also to subordinate authorities.

(4) Should any deficiencies that the Federal Government has found to exist in the execution of federal statutes by the Länder not be corrected, the Bundesrat, at the request of the Federal Government or of the Land concerned, shall decide whether such Land has violated the law. The decision of the Bundesrat may be challenged in the Federal Constitutional Court.

(5) With a view to the execution of federal statutes, the Federal Government may be authorized by federal statute requiring the consent of the Bundesrat to issue individual instructions for particular cases. They shall be addressed to the highest Land authorities unless the Federal Government considers the matter urgent.

Article 85 (Execution by the Länder as agents of the Federation)

(1) When the Länder execute federal statutes as agents of the Federation, the establishment of the requisite agencies shall remain the concern of the Länder, except insofar as federal statutes enacted with Bundesrat consent otherwise provide.

(2) The Federal Government may, with the consent of the Bundesrat, issue general administrative rules. It may regulate the uniform training of civil servants and other salaried public employees [der Beamten und Angestellten]. The heads of agencies at the intermediate level shall be appointed with its agreement.

(3) The Land authorities are subject to instructions of the appropriate highest federal authorities. Such instructions shall be addressed to the highest Land authorities unless the Federal Government considers the matter urgent. Execution of the instructions shall be ensured by the highest Land authorities.

(4) Federal supervision extends to the lawfulness and appropriateness of execution. For this purpose the Federal Government may require the submission of reports and documents and send commissioners to all Land agencies.

Article 86 (Direct federal administration)

When the Federation executes statutes by means of direct federal administration or of federal corporate bodies or institutions established under public law, the Federal Government shall, insofar as the statute concerned contains no special provision, issue general administrative rules. The Federal Government shall provide for the establishment of the requisite agencies insofar as the statute concerned does not otherwise provide.

Article 87[58] (Subjects of direct federal administration)

(1) The foreign service, the federal financial administration, the federal rail-roads, the federal postal service and, in accordance with the provisions of Article 89, the administration of federal waterways and of shipping shall be conducted as matters of direct federal administration with their own administrative substructures. Federal legislation may be enacted to establish Federal Border Guard authorities and central offices for police information and communications, for the criminal police, and for the compilation of data for purposes of protection of the constitution and of protection against activities within the federal territory which, through the use of force or acts preparatory to the use of force, endanger the foreign interests of the Federal Republic of Germany.[59]

(2) Social insurance institutions whose sphere of competence extends beyond the territory of one Land shall be administered as federal corporate bodies under public law.

(3) In addition, autonomous federal higher authorities as well as new federal corporate bodies and institutions under public law may be established by federal legislation for matters on which the Federation has the power to legislate. When new functions arise for the Federation with respect to matters on which it has the power to legislate, federal authorities at the intermediate and lower levels may be established, in case of urgent need, with the consent of the Bundesrat and of the majority of the members of the Bundestag.

Article 87a[60] (Establishment and powers of the Armed Forces)

(1) The Federation shall establish Armed Forces for defense purposes. Their numerical strength and general organizational structure shall be shown in the budget.

(2) Apart from defense, the Armed Forces may be employed only to the extent expressly permitted by this Basic Law.

(3) While a state of defense or a state of emergency exists, the Armed Forces shall have the power to protect civilian property and discharge functions of traffic control insofar as necessary for the performance of their defense mission. Moreover, when a state of defense or a state of emergency exists, the Armed Forces may also be entrusted with protection of civilian property in

---

[58] Inserted by federal statute of March 19, 1956 (BGBl. I S. 111), and amended by federal statute of June 24, 1968 (BGBl. I S. 711).

[59] Second sentence added by federal statute of July 28, 1972 (BGBl. I, S. 1305).

[60] Inserted by federal statute of March 19, 1956 (BGBl. I S. 111).

support of police measures; in this event the Armed Forces shall cooperate with the competent authorities.

(4) In order to avert an imminent danger to the existence or to the free democratic basic order of the Federation or of a Land, the Federal Government, should conditions as envisaged in paragraph (2) of Article 91 obtain and the police forces and the Federal Border Guard prove inadequate, may employ the Armed Forces to support the police and the Federal Border Guard in the protection of civilian property and in combatting organized and militarily armed insurgents. Any such use of the Armed Forces shall be discontinued whenever the Bundestag or the Bundesrat so demands.

Article 87b[61] (Administration of the Federal Armed Forces)

(1) The Federal Armed Forces Administration shall be conducted as a direct federal administration with its own administrative substructure. Its function shall be to administer personnel matters and directly to meet the material requirements of the Armed Forces. Tasks connected with benefits to injured persons or with construction work shall not be assigned to the Federal Armed Forces Administration except by federal legislation requiring the consent of the Bundesrat. Such consent is also required for any statutes to the extent that they empower the Federal Armed Forces Administration to interfere with rights of third parties; this requirement, however, does not apply in the case of statutes concerning personnel matters.

(2) Moreover, federal statutes concerning defense, including recruitment for military service and protection of the civilian population, may, with the consent of the Bundesrat, provide that they shall be executed, wholly or in part, either by means of direct federal administration with its own administrative substructure or by the Länder acting as agents of the Federation. If such statutes are executed by the Länder acting as agents of the Federation, they may, with the consent of the Bundesrat, provide that the powers vested in the Federal Government or appropriate highest federal authorities by virtue of Article 85 be transferred wholly or in part to higher federal authorities; in such an event it may be enacted that these authorities shall not require the consent of the Bundesrat in issuing general administrative rules as provided in the first sentence of paragraph (2) of Article 85.

Article 87c[62] (Administration in the field of nuclear energy)

Statutes enacted under clause 11a of Article 74 may, with the consent of the Bundesrat, provide that they shall be executed by the Länder acting as agents of the Federation.

---

[61] Inserted by federal statute of March 19, 1956 (BGBl. I S. 111).

[62] Inserted by federal statute of December 23, 1959 (BGBl. I S. 813).

Article 87d[63] (Aviation administration)

(1) Aviation administration shall be conducted as a direct federal administration. Whether it shall be organized under public or private law shall be determined by federal statute.[64]

(2) By federal legislation requiring the consent of the Bundesrat, functions of aviation administration may be transferred to the Länder acting as agents of the Federation.

Article 88 (Federal Bank)

The Federation shall establish a note-issuing and currency bank as the Federal Bank [Bundesbank]. Its functions and powers may, within the framework of the European Union, be transferred to a European Central Bank that is independent and committed to the overriding goal of assuring price stability.[65]

Article 89 (Federal waterways)

(1) The Federation shall be the owner of the former Reich waterways.

(2) The Federation shall administer the federal waterways through its own authorities. It shall exercise those governmental functions relating to inland shipping which extend beyond the territory of one Land, and those governmental functions relating to maritime shipping which are conferred on it by statute. Upon request, the Federation may transfer the administration of federal waterways, insofar as they lie within the territory of one Land, to that Land as its agent. If a waterway touches the territories of several Länder, the Federation may designate one Land to be its agent if so requested by the affected Länder.

(3) In the administration, development, and new construction of waterways, the requirements of land improvement and of water economy shall be safeguarded in agreement with the Länder.

Article 90 (Federal highways)

(1) The Federation shall be the owner of the former Reich expressways [Reichsautobahnen] and Reich highways.

---

[63] Inserted by federal statute of February 6, 1961 (BGBl. I S. 65).

[64] Second sentence inserted by federal statute of July 14, 1992 (BGBl. I S. 1254).

[65] Second sentence inserted by federal statute of December 21, 1992 (BGBl. I S. 2087).

(2) The Länder, or such self-governing corporate bodies as are competent under Land law, shall administer the federal expressways and other federal highways used by long-distance traffic as agents of the Federation.

(3) At the request of a Land, the Federation may place federal expressways and other federal highways used by long-distance traffic under direct federal administration insofar as they lie within the territory of that Land.

Article 91[66] (Internal emergency)

(1) In order to avert an imminent danger to the existence or to the free democratic basic order of the Federation or a Land, a Land may request the services of the police forces of other Länder, or of the forces[67] and facilities of other administrative authorities and of the Federal Border Guard.

(2) If the Land where such danger is imminent is not itself willing or able to combat the danger, the Federal Government may place the police in that Land and the police forces of other Länder under its own orders and employ units of the Federal Border Guard. This order shall be rescinded after removal of the danger, or at any time on the demand of the Bundesrat. If the danger extends to a region larger than a single Land, the Federal Government may, insofar as is necessary for effectively combatting such danger, issue instructions to the Land governments; the first and second sentences of this paragraph are unaffected by this provision.

VIIIa.[68] JOINT TASKS

Article 91a[69] (Participation of the Federation by virtue of federal legislation)

(1) In the following areas the Federation shall participate in the discharge of responsibilities of the Länder, provided that such responsibilities are important to society as a whole and that federal participation is necessary for the improvement of living conditions (joint tasks):

---

[66]As amended by federal statute of June 24, 1968 (BGBl. I S. 711).

[67] [E.g., civil defense corps, emergency civil engineering corps, fire brigades.]

[68] Inserted by federal statute of May 12, 1969 (BGBl. I S. 359).

[69] Inserted by federal statute of May 12, 1969 (BGBl. I S. 359).

1.[70] extension and construction of institutions of higher education, including university clinics;

2. improvement of regional economic structures;

3. improvement of the agrarian structure and of coast preservation.

(2) Joint tasks shall be defined in detail by federal statute requiring the consent of the Bundesrat. Such legislation shall include general principles governing the discharge of joint tasks.

(3) Such legislation shall provide for the procedure and the institutions required for joint overall planning. The inclusion of a project in the overall plan shall require the consent of the Land in which it is to be carried out.

(4) In cases to which items 1 and 2 of paragraph (1) of this Article apply, the Federation shall meet one half of the expenditure in each Land. In cases to which item 3 of paragraph (1) of this Article applies, the Federation shall meet at least one half of the expenditure, and such proportion shall be the same for all the Länder. Details shall be regulated by statute. Provision of funds shall be subject to appropriation in the budgets of the Federation and the Länder.

(5) The Federal Government and the Bundesrat shall be informed about the execution of joint tasks, should they so demand.

Article 91b[71] (Cooperation between the Federation and the Länder by virtue of agreements)

Pursuant to agreements, the Federation and the Länder may cooperate in educational planning and in the promotion of institutions and projects of scientific research of supraregional importance. The apportionment of costs shall be regulated in the relevant agreements.

IX. THE ADMINISTRATION OF JUSTICE

Article 92[72] (Court organization)

The judicial power shall be vested in the judges; it shall be exercised by the Federal Constitutional Court, by the federal courts provided for in this Basic Law, and by the courts of the Länder.

---

[70] As amended by federal statute of July 31, 1970 (BGBl. I S. 1161).

[71] Inserted by federal statute of May 12, 1969 (BGBl. I S. 359).

[72] As amended by federal statute of June 18, 1968 (BGBl. I S. 657).

Article 93 (Federal Constitutional Court: jurisdiction)

(1) The Federal Constitutional Court shall decide:

1. on the interpretation of this Basic Law in the event of disputes concerning the extent of the rights and duties of a supreme federal body or of other parties vested with rights of their own by this Basic Law or by the rules of a supreme federal body;

2. in case of differences of opinion or doubts respecting the formal or material compatibility of federal law or Land law with this Basic Law, or the compatibility of Land law with other federal law, at the request of the Federal Government, of a Land government, or of one third of the members of the Bundestag;

3. in case of differences of opinion respecting the rights and duties of the Federation and the Länder, particularly in the execution of federal law by the Länder and in the exercise of federal supervision;

4. in other disputes involving public law, between the Federation and the Länder, between different Länder, or within a Land, unless recourse to another court exists;

4a.[73] on complaints of unconstitutionality, which may be filed by any person who claims that one of his basic rights or one of his rights under paragraph (4) of Article 20 or under Article 33, 38, 101, 103, or 104 has been violated by public authority;

4b.[74] on complaints of unconstitutionality filed by communities or associations of communities on the ground that their right to self-government under Article 28 has been violated by a statute other than a Land statute subject to complaint in the respective Land constitutional court;

5. in other cases provided for in this Basic Law.

(2) The Federal Constitutional Court shall also act in such other cases as may be assigned to it by federal legislation.

Article 94 (Federal Constitutional Court: composition)

(1) The Federal Constitutional Court shall consist of federal judges and other members. Half the members of the Federal Constitutional Court shall be elected by the Bundestag and half by the Bundesrat. They may not be mem-

---

[73] Inserted by federal statute of January 29, 1969 (BGBl. I S. 97).

[74] Inserted by federal statute of January 29, 1969 (BGBl. I S. 97).

bers of the Bundestag, of the Bundesrat, of the Federal Government, or of any of the corresponding bodies of a Land.

(2) The constitution and procedure of the Federal Constitutional Court shall be regulated by federal statute, which shall specify in what cases its decisions shall have the force of law.[75] Such statute may require that all other legal remedies be exhausted before a complaint of unconstitutionality can be filed, and may make provision for a special procedure as to acceptance of the complaint.

Article 95[76] (Supreme Courts of the Federation; Joint Panel)

(1) For purposes of ordinary, administrative, fiscal, labor, and social jurisdiction, the Federation shall establish as supreme courts of justice the Federal Court of Justice, the Federal Administrative Court, the Federal Finance Court, the Federal Labor Court, and the Federal Social Court.

(2) The judges of each of these courts shall be selected jointly by the competent Federal Minister and a committee for the selection of judges consisting of the competent Land ministers and an equal number of members elected by the Bundestag.

(3) In order to preserve uniformity of decisions, a Joint Panel [gemeinsamer Senat] of the courts specified in paragraph (1) of this Article shall be established. Details shall be regulated by federal statute.

Article 96[77] (Other federal courts; exercise of federal jurisdiction by courts of the Länder)

(1) The Federation may establish a federal court for matters concerning industrial property rights.

(2) The Federation may establish military criminal courts for the Armed Forces as federal courts. They may exercise criminal jurisdiction only while a state of defense exists, and otherwise only over members of the Armed Forces serving abroad or on board warships. Details shall be regulated by federal statute. These courts shall be within the competence of the Federal Minister

---

[75]Inserted by federal statute of January 29, 1969 (BGBl. I S. 97).

[76] As amended by federal statute of June 18, 1968 (BGBl. I S. 657).

[77] The original Article 96 was repealed by federal statute of June 18, 1968 (BGBl. I S. 658). The present Article 96 is the former Article 96a as inserted by federal statute of March 19, 1956 (BGBl. I S. 111) and amended by federal statutes of March 6, 1961 (BGBl. I S. 141), June 18, 1968 (BGBl. I S. 658), May 12, 1969 (BGBl. I S. 363), and August 26, 1969 (BGBl. I S. 1357).

of Justice. Their full-time judges shall be persons qualified to hold judicial office.

(3) The highest court of justice for appeals from the courts mentioned in paragraphs (1) and (2) of this Article shall be the Federal Court of Justice.

(4)[78] The Federation may establish federal courts for disciplinary proceedings against, and for proceedings in pursuance of complaints by, persons in the federal public service.

(5)[79] With respect to criminal proceedings under paragraph (1) of Article 26 or involving the protection of the State, a federal statute requiring the consent of the Bundesrat may provide that Land courts shall exercise federal jurisdiction.

Article 96a [80]

Article 97 (Independence of the judges)

(1) The judges shall be independent and subject only to the law.
(2) Judges appointed permanently on a full-time basis in established positions cannot, against their will, be dismissed or permanently or temporarily suspended from office or given a different position or retired before the expiration of their term of office except by virtue of judicial decision and only on the grounds and in the manner provided by statute. Legislation may set age limits for the retirement of judges appointed for life. In the event of changes in the structure of courts or in their districts, judges may be transferred to another court or removed from office, provided they retain their full salary.

Article 98 [81] (Legal status of judges in the Federation and the Länder)

(1) The legal status of federal judges shall be regulated by a special federal statute.

(2) If a federal judge infringes the principles of this Basic Law or the constitutional order of a Land in his official capacity or unofficially, the Federal Constitutional Court, upon the request of the Bundestag, may decide by a two-thirds majority that the judge be given a different office or retired. In a case of intentional infringement, his dismissal may be ordered.

---

[78] As amended by federal statute of May 12, 1969 (BGBl. I S. 363).

[79] Inserted by federal statute of August 26, 1969 (BGBl. I S.1357).

[80] See note 77 supra.

[81] As amended by federal statute of March 18, 1971 (BGBl. I S. 206).

(3)[82] The legal status of judges in the Länder shall be regulated by special Land statutes. The Federation may enact framework provisions, insofar as paragraph (4) of Article 74a does not otherwise provide.

(4) The Länder may provide that the Land Minister of Justice together with a committee for the selection of judges shall decide upon the appointment of judges in the Länder.

(5) The Länder may enact provisions for Land judges that correspond with those of paragraph (2) of this Article. Existing Land constitutional law is unaffected. The decision in a case of impeachment of a judge shall rest with the Federal Constitutional Court.

Article 99[83] (Decision by the Federal Constitutional Court and the highest courts of the Federation in disputes concerning Land law)

The decision of constitutional disputes within a Land may be assigned by Land legislation to the Federal Constitutional Court, and the decision at last instance in matters involving the application of Land law to the supreme courts of justice specified in paragraph (1) of Article 95.

Article 100 (Compatibility of statutory law with the Basic Law)

(1) If a court considers that a statute on whose validity the court's decision depends is unconstitutional, the proceedings shall be stayed, and a decision shall be obtained from the Land court with jurisdiction over constitutional disputes when the constitution of a Land is held to be violated, or from the Federal Constitutional Court when this Basic Law is held to be violated. This shall also apply when the Basic Law is held to be violated by Land law or where a Land statute is held to be incompatible with a federal statute.

(2) If, in the course of litigation, doubt exists whether a rule of public international law is an integral part of federal law and whether such rule directly creates rights and duties for the individual (Article 25), the court shall obtain a decision from the Federal Constitutional Court.

(3)[84] If the constitutional court of a Land, in interpreting this Basic Law, intends to deviate from a decision of the Federal Constitutional Court or of the constitutional court of another Land, it shall obtain a decision from the Federal Constitutional Court.

---

[82] As amended by federal statute of March 18, 1971 (BGBl. I S. 206).

[83] As amended by federal statute of June 18, 1968 (BGBl. I S. 658).

[84] As amended by federal statute of June 18, 1968 (BGBl. I S. 658).

Article 101 (Ban on extraordinary courts)

(1) Extraordinary courts shall not be allowed. No one may be removed from the jurisdiction of his lawful judge.

(2) Courts for special fields of law may be established only by legislation.

Article 102 (Abolition of capital punishment)

Capital punishment is abolished.

Article 103 (Hearing in accordance with law; ban on retroactive criminal legislation and on repeated punishment)

(1) In the courts everyone shall be entitled to a hearing in accordance with law.

(2) An act may be punished only if it was defined by law as a criminal offense before the act was committed.

(3) No one may be punished for the same act more than once under general criminal legislation.

Article 104 (Legal guarantees in the event of deprivation of liberty)

(1) The liberty of the individual may be restricted only on the basis of a formal statute and only in compliance with the procedures prescribed therein. Detained persons may not be subjected to mental or physical ill-treatment.

(2) Only judges may rule upon the permissibility or continuation of any deprivation of liberty. If such a deprivation is not based on the order of a judge, a judicial decision shall be obtained without delay. The police may hold no one in custody on their own authority beyond the end of the day after the day of apprehension. Details shall be regulated by legislation.

(3) Any person provisionally detained on suspicion of having committed an offense shall be brought before a judge no later than the day following the day of apprehension; the judge shall inform him of the reasons for detention, examine him, and give him an opportunity to raise objections. The judge shall, without delay, either issue an arrest warrant setting forth the reasons therefor or order his release from detention.

(4) A relative or a person enjoying the confidence of the person detained shall be notified without delay of any judicial decision imposing or ordering the continuation of his deprivation of liberty.

X. FINANCE

Article 104a[85] (Apportionment of expenditures between the Federation and the Länder)

(1) The Federation and the Länder shall separately meet the expenditures resulting from the discharge of their respective tasks insofar as this Basic Law does not provide otherwise.

(2) When the Länder act as agents of the Federation, the Federation shall meet the resulting expenditures.

(3) Federal statutes to be executed by the Länder and granting money payments may make provision for such payments to be met wholly or in part by the Federation. If any such statute provides that the Federation shall meet one half of the expenditure or more, it shall be implemented by the Länder as agents of the Federation. If any such statute provides that the Länder shall meet one quarter of the expenditure or more, it shall require the consent of the Bundesrat.

(4) The Federation may grant the Länder financial assistance for particularly important investments by the Länder or communities or associations of communities, provided that such investments are necessary to avert a disturbance of the overall economic equilibrium or to equalize differences of economic capacities within the federal territory or to promote economic growth. Details, especially concerning the kinds of investments to be promoted, shall be regulated by federal statute requiring the consent of the Bundesrat or by administrative agreements under the federal budget law.

(5) The Federation and the Länder shall meet the administrative expenditures incurred by their respective authorities and shall be responsible to each other for ensuring proper administration. Details shall be regulated by federal statute requiring the consent of the Bundesrat.

Article 105 (Legislative powers)

(1) The Federation shall have exclusive power to legislate with respect to customs duties and fiscal monopolies.

(2)[86] The Federation shall have concurrent power to legislate with respect to all other taxes the revenue from which accrues to it wholly or in part or as to which the conditions provided for in paragraph (2) of Article 72 apply.

---

[85] Inserted by federal statute of May 12, 1969 (BGBl. I S. 359).

[86] As amended by federal statute of May 12, 1969 (BGBl. I S. 359).

(2a)[87] The Länder shall have power to legislate with respect to local excise taxes so long and insofar as they are not identical with taxes imposed by federal legislation.

(3) Federal laws relating to taxes the receipts from which accrue wholly or in part to the Länder or to communities or associations of communities shall require the consent of the Bundesrat.

Article 106[88] (Apportionment of tax revenue)

(1) The yield of fiscal monopolies and the revenue from the following taxes shall accrue to the Federation:

1. customs duties;

2. excise taxes insofar as they do not accrue to the Länder pursuant to paragraph (2) of this Article, or jointly to the Federation and the Länder in accordance with paragraph (3) of this Article, or to the communities in accordance with paragraph (6) of this Article;

3. the road freight tax;

4. capital transaction taxes, the insurance tax, and the tax on bills of exchange;

5. nonrecurrent levies on property, and contributions imposed for the purpose of implementing the legislation respecting equalization of burdens [Lastenausgleich];[89]

6. income and corporation surtaxes;

7. charges imposed within the framework of the European Communities.

(2) Revenue from the following taxes shall accrue to the Länder:

1. the wealth tax;

2. the inheritance tax;

3. the motor vehicle tax;

---

[87] Inserted by federal statute of May 12, 1969 (BGBl. I S. 359).

[88] As amended by federal statutes of December 23, 1955 (BGBl. I S. 817), of December 24, 1956 (BGBl. I S.1077), and of May 12, 1969 (BGBl. I S. 359).

[89] [I.e., contributions imposed on persons having suffered no war damage and used to indemnify persons having suffered such damage.]

4. such taxes on transactions as do not accrue to the Federation pursuant to paragraph (1) of this Article or jointly to the Federation and the Länder pursuant to paragraph (3) of this Article;

5. the beer tax;

6. the gaming casinos levy.

(3) Revenue from income taxes, corporation taxes, and sales taxes shall accrue jointly to the Federation and the Länder (joint taxes) to the extent that the revenue from the income tax is not allocated to the communities pursuant to paragraph (5) of this Article. The Federation and the Länder shall share equally the revenues from income taxes and corporation taxes. The respective shares of the Federation and the Länder in the revenue from the sales tax shall be determined by federal statute requiring the consent of the Bundesrat. Such determination shall be based on the following principles:

1. The Federation and the Länder shall have an equal claim against current revenues for the purpose of meeting their respective necessary expenditures. The extent of such expenditures shall be determined with due regard to financial planning for several years ahead.

2. The requirements of the Federation and of the Länder shall be coordinated in such a way that a fair balance is struck, any overburdening of taxpayers precluded, and uniformity of living standards in the federal territory ensured.

(4) The respective shares of the Federation and the Länder in the revenue from the sales tax shall be apportioned anew whenever the relation of revenues to expenditures in the Federation develops substantially differently from that of the Länder. If federal legislation imposes additional expenditures on or withdraws revenue from the Länder, the additional burden may be compensated for by allocation of federal grants pursuant to federal statute requiring the consent of the Bundesrat, provided such additional burden is limited to a short period of time. Such statute shall lay down the principles for calculating such grants and distributing them among the Länder.

(5) A share of the revenue from the income tax shall accrue to the communities, to be passed on by the Länder to their communities on the basis of income taxes paid by the inhabitants of the latter. Details shall be regulated by federal statute requiring the consent of the Bundesrat. Such statute may provide that communities shall establish the rate applicable to this communal share.

(6) Revenue from taxes on real estate and on local industry and trade shall accrue to the communities; revenue from local excise taxes shall accrue to the communities or, as may be provided for by Land legislation, to associations of communities. Communities shall be authorized to establish, within the framework of the relevant statutes, the rates at which the taxes on real es-

tate and on local industry and trade are levied locally. If there are no communities in a Land, revenue from taxes on real estate and on local industry and trade as well as from local excise taxes shall accrue to the Land. The Federation and the Länder may participate, by virtue of an apportionment, in the revenue from the tax on local industry and trade. Details regarding such apportionment shall be regulated by federal statute requiring the consent of the Bundesrat. In accordance with Land legislation, taxes on real estate and on local industry and trade as well as the communities' share of revenue from the income tax may be taken as a basis for calculating the amount of apportionment.

(7) An overall percentage of the Land share of total revenue from joint taxes, to be determined by Land legislation, shall accrue to the communities or associations of communities. In all other respects Land legislation shall determine whether and to what extent revenue from Land taxes shall accrue to communities or associations of communities.

(8) If in individual Länder or communities or associations of communities the Federation causes special facilities to be provided that directly result in an increase of expenditure or a loss of revenue (special burden) to these Länder or communities or associations of communities, the Federation shall grant the necessary compensation if and insofar as such Länder or communities or associations of communities cannot reasonably be expected to bear such special burden. In granting such compensation, due account shall be taken of third-party indemnities and financial benefits accruing to the Länder or communities or associations of communities concerned as a result of provision for such facilities.

(9) For the purpose of this Article, revenues and expenditures of communities or associations of communities shall be deemed to be Land revenues and expenditures.

Article 107[90] (Financial equalization)

(1) Revenue from Land taxes and the Land share of revenue from income and corporation taxes shall accrue to the individual Länder to the extent that such taxes are collected by revenue authorities within their respective territories (local revenue). A federal statute requiring the consent of the Bundesrat may provide in detail for the delimitation as well as the manner and scope of allotment of local revenue from corporation and wage taxes. Such statute may also provide for the delimitation and allotment of local revenue from other taxes. The Land share of revenue from the sales tax shall accrue to the individual Länder on a per capita basis; a federal statute requiring the consent of the Bundesrat may provide for supplementary shares not exceed-

---

[90] As amended by federal statutes of December 23, 1955 (BGBl. I S. 817), and of May 12, 1969 (BGBl. I S. 359).

ing one quarter of a Land share to be granted to Länder whose per capita revenue from Land taxes and from the income and corporation taxes is below the average of all the Länder combined.

(2) Such statute shall ensure a reasonable equalization between financially strong and financially weak Länder, due account being taken of the financial capacity and financial requirements of communities or associations of communities. Such statute shall specify the conditions governing equalization claims of Länder entitled to equalization payments and equalization liabilities of Länder owing equalization payments as well as the criteria for determining the amounts of equalization payments. Such statute may also provide for grants to be made by the Federation from federal funds to financially weak Länder in order to complement the coverage of their general financial requirements (supplementary grants).

Article 108[91] (Revenue administration)

(1) Customs duties, fiscal monopolies, excise taxes subject to federal legislation, including the import sales tax, and charges imposed within the framework of the European Communities shall be administered by federal revenue authorities. The organization of these authorities shall be regulated by federal statute. The heads of authorities at the intermediate level shall be appointed in consultation with the respective Land governments.

(2) All other taxes shall be administered by Land revenue authorities. The organization of these authorities and the uniform training of their civil servants may be regulated by a federal statute requiring the consent of the Bundesrat. The heads of authorities at the intermediate level shall be appointed in agreement with the Federal Government.

(3) To the extent that taxes accruing wholly or in part to the Federation are administered by Land revenue authorities, those authorities shall act as agents of the Federation. Paragraphs (3) and (4) of Article 85 shall apply, the Federal Minister of Finance, however, being substituted for the Federal Government.

(4) With respect to the administration of taxes, a federal statute requiring the consent of the Bundesrat may provide for collaboration between federal and Land revenue authorities, or in the case of taxes under paragraph (1) of this Article for their administration by Land revenue authorities, or in the case of other taxes for their administration by federal revenue authorities, if and to the extent that the execution of revenue statutes is substantially improved or facilitated thereby. As regards taxes whose revenue accrues exclusively to communities or associations of communities, their administration may wholly

---

[91] As amended by federal statute of May 12, 1969 (BGBl. I S. 359).

or in part be transferred by the Länder from the appropriate Land revenue authorities to communities or associations of communities.

(5) The procedure to be applied by federal revenue authorities shall be laid down by federal legislation. The procedure to be applied by Land revenue authorities or, as envisaged in the second sentence of paragraph (4) of this Article, by communities or associations of communities may be laid down by a federal statute requiring the consent of the Bundesrat.

(6) The jurisdiction of revenue courts shall be uniformly regulated by federal legislation.

(7) The Federal Government may issue appropriate general administrative rules which, to the extent that administration is entrusted to Land revenue authorities or communities or associations of communities, shall require the consent of the Bundesrat.

Article 109[92] (Budget management in the Federation and the Länder)

(1) The Federation and the Länder shall be autonomous and independent of each other in their budget management.

(2) The Federation and the Länder shall have due regard in their budget management to the requirements of overall economic equilibrium.

(3)[93] By federal legislation requiring the consent of the Bundesrat, principles applicable to both the Federation and the Länder may be established governing budgetary law, responsiveness of budget management to economic trends, and long-term financial planning.

(4) With a view to averting disturbances of the overall economic equilibrium, federal legislation requiring the consent of the Bundesrat may be enacted providing for:

1. maximum amounts, terms and timing of loans to be raised by territorial entities [Gebietskörperschaften] or special purpose associations [Zweckverbände], and

2. an obligation on the part of the Federation and the Länder to maintain interest-free deposits at the Deutsche Bundesbank (reserves for counter-balancing economic trends).

Authorizations to issue the relevant regulations may be conferred only on the Federal Government. Such regulations shall require the consent of the Bun-

---

[92] As amended by federal statute of June 8, 1967 (BGBl. I S. 581).

[93] As amended by federal statute of May 12, 1969 (BGBl. I S. 357).

desrat. They shall be repealed insofar as the Bundestag may so demand; details shall be regulated by federal legislation.

Article 110[94] (Budget and budget law of the Federation)

(1) All revenues and expenditures of the Federation shall be included in the budget; in respect of federal enterprises and special assets, only allocations thereto or remittances therefrom need be included. The budget shall be balanced as regards revenue and expenditure.

(2) The budget shall be laid down in a statute covering one year or several fiscal years separately before the beginning of the first of those fiscal years. Provision may be made for parts of the budget to apply to periods of different duration, but divided into fiscal years.

(3) Bills within the meaning of the first sentence of paragraph (2) of this Article as well as bills to amend the budget statute and the budget shall be submitted simultaneously to the Bundesrat and to the Bundestag; the Bundesrat shall be entitled to state its position on such bills within six weeks or, in the case of amending bills, within three weeks.

(4) The budget statute may contain only such provisions as apply to revenues and expenditures of the Federation and to the period for which the budget statute is being enacted. The budget statute may stipulate that these provisions shall cease to apply only upon the promulgation of the next budget statute or, in the event of an authorization pursuant to Article 115, at a later date.

Article 111 (Interim budget management)

(1) If, by the end of a fiscal year, the budget for the following year has not been established by statute, the Federal Government may, until such statute comes into force, make all payments which are necessary:

(a) to maintain statutory institutions and to carry out measures authorized by statute;

(b) to meet the Federation's legal obligations;

(c) to continue building projects, procurements, and other services, or to continue to grant subsidies for these purposes, provided that amounts have already been appropriated in the budget of a previous year.

(2) To the extent that revenues provided by specific legislation and derived from taxes or duties or any other sources, or the working capital reserves, do not cover the expenditures referred to in paragraph (1) of this Article, the

---

[94] As amended by federal statute of May 12, 1969 (BGBl. I S. 357).

Federal Government may borrow the funds necessary for the conduct of current operations up to a maximum of one quarter of the total amount of the previous budget.

Article 112[95] (Expenditures in excess of budgetary estimates)

Expenditures in excess of budgetary appropriations and extrabudgetary expenditures shall require the consent of the Federal Minister of Finance. Such consent may be given only in the case of an unforeseen and compelling necessity. Details may be regulated by federal legislation.

Article 113[96] (Consent of the Federal Government to increases in expenditures or decreases in revenue)

(1) Statutes increasing the budget expenditures proposed by the Federal Government or involving or likely in the future to cause new expenditures shall require the consent of the Federal Government. This requirement also applies to statutes involving or likely in the future to cause decreases in revenue. The Federal Government may demand that the Bundestag postpone its vote on such bills. In this case the Federal Government shall state its position to the Bundestag within six weeks.

(2) Within four weeks after the Bundestag has adopted such a bill, the Federal Government may demand that it vote on that bill again.

(3) If the bill has become law pursuant to Article 78, the Federal Government may withhold its consent only within six weeks and only after having initiated the procedure provided for in the third and fourth sentences of paragraph (1) or in paragraph (2) of this Article. Upon the expiration of this period such consent shall be deemed to have been given.

Article 114[97] (Rendering and auditing of accounts)

(1) The Federal Minister of Finance, on behalf of the Federal Government, shall submit annually to the Bundestag and to the Bundesrat for their approval an account, covering the preceding fiscal year, of all revenues and expenditures as well as of property and debt.

(2) The Federal Audit Office, whose members shall enjoy judicial independence, shall audit the account and examine the management of the budget and the conduct of business as to economy and correctness. The Federal Audit

---

[95] As amended by federal statute of May 12, 1969 (BGBl. I S. 357).

[96] As amended by federal statute of May 12, 1969 (BGBl. I S. 357).

[97] As amended by federal statute of May 12, 1969 (BGBl. I S. 357).

Office shall submit an annual report directly to the Federal Government as well as to the Bundestag and to the Bundesrat. In all other respects the powers of the Federal Audit Office shall be regulated by federal legislation.

Article 115[98] (Procurement of credit)

(1) The borrowing of funds and the assumption of pledges, guarantees or other commitments, as a result of which expenditure may be incurred in future fiscal years, shall require federal legislative authorization indicating, or permitting computation of, the maximum amounts involved. Revenue obtained by borrowing shall not exceed the total of expenditures for investments provided for in the budget; exceptions shall be permissible only to avert a disturbance of the overall economic equilibrium. Details shall be regulated by federal legislation.

(2) With respect to special assets of the Federation, exceptions to the provisions of paragraph (1) of this Article may be authorized by federal legislation.

Xa.[99] STATE OF DEFENSE

Article 115a (Concept and determination of a state of defense)

(1) The determination that federal territory is being attacked by armed force or that such an attack is directly imminent (state of defense) shall be made by the Bundestag with the consent of the Bundesrat. Such determination shall be made at the request of the Federal Government and shall require a two-thirds majority of the votes cast, which shall include at least the majority of the members of the Bundestag.

(2) If the situation imperatively calls for immediate action and if insurmountable obstacles prevent the timely assembly of the Bundestag, or if there is no quorum in the Bundestag, the Joint Committee shall make this determination with a two-thirds majority of the votes cast, which shall include at least the majority of its members.

(3) The determination shall be promulgated in the Federal Law Gazette by the Federal President pursuant to Article 82. If this cannot be done in time, the promulgation shall be effected in another manner; it shall subsequently be printed in the Federal Law Gazette as soon as circumstances permit.

(4) If the federal territory is being attacked by armed force and if the competent bodies of the Federation are not in a position at once to make the de-

---

[98] As amended by federal statute of May 12, 1969 (BGBl. I S. 357).

[99] Entire section Xa inserted by federal statute of June 24, 1968 (BGBl. I S. 711).

termination provided for in the first sentence of paragraph (1) of this Article, such determination shall be deemed to have been made and promulgated at the time the attack began. The Federal President shall announce such time as soon as circumstances permit.

(5) If the determination of the existence of a state of defense has been promulgated and if the federal territory is being attacked by armed force, the Federal President may, with the consent of the Bundestag, issue declarations under international law regarding the existence of such state of defense. If the conditions mentioned in paragraph (2) of this Article apply, the Joint Committee shall act in place of the Bundestag.

Article 115b (Transfer of command to the Federal Chancellor during a state of defense)

Upon the promulgation of a state of defense, the power of command over the Armed Forces shall pass to the Federal Chancellor.

Article 115c (Extension of legislative powers of the Federation during a state of defense)

(1) The Federation shall have the right to legislate concurrently with respect to a state of defense even on matters within the legislative powers of the Länder. Such statutes shall require the consent of the Bundesrat.

(2) Federal legislation to be applicable upon the occurrence of a state of defense to the extent required by conditions obtaining while such state of defense exists may make provision for:

1. preliminary compensation to be made in the event of property being taken, notwithstanding the second sentence of paragraph (3) of Article 14;

2. provision for a time limit other than that referred to in the third sentence of paragraph (2) and the first sentence of paragraph (3) of Article 104 with respect to deprivations of liberty, but not exceeding four days at the most, in a case where no judge has been able to act within the time limit applying in normal times.

(3)[100] Federal legislation to be applicable upon the occurrence of a state of defense to the extent required for averting an existing or directly imminent attack may, subject to the consent of the Bundesrat, regulate the administration and the financial system of the Federation and the Länder notwithstanding Sections VIII, VIIIa and X, provided that the viability of the Länder, communities, and associations of communes is safeguarded, particularly in financial matters.

---

[100] As amended by federal statute of May 12, 1969 (BGBl. I S. 359).

(4) Federal statutes enacted pursuant to paragraph (1) or subparagraph 1 of paragraph (2) of this Article may, for the purpose of preparing for their enforcement, be applied even prior to the occurrence of a state of defense.

Article 115d (Legislative process in the case of urgent bills)

(1) While a state of defense exists, the provisions of paragraphs (2) and (3) of this Article shall apply with respect to federal legislation, notwithstanding the provisions of paragraph (2) of Article 76, the second sentence of paragraph (1) and paragraphs (2) to (4) of Article 77, Article 78, and paragraph (l) of Article 82.

(2) Bills submitted as urgent by the Federal Government shall be forwarded to the Bundesrat at the same time as they are submitted to the Bundestag. The Bundestag and the Bundesrat shall debate such bills together without delay. Insofar as the consent of the Bundesrat is necessary, the majority of its votes shall be required for any such bill to become law. Details shall be regulated by rules of procedure adopted by the Bundestag and requiring the consent of the Bundesrat.

(3) The second sentence of paragraph (3) of Article 115a shall apply with respect to the promulgation of such statutes.

Article 115e (Powers of the Joint Committee)

(1) If, during a state of defense, the Joint Committee determines by a two-thirds majority of the votes cast, which shall include at least the majority of its members, that insurmountable obstacles prevent the timely assembly of the Bundestag or that there is no quorum in the Bundestag, the Joint Committee shall have the status of both the Bundestag and the Bundesrat and shall exercise their rights as one body.

(2) The Joint Committee may not enact any statute to amend this Basic Law or to deprive it of effect or application either in whole or in part. The Joint Committee shall not be authorized to enact statutes pursuant to the second sentence of paragraph (1) of Article 23, paragraph (l) of Article 24, or Article 29.[101]

Article 115f (Powers of the Federal Government)

(1) While a state of defense exists, the Federal Government may, to the extent necessitated by circumstances:

    1. employ the Federal Border Guard throughout the federal territory;

---

[101] Last sentence amended by federal statute of December 21, 1992 (BGBl. I S. 2086).

2. issue instructions not only to federal administrative authorities but also to Land governments and, if it deems the matter urgent, to Land authorities, and may delegate this power to members of Land governments to be designated by it.

(2) The Bundestag, the Bundesrat, and the Joint Committee shall be informed without delay of the measures taken in accordance with paragraph (1) of this Article.

Article 115g (Status and functions of the Federal Constitutional Court)

The constitutional status and the performance of the constitutional functions of the Federal Constitutional Court and its judges shall not be impaired. The Federal Constitutional Court Act may not be amended by a statute enacted by the Joint Committee except insofar as such amendment is required, also in the opinion of the Federal Constitutional Court, to maintain the capability of the Court to function. Pending the enactment of such a statute, the Federal Constitutional Court may take such measures as are necessary to maintain the capability of the Court to carry out its work. Any decisions by the Federal Constitutional Court in pursuance of the second and third sentences of this Article shall require a two-thirds majority of the judges present.

Article 115h (Functioning capability of constitutional organs)

(1) Any legislative terms of the Bundestag or of Land parliaments due to expire while a state of defense exists shall end six months after the termination of such state of defense. A term of office of the Federal President due to expire while a state of defense exists, and the exercise of his functions by the President of the Bundesrat in case of the premature vacancy of the Federal President's office, shall end nine months after the termination of such state of defense. The term of office of a member of the Federal Constitutional Court due to expire while a state of defense exists shall end six months after the termination of such state of defense.

(2) Should the necessity arise for the Joint Committee to elect a new Federal Chancellor, the Committee shall do so by the majority of its members; the Federal President shall propose a candidate to the Joint Committee. The Joint Committee can express its lack of confidence in the Federal Chancellor only by electing a successor by a two-thirds majority of its members.

(3) The Bundestag shall not be dissolved while a state of defense exists.

Article 115i (Powers of the Land governments)

(1) If the competent federal bodies are incapable of taking the measures necessary to avert the danger, and if the situation imperatively calls for immediate independent action in individual parts of the federal territory, the Land governments or the authorities or commissioners designated by them shall be

authorized, within their respective spheres of competence, to take the measures provided for in paragraph (1) of Article ll5f.

(2) Any measures taken in accordance with paragraph (1) of the present Article may be revoked at any time by the Federal Government, or, in relation to Land authorities and subordinate federal authorities, by minister-presidents of the Länder.

Article 115k (Duration of extraordinary legal provisions)

(1) Statutes enacted in accordance with Articles ll5c, ll5e and ll5g, as well as regulations issued on the basis of such statutes, shall suspend laws that are inconsistent with such statutes or regulations for the duration of their applicability. This provision shall not apply to earlier legislation enacted by virtue of Articles 115c, 115e or 115g.

(2) Statutes adopted by the Joint Committee, as well as ordinances issued by virtue of such statutes, shall cease to have effect not later than six months after the termination of a state of defense.

(3)[102] Statutes containing provisions that diverge from Articles 91a, 91b, 104a, 106, and 107 shall apply no longer than the end of the second fiscal year following upon the termination of a state of defense. After such termination they may, with the consent of the Bundesrat, be amended by federal legislation so as to return to the provisions made in Sections VIIIa and X.

Article 115l (Repeal of extraordinary statutes and measures; termination of a state of defense; conclusion of peace)

(1) The Bundestag, with the consent of the Bundesrat, may at any time repeal statutes enacted by the Joint Committee. The Bundesrat may demand that the Bundestag make a decision on such matter. Any measures taken by the Joint Committee or the Federal Government to avert a danger shall be revoked if the Bundestag and the Bundesrat so decide.

(2) The Bundestag, with the consent of the Bundesrat, may at any time declare a state of defense terminated by a decision to be promulgated by the Federal President. The Bundesrat may demand that the Bundestag make a decision on such matter. A state of defense shall, without delay, be declared terminated if the prerequisites for the determination thereof no longer exist.

(3) The conclusion of peace shall be the subject of federal statute.

---

[102] As amended by federal statute of May 12, 1969 (BGBl. I S. 359).

XI. TRANSITIONAL AND CONCLUDING PROVISIONS

Article 116 (Definition of "German"; regranting of citizenship)

(1) Unless otherwise provided by statute, a German within the meaning of this Basic Law is a person who possesses German citizenship or who has been admitted to the territory of the German Reich within the frontiers of 31 December 1937 as a refugee or expellee of German stock [Volkszugehörigkeit] or as the spouse or descendant of such person.

(2) Former German citizens who, between 30 January 1933 and 8 May 1945, were deprived of their citizenship on political, racial, or religious grounds, and their descendants, shall be regranted German citizenship on application. They shall be considered as not having been deprived of their German citizenship if they have established their domicile [Wohnsitz] in Germany after May 8, 1945 and have not expressed a contrary intention.

Article 117 (Temporary provision respecting Article 3 paragraph (2) and Article 11)

(1) Laws inconsistent with paragraph (2) of Article 3 shall remain in force until adapted to that provision of this Basic Law, but not beyond March 31, 1953.

(2) Statutes that restrict the right of freedom of movement in view of the present housing shortage shall remain in force until repealed by federal legislation.

Article 118 (New delimitation of the Länder of Baden, Württemberg-Baden, and Württemberg-Hohenzollern)

A new delimitation of the territory comprising the Länder of Baden, Württemberg-Baden and Württemberg-Hohenzollern may be effected, notwithstanding the provisions of Article 29, by agreement between the Länder concerned. If no agreement is reached, the reorganization shall be effected by federal legislation, which shall provide for a plebiscite.

Article 119 (Regulations having statutory effect in matters relating to refugees and expellees)

In matters relating to refugees and expellees, in particular as regards their distribution among the Länder, the Federal Government may, with the consent of the Bundesrat, issue regulations having the force of law, pending settlement of the matter by federal legislation. The Federal Government may be authorized to issue individual instructions for particular cases in this matter. Except when danger would result from any delay in taking action, such instructions shall be addressed to the highest Land authorities.

Article 120[103] (Occupation costs and burdens resulting from the war)

(1)[104] The Federation shall meet the expenditures for occupation costs and other internal and external burdens caused by the war, as regulated in detail by federal legislation. To the extent that these costs and other burdens have been regulated by federal legislation on or before October 1, 1969, the Federation and the Länder shall meet such expenditures between them in accordance with such federal legislation. Insofar as expenditures for such of these costs and burdens as neither have been nor will be regulated by federal legislation have been met on or before October 1, 1965 by Länder, communities, associations of communities, or other entities performing functions of the Länder or the communities, the Federation shall not be obliged to meet an expenditure of that nature even if it arises after that date. The Federation shall pay the subsidies toward the burdens of social insurance institutions, including unemployment insurance and public assistance to the unemployed. The division between the Federation and the Länder of costs and other burdens caused by the war, as regulated in this paragraph, shall not affect any statutory regulation of claims for indemnification in respect to the consequences of the war.

(2) Revenue shall pass to the Federation at the time it assumes responsibility for the expenditures referred to in this Article.

Article 120a[105] (Implementation of legislation respecting equalization of burdens)

(1) Statutes serving to implement the equalization of burdens may, with the consent of the Bundesrat, stipulate that they shall be executed, as regards equalization benefits, partly by the Federation and partly by the Länder acting as agents of the Federation, and that the relevant powers vested in the Federal Government and the competent supreme federal authorities by virtue of Article 85 shall be wholly or partly delegated to the Federal Equalization Office. In exercising these powers, the Federal Equalization Office shall not require the consent of the Bundesrat; with the exception of urgent cases, its instructions shall be given to the highest Land authorities (Land Equalization Offices).

(2) The provisions of the second sentence of paragraph (3) of Article 87 shall not be affected hereby.

---

[103] As amended by federal statutes of July 30, 1965 (BGBl. I S. 649), and of July 28, 1969 (BGBl. I S. 985).

[104] As amended by federal statute of July 28, 1969 (BGBl. I S. 985).

[105] Inserted by federal statute of August 14, 1952 (BGBl. I S. 445).

Article 121 (Definition of "majority of the members")

Within the meaning of this Basic Law, a majority of the members of the Bundestag and a majority of the members of the Federal Convention [Bundesversammlung] shall be the majority of the respective statutory number of their members.

Article 122 (Transfer of legislative powers hitherto existing)

(1) From the date of the assembly of the Bundestag, statutes shall be enacted exclusively by the legislative bodies recognized in this Basic Law.

(2) Legislative bodies as well as those bodies participating in legislation in an advisory capacity, whose competence ends by virtue of paragraph (1) of this Article, shall be dissolved effective that date.

Article 123 (Continued validity of preexisting law and treaties)

(1) Law in force before the first assembly of the Bundestag shall remain in force insofar as it does not conflict with this Basic Law.

(2) Subject to all rights and objections of the interested parties, the treaties concluded by the German Reich concerning matters which, under this Basic Law, are within the legislative competence of the Länder, shall remain in force, provided they are and continue to be valid in accordance with general principles of law, until new treaties are concluded by the agencies competent under this Basic Law, or until they are in any other way terminated pursuant to their provisions.

Article 124 (Applicability as federal law within the sphere of exclusive legislative power)

Law affecting matters subject to the exclusive legislative power of the Federation shall become federal law in the area in which it applies.

Article 125 (Applicability as federal law within the sphere of concurrent legislative power)

Law affecting matters subject to the concurrent legislative power of the Federation shall become federal law in the area in which it applies:

1. insofar as it applies uniformly within one or more zones of occupation;

2. insofar as it is law by which former Reich law has been amended after May 8, 1945.

Article 126 (Differences of opinion regarding the applicability of law as federal law)

Differences of opinion regarding the applicability of law as federal law shall be resolved by the Federal Constitutional Court.

Article 127 (Legislation of the Bizonal Economic Administration)

Within one year of the promulgation of this Basic Law the Federal Government may, with the consent of the governments of the Länder concerned, extend to the Länder of Baden, Greater Berlin, Rhineland-Palatinate and Württemberg-Hohenzollern any legislation of the Bizonal Economic Administration, insofar as it continues to be in force as federal law under Article 124 or 125.

Article 128 (Continuance of authority to give instructions)

Insofar as law continuing in force provides for authority to give instructions within the meaning of paragraph (5) of Article 84, these powers shall remain in existence until otherwise provided by statute.

Article 129 (Applicability of authorizations)

(1) Insofar as legal provisions that continue in force as federal law contain authorizations to issue regulations or to issue general administrative rules or to perform administrative acts, such authorizations shall pass to the agencies henceforth competent in the matter. In cases of doubt, the Federal Government shall decide in agreement with the Bundesrat; such decisions shall be published.

(2) Insofar as legal provisions that continue in force as Land law contain such authorizations, they shall be exercised by the agencies competent under Land law.

(3) Insofar as legal provisions within the meaning of paragraphs (1) and (2) of this Article authorize their amendment or supplementation or the issue of regulations instead of statutory provisions, such authorizations shall be deemed to have expired.

(4) The provisions of paragraphs (1) and (2) of this Article shall also apply when legal provisions refer to regulations no longer valid or to institutions no longer in existence.

Article 130 (Control over existing institutions)

(1) Administrative agencies and other institutions that serve the public administration or the administration of justice and are not based on Land law or treaties between Länder, as well as the Administrative Union of South West German Railroads and the Administrative Council for the Postal Services and Telecommunications of the French Zone of Occupation, shall be

placed under the control of the Federal Government. The Federal Government, with the consent of the Bundesrat, shall provide for their transfer, dissolution, or liquidation.

(2) The highest disciplinary superior of the personnel of these administrative bodies and institutions shall be the appropriate Federal Minister.

(3) Corporate bodies and institutions under public law not directly subordinate to a Land nor based on treaties between Länder shall be under the supervision of the competent supreme federal authority.

Article 131 (Legal position of persons formerly employed in the public service)

Federal legislation shall be passed to regulate the legal position of persons, including refugees and expellees, who, on May 8, 1945, were employed in the public service, have left the service for reasons other than those arising from civil service regulations or collective agreement rules, and have not until now been reinstated or are employed in a position not corresponding to their former one. The same shall apply to persons, including refugees and expellees, who, on May 8, 1945, were entitled to a pension and who no longer receive any such pension or any commensurate pension for reasons other than those arising from civil service regulations or collective agreement rules. Until the pertinent federal statute comes into force, no legal claims may be made, unless Land legislation otherwise provides.

Article 132 (Temporary revocation of rights of persons employed in the public service)

(1) Civil servants and judges who, when this Basic Law comes into force, are appointed for life, may, within six months after the first assembly of the Bundestag, be retired or temporarily retired or be given a different office with lower remuneration if they lack the personal or professional aptitude for their present office. This provision shall also apply to salaried public employees, other than civil servants or judges, whose service cannot be terminated by notice. If, however, such service can be terminated by notice, periods of notice in excess of the periods fixed by collective agreement rules may be cancelled within the six months referred to above.

(2) The preceding provision shall not apply to members of the public service who are not affected by the provisions regarding the "Liberation from National Socialism and Militarism" or who are recognized victims of National Socialism, except on important grounds relating to themselves as individuals.

(3) Those affected may have recourse to the courts in accordance with paragraph (4) of Article 19.

(4) Details shall be specified by regulations of the Federal Government requiring the consent of the Bundesrat.

Article 133 (Bizonal Economic Administration: succession to rights and obligations)

The Federation shall succeed to the rights and obligations of the Bizonal Economic Administration.

Article 134 (Reich property to become federal property)

(1) Reich property shall basically become federal property.

(2) Insofar as such property was originally intended to be used predominantly for administrative tasks that are not those of the Federation under this Basic Law, it shall be transferred without compensation to the agencies now charged with such tasks, and to the Länder insofar as it is being used at present, and not merely temporarily, for administrative tasks that under this Basic Law are now within the administrative competence of the Länder. The Federation may also transfer other property to the Länder.

(3) Property that was placed at the disposal of the Reich by Länder or communities or associations of communities without compensation shall again become the property of such Länder or communities or associations of communities, insofar as it is not required by the Federation for its own administrative tasks.

(4) Details shall be regulated by a federal statute requiring the consent of the Bundesrat.

Article 135 (Succession to property of previously existing Länder and corporate bodies)

(1) If after May 8, 1945 and before the coming into force of this Basic Law an area has passed from one Land to another, the Land to which the area now belongs shall be entitled to the property located therein of the Land to which it previously belonged.

(2) Property of Länder or corporate bodies or public-law institutions that no longer exist, insofar as it was originally intended to be used predominantly for administrative tasks or is being so used at present and not merely temporarily, shall pass to the Land or the corporate body or public-law institution that now discharges those tasks.

(3) Real estate of Länder that no longer exist, including appurtenances, shall pass to the Land within which it is located, insofar as it is not included among property within the meaning of paragraph (1) of this Article.

(4) If an overriding interest of the Federation or the particular interest of an area so requires, a settlement other than in paragraphs (1) to (3) of this Article may be effected by federal legislation.

(5) In all other respects, the succession in title and the settlement of the property, insofar as it has not been effected before January 1, 1952 by agreement between the affected Länder or corporate bodies or institutions established under public law, shall be regulated by federal legislation requiring the consent of the Bundesrat.

(6) Interests of the former Land of Prussia in enterprises established under private law shall pass to the Federation. A federal statute, which may also diverge from this provision, shall regulate details.

(7) Insofar as property that on the effective date of this Basic Law would devolve upon a Land or a corporate body or institution established under public law pursuant to paragraphs (1) to (3) of this Article has been disposed of through or by virtue of Land law or in any other manner by the party thus entitled, the transfer of the property shall be deemed to have taken place before such disposition.

Article 135a[106] (Old liabilities)

(1) The legislation reserved to the Federation in paragraph (4) of Article 134 and in paragraph (5) of Article 135 may also stipulate that the following liabilities shall not be discharged, or not to their full extent:

1. liabilities of the Reich or liabilities of the former Land of Prussia or liabilities of such corporate bodies and institutions under public law as no longer exist;

2. such liabilities of the Federation or corporate bodies and institutions under public law as are connected with the transfer of properties pursuant to Article 89, 90, 134, or 135, and such liabilities of these entities as arise from measures taken by the entities mentioned under clause 1;

3. such liabilities of Länder or communities or associations of communities as have arisen from measures taken by these entities before August 1, 1945 within the framework of administrative functions incumbent upon or delegated by the Reich to comply with regulations of occupying powers or to put an end to a state of emergency due to the war.

(2)[107] Paragraph (1) above shall also be applied to liabilities of the German Democratic Republic or its legal entities as well as to liabilities of the Federation or other corporate bodies and institutions under public law that are connected with the transfer of properties of the German Democratic Republic to

---

[106] Inserted by federal statute of October 22, 1957 (BGBl. I S. 1745).

[107] Inserted by the Unification Treaty of August 31, 1990, and federal statute of September 23, 1990 (BGBl. II S. 885).

the Federation, Länder, and communities, and to liabilities arising from measures taken by the German Democratic Republic or its legal entities.

Article 136 (First assembly of the Bundesrat)

(1) The Bundesrat shall assemble for the first time on the day of the first assembly of the Bundestag.

(2) Until the election of the first Federal President, his powers shall be exercised by the President of the Bundesrat. He shall not have the right to dissolve the Bundestag.

Article 137 (Right of civil servants to stand for election)

(1)[108] The right of civil servants, of other salaried public employees, of professional soldiers, of temporary volunteer soldiers, or of judges to stand for election in the Federation, in the Länder or in the communities may be restricted by legislation.

(2) The electoral statute to be adopted by the Parliamentary Council shall apply to the election of the first Bundestag, of the first Federal Convention, and of the first Federal President of the Federal Republic.

(3) The function of the Federal Constitutional Court pursuant to paragraph (2) of Article 41 shall, pending its establishment, be exercised by the German High Court for the Combined Economic Area, which shall decide in accordance with its rules of procedure.

Article 138 (Southern German notaries)

Changes in notarial institutions as presently existing in the Länder of Baden, Bavaria, Württemberg-Baden, and Württemberg-Hohenzollern shall require the consent of the governments of these Länder.

Article 139 (Continued validity of denazification provisions)

The legislation enacted for the "Liberation of the German People from National Socialism and Militarism" shall not be affected by the provisions of this Basic Law.

Article 140 (Law respecting religious bodies)

The provisions of Articles 136, 137, 138, 139, and 141 of the German Constitution of August 11, 1919 shall be an integral part of this Basic Law.[109]

---

[108] As amended by federal statute of March 19, 1956 (BGBl. I S. 111).

[109] See Appendix to the Basic Law, infra.

Article 141 ("Bremen Clause")

The first sentence of paragraph (3) of Article 7 shall not be applied in any Land in which different provisions of Land law were in force on January 1, 1949.

Article 142 (Basic rights in Land constitutions)

Notwithstanding the provision of Article 31, such provisions of Land constitutions shall also remain in force as guarantee basic rights in conformity with Articles 1 to 18 of this Basic Law.

Article 142a [110] (Repealed)

Article 143[111] (Deviations from the Basic Law)

(1) Law in the territory specified in Article 3 of the Unification Treaty may deviate from provisions of this Basic Law at the latest until December 31, 1992 insofar and as long as, owing to differing conditions, no complete accommodation to the order of the Basic Law [grundgesetzliche Ordnung] can be achieved. Deviations may not violate Article 19(2) and must be compatible with the principles specified in Article 79(3).

(2) Deviations from sections II, VIII, VIIIa, IX, X, and XI are permissible, at the latest, until December 31, 1995.

(3) Notwithstanding paragraphs (1) and (2), Article 41 of the Unification Treaty and the rules for its implementation shall remain valid insofar as they provide for the irreversibility of incursions on property rights in the territory specified in Article 3 of the said Treaty.

Article 144 (Ratification of the Basic Law)

(1) This Basic Law shall require ratification by the parliaments of two thirds of the German Länder in which it is for the time being to apply.

(2) Insofar as the application of this Basic Law is subject to restrictions in any Land listed in Article 23 [since repealed] or in any part thereof, such Land or part thereof shall have the right to send representatives to the Bundestag in accordance with Article 38 and to the Bundesrat in accordance with Article 50.

---

[110] Inserted by federal statute of March 26, 1954 (BGBl. I S. 45) and repealed by federal statute of June 24, 1968 (BGBl. I S. 714).

[111] Inserted by the Unification Treaty of August 31, 1990 and federal statute of September 23, 1990 (BGBl. II S. 885).

Article 145 (Promulgation of the Basic Law)

(1) The Parliamentary Council, with the participation of the deputies of Greater Berlin, shall confirm in public session the ratification of this Basic Law and shall certify and promulgate it.

(2) This Basic Law shall take effect at the end of the day of promulgation.

(3) It shall be published in the Federal Law Gazette.

Article 146[112] (Duration of validity of the Basic Law)

This Basic Law, which is valid for the entire German people following achievement of the unity and freedom of Germany, shall cease to be in force on the day on which a constitution adopted by a free decision of the German people takes effect.

APPENDIX TO THE BASIC LAW[113]

Extract from the Weimar Constitution of August 11, 1919: Religion and Religious Associations

Article 136 (Weimar Constitution)

(1) Civil and political rights and duties shall be neither dependent upon nor restricted by the exercise of the freedom of religion.

(2) Enjoyment of civil and political rights and eligibility for public office shall be independent of religious denomination.

(3) No one shall be bound to disclose his religious convictions. The authorities shall not have the right to inquire into a person's membership in a religious body except to the extent that rights or duties depend thereon or that a statistical survey mandated by law so requires.

(4) No one may be compelled to perform any religious act or ceremony, to participate in religious exercises, or to take a religious form of oath.

Article 137 (Weimar Constitution)

(1) There shall be no state church.

---

[112] As amended by the Unification Treaty of August 31, 1990 and federal statute of September 23, 1990 (BGBl. II S. 885).

[113] See Article 140 above.

(2) Freedom of association to form religious bodies is guaranteed. The union of religious bodies within the territory of the Reich is subject to no restrictions.

(3) Every religious body shall regulate and administer its affairs autonomously within the limits of the law valid for all. It shall confer its offices without the participation of the state or the civil community.

(4) Religious bodies shall acquire legal capacity according to the general provisions of civil law.

(5) Religious bodies shall remain corporate bodies under public law insofar as they have been in the past. Other religious bodies shall be granted like rights upon application, if their constitution and the number of their members offer assurance of their permanency. If two or more religious bodies established under public law unite into a single organization, that organization shall also be a corporate body under public law.

(6) Religious bodies that are corporate bodies under public law shall be entitled to levy taxes in accordance with Land law on the basis of the civil taxation lists.

(7) Associations whose purpose is the common cultivation of a philosophical persuasion shall have the same status as religious bodies.

(8) Such further regulation as may be required for the implementation of these provisions shall be a matter for Land legislation.

Article 138 (Weimar Constitution)

(1) State contributions to religious bodies, based on law or contract or special legal title, shall be redeemed by means of Land legislation. The principles governing such redemption shall be established by the Reich.

(2) The right to own property and other rights of religious bodies or associations with respect to their institutions, foundations, and other assets destined for purposes of worship, education or charity shall be guaranteed.

Article 139 (Weimar Constitution)

Sunday and the public holidays recognized by the state shall remain legally protected as days of rest from work and of spiritual edification.

Article 141 (Weimar Constitution)

To the extent that there exists a need for religious services and spiritual care in the army, in hospitals, in prisons, or in other public institutions, religious bodies shall be permitted to provide them; in this connection there shall be no compulsion of any kind.

Index

413